Women in the Muslim World

Women in the Muslim World

Edited by

Lois Beck and Nikki Keddie

HARVARD UNIVERSITY PRESS
Cambridge, Massachusetts
and London, England 1978

Printed in the United States of America

Library of Congress Cataloging in Publication Data
Main entry under title:
WOMEN IN THE MUSLIM WORLD
Bibliography: p.
Includes index.
1. Women, Muslim—Addresses, essays, lectures.
I. Beck, Lois, 1944– II. Keddie, Nikki R.
HQ1170.W59 301.41′2′0917671 78–3633
ISBN 0–674–95480–7

To the women of the Muslim world

Preface

In editing this volume of original essays on women in the Muslim world, we have received the assistance of many colleagues, students, and friends. In addition to those mentioned in the notes to the Introduction and to individual chapters, we wish to thank Margot Badran, Margaret Fallers, Elizabeth Fernea, Ernest Gellner, Judith Gran, Şerif Mardin, Ann Mayer, Paul Rabinow, and Louise Sweet for their useful suggestions. Sam Beck, Selma Brandow, Gloria Cook, Hollis Granoff, Ursula Hanly, Ronald Holt, Ronald Jennings, Nancy Klepper, June McCartney, Amal Rassam, and John Shoup were also very helpful. We wish to acknowledge the aid of the Department of Anthropology and the Middle East Center of the University of Utah, the Anthropology-Sociology Department of Amherst College, and the History Department and the Gustave E. von Grunebaum Center for Near Eastern Studies of the University of California at Los Angeles. We are grateful to Aida Donald and Laura Margolis of Harvard University Press for their valuable suggestions. The photographs of the volume were taken by the book's authors, with the exception of those taken by Dorothy Grant.

The book mainly covers the Middle East, but the submission of some valuable essays dealing in whole or in part with other areas precluded the use of "Middle East" in the title. Considerations of time and space prevented us from including essays on Muslim women everywhere.

Both editors read and edited all essays, but Lois Beck took on the burden of doing much of the work that remained after the manuscript was submitted, when Nikki Keddie went to teach in Paris for two years.

Salt Lake City, Utah Lois Beck
Paris, France Nikki Keddie

Contents

PART TWO

PART THREE

PART FOUR

Women in the Muslim World

Introduction

Nikki Keddie and Lois Beck

The serious study of women in the Third World is still in its infancy, sparked largely, in the West at least, by movements here for the liberation of women. Women's studies is still seen by some scholars as an artificial separation of one segment of society from the rest, or an exercise in building self-esteem. While women's studies, like other fields, may include some of these elements, it is aimed primarily at shedding a clear analytical light on that half of humanity whose mode of life, contributions, and very existence have too often been neglected by the most serious of scholars. In the past, it was rarely suggested that the kind of social science that dealt almost exclusively with men was designed to bolster the ideology of male dominance and was made to focus on areas like politics and warfare in which men excelled. However, these charges are as just and as partial as those made about women's studies.

Behind the scholarly neglect of women are a number of unspoken assumptions that still function in nearly all societies. Some of these are that predominantly male activities—such as war, politics, economic and religious leadership—are the important ones, the ones worth studying, while activities that are mainly female—like childbearing, childrearing, cooking, women's work in agriculture

Although the Introduction is not a summary of the chapters of the book, it owes a great deal to the careful reading and assimilation of them, and we offer appreciation to their authors. For their helpful criticisms of working drafts, we would like to thank Barbara Aswad, Natalie Davis, Michael Fischer, Peter Gran, Fadwa al-Guindi, John Gulick, Temma Kaplan, Louise Lamphere, Maxime Rodinson, Eleanor Searle, Lucette Valensi, and Nadia Youssef.

and husbandry, nursing and midwifery, magic, folk art and tradition—are unimportant and not worthy of study. In history, the powerful and prominent have had by far the most coverage, and these are mostly men, although interest in those who left few direct records is growing. Until recently, female social scientists have usually gone along with the dominant trend in their professions and concentrated on men, whose activities seemed more important and appeared more structured. The result was to reinforce the idea that the important activities—those worthy of study and theorization—were those carried on exclusively or predominantly by men. There seems little doubt that a social science that virtually ignored or distorted the role of women was (and often still is) a social science yielding a distorted picture of society as a whole—just as a social science that spoke predominantly of the achievements of ruling classes and ethnic groups and said little of workers, peasants, nomads, ethnic minorities, slaves, and serfs gave a distorted picture of society's functioning.

Some who have not read serious works in women's studies say that it separates women from society as a whole, unnaturally dividing social groups. One may affirm from reading this book alone that the opposite is true: many of its essays deal with women's interactions with the family and all its members. A focus on Middle Eastern women greatly broadens our perspective on the Middle Eastern traditional family. The tremendous importance given to a bride's virginity, the preference for early marriage, the overwhelming evaluation of the wife as a producer of sons and hence maltreatment of a (presumed) sterile or exclusively daughter-producing wife, and the relatively freer roles for women when they are not sexually vulnerable—in early childhood or after menopause—are all explained in a variety of essays herein, as are the nature of a girl's relations with her parents and brothers, and later with her husband and in-laws. So, instead of a "narrow" focus on women cut off from men or from male-dominated society, there is a deepened picture of male and female interrelationships at different stages of their lives, in different roles, and among different social classes.

It is sometimes held that women should be studied almost exclusively as a part, if perhaps the most important part, of the family complex. But this is a distortion that diminishes the numerous roles of women and puts blinders on scholars, limiting the multiple perspectives from which women, often even the same women, may be seen. Leaving aside those large areas in Africa, the Caribbean, and elsewhere where women do most of the agricultural work and carry out long-distance as well as local trading, even in far more "usual" societies women are involved in activities that are not to be studied primarily from the point of view of the family. First, nearly all women *work,* often from early childhood. This simple fact has been obfuscated by the tendency of Western industrial societies to regard as work only what is directly paid, and to adopt this definition in censuses throughout the world. Yet in precapitalist societies and even in parts of Third World societies today, such a distinction makes no sense, however widely it is used. A man whose main occupation is raising grain for his own family and who must either give part of the crop to a landlord or sell it below value is generally listed in a census as a *full-time worker,* while his wife who raises and tends the domestic animals, helps in weeding, harvesting, and gleaning, grinds the grain, processes products for market, cleans house, gives birth and raises the children, and perhaps produces handicrafts that are sold by her husband is often listed as *economically inactive* even though these tasks are as crucial to the perpetuation of family and society as are his. Even if we bow to the current fashion that housework, childbearing, and childrearing are not work, all careful observers note the heavy labor in connection with agriculture and domestic animals carried out by women. And yet, for the Middle East at least, this work never appears in censuses (except in Turkey) to approach anywhere its true extent. Finally, there are other forms of work, too. There are workers in traditional occupations, such as hired fieldworkers, weavers and craftspeople, midwives and curers, dancers and singers, prostitutes, domestic servants, and others. In modern times women initially entered roles that most closely resembled their traditional tasks—teachers, nurses (although these were at first low-ranked), workers in segregated handicraft shops and factories. From the upper classes, as small numbers began to be educated at home and abroad, women entered the fields of literature, art, and various professions, and gradually were found in almost every field in the more economically developed countries. In both traditional and modern milieus it appears true in the Middle East, as in most parts of the world, that women, on the average, work longer hours than men, usually receiving little or nothing in wages.

Family and Lineage Patterns

Family and lineage ties are of great importance in most milieus, especially in villages, among nomads, and among the traditional urban upper classes. Village and tribal groups tend to consist of related families and lineages. Many are subject to control by landlords or government representatives whose interest is to forestall unified action and demands. Lineage factions, which on the one hand arise from within the lineage system, are, on the other, often encouraged by powerful outsiders in order to divide and rule. With frequent local disputes over land, water, outside favor, and rights, it is in each family's and lineage's interest to be as strong as possible, and strength has long been largely equated with number of sons.[1]

Family and lineage solidarity is strengthened by preferred endogamous marriages, although the theoretical preference for marriage between a male and his father's brother's daughter is met only in a minority of cases. Marriage is, as in other traditional societies, a social and not an individual or romantic proposition. The bride must be a virgin, not only to preserve family (and often lineage or tribal) honor, of which she is a symbol, but to try to ensure that her children will be fathered only by her husband. From an early age, a girl's mother, father, brothers, and perhaps others in the patrilineal group control her movements and activities. Her family tries to marry her off as soon as possible after puberty, and sometimes before. Groom and bride are supposed to give consent in marriage, but in most cases their parents have means to force consent. In addition to preferences for marriage between kin (other considerations sometimes predominate), the bridewealth that a groom or groom's family can pay is an important factor in his acceptability as a spouse. Part of this is paid before or on marriage, and it may only cover the bride's trousseau. The rest is held back in case of divorce or the husband's death, but despite the legality of the custom and the contract embodying it, it is often not paid when due. The bride is desired primarily as a producer of sons, although her personal characteristics are a feature. (In villages and nomadic groups the groom has often seen her before from a distance, or as part of his kin or neighborhood group.) If the bride does not produce sons, it is seen, in both countryside and town, as her fault, and the husband is more likely than he would be otherwise to exercise his option to divorce her or take a second wife.

The desire for many sons is not irrational, even today. The strength of both family and lineage depends largely on the number of its males, and even if some must find all or part of their work away from home, they send back money that helps the family. High infant mortality makes several sons an insurance that at least one will survive to carry on the family, which in these patrilineal societies is counted only in the male line. Since daughters usually join a different family upon marriage, it is primarily sons who provide economic help to their parents after marriage and especially during their parents' old age. A mother gains status and power through her sons, whom she attaches to herself and who support and protect her. After a number of children the woman may wish to cease childbearing, but she rarely talks to her husband of such matters, and is frequently prejudiced by midwives and others against birth control.

Villagers

The literature on the Middle East suggests that different forms of production lead to typically different forms of working life and family and to different ideas of proper behavior for both women and men. What follows is an "ideal typical" picture of the Muslim Middle East—not an exact description of any group but a distillation of a number of studies which often reveal remarkably similar patterns in similar surroundings.

Most villagers concentrate on agriculture, with stockraising and handicrafts as secondary occupations. Before the impact of the world market, capitalism, and imperialism, which began before the nineteenth century but increased rapidly from then on, villages were both more self-sufficient and less class-stratified than they are today. This meant that families, and particularly women, were occupied with jobs like weaving, sewing, and food processing for domestic needs, producing goods that are now mostly purchased. In most areas the agricultural surplus went primarily to taxes and/or a landlord, rather than being sold in sometimes distant markets, as is true today. The complementarity of men's and women's tasks was clear in the traditional village, and there were rarely alternative models to challenge existing sex roles. Occasionally, heresies or Sufi orders appealing to villagers as well as city people advocated and practiced a more egalitarian status between sexes, thus rejecting parts of the traditional pattern.

With the introduction of cheap Western manufactured imports to the Middle East, aided by Western-enforced low tariffs, and of Western demand for Eastern goods, villages became increasingly commercialized and class-stratified, and also increasingly controlled by, first, commercially oriented landlords and moneylenders, and, second, by the government bureaucracy. The growth of Western manufactured imports removed many of the tasks of both women and men, and if local income was insufficient to meet needs, men or entire families increasingly had to migrate from the village, temporarily or permanently. Capitalist market relations, as elsewhere, led to greater village stratification, with those at the bottom often reduced to the status of seasonal migrants or laborers and those at the top imitating town ways, recently including veiling—a sign that the family's women did not have to work or expose themselves to circumstances that would threaten their honor. Lineage solidarity began to break down and class divisions were felt, although the continuation of (externally encouraged) factions has helped prevent class feeling from becoming too highly developed in most cases. What exists now in most villages, for both women and men, is some mixture of traditional and modern ways.

One example may suggest how complex this mixture can be. Carpets in Iran used to be produced primarily in the home (or tent area), mainly for domestic use. With the rise in Western demand for Persian carpets, which grew from the late nineteenth century, Western and Iranian businessmen began producing carpets on a commercial basis, either by setting up large workshops in towns or using a "putting out" system, whereby they supplied looms and dyed wool and paid those who worked at home on a piecework basis. For a time the number of large workshops grew, but in recent years the trend has reversed. Factory legislation, compulsory employer welfare contributions, a law against employing children under twelve (often enforced in large workshops), and the declining profitability of carpets as compared with other investments have led to a drastic reduction in large workshops and a return to the putting out system, employing mainly village women and girls, whose labor is the cheapest. Although those villagers who own their own looms and can afford the raw material, and who can wait until their carpets are finished to sell are better off, those who work for others or must borrow often receive minimal compensation, and the rooms in which women and small girls work are often dark, damp, and unhealthy. In addition, the husband sells the carpet and controls its profits. Small girls suffer from this employment, although the advance of universal education, more than the child labor law, is reducing the hours spent by young girls on the loom. Wages, although very low, are rising, and the beginnings of carpet cooperatives in Iran are a hopeful sign.

Nomadic Pastoralists

Many features of village society are also found in the nomadic societies that once covered vast areas, but whose territories have been shrinking. In ecologically marginal areas of the Middle East and on its periphery, nomadic tribes, often speaking minority languages, ignoring various orthodox customs, and exhibiting a posture of pride and independence, continue to flourish, although with economic and political change, new relations between tribes and states have emerged.

Nomadic and seminomadic tribes are distinguished by their concentration on stock-raising (sheep, goats, camels) and, because of their marginal environment, by their need to migrate among pasture areas to find sufficient pastoral resources for their stock. They often carry on some agriculture (and they have close relations with agriculturalists), but this is often subsidiary to their main mode of production. Like village women, nomadic women work very hard—they milk and care for numerous animals; process pastoral products such as cheese and butter; weave tents, tent furnishings, and sometimes carpets; make clothing; and, of course, do domestic and maternal chores. In some areas the women, after the male occupations of fighting and raiding died out, do nearly all the physical labor; to the men are left the tasks associated with political relations and contacts with tribal leaders and the sedentary community. Family and lineage ties, bridal virginity, and numerous sons are as important to nomads as to villagers—family and lineage strength perhaps even more so. Outside observers, seeing nomadic women unveiled and striding about with apparent freedom, may get the impression that social intercourse between males and females is much freer among nomads than among others, but this should not be exaggerated. Boys and girls do not generally play together, and men and women do not really mix—and the same may be said of those villagers who remain unveiled. Contacts between women and unrelated men are quite limited. However, the tent schools of the nomadic Qashqa'i of Iran have had success in attracting girls to mixed classes led by male and female teachers, and it is probably true that barriers to sexual desegregation are fewer among such tribes than elsewhere, and women somewhat more independent.

As with villagers, nomads have been affected by the rise of capitalist market relations and the related growth of government power. The most obvious effect has been the settling of many nomads and their conversion into agriculturalists, which was often encouraged or forced by centralizing governments who found armed, mobile, and independent tribes a threat. Even in tribes that continue to be nomadic, however, there is greater dependence on market exchange than before: nomads sell meat, wool, hides, milk products, carpets, woven goods, and agricultural products in greater amounts than previously, and in return buy more foods, machine textiles, and other manufactured goods. As in villages, stratification has probably grown and lineage solidarity decreased; the wealthy men (and sometimes women) of the tribe may receive a modern education in the city or abroad and adopt Western ways, visiting the tribe infrequently, if at all. The ordinary tribeswoman may produce handicrafts on a time schedule and out of a family's need for money rather than primarily for the tent. As with the village woman, a middleman usually gets much of the profit, and the husband sells the goods and controls the money.

Town and City Dwellers

The situation in the towns and cities is harder to characterize because of greater class divisions, diversity of occupations, importance of state institutions, and so forth. In peasant villages and in pastoral tribes, where men are involved with subsistence production, most women have complementary tasks associated with this production. As noted, women may do more of the work connected with subsistence than do men, who become increasingly involved with extradomestic economic and political relationships, which often draw them away from the home for long periods.

As soon as the male becomes involved in wage labor, as in Middle Eastern towns and cities, production is almost always drawn away from the domestic unit and into the marketplace or an occupational center, thus severing the woman from association with this work. Although she is relieved of the backbreaking tasks of agriculture or animal husbandry, she is also denied the fruits of this labor, in the form of products to prepare, to sell perhaps, and, importantly, to use in reciprocal exchanges with kin, neighbor, and friend. Some women in towns and cities produce and market various goods and services, but on the whole their access to the public domain of economic and political systems is restricted, largely because of ideological beliefs relating to sexual segregation and female seclusion.

Traditionally limited to urban upper and middle classes, severe veiling and seclusion were signs that a man could afford to have servants do the household shopping and errands and that he occupied an economic position that allowed him to protect the honor of his family from abuse. Recently, veiling and seclusion have become much more complex social phenomena. While the wealthier classes educated in Western ways have increasingly abandoned veiling and seclusion, these practices, ironically, have spread among the lower-middle and lower classes. In Turkey (where Ataturk never outlawed the veil, despite frequent statements to the contrary, but did discourage it very strongly), the post-world War II period has seen a rapid spread of the veil in small towns, and even villages, where it had scarcely existed before. This was partly a sign of status—the lower classes imitating the bazaar bourgeoisie, and men showing themselves capable of "inconspicuous consumption." It was also due to the breaking forth of religious and traditionalist values that had been strongly discouraged under Ataturk. In Iran, which was, to our knowledge, the only non-Communist country ever to outlaw the veil (and its enveloping *chador*)—under Reza Shah in 1936—there was a strong revival of the chador after his abdication in 1941. Today, although the best-educated classes and those who work in Western-style offices, especially in Tehran, have abandoned the chador, it has spread rapidly in the countryside.[2] Some villagers in North Africa seclude and veil their wives as soon as they accumulate a little economic surplus.[3] In postindependence Algeria and Morocco, the veil has both spread to new classes and continued among the urban bourgeoisie, among whom it is felt to be in part a nationalist or "Islamic" reaction against French ways and Western denigration of Islamic customs.[4] In the past decade, however, veiling has noticeably decreased in Morocco.

In sum, although it is often loosely said by people who visit only the major Middle Eastern cities or who do not know what things were like some forty years ago, that the veil is disappearing, it is our impression that currently the veil, if one considers the entire Middle East, is probably spreading. This is not necessarily a cause for discouragement since, in itself, the veil is probably much less important in women's lives in many contemporary environments than most people think. Also, history moves in contradictory waves, not in straight lines, and there is little doubt that the growing forces of education and employment, plus the increase in women's activity on their own behalf, will eventually cause the elimination of the *forced* use of the veil—leaving it as at most a variable item of women's choice, like the lacy, transparent chadors sometimes worn over miniskirts in Iran. Ironically, the property and inheritance rights of veiled urban women have often been better complied with than those of unveiled rural and tribal women.[5]

An urban group with special problems, often discussed in literature, are women whose origins may be village or town lower or middle bourgeoisie, but who are married to urban men with whom and with whose families they had no previous contact. This man often keeps his wife strictly veiled and secluded to proclaim his status and hers; by tradition she cannot go out without his permission, which he seldom grants. Unlike the village or tribal girls who, after marriage, often live near and frequently visit their natal families and women of their lineage and neighborhood, this young wife may be almost without company; if her in-laws are present, it is rather as masters than as friends. Although we need more evidence, it seems that these young women are in a more trying position than those of their class would have been some time ago, when seclusion was not as strict. It should be noted that the literature describing them comes mostly from North Africa, one of the strictest areas of seclusion today, and the images provided in this volume of women of the same or lower social classes show much more sociability. The phenomenon exists outside North Africa, however, and it has been suggested that such women evince a high rate of mental illness. Permitted neither to work nor to visit, they are kept *purely* as mothers, sexual objects, and representatives of men's honor—roles played by most other women who also have, however, the advantages of friends, families, visiting, and ceremonies.

Another group that often appears in the literature as unhappy and frustrated are those who have had a taste of what a freer, more modern life could be, but who then must return to traditional patterns. These are primarily girls who are sent to modern schools and may have friends from modern families, but who are then pulled from school soon before or upon puberty (as are a large proportion of Muslim schoolgirls), secluded more closely than before, and married off to men with whom they may not be acquainted, with childhood freedoms and career plans crushed. Whether these girls enter the ranks of the near solitaries mentioned above, or whether they continue to have some contact with friends and families, they return to a traditional pattern of subordination to husband and mother-in-law, breeding and childcare, and strict limits on outside activities.

There are increasing numbers of women in a variety of urban jobs, but, as Nadia Youssef has shown, the percentages of Middle Eastern Muslim women in such jobs are among the lowest in the world.[6] Discrimination on the job and at home is least at the top levels. Female doctors, lawyers, artists, professors, teachers, nurses, secretaries, other professionals, and even high-level government personnel are to be found in the Muslim countries significantly influenced by modernization, though their absolute numbers may be small. Beginning with the late nineteenth century, it has been the upper- and middle-class groups with the most ties to the West and to Westerners who have adopted Western life styles, including greater freedom and education for women.

On the working-class level, textile workers predominate in both machine and hand workshops, and in both they are usually segregated by sex. Other working-class jobs exist and, as in much of the world, nearly all working-class and lower professional jobs for women are distinguished by significantly lower salaries than those in which men are employed. Nor can "work" be automatically equated with "liberation." The professional woman whose family has a relatively high income can afford servants to cook, clean, and care for children, and her burden at home is reduced. This is not true of most working-class women, who at best may have female relatives with whom to leave small children, but who still do much household work. Traditional Middle Eastern men, aside from those who do the shopping mainly to keep their wives from straying far from home, do not take on household work to any degree, even if their wives work full-time—the same, of course, can be said of men elsewhere. However, some real progress has been shown in many countries in women's education and their increasing entry into better and better-paid jobs. Where upper-class women might once have been content with self-beautification and gossip, they are more frequently entering jobs and professions where they have contact with both men and women, and their husbands, who are also exposed to modern ways, are increasingly accepting and even encouraging this.

Western and Indigenous Capitalism

Many of the phenomena noted above, such as the removal of many women from some of their productive activities as more goods and services came to be purchased, were a result of capitalism and often of imperialism. In the Third World, as probably also in the West, a long "early" period of capitalist development was generally (and for much of the Third World still is) characterized by the rich getting richer and the poor poorer. In both areas this early capitalist period was also characterized by many nonelite women losing employment and status. In the Middle East, as elsewhere, the impact of capitalism has thus been differential for men and women, and the changes for women require separate study from those for men.

The Western impact often benefited existing middle and upper classes, and also created new classes involved in foreign trade or professions that closely tied them to Westerners, especially, but not exclusively, in the colonized countries. Such Westernized middle- and upper-class elements were generally represented ideologically by thinkers who advocated moderate political reformism along Western lines, and often spoke out for women's rights, as did the Egyptians Muhammad ʿAbduh, Qasim Amin, and also various twentieth-century liberal nationalist thinkers. The centrality in the minds of such thinkers of the idea that women must be educated primarily in order to educate their families is one found among early advocates of women's rights the world over, and it is no accident that early feminism everywhere seems to have followed the early development of capitalism. The education of boys and girls by modern schools and by mothers with a modern education is increasingly needed in a variety of positions to instill habits and values needed by capitalism: punctuality, the ability to stay in one place for hours doing dull tasks according to a strict schedule, willingness to take orders from a stranger, a scientific rather than superstitious approach to life, and so forth. Capitalism also requires some women in the labor force in specific jobs: teachers, nurses, doctors, and social workers for women, and also low-paid factory and workshop workers. The role of intellectuals who appealed to the Western-tied upper- and middle-class groups in pushing for increased women's rights was thus not based purely on imitation of the West, but had indigenous bases in the needs of capitalism. They were at first opposed by some in their own class group, as ideas favorable to a nascent socioeconomic system are generally favored at first by a small minority.

The differential impact of capitalism on different groups helps explain the diverse ideas and actions of different socioeconomic classes regarding the issues of women's rights. If the Western impact, and even Western rule, was advantageous to an important section of the upper and new middle classes, it was often harmful to the traditional or bazaar bourgeoisie, petty bourgeoisie, and manual workers in both town and countryside. This is one reason why the traditional groups were less inclined to admire and emulate Western ways than the upper and new middle classes. Another is that Western ways were, at least until very recently, less advantageous to the traditional groups. Rural and nomadic children could learn in the home and community environment all they needed for economic and social functioning; literacy and modern ideas were not helpful to those who, for the most part, could not afford the investment needed to do their work in more modern ways, even had there been specialists around to teach them how. In the traditional rural or nomadic environment women's schooling and modern rights could not be seen as serving any useful function. Bazaar merchants and artisans often felt directly the ruinous competition of Western goods, and, later on, of the larger commercial and industrial enterprises of their own Westernized upper class. They and the urban workers therefore frequently turned against the Western liberal ideology associated with Western and Westernized oppressors and competitors, and adopted nationalist ideologies that were anti-imperialist and stressed the values of the Islamic past. The de facto antifeminism of Mustafa Kamil and the Muslim Brethren in Egypt, and of the current leadership in Algeria and Libya, is based largely on this type of urban following. This "neotraditionalist" attitude, with its strong anti-Western component, is more likely to appear in countries that have been colonies and hence have developed the most persistent anti-imperialist ideologies, than in those that have not, like Iran, Turkey, and China, where women's liberation has moved more rapidly than in most of the ex-colonies.[7] Only where there have been efforts by leftist movements to mobilize masses of women and men around women's emancipation, as in South Yemen, Dhofar (Oman), and sections of the Sudanese and Palestinian movements, has there been effective education and action by women and men of the lower classes in favor of a radical improvement in status for women of all classes. Thus far, there has been little scholarly discussion of the impact of capitalism and imperialism on women of different social classes, and on ideologies regarding women.

Tradition and Change

Among urban workers, peasants, and nomads, traditional familial relations and attitudes still hold sway, for reasons that some of the essays begin to discuss, but that no one has yet fully explained. Briefly, one may say that the desire for many sons still appears functional to the rural classes, where child labor is needed in peak agricultural seasons and where sons increase the power of family and lineage. The lack of direct experience of such novelties as the utility of female education, the possibility that men and women can be alone together without having sexual relations, or the increased prosperity of a family with fewer children makes rural people understandably skeptical of those who advocate such ideas. "Religion" and "what is right" are inextricably mixed with tradition, and religious leaders tend to propagandize for the old ways as the only ones compatible with religion and virtue. And, indeed, "innovation" is traditionally evil in Islam, so that people are likely to heed their religious leaders. This is not merely a matter of rural conservatism: many practical experiments have demonstrated that, when peasants can be shown that a particular innovation will be directly beneficial to them, they adopt it. The problem with changes in family structure and childbearing is that such demonstrations have rarely been made, and in many countries could not be made without social changes too radical to be desired by existing governments. An improvement in the position of women might involve encouraging women to organize independently, which could temporarily alienate many men until they find how little they really gained from their previous privileges. It might involve governments' enforcing laws on minimum marriage ages, limiting men's rights to divorce and free repudiations, and so forth, not only in the cities but also in the towns and countryside—which again would be temporarily unpopular with the men. It could involve major programs to train village girls as nurses, midwives, paramedics, teachers, and agricultural specialists, on condition that they spend some years back in their own villages so that villagers could see at first hand the advantage to them of educating girls. Some of these are only tentative ideas, others based on programs now being tried in various Middle Eastern countries. The force of tradition is not simply a self-perpetuating hesitancy to change, but is based on positive values that traditional ways have provided, particularly for the male and dominant members of society, but also for many women who get satisfaction from their children, relatives, and communities. To break with tradition so that the majority of women, children, and also men become freer than they are today, programs must be sought in which those now tied to tradition can actively and willingly participate. This not only could modify current value systems, but in many areas is a prerequisite to material improvements and rising incomes.

Muslim countries now have the world's highest rate of population increase on record, and in most, these rates are still rising.[8] Except for the few oil-rich countries (which, as long as their oil holds out, can increase their per capita gross national product), such rapid population rate increases, along with the resultant huge population of children who consume more than they produce and of mothers of many babies who contribute little to production, mean that per capita GNP is rising painfully slowly, remaining stationary, or even falling. Thus, the position of women and attitudes toward women as early and continuous childbearing instruments radically affect living standards and the entire economy. The correlation of family law reform and female education with women's employment and lower birth rates indicates that educational opportunities and legal reform can help to change traditional ways. The striking legal changes and encouragement of women's organization in revolutionary South Yemen suggest what can be accomplished by a dedicated government and women's movement.

If such data seem to point to future change, other facts suggest the painful slowness of change in many areas, particularly if we focus, as does this book, on the lower-class majority, rather than the upper-class and professional elite. In the 1920s and 1930s Ataturk launched in Turkey a series of reforms that has yet to be matched for Muslims anywhere outside the Communist world. Completely replacing the *sharia* (Islamic law) with the Swiss Civil Code in matters of family and personal status, he thereby outlawed polygamy and man's right to unilateral repudiation of his wife, and established civil marriage as the only legally recognized form. As a revolutionary hero who had led the rescue of Turkey from its European foes and as the inheritor of over a century of Ottoman reforms, Ataturk was in a position of strength unmatched by any subsequent Muslim leader. What was not widely realized outside Turkey until after World War II was that Ataturk's family reforms have not to this day been completely carried out, especially in eastern rural areas.[9] Thus, many marriages are performed only according to Muslim rules and not registered; some husbands still repudiate their wives and others take second wives, so that the Turkish Assembly has had to legitimize millions of civilly illegitimate children. There has also been a revival of the veil and of seclusion in towns and some villages since World War II, along with the increasing influence of the Muslim *ulama* (religious scholars) in those areas and of their propaganda for seclusion. Despite these negative features, however, education for women continues to expand, as does the range and number of jobs open to them.

Similar contradictions may be noted in the Muslim country with the next most radical laws concerning women (outside the Communist world), Tunisia. President Bourguiba did not take Ataturk's path of scrapping the sharia, which might have been difficult in an Arab country, given the Arabs' special identification with Islam, but rather took the route of the radical reinterpreters of Islam and the Quran. Polygamy was outlawed (making Tunisia and Turkey the only non-Communist countries yet to do this) on the grounds that the Quran's demand that all co-wives be treated equally, being impossible to fulfill, had really intended to negate polygamy. Tunisia was also ahead in marriage and divorce reform, in efforts to educate and unveil girls, and in setting up active women's organizations. As with Turkey, much was accomplished, but again as with Turkey, the reforms were not pushed hard enough in the countryside, and there has been a move backward as the radical element was dismissed from Tunisia's government and the president himself became a less forceful reformist. Yet in both Tunisia and Turkey some loss in government impetus is counteracted by the force of events—the growth of education, temporary migration abroad, industrial enterprises, the need for skilled labor, and so on, all of which lead gradually to some improvement in the position of women and to a growth of urbanization which, if it does not improve women's status immediately, tends to do so in the long run.

Somewhat parallel to the cases of official rapid advance followed by later backsliding, is that of Algeria, where women's hopes were aroused not so much by egalitarian laws as by the role played by women fighters in the Algerian revolution, followed by the sexually egalitarian words of the Algerian Constitution. These words were not followed by serious laws or actions, however, as the governments of Ben Bella and, even more, Boumedienne catered to the beliefs of their petty-bourgeois male supporters and propagandized for the return of women to the home and to old ways. The existence of huge unemployment in postindependence Algeria (paralleled on a somewhat smaller scale elsewhere in the Maghreb and the Middle East) made many men hostile to the idea of women as competitors for jobs and open to the easy arguments of "back to the home," rather than to more radical or socialist attempts at solution.[10]

It is not only the Middle East that has seen backward steps on the tortuous road to women's freedom, however, as indicated by the multifaceted and successful campaign in the United States for a return to home and large family after World War II. The poignancy of the Middle Eastern situation, however, is that, today at least, Muslim women can be shown to be behind the rest of the world by most of the indexes generally used for advance in human rights. Fewer women are educated in the Muslim world than in other culture areas, and although the absolute number of women educated is growing, so is the gap between women and men. The percentage of women working other than in agriculture is probably the smallest in the world, the birth rate the highest, and the laws regarding marriage and related matters most unequal. Nor do the life situations faced by that majority of women with little education or wealth modify this picture significantly, despite the positive elements found in many women's domestic and social lives.

On the other hand, there is no doubt that there have been very significant advances, made particularly by urbanized and educated women, in most Middle Eastern countries. This is clearly true in Turkey and Tunisia, in Egypt (despite its lag in legal reform), in Iran, and to a varying degree in Arab Asia and the Maghreb. It seems reasonable to hope that the continued spread of education, legal reform, urbanization, and industrialization, along with more serious birth control and extension programs, vocational training, literacy programs, and the demand for labor in a variety of modern jobs (many of them requiring contact between the sexes), will lead to further positive changes in women's roles and sexual relationships.

The activities of women's rights movements of various kinds in many countries and the role of women in revolutionary and political movements demonstrate the political, intellectual, and organizing capabilities of women and their courage and strength in the face of adversity and danger. These forces apply pressure on often reluctant governments and individuals to bring about changes. The radical socialist regime in South Yemen has not only put through legal reforms about as sweeping as Tunisia's but has encouraged women's organizing for their rights. Women have also played important roles in leftist and revolutionary movements in the Sudan, among Palestinians, in Dhofar (Oman), and in other places.

The present volume contains numerous in-depth studies of many aspects of the lives of those women who make up the majority of women in society—peasants, nomads, lower- and lower-middle-class town and city women—but it leaves much room for further studies of elite women, of women's movements, and of women in politics and the public domain. The emphasis on the former groups of women, so often neglected in the past, is healthy, but the latter groups must also be studied more if a balanced picture of not only women's past and present, but also their probable future, is to be achieved. Today the elite Westernized woman may be worlds, and seemingly centuries, away from her village compatriot, and the picture presented of a rural or nomadic Middle Eastern woman is not valid for women as a whole. To take an obvious and easily duplicated example, one need only note the number of Middle Eastern authors from many countries contributing to this volume and other academic works.

The story of Middle Eastern women, like most historical and social phenomena, is a highly mixed and dialectical one: amazingly rapid change in formerly traditional, now revolutionary, South Yemen and in Kuwait, which lacks a strong conservative rural hinterland or a powerful ulama; explicitly conservative sexual ideologies in Saudi Arabia (which, however, is slowly changing) and Libya (also a country with contradictory features); less dramatic trends in most of the Middle East, which thus far have affected mostly the upper classes, and have included partial steps backward from more dramatic changes, as in Tunisia, Turkey, and Algeria. With industrialization, as with the West's own industrial revolution, some developments are initially negative for women, but contain the seeds for further advance. Putting women into large carpet workshops or mechanized factories with low pay and long hours probably makes the lives of most of them worse than when work was done at home. On the other hand, industrialization has now begun to foster factory and maternity laws in many countries, and over time compliance with law grows. Increased enforcement of laws establishing factory literacy classes, minimum wages, and child care facilities may bring a situation where a female wage worker can be better off than a woman who does not work for wages. Such changes, along with increased education and urbanization, should also lead to lower birth rates, which will benefit both family and region.

Such optimistic possibilities will not, however, occur automatically. The struggles and activities of women, as well as the foresight and understanding of some men—not only the obvious Ataturks and Bourguibas, but a variety of planners, rural workers, trade unionists, and political progressives—have been needed to achieve the progress attained to date and will be even more necessary in the future.

The "value-free" social scientist may object to the use of "value-laden" words in the above discussion, but it seems impossible to read many of the essays herein without concluding that there is, by current Western standards and possibilities, something lacking in the lives of most Middle Eastern women, whatever satisfactions and positive features these lives may often contain. The lack of material satisfactions for most men and women is clear, but this is not the place to discuss it. What most Middle Eastern women lack when compared either with their wealthier and better educated compatriots or with Western women of many social classes, is freedom of choice regarding basic life decisions. In most cases, a girl's parents decide whether and for how long she goes to school; the parents of both parties decide on the marriage partner (this limits the boy too, but he often can turn to other sexual partners or repudiate his spouse, which she cannot easily do) ; the mother-in-law and husband rule over much of the young wife's life, and the husband can, de jure or de facto, decide if the wife can work for wages, at what kind of job, and whether she can use any of her wages if she works. The husband, according to religious law, receives custody of children (after a certain age) after divorce; women are thereby suddenly cut off from those by whom their role as females is defined, and are denied the continuing satisfactions of the maternal role. Most women are not allowed to remain unmarried, even after an early divorce, or to live alone. Women are threatened with repudiation or with a second wife being brought into the house if they do not bear sons. Many women find considerable satisfactions in traditional family life, but their legal and customary status is often precarious.

Other means of control include the physical and psychological domination of the male over the female. Some Middle Eastern men are diverted from larger economic and political struggles by venting frustration and aggression at home. In North Africa woman is widely believed to be the "rope of Satan" (just as Eve induced Adam to eat of the apple of evil proffered by the serpent Satan). Troubles may be blamed on women's evil or witchcraft instead of analyzed rationally. A man's frustrations on the job can be taken out by beating his wife—a legitimate activity in traditionalist circles, although far from universal.

Even subject to the contraints of male-dominated society, women are not completely subject to forces outside their control, and they have a variety of strategies enabling them to mitigate the effects of male control. To the female belongs the domestic domain, and the tasks she performs there are by right exclusive to her. In controlling much of this domain, she partially controls its inhabitants, including men. She largely determines the quality of care she offers, which she manipulates according to her attitudes. "Poison in the stew" is the extreme female response to male oppression, but is reflected in dozens of less dramatic acts: an unkept house, noise when the husband is entertaining, insufficient food for guests, unruly children, and so forth, all of which cast uncomplimentary light on the husband and his supposed control over her. Part of his honor is defined by the degree of this control, and a woman by subtle means can undermine it.

Another traditional response by females to subordination is manipulation of sexuality. The woman, through alluring stance and suggestive remark (traditionally a tendril of hair or the jingling of jewelry was said to be sufficient to drive a man to distraction), can entice a man away from the "rational" world of men, into the uncontrolled and unpredictable world of sensuality. Equally, she can deprive him of pleasure by refusing sex or by making sex impossible by attacking his virility. If she can demean him in the public eye, especially by showing interest in another man, she has cast doubt on his masculinity, a symbol of his powers in the secular world.

Female associations, powerful in cultures where social institutions and values inhibit most efforts by women to establish solidarity in one another, can challenge male domination. Lasting female contacts challenge the idea that women are subject to the exclusive control of men. Women's position and roles in neighborhood associations and bilateral kinship networks also have potential for women's communications and interactions. Women exercise some control over men's affairs through gossip, intrigue, and ridicule;

through similar techniques they influence the maintenance of behavioral standards among women. Women thus support their own position by controlling those who are "deviant" and threatening. Such self-policing prevents males from punishing all women because of the actions of a few, and keeps men from knowing the facts of female behavior and interaction.

Another exercise of power is through religion and the supernatural. Attendance at saints' tombs, ecstatic performances, and curing and life crisis rituals serve to detach the female from the control of the male. Men may doubt the efficacy of some such acts by women, yet fear the dangers that meddling with their powers might bring. Mental and physical illness, too, is a way of (temporarily) alleviating the stresses of subordination. A man prohibited by cultural beliefs from performing domestic and child care tasks, and unknowledgeable in them, cannot cope with an incapacitated wife and may ply her with attention, favors, and even wealth to secure her well-being.

For the nonelite classes and increasingly for the elite, the achievement of equality and greater freedom of choice requires successful struggles for daycare centers, for creative ways to share housework and child care, for good part-time jobs, for planned fuller employment, for a reduction in the growing income gap between the rich and poor in both the oil and nonoil countries, and for planning for the general social good, with the involvement in local and central planning of those whose lives are to be affected, male and female. These are goals that have yet to be achieved in most of the West. Insofar as Western or indigenous capitalists and governments profit from cheap Middle Eastern labor and goods, including cheap female and migrant labor, and from unusually profitable investments and sales, the fight for a more humane society for women and men involves continuing political and social struggles against those with a large stake in the status quo.

As women's liberation movements and their male allies in the West have begun to point out, women's liberation will also mean men's liberation. The man who cannot choose his wife, who wants a wife not sexually knowledgeable, who prefers that she contribute little or nothing to the family income, who cannot freely talk with women outside his family and has little social contact even with his wife, and who must maintain a macho image surrounded by the requirements and taboos of masculine behavior is surely less free and has a less rich life than one with freer choices. In widening the areas of free choice for both men and women both East and West have far to go; but the directional signs are not discouraging.

The Historical Context

In a book that deals partly with history, and almost in toto with institutions that have evolved over a long period, it seems useful to discuss some historical and even prehistorical questions about how women's status in the Middle East arose, even though much of this is necessarily speculative. Research on women's history in the Middle East has been scarce, not because historians are more male-oriented than other social scientists, but because documentation, particularly for the premodern period, is harder to find than are the living documents of anthropology and sociology. The historical papers included in this volume suggest what might be done, and much more evidence remains to be culled in legal records, censuses, tax records, wills, biographical dictionaries, literature, and the arts, to name only a few sources. What follows does not attempt to summarize what little is known about women's past in the Islamic Middle East, but rather to raise, and try tentatively to answer, some rather theoretical questions. These questions are: Why and how did male dominance arise in human society? Did male dominance increase when society became city-centered and class-divided, and, if so, how and why? To what extent is and was male dominance in the Islamic Middle East similar to many other parts of the world; to what extent did Islam contribute something unique?

The question of how and why male dominance arose in human society is, in a sense, purely theoretical: it is very doubtful that we will have proof of an answer. It may be noted, however, that although there were and are numerous preliterate societies where the position of women is relatively high (women occasionally entered into political councils or even became rulers; sexual and associational freedoms were sometimes allowed; women's economic contributions to society could be both great and recognized), there has never been proof of a matriarchy (a society where women as a group actually and consistently rule). Some societies have myths of matriarchy, which along with particular customs formed the foundation of various past scholarly theories of matriarchy, but unless more evidence is forthcoming, the idea of matriarchy, stricto senso, cannot be taken as a point of scholarly departure. What can be said is that in nearly all preliterate societies, which means societies without large economic surpluses to support cities or ruling classes, the basic division of labor has been between men and women. Men's work is nearly always valued above women's work, although often not to the degree found in class societies. Why a sexual division of labor should have arisen is not hard to imagine: the woman's role as childbearer and nurser kept her close to the home and to the tasks necessary for childrearing. Because of his freedom from pregnancy and nursing, and probably because of his greater physical strength, man became the trader, explorer, hunter, and fighter. Man's mobility, his travels, his superior ability to defend the home and to face predators and enemies must have been factors in early male dominance, despite women's frequent provision of a major portion of family subsistence through food-gathering. Men, not tied to the hearth or childrearing, were able to engage in extrafamily and extragroup contacts that helped to build economic, political, and military systems. These male-dominated systems netted the male not only prestige and status but much of society's economic surplus, which he used to further his domination of the family.

Preclass societies have a range of attitudes on virginity, fidelity, polygamy, and so forth, but in general seem less concerned with these issues than are class societies. Many of the features relating to attitudes about women noted as typical of Middle Eastern society, particularly in its rural areas, are not peculiar to the Middle East. Many have existed in southern Europe, parts of eastern Europe, China, India, and elsewhere. These areas have contained most of the following features: boy babies are valued more highly than girl babies, even on occasion to the point of female infanticide or sale. Girls are brought up to fill maternal and domestic roles: as they grow older they often mix less with boys, are more protected, and are very rarely educated. Marriages are controlled by the family: the girl may be engaged as an infant, she is married near puberty, and is expected in most cases to be a virgin. She goes to live with her in-laws, where she is subject first to her mother-in-law, and next to her husband and his relatives. She gains status only after the birth of a son, the husband may beat her, a barren marriage is a tragedy that is her fault, and so forth. Regarding urban life, situations vary more, but the major fact of male dominance is consistent. Few women achieved formal political power, and though women worked very hard both in city and countryside, their work was almost always valued less than that of men.

The coming of a class-divided society increased the gap in power between men and women and furthered the asymmetrical evaluation of the sexes. It can be surmised that with the growth of settled agriculture, coming after the Neolithic Revolution's domestication of grain and animals, with male-controlled animal-drawn plows and the consequent increase in crops and demarcation of private plots (this took place in different ways and sequences in different areas), the private property of a family or a lineage came to have more importance than in preclass societies. This was so even where land was not privately owned, because "possession," whether in the form of land, money, animals, or titles, was a new social value in the recently stratified society. Increasing its private property and passing it on became a key function of the family or lineage. Another function was to become as large, strong, and united as possible, and for this many sons were necessary, especially with high infant mortality. A large and united family or lineage might not only possess group strength but might also, in those periods when unworked land was widely available in many parts of the world, spread and take over new property. These conditions provide reasons for the treatment of females that we have described above as being so widespread in the rural parts of many city-centered cultures. If, as is typical, a family or lineage regards its strength as coming largely from the purity of its line of descent, it will want to be sure that the girls its sons marry stem from established and honorable families. Sexual purity is part of this: the paternity of the children produced by the new union must be certain. Any prior sexual relations by the woman, in addition to the emotive-ideological role this comes to play, can cast doubt both on the paternity of the first child and on the wife's future conduct, which would affect the son's (and heir's) reputation. Family and lineage inheritance, status, and solidarity are key parts in the sexual ideology regarding women that emerges particularly in class societies, both in the countryside and in cities. The social control exercised by the mother-in-law and the husband helps to keep the wife in line regarding her wifely duties, and prevents her from doing anything that might cause gossip, since often not only actual relations with other men matter, but also dawdling, smiling, or conversation, which might give rise to talk.

The family or lineage might be slightly less significant in the traditional city than among peasants or nomads, but this was not always so, and among the wealthy, large families and lineages were very important. The traditional ideology of the female role, bolstered by religion and folk wisdom, retained potency in the world's cities. Many traditional ideologies stated that women are lustful and deceitful, and that they lack the rational control necessary to restrain their sexual desires if faced by opportunities. Many traditional ideologies also posited that a man and a premenopausal woman left alone together would almost surely indulge in sexual relations—any other kind of relations between nonkin male and female being nearly impossible to imagine—an idea still found in parts of Mediterranean Europe and Asia. Additional features are found in the urban upper classes. In wealthy families in many parts of the world, wives become possessions whose demonstrable nonlabor becomes more valued than their labor, while other women are used increasingly as sexual, or partially sexual, playthings. Thus, total seclusion of Muslim wives of the highest classes and footbinding of Chinese women, as well as tight corsets and hoop or hobble skirts in the West, were all, in part, signs that a woman did not and could not engage in significant physical labor. The large polygamous establishment, whatever its combination of wives, concubines, and slave girls, was not an exclusively Islamic institution, although it was probably more widespread in Islam than elsewhere; it was, however, an upper-class institution, and provided the wealthy man, according to his means, with status, with a ready-made collection of female servants, entertainers, sexual partners, and mothers for a progeny so numerous that his family group would be sure to outnumber nearly all his fellows'. In the cultures where it existed, polygamy (generally bigamy) at lower levels might have more prosaic causes: the desire to have children, or more children, to have more women as workers, to get a young wife to supplement the one grown older, and so forth. Fidelity was as much demanded in the huge polygamous household as in the monogamous one, although stories, sometimes documented, of lesbian attachments, of relations with eunuchs, and of other intrigues abound.

That the treatment of women centers on their sexual role and on paternity is indicated by the woman's varying treatment in the course of her life cycle, which revolves around her relationship to sex and reproduction. Small girls are often given some freedom, but the more they approach puberty the more they are restricted and kept from contact with males. Restriction, along with a rush to marry girls off, reaches its height with puberty, and marriage is often tentative until, first, virginity is proven and, second, a son is produced. While at first subordinate to her mother-in-law and scarcely in contact with her husband, a wife who has produced a few children may, either indirectly or through arguing with her husband, succeed in getting him to break off and form a separate household in which she has some power, even though the husband is still dominant. With the onset of menopause the woman is assumed no longer to be a sexual being—an idea that goes against physiology but fits well with traditional ideologies' central concern with a pure family line. Postmenopausal women can thus often mix more freely with men, and can have and express views on subjects they could never have broached before.[11] As mother-in-law, the middle-aged woman may have the chance to become household tyrant and relieve herself of the most unpleasant household chores

—once she has lost the possibility of staining the family line her status in many ways approaches more closely that of the man.

The Impact of Islam

In the light of patterns that are found in many traditional societies around the world, although with numerous variations, one comes to question the view that attributes these patterns to Islam or its laws and customs. Such an attribution could only be made by those (all too numerous) persons who know only modern Western society and some Islamic societies, but not what has gone on in other countries or periods. The basic patterns of male domination, the virginity-fidelity-son producing ethos, a sexual double standard, and so on, existed in the Middle East and in other parts of the world long before Islam was born. Even veiling is not original to Islam: the earliest iconographic depiction of it dates from Palmyra in the first century A.D., and it was practiced in the Byzantine Empire and adjacent areas before Islam, although it is not known to what degree.[12] As Muslim converts and Arabs extended this Near Eastern custom, they interpreted certain Quranic passages as referring to veiling, and Islam spread the practice further in territory, and possibly also in class, than before. Probably because of the religious associations it took on, it has been harder to discard veiling in Muslim countries than it has been to get rid of it or parallel customs in non-Muslim countries. Thus Hindu women, who took on *purdah* (veiled seclusion) after the Muslim invasions of India, were able to drop it relatively quickly, while Chinese footbinding (a far more crippling custom than veiling) disappeared with rapidity when outlawed.

What is special about Islam in regard to women is the degree to which matters relating to women's status have either been legislated by the Quran, which believing Muslims regard as the literal word of God as revealed to the Prophet, or by subsequent legislation derived from interpretations of the Quran and the traditional sayings of the Prophet. Thus, innovators in this, as in many other matters, have to deal not merely with some customary belief that may be relatively easily replaced by another, once the newer one becomes more functional, but with the heart of religion, which is the holy law or sharia. The legitimacy of marrying up to four wives is enshrined in the Quran. The exact inheritance shares of family members, which give women half the share of men, is similarly Quranic, as are injunctions of obedience of women to men, and to the proper dress and modest behavior of women. In Islamic law women have male guardians; woman's testimony is worth half that of a man; women are considered to have less reason than men; men are allowed to divorce unilaterally but women only for limited causes, before courts, and with difficulty; and child custody, after an age that varies with the legal school, goes to the man. Other customs involving male domination widely regarded as "Islamic" and "religious" are also followed and may even be upheld in court when there is no specific Islamic text.

While it is probable that the Quran by and large improved the position of Arabian women (although some scholars say that women in different tribes and towns had varied positions and marriage customs, some of which became less free through Quranic law), it does not seem that that the Quran meant any dramatic upward change for women. Nor were Quranic rules favorable to women always followed. With the Arab Muslim conquest of the Middle East, followed by the spread of veiling and the development of a body of Islamic law that combined Quranic, interpretative, and older Near Eastern concepts, the subordinate position of women was codified into law, as well as embodied in customs, many of which predated Islam. To be sure, the picture was not as bad as Westerners often used to paint it; many women legally inherited and controlled their own property, and were entitled to a sum agreed upon in the marriage contract in case of divorce—and the latter, when honored, was an obstacle to free repudiation. Yet recent studies have demonstrated that women's right to inheritance and property often remained and remains theoretical—especially in rural and tribal areas—and male family members often take over the inheritance in return for support of the sister, or even without any real return, while the husband does not always respect a woman's right to control and dispose of her property.[13] Regarding property the legal and de facto situation for many urban and a few rural women was certainly better than it was in the West until quite recently, but it was hardly as ideal or absolute as is suggested by those scholars who take the letter of Islamic law for reality. On the other hand, a minority of Muslim women were able to take advantage of the law to mitigate prevailing Islamic practices: in some areas it was, for example, possible, although generally rare, to insert into the marriage contract protective provisions (such as one allowing a woman to divorce her husband should he take a second wife), provided they were not openly contrary to the sharia. This feature was taken advantage of in the reforming Iranian Family Protection Act of 1967, which inserted parts of the Act into every marriage contract, thus giving it Islamic justification. Women also had some access to legal redress and to the courts, but they used courts much less frequently than men.

If the embedding of the position of women in Islamic texts and law may largely account for the conservatism of Islam regarding women's position as compared with other parts of the Third World where such religious embedding is less deep, we are still left with the question of why it was precisely the family and personal status aspects of Islamic law and custom that have been held onto most tenaciously. Whereas Islamic civil and commercial codes have often been swept away with a virtual stroke of the pen, the same has been true of family law only in Turkey, and even there old practices, now illegal, long outlived the legal change. In most other countries legal change in this area has been very gradual, and has been careful to emphasize its Islamic nature, either by taking the most liberal rulings on various matters from different schools of law (a mixture that would not have been made in traditional times), by combining schools on a single question, by providing a modernist or forced exegesis of the Quran or of law (as in Tunisia's outlawing polygamy through Quranic interpretation), by inserting new provisions in all marriage contracts (Iran's 1967 law), and so forth. The exceptional resistance and slowness in this one area, despite the real progress achieved to date, coupled with the nonlegal problems of high birthrates, low urban labor force participation rates, low literacy rates, and so on, suggest that the majority of Muslim women, if not the horribly oppressed and faceless creatures suggested by some earlier Western accounts, do, on the average, fall near the end, in terms of rights and freedoms, of a continuum of societies that were once more similar in their treatment of women of various social classes. In these past societies Muslim women were disadvantaged in terms of greater veiling and seclusion, but they were probably somewhat advantaged in property rights (although both veiling and de facto property rights were mainly urban phenomena).

We end, therefore, on a new question. The question is not why traditional Islamic culture has been more discriminatory toward women than other major cultures, since the similarities in several city-centered, rural-majority cultures suggest that Islam was not radically different from the others, at least for the majority of its women. The real question, which contains policy implications for population control, improved childrearing, educational development, and economic change, is why Islamic society has been more conservative in its maintenance of old laws and traditions in this area than have other societies—although the others have not lacked conservatism. The embedding of personal status and other questions relating to women in the Quran and Islamic law have been noted, with more key points concerning women than on most other questions found in the Quran itself. However, other parts of Quranic and sharia tradition have been overcome in many countries with much greater ease. We have also noted the strength of Islam as an ideological system throughout the vast region and among the various socioeconomic classes. The limits posed on male freedom by religion and tradition and by the modern power of employers, government institutions, and Western incursions, may encourage men lacking wealth and power to keep control in the only area they can—that of women and children. Changing commercial and civil codes was of obvious advantage to increasingly powerful bourgeois and governmental classes, and often a prerequisite, along with criminal code changes, to throwing off Western extraterritorial privileges, whereas the reform of personal status codes appears to many men not as an advantage but as a loss of rights and powers and, if they believe the folklore of their society, an encouragement to marital infidelity and sexual freedom for women.[14] The recent revival of nationalist and anti-Western Islamic ideologies among some governments and intellectuals reinforces traditional views on the status of women. Here deep psychological biases and fears mesh with religion and tradition and with the total organization of society to form a barrier which is, however, being steadily breached by the efforts on every level of women and men of contrary persuasion.

Organization of the Volume

The chapters in this volume are organized into four parts: general perspectives on legal and socioeconomic change; historical perspectives; specific case studies on nomads, villagers, and town and city dwellers; and ideological, religious, and ritual systems.

The section considering legal and socioeconomic change begins with a discussion by Noel Coulson and Doreen Hinchcliffe of women's legal position in Islam, according to the various schools of legal interpretation, and their summary of the extent of legal reform in Muslim nations. Elizabeth H. White follows with an essay correlating the degree of legal reform in various Muslim countries with the status of women in these countries. Nadia H. Youssef analyzes women's status in the family and in education and employment, in the context of women's fertility patterns. The three chapters are complementary in subject and scope. The next two chapters demonstrate the importance of analyzing the position of women in individual countries in terms of socioeconomic variables, rather than as a homogeneous entity. Vanessa Maher on Morocco and Fatma Mansur Cosar on Turkey give separate treatment to women in each of the various socioeconomic levels and class groups of society.

The next five chapters discuss the factors behind contemporary legal reform and social change in individual Middle Eastern countries. Mark A. Tessler with Janet Rogers and Daniel Schneider look at the situation in Tunisia, where liberal reforms were followed by a partial retreat. Juliette Minces presents the case of Algeria, where women's participation in revolutionary struggle temporarily changed their role; this was followed, however, by a return to prerevolution conditions when the conflict ceased. The rapid improvement in women's status in Kuwait, presented by Kamla Nath, is related to changes in society brought about largely by a booming, oil-rich economy. For Iran, Michael M. J. Fischer demonstrates the complexity of women's position within changing social and cultural contexts. Behnaz Pakizegi, also dealing with Iran, is interested in both change and resiliency in the patterns of women's life cycle.

These essays provide backgrounds for the more specific time periods, social groups, and issues dealt with in the remainder of the collection.

The five chapters that comprise the second part of the book, through historical reconstruction, shed much-needed light on the roles of women in the past. Two essays discuss Turkey: Ian C. Dengler covers the range of activities and occupations of women in Ottoman times; Ülkü Ü. Bates discusses the importance of women as patrons of architecture, and as political figures, among the Ottoman ruling elite. Two chapters discuss women in modern Egyptian history. Afaf Lutfi al-Sayyid Marsot presents an overview of the changes in women's lives in nineteenth and early twentieth century Egypt, based in part on personal knowledge of some of the leading figures. Thomas Philipp documents the relationship between nationalist thought and the feminist movement in Egypt preceding the revolution of 1919. The material presented by Mangol Bayat-Philipp for Iran in the period of 1905 to 1911 documents the earliest known revolutionary activity by women in the modern Middle East.

The importance of separating out socioeconomic factors, demonstrated in the chapters by Maher and Coşar, and of assessing the degree of female participation in productive, economic, and political activity, is demonstrated in the next set of chapters, where specific case studies of nomads, villagers, and town and city dwellers are presented.

Emrys L. Peters details the integration of women in bedouin society in Cyrenaica (Libya) and compares this society with three non-nomadic Middle Eastern communities. Lois Beck analyzes the factors behind a high degree of symmetry in the relations between women and men in a pastoral nomadic society in Iran. For another group of Iranian nomads, Nancy Tapper presents material on the structure and function of a women's subsociety. Dawn Chatty discusses the changes in women's and men's lives brought about by the recent introduction of the truck to camel-herding bedouin of Syria and Lebanon.

Susan Schaefer Davis analyzes the multifaceted nature of work opportunities for women in a Moroccan village. Carroll McC. Pastner outlines the complexity of property ownership and control in an oasis in Baluchistan, Pakistan. Paul Vieille discusses marriage alliance and sexual politics among Iranian peasants and industrial workers, in a theoretical presentation relevant to much of traditional Middle Eastern society. (The essays by Erika Friedl on folklore in an Iranian village and by Soheir Morsy on folk illness in an Egyptian village are included in the fourth section.)

Two studies of women's associations in towns follow: one by Barbara C. Aswad for Turkey and the other by Mary-Jo DelVecchio Good for Iran and Turkey. Both studies discuss the complex issue of social class; they demonstrate the internal structure and functioning of women's groupings as well as the nature of the connection between women's status hierarchies and those of men.

The lives of city women are discussed in three chapters. John Gulick and Margaret E. Gulick look at the attitudes and domestic organization of urban and recent migrant women in the Iranian city of Isfahan. Sawsan el-Messiri analyzes the self-image of women in a traditional district in Cairo. Suad Joseph discusses female interaction in a neighborhood street in Lebanon's Beirut.

The role of ideology in stating the qualities and capabilities of women and men and in perpetuating these beliefs through time is of major concern in the study of women, as is the study of the incorporation of sexual ideologies in religious systems. These considerations are taken up in the book's fourth section. As the earlier part of the Introduction demonstrates, the general legal and socioeconomic changes typical of the modern period do not necessarily involve improved conditions for women, and much of the hesitancy to alter the bases of sexual inequality rests in ideological systems and religious beliefs.

Lawrence Rosen provides an analysis of the ideological bases of male-female relations; although his material comes from an urban Moroccan context, the discussion is more broadly applicable. Daisy Hilse Dwyer describes the affiliatory patterns of women in Sufi orders in Morocco and their interplay with men's affiliatory patterns. Addressing the subject of ritual, Soheir A. Morsy looks at the attempts of women in rural Egypt to deal with sex-role dilemmas through the symptomology of folk illness. Evelyne Accad discusses sexual oppression in North Africa as represented in literature. Through a discussion of the roles of and attitudes towards women and men as expressed in the folktales of an Iranian peasant community, Erika Friedl's essay provides an analysis that integrates the social and ideological components of sexual asymmetry. For a final paper it seems appropriate to include one perspective on Muslims outside of the Middle East, where, ironically, Muslim women have greater institutional support for religious activity than most of them have had in Muslim countries. For this, Barbara L. K. Pillsbury presents original material on China.

Notes

1. Michael Fischer cautions us against applying too strictly the lineage model to village society on the basis that urban and bilateral patterns are also of great significance. A few others, including Constance Cronin in a personal communication, are questioning the presence of lineages in any meaningful sense among some traditional urban upper classes. For a recent discussion of this issue see Emrys L. Peters, "Aspects of Affinity in a Lebanese Maronite Village," in *Mediterranean Family Structures,* ed. J. G. Peristiany (Cambridge, 1976).

2. One well-informed Iranian anthropologist said that when he last traveled through the Iranian countryside the chador was limited to women of the village elite, but the authors' recent experiences in Iranian villages indicate that the nonelite are now veiled. Settled Baluch, who reportedly had not worn chadors a few years ago, were now, in areas observed, completely so dressed. Settled Qashqa'i and Bakhtiyari tribeswomen do not generally wear the chador, except when going to towns and to religious shrines, but in most regions nontribal village women wear chadors.

3. For the spread of veiling in rural Tunisia, see Nadia Abu Zahra, "Inequality of Descent and Egalitarianism of the New National Organizations in a Tunisian Village," in *Rural Politics and Social Change in the Middle East,* ed. R. Antoun and I. Harik (Bloomington, Ind., 1972).

4. On the spread of veiling in the North African countryside, see the suggestive book by Germaine Tillion, *Le harem et les cousins* (Paris, 1966), chap. 9, "Les femmes et le voile."

5. Tillion, *Le harem.*

6. See Nadia Youssef, *Women and Work in Developing Societies* (Berkeley, 1974), table 1, p. 10; table 9, p. 27; pp. 34–36.

7. Several points in this discussion were suggested by Judith Gran, Peter Gran, and Carlo Poni and by an unpublished paper on Egypt by Hollis Granoff. On the growth of neotraditionalism in colonies, see N. Keddie, "Western Rule Versus Western Values: Suggestions for a Comparative Study of Asian Intellectual History," *Diogenes*, 26 (1959): 71–79.

8. According to the "World Population Sheet" of the *Population Reference Bureau* (Washington, D.C., 1976), the crude birth rate in Latin America was 37 per 1000 in 1976, whereas that of North Africa was 43.2 and of the Near East 45.

9. See, for example, Paul Stirling, *Turkish Village* (New York, 1965).

10. See F. M'Rabet, *La femme algérienne, suivi de les algériennes*, rev. ed. (Paris, 1969).

11. When talking with village carpet-weavers in 1974, N. Keddie was struck with how well-informed and "intelligent" middle-aged women suddenly became about the economics of carpet-weaving, while younger women expressed ignorance and referred to their husbands.

12. Strabo (early 1st cent. A.D.) refers to total, including facial, veiling as a custom brought in by Medea, described as a Mede. Thanks to James Reid for this reference (*The Geography of Strabo*, trans. H. L. Jones [London and New York, 1928], 5, pp. 313–318). Discussion of pre-Islamic veiling, including probable references to facial veiling in Assyrian codes of 1500–1200 B.C., is found in R. de Vaux, "Sur le voile des femmes dans l'orient ancien," in his *Bible et Orient* (Paris, 1967).

13. Tillion, *Le harem*, p. 179, notes that the (urban) area of veiling corresponds quite closely to the area where women inherit as the Quran and Muslim law say they should. In Tillion's experience, mostly in North Africa, women very rarely inherit anything significant in rural or tribal areas, although they get the financial support of their agnatic family when needed. This urban-rural difference helps account for the difference between urban court records that report women inheriting as they should, and numerous village and tribal studies that show them not inheriting. For urban court records, see Ronald Jennings, "Women in Early Seventeenth Century Ottoman Judicial Records: The Sharia Court of Anatolian Kayseri," *Journal of the Economic and Social History of the Orient*, 28, part 1 (1975):53–114.

14. See Hanna Papanek, "Purdah: Separate Worlds and Symbolic Shelter," *Comparative Studies in Society and History*, 15 (1973):289–325.

Bibliography

ʿAbd ar-Raziq, Ahmad. *La femme au temps des Mamlouks en Egypte*. Cairo, 1973.

"Appearance and Reality: Status and Roles of Women in Mediterranean Societies." Special issue of *Anthropological Quarterly*, 40 (July 1967).

Audiburt, G., trans. and annot. *La femme persane jugée et critiquée par un persan*. Paris, 1889.
Bamdad, Badr ol-Molk, and F. R. C. Bagley, ed. and trans. *From Darkness into Light: Women's Emancipation in Iran*. Hicksville, N.Y., 1977.
Bittari, Zoubeida. *O mes soeurs musulmanes, pleurez!* Paris, 1964.
Boserup, Ester. *Women's Role in Economic Development*. London, 1970.
Bousquet, J. H. *L'Ethique sexuelle de l'Islam*. Paris, 1966.
Clark, Alice. *Working Life of Women in the Seventeenth Century*. New York, 1968 (reprint).
Fernea, Elizabeth Warnock. *Guests of the Sheik*. Garden City, N.Y., 1969.
———. *A Street in Marrakech*. Garden City, N.Y., 1975.
Fernea, Elizabeth, and Basima Bezirgan, eds. *Middle Eastern Muslim Women Speak*. Austin, Tex., 1977.
Fernea, Robert, and Elizabeth Fernea. "Variations in Religious Observance among Islamic Women." In *Scholars, Saints, and Sufis: Muslim Religious Institutions in the Middle East since 1500*, ed. Nikki R. Keddie. Berkeley and Los Angeles, 1972.
Goody, Jack, and S. J. Tambiah. *Bridewealth and Dowry*. Cambridge, 1973.
Gordon, David. *Women of Algeria: An Essay on Change*. Cambridge, Mass., 1968.
Granqvist, Hilma. *Marriage Conditions in a Palestinian Village*, 2 parts. Helsingfors, 1931, 1935.
———. *Birth and Childhood among the Arabs: Studies in a Muhammadan Village in Palestine*. Helsingfors, 1947.
Hansen, Henny. *The Kurdish Woman's Life*. Copenhagen, 1961.
Helmstrom, Engin Inel. "Changing Sex Roles in a Developing Country." *Journal of Marriage and the Family*, (August 1973) :546–553.
Layish, Aharon. *Women and Islamic Law in a Non-Muslim State*. New York and Jerusalem, 1975.
Lewis, Bernard. *The Emergence of Modern Turkey*. London, 1961.
Levy, Marion. *The Family Revolution in Modern China*. New York, 1963.
Maher, Vanessa. *Women and Property in Morocco*. Cambridge, 1974.
Massell, G. *The Surrogate Proletariat: Moslem Women and Revolutionary Strategies in Soviet Central Asia, 1919–1929*. Princeton, 1974.
M'Rabet, Fadéla. *La femme algérienne, suivi de les algériennes*. Paris, 1969.
Musallam, Basim F. "The Islamic Sanction of Contraception." in *Population and its Problems*, ed. H. B. Parry. Oxford, 1974.
O'Faolain, Julia, and Lauro Martines, eds. *Not in God's Image: Women in History from the Greeks to the Victorians*. New York, 1973.
Peristiany, J. G., ed. *Mediterranean Family Structures*. Cambridge, 1976.
Pomeroy, Sarah B. *Goddesses, Whores, Wives, and Slaves: Women in Classical Antiquity*. New York, 1975.
Power, Eileen. *Medieval Women*, ed. M. Postan. Cambridge, 1975.
Rice, C. Colliver. *Persian Women and Their Ways*. Philadelphia, 1923.
Rosaldo, Michelle Z., and Louise Lamphere, eds. *Woman, Culture, and Society*. Stanford, Calif., 1974.

Stirling, Paul. *Turkish Village.* New York, 1965.

Tillion, Germaine. *Le harem et les cousins.* Paris, 1966.

Tomiche, Nada. "The Situation of Egyptian Women in the First Half of the Nineteenth Century." In *Beginnings of Modernization in the Middle East,* ed. W. R. Polk and R. L. Chambers. Chicago, 1968.

———. "La femme en Islam." In *Histoire mondiale de la femme,* ed. Pierre Grimal. Paris, 1967.

"Visiting Patterns and Social Dynamics in Eastern Mediterranean Communities." Special issue of *Anthropological Quarterly,* 47 (January 1974).

Wikan, Unni. "Man Becomes Woman: Transsexualism in Oman as a Key to Gender Roles." *Man,* 12 (August 1977):304–319.

Wolf, Margery, and Roxane Witke, eds. *Women in Chinese Society.* Stanford, Calif., 1975.

Woodsmall, Ruth F. *Moslem Women Enter a New World.* London, 1936.

———. *Women and the New East.* Washington, D.C., 1960.

Youssef, Nadia H. *Women and Work in Developing Societies.* Berkeley, 1974.

Part One | General Perspectives on Legal and Socioeconomic Change

Daughter and mother of al-Fadl nomadic tribe in Syria-Lebanon. Courtesy of Dawn Chatty.

1 Women and Law Reform in Contemporary Islam

Noel Coulson and Doreen Hinchcliffe

A central feature of the rules of conduct contained in the Quran, the primary source of Islamic religious law, is the intent to improve the social position of women. Under the customary tribal law existing in Arabia at the advent of Islam, women as a general rule had virtually no legal status. They were sold into marriage by their guardians for a price paid to the guardian, the husband could terminate the union at will, and women had little or no property or succession rights.[1]

This tribal law was radically modified by various concrete provisions of the Quran. For example, the dower—the payment made in consideration of marriage by the husband—was now to belong to the wife alone, so that marriage became a contract between husband and wife instead of a contract between husband and guardian with the wife as the sale-object. The husband's power to terminate the marriage (immediately and at will) by repudiation (*talaq*) was now curtailed by the introduction of the *'idda*—a waiting period of some three months after the pronouncement of talaq before it became an effective divorce. Rights of inheritance, expressed basically as fractional shares of the estate, were given to the wife, the mother, the daughter, and the sisters of the deceased.

Insofar as it prescribes rules of behavior, however, the Quran is not primarily a legislative document, but rather the declaration of the fundamental Islamic ethic—the general moral norms it lays down with regard to the position of women are undoubtedly of equal or even greater importance than its specific legal rules. Thus, injunctions that wives should be treated fairly and equitably, that

Left:
Workers in government workshop for spinning and weaving, Birjand, Iran. Courtesy of Nikki Keddie.

divorce should take place only with due consideration, and that in general women's rights should be respected, abound.

But a considerable step—a process of juristic development extending over more than two centuries—separates the Quran from the classical formulation of Islamic law according to the different Sunni and Shiite schools, and the general Quranic norms and injunctions suffered progressive dilution during this time. The hallmark of early Muslim jurisprudence, or at least the jurisprudence of the Sunni majority, was the principle that the status quo remained valid unless and until it was expressly superseded by the dictates of Islam. Hence the standards and criteria of pre-Islamic customary law were carried over into Islam and exercised a dominant influence in the development of the Islamic legal system. The modicum of explicit Quranic legal rulings on the status of women were naturally observed, but outside this the tendency was to interpret the Quranic provisions in the light of the prevailing standards of the tribal law. In particular, the general ethical injunctions of the Quran were rarely transformed into legally enforceable rules, but were recognized as binding only on the individual conscience.

Thus, for example, a husband was never required to show that he had any reasonable or proper motive before exercising his power to repudiate his wife. And while the Quran might insist upon the impartial treatment of co-wives in polygamous unions, classical Islamic law did not elevate this requirement into any kind of legal restriction upon a husband's entrenched right to have four wives. The result was that the Quranic provisions concerning women's status and position in the family were dissipated and largely lost. Islamic law continued to reflect the patriarchal and patrilineal nature of a society based upon the male agnatic tie. Within the scheme of family law which developed in this way, woman, whether as daughter, wife, or mother, occupied an inferior position.

In the course of the present century the impetus for legal reform has derived basically from the breakdown of the traditional social unit of the extended agnatic family group. Today, at least in urban areas, society is based on the much smaller unit of what is often called the nuclear family, consisting of the husband, wife, and their lineal descendants. Within this group the woman naturally occupies a much more important and responsible position. This situation, buttressed by the general emancipation and increasing education of women, has produced the favorable climate for improving the legal status of women in a manner consonant with their new role in society.

Of course fundamental problems of principle were involved in the reform of a religious law so long regarded as immutable. Precisely how these juristic problems were surmounted is not our concern here—suffice it to say that they were surmounted.[2] The major results of the reforms achieved to date may be summarized in relation to five principal topics: capacity to marry, polygamy, divorce, custody of children, and succession. We shall be dealing with the developments that have taken place throughout the Muslim Middle East and in the Indian subcontinent.[3]

Capacity to Marry

All schools and sects of Islam recognize the right of certain "marriage guardians" to contract their infant wards of either sex in marriage without their consent. In such cases Hanafi law allows only the ward who has been contracted in marriage by a guardian other than the father or paternal grandfather the right to repudiate the marriage when he or she attains puberty. The position of non-Hanafi women is even more unfortunate for, until they have once been married, they may be contracted in marriage without their consent and against their will even when they are of adult years.

Most Muslim countries have now sought to introduce minimum ages for marriage. In most of these countries the minimum age for marriage in the case of boys is now eighteen. For girls the minimum age is fifteen in Tunisia and Morocco, sixteen in Egypt and Pakistan, and seventeen in Jordan and Syria. However, with few exceptions, marriages contracted between parties below the minimum age are still recognized as legally valid, although in some instances they attract penal sanctions. There is, in fact, a considerable amount of case law from India and Pakistan concerned with cases where children have been contracted in marriage contrary to the express provisions of the 1929 Child Marriage Restraint Act.

Traditional Hanafi and Shiite law allows women who have reached the age of majority (that is, puberty, which the law holds may occur from the age of nine onwards and which will be conclusively presumed to have occurred by the age of fifteen) to contract their own marriages. They have no such right under the law of the other schools. Accordingly, in 1956 Tunisia, a predominantly Maliki country, enacted that the consent of both spouses was an essential condition of marriage and that women could henceforth conclude their own contracts. In Morocco, however, a woman must still have a marriage guardian to act for her, but no adult woman may be contracted in marriage without her consent unless the court accepts the guardian's application to marry her on the grounds that he is concerned about her moral welfare.

Polygamy

Traditional Islamic law permits a man to have up to four wives at any one time and, if he is an Ithna ʿAshari Shiite, any number of *mutʿa* or temporary wives. The law does not require a husband to obtain the permission of the court or of his current wife before contracting an additional marriage. As we have seen, although the Quran stresses that a man should not marry a second wife if he does not feel able to treat his several wives equally, the law regards this purely as a matter for a man's own conscience and one in which judicial intervention is unnecessary.

In recent years many countries in the Muslim world have sought to restrict the practice of polygamy, but, apart from a decree issued in 1962 by the Aga Khan that forbade the practice of polygamy by the Ismaʿilis of East Africa, so far only Tunisia, Israel, Turkey, and the Soviet Union have prohibited it altogether and have declared polygamous marriages contracted subsequent to the prohibition to be void. In Iran, article 16 of the 1975 Family Protection Act provides that a husband who wishes to take a second wife must first seek the permission of the court, which will not be granted unless his first wife agrees or is unable or refuses to cohabit, becomes insane, contracts an incurable disease, becomes addicted to drugs, drink, or gambling, is sentenced to five or more years' imprisonment, abandons the family, or becomes sterile.

In Iraq, Singapore, and two of the Malay states, a husband who wishes to marry a second wife must first obtain the permission of the court. In Pakistan such permission must be obtained from an arbitration council consisting of the chairman of the local union council and representatives of the husband and of the wife. However, second marriages contracted in contradiction to these various statutory provisions are still valid, although the husbands concerned are liable to criminal prosecution and, in Iran and Pakistan, the first wife may obtain a dissolution of her marriage and may also, in Pakistan, demand the full dower due her. Furthermore, in Iran, even if the court grants permission to a husband to take a second wife, the first wife may still petition for divorce on the grounds that she herself did not consent to the second marriage.

Morocco and Lebanon have not restricted polygamy directly, but a woman is allowed to insert stipulations into her marriage contract that her husband will not take a second wife, and that if he does she will have the right to seek a dissolution of their marriage on the grounds that the stipulation has been broken. Stipulations of this type are valid under traditional Hanbali law but not under the law of the other schools. The other schools hold that all the obligations and rights (of which polygamy is one) that arise out of the contract of marriage have been laid down once and for all by the religious law and are not therefore subject to variation by the agreement of the parties. The Hanbalis, on the other hand, relying upon the Quranic verse, "O you who believe, abide by your contracts," adopted a more liberal approach and held that all stipulations except those that contravened the essential nature of marriage itself were valid. This Hanbali view has found favor with Muslim reformers; in many Muslim countries today a wife is permitted to insert stipulations into her marriage contract not only restricting her husband's right to marry additional wives but also guaranteeing, for example, her freedom of movement and the right to work outside the home—a right which under the traditional law of the majority of schools she was denied.[4]

Divorce

Undoubtedly, it was the traditional law of divorce in its various aspects that posed the greatest problem for the reformers in the Muslim world. A prominent aim of the reforms enacted since 1915 has been to improve the position of women by granting them the right to obtain a dissolution of their marriage, a right that was denied to them under traditional Hanafi law no matter how ill-treated they had been. Most of the reforms enacted have been based upon Maliki principles, for Maliki law was the most liberal regarding women's right to obtain a judicial decree of divorce.

Today in most parts of the Muslim world a woman may obtain a divorce if her husband is insane or afflicted with a disease that makes the continuation of married life dangerous to her or if he fails to maintain her, deserts her, or treats her cruelly. In Tunisia and Algeria the reforms have been even more far-reaching, and women are now permitted to insist on divorce without proving any grounds, provided they are prepared to pay financial compensation to their husbands. In Pakistan the Supreme Court has extended the right of women in divorce matters by granting a dissolution on the grounds of incompatibility of temperament. In such cases, however, the wife is required to return to her husband all benefits she has received from the marriage.

Wherever Islamic law applies, the wife remains under a duty to obey her husband in certain matters, but it is uncertain whether husbands still hold the right to administer personal chastisement to disobedient wives. In most countries a wife may obtain a dissolution of her marriage on the grounds of cruelty, but the question arises whether a distinction can be made between personal chastisement and cruelty. The formula adopted by Egypt is that the wife may obtain a decree of dissolution on the grounds of cruelty where the treatment to which she is subjected is "intolerable to persons of her social status." This of course represents a variable standard inasmuch as a blow from her husband, for example, might be intolerable to a middle-class wife but acceptable to a woman of the poorer classes.

In India and Pakistan a wife may petition for divorce on the grounds of cruelty, among other things, if "her husband habitually assaults her or makes her life miserable by cruelty of conduct, even if such conduct does not amount to physical ill-treatment." Clearly, then, a single assault by a husband on his wife would not constitute a ground for dissolution under the first part of this subclause; nor if it were a trifling as opposed to a grievous assault could it be alleged that he had made her life miserable by cruelty of conduct in accordance with the provision of the second part of the subclause. However, it is submitted that even if the assault were trifling, it would, if made in circumstances that humiliated the wife, constitute a ground for dissolution. It appears clear that in such circumstances the court would have to adopt the standard of a "reasonable woman," and only if it were satisfied that an assault of the type complained of would cause misery to a "reasonable woman" would it grant relief.

The most urgently needed reform, however, was to restrict the husband's unfettered power to repudiate his wife at will, for this power represented an even more serious threat to the welfare of the Muslim woman than her own lack of the right to seek a dissolution of her marriage. It is a fundamental principle of Islamic law that the power of divorce is in the hands of the husband and may be exercised at will, however blameless she may be, without having recourse to a court of law. It is true that it is considered to be morally reprehensible for a husband to divorce his wife without good cause, but this is merely a matter for the husband's conscience: the divorce so effected will be legally valid. Even repudiations uttered in jest, as a threat, or even, according to some jurists, while the husband is drunk or under duress, are binding. Thus, a wife could find herself effectively repudiated even though her husband had no desire to divorce her.

Sunni Islam recognizes two forms of divorce by repudiation, or talaq. The first form is said to be in accordance with the *sunna*. Here the husband may either pronounce a single talaq which will become effective when the wife has completed her ʿidda (waiting period of three menstrual cycles, or, if she is pregnant, until she is delivered of the child), or he may pronounce three talaqs in three successive months. If a husband adopts a form of talaq in accordance with the sunna, he gives himself a chance to have second thoughts on the matter, and interested parties may make efforts to reconcile the spouses. Unfortunately, however, the form of divorce most commonly employed is the *talaq al-bid'a*—the talaq of innovation. This form is regarded as sinful but it is nonetheless legally effective. Here the husband pronounces three talaqs at the same time, thus immediately dissolving the marriage irrevocably and, moreover, making remarriage between himself and his divorced wife impossible until she has consummated a marriage with another man and this intervening marriage is, of course, duly terminated. Talaq al-bid'a is not recognized by the Ithna 'Ashari sect of the Shiites.

Upon divorce the wife is entitled to claim any unpaid portion of the dower, although if the husband is reluctant to pay it she will have to bring a civil suit to recover it. Her right to maintenance, however, continues only while she is observing the 'idda. All schools are agreed that women observing the 'idda following a revocable talaq (that is, one that does not become effective until the end of the 'idda) are entitled to maintenance, but there are divergent views regarding the right to maintenance in the 'idda following an irrevocable, or immediately effective, talaq. Only the Hanafi school allows women this right in all cases, the other schools restricting the right to women who are pregnant. The divorced woman has no right to apply to the court for ancillary relief in the form of a lump sum or periodic payments. The husband's responsibility for his wife terminates with the pronouncement of the talaq, or at the expiration of the 'idda, as the case may be.

Today, reforms designed to curtail the husband's freedom to terminate the marriage unilaterally have been enacted in most Muslim countries. The husband's motive for divorcing his wife was first made the subject of judicial scrutiny by the 1953 Syrian Law of Personal Status. This law provided that where the husband divorced his wife without good cause, he should pay her financial compensation up to the equivalent of one year's maintenance. In 1956 a similar provision was enacted by Tunisia but no legal limit was placed on the amount that could be awarded as compensation.

In Pakistan no repudiation becomes effective until ninety days have elapsed from the date the necessary notice of the repudiation is given to the chairman of the local union council. Upon receipt of the notice the chairman must set up an arbitration council. This council must attempt to reconcile the parties, and it is only when all such attempts have failed that the repudiation takes effect. In Singapore the courts are forbidden to register a repudiation if the wife does not consent. If she refuses to agree to the dissolution of the marriage, the case is referred to the *sharia* court, which will attempt to reconcile the parties with the aid of social workers in relevant cases. But if the husband persists in his determination to divorce his wife, the court is bound to register the repudiation.

The law of Tunisia, Iraq, Iran, and South Yemen is much more progressive, inasmuch as it now requires that all pronouncements of divorce be made in a court of law. The Iraqi law, however, while stating that the husband who wishes to repudiate his wife must commence proceedings in the sharia courts, contains a provision that if the husband is unable to take the matter to court he may register the repudiation during the ʿidda period; and the courts have subsequently held that even failure to register the repudiation during the ʿidda does not render it invalid per se. Therefore, while these reforms are to be welcomed, it is quite apparent that even under the modern law the power to dissolve the marriage tie remains in the control of the husband, and a determined husband may still divorce his wife however blameless she may be.

In Iran and South Yemen, however, the husband's power of unilateral repudiation has been totally abolished. Like the Tunisian law of 1956, the new Iranian Family Protection Law, promulgated in 1975, put the spouses on an equal footing in the matter of divorce. But, unlike the Tunisian law, it did so not by giving the wife a virtual power of talaq, but by removing the power of talaq from the husband. Following the enactment of this statute, the sole ground for dissolution is "irretrievable breakdown of marriage," which may be established in a variety of ways, notably when one of the spouses "abandons family life." In South Yemen, also, no divorce may be obtained by either spouse unless the court is satisfied that the marriage has irretrievably broken down. Because the restriction of talaq is undoubtedly the most critical problem facing reformers in Islamic divorce and, indeed, family law, the passage of the two statutes has put Iran and South Yemen in the forefront of law reform in this sphere. It remains to be seen to what extent the radical Iranian and South Yemen statutes will influence future reforms in other parts of the Muslim world.

Custody of Children

Rigidity is the outstanding characteristic of the traditional law relating to the custody of children. The woman who is divorced or widowed retains the custody of her children for only a limited period of time, after which they pass automatically into the care of their father or nearest male agnate relative. Thus in Ithna ʿAshari law a mother has the right to the custody of her sons only until the age of two (which is the recognized age of weaning) and of her daughters until the age of seven. In Hanafi law the mother's custody continues until her sons are seven and her daughters are nine, while in Maliki law, which lays most emphasis on the mother's right in this regard, the mother is allowed to keep her children until her sons have reached puberty and her daughters have reached puberty and are married. In Shafiʿi law children are given the choice at the age of seven as to which parent they will live with. Hanbali law accords the same right to boys, but girls at the age of seven pass automatically into the custody of the father.

During the mother's period of custody, however, the father or the nearest male agnate relative remains the guardian of the child. He has the right not only to control the child's education but also, as we have seen, to contract the child in marriage without the consent of the mother. Nor is the mother's right to custody absolute. She loses the right not only if she becomes unfit, physically or morally, to take care of the child but also if she marries a man who is not related to the child within the prohibited degrees, or, in Ithna ʿAshari law, if she remarries at all, even to a close relative of the child.

Today, throughout the greater part of the Muslim world, these traditional rules regarding custody of children have been relaxed. The principle underlying the recent reforms has been that the welfare of the child is paramount. Thus, the Egyptian law of 1929 provides that the court has the right to decide which parent should have custody of girls after the age of nine and boys after the age of seven. However, the mother may not have custody of her girls once they have reached the age of eleven or of her boys once they have reached the age of nine. Sudanese law allows the court a similar discretion up to the age of puberty in the case of boys and until marriage in the case of girls. The law in Syria, Tunisia, Iraq, Iran, and South Yemen now expressly provides that the interests of the child are of prime importance, and custody may be granted to either parent at the court's discretion. In India and Pakistan the same results have been achieved by means of judicial decisions. The principle that emerges from the case law is that the welfare of the child is paramount, and although there is a presumption that the welfare of the child is best served by applying the strict rules of the traditional law, the presumption is rebuttable.

Succession

One of the most important reforms introduced by Islam into the law of Arabia was the recognition of the right of women to inherit on an intestacy. This is not to say, however, that the position of women was equated with that of men. A wife whose deceased husband is survived by descendants inherits a mere one-eighth of his estate, while if her husband is not survived by descendants her share is increased to one-quarter. In the case of polygamous unions the several surviving widows divide this one-eighth or one-quarter share equally. Further, the wife's share is liable to be reduced if the doctrine of *ʿawl,* or proportionate reduction, has to be applied because the estate is oversubscribed; but if the estate is undersubscribed, the wife's share is not augmented, as are the shares of the other heirs, by the application of the doctrine of *radd,* or return. A husband who considers that the share his wife will inherit on his death is too small can make provision for her only by gift *inter vivos*, since a testamentary disposition to an heir is held by Sunni law to be *ultra vires* and ineffective unless the other heirs consent to it.

The allotted Quranic share of a daughter is one-half the estate of her parent, while the share of a plurality of daughters is two-thirds. If, however, the deceased is survived by both a son and a daughter, the daughter ceases to be a Quranic heir and is instead converted into a residuary heir by her brother, taking half as much as he does. The law of pre-Islamic Arabia recognized only the male agnates as entitled legal heirs, and Sunni Islam gives preference to the agnates in matters of succession. Thus, if the sole heirs are a daughter and a distant male agnatic cousin, the daughter will be restricted to one-half the estate of her parent and the remaining half will go to the distant cousin as residuary agnatic heir, although he might, at least in the circumstances of present-day society, have had no real contact at all with the deceased.

Shiite law, on the other hand, gives no such precedence to male agnates. It divides all heirs, excluding the spouse relict (widow or widower) who inherits in all cases, into three classes. Class I comprises parents and all lineal descendants; Class II, grandparents and collaterals and their issue; and Class III, uncles and aunts and their issue. Any heir in Class I excludes all those in Class II, so that a daughter will exclude not only brothers and uncles and any male agnate of lower priority but also the grandfather. Thus, while the Sunni notion of the family is that of a unit based on tribal ties, the Shiite concept is one of a smaller unit consisting basically of parents and children. Within this unit the male still inherits twice the share of the female, but clearly the position of the Shiite woman in matters of inheritance is much more favorable than that of her Sunni sister.

Reforms in the law of inheritance have been less far-reaching than those effected in other branches of Islamic family law, although a recent decree in Somalia has provided that men and women have equal rights of inheritance. The extremely controversial nature of this decree is obvious, for it is the Quran itself that prescribes that the male shall take double the share of the female relative who has the same blood relationship with the deceased.

In other parts of the Muslim world less radical, but at the same time greatly significant, reforms have taken place. In Tunisia the law has changed to allow daughters to exclude collaterals and other more remote male agnates from inheritance. It may be observed that the Quran itself expressly states that a brother is excluded from inheritance in the presence of a *walad* (child) of the deceased. Traditional Sunni law, however, maintained that in this instance the word walad meant male child. The same Tunisian law also provides that the spouse relict should share equally in radd along with other entitled heirs. In Iraq the law of 1963 enacted an order of priorities identical to the basic provisions of the Shiite law to apply to both the Sunni and the Shiite communities, with the result that any child of the deceased, male or female, would totally exclude from inheritance collaterals and, of course, other more remote relatives. Finally, in the Sudan, Egypt, and Iraq, a bequest within the traditional limit of the bequeathable third of the estate made to an heir is no longer *ultra vires,* which means that the share of a wife or a daughter may be augmented if her husband or father makes a testamentary disposition in her favor.

Such, then, have been the major advances achieved recently in women's legal status in the Muslim countries of the Middle East and elsewhere. There is no doubt that they represent, in toto, a radical departure from traditional Islamic doctrine and draw, perhaps, the blueprint of a totally new philosophy of family law. In substance the changes in some countries are hardly less fundamental than those effected in Turkey in the 1920s by the complete abandonment of the religious law and its replacement by the secular Swiss Civil Code. But of course the juristic basis of the reforms discussed here is entirely different. They are put forward as a new interpretation of the religious law, an expression of it manifestly different from that of the traditional authorities but nonetheless equally legitimate in the context of the current social climate. The basic tenet of Muslim jurisprudence that law is the expression of the divine will is preserved, and there is considerable force and merit in the view that these present laws preserve and reflect, to a much greater extent than the traditional doctrine, the essential spirit of the original precepts of the Quran and particularly its general ethical injunctions relating to the treatment and position of women.

Impressive though the terms of this paper legislation may be, however, the vital question is whether they apply in practice and whether they are proving to be an effective remedy for the social mischiefs that the reformers set out to cure. In this respect it must be admitted that from the present circumstances of Muslim state and society stem two principal difficulties.

In the first place there is a considerable rift between the standards and values current in urban society and those obtaining in rural communities. While there is little doubt that the reforms reflect the ideals and aspirations of the urban population—the chief architects of the reforms have, of course, been the educated, Western-orientated, urban elite—there is equally little doubt that in the much more traditional and conservative atmosphere of the rural areas the same reforms are viewed with considerable hostility and suspicion. They meet with the particular opprobrium always reserved in traditional Islamic society for an innovation *(bidʿa)*. Consequently, because of their customary seclusion, women are quite likely to be totally ignorant of their rights under the new legislation; and even if they should be aware of them it would take a good deal of courage to run the gauntlet of the various social pressures and sanctions that would undoubtedly face any woman insisting upon these rights in a court of law.

The second major barrier against the effective implementation of the reforms lies in the attitude of the judiciary. Liberal and enlightened *qadi*s (religious judges) there certainly are. But equally, and again especially in the rural communities, a great number of the Muslim judiciary remains deeply loyal to the traditional doctrines and values that formed the exclusive basis of their education in the law. It is hardly surprising, therefore, that there has been a latent opposition to the new legislation on the part of the more conservative judiciary, and that this has resulted in the clear intentions of the reformers being minimized and whittled away by judicial interpretation. Even in the relatively progressive climate of Tunisia, for example, it was not until 1964, some eight years after the Code of Personal Status had expressly prohibited polygamy. that the courts were prepared to declare that a polygamous marriage contracted in defiance of this provision was invalid. So too in Iraq, where the judiciary has proved particularly conservative, the new law of succession promulgated in 1963, which imposed a wholly new order of priorities in inheritance, has been so progressively diluted by judicial interpretations that the order of priorities under traditional Sunni law today continues to apply to the estates of deceased Sunni Muslims.

It is clear that the paper legislation in many respects does not represent the social reality. The legal machinery for the advancement of women's status exists, but it does not yet function effectively everywhere. For Muslim women today the problem, in the current jargon of industrial economy, is the utilization of existing plant. To the legal historian the problem is not a new one. Like many other societies in the past and, doubtless, in the future, Muslim society today is experiencing the truism that any law, to be an effective instrument of social change, must be supportable by the generality of the society to which it applies, and that any law, ultimately, is only as strong as the courts whose responsibility it is to administer it.

Chronological Table of Reforms

1917 Ottoman Law of Family Rights, now applicable in Lebanon and Israel, reforms some aspects of marriage and divorce.

1920–1929 Egypt and Sudan enacted a series of laws that regulate the age of marriage, give women the right to divorce on specified grounds, and restrict talaq.

1939 Passage of the Dissolution of Muslim Marriages Act in India and Pakistan (with modifications) gave women the right to divorce on specified grounds.

1946 Egypt enacted the Law of Obligatory Bequests, providing for inheritance by orphaned grandchildren.

1951 Jordanian Law of Family Rights was reformed to allow stipulation in marriage contracts against polygamy, give women the right to divorce on certain specified grounds, and restrict talaq.

1953 Syria enacted the Law of Personal Status which lay down minimum ages for marriage, restricted polygamy and talaq, and provided for maintenance for divorced wives.

1956 Tunisia enacted the Code of Personal Status, providing for minimum ages for marriage, abolishing polygamy, providing that no divorce may be pronounced outside a court of law, and giving women the same right of talaq as men.

1958 Morocco enacted the Code of Personal Status, laying down minimum ages for marriage and restricting talaq.

1959 Passage of the Iraqi Law of Personal Status (amended in 1963) laid down minimum age for marriage, introduced restrictions on polygamy and talaq, and provided reforms in the Sunni law of inheritance.

1959 Algeria enacted the Marriage Ordinance prohibiting divorce outside a court of law and permitting alimony to be granted to a divorced wife.

1961 Pakistan Muslim Family Laws Ordinance was enacted restricting talaq and polygamy and providing for inheritance by orphaned grandchildren.

1967 Iran enacted the Family Protection Act (repealed 1975), which abolished talaq and restricted polygamy.

1974 South Yemen acted to restrict polygamy and to prohibit divorce except on specified grounds when marriage has irretrievably broken down.

1975 Iran enacted a second Family Protection Act, after repealing the first. Further restriction on polygamy.

Notes

1. Although this is a controversial point, the weight of the evidence in our view supports our statement.

2. The methods of achieving reform are discussed comprehensively in N. J. Coulson, *A History of Islamic Law,* Edinburgh (1964), pp. 174ff.

3. We do not consider Turkey, although the first reforms which took place in Islamic family law occurred there, since *sharia* law has been totally abandoned and replaced by the Swiss Civil Code. Countries such as Albania, Yugoslavia, and the Soviet Union are not included, despite their significant numbers of Muslim inhabitants, since their law can no longer be considered in any way Islamic.

4. It is interesting to note that article 17 of the original Iranian Family Protection Act of 1967 provided that its provisions relating to circumstances in which a certificate of reconciliation could be sought from the court should henceforth be included as stipulations in all marriage contracts. At first sight this article appears to serve no useful purpose, but it is in fact a legal strategy. By its insertion a complete break with the sharia was avoided, for the effect of the article was to give the impression that divorce was still the right of the husband and that the wife had a comparable right only when it was delegated to her.

Bibliography

Anderson, J. N. D. *Reforms in Islamic Law*. London, 1977.

Coulson, N. J. *Conflicts and Tensions in Islamic Jurisprudence*. Chicago, 1969.

———. *A History of Islamic Law*. Edinburgh, 1964.

———. *Succession in the Muslim Family*. Cambridge, 1971.

de Bellefonds, Y. Linent. *Traité de droit musulman comparé*, vols. I–III. Paris, 1965–1973.

2 Legal Reform as an Indicator of Women's Status in Muslim Nations

Elizabeth H. White

In comparison with other major culture areas, the Muslim-majority nations of the world have low rates of reported economic activity by women, low female literacy, and low female school enrollment at all levels. Female education in the Muslim world has shown only slight improvement in recent years, and the gap between female and male literacy rates is increasing. During the decade from 1960 to 1970, female literacy in the Arab world improved by 5 percent, from 90 to 85 percent illiterate, while male rates improved by over 10 percent, from 71 to 60 percent illiterate (UNESCO 1972). In the Arab area, which includes most of the Muslim countries of the Middle East, the gap between female and male rates increased from 19 percent in 1960 to 25 percent in 1970. Age-specific literacy rates for individual countries reveal that the traditions that limit women's access to education are still very strong: illiteracy among younger women is not substantially less than among the elderly. For example, in Pakistan 85 percent of the 10- to 14-year-old girls are illiterate; in Iran, 70 percent of that age are illiterate; in Libya, 84 percent. In all three countries more than 95 percent of women over 60 are illiterate. Though there has been some increase in the number of literates over the years, it is far less than the change in Latin American countries where illiteracy has declined from over half the 60-year-old women to generally less than one-fourth of the 15- to 19-year-olds. Throughout the world, the poor, the rural, and the female half of the population are least likely to be educated. The restrictive nature of the Muslim social system further reduces the chances that women will become educated.

In most Muslim countries, the reported rate of female participation in economic activity is very low, in comparison with other countries at similar levels of economic development. Although Iran, Morocco, Syria, and Tunisia, for instance, are at about the same level of economic development as Mexico, Peru, and Ecuador, the rate of women's employment in the Muslim countries is less than half that of the Latin American countries (Youssef 1974:10). Some of this contrast is due to differences in the criteria for the statistics; it is also due to different attitudes towards women's work. Muslim women are not idle, but their labor is generally confined to the home and cottage industries which are not considered worthy of reporting in national statistics. In the Muslim world, economic dependency, not active participation in economic activities, is the ideal for women.

Statistical evidence suggests that low levels of female education and female employment are typical of Muslim societies. It can be further inferred that among Muslim societies, those that are the "most" Muslim, in the sense of enforcing the traditional restrictions on women, will have the lowest rates of female education and employment. The problem can be stated in the form of the hypothesis: women's educational achievement and participation in economic activity in Muslim countries varies with the enforcement of Islamic restrictions on women.

Two types of restrictions operate to affect women's status in Muslim societies: first, the legal restrictions and inequalities mentioned in the Quran, *hadith, sunna,* and *sharia* law codes. These include inequality in inheritance, marriage, divorce, child custody, and the ability to serve as witnesses. The second type of restriction is that imposed by the practice of *purdah* or seclusion. In this study, only the first type of restriction, legal inequality, will be used to create a scale upon which Muslim nations may be ranked, according to the extent of reform up to January 1974. The information on enforcement of traditional laws has been obtained from several articles and books about individual countries and the comparative works of J. N. D. Anderson (1959), N. J. Coulson (1964), and Tahir Mahmood (1972). Mahmood's work is the most recent and helpful summary of reform in laws affecting women and the family in the Muslim world. The following indicators are used to create a scale of relative improvement in women's status in Muslim countries: the establishment of a minimum legal age for marriage, the establishment of a registration requirement for marriage, the provision for women to request dissolution of marriage, reform in inheritance laws, regulation of polygamy, abolition of men's right of unilateral divorce, abolition of polygamy, establishment of secular inheritance law to replace religious inheritance law, and secularization of all personal law through establishment of a civil code that is not based upon religion.

It is possible to rank Muslim countries on a scale based on these indicators of reform. However, there are a number of countries in which there has been no effort to reform or codify traditional law as it applies to women and the family. This was the case for Somalia until very recently. Saudi Arabia, Mauritania, and Yemen (YAR) are among the nations which up to 1972 had not reformed or codified any aspect of personal or family law. In those nations, there is no limitation upon a man's right to contract several marriages, to repudiate wives, to arrange the marriage of his underage daughter without her consent, or to keep his wives' and daughters' share of his estate to the minimum. These countries, therefore, are at the most restricted end of the scale of countries ranked on the basis of reform in laws affecting women (Mahmood 1972:272).[1]

In those countries where personal law has been neither codified nor reformed, there is lack of uniformity in its application to individual cases. Local custom and the limited knowledge of local judges may affect decisions as much as the words in the Quran or sharia. For instance, in many areas daughters are not permitted to inherit land in spite of the specific advice in the Quran that they have a share in the father's estate. In addition to local variation, there is variation among the schools of legal interpretation. The Hanafi school allows an adult woman to contract her own marriage, while according to the Shafiʿi school every woman must have the consent and cooperation of her father or guardian (*wali*) in order to contract a marriage (Coulson 1964:183). Although there is considerable variation among the countries whose laws remain uncodified and unreformed, they are given the same rank on the scale used in this study. It can be assumed that they apply traditional restrictions and inequalities more severely than those countries that have instituted one or more reforms.

The first reform used as an indicator of decreasing restrictiveness is the establishment of a minimum age for marriage. The first Muslim ruler to introduce such a reform was the Emperor Akbar of India (1556–1605) who required men to be sixteen and women fourteen before marriage. The reform was not enforced by his successors, however (Mujeeb 1967:263). Minimum age for marriage is desired by Muslim women themselves; at a conference of Arab women in Kuwait in December 1972, there was a unanimous call for abolition of marriage under the age of sixteen, along with equal rights, the franchise, and abolition of brideweath (*Arab Report and*

Record 1972:2). Where there is no legal age for marriage, girls are often married in late childhood or at puberty, according to local custom. Their chances of being educated or having a choice in life roles is limited. Introduction of age requirements for marriage is a limited step in freeing women from traditional restrictions. Along with registration of marriage, it has been introduced in conservative countries, such as Libya. Where minimum marriage age has been introduced, it is rarely enforced or widely publicized. In Turkey, the legal age was eighteen for men and seventeen for women according to the Family Law of 1926, but the minimum was lowered to seventeen and fifteen years when it became evident that few people complied with the age requirement.

Because there is no uniform system of birth registration in most of these countries, proof of age is difficult to obtain; a bride might not be aware of her exact age, making enforcement of the law difficult. The Syrian law avoids this problem by requiring puberty and sanity, rather than a specific age, for marriage. In most countries there are few sanctions against underage marriage. Fairly typical is Pakistan's Family Laws Ordinance which raises the marriage age to sixteen but specifies no punishment for marriage of persons under sixteen. The marriage of underage persons is not void unless the bride or groom who is underage reports the marriage to the authorities prior to consummation. Only the Soviet Union in its Muslim territories has punishment, including prison terms, for "marriage or conjugal relations with persons under eighteen" (Coulson 1964:248; Mahmood 1972:20, 48). The relevant provisions in the Turkmen Criminal Code was restated in harsher terms in 1960, indicating that the minimum marriage age introduced in 1926 was not uniformly observed. Although enforcement of minimum age is rarely uniform among economic classes and geographic areas, or genuinely effective, the fact that such a law has been introduced indicates an official concern for the rights of children, particularly girls, who are usually married at a younger age than boys.

The second reform that serves as an indicator of decreasing severity of restrictions is the requirement of civil registration of marriage. This reform is usually introduced along with the minimum age requirement. Again, there is considerable variation concerning its enforcement. In Pakistan registration is required by law, but lack of registration carries no fine and does not invalidate the marriage. In Turkey, where civil marriage registration has been required for many years, there is still resistance to it, in rural communities particularly. There are objections to the requirement of medical examinations which violate the modesty of the bride and difficulty in securing documents for proof of age and identity. For any, the civil marriage and registration is not considered as important to the legitimacy of the union as the signing of a traditional marriage contract (Reed 1957:68). The Turkish Assembly periodically legitimizes the children of all unregistered and polygamous marriages, indicating that large numbers of people do not comply with the legal requirements of registration and monogamy.

Some of the registration of marriage laws include the requirement that both bride and groom give consent for marriage, but except in the countries that have completely secularized personal law, the bride's silence is still considered the equivalent of consent (Levy 1965:56, Mahmood 1972:64). Registration of marriage can improve women's status by giving the wife legal basis for asserting her rights in disputes over inheritance, divorce, and child custody. Ideally, the religious *nikah* contract, which is required by Islam and binding on both parties, should accomplish the same protection of women's rights, but the nikah is subject to the whims of interpretation of religious authorities who are likely to be extremely traditional. Minimum marriage age and reforms in divorce and polygamy depend upon registration of marriages for enforcement; therefore, requiring registration is an appropriate indicator of intention to limit the traditional restrictions on women.

The third most frequent reform affecting women's rights is the provision that wives may request divorce. In some schools, it has been possible for a bride's family to include in the marriage contract specific situations that will be grounds for divorce initiated by the wife, particularly if those grounds do not impinge upon the husband's rights of divorce and polygamy and if the wife is willing to give up her claim to *mahr,* or dower, pledged at the time of marriage (Coulson 1964:191). The earliest divorce reform was the Ottoman Family Law of 1917, which permitted women to ask for separation without limiting the husband's right to repudiate wives without cause. The modern reforms generally permit women to request divorce on specific grounds, either those mentioned in the marriage contract or others considered generally valid. For instance, in Iran the grounds for divorce by the wife include disappearance, imprisonment, impotence, and failure of the husband to maintain the wife financially. In Pakistan, a wife can request divorce on the grounds of an improperly registered polygamous marriage, but in Indonesia polygamy is grounds for divorce only if it was specifically mentioned in the marriage contract. In Egypt, a wife can request dissolution of marriage only on the grounds of desertion, disappearance, failure to maintain, cruelty, and disease.

Those reforms that only grant women limited rights to request separation or divorce do not change the Muslim husband's right to repudiate wives, which is known as *talaq*. The husband can simply pronounce the talaq formula, "I divorce thee," and inform authorities later, if at all, while a woman must present her request for divorce before a civil or family court (Mahmood 1972:193, Vreede-de-Stuers 1968:31). Even where women have been granted the right to request divorce, few take advantage of it. Many illiterate women are unaware of the law, and social pressure prevents the exercise of the new rights. Nevertheless, where the reform has been introduced, women's lives are not quite so restricted by traditional social regulations.

Another indicator of willingness to remove traditional inequalities is reform of inheritance law. Under all schools of Islamic law, women's inheritance is limited and unequal to men's. A childless widow may inherit one-fourth of her husband's estate, one-eighth if she has children; a widower, however, may inherit half his childless wife's estate, one-fourth if there are children. A daughter's inheritance is half that of a son. In the Quran it is mentioned that a male shall always inherit twice as much as a female. This inequality is based on the assumption that males will provide for the material needs of females throughout their lives. In many parts of the Muslim world, women do not inherit even their legal share of parents' estates. In those areas, enforcement of Islamic law could increase women's property rights. The first step in most reforms of inheritance law is to permit orphaned grandchildren to inherit from grandparents. Ten countries have introduced this reform. Other reforms permit wives and daughters to inherit more than the traditional share of their fathers' or husbands' estates. Reform of inheritance law indicates a willingness to replace arbitrary rules concerning the division of property with increased equality and appropriateness to modern economic situations.

The two aspects of Islamic law that are most inequitable to women are those concerned with polygamy and talaq. Few Muslim countries have been willing to eliminate these rights which favor men: only Tunisia, Turkey, Albania, and the Muslim states of the Soviet Union have done so. Several other nations have introduced regulations concerning polygamy, but frequently these laws merely give sanction to the existing practice without limiting or controlling it. For example, in Syria court consent is required for polygamy, determined by the husband's presentation of proof of ability to support more than one wife. The wife's approval is not required. The Moroccan law forbids unequal treatment of wives, but does not stipulate a means of determining inequalities. Pakistan's family laws require only that the polygamous marriage be approved by the local union council (an elected body of local leaders which existed during the Ayub Khan regime); it does not limit the right of men to enter polygamous marriages. President Sadat of Egypt in 1972 declared a "war on polygamy," but no legal limitation has been placed on the practice in that country (Mahmood 1972:105). In Iran, polygamy is permitted only under limited circumstances and with proof that the first wife has been informed. Regulation of polygamy that does not limit its practice does little to remove the inequity of the situation wherein men are allowed four spouses and women one. The practice of polygamy is actually fairly low (less than 10 percent of marriages are polygamous in most areas), but as long as the threat of polygamy remains, women are constrained to agree with the husband and his family. If a woman disagrees or falls into disfavor, another wife may enter the home to divide the resources and affection of the husband. Continued legality of polygamy may affect birth rates considerably. A wife is under pressure to produce sons quickly after marriage to avoid replacement by a co-wife. Regulation of polygamy is an indication of interest in removing its effect on women's status, but where it is not actually abolished, the possibility of polygamy can affect every woman's role as wife and mother.[2]

Actual abolition of polygamy and talaq has only been effected in four of the countries included in this study. Two small but influential Muslim sects, the Druze and the Isma'ilis, have also abolished polygamy for their members (Coulson 1964:211). Where talaq has not been abolished, it is practiced with varying frequency by Muslim husbands. In Indonesia, the talaq rate is 52 percent of the marriage rate; in Egypt 26 percent; and in Syria only 5 percent of the marriage rate (Vreede-de-Stuers 1960:127). Like polygamy, the frequency of practice is not so important as the existence of this arbitrary right that husbands can exercise over wives. There is reluctance to eliminate these two practices which are essential to the concept of the husband's superiority.

Turkey and the Communist Muslim states eliminated polygamy and talaq when replacing religious law with a complete code of civil law based on European legal codes. Tunisia took the more unusual step of abolishing these practices within the framework of an Islamic explanation. The abolition of polygamy was explained as being based upon the Quranic stipulation that men must treat wives equally even though no mortal is capable of being so fair. The contradiction is interpreted to mean that Muhammad was not in favor of polygamy under general circumstances. Abolition of talaq was also explained in Islamic terms. There are verses that state that divorce is undesirable and arbitration is required whenever there is discord between the spouses. Tunisia's jurists assumed that a husband's desire to pronounce talaq was evidence of discord and therefore required intervention of the court for arbitration. Requiring court arbitration in all divorce cases could be interpreted as correction of customary abuses in Islamic traditions, not destruction of the Islamic character of the society (Coulson 1964:215). President Bourguiba is quoted as having said that Tunisia had done all that was possible in terms of reform of personal law, while still remaining a Muslim state. Although Tunisia has taken the radical steps of eliminating polygamy and talaq, it has not replaced inheritance law with a secular inheritance law. The pattern of inheritance remains basically Maliki, with some adjustment to permit inheritance by orphaned granddaughters (Mahmood 1972:109).

The only countries that have eliminated the Muslim inheritance pattern and introduced secular personal law in all spheres are those that have undergone revolutions: Turkey, Albania, and the Soviet states of Central Asia. Among these nations, there is variation in the length of time since the introduction of reforms. There is also considerable regional and class variation in compliance with reformed laws within each country.

Other indicators that might have been useful in this scale are data concerning women's economic rights. In some countries women are permitted to sue and enter contracts without their husband's authorization; in others employment of women is restricted by the need to obtain the husband's permission. Unfortunately, data on women's economic restrictions are not available for many of the Muslim countries (United Nations Commission on the Status of Women 1968:76, 90). One can assume that in Saudi Arabia, where there have been no reforms to reduce restrictions on women in traditional law, there would also be no removal of traditional restrictions on women's rights to engage in employment or enter contracts.

The nine indicators arranged in order of decreasing restrictiveness form a scale upon which twenty-one Muslim countries can be ranked. Beginning with the rank of one at the bottom of the scale are the countries that are most restrictive and have reformed none of the laws discussed here. The countries that have introduced the largest number of reforms are at the top, the "emancipated" end of the scale. The scale has acceptable coefficients of reproductibility (0.98) and scalability (0.95) for use as a measure of variations

Table 2.1. Reform in restrive laws affecting women's status (to January 1974).

Rank and country	Minimum marriage age	Marriage registration	Dissolution of marriage	Inheritance reform	Polygamy regulation	Abolition of talaq	Abolition of polygamy	Secular inheritance law	Civil code replacing all religious law
10. Albania	+	+	+	+	+	+	+	+	+
10. Soviet Central Asia	+	+	+	+	+	+	+	+	+
10. Turkey	+	+	+	+	+	+	+	+	+
8. Tunisia	+	+	+	+	+	+	+	—	—
6. Syria	+	+	+	+	+	—	—	—	—
6. Morocco	+	+	+	+	+	—	—	—	—
6. Iraq	+	+	+	+	+	—	—	—	—
6. Iran[a]	+	+	+	+	+	—	—	—	—
5. Egypt	+	+	+	+	—	—	—	—	—
4. Pakistan	+	+	+	—	—	—	—	—	—
4. Jordan	+	+	+	—	—	—	—	—	—
4. Indonesia	+	+	+	—	—	—	—	—	—
4. Algeria	+	+	+	—	—	—	—	—	—
4. Sudan	+	—	+	—	—	—	—	—	—
3. Libya	+	+	—	—	—	—	—	—	—
3. Mali	+	+	—	—	—	—	—	—	—
1. Afghanistan	—	—	—	—	—	—	—	—	—
1. Saudi Arabia	—	—	—	—	—	—	—	—	—
1. Mauritania	—	—	—	—	—	—	—	—	—
1. Somalia[a]	—	—	—	—	—	—	—	—	—
1. Yemen (Arab Republic)	—	—	—	—	—	—	—	—	—

a. Reforms since January 1974 change the place of Somalia and Iran in this table—*eds.*

among Muslim countries. Table 2.1 provides the positions of the twenty-one countries on the scale. The list includes all the Muslim-majority nations except Kuwait and a number of other extremely small states in the Arabian peninsula. All the latter would have scores of one on the scale as they have not introduced any reforms in personal or family law. The large minority of Muslims who live in India also retain traditional laws concerning polygamy, inheritance, and divorce; the Indian marriage acts specifically exclude Muslims from their jurisdiction (Smith 1970:420).

Using the scale as an indicator of variation in the enforcement of traditional Muslim restrictions on women, it is possible to test the hypothesis that the educational achievement of women will vary with the enforcement of traditional Muslim restrictions. The indicators of educational achievement of women used to test this hypothesis are: female enrollment in elementary school as a percentage of total elementary enrollment, female enrollment in secondary school as a percentage of total secondary enrollment, female primary school enrollment as a percentage of the total population of females of primary school age, female primary school enrollment (as a percentage of total girls of school age) in proportion to male primary school enrollment (as a percentage of total boys of school age), literacy of females over fifteen years of age, and the ratio of adult female literacy to male literacy. Data on literacy and school enrollments were obtained from United Nations yearbooks and other publications (UNESCO 1970:13). School enrollment figures are available for all the countries on the scale, but adult literacy rates, which depend upon census data, are not available for Saudi Arabia, Mauritania, or Somalia. Considering the low female enrollment rates in those countries, one can expect that adult female literacy rates are extremely low, certainly below 10 percent. School enrollment figures are likely to be the most accurate as they are gathered annually by the education departments in the countries concerned. The proportion of girls in school to total population of girls of school age is more subject to error, as it depends upon recent accurate age-group census data, as does the adult literacy rate. Particularly in the more conservative countries, there is likely to be underreporting of females of all ages, owing to reluctance to reveal the identity or existence of female family members to the census taker. The use of several indicators of educational achievement may decrease the problem of errors in any single indicator.

There is a wide variation in educational achievement by women among the countries under consideration. The proportion of girls in the elementary student population ranges from over 50 percent in Tunisia, where an effort is being made to make up for low female enrollment in the past, to Yemen where only 2 percent of the elementary students are female. At the secondary level female enrollment varies from 1 percent in Yemen to 40 percent in Albania. Ideally, half the school population should be female in any area. The indicator with the greatest variation is the proportion of girls of school age who are actually enrolled in school. In those countries where girls make up the smallest proportion of students, students of both sexes are only a tiny fraction of the total population of school-age children. The educational systems of these countries are very underdeveloped. In Yemen and Somalia, for instance, only 8 percent of the boys of school age are enrolled in school and less than 3 percent of the girls. Jordan and Indonesia evidently have well-developed educational systems as both countries report over 40 percent of the primary enrollment as female. This represents over three-fourths of the girls of school age in the population of Jordan and Indonesia.

Table 2.2 illustrates the variation in the education indicators. The nations that are most conservative in terms of legal reforms affecting women have the lowest female enrollment at all levels and the lowest adult female literacy rates. Analysis of the data reveals that there is a strong statistical relationship between the variables *legal reform* and *women's education.* The relationship is linear; that is, increasing reforms affecting women correspond with increasing female educational achievement.

The strongest statistical relationship is of the legal reform ranking and the percentage of primary school-age girls who are in school. Evidently, those countries that have made little effort to improve women's legal status provide few schools for girls and do not encourage their enrollment in existing schools. The relationship is almost as strong when the percentage of primary enrollment that is female is used as an indicator of female educational achievement. This measure is likely to be more accurate as it is based upon current enrollment and does not depend upon knowledge of the age distribution of the total population.

It is surprising and discouraging to find that the effect of restrictiveness operates strongly even at the primary level to limit the opportunities for girls in school. The most restrictive countries have fairly low enrollment rates for boys also, but the disparity between girls' and boys' enrollment rates decreases with the decreasing restrictiveness as indicated by rank on the reform scale. There is also a strong relationship between restrictiveness and the proportion of female secondary students enrolled. Higher education for both sexes is limited in the poorer countries, but there are fewer opportunities for girls. Desire to keep girls at home after puberty, although there are schools available, is typical of Muslim society. Even in the Soviet Union, the custom of withdrawing girls from school at about eleven years of age is reported among the Uzbek and other Muslim people (Bacon 1966).

Table 2.2. Women's educational achievement and economic activity (to 1973).

Reform rank	School-age girls in school (primary) (%)	Female school enrollment (primary) (% of total enrollment)	Female school enrollment (secondary) (% of total enrollment)	Females over 15 literate (%)	Adult females economically active: Total (%)	Adult females economically active: Nonagricultural (%)
10. Albania	99	46	40	33	36.3	—
10. Soviet Central Asia	99	48	40	94	40.0	20.0
10. Turkey	61	41	28	28	33.4	6.68
8. Tunisia	83	55	27	18	3.0	2.61
6. Syria	57	37	24	13	5.4	0.54
6. Morocco	36	33	26	6	5.9	3.89
6. Iraq	50	29	26	6	2.3	1.73
6. Iran	44	36	33	13	8.3	6.23
5. Egypt	55	38	31	9	4.8	3.60
4. Pakistan	25	29	22	8	8.8	0.97
4. Jordan	85	43	30	16	2.6	1.72
4. Indonesia	72	45	30	27	19.0	10.00
4. Algeria	54	38	29	8	1.8	1.35
4. Sudan	21	33	23	3	26.4	3.96
3. Libya	54	29	16	4	2.7	2.24
3. Mali	12	32	23	1	—	—
1. Afghanistan	5	13	13	2	—	—
1. Saudi Arabia	18	28	14	—	—	—
1. Mauritania	1	28	9	—	—	—
1. Somalia	3	22	19	—	—	—
1. Yemen (Arab Republic)	1	2	1	6	—	—

Source: International Labor Organization, *Statistical Yearbook* (Geneva, 1973); UNESCO, *Literacy 1969 to 1971* (Paris, 1972).

Low adult female literacy rates are also associated with variations in restrictiveness. Where Islamic restrictions are maintained, women's literacy is low and lags behind men's. All the indicators of female educational achievement support the hypothesis that enforcement of Muslim restrictions on women limits their educational achievement.[3]

There is a possibility that economic development could affect women's educational achievement, but statistical tests reveal little relationship among per capita gross national product, restrictiveness, and women's education. Relatively poor Muslim states, such as Turkey and Tunisia, have reformed many laws affecting women and encouraged female education, while some of the wealthier countries, such as Libya and Saudi Arabia, have introduced few or no reforms and report low educational achievement of women. Some of the most conservative countries are now experiencing rapid increases in wealth owing to the exploitation of oil; the effect of this prosperity on the status and achievements of women will be an interesting area for further research.

Relatively few women are employed outside the home in Muslim countries. Even in the agricultural sector, the employment rate of women is less than in neighboring areas of different religious persuasion (Boserup 1972:71). There is a strong tendency to underreport women's employment and participation in economic activities, as indicated by the data in table 2.2. Seclusion of women is the ideal in most Muslim societies, so their contribution to production is not recognized in national statistics. The discrepancy in reporting methods is illustrated by Turkey which reports that 33 percent of its adult female population is economically active, while Iran reports only 8 percent. The Turkish figure includes many women employed on family farms, while in Iran such labor on family farms and local crafts is probably not reported. Pakistan reports that only 8.8 percent of adult women are economically active but a survey I conducted in 1974 revealed that almost 20 percent of adult women were employed outside the home and therefore "economically active." Employment of women in commercial, industrial, and clerical jobs is rare in Muslim areas, although in non-Muslim parts of Asia and in Catholic South America women are active in these fields of employment. Highly educated women in the Muslim world pursue professional careers within the all-female, secluded institutions which purdah necessitates. Opportunities for women to serve as hospital administrators, school and college principals, as well as teachers and doctors, may be greater in Muslim areas than in areas where mixed institutions are acceptable. However, these professionals are a small percentage of the total female population.

Low female participation in the labor force affects the economic development of the Muslim world by limiting the labor pool and by encouraging high dependency ratios and population growth. The governments of these countries recognize that superstitions, social prejudice, and women's own attitudes are obstacles to their participation in the labor force. Iran, Iraq, Libya, Pakistan, Somalia, and Egypt are among the countries that report to the United Nations that social constraints limit the roles of their women in economic development (United Nations Commission on the Status of Women 1970:49).

The indicators of women's employment used to test the hypothesis are the percentage of women economically active and the percentage of women active in the nonagricultural sector, as reported in the International Labor Organization *Statistical Yearbook, 1972.* The percentage of women economically active ranges from 1.8 to 40. Turkey and the Soviet Central Asian areas report the highest participation. Only two countries that rank below eight on the reform scale report economic activity rates over 9 percent: these are Indonesia and the Sudan. Geographic location may explain these exceptions: there is a strong tradition of women's activity in agriculture and petty trade in both Africa and southeast Asia that may counteract the expected restrictiveness of Islam. Several nations, including Mali, Afghanistan, Saudi Arabia, Mauritania, and Somalia, do not report women's economic activity or employment. Women's participation in the nonagricultural sector is lower than total female participation, ranging from 0.54 to 20 percent. There is likely to be more accurate and comparable data for the nonagricultural sector, although domestic service and cottage industry occupations may be underreported. Statistical tests of the employment levels and reform scale rankings indicate that there is a close relationship between these two variables, though slightly less strong than the relationship of educational achievement and reform scale ranking.[4]

In conclusion, the evidence supports the hypothesis that variations in the severity of enforcement of traditional Islamic restrictions on women are associated with variations in the educational achievement and employment of women. Although Islamic laws do not prohibit female education or participation in economically productive activities, those nations that are unwilling to reform those laws are also apparently unwilling to provide equal educational facilities for women or to encourage the entry of women into the labor force. The nations that have reformed the laws most inequitable and restrictive to women have higher female literacy, school enrollment, and reported female participation in economic activities. Although Muslim nations as a group have some of the lowest levels of female literacy and school enrollment in the world, there is considerable variation among them. Analysis of data of the early 1970s indicates that over half the variation in educational achievement is statistically related to the variation in legal reforms. Just under half the variation in employment rates is related to the variation in legal reforms. This supports the hypothesis of this study strongly, and refutes the notion of the so-called apologists of Islam who argue that the existence of legal inequities is unimportant. Differences in legal restrictions are important variables in determining behavior patterns.[5]

This conclusion has important implications for administrators and political leaders of Muslim countries that are striving to achieve the levels of literacy and employment associated with economic development. Other studies have indicated that women's fertility varies inversely with their education; those Muslim nations that wish to limit population growth have a further incentive to encouraging women's education. Improvement of women's educational achievement may be impossible without accompanying reforms in the restrictive legal and social structures of these countries. Conservative religious and political elements in the population frequently resist such reforms. There was violent resistance to reform in Soviet Central Asia and in Afghanistan in the 1920s, but in Turkey the enthusiasm of the national revolution facilitated the acceptance of reform. Strong, relatively popular regimes, such as those in Iran and Tunisia, have been able to introduce reforms in an Islamic context without causing widespread protest or violence.[6]

Reforms that reduce the inequalities in traditional Islamic law affecting women are apparently an essential aspect of the process of social development. Without such reforms, the high literacy, low birth rates, and high participation of women in the labor force that are characteristic of economic and social development are not likely to appear.

Notes

1. Uncodified Islamic law also applies to the large Muslim minorities of Thailand, Burma, Greece, Yugoslavia, Ethiopia, Ghana, Uganda, and Sierra Leone.

2. There is some controversy over the physiological effect of polygamy

on birth rates. Polygamous husbands have more children than monogamous husbands, but the women in polygamous marriages have fewer children than women in single unions.

3. Correlation values and regression equations for the education indicators and the reform scale rankings (significant at 0.01 or better) are as follows:

Restrictiveness and the percentage of primary-age girls in school:	$R^2 = .62$	$y = 4.09 + 8.42 \times$
Restrictiveness and females as a percentage of total primary enrollment:	$R^2 = .56$	$y = 22.9 + 2.44 \times$
Restrictiveness and females as a percentage of total secondary enrollment:	$R^2 = .59$	$y = 13.5 + 2.1 \times$
Restrictiveness and the percentage of literate females over fifteen:	$R^2 = .46$	$y = 7.0 + 4.93 \times$

4. Correlation values and regression equations for the employment indicators (significant at 0.01 or better) are as follows:

Restrictiveness and the percentages of women economically active:	$R^2 = .43$	$y = -9.18 + 3.76 \times$
Restrictiveness and the percentage of women active in the nonagricultural sector:	$R^2 = .42$	$y = -2.68 + 1.29 \times$

5. Additional tests of the hypothesis using data on legal reform, education, and employment of women at different periods in the past, such as 1950 or 1960, would probably support the findings of this study. A test in the future, at the end of this decade of change and economic development, is planned.

6. In 1977 there were violent protests in Iran, partly against coeducation and women's equal rights—ed.

Bibliography

Anderson, J. N. D., ed. *Changing Law in Developing Countries.* New York, 1961.

———. *Islamic Law in the Modern World.* New York, 1959.

Bacon, Elizabeth E. *Central Asia under Russian Rule.* Ithaca, N.Y., 1966.

Boserup, Ester. *Women's Role in Economic Development.* London, 1972.

Conference of Arab Women, Kuwait. *Arab Report and Record,* 11 (1972): 31.

Coulson, N. J. *A History of Islamic Law*. Edinburgh, 1964.

———. "Islamic Family Law: Progress in Pakistan." In *Changing Law in Developing Countries*, ed. J. N. D. Anderson. New York, 1963.

International Labor Office. *Statistical Information on Women's Participation in Economic Activity*. Geneva, 1970.

International Labor Organization. *Statistical Yearbook, 1972*. Geneva, 1973.

Levy, Reuben. *The Social Structure of Islam*. London, 1965.

Mahmood, Tahir. *Family Law Reform in the Muslim World*. Bombay, 1972.

Mujeeb, M. *The Indian Muslims*. Montreal, 1967.

Papanek, Gustav F. *Pakistan's Development: Social Goals and Private Incentives*. Cambridge, Mass., 1967.

Reed, Howard. "The Religious Life of Modern Turkish Muslims." In *Islam and the West*, ed. Richard Frye. The Hague, 1957.

Reed, J. S. "Women's Status and Law Reform." In *Changing Law in Developing Countries*, ed. J. N. D. Anderson. New York, 1963.

Smith, Donald Eugene. *Religion and Political Development*. Boston, 1970.

United Nations Commission on the Status of Women. *Constitutions, Electoral Laws, and Other Instruments Relating to the Political Rights of Women*. New York, 1968.

———. *The Participation of Women in the Economic and Social Development of Their Countries*. New York, 1970.

United Nations Educational, Scientific and Cultural Organization. *Comparative Study of Co-Education*. Paris, 1970.

———. *Literacy 1969 to 1971: Progress Achieved throughout the World*. Paris, 1972.

Vreede-de-Stuers, Cora. *The Indonesian Woman: Struggles and Achievements*. S'Gravenhage, 1960.

———. *Parda: A Study of Muslim Women's Life in Northern India*. Assen, 1968.

Youssef, Nadia Haggag. *Women and Work in Developing Societies*. University of California Population Monograph Series, no. 15. Berkeley, 1974.

3 The Status and Fertility Patterns of Muslim Women

Nadia H. Youssef

This essay relates available information on the fertility patterns of Muslim countries in North Africa, the Middle East, and Asia—Algeria, Tunisia, Morocco, Libya, Egypt, Syria, Jordan, Iraq, Iran, Turkey, Pakistan, and Indonesia—to the status and position of women in Muslim social structure. The analysis relies chiefly on the latest census data, United Nations publications, and sample surveys conducted in the countries concerned.

Table 3.1 presents the distribution of fertility levels as measured by the gross reproduction rate, the crude birth rate, and the child/woman ratio for the individual Muslim countries and the regional averages of these fertility variables for the Muslim world, for non-Muslim Asia (excluding Japan and Israel), and for the Central and South American countries. The individual figures for the Muslim nations should not be regarded as highly accurate since official statistics are generally not complete enough to provide reliable measures of natality.[1] The lack of accuracy is reflected, for example, in considerable discrepancies between the values of the crude birth rate and the gross reproduction rate, the crude birth rate and the child/woman ratio, and the gross reproduction rate and the child/woman ratio within and across individual countries that cannot be

---

This article is a portion of a larger paper entitled "Women's Status and Fertility in Muslim Countries of the Middle East and Asia," prepared for the Symposium on Women's Status and Fertility around the World, sponsored by the American Psychological Association, August 1974, New Orleans, Louisiana. I wish to thank Professor David Heer for his evaluation of the larger version of this paper and the valuable criticism and helpful suggestions he offered.

Table 3.1. Fertility profile of Muslim populations, c. 1960.

Country	Population Muslim (%)	Gross reproduction rate (est.)	Crude birth rate	Child/woman ratio[a]
Pakistan	88	3.7	51	832
Syria	82	3.5	48	956
Iraq	95	3.5	49	840
Morocco	95	3.4	50	845
Algeria	99	3.4	50	940
Tunisia	97	3.4	38	880
Jordan	88	3.4	48	815
Libya	96	3.3	46	857
Egypt	91	3.2	37	702
Iran	98	3.1	45	851
Turkey	99	2.9	40	700
Indonesia	90	2.8	47	—
Regional Averages				
Muslim countries		3.3	46	838
Asian countries		2.6	35	644
Central American countries		2.7	37	772
South American countries		2.6	37	670

Sources: A. R. Omran, *Egypt: Population Problems and Prospects* (Chapel Hill, N.C., 1973), p. 166; Department of Economic and Social Affairs, *Demographic Yearbook 1969* (New York, 1970), tables 8, 15, 18, 31; *1973 World Population Data Sheet* (Washington, D.C., 1974); Charles Nam, *Population and Society* (Boston, 1968), p. 232; Department of Economic and Social Affairs, *Demographic Yearbook 1968* (New York, 1969), table 8.

a. Number of children under 5 years of age per 1000 females of reproductive age (15–49 years).

accounted for by country differences in the age composition of the female population or infant/childhood mortality statistics.[2]

Within the data limitations, there is, nevertheless, reasonably reliable information, when taken collectively, to enable us to identify distinctive features of Muslim fertility. For the purpose of the following discussion, the gross reproduction rate will be considered as the most accurate and sensitive indicator of fertility performance; the child/woman ratio as reflecting, at best, the extent to which women in each society are burdened with child care. The latter measure is of particular importance to the subject of women's status. Instead of births, this ratio is based on the survivors of past births and thus includes the effects of infant/childhood mortality.

The two poignant observations of this study are, first, that all Muslim countries exhibit a very high fertility, despite pronounced diversities in ethnic background, economic infrastructure, and political ideology. Second, Muslim fertility levels on all variables are higher than those of non-Islamic countries currently at comparable levels of economic-industrial development. The gross reproduction rate in the Muslim countries, which averages 3.3, corresponds to an average crude birth rate of 46, and an average of 838 children aged under five per 1000 females of reproductive age. Fertility appears to be highest in Pakistan, Syria, and Iraq (GRR = 3.6) and lowest in Turkey and Indonesia (GRR = 2.9). The child/woman ratio is highest in Syria and Algeria and lowest in Turkey and Egypt. Such high fertility characteristics are not found in other countries associated with economic and social modernization. Women in neighboring Asia bear fewer children (GRR = 2.6; the child/woman ratio averages 644). The same is true of the Central and South American countries where the average gross reproduction rate is also 2.6 and where the number of children aged less than five per 1000 women (15–49) averages between 670 and 772.

The possibility of a specific pronatalist force in Muslim cultures is suggested by a comparison of the natality statistics of Muslim populations with those of their non-Muslim neighbors.[3] In Europe and in the Soviet Union, Muslims have shown a consistently higher fertility than Christians and other non-Muslim groups. This is evident when one looks at the natality statistics for Albania, the Muslim districts of Yugoslavia, and the Muslim republics in the Soviet Union. In the Near and Middle East the sharp differential is suggested by the birth rate in Turkey (GRR = 2.9) and Greece (GRR = 1.2), and by the by far higher natality of Muslims in North Africa when compared with resident Europeans, in Israel when compared with Jews, in Lebanon when compared with the indigenous Maronite population, and in Egypt when compared with the native Christian population. Studies in India and in Malaysia have also shown Muslim fertility to be higher than the fertility of Hindu and Buddhist religious groups.

Correlates of Fertility

Demographic studies have sought to distinguish the relative importance of a variety of economic, demographic, social, and cultural factors that are associated with particular fertility patterns. In light of previous findings, the high fertility characteristic of Muslim societies should come as no surprise. Not only do Muslim nations exhibit a general positive valuation to high fertility, they are also distinguished by a composite of economic, demographic, and social variables that have been consistently highly correlated with high fertility in other parts of the world.

Fortunately, there are some variations in the values of these variables among Muslim countries that enable us to examine the relationship between fertility behavior and other economic and social characteristics. Although the variation in the dependent variable (the gross reproduction rate) is numerically not very large, slight variations in this rate are very significant demographically. Furthermore, there is sufficient range of variation in the economic and social correlates of fertility to justify a search for the predictors of Muslim natality levels.

In line with the general contention that fertility levels correlate negatively with advanced economic-industrial development and a decline in the actual experience/expectation of death, four indicators of these correlates have been compiled for the individual Muslim countries and presented alongside the fertility measures: the per capita gross national product, to reflect standards of living; the percentage of adult males in nonagricultural activities, to indicate industrialization level; and the general death and infant mortality rates (table 3.2).

Classifying the twelve countries into four developmental levels ranked in order of per capita GNP identifies oil-producing Libya as the most advanced economically, the Group II countries the average of the Muslim region, and Pakistan and Indonesia as the least developed. This classification corresponds closely to variations in the level of industrialization in each society, with the exception of Jordan and Turkey.

A glance at the corresponding fertility variables for each country does not indicate that the reproductive behavior of Muslim women has reacted to changes and/or differences in economic-industrial conditions. Theoretically, we expect fertility in Libya and in Iran to be lowest and in Pakistan and Indonesia to be highest. Instead we find that the highest fertility countries (Pakistan, Syria, Iraq) are spread along three different developmental stages; that Indonesia and Pakistan, though similar in their low level of economic development, typify the extremes of high and low gross reproduction rates; and, conversely, that the lowest fertility reported (Turkey, Indonesia) is characteristic of countries that differ considerably in developmental terms.

Table 3.2. Fertility levels in Muslim countries in relation to economic and demographic variables, c. 1960.

	Economic Variables		Demographic Variables		Fertility Levels	
Development level/ country	Per capita GNP (US $)	Males in nonagricultural work (%)	General death rate/ 1000	Infant mortality rate/ 1000	Gross reprod. rate	Child/ woman ratio[a]
Group I						
Libya	1,770	51.2	16	—	3.3	857
Group II						
Iran	380	39.6	17	—	3.1	851
Iraq	320	44.6	15	104	3.5	840
Algeria	320	40.8	17	86	3.4	940
Turkey	310	36.4	15	119	2.9	700
Group III						
Syria	290	35.0	15	—	3.5	956
Jordan	250	51.2	16	115	3.4	815
Tunisia	250	34.9	16	120	3.4	880
Morocco	230	38.4	16	149	3.4	845
Egypt	210	40.1	16	118	3.2	702
Group IV						
Pakistan	100	26.4	18	142	3.7	832
Indonesia	80	26.9	19	125	2.8	—
Mean	374	38.7	16	120	3.3	838

Sources: *1973 World Population Data Sheet* (Washington, D.C., 1974); International Labor Office, *Yearbook of Labor Statistics 1972* (Geneva, 1973), table 2A; Department of Economic and Social Affairs, *Demographic Yearbook 1972* (New York, 1973), tables 1, 2; Department of Economic and Social Affairs, *Demographic Yearbook 1969* (New York, 1970), tables 15, 18, 31; Department of Economic and Social Affairs, *Demographic Yearbook 1968* (New York, 1969), table 8.

a. Number of children under 5 years of age per 1000 females of reproductive age (15–49 years).

The relationship between economic development level and the child/woman ratio is likewise unclear. Algeria and Turkey, similar in terms of the GNP variable, report respectively the highest and the lowest child/woman ratio. Conversely, the same ratio is obtained in Libya, Morocco, and Pakistan, which rank first, ninth, and eleventh in terms of their per capita GNP. Syria, with the highest child/woman ratio (956), ranks sixth in developmental level, while countries reporting the lowest child/woman ratio (Egypt, Turkey) differ markedly in terms of their living standards.

The failure of the birth rates to respond to economic influences is mostly accounted for by the weakness of the per capita GNP variable in reflecting the *actual* standards of living in the Muslim world. What lends poignancy to the economic situation in which most Muslim countries find themselves is not merely their relatively low per capita income, but its uneven distribution among their citizens. The lowest incomes (well below the reported per capita) are assigned to the bulk of the population, while a minute proportion of earners are able to accrue the larger share of the total income. Inequality in income distribution is undoubtedly as high in Libya and in Iran as in the rest of the Muslim countries.

The actual experience with or expectation of death has been found to be strongly and positively correlated with fertility.[4] Except for Pakistan and Indonesia, the general mortality level is uniform in all Muslim societies (16 per 1000). Indication of a positive relationship between the general death rate and the fertility rate is obtained only in Pakistan (GRR = 3.7; CDR = 18 per 1000). Indonesia, however, appears to sustain the highest death rate (19 per 1000) together with the lowest fertility rate (GRR = 2.8). The influence of the infant mortality variable upon the fertility level is likewise ambivalent. It is expected that as the number of child deaths per family increase, so would the number of children ever born. The validity of this contention is only partially true in Muslim countries. Although there are individual cases where a correspondence between the two variables emerges, there are other cases where the expected relationship between fertility and infant mortality rates is not obtained (Algeria, Turkey, and Indonesia).

The critical point is to relate the fertility levels of Muslim populations to women's status and position. The latter are indicated by five measurable indicators: the female literacy rate, the sex differential in literacy rates, the female activity rate in income-earning economic activities, the timing of marriage, and the incidence of marriage (table 3.3). When multiple regression analysis was used to determine the relative effectiveness of women's status indicators as predictors of the fertility rate, the following results were obtained. The predictor variables accounted for 65.7 percent of the variance in gross reproduction rate (Mult. R. = 0.81061). The greatest contribution came from the female literacy variable, with female activity rate in nonagricultural work second in prediction ability. Both are negatively correlated with the gross reproduction rate. Neither the timing nor the incidence of marriage adds significantly

Table 3.3. Fertility levels in Muslim countries in relation to women's status and position, c. 1960.

Country	Fertility level GRR[a]	Indicators of Women's Status: Literacy rates	Sex differential in literacy rates	Activity rate, nonagricultural work (%)	Married, age 15–19 (%)	Never married, age 45–49 (%)
Pakistan	3.7	7.5	21.5	2.3	74.5	.8
Syria	3.5	12.7	35.7	5.4	40.3	2.6
Iraq	3.5	5.3	18.1	3.1	31.3	3.0
Morocco	3.4	2.8	17.2	6.1	54.1	2.1
Algeria	3.4	8.0	21.9	3.2	46.4	1.1
Tunisia	3.4	17.6	28.7	4.8	19.0	2.6
Jordan	3.4	15.2	36.4	1.8	30.6	2.9
Libya	3.3	4.2	33.3	4.1	73.5	.7
Egypt	3.2	12.4	27.6	5.0	34.6	1.1
Iran	3.1	12.2	20.6	12.1	45.9	.7
Turkey	2.9	27.4	37.1	3.3	32.6	1.4
Indonesia	2.8	26.1	26.9	11.9	—	1.5
Mean	3.3	12.6	27.1	5.2	43.9	1.7

Sources: Department of Economic and Social Affairs, *Demographic Yearbook 1969* (New York, 1970), table 31; Department of Economic and Social Affairs, *Demographic Yearbook 1971* (New York, 1972), tables 10, 11; International Labor Office, *Yearbook of Labor Statistics 1972* (Geneva, 1973), table 2A; Department of Economic and Social Affairs, *Demographic Yearbook 1972* (New York, 1973), tables 1, 2.

a. Gross reproduction rate.

to the prediction once the literacy rate and the activity rate are considered. The sex differential in literacy attainment has less predictive value than the female literacy rate variable.

The Status of Women

The subject matter of women's status can be approached from several different angles. One predominant trend is in terms of woman's ability to exercise her rights, such as in the decision to marry, choice of spouse, time of marriage, and dissolution of marriage; and in rights pertaining to education, economic independence through work, and participation in public life.[5] Operationally, this approach has distinct advantages in that it lends itself to measurement and easy comparison. Methodologically, however, it contains an intrinsic evolutionary bias in that it views "emancipation" and "rights" in terms of modern ideas, values, and behavior characteristic of the Western world. "Women's status" can also be seen to have two different components: the *rights* given to women and the *respect* given to them. Confusion ensues because the two distinct factors are erroneously used interchangeably, when in reality they are often inversely correlated. Thus, women receive great respect in certain societies that give them few rights; they receive equality of rights in societies in which they compete with men but have relatively low respect.[6]

A more universalistic approach and by far the most difficult to subject to measurement stems from Safilios-Rothschild's definition of *individual modernity,* which I see to have specific applicability to the status of women. She defines this concept as "the degree to which an individual is aware of the range of available options and the degree to which he holds values that permit him to choose which option is best suited to his abilities, talents, skills, interests and preferences."[7] From the outset it should be emphasized that the gap between the legally available options and rights and those that are accessible to Muslim women in actuality is very large. This is not only because of structural barriers, but because of prevailing cultural ideals that render many options in different life sectors totally unacceptable for women. Hence, Muslim society contains few explicit official and legal injunctions discriminating against women in public life. Even when these exist, they are of minimal importance when compared with censorship and control in the form of social stigmatization penalizing women who threaten to violate morality taboos.

An evaluation of the Muslim woman's marital, reproductive, educational, and occupational behavior must thus be understood as basic choices made in the context of the combined effects of the tradition of seclusion and exclusion patterns. The former refers to the volitional response of women to "resist" the forces of social modernity, the personally motivated avoidance of higher education, economic independence, and participation in public life, as distinct from exclusion, by which is meant the sanctioned prohibitions and limitations imposed by males.

Two interrelated considerations are of importance in understanding how kinship and family organization affect the status of women in Muslim society. One is the stipulation that a woman belongs to her agnatic group. This originally tribal concept has several structural ramifications. First, explicit provisions are made within the kinship unit for a male relative from the agnatic line to be economically, legally, and morally responsible for a kinswoman regardless of her marital status. The second consideration pertains to the criterion of familial pride and ratification of male identity in the Muslim community, which depend largely if not exclusively upon conformity to behavioral norms that are conceived as having to do with male "honor." The honor is realized critically and importantly through the chaste and discreet sexual behavior of womenfolk in a particular man's life: premarital chastity of the daughter and sister, fidelity of the wife, and continence of the widowed and divorced daughter or sister. These are basic principles upon which a family's reputation and status in the community depend. Such principles of honor are at the highest level of cultural valuation and have a clear structural meaning. They reflect a solid corpus of cultural strictures that control behavior and act as effective checks on social relationships.[8]

The interaction between the acknowledgment of economic and moral responsibility toward all kinswomen as prescribed by kinship institutions, on the one hand, and principles of familial honor which depend upon attributes of female sexual purity, on the other, has consolidated the structure of control over women into the exclusive hands of male members of the kin group. That in performing such a function, male family members receive the full institutional support of the religious and judicial systems has meant that the sanctions invoked against women can be very strong, particularly when the principle of legitimacy is couched in terms of family honor. Honor alone, however, is not sufficient as a cultural ideal to implement control. For kinship sanctions to become fully effective, it becomes incumbent upon the kinship group to provide economic support for its women at all times. This is exactly what has happened up until now in most Muslim societies: the perpetuation of the status of women as economic dependents. Few women have felt the need to be self-sufficient through education or employment because of the availability of economic support. It is only when family responsibilities for the economic support of female relatives begin to be questioned that the present structure of control and the prerogative of male family members to impose restrictions on their women will become nebulous.

Let us see how such a system of control has affected the institutional position of Muslim women and clarify some of the ways in which it operates in a pronatalist direction. Because kinship control over women is expected to differ according to marital status, the position of the nonmarried and the married woman in Muslim social structure are discussed separately. Women's experiences, aspirations, and range of options prior to and in between marital unions play a crucial role in explaining their high fertility within marriage. The position of the single woman in Muslim society is most precarious since any suspicion or mistrust of her moral conduct can stigmatize her and her family for life. It is self-evident that a social system wherein men have continually to safeguard against a woman's sexual misconduct or suspicion thereof requires a strong machinery of social control geared to secure the segregation of the sexes and to guarantee nonexposure to viable alternatives to marriage. Thus, Muslim societies are characterized by numerous and highly effective institutional mechanisms that preclude contact with the opposite sex. To mention only a few: sex segregation in most public and private schools, rigid sex segregation at work, and informal separation of the sexes in most recreational and often familial activities.

Tight control through an early and parentally supervised/controlled marriage, as well as strict seclusion before that event, instill the idea that only one life exists for the woman. Motivation is channeled in the direction of marriage by creating desires for familial roles, by extolling the rewards accruing from the wife-mother status, and by severe community censure of spinsterhood. Alternatives to marriage are seen as compromising a girl's sex ethics and as potential threats to her eventual chances of marriage. The mere fact that a girl may be highly educated or employed will often jeopardize her chances of a good match. In the marriage market the working girl is still judged by many as loose, immoral, and, in certain cases, promiscuous, in contrast to those girls who are secluded in their homes and thereby considered paragons of virtue and chastity.

Given these circumstances, it is not surprising that very few young women continue their schooling beyond age fifteen, however late they may actually marry. It is also understandable why the number of single women employed outside the home is so minute. In Turkey, Syria, and Egypt, for example, among every one hundred single women only six, eight, and ten, respectively, are employed in income-earning activities in the industrial and service sectors. Among these, there are many from the ranks of the more highly educated segment. For example, 42 percent of all the single women employed in Egypt, and 35 percent of those employed in Syria, hold either professional or white collar jobs. Such women represent the urban elite minority who, because of their location in the stratification system, are spared much of the moral censure imposed on other social groups. It is important to realize, however, that the progressive attitude of this minority and their families does not imply a general acceptance of permanent legitimate alternatives to marriage. In Muslim society modernity is often a struggle to incorporate higher female education and occupational emancipation within the traditional boundaries that define roles in terms of marriage and motherhood,[9] rather than an attempt to restructure relationships between the sexes in relation to society.

Societal mechanisms have succeeded well in channeling young girls into marriage by penalizing the single status. This is done in several ways. Whereas in other societies an unmarried girl who is educated or working enjoys emancipation from parental control, a more favorable position in the marriage market, and economic independence, in Muslim society she accrues none of these advantages. Her education, her employed status, and even her professional standing will not liberate her from traditional family restraints. The kind of freedom in decision-making that employed Western women know is practically unknown to employed unmarried women in the Muslim world.[10] Working girls are expected to continue to live with their parents until marriage, to contribute their earnings to the family budget, to be restricted in their social life, and in many cases to be denied the right to choose when and whom to marry. Because activities involving the public are so easily linked with suspicions of promiscuous behavior, women who attend the university or go to work are likely to come under the continual scrutiny of their family in every move they make outside the home. It is precisely because of this strict control that marriage comes into perspective for the single woman as an avenue of greater freedom.[11]

Yet Muslim girls are not legally compelled to seclude themselves prior to marriage; neither can they be legally forced into an early marriage. Such decisions often involve self-choices that could not have been sustained for long unless powerful mechanisms were operating in Muslim society to motivate the woman herself. That her individual goals tend to coalesce with a familial role stems from a firm realization that a woman's ultimate status within the social framework is derived exclusively from her ability to meet societal and familial expectations. Institutional arrangements, in this regard, are highly effective not only in preventing women from seeking extrafamilial options but, more importantly, in withholding all inducements that would make the typical Muslim woman seek—even if only temporarily—an alternative life-style to marriage and motherhood.

The latest statistics available show that on the average 45 percent of all Muslim girls aged 15–19 are already married; in some countries as many as 5 percent are already divorced or widowed before reaching age 20. Early marriage is particularly striking in Libya and Pakistan where, among the 15–19-year-old group, three girls in every four have already married. Nuptiality age is higher in Turkey, Jordan, Iraq, and Egypt (where one woman in every three is married by age 19). The late age at marriage reported by Tunisia is very atypical and is disapproved by Bourguiba.

Despite these variations in the timing of marriage, all Muslim societies are almost totally married societies. Singleness disappears from the female population before age thirty. By the time women reach the end of their reproductive period, less than 1 percent in Pakistan, Libya, and Iran; between 1 and 2 percent in Morocco, Algeria, Egypt, Turkey, and Indonesia; and close to 2.7 percent in Iraq, Tunisia, and Jordan are still unmarried. For the region as a whole, the proportion of unmarried women does not even reach two in a hundred (table 3.3).

The position of the single woman has been somewhat lengthily elaborated upon in order to stress that it is these early years that shape the opportunity structure in which subsequent decision-making on fertility occurs. On balance, the sociocultural context surrounding the single girl creates strong parental and community pressures for an early and parentally supervised (if not arranged) marriage. More critical is the socialization that so effectively channels the quest for satisfaction in the direction of the home and the feeling of guilt in the direction of education and work. Adolescent girls are virtually stripped of any other source of self-identity outside that of marriage and motherhood. The impact of all this upon woman's subsequent position and reproductive behavior is compounded by the fact that young women realistically lack the resources necessary (education/employability) to assume any but the traditional role even if they desired to perform other roles prior or subsequent to marriage.

In assessing the effect of the position of the Muslim woman at the time of her marriage on fertility, we must realize that the young age at marriage is only one of the components involved in producing high natality in the Muslim world. Implementing in practice the already legislated legal minimum age of marriage to fifteen or sixteen, or even raising nuptiality age to sixteen or eighteen, is not likely to have a significant impact on the birth rates unless accompanied by a concurrent restructuring of the social and economic system of rewards and opportunities. Given the present positive valuation of high fertility, a later age at marriage might only serve to reduce the incentive to restrict births in later years among those who utilize contraceptives.

It is imperative to counteract the effective socialization young Muslim girls are subjected to, through educational and occupational enticements that would influence the desirability of marriage and motherhood, particularly at the young ages. However, any attempt to redefine the desirability of marriage will also have to recognize the parentally controlled marriage structure that prevails in most of the Muslim world. The gut issue here is how to release parents from the intensive compulsion to marry off their children, particularly at such young ages. Muslim parents as decision-makers have strong vested interests in their children's marriage—particularly the daughters' marriage since this constitutes an independent source of prestige and honor. Such a reward will not be relinquished easily unless it is replaced by an equally powerful and socially supported set of benefits and advantages. The kind of restructuring that is urgently needed requires manipulation of the social framework in such a way that "parents can indulge themselves by personally consuming the economic and social goods that their children may offer them, rather than pushing the offspring to devote their principal energies to a new generation."[12]

Until now the social advantages derived from a daughter's early marriage have outweighed the possible economic benefits that could have accrued from her income-earning activities. With the advent of higher levels of economic development in the Muslim world, rising levels of expectations and aspirations may well create a situation where families will need to depend upon additional sources of income that a well-trained and employable unmarried daughter can provide.

Provision for the consequences of divorce are particularly important in Muslim society because of the high frequency of legal dissolution and because the right to initiate such proceedings is a prerogative granted chiefly to men. It is not surprising that kinship institutions prescribe a distinct set of moral and financial obligations that provide the divorced female relative with status placement and economic support. The divorced woman's right to return to her parental home is undisputed. The legal codes relieve her of a considerable portion of child care responsibilities since religious family law assigns guardianship to either the maternal or the paternal grandparents, until such time as the ex-husband uses his prerogative to claim custody rights over his children.

These factors combined trigger a system of expectation by virtue of which the divorced woman is emboldened to compete with the single girl in the marriage market. This is relatively easy because divorced women are typically young, and since legal dissolution is a religious institution, the social stigma attached to the status is imperceptible. To enhance the possibility of a good match, however, the divorcée is often subjected to the same family restrictions and controls as are imposed upon the single girl so as to secure a remarriage that will reflect favorably on her own standing and that of her family.

The situation differs considerably for the widow who, together with her children, is expected to return to her family where she is fully provided for financially, but is not usually expected to remarry, as is her divorced counterpart. Her older age, the presence of several children, and the cultural superstitions that label her as a "bad omen," all combined, represent a deficit in the marriage market. They also provide sufficient rationalization to seclude the widowed relative in her parental home where a life of chastity and continence dedicated to the memory of her late husband and devotion to her children are the only activities deemed appropriate for her to pursue.

This composite reflects traditional attitudes in Muslim society toward the divorcée and the widow. The acknowledgment of economic obligations for their care is considered an unquestionable duty, which in the eyes of many Muslim jurists was the justification of the bridal gift paid by the husband at the time of the marriage contract. With respect to the divorced woman, the initial expectations of remarriage are definitely being met. Despite the high divorce rate in all Muslim countries, the proportion of adult women reported in any census count as currently divorced does not exceed 3 percent. The same is not true for widows whose remarriage rate is considerably lower.

With respect to the legal and religious codes that stipulate the responsibility of the kinship unit to provide for a kinswoman, there is fragmented evidence in recent years that the legal dissolution of a marriage permits a wider latitude in the acknowledgment of these obligations and apparently even in the exercise of family control. The cross classification of women workers by marital status shows a considerably higher percentage of divorced women in the labor force as compared with the widowed and the single. This seems to suggest that divorced female relatives are not receiving the same kind of economic support that is granted the other nonmarried statuses. Whereas the work participation rates of divorced women exceed those of single females, the percentage of employed widows is as low as that of married women. If we compare the rates of the divorced and the widowed groups, we find that the percentage of divorcées employed in income-earning activities outside agriculture is three times as high as for widows in Egypt, four times as high in Syria, and seven times as high in Turkey.

A conceivable explanation of why divorced women in particular have been somewhat released from traditional restrictions is related to the high expectations initially placed upon their remarriage. The divorcée who fails to contract a new union falls short of both societal and familial expectations: economically, she has become a continual burden that was expected to be borne for only a limited period of time. If this interpretation is correct, the relatively high number of divorced women in the labor force would represent those who have been unsuccessful in finding a husband and, consequently, have been pressured by their families into work. Unfortunately, it is not possible to substantiate this explanation categorically because the census data fail to classify the labor force by age and by marital status simultaneously. Evidence in favor of this argument would be compelling, however, if an overrepresentation of divorced women appeared in the nonagricultural labor force at the older ages.

Whatever the explanation is, it is important to note that the labor force behavior of the divorcée may be the first indication we have of the incipient disintegration of traditional family obligations. Because of her youth, her right to forge a new life, and her absolution from the need to prove her chastity, the divorced woman may have become the first target in the conflict between the continued extension of family support and increasing economic demands. If this is in fact the case, we may expect that in the future the institutional position of the divorced woman will be considerably redefined.

Turning to a consideration of the impact that divorce has had up to now upon the position of women in Muslim society, it can only be emphasized that the sociocultural context in which the divorcée has been functioning has reinforced her traditional status. This occurs through relieving her of any economic pressure that might encourage her to evolve out of her dependency status, defining her status as a purely transitory one (between one marital union and the next) and providing her with structural facilities that encourage her to continue childbearing activities once remarriage takes place.

The expectations placed upon the prompt and quasi-universal remarriage of the divorcée are very strong. They have been forceful enough to elicit from the kin group the necessary economic and social support to enable the divorced relative to engage in a new contractual union. The divorced status, as such, is perceived as a temporary one. Women are not allowed, least of all pressured, to think of themselves in any other terms except as "expectant wives." Given the availability of economic support, divorced women, until very recently, have not felt the need to further their education or seek employment after they divorced in order to become self-sufficient—a process which in fact might delay remarriage. It is doubtful whether it would eventually lower the remarriage rate itself.

The institutional position of the divorcée operates in a pronatalist direction. This is through the legal codes that absolve the divorced mother of both financial and child care responsibilities, thereby lifting from her all restraints identifying her with her past. In this manner her situation is made to approximate very closely that of the single girl, with whom she competes, quite successfully, in the marriage market. The disadvantage of her years and nonvirginal status is partially outweighed by the tradition that divorced women command a considerably lower bridewealth than the virgin, which makes them attractive to the potential wife-seeker.

That relieving the divorced woman of the burden of her children increases her chances for remarriage is self-evident. What is far more critical is the opportunity thereby provided for the remarried woman to engage in as abundant childbearing as the single woman does upon her first marriage. For the divorcée this reproductive activity is her second, or perhaps even her third, time around. The lack of built-in restraints in the divorce situation brought by the presence/burden of children is equally applicable to the divorced man. Until he can claim custody of his children (in Egypt at nine for boys, eleven for girls), the guardianship rights are assumed by the maternal or paternal grandparents. At this point, if he remarries it is customary for the man to relegate his children to the care of his own parents (if alive) or an older sibling.

The status and position of the married woman in Muslim social structure is most difficult to define. Traditionally, her inferior status has been underlined within the context of rigid systems of marital role allocation that uphold separate male and female worlds. The monopoly of suprafamilial activities is in the hands of the husband; wives are secluded and related to home care and children. This division of labor is supported by the age gap (typically 8–10 years) and the educational disparities between husband and wife.

There exist more critical aspects, related to the religio-legal prescriptions under which the Muslim wife functions, that provide grounds to argue for her subordinate position in the institutional structure. The principle of sex equality within the family and upon marriage is not provided by Islamic law, which governs Muslim family institutions in nearly all Islamic countries. In defending Islam against the accusation that it discriminates against women, apologists argue that Islamic law has always granted married women independent legal and property rights—a privilege only recently acquired by women in the Western world. We know well that such legal rights are often not implemented, for male family members appropriate their daughters'/sisters' property holdings on the grounds that these women will need economic support in case of divorce, separation, or widowhood. Even when a property right is protected, by itself it hardly outweighs the patriarchal arbitrariness of many of the legal codes regulating family behavior. By twentieth-century standards, the religio-legal sanctioning of polygamy; the husband's unilateral power in divorce, in custody over his children, and in enforcing the return of a rebellious wife; unequal female inheritance; and unequal weight to a woman's legal testimony can hardly be viewed as congruent with a married woman's equal position. Not all Muslims take advantage of these privileges. Nevertheless, their mere legal endorsement functions as a constant source of anxiety to many married women.

That Muslim women lack social and economic options outside marriage (which obviously constrains their behavior within marriage), often lack the freedom to marry the man of their choice, and are discriminated against by family and marriage laws mean that the Muslim wife occupies a subordinate status. However, within her domain—the women's world—the Muslim wife is given great respect and a considerable degree of real familial power. This is shown in her relationship with her husband, her strong influence over her children even when they are adults, and her special position within her parental home by virtue of her having attained the marriage and motherhood position. Women can draw on many sources of valuation for two reasons: one is that marriage and motherhood roles are greatly valued in the community and hence given very high status and respect, and two, that such high roles can be filled only by women.

This does not imply that the degree of patriarchy, male dominance, and male control of suprafamilial activities is thereby reduced. The high status held by women derives exclusively from marriage- and maternal-related roles and is grounded in the separation between familial and suprafamilial activities and power. Thus, the respect and power that she commands depend on the male's suprafamilial orientation. Similarly, women have very few possibilities of becoming involved with the activities of the larger world, and they are often excluded from entering into areas whence men derive their status and prestige.

Until recently, the Muslim wife has tended to accept her world. Outside of a highly educated and politicized minority, I have not found Muslim wives to perceive their status and role within the home and in relation to their husband as "subordinate," "oppressed," "inferior," or "powerless." Women's acceptance of their world reflects the combined effects of "false consciousness" and a highly effective socialization process. It may also indicate a volitional avoidance by the average wife of entering the mainstream of "modern life" at the risk of threatening the security and power she has accrued in her "own" world.

According to Steven Goldberg, women's desire to attain status (that is, rights) in areas from which men derive their authority and prestige can be achieved only at the expense of a reduction in the status (respect) given to roles only women can fulfill.[13] If this is correct, it is understandable why the average Muslim wife, who is so poorly prepared to engage in extrafamilial activities, would not want to risk changing her situation from one where she cannot lose to one where she may be unable to win.[14] The conspicuous absence in all Muslim countries of married women in the occupational world (an average of only 1 percent of all married women work in nonagricultural sectors of the economy) and in public life could very well be due, in part, to their own assessment of the gains and losses involved.

What inferences can be drawn from this discussion concerning fertility in Muslim society? As the situation is now, all seems to point to the maximization of natalist tendencies. Muslim women are fully cognizant of the need to attain marital position and motherhood for commanding respect and status in their own kin group and community. They are not about to deemphasize willingly the only role that now gives them a bargaining position in the social structure. Children represent much more than a form of social insurance against the threat of divorce or polygamy, for women derive status from motherhood even when divorced or rejected for a second wife. Offspring guarantee to the woman status and respect that extends far beyond her position in the conjugal home and reaches into the heart of her own family's and the community's valuation of her. Hence we may expect women to continue childbearing activities throughout their reproductive years—whether they are happy in their marriage or not. When Muslim countries report an average of seven live births per married woman and the extension of reproductive behavior to more advanced ages beyond thirty-five years, we should be able to appreciate the importance of maternal-related roles.

The highly educated Muslim wife is often ready to explore external sources of prestige and satisfaction, but not, however, to the exclusion of her maternal role. There is evidence that higher female education (particularly university) is accompanied by considerably reduced fertility and a relatively high proportion of employment in professional jobs.

The optimistic expectation of most demographers that an increased participation of married women in the work force will reduce reproduction within marriage has, however, to be approached with caution, as many Muslim working wives are able to escape the contradiction between the economic and familial role, which is a prerequisite for labor force participation to affect fertility. The availability of inexpensive domestic help and accessibility to baby-sitting provided by family members enable many working wives to combine the activities without much strain or guilt. Hence it is doubtful that the supply of female labor in Muslim countries is influenced by the number, spacing, and ages of children or that a substantial entry of married women into the work force will mean a reduction in fertility. Women who work have adjusted themselves to selecting occupations that allow some flexibility in work conditions: specifically, lower-class wives are mostly involved in cottage-type manufacturing, while upper-class wives choose careers in teaching, which enable them to plan childbirth during the three months' summer vacation.

Pronatalism in Islamic Doctrine

Another matter related to marital fertility in the Muslim world concerns pronatalist tendencies contained within Islam. Several writers have maintained that this orientation in Islam stems less from direct injunctions to procreate than from the support of conditions that produce high fertility.[15] There is some controversy as to whether Islam encourages large families, for example. The Prophet's famous statement, "Marry and reproduce so that I may be proud of you before God," is not borne out by any direct reference in the Quran. Children are viewed as among the richest blessings granted by Allah, but they do not constitute the primary values. Surrender and Obedience surpass by far the importance of Wealth and Children. High fertility patterns may, however, have been encouraged by the fatalistic streak in Islam which stems from the strong belief in the active providence of God. For example, it is

Allah who creates sexuality and determines procreation and barrenness.

By contrast, the Quran is not ambivalent with respect to the importance of marriage as a universal institution for Muslims. Specific institutional and religious prescriptions comprise the following injunctions: all Muslim males are enjoined to marry to "complete half their religion," the early and universal remarriage of widowed and divorced women is highly encouraged, and the purpose of marriage is explicitly stated to be not only procreation but the gratification of spiritual and physical needs. This means that sexual intercourse within marriage has positive value independent of reproduction itself.

On the other hand, fertility control is not prohibited in Islam. The Quran has historically been interpreted as justifying coitus interruptus to protect the male's property, to preserve the wife's health, and to allay anxiety over numerous children. Modern legal opinions support measures to prevent conception, and in several Muslim countries religious leaders have endorsed family planning programs by declaring them to be sanctioned by Islamic doctrine. Only abortion and permanent sterilization are still met with strong opposition from religious authorities.

The lack of doctrinal injunctions against most methods of birth control may prove to be a double-edged sword. One might hope that the lack of prohibition will allow the introduction and acceptance of contraceptive techniques. The absence of an organized clergy in Islam, however, has meant that every parochial leader can assume the right to interpret the faith as he understands it. Individual definitions of the situation and variations in interpreting what may be acceptable practices in Islam could conceivably have a backlash on the implementation of fertility control programs.[16]

Fertility and Women's Education and Employment

During the 1960s, for the Muslim group of countries under study, the average percentage of adult women (15 and over) who were literate was only 13 percent, the range spreading from a low of 4 percent (Algeria, Libya, Morocco, and Pakistan) to a high of 30 percent (Indonesia and Turkey). In the total population of these countries, women are less likely than men to be able to read and write by 30 percent. Considering current attendance rates, girls aged 5–14 average about 60 percent of the attendance rate of boys; this declines to 34 percent when the age group 15–19 is considered. The decline in women's enrollment is most drastic around age 15 when the bulk withdraw from school. Around 1970 the Muslim woman's share of the total enrollment in secondary and higher education was 27 and 25 percent, respectively. Of what significance are such educational standards to the subject of Muslim fertility?

Generally, the most relevant aspects of education for fertility regulation are delaying marriage and increasing the probability of non-marriage; reducing desired family size by creating aspirations for higher levels of living and stimulating women's interest and involvement in extrafamilial activities; and exposing women to knowledge, attitudes, and practices favorable to birth control communication.

It is doubtful whether in Muslim societies additional years of schooling—even the completion of a degree—will increase the probability of nonmarriage. The educated Muslim woman is not ready to give up marriage for a career, however stimulated her nonfamilial interests may be. Nor can we expect her to fare poorly in the marriage market because of her high educational standing. Muslim men are *not* reluctant to marry a highly educated woman, as neither her earnings nor the social recognition she derives from work threatens the status and authority of the Muslim husband in the way that it does in the United States.[17] Suprafamilial activities have not yet been legitimized as sources from which women in the Muslim world can derive prestige and status. Hence the husband's power and authority are not affected. Also, owing to the large sex differential in educational standards, the educated Muslim female is guaranteed a pool of potential mates of similar, if not higher, educational position.

Continued educational involvement of Muslim women throughout their teens will, however, mean a delay in marriage (and consequent postponement of first birth), primarily because the practice of women's continuing education after marriage is not culturally accepted. Also, there is evidence in some Muslim countries of the value of female education in secondary and higher levels in significantly reducing fertility within marriage and accelerating women's involvement in employment outside the home.

The cultural pressures within Muslim society directed toward protecting the sexual purity of women make the delay of marriage very difficult and account for two interrelated factors: formal education for women is not socially valued, and women are withdrawn from the educational process by puberty. Such a withdrawal seems to occur systematically in Muslim societies irrespective of the nuptiality age in the individual countries. In Pakistan, the relationship is blatant between the minute percentage (2 percent) of girls aged 15–19 who are enrolled in school and the high proportion within this age group (75 percent) who are already married. In Tunisia and Jordan, however, where women marry comparatively much later, there is still an excessive drop in the female enrollment rates (at age 15 and onwards) that is not explainable by marital patterns. Hence we find that the educational lifespan of the average Muslim woman is cut short even by the anticipation of a future marriage.

It is the indirect effect of women's higher educational status upon fertility that is most significant. This is due to the inverse relationship between education and reproduction within marriage. The most detailed information available is from sample surveys and census analyses from Turkey and Egypt during the 1960s. These show that the fertility level decreases monotonically as female educational status rises, with the standardized average parity of university degree holders between one-half (Egypt) and one-third (Turkey) that of all literate women. For example, for each one hundred Egyptian wives, those with university education had 394 children; with secondary schooling, 583; with primary education, 703; with no education whatever, 708 children. Stated in other terms: for every 100 children born to the illiterate Egyptian female, 87 were born to women who could only read and write, 63 to women with secondary schooling, and 53 to women holding university degrees.[18] Similarly, the Turkish study, in which 3,200 currently married women under age forty-five were interviewed, indicated that university graduates averaged 1.4 children; high school graduates, 2.0 children; women with five years schooling, 3.8 children; and illiterate women, 4.2 children.[19]

The lack of education among Muslim women has crucial implications for other points related to fertility regulation. I refer to the propensity of educated women to seek employment and become economically independent. The relationship between female educational levels and nonagricultural employment is particularly important in Muslim countries because the female activity rates accelerate markedly at each successive educational level. For example, in Turkey, Syria, and Egypt, less than 4 percent of all women who had partial/completed primary education were working during the 1960s, as compared with those women with secondary schooling, among whom the proportion employed in the nonagricultural sector was 21 percent. The positive effect of education upon the employability of Muslim women is even more striking at the highest educational levels: among university trained Egyptian women, an average of two in every three were employed in the upgraded occupations.[20] Interviews in West Pakistan showed that 79.6 percent of the women graduates of the University of Karachi and 65.0 percent of the women graduates of Lahore University were in the labor force—and Pakistan is one of the most conservative of all the Muslim countries.[21]

In terms of comparative quantitative data, Muslim societies consistently report the lowest female participation rates in economic activities outside of agriculture. In addition, there is evidence of a failure by the female work force to respond to higher stages of economic development by a parallel increase in the number of women employed in nonagricultural activities.[22] If we consider work participation in the industry and service sectors of the economy we find that the average number of adult Muslim women (over fifteen) who are employed is 5 percent; the proportion is highest in Indonesia and Iran (12 percent) and lowest in Jordan and Pakistan (2 percent).

Let us now interpret the above statistics by relating the work patterns of Muslim women to the broader social context in which female labor force participation takes place. First, until recently there has been clear evidence of a lack of participation among Muslim women in the world of work. Secondly, there has been a traditionally established closed occupational opportunity structure that restricts women from employment sectors that presuppose contact with men. This much has been measurable. What we do not know is the extent of interplay that occurs to produce these patterns between sanctioned prohibitions and limitations imposed by males and women's volitional negative and/or selected response to labor market demands.

Sociologists concerned with women's status and position in society often assume that all women desire to work but are constrained from so doing by an external system of male- or public-induced constraints. Few studies have probed how Muslim women themselves define their relationship to their work. All we can do is ask ourselves, within the present sociocultural context, what would motivate the average Muslim woman to want to work.

A realistic part of the context in which the Muslim woman functions relates to the suspicion, mistrust, and fear that paid employment outside the home has traditionally represented for the family and the community. The issue at stake for the family head has involved in the past more than a challenge to his ability to provide economically for his relatives; more critically, it has been a challenge to his control over the whereabouts and behavior of his women. This challenge has affected the Muslim male in his role of father, brother, or husband, which explains why kinsmen feel compelled to assume economic responsibility for all their women regardless of whether these are single, divorced, or widowed.

In some Islamic countries resentment against the work participation of women has been intense and expressed by men and women alike. The most frequent criticism leveled against the working woman, especially working wives, revolves around the so-called dangers of promiscuity. Moroccans tend to view work as a locus providing free access for women to "play around with men";[23] Pakistani parents fear that employment will compromise their daughter's reputation and damage her marriage prospects.[24] Educated Muslim men admitted that their objection to female employment rested in their lack of confidence in married women. The persistent mistrust was explained as resulting from the arranged-marriage system, where family pressure often prevails over the will of either spouse. In the men's own words, "there is no reason for having confidence in a woman whom you know has married you in obedience to her parents' wish, or because there was nothing else for her to do."[25]

But even among upper-middle-class Muslim males who hold "liberal" views about the right of women to work, appropriate jobs are circumscribed and only those guaranteeing segregated employment are accepted. The medical (pediatrics, gynecology) and teaching (preuniversity) professions are particularly favored because women are confined in their professional contacts to members of their own sex. These men are able to overcome traditional scruples about working wives, as long as their women have enough education to gain a position of prestige; however, the importance of segregated employment still remains crucial.

In attributing motives and desires to the women themselves, it is important to remember that until now the acknowledgment of kinship support has sustained a situation that has eliminated from the Muslim woman's existence the need to work for economic survival. Few other cultures can claim such an achievement on their balance sheet. The question today is to what extent such traditional obligations can continue in the face of impending changes in the economic structure that may be accompanied by considerable economic pressures and constraints. For if and when economic responsibilities begin to be neglected or postponed by kinship groups, a considerable restructuring in the meaning of and structural accessibility to work will take place in a woman's life.

Confirmation from various sources indicates that in some of the Muslim countries where economic constraints have recently emerged, there has been considerable change in the structural position of the woman. Unfortunately, the magnitude of such changes as demonstrated in behavior cannot be empirically verified for large parts of the population, either because census data are lacking or because the changes so far have not been large enough to be felt statistically at the aggregate level.

In Egypt and a few other states, it appears that a more positive attitude has emerged regarding the employability of urban single and widowed women. Likewise with respect to the married woman, there is clearly the beginning of definite signs of social recognition and rewards in terms of the higher education she pursues and the professional level she attains. True, this is mostly felt among the urban upper-middle classes.

Economic pressures have undoubtedly induced changes in the attitude of young men. The implicit atmosphere of mistrust and suspicion that traditionally surrounded the working woman is lessening considerably. In Egypt young educated males now seek wives who have jobs because of the economic advantages that a double salary can provide. Such economic incentives are bound to spread to other parts of the Islamic world, if they have already not done so. One immediate effect that may be expected to emerge from such a situation is a gradual desegregation in the labor market. Areas of work that have traditionally been closed to Muslim women because working conditions entailed intermingling with the opposite sex will disappear. Egyptian officials claim that in that country, at least, women are being accepted not only in the clerical ranks in the factories, side by side with males, but also as skilled laborers in the heavy industries.

Future Influences

The current status of women in Muslim society has its impact on their reproductive behavior by way of the interplay between prohibitions imposed informally by males, which restrict women to marital and maternal roles, and the resistance of women to claiming their "rights" in the suprafamilial world. This interplay has persisted, despite initial breakthroughs in economic modernization, for two important reasons: the strong control exerted over women by the kinship group and the respect and socio-psychological rewards derived by women from their traditional status, which have until now militated against the eruption of protest and rebellion. Retrospectively, the thrust of my argument throughout the entire essay has been to emphasize the importance of social arrangements and their cultural adjuncts related to the criterion of family honor as a powerful variable explaining why the control over women by kinsmen in the agnatic line has been so successful. The question that now stands is, if this observation is in fact correct, what realistic prospects exist in Muslim society to challenge the persistence of this deeply entrenched cultural ideal?

An important consideration in understanding the traditional importance of the criterion of family honor, as well as its possible demise in the future, is the strong symbiotic relationship that it bears to the high valuation of children in Muslim culture. Rather than having women reap the direct benefits of such a positive valuation, males have been able to utilize the importance of women's reproductive role to achieve and perpetuate social recognition and prestige for themselves. Daughters, sisters, all female relatives, in fact, have become an independent source of honor and prestige for their kinsmen because they represent a highly valued commodity and element of wealth. Viewed from this perspective, the imposition of chastity norms and the continual anxiety surrounding the subject of woman's sexual misconduct, or suspicion thereof, can be interpreted as the most effective way by which kin groups protect their "investment" and guarantee the kind of marriage for their daughters and sisters that will reflect favorably upon their own status and position.

The high appreciation of children in Muslim society is said to rest on strong religious grounds. More realistically, it is a function of the actual experience with or expectation of child deaths that has caused much of economic insecurity. For centuries now, excessive infant/childhood mortality, particularly within the context of a subsistence-type economy, has interacted to attach great value to children (particularly males) and to create a need for women to bear surplus children to ensure a sufficient number of survivors, particularly males.[26] From here stems the interrelatedness of traditional high valuation of children and the desire for large families.

Given the sweeping change of economic and political modernization characterizing the modern Muslim world, the most prominent undercurrent of the high valuation of children, particularly on the part of men, is the incipient decline in infant mortality rates that inevitably accompanies economic development. If until very recently the relative improvement in childhood/infant survival has had no marked effect on the value system, this is because under current economic conditions children are still perceived in Muslim societies as economic assets, cheap labor, and a form of social security for aged parents. Successive increases in national productivity levels, particularly if accompanied by an equitable distribution of national income, will bring about a considerable range of structural changes. Rising levels of individual expectations and of parental aspirations, together with new systems of economic production that reduce drastically the opportunities for unskilled workers and demand for child labor, will effect a significant reshuffling in and reevaluation of values and attitudes related to childbearing. Supportive of this shift will be the demographic revolution which, when set in motion, will increasingly guarantee the survival of most births.

As children in Muslim society become more difficult and more expensive to raise, a reduction in the male demand for children will occur. This is, of course, the very cornerstone of the demographic transition that has occurred in so many countries of the world. References abound in the literature as to the immediate effect this phase of the transition has had upon the fertility levels. Not much systematic research has been done, however, on the effects of a decline in the value of children upon role-related behavior and concepts of self-identity among women.

With respect to the Muslim female, the structural ramifications of a reduction in the value attached to children, and consequent lower appreciation of the only role and function from which she derived status for so long, could be severe. The danger lies in the particular mechanisms of adjustment that will be made available to women during the transition represented by a loss in the value of roles which only women can fulfill, to a restructured and redefined situation that supports and honors women's status in terms of their accomplishments in areas from which men derive their authority and prestige.

In some Islamic societies there have been structural "facilitators" to allow for the restructuring of women's role options. The beginnings of female modernism in the Muslim world cannot be traced to a feminist movement; rather it is symbiotically related to intrinsic tensions generated by rapid economic change, on the one hand, and political conditions accompanying a postcolonial era, on the other. Granted that the official stance in Muslim society toward the full participation of women in political life has been less than wholehearted, still political leaders have recently vocalized the need to mobilize womanpower for social and economic development goals. Whether official action thus far on issues relating to the status and roles of women has been primarily symbolic, statements supporting greater equality of women, the enfranchisement of women, and even in certain cases (Egypt and Iran) the appointment of women to cabinet office, have all provided a form of legitimation to any future strides women may make in the direction of greater participation in social, economic, and political activities.

But can woman's desire for greater participation in such extra-familial activities be guaranteed? Does Islamic society provide fertile ground for the birth and growth of a feminist movement in which women would be organized to protest and rebel against their secluded position? What realistic prospects exist for a challenge to the deeply entrenched cultural ideal related to the criterion of family honor in the Muslim community, which has thus far legitimated the exclusion and seclusion of women from participation in public life? Answers to such motivational and structural issues would seem to be more important in predicting future influences upon the status of women than are those related to the attitudes of the government and the Muslim clergy.

I do not foresee in the immediate future the growth of a multi-class feminist movement in the Muslim world. The very women who could provide the leadership for a feminist movement, those with education and high social standing, generally are little inclined to do so since they suffer the fewest disabilities at present.

Rather, I would tend to locate the most crucial determinant for the continuing demise of the traditionally subordinate position of the Muslim woman in the economic constraints currently emerging in Islamic countries that are intrinsic to the process of economic modernization itself. Such constraints will increasingly challenge the control exercised by male members of the kinship group over their womenfolk and will lower the valuation of maternal related roles.

Muslim families are already facing the conflict between the continued extension of family support to female relatives and increasing economic demands, so that it will become increasingly difficult for male members to meet their obligation to provide economically for all their womenfolk in case of need. Lack of economic support from the kin unit will mean the beginning of the end of the woman's economic dependency upon the male. More importantly, it will also mean a decline in the power of male members of the kinship group to subject women to their demands and restrictions. Reference has been made to the incipient disintegration of traditional family responsibilities toward divorced female relatives. Single women may soon follow suit. With the advent of higher levels of economic development, rising expectations and aspirations may well create a situation where Muslim families will need to depend upon additional sources of income that a well-educated daughter can provide.

There are scattered indications that women in certain Muslim societies are beginning to question, if not actually reject, the acceptance of traditional pronatalist prescriptions. The counteraction to the strongly entrenched pronatalist trends is reflected in steps taken by some Muslim women voluntarily to restrict childbearing through use of contraceptives and, more significantly, through abortion.[27]

Most Islamic countries (except Algeria and Afghanistan) have government-sponsored population policies. The statistics (questionable as they may be) indicate that over the past ten years there is a growing trend among certain Muslim women to curtail reproduction through contraceptive usage. Receptivity to birth control has been particularly good among women in Tunisia, Egypt, and Iran, although admittedly the population in question tends to be heavily represented by the urban upper and middle classes.

Recent statistics on the incidence of induced abortion in Muslim countries is even more indicative of the strong motivation among some Muslim women to curb childbearing. The figures, considered to be a gross underestimation of the actual occurrence of induced abortion, are highest, relatively, for Iran, Egypt, and Turkey. Again, the phenomenon as recorded is an urban one, closely associated with other indexes of modernism. At this point of writing, Tunisia and Iran are the only countries to have legalized abortion.

The intensity of the desire to limit reproduction is not fully reflected in the number of contraceptive users or abortions (even if and when the statistics would be correct). Recent survey information, obtained from urban Morocco and Iran,[28] indicates clearly that both urban women *and* men, a significant proportion of whom are not of high social status, genuinely desire to limit their family size but object to the poor ways women are treated at birth control clinics and dislike the birth control methods they are offered. I would venture to state that in a social structure that has heretofore allowed women to derive status, power, and identity almost exclusively from their maternal-related roles, the recent moves to avoid and particularly to terminate pregnancy are very significant.

Theoretically, one may conceptualize a smooth progression from the time when men begin to value children less and less, to the development of conditions in which, first, the male's valuation of woman's traditional role declines, and, second, women themselves begin to manifest significant interest in suprafamilial activities and functions. In the experience of the now-industrialized Western world, women were culturally prepared to cope with the structural ramifications of the demographic transition that resulted in a lower value attached to children. Institutional arrangements in Islamic society have, unfortunately, not provided sufficient mechanisms to permit women to prepare themselves gradually for such a drastic transformation. I can foresee considerable difficulty within Islamic society for some time to come in redefining what specific types of extrafamilial activities will be appropriate or acceptable for Muslim women to pursue, even when women are granted the right to work and the right to be educated.

Notes

1. Dudley Kirk, "Factors Affecting Moslem Natality," in *Population and Society,* ed. Charles Nam (Boston, 1968), p. 231.

2. The exception is Indonesia where the discrepancy between the CBR and the GRR is explained by distortions of the age structure owing to war and internal strife, resulting in birth deficits in the 1940s and relatively small numbers of older children in 1960 (see Kirk, "Factors," p. 233).

3. Kirk has summarized these patterns very well, and the following discussion draws upon his work (ibid., pp. 230–235).

4. Shafick S. Hassan, "Childhood Mortality Experience and Fertility Performance," in *Egypt: Population Problems and Prospects,* ed. Abdel Omran (Chapel Hill, N.C., 1973), p. 356.

5. Refer, for example, to United Nations Economic and Social Council, Commission on the Status of Women, *Study on the Interrelationship of the Status of Women and Family Planning* (New York, 1974), p. 356.

6. Steven Goldberg, *The Inevitability of Patriarchy* (New York, 1973), pp. 68–70.

7. Constantina Safilios-Rothschild, "Toward a Cross Cultural Conceptualization of Family Modernity," *Journal of Comparative Family Studies,* 1 (1970):19.

8. Sania Hamady, *Character and Temperament of the Arabs* (New York, 1960), p. 50; Charles Issawi, *Egypt: An Economic and Social Analysis* (London, 1947), p. 59; Peter C. Dodd, "Family Honor and the Forces of Change in Arab Society," *International Journal of Middle East Studies,* 4 (1973):42–47.

9. Carmel Camilleri, "Modernity and the Family in Tunisia," *Journal of Marriage and the Family,* 29 (1967):592–594.

10. J. Henry Korson, "Career Constraints among Women Graduate Students in a Developing Country: West Pakistan," *Journal of Comparative Family Studies,* 1 (1970):89.

11. Morroe Berger, *The Arab World Today* (New York, 1964), chap. 4.

12. Judith Blake, "Parental Control, Delayed Marriage and Population

Policy," *Proceedings of the World Population Conference, 1965,* vol. 2 (1967), p. 135.

13. Goldberg, *Inevitability,* p. 72.

14. Ibid.

15. Dudley Kirk, "Factors," pp. 235–240; Mahmud Sklani, "La fecondité dans les pays arabes," *Population,* 15 (October-December 1960) :831–836; William Goode, *World Revolution and Family Patterns* (New York, 1965), chap. 3.

16. Nusret Fisek, "Prospects for Fertility Planning in Turkey," in *Fertility and Family Planning,* ed. S. J. Behrman et al. (Ann Arbor, Mich., 1969), pp. 467–477.

17. Talcott Parsons, "Age and Sex in the Social Structure," in *The Family: Its Structure and Function,* ed. Rose Coser (New York, 1965), p. 225.

18. M. A. El Badry and Hanna Riz, "Regional Fertility Differences among Socio Economic Groups in the United Arab Republic," *Proceedings of the World Population Conference, 1965,* vol. 2 (1967), p. 138.

19. United Nations Economic and Social Council, *Women and Family Planning,* p. 56, citing Serim Temur, "Socio Economic Determinants of Differential Fertility in Turkey," *The Second European Population Conference* (Strasbourg, 1971).

20. Nadia Youssef, *Women and Work in Developing Countries,* Population Monograph Series, no. 15 (Berkeley, 1974), p. 59.

21. J. Henry Korson, "Career Constraints," p. 89.

22. Nadia Youssef, "Social Structure and the Female Labor Force: The Case of Women Workers in Muslim Middle Eastern Countries," *Demography,* 8 (1971) :431.

23. Nelly Forget, "Attitude towards Work by Women in Morocco," *International Social Science Journal,* 14 (1962) :105–123.

24. Korson, "Career Constraints," p. 94.

25. Forget, "Attitude towards Work," p. 104.

26. See David Heer, "Births Necessary to Assure Desired Survivorship of Sons under Differing Mortality Conditions," Paper presented to Population Association of America, New York, 1966; David Heer and Dean Smith, "Mortality Level, Desired Family Size, and Population Increase," *Demography,* 5 (1968) :104–121, and "Mortality Level, Desired Family Size and Population Increase: Further Variations on a Basic Model," *Demography,* 6 (1969) :141–149.

27. Isam Nazer, *Induced Abortion: A Hazard to Public Health* (Beirut, 1972). For statistics on contraceptive usage and induced abortion, refer specifically to pp. 91–92, 98–99, 136–168, 199, 255–260, 264–271.

28. Survey information from Morocco; see chapter 25 by Gulick and Gulick.

4 Women and Social Change in Morocco

Vanessa Maher

Until very recently the real experience and activity of women have been generally ignored in studies of social change.[1] For a long period diplomatic and political historiography neglected economic and social factors, attributing political events to the intrigues of the powerful rather than to the complex interaction of social forces. Such a version enhanced the role of elites who claimed the lion's share of dynamism and intelligence as a justification for their political dominance.

When women have not been ignored, they have been regarded only as the point at which history and male activity begin, or, in other cases, as an obstacle to desirable social change and as an impediment to male activity. There is a parallel to be drawn here with the way many students of "modernization" regard peasants. Both peasants and women are seen as representatives of traditional society. They are conservative, passive, and uneducated, and they obstruct the efforts of their urban male counterparts who are modern, active, and educated. Thinking in terms of binary oppositions leads to exaggeration and caricature, but it is true, in North Africa, that it is the land of peasants and the labor of women that are refused to the market, and it is the spread of market relationships that interests most advocates of "modernization."

The field work on which this article is based was carried out between 1969 and 1971 (eleven months) in the Middle Atlas of Morocco. It was financed by the Wenner-Gren Foundation for Anthropological Research. An earlier and different version of this paper was published in Italian: "Il problema della donna e il cambiamento sociale nel Marocco," *Affari sociali internazionali,* 3, no. 3 (Autumn 1975) : 28–61. All translations of French quotations are mine.

I suggest that these stereotypes tend to legitimize the subordination of the supposed representatives of traditional society, peasants and women, to the ostensibly dynamic elements of society. Ida Magli suggests most plausibly that to see women as agents of social transformation would upset the arrangements that have invested women with deep symbolic value (such as the source of fertility, or as gifts sealing an alliance) and have transformed them into the objects rather than the subjects of culture (1974).

I have drawn an analogy between the stereotypes that are held about traditional society (usually rural) and those that are held about women because it seems that in times of social upheaval, when economic and power relations are convulsed and ill-defined, women and their roles become doubly invested with symbolic significance for the relationships among men, but that these symbols are drawn from the moral context believed to be proper to the traditional society, which is itself an ideological abstraction. In other words, in Morocco too, women have been forced to *represent* a traditional model of social reality for the purposes of men.

Town and Country

Moroccan society, especially in the south, is marked by a sharp cultural discontinuity between town and countryside. To a certain extent, this situation is a result of recent local history in that the town, to which I refer as Akhdar, like many in the Middle Atlas, did not exist until the French established a military garrison there in 1917 and transferred to it the local tribal market and some of the population from their hamlets. However, the establishment of such *postes* meant that state authority, against which the tribes had struggled for centuries, was at last to take root in the countryside. Organized into autonomous territorial units within a segmentary tribal structure that allowed for shifting alliances and confederations, the tribes had maintained an armed and ordered "anarchy" and refused to pay taxes or to accept the temporal authority of the sultan and his government (the *Makhzen*), though they acknowledged him as their spiritual leader. Thus, in pre-Protectorate times the sultan's authority and the scope of his administrative apparatus were limited to the towns and some tribes under their aegis (*gish* tribes) which were rewarded for their administrative and military services with grants of land. The towns were the centers of commercial and craft activities, were patronized by absentee landlords and a tax-supported upper class, and were integrated by a common adherence to orthodox Maliki Islam with its complex legal system and body of tradition.

It could be said that town and country were linked not only through an exchange of personnel and goods, but, because each represented an ideal type, were defined in function of each other. The towns were seen as places of high culture and enviable riches, the countryside as epitomized by a devotion to the values of group loyalty that bound peasants and nomads to the land by a sacred link. The frugal, naive ways of the warrior and nomad were contrasted with the luxury-loving and profit-oriented ways of city life. Needless to say, such stereotypes served to legitimize the exploitation of "stupid" peasants by urban notables, as well as the periodic attacks by which tribal armies attempted to remove ostensibly corrupt town-based dynasties. That the new regimes set up by the invaders quickly came to resemble their predecessors was not taken to suggest that the stereotypes could not hold, or that there were elements in both town and country populations that were equally eager for power and booty. The stereotypes as charters for behavior persist still.

The Relation of Women to Property

Women in the town live secluded, to a greater or lesser extent according to whether they are of higher or lower status. According to Islamic law, women may inherit half a male share in any legacy, but since they are legal minors, their property should be managed by a male kinsman, or, when they marry, by their husband. In the countryside, where land and labor are often unsalable, women are generally deprived of their inheritance in order to avoid its transfer to another lineage when they marry; for similar reasons only a token bridewealth is paid on marriage and patrilateral parallel cousin marriage is preferred. In the town, however, where property can be bought and sold on the market and its equivalent in movable goods estimated, women can be given their fair share. Marriage becomes complicated by economic considerations, and women, as bearers of capital and political connections, have to be strictly controlled. Marriages are arranged between families of equal status and involve the payment of bridewealth from groom to bride. In elite circles the woman's family may also give her a dowry to bring to the marriage.

It is the payment of bridewealth that confers the status of Arab on a tribesman, with all that it entails in terms of the passage from the rural cultural and political context to the urban one. "Amongst non-Arab Muslims, a man was by birth the equal of an Arab if both his father and his grandfather had been Muslims before him, but only then if he were sufficiently wealthy to provide an adequate *mahr* or marriage endowment" (Shaybani, as quoted in Levy 1957:63). The bridewealth is used by the bride to furnish the new household, and is forfeit on divorce by whichever party is legally held responsible for the breakdown of the marriage. This general pattern is still typical of the Middle Atlas.

The payment of bridewealth in itself confers on a husband the right to interrupt the relations of his wife with her kin group. Instead of paying the bridewealth to her male guardians, the husband gives it directly to the bride, so that by renouncing their right to the bridewealth, her kin fulfill for the present their material duty toward her. Rosenfeld has observed that a woman in accepting bridewealth gives up the protection of her patrilineage (1960).

In the countryside, on the other hand, where women do not inherit or receive bridewealth, it is recognized that they retain rights in their kin group. Such rights are acknowledged in the token share of the harvest that a married woman receives from her kin and in her right to be maintained by them whenever she sees fit. I have argued elsewhere that this fact gives rise to an intense exchange of services between female kin and reduces the economic and social relevance of the conjugal relationship, thus facilitating the return of women to their natal family and favoring a high rate of divorce (1974b:180).

Women as Ramparts against the Market

The contrast between town and country is between a social system governed by the market, where land, labor, and their products can be bought and sold, so that chance, cunning, and political alliances separate men's fates and offer to them the mirage of profit, social mobility, and power; and a system in which land, labor, and their products are the foci of social relationships, which are defined in kinship terms so that definite rights and duties are assigned to them. The nonobservance of these rights and duties would result in the dissolution of the relationships. Marriage and the inheritance of women are manipulated differently in each of these contexts.

The Kabyle (Algerian Berber) concept of *niya,* discussed perceptively by Bourdieu and Sayad (1964:87), derives from the necessities of the second of these social systems. All peasant virtues are comprised in the word niya (sobriety, uprightness, ingenuousness). *Bu-niya* is the man who makes provision against the future but does not speculate for gain. Money does not figure in his exchanges with other peasants, especially when it is a matter of food to be consumed immediately, such as milk, butter, or fruit.

Lacoste du Jardin (1970) remarks that the survival of the patrilineal group which the idea of niya serves to keep together is always linked to the problem of sterility. The importance of compelling women to marry as their elders choose and of their producing male children for their husband's patrilineal group cannot be overstated. The son-father relationship is the basis of production and group cohesion, and sterility threatens to replace it by that of employer-employee. Clearly, women cannot be permitted to perceive alternative roles such as those offered by the market. They must be maintained in a position of economic and political dependence on men. So they are married young, secluded, and prevented from working for wages, taking part in commerce, or holding political power.

In the town, where fertility is less important, these values still hold, for it is through them that a man manages to assimilate his wife's status to his own. In the countryside they result in a contradictory situation, for women can use their fertility to a certain extent to gain bargaining power (Lacoste du Jardin 1970:485). That a woman does not choose her own spouse and that she can divorce easily are factors that turn even her beauty into a threat for her husband, for she can leave him at any moment for another man. This theme recurs in the Kabyle folktales Lacoste du Jardin analyzes (1970:322).

French Colonialism

The colonial penetration at the end of the nineteenth and the beginning of the twentieth century convulsed the social and ecological environment to which the value system of niya corresponded. By seizing extensive tracts of pastureland, the French undermined the viability of the rural economy based on transhumance or nomadism. By introducing the registration of land, they opened the way to the expropriation of illiterate peasants by powerful notables. By imposing taxes, they exacerbated the difficulties of many Moroccan households, which already had to face the fact that they had to buy many consumer goods that had previously been produced at home (such as clothes), and that they could no longer derive a living from their reduced landholdings. The scarcity was answered only by a flood of French products, and Moroccans were forced to seek work in mines, in factories both at home and abroad, and on *colons'* farms.

One of the most notorious aspects of French colonial strategy was the so-called Berber policy, which attempted to turn the Berbers into allies of the French. Their strategy was, on the one hand, to emphasize the supposedly European origin of the Berbers, their separateness in ethnic, cultural, and therefore legal terms from the Arabs (perhaps 40 percent of the Moroccan population speaks Berber) ; and on the other, to assure them of the French respect for their customs, in spite of the fact that, as we have observed, they had destroyed the socioeconomic infrastructure on which these customs were based. In this way they hoped to create a Berber bloc that could be used against the Arabs in the cities, from whom came the most articulate political opposition to the French presence. Thus, Lyautey instructed, "We should try to pass directly from Berber to French. Arabic tends to Islamise because it is the language of the Koran. It is in our interest to educate the Berbers outside the framework of Islam" (Bidwell 1973:52) , and de Caix remarked that Arabic was a language "which can transmit hostile ideas" (Bidwell 1973:55) .

As far as women were concerned, we should not forget that the French attempted to prevent change in the private life of the rural populations, and especially to defend them against Arab nationalism or emancipatory movements. Thus, Lyautey claimed, "the secret of my conquest was that I protected the Berber against any violation of the intimate spheres of his life, or his clan custom, or his traditions" (Bidwell 1973:51) . More brutally, the *Bulletin d'Enseignement Public* declaimed in 1920, "Politics, in the current European sense of the word, cannot favor our attempts to bring about progress here. Therefore, let us not dream of emancipating the Moroccan citizen, or of freeing the slave, or of liberating the women" (Bidwell 1973:248) . Thus, the colonization of Morocco was not likely to lead to improvements in the position of women—on the contrary. Indeed, Christiane Souriau (1969) , writing on Libyan women, suggests that attitudes to women in France are still far from advanced and have much to learn from developments in the Third World.

Women in Contemporary Morocco

Among the tendencies both structural and contingent that have characterized independent Morocco, the following have been singled out as having particular relevance to the discussion of women: first, the spread of the nationalist ideology that was forged during the struggle for independence with its rival tendencies, the first in favor of a new puritan Muslim orthodoxy, the latter socialist in tone; second, the growth and influence of a new and expanding state-employed class; third, a high rate of population growth which, together with the depredations of the market economy, has reduced the viability of rural household and stimulated mass emigration from the countryside to the cities; fourth, the slow development of industry or of other productive sectors of the economy that could provide work and a living for the vast numbers of unemployed and underemployed; and fifth, the spread of money transactions.

In the discussion to follow, eight main categories of women, who nevertheless share many common features, demonstrate the variety of social circumstances in which women live their lives. These categories are labeled: elite women, educated working women, women of the old urban bourgeoisie, women dependent on state-employed men, country women, "free" women, migrant women, and women factory workers.

Elite Women

First, there is a tiny elite who, by virtue of their high bourgeois origin, their strength of character, or both, have been able to acquire a secondary education and to use it to acquire both economic and political autonomy. However, education does not necessarily bring about autonomy.

Educated Working Women

Second is a category of "new women." Most of them are the first in their families to exercise a profession—nearly all of them are teachers (primary), nurses, or secretaries. They hold strongly to the national ideals of the new state-employed class and are exemplary Muslims, but because of their humble social origin (most are of petty bourgeois or peasant origin) and their small numbers risk severe censure if they step outside the norms of acceptable female behavior. All of them make vital contributions to the livelihood of their family of origin, and although this gives them a prestigious role within it and confers on them the role of mediator between the private and public sphere (many of them become peacemakers and advisers in the quarter where they live), it ties them closely to the norms that govern other women.

The single women in this category often regard marriage as a threat which, by reinforcing those aspects of their social personality that link them with other women, would subject them to the arbitrary power of a husband and to the authority of his female kin. This is particularly so because they expect the husband to be chosen for them, within the framework of a family alliance. However, most women of this kind have great self-esteem, and hold out for a match that they consider worthy of them. Indeed, to complete a professional course at all, considering the odds against them, is a rare achievement for women.

In 1960 there were still only 2,352 women primary school teachers, of which 1,566 were "unqualified" (Forget 1964:146), and 311 nurses (Zeghari 1962). But when this figure is compared with that of 1954 (98 women teachers), the change is considerable, although it should be noted that women have access, as in Western industrial societies, mainly to professions that are coextensive with their domestic ones (care of children and the sick) and are generally the executors of male decisions.

Women of the Old Urban Bourgeoisie

The third category of women is composed of the wives, daughters, and sisters of the established bourgeoisie and petty bourgeoisie of the old towns (Fez, Rabat, Salé, Tetouan) where strict control of women has been one of the means by which the family, under the control of its male head, was able to act as a corporation. Its human and material assets could be used to create judicious new alliances of an economic or political kind or to recreate old ones, thus enlarging the scope of the original corporation and multiplying the links within it. Lahlou comments of such families in Fez, "Before being himself, the individual belongs to his family. This is even truer for women" (1968:422).

In this milieu, there is a strong preference for marriage between the children of brothers which tends to perpetuate and reinforce the cohesion of the corporation. In the 1966 survey cited by Lahlou, 95 out of 135 family heads in Fez were in favor of this marriage arrangement (1968). The few women interviewed were, interestingly enough, in favor of considering the wishes of the couple. Women of this milieu were also very critical of attempts on the part of the parental generation to absorb the young couple into the household of the groom's father. Such extended households generally tend to split up fairly quickly, apparently as a result of conflict between daughter-in-law and mother-in-law. However, this is a formulation that camouflages the son's struggle for autonomy and the threat of a conflict within the father-son unit which lies at the core of property and power relations.

Women inherit and sometimes even receive dowries in this milieu. In some families, prosperous brothers give up property in favor of a less successfully married sister. Such a gesture indicates the close cooperation between brothers-in-law which lies at the origin of arranged marriage. Women are closely secluded; this is the milieu par excellence of the use of *djellaba* (wide robe, originally a male garment) and veil, used especially by older married women to go out and move around the town. Younger women tend to stay at home. Unmarried girls are secluded in order to prevent them from finding their own husbands, as are young wives whose identification with their husband's group is considered suspect until they have had many children.

Only a certain level of income can guarantee the complete seclusion of women. Many tasks, such as shopping, washing clothes at the stream, and taking bread to and from the public oven, make it necessary for women to leave the house, as it would be considered undignified for men to do domestic chores. In the past richer women had slaves; today they employ servants or delegate outside tasks to foster children, poor relatives, or clients. But complete seclusion is inconvenient even for the state-employed class that attaches such importance to it as a symbol of urban bourgeois status. It is achieved partly by a heavy emphasis on male authority combined with the threat of repudiation or even violence, in part by gifts of clothes and jewelry and the attractions of high status—the stick and the carrot.

The urban wife is anxious to distinguish herself from her free but laborworn, "uncouth" rural sisters. One urban woman from Akhdar asked another why she didn't come to visit. "I haven't got *henna* up to my ankles, have I?," was the response, thus referring with some contempt to the customs of rural women, who stain their hands and feet all over with henna, whereas bourgeois women have dainty patterns applied on special occasions.

Women Dependent on State-Employed Men

The fourth category is that of peasant or petty bourgeois women who are the wives, sisters, and daughters of the state-employed class. The members of this class generally get wives from their home region as a result of the mediation of their kinswomen. The wives may have completed three or four years of primary school but rarely know French. They are subject to strict seclusion, for their husbands are keen to follow the urban customs to the last detail. They are able to achieve this seclusion by maintaining a foster child or a poorer female relative to help with labor-intensive tasks or to run essential errands involving contact with the outside world. Most of the men, especially in the south, are teachers, policemen, soldiers, or petty officials of the administration. Such men see themselves as upwardly mobile and maintain competitive relations with others of their kind. Since they are not rich enough to engage in conspicuous consumption, for they earn on the whole about $120 a month, their claim to high status is manifested in a close adherence to traditional urban bourgeois behavior, and especially in the strict control of women.

They maintain this stance with such rigidity because other models of behavior, represented by their milieu of origin and that of their wife, challenge it continuously. Such men appear to be especially haunted by the idea of promiscuity in the sense of "mixing with dishonorable strangers." In the countryside, when women leave the house, or in their contacts with neighbors and friends, they inevitably remain among "kinswomen" or the wives of "kinsmen" (for all relationships implying common interests and solidarity would be couched in these terms). Women's and men's activities are organized in time and space so that they never coincide. In the countryside, women move around more easily, not only spatially but also from kin to spouse and from marriage to marriage, maintaining constant only their kinship ties, especially those with mother, sisters, and daughters, with whom they continue to exchange visits, goods, and services all their lives. This kind of independence of the conjugal tie is threatening to state-employed men.

As was indicated, the fiercest expressions of male authority are to be found in this milieu. For example, a teacher said, "If my wife stepped over the threshold without my permission I would divorce her." Men, fearing rightly enough the psychological and social independence of their spouses, tend to cut them off as far as possible from their female kin and indeed from other women in general. Husbands attempt to supply their wives with helpers and companions from among their own women kin or at most from among the wives of their own reference group.

Thus, women who advance socially tend to forfeit their links with poorer kin and with the countryside and to become more dependent on their kin by marriage. The implications of this emerge in the second generation, whose members are generally more closely linked to their father's kin than to their mother's. The family with its strongly agnatic framework resembles more closely other urban bourgeois families than it does those of the spouses' parents or those of the urban or rural proletariat in which links through women are very important.

Country Women

This category, containing about 60 percent of all Moroccan women, consists of those who live and work in the countryside, more or less secluded according to the extent to which their husbands can dispense with their labor. As mentioned earlier, such women, who neither inherit their due share of land nor receive bridewealth, are more closely tied by rights and duties to their own kin than to their conjugal unit. This situation results in a high level of divorce. In fact, 50 percent of the marriages ever made by the inhabitants of one village in the Middle Atlas had ended in divorce, most of them within the first few years of marriage. This figure should be compared with the 28 percent among the urban employed class and 40 percent among migrants who themselves tend to conform to the marriage patterns of the countryside from which they had recently come (Maher 1974b:194).

Although rural women do not generally work for wages, some of them may be employed by other peasants or help other women within the framework of a patron-client relationship. In a survey conducted by Belghiti in the Tessaout area near Marrakech, it was found that 14 percent of a sample of peasant women was engaged in paid work (1971:310). However, there was no fixed rate of payment and they were paid as often in meals and clothes as in cash. Further, as the women themselves observed, such activities could not provide them with a living as they were occasionally and badly paid. In an area of the Middle Atlas, many women picked fruit in season for the more wealthy peasants who owned orchards. Country women are expected to cut hay and care for animals, fetch water, weed the crops, harvest beans and peas, manage supplies of grain, harvest maize, and sometimes bring loads of firewood from the mountains. They should also process food, carry out all domestic services, and bear and rear preferably male children. In return, they receive subsistence (food, clothes, and shelter), but anything else, such as medical care, should be supplied by their kin. Men plow, irrigate, and sow the crops, but hire laborers to harvest and sometimes thresh the grain. Indeed, more and more male tasks are assumed by wage laborers, but some, such as winnowing the wheat, are taken over by women to whom at one time all contact with the harvest would have been taboo for fear of mystical contamination. Agricultural tasks have been redistributed in such a way as to increase the workload of women. Similarly, women, in the absence of their men, are often forced to go to market although this is theoretically forbidden. Thus, in Belghiti's sample, 13 percent attended the market in the husband's absence and another 11 percent went regularly (1971:351).

After the menopause or as widows, country women may play an influential role in the community, particularly as they are often left to take care of the land, which in times past would have been managed by a male relative; today, sons and brothers-in-law tend to emigrate in search of wage work. In the countryside, the segregation of the sexes is less severe than it is in the town, and women often move around the village unveiled. Although great importance is attached to virginity and to female submission, two values which are served by the early marriage (age 10–14) of girls, women may enjoy considerable autonomy and even sexual freedom between marriages. Some may temporarily join the ranks of the *huryin* (free women), who prefer the life of the courtesan to the yoke of marriage and subordination to men.

"Free" Women

The concept of *hurya* is not a simple one, for it is used for women with different social personalities. The most important and self-conscious category are the *shikhat* or dancers to whom being a free woman is a profession. They live alone or in groups, having in common the characteristic that they have left or been repudiated by their kin, and have thus forfeited lineage and male tutelage. They are popularly defined as "women who do not want men to tell them what to do." Gellner describes a meeting with such a woman: "I once had a fascinating conversation with a village tart in a tribal society, which made me comment in my notes that I had met a suffragette: she explained her choice of calling precisely in terms of desire for equality, for only in this profession could she talk with men sensibly and as an equal, instead of being constrained to act in a 'feminine' manner" (1973:147–148).

Such women are called to sing and dance at weddings and other feasts (one contacting the others). They perform in the room where only men are gathered, and their behavior, in its detailed reversal of proper behavior for women, seems to have a ritual value. They smoke, drink heavily, joke, talk boldly, and fondle male guests in a way that would be taboo for women in other contexts. However, that they are taking upon themselves the burden of ritual license is suggested by the fact that at weddings of people too poor to employ professional dancers, it is the young unmarried village women (the boldest ones) who go in to dance to the men. Their matronly sisters cry "Shame!" but receive them equably when they come back. The mother of the bride may herself engage in licentious dancing. On such occasions, the values inherent in the "normal" restrained relationship between the sexes are made explicit.

The category of "unmarriageable" shikhat shades into that of "once-married woman," who is her own mistress and may engage in casual sexual relationships and other behavior which "women of honor" condemn. Such women "talk to men," drink with them in bars, and may even live in common law union in the prostitutes' quarter. Such women are not generally kinless, may inherit property, and eventually marry. Indeed, a number of women in one area of the Middle Atlas turned out to be "bad women" between marriages, but this did not prevent them from receiving all the signs of community acceptance when they married, nor from assuming privileged (and sexually loaded) roles at rites of passage. They were less like courtesans than the shikhat in that their "freedom" was temporary in most cases, but they tended to share with them the essential qualifications of freedom from male tutelage, sexual availability, and independence of spirit.

A few points concerning the resistance and resignation of women can be inserted at this point. The existence of the huryin who are generally of rural origin, although they live in towns, is but one symptom of many women's growing resentment of their situation. These are especially the poorer and younger ones, and those married to elderly husbands, for older men increasingly tend to consider their work life over at about fifty-five and, disillusioned both with the labor market and agriculture, retire to a life of inactivity and dependence on their wives' energies.

A woman in Belghiti's sample reveals a clear awareness of exploitation: "You never stop cooking and washing clothes. Working for men without pay" (1971:305). Another saw seclusion as a threat to her capacity to survive, a feeling that must be becoming more current as men find it increasingly difficult to maintain their families without emigrating (and even emigration cannot guarantee an income). If emigration is added to the high rate of divorce in this milieu and the tendency for husbands to be ten to thirty years older than their wives, even the most submissive woman must see that male support is unreliable and that it is essential to know how to stand on her own two feet. One woman expresses this view with great clarity: "If ever he [husband] dies, I'll be in a fine pickle. I'll have to see to everything though I have always been kept blindfolded, blinded. Nobody has ever let me see the world, but I want to see how things are, go with him to sell a cow, watch how he goes about it and learn in my turn to deal with life" (Belghiti 1971:352).

It is these poorer women who, for example, by taking part in village feasts, are able to maintain active relationships with other women, to compare and relativize their situation, and to achieve a certain breadth of outlook and awareness of exploitation. However, it is interesting that such women never make any attempt to claim their inheritance, for as Rosenfeld has observed, to claim one's inheritance means to forfeit the protection of one's patrilineage (1960). On the other hand, women who derive economic and social advantages from their conjugal situation (that is, those who are married to richer men and who are relieved from agricultural labor and derive prestige from this and are less likely to divorce) tend to make a battle for their inheritance rights. They rarely appear to be successful, and their attitude brings about enduring family feuds. Belghiti confirms this analysis for Tessaout: "Most poor women give in. Only at a certain economic level do you find women who fight for their rights" (1971:335).

Migrant Women

It is in this context of progressive impoverishment in the countryside with its particularly devastating consequences for women and children, as a result of their subordination to men and their exclusion from the labor market, that the next category of women is considered: women migrants, and the wives, daughters, and sisters of migrants. Sisters are included even if they do not necessarily migrate because the women of this group are in constant communication with one another, whether they live in the countryside, in shantytowns outside the city, or in hamlets near small towns. Further, the community of putative or classificatory kin, linked more by their common geographical origin than by real blood ties, is perpetually reconstituted by community-endogamous marriages that are arranged by women. Adam points out that in a Casablanca shantytown, 64 percent of the men had married girls from their home region and 33 percent had married relatives (1968:739). In one hamlet in the Middle Atlas 78 percent of hamlet members over three generations had married spouses living less than five kilometers away, and 22 percent had married relatives.

Through such networks of classificatory kin and affines, women arrange marriages, celebrate family rituals, and take care of the children of broken marriages and of elderly relatives. Migrant women continually revitalize the links, returning to their home region to have their children, to visit their mothers, to celebrate weddings and funerals, and to look for prospective brides for their sons. Country women send their sons to stay with relatives in town so that they can go to school and their daughters to help in the households of richer relatives. Divorcées travel from town to town staying with female relatives. Town children spend the summer in the countryside and country children are scattered among the households of their town kin.

There is a constant flow of money and goods from richer to poorer women of the network against a reverse flow of services and visiting. Women whose husbands have jobs are thus placed, if they have been married long enough to be trusted with money, in the role of patrons with respect to their poorer friends and kinswomen, although they may continue to call each other *sister* and adhere to the values of mutual loyalty typical of the tribal context. More concretely, poorer and less secluded women keep their prosperous and less mobile counterparts in touch with the outside world and with other women, do errands and household chores, bring news and visitors from the home region, and receive in exchange invitations to meals, loans, cast-off clothes, and mediation with the bureaucracy (through their patrons' menfolk).

Women Factory Workers

There is a small but significant number of women working in factories in the cities. In 1952, about 100,000 women worked in textiles and food-processing; this figure must have doubled since independence (Forget 1964:140). Further, many rural women are seasonally employed in the nearest large city (as, for example, in sardine-packing on the west coast), returning to the countryside between seasons. Such women camp with their children in deplorable conditions on the fringes of the city, and some are forced to supplement their miserable wages by prostitution. Factory work seems to be in most cases the last resort of women who have no other resources, and paradoxically often indicates a state of extreme social isolation such as that of divorced or widowed women whose kin cannot help them. In the shantytowns of Casablanca, according to Baron and Pirot, the woman living alone is a strikingly common figure (as cited in Forget 1964).

The proportion of women living alone as heads of households increases as one goes down through the layers of the proletariat—42 percent (against 58 percent of male household heads) in the poorest households (Forget 1964:173). Baron and Pirot attribute this to the fact that divorcées and widows (134 out of 900 women workers living in the shantytowns of Port Lyautey) can only rarely be absorbed into their families of origin (Forget 1964:173). Besides the husbandless women, 50 percent of working women in Casablanca shantytowns had old, ill, or unemployed husbands.

Attitudes about Fertility

As might be expected, Moroccans no longer express unqualified approval of large families. A recent government inquiry into

Moroccan attitudes toward family planning revealed that 75 percent of men and 75 percent of women thought that the ideal family was composed of fewer than five children, yet 31 percent of women had borne five or more. Seventy-four percent of women whose husbands had received more than a primary education were in favor of birth control, and 57 percent of women whose husbands were less educated were in favor of it. Husbands were generally less favorable than their wives, but at least 50 percent of those in the sample wanted their wives to know about contraceptive methods (Enquête d'opinion 1967). From these facts, we may deduce that children are more useful to country women and female relatives of migrants, and not unexpectedly that they cost more than they yield in the towns.

Large families are an insurance against a tragically high infant mortality rate (186 per 1000 in rural Morocco and 100 per 1000 in the towns; seventy percent of deaths occur among children under fourteen [*Resultats de l'enquête à objectifs multiples* 1964:76]) and against the vagaries of the economic system, for children may be placed in various economic niches, rural and urban, and therefore at least one may be able to maintain the family. Finally, they are a precaution against an indigent old age. So contraception is rarely practiced, although in the country women sometimes resort to traditional methods without their husband's knowledge, as may women with large families in the town.

Paternity is no longer so avidly desired by men since it has fewer economic and political advantages. Indeed, 3 percent of a sample of young unmarried men of peasant families wished to have no children at all, which would have been social suicide a few generations ago (Pascon and Bentahar 1971:264). One consequence of this attitude is that women's reproductive faculty is less valued, their bargaining power is reduced, and they are more effectively subordinated to men. Men tend not to claim the children of a broken marriage, but rather to leave them in the hands of the mother and her uterine kin. This is in contrast to the situation described by Mareuil in 1948 among the Ait Morghad Berbers, where he states that most men claimed their children, especially the boys, once they were weaned. Today, women are left with the added burden of children when they cannot support themselves from the land, so that the transfer of children from poorer to richer women kin or members of the migrant network has probably increased in importance. (One in four households in my Middle Atlas town sample contained a foster child.)

Indeed the difference between urban and rural households seems to consist mainly in the fact that while rural households are overwhelmingly nuclear (72 percent in a village sample contain just parents and children), urban households more often contain relatives (only 43 percent in a town sample were nuclear). These relatives were mainly foster children or divorced women (Maher 1974b:68–69).

The myth that rural households are patriarchal and extended and urban ones nuclear and companionate is not helpful in Morocco, where rural households seem to have been nuclear at least during the last century and a half, except for certain short phases of their developmental cycle, and where male authority seems to have been less absolute than in the town (if we exclude certain elite town families). Today, extended households, consisting of a man and his wife and their married sons, are to be found only rarely in either town or country, and then they are among richer families attempting to set themselves up as solidary corporations. Poorer families have no reason to stay together since the family is embedded in a cooperative village community and sons are expected to migrate before they marry.

Contradictions between Ideology and Reality

It is not clear whether the conscientious adherence of many Moroccans, and especially of the new state-employed class, to reformist Islam will change people's view of women for better or for worse. For strict adherence to Quranic dictates might have different implications for different parties. Thus, some might follow Baydawi —indeed his interpretation appears to resemble the opinions of most Moroccan men.

> Allah has preferred the one sex over the other . . . in the matter of mental ability and good counsel, and in their power for the performance of duties and for the carrying out of [divine] commands. Hence to men have been confined prophecy, religious leadership, saintship, pilgrimage rites, the giving of evidence in law courts, the duties of the holy war, worship in the mosque on the day of assembly [Friday], etc. They also have the privilege of electing chiefs, have a larger share of inheritance and discretion in the matter of divorce (Levy 1957:98).

Such a view would find Quranic legitimation for most of its claims. For example, "Men stand superior to women in that God hath preferred the one over the other . . . Those whose perverseness ye fear, admonish them and remove them into bed-chambers and beat them; but if they submit to you then do not seek a way against them" (Sura IV:38).

On the other hand, a woman professional making a campaign for women's education (Zeghari 1962) insists that women and men are equal before God, quoting the Quran: "And whosoever does a righteous deed, be it male or female, believing, We shall assuredly give him to live a godly life" (Sura XVI:95) (note that this suggests moral not political equality). She quotes the Quran even to combat polygamy (which only affects 3 percent of Moroccan households, most of them petty bourgeois): "You will not be able to be equitable between your wives, be you ever so eager" (Sura IV:125), pointing out that earlier in the sura the Prophet commands, "but if you fear not to be equitable, then [marry] only one [wife]" (Sura IV:3).

However, she notes that justice for women must involve non-Quranic claims such as that of Mlle. Souad, "Nous réclamons l'égalité de l'homme et de la femme devant l'héritage" (*Démocratie,* February 1957, as cited in Zeghari 1962), which was answered by the Istiqlal leader Allal al Fassi who said that women did not have to support a household. This statement is somewhat unrealistic, as we have seen.

On the whole, it appears that the attitudes both of peasants, especially those who are young, ambitious, and frustrated, and of townsmen of all strata hold to the subordination of women and their exclusion from public life for social structural (though diverse) reasons, and that they can find Quranic legitimation for this position. For the mass of the population, the claustration of women might be seen as a defense mechanism that maintains women's dependence on and reactivation of those kin and community ties that the market economy tends to destroy. Such networks are essential to the survival of both men and women, especially the very young and the very old. As seclusion is undermined by the growing necessity for women to fend for themselves, the ferocity with which men defend their prerogatives is accentuated. As Bourdieu and Sayad observe, "The importance of *niya* as a value is accentuated as people become aware of behavior which tends to undermine it" (1964:91).

The ideology to which men adhere expresses this contradiction in three ways: first, in the belief that women are impressionable, lacking in judgment, and treacherous, and must be rigidly controlled; second, in the fear that any contact of women with the labor or commodity market will result in the dissolution of their family ties; and third, in an intransigent opposition to education or any extradomestic experience that might offer to women economic and political independence or a sense that there are alternatives to their present situation. Men attempt to depreciate the work done by women. Peasant men when asked about women's work answer that it is "those tasks which can be performed sitting down" or "women just cook" (Pascon and Bentahar 1971), although, for example, 80 percent of Belghiti's sample worked in the fields, 79 percent reared chickens or rabbits, 67 percent spun or wove, and 6 percent practiced other crafts (1971:306, 296). This male view conforms to the urban petty-bourgeois ideal of female passivity, certainly unattainable for most peasants. Further, by playing down the value of women's work, men play down also the rewards that women can claim. One young peasant protests: "If women were to go to the market they would want pricey clothes. They aren't reasonable. And it is the man who earns the money, so it is fair that he should spend it" (Pascon and Bentahar 1971).

Above all, women must be kept away from the market for they would abandon their family roles. Another peasant: "Take a woman to market? She'll see other men, or get lost, or find someone better. And if she goes out, she won't come back home, that's certain." It is significant that this claustration is selective, and does not apply to leaving the house to get medicines for children, to visiting saints' tombs, or, above all, to working in the fields (Belghiti 1971:349). It is commercial exchange, the value of commodities and their desirability—and the possibility of undertaking paid work in order to buy them—that women must not discover.

Women must be kept from "understanding" their relation to the world, or realizing their real capacities or opportunities. The emphasis on trammeled perception of which the Tassaout woman, who was cited earlier, complains—"I have always been kept blindfolded, blinded"—is a recurrent theme. "Girls should be married off before their eyes open" (50 percent of the women in the Tassaout sample were married before puberty, 40 percent just after). Another woman says, "Girls should be married off young so that they are not too wide awake, nor do they know too much about life. That way, a husband can control his wife easily; otherwise, she is hard to manage" (Belghiti 1971:313).

Consonant with this view is the opposition to the education of women both in town and countryside. Educated women are liable to become *chiki* (cheeky or osée), a word used to describe women who are immodest or wear European clothes. The association that Moroccans (and others) make between "knowledge of the world," whether derived from experience or education, and sexual license is a complex one. Here I would point out only that they recognize the fragility of the marriage tie and that it is linked with a woman's continuing emotional and economic interest in her family of origin throughout her lifetime, and her initial and sometimes permanent lack of status in her husband's home.

What is not overtly recognized is that her reproductive powers are the means by which heirs to property are produced in the town and by which a man makes a place for himself, economically and politically, in the countryside. Legitimate filiation is vital in both contexts, and can only be achieved by assuring complete control over the woman's sexuality. The need to put women's sexuality to the service of property or the lineage means that the experience of women's sexual subjectivity and autonomy (epitomized in the huryin) is a threatening one. Women are thought of as naturally lascivious temptresses, without moral sense, and so on.

Education of Women

In the province where research was undertaken, 8 percent of girls of primary school age are at school (see Maher 1974b:83–86). One town provides the majority of these girl pupils, for in the southern half of the province no girls at all go to school. In rural schools there is on the average one girl to four boys, but this proportion rises to one in three for semiurban and urban schools. The proportion of girls to boys in the first year of secondary school (*classe d'observation*) is one to five; there is a sharp fall in the number of girls attending college after the first year relative to boys (one to seven), and only a negligible proportion carry on after the *certificat d'etudes secondaires,* which is taken in the fourth year. On the whole about 50 percent of town girls and 10 percent of rural ones are at school (Zeghari 1962).

It is the opinion of Arabs as well as Berbers, in the town as in the country, that education is wasted on girls and is proper only if it does not disturb traditional relationships. "A woman kneads bread, she cooks, she carries children on her back" (*ta-ju, ta-ib, ta-rkib ulad*). Thus parents are more ready to allow girls to attend the schools of housecraft run by the Union Nationale des Femmes Marocaines, than to let them pursue academic or technical studies at a secondary school. Men in particular regard schools as having a corrupting influence on girls, causing them to lose their virginity, to feel dissatisfied with the constraints of married life, and to commit adultery.

At home, girls are kept too busy with domestic chores to have time to study. They look forward to breaking the monotonous round by traveling, for example to see richer relatives, in the summer months. Women and girls begin discussing where they will go in the summer months before winter has set in. Marriage, too, offers a change of scene and a different round of visits.

Few women expect to shape their lives by their own efforts but most hope to take advantage of the variety of stimuli offered within their networks of kinship and affinity.

Summary

Women in the countryside and among urban migrants, through the marriages they arrange, the children they foster, the feasts they celebrate, the visits they make, and the goods and services they exchange outside the framework of the market, tend to recreate in a modified form the society and the community of clansmen based on "personal loyalty and good faith" (Bourdieu and Sayad 1964:89). But in the towns and particularly among the new class of state employees, an attempt is made to inhibit the social relationships of women, and to make of them the symbols of social differentiation (that is, of status differentiation) rather than of social cohesion. This situation should be referred to the socioeconomic conditions of the two categories. The former, although unable to get a living from their land, cannot be assured of employment within the market economy (20 percent of all males between twenty and sixty are unemployed), and only outside it can they find a minimum of security and social satisfactions. The latter are attempting to achieve social mobility within the framework of the market, where competitiveness, individualism, and the desirability of controlling the services of others are more valid than the principle of reciprocity.

However, both peasants and urban migrants are aware that the progressive monetarization of labor and its products is liable to make inroads into their patrimony in land (since agricultural prices and productivity fall continuously in relation to those of the manufactured products they are forced to buy), already meager because of colonial depredations and the phenomenal population growth of recent decades. But their property in land and houses is the basis for the cohesion of the community of clansmen on which they depend.

Since this land and the relationships associated with it (involving kinship, affinity, reciprocal exchanges of labor, and the sharing to some extent of the means of subsistence) are mostly mediated by women, it is they who must be prevented from entering the market economy and from disposing of any property. If women were to become economically or politically independent of men, they would no longer bend so readily to those matrimonial and reproductive roles that link men to one another through affinity and descent, but that separate women from their kin and reduce them to instruments of production and reproduction. One example of the many ideological mechanisms that tie women to male-oriented roles is the fact that married women in Morocco are accorded higher status than unmarried women, that women with children enjoy higher status than those without, that those with male children are considered fortunate (especially in the countryside), and that those with numerous male children seem to be the most honored of all. It is in the interactions among women that these distinctions become apparent. A woman learns to evaluate her roles and those of other women according to their efficacy in perpetuating a male-dominated social structure.

Significantly, peasants and men of recent peasant origin living in the towns tend to attribute to women ideal roles (seclusion, exclusively domestic work, virginity or fidelity, subordination to male authority) that emphasize their dependence on men, but which are in sharp contrast with the facts of women's existence in these classes. Peasant women carry out heavy agricultural or seasonal factory work and they are involved in intense extradomestic activity in maintaining a network of relationships among women that guarantee their survival in the face of frequent divorce, the absence of men, or the incapacity of men through unemployment or age to see to their needs or those of their children. The forms of women's rebellion (high divorce rate, casual prostitution, intrigue, solidarity among women, ritual ridicule, ecstatic religion's validating nonsexual roles) tend to undermine those institutions, such as the conjugal relationship, in which their oppression and subordination to men is most apparent. Women's activities and attitudes give rise to a deep fear and mistrust on the part of men toward women, and to a certain psychological independence on the part of those women whose activities are most in contradiction with the image and ideal presented to them by men.

Women who have married salaried townsmen (such a new social category that to marry into this class usually represents a social advance for the woman and a relief from labor) are generally more ready to accede to male authority, particularly since the male ideal corresponds to the woman's real experience, which is "sedentary" and limited. Further, the work carried out by the male appears to give him the right to dispose of his salary, and seclusion limits that association with other women that could confer a certain degree of psychological independence. Divorce in this milieu is much rarer than among migrants or in the countryside and is more often initiated by the man.

Most women cannot escape the dilemma: either psychological independence, conditioned by patrilineal protection and control, poverty, and heavy labor; or physical ease at the price of social isolation, passivity, and total subordination to male authority. The few who, by virtue of their advanced education or wide experience, can be at least potentially autonomous as workers and thinkers face other problems. They frequently live lives of conflict and frustration but undoubtedly supply a model with which many younger women can identify. Their choices are watched critically and attentively by women who hope to make them their own, even if such hopes are objectively unrealistic. They mediate among the women of their neighborhood and kin groups. If their willingness to resist the pressures "to be as other women are" and their determination to shape their own future are combined, as I have seen it to be in many cases, with tact and political sensibility, such that they remain in close contact with the masses of women whose struggles and oppression are intimately linked with their own, this group may play an important role in determining the direction of social change in Morocco.

Note

1. For example, *The Politics of Social Change in the Middle East and North Africa* (Halpern 1963) devotes only three sentences out of 450 pages to women.

Bibliography

Adam, A. *Casablanca,* vols. I and II. Paris, 1968.

Amin, S. *The Maghreb in the Modern World.* London, 1970.

Belghiti, M. "Les relations féminines et le statut de la femme dans la famille rurale dans trois villes de la Tessaout." In *Etudes sociologiques sur le Maroc,* ed. A. Khatibi. *Bulletin Economique et Sociale du Maroc* (1971) : 289–361.

Bidwell, R. *Morocco under Colonial Rule.* London, 1973.

Bourdieu, P., and A. Sayad. *Le déracinement: la crise de l'agriculture traditionelle en Algérie.* Paris, 1964.

"Enquête d'opinion sur la planification familiale." *Bulletin Economique et Sociale du Maroc,* 29, no. 104–105 (January–June 1967) :95–149.

Forget, N. "Femmes et professions au Maroc." In *Images de la femme dans la société,* ed. P. Chombart de Lauwe. Paris, 1964.

Gellner, E. *Cause and Meaning in the Social Sciences.* London, 1973.

———. "The Unknown Apollo of Biskra: The Social Base of Algerian Puritanism." *Government and Opposition,* 9, no. 3 (Summer 1974) : 277–310.

Halpern, M. *The Politics of Social Change in the Middle East and North Africa.* Princeton, 1963.

Lacoste du Jardin, C. *Le conte Kabyle.* Paris, 1970.

Lahlou, A. "Etude sur la famille traditionelle de Fez." *Revue de l'Institut de Sociologie,* 3 (1968) :407–441.

Levy, R. *The Social Structure of Islam.* Cambridge, 1957.

Magli, I. *La donna: un problema aperto.* Firenze, 1974.

Maher, V. "Divorce and Property in the Middle Atlas of Morocco." *Man,* 9 (1974a) :103–122.

———. *Women and Property in Morocco.* Cambridge, 1974b.

de Mareuil, M. B. "Notes sur la condition des femmes en Assoul." Unpublished. Paris, 1948.

Ministre du plan, Division statistique. *Resultats de l'enquête à objectifs multiples, 1961–1963.* Rabat, 1964.

Pascon, P., and M. Bentahar. "Ce que disent 296 jeunes ruraux." In *Etudes sociologiques sur le Maroc,* ed. A. Khatibi. *Bulletin Economique et Social du Maroc* (1971) :145–287.

Rosenfeld, H. "On Determinants of the Status of Arab Village Women." *Man,* 15 (1960) :66–70.

Souriau, C. "La société féminine en Libye." *Revue de l'Occident Musulman et de la Méditerranée,* 6, nos. 1–2 (1969) :127–155.

Zeghari, El Hassan L. "La femme marocaine et sa préparation à la vie familiale et professionelle." *Confluent,* 23–24 (September–October 1962) .

5 Women in Turkish Society

Fatma Mansur Coşar

Turkey as a republic is just over fifty years old. It is therefore inevitable that the nature of Turkish society, and the position of women who make up a little more than half of it, are the result of the interplay of historical and other factors that operate within a changing society bent on a difficult process of socioeconomic development. Turkish society experienced an enormous upheaval in the 1920s, and the result was consciously introduced changes in motivation, direction, and function. The proclamation of the republic, abolition of the sultanate and caliphate, introduction of secularization, adoption of Western law, liberal capitalism, and industrialization became signposts on the road the Turks were told they would travel henceforth. Development within the new boundaries was the password. In this way, the centuries-old Ottoman structure collapsed, taking with it its underpinnings. In Turkey, as against many Western nations, the legal system is no obstacle to the emancipation of women, although it needs improvement. But the basic framework was put in place by Ataturk: the right to vote and be elected, the compulsion to be sent to school at least until the age of eleven, monogamy, proper divorce proceedings, equal inheritance and property rights, and equal pay for equal work, equal social security, and so forth. And yet . . .

My examination of the extent to which the position of women has been affected by the republican laws, changes in social attitudes, and changes in functions is based upon an assumption: that it is a good thing for a woman to have a choice of functions available to her, to be free to choose and not to be impeded by factors at odds with the general direction in which the society as a whole is moving.[1] In Turkey it must be borne in mind that poverty and tradition increase as one proceeds from west to east and to a lesser extent from south to north. Also, as a result of the geographic situation of Turkey, there are cultural and ethnic differences within the population.[2]

Turkey is still an agricultural country, in that 70 percent of its population still lives on the land and agriculture still contributes more to the gross national product than the industrial sector.[3] This means that two-thirds of the women of Turkey live and work on the land. The remainder live in a large number of small towns and in a half dozen cities. However, it has been repeatedly shown that owing to a very rapid population increase, an inheritance law that divides property equally among children, and a far from efficient agricultural and industrial policy, the majority of people in the largest cities and towns are immigrants from the villages. These newcomers are first and second generation city dwellers and tend to live in neighborhoods where they recreate the social mores of the villages and small towns from which they came. This bears special significance for the women. These women, who had a certain amount of social and familial authority in the village because of the part they played in the economic life, find themselves deprived of it while still remaining under the social pressure of their male relatives.

It therefore seems logical to discuss the position of village women before that of urban women. However, there are factors that play a role in women's lives and development regardless of social setting. A Turkish woman is branded at birth because she is not born a boy. The imperial Islamic mentality that needed soldiers—men—is still widely present. In villages remote from larger centers a girl's birth is often registered very late, or together with another birth in the family, or even not at all. The mother, after having gotten over the first disappointment of not having "given a son" to the father, takes cheer in the fact that a daughter will help her in work and take care of her when she is ill. The girl child is called a "guest" in popular parlance, meaning that she will eventually leave the paternal roof. Underlying this is the thought that too much trouble will not be taken, or is not worth taking, in her upbringing. This attitude is gradually qualified to the girl's advantage as higher socioeconomic levels are reached and as one approaches the cities.

The socialization of girl children is overwhelmingly similar in all strata under consideration. She is taught the "womanly virtues" of discretion, chastity, and obedience, and from the age of six onward she is largely segregated from boys except at school. This coincides with the age at which she is put to work in an agricultural setting. In the towns and cities she only helps with the housework. She is allowed to cry whereas boys are not, and discouraged from quarreling and fighting whereas boys are actively encouraged in these activities. Boys must learn to defend themselves; girls rely on their parents and brothers to defend them.

Schooling, which is legal but not in fact compulsory for all children until the age of eleven, is not taken as seriously for girls as it is for boys. The assumptions here are that it is more important for a girl to be a good mother and homemaker and a good field worker. The attitude toward schooling becomes more positive, again, as one proceeds up the socioeconomic scale and from village to city. In the remote and poorest districts, although male literacy is nothing to boast about, female illiteracy is nearly total. In the more prosperous regions, female literacy is not quite up to the 55 percent mark. The social groups that seem keenest on girls' education are the second generation immigrants in the large cities, the groups engaged in the service sector, government service including schoolteachers, and all income groups above the lowest. This holds true for higher educational levels even though higher education is practically free of charge.

As in all societies, marriage, which provides a socioeconomic framework for the biological function of women, is regarded as the culmination of a girl's development. The attributes of chastity, discretion, and obedience will now be part of the package deal displayed to prospective husbands. Whatever economic advantages exist play an important role, but it may be said with some confidence that these are secondary. The most significant consideration is virginity: the marriageable girl should be known as "untouched by any hand." This is considered so important that even in the most sophisticated social sets, surgeons are asked to restore a damaged hymen. There is a legal reason for such a drastic medical remedy: a man may claim that he was kept in ignorance of the fact that his wife was not a virgin and may be granted a divorce. Virginity is so central to the rites of marriage that the virginity of a bride is scrutinized the morning after the first night of marriage by female relatives of the husband, and her premarriage virginal state announced publicly to the community. In some areas rifles are discharged into the air on the occasion. In all these happenings the girl arrives at the marriage bed ignorant of what exactly will happen. In the countryside she has seen animals copulating and is less ignorant; in the towns and cities a girl gets information through gossip and more recently through the media.

The premium put by the society on virginity and chastity affects men as well: a man who has been named as a seducer is honor-bound to marry the girl he has seduced, since she is now considered to be "soiled merchandise" whom no other man will marry. This attitude has given rise to a widespread custom: that of elopement. Marriage through elopement is very common in the countryside because it serves as an escape valve from rigid custom and from family and economic pressure. Two young people who want to get married and who are prevented from doing so by their families or by one of the families (because the young man is too poor to provide the bridewealth or comes from a family that is not approved of by the girl's side or comes from outside whatever kin group is acceptable to the girl's family), will stage an elopement. Usually, however, the young girl is untouched by the young man and is given in keeping to an aged relative until the marriage ceremony occurs. This is done because once the young girl has spent a night away from the parental roof and in company of a young man, it is assumed automatically that she has been defiled and there is no solution but marriage. Elopement is one of the ways by which rigid sexual and social mores break down.

Another manifestation of the double standard is what has been termed the "religious wedding." The Republican Civil Code abolished polygamy and gave property and inheritance rights only to children issued from a marriage performed by the secular authorities. However, the Islamic polygamous tradition is still rife. In the villages and small market towns, where economic life is based upon agricultural work and produce, men are in the habit of taking one or more wives after their first secularly married wife ceases to be sexually attractive or has failed to produce a male child. The number of wives depends upon the economic importance of the man in question. Here, however, another social control mechanism comes into play: social acceptance for each of the succeeding wives is gained by performing only the "religious wedding." Children issued from such a marriage are considered illegitimate by the civil code and it is entirely up to their father to see that they are treated fairly, financially. Numerous first marriages are also religious only and not registered. To show the extent to which these customs prevail, it is enough to point out that by 1950, 8 million children were given legal status by the civil authorities. This was at a time when the population was at the 21 million mark.

From the point of view of women, polygamy creates conflict and insecurity. The first wife has to accept what is customarily done and the younger wives have to bow to the wishes of their fathers and elders. Again, as in everything else, this custom is wider spread in east Turkey than in west Turkey. It is enough to say that it is another indication that men are still sexually privileged in Turkish society.

Upon marriage the girl leaves her parental home for good. She is now said to "belong" to her husband and his family. They take over the tutelage functions which will be differently interpreted according to the social situation. In the village she will be left to her husband's family while he is off for his two years of military service, so that they can watch over her actions. This is the case for all but the highest income groups in the large towns and cities where men do not usually marry before they have done their military service.

Once married, a woman is expected to be a good homemaker. Even in the most sophisticated social sets a perfect homemaker will be mentioned with admiration by men and women alike. She is expected to be thrifty: "the nest is made by the female bird," goes the saying. In the countryside she will do her share of the work for the fields and animals of the husband's family, and in the towns she will be expected to make other economic contributions to the family's budget like making the clothes of the family, making some of the food, and perhaps taking in sewing or knitting or working as a maid or in a factory. This is possible because even the nuclear family in Turkey almost always includes some aged relative or unmarried aunt who can look after the children and the home while the woman goes out to work.

In addition to being good housewives, women are expected, as elsewhere, to be good mothers. A good mother in the popular understanding is a mother who "sacrifices" herself to her children. The adjective *self-sacrificing* is as current as *chaste* and *neat*. They constantly recur in conversations and gossip sessions. Self-sacrifice is a virtue that is praised by men also, but, like chastity, it is never mentioned in connection with men. Public morality accepts the double standard in sexual matters and either winks at or tacitly accepts laxity of sexual morals in men. This attitude clearly cuts across socioeconomic boundaries: it goes for a peasant who visits a bawdyhouse on market days, for a small craftsman on a trip to a larger town where he goes to buy parts or goods, as well as for a businessman on an Istanbul or European business trip. It is only in the high social sets that women are openly allowed to have lax sexual-marital morals in the sense that no penalties attach to their actions. Anywhere below that level the penalty ranges from ostracism to murder. In the latter case the law is more lenient than for murders committed for purposes such as blood vendettas or material gain. Moreover, in the matter of adultery, the civil code favors men over women because it requires less conclusive evidence as far as women are concerned.[4]

The above is a succinct and sketchy summary of a social and legal situation, but it is clear that the traditions of Islam concerning women are still too strong to be termed a mere residue. They permeate Turkish society in breadth and in depth and are at the bottom of male-female relationships even in such Westernized social institutions as hospitals, universities, and government departments. They confirm Turkish women in their subservient role relative to men and encourage them to remain passive about, and insensitive to, their social situation. It can be said that Turkish women, when considered from the point of view of their biological function only, are required by social mores and to some extent by law to lead a life of service and obedience, first to their male relatives and then to their husbands and even their grown sons. Compliance brings social approval, while deviation brings social censure and heavy penalties.

What customs, institutions, and developments provide for variation in the pattern and enough elasticity to ensure the viability of the system? It is here that the other roles played by women come into play. The legal reforms introduced by Ataturk provide equal opportunities for women provided they are able and willing to make use of them and the tradition of work. The laws are self-explanatory and are in many of their aspects among the most advanced in the world. They relieve women of the fight for the acquisition of rights and leave them free to fight for the enjoyment of those rights.

It is at this point that the economic function of the Turkish woman provides a base upon which the independence she has can be built and enlarged. At first glance the usual socioeconomic pattern of a developing country provides a clue. Seventy percent of the female population lives and works on the land and the rest of the women are distributed extremely unevenly among small market towns, large towns, small cities, and very large cities.

The life led by peasant women is so different that it must be considered separately, for this is no mere case where women play an economic role as well as other roles. The difference lies in the fact that for peasant women farm work is compulsory through tradition, completely integrated within home and family life, and *inevitable*. If one bears in mind that the bulk of Turkish agricultural production is performed by women, the magnitude of the phenomenon is better appreciated. Suffice it to say that for every one hundred working persons in the towns, only eight are women, while for every one hundred working persons on the land, forty-nine are women

(Çinar 1975:2). To quote Seniye Çinar, who is an agricultural engineer:

> In the Black Sea region the hazelnut and tea crops are entirely produced by women. In Central Anatolia wheat is worked by women, from the planting until the harvest, and it is women who carry it to the mills. In the Southeast region of Cukurova most of the work connected with the production of sugar beets and tobacco is done by women. Cotton in the hot and primitive region of Cukurova in the Southeast is picked by women and girls. Girls and small boys walk for miles on the plateaux of Eastern Anatolia watching the cattle and gathering their droppings (1975:5).

Çinar could have added that it is the women who turn the result into bricks for fuel and building, that the care of all animals is women's province, and that in the west it is the women who pick and process almonds, olives, citrus, and figs. By and large, the men only do the plowing. In addition, the peasant woman bears children and is often delivered in a field, she weaves cloth and furnishings, sews and darns, makes flour and cereals for the home, pickles and preserves, and is in charge of all dairy work and of all catering arrangements for the constantly recurring festivals, weddings, and circumcision and other feasts. In the poorest areas she will emigrate with her children and a baby strapped to her back to alien regions and work as a migrant laborer, paid a minimum wage, uninsured and unprotected.

The constitution, which is pledged to protect the family, mothers, and children, and to ensure a decent standard of living for all, is directly at odds with a country where the budget cannot bear the enormous burden that would result if and when social insurance is extended to agricultural workers.

In areas where large property is the rule, a quasi-feudal system bears even more heavily upon women: in these regions the extended family is the prevalent form, and, in addition to hard farm work, women have to look after a great number of children, put up with one or more wives, obey each male relative in descending order of importance and each older female relative as well. In these regions, the rate of literacy is at its lowest, and there is no way for a woman to escape her lot, for even if she were able to migrate, her skills would not be enough to gain her employment elsewhere.

In regions where small landholdings predominate, women still work very hard but are free from a quasi-feudal social and familial setup. But in all cases, the bulk of the agricultural work rests upon women's shoulders. Once the plowing season is over, the men congregate daily in the coffeehouses.

In some situations women acquire a considerable amount of authority because of the responsibilities they undertake. In the Black Sea region, for instance, where men are mostly sailors, most decision-making devolves upon the women. In other regions, running a large holding or being a first wife carries with it authority and prestige. However, for hundreds of thousands of peasant women, life is a never-ending succession of hard labor and child-bearing and rearing, in an environment where such amenities as running water and electricity are the exception rather than the rule. It is against such a background that the position of the majority of Turkish women must be viewed and Turkish sexual morality appreciated.

For these women the society as a whole, in its legal, cultural, and institutional aspects, is a closed book. Remoteness, lack of communications, and illiteracy discourage an interest in anything but the village itself. Politics are left to the men. Political and, for that matter, other rights which were given to women with the formation of the republic are unknown and unused. The only relief is provided by religious festivals and ceremonies and by wandering preachers, and the only consolation is the hope of Paradise.

It is not that men are much better off. They also suffer from ignorance and isolation, but they do not have the same work burden and they are free to come and go. Freedom of movement, which is a constitutional right, does not exist for women. Work and custom tie them to the home unless they are so poor that they have to hire themselves out as migrant laborers. Even then they are not free of social control, because whole villages migrate together, under the leadership of an "uncle," and social control is severely maintained.

As one proceeds westward, the situation of women improves with the general socioeconomic situation. The climate becomes increasingly better and milder, the roads and other means of communication more numerous, landholdings become smaller, and the extended family turns into a modified form of nuclear family. Women are freed from the harshest types of work and the harshest types of family and social control. Religious superstition loses its intensity, and religious life acquires a more sociable character. Since agriculture is more mechanized and other industries have begun to appear, more men go to work and women are able to devote more time to their homes and children.

It is in these regions and in the small towns of Anatolia that the status of women is beginning to change. It was mentioned above that economic pressure on the land has created a movement of internal migration. The pattern of this migration leads from the villages to the small towns and eventually from the small towns either to the large cities or to foreign industrialized countries. Men who have no land to work and no other means of employment migrate with their families to towns where they hope to find work of some sort. Often the small town acts as a social workshop where the man learns the elements of a trade and his wife learns how to become a town dweller.

The migrating family usually joins relatives who have migrated before and thus is spared the harshest problems attendant upon such moves. For the women this means a sudden change, because, while she is all at once relieved of agricultural work, she is confined by her ignorance to the home. The larger the town, the more frightened she will feel or be made to feel by her social group about possible dangers to her chastity. She will not be allowed out at all, except under the escort of her husband, a male relative, or even a younger brother, while her husband will be free to explore the possibilities for enjoyment under the guidance of the older migrants. This means that in return for less work and a little more comfort, women will have a social life even more narrow in physical and psychological terms than they had in the village. The new migrants will henceforth live the life that the second largest group of women live in Turkey: the group that inhabits all but the three largest cities of Istanbul, Izmir, and Ankara.

The position of these women cannot be said to be a transitional one between the peasant woman and the fully emancipated urban woman. On the contrary, women in small towns live a life that is nearer to the segregated "harem" life than that of peasant women. Before the veil was actively discouraged by Ataturk, women in the countryside did not wear the veil because they could not work in the fields with a veil on. At most, they would turn their head when meeting a strange man on the village street. But urban women were strictly veiled and lived a strictly segregated life in their homes. Today, with the resurgence of religiosity, the largest number of women who have started to cover their heads and limbs are found in the smaller urban centers. They are not allowed to go to work, rarely go out singly, and are always back in their homes before nightfall. Their shopping is done by their husbands and they cook what is brought to the house that day. They may or may not buy their own clothes, but they usually make them out of materials bought by their husbands. They are taken, as peasant women are, to the doctor or the dentist by their husbands, and preferably to a woman practitioner. They do not know what the family income is and are not consulted when the acquisition of new assets is planned. They may or may not eat with their husbands. The latter will do whatever entertaining of other men they have to do outside the home and will spend a few evenings a week with other men in a restaurant. For these women television has proved a boon for the evenings.

Sexual mores are strictest in these environments. The realities of country life did allow for hurried marriages now and again. In the small urban centers girls are severely segregated from the age of eleven onward. The strictness about sexual relationships is illustrated by the fact that 63 percent of the girls who live in small towns see their husband for the first time on their wedding day, while the proportion for the three large cities and the villages are 16 and 19 percent, respectively. It is in hundreds of these little urban centers that women lead the most segregated life and are most reduced to their traditional biological function. As compensation, they have the lightest burden of work and the most help in housework and childrearing.

Turkey is a centrally administered country, which means that in every small town there are a number of government officials, with their families, temporarily in residence before being transferred to another post. The wives of these officials—who may also work in the town as schoolteachers or other government employees—represent the most emancipated type of woman in the provinces, but communication between them and the local women, as between their male counterparts, is minimal. Local women are aware of the relative freedom of the government wives but do not seek to imitate them any more than they would imitate a foreign tourist. "Our ways are different," is the way they would put it. They display the same reaction when they see Turkish actresses on television or listen to programs produced and presented by women. The peasant woman does not have many opportunities to see and observe these other types of Turkish women, but the small-town woman does, and so great is tradition and male pressure that she divorces herself from the experience.

What is happening very slowly is that more and more girls from this group are being educated or demanding to be and that economic change creates greater mobility for men, so that in the more technologically developed areas of Turkey, even these women are beginning to move more freely, go with their neighbors to the cinema at night unaccompanied by a male relative, shop in the market by themselves, or even travel to another city to see a relative.

It is in the large cities that the Ataturk reforms concerning women are being worked out: the Turkish woman here is given and/or takes the opportunity to become a full member of society in fields other than the strictly biological one. Whereas the peasant woman is made to work at compulsory labor for no wages and the small-town woman is prevented from playing any but a biological role, the woman in the large city is given an opportunity to function in any capacity she chooses. It is true that opportunities depend on her education and training and on the socioeconomic background that she has, but the anonymity which pervades relationships in large cities works largely on the side of the woman. It helps to diminish her shyness in public and makes her menfolk less conscious of social pressure from their peers.

Other factors that have been decisive in emancipating women and taking them away from the home into the hurly-burly of life are the growth of job opportunities and a constant rise in prices which has degenerated into a more or less continuing inflation. Faced with severe economic pressure, women have to go to work whether they or their husbands want it or not.[5] Prejudices and fear of the outside world give way to necessity and necessity turns into habit. For another category of women, work becomes a means by which to satisfy increasingly rising expectations and gives women a feeling of exercising a certain amount of choice: they do not have to work, but rather choose to. For a third category, work provides self-fulfillment in the form of a career. Whereas the first two categories contribute to the economic life of society, the third category can be said to exercise the most choice: women in it can choose to play a social and economic role in conjunction with, or to the exclusion of, their biological role.

Whether city women are factory workers, typists, government officials, or professionals, they are integrated into a type of life where legal, economic, and political rights are clearly spelled out and widely known. In this sense, city women benefit to the largest extent from the Ataturk reforms. The only exceptions are what may be termed social rights: it can safely be said that outside working hours women are less free and more dependent upon men the lower one goes on the socioeconomic ladder. The social life led by the newly arrived peasant woman is not very different than the life led by her small-town sister, except that she works harder. The life led by a full-fledged professional woman is not very different than the life led by her Western sister. The latter has to put up with residues of male prejudice, but not with overt censure or vetoes from men.

A peasant woman not only is not aware of her rights but she has to rely upon her husband or male relatives to go to the law for her. City women know and can fight by themselves. Lawyers will take up their cases directly, without referring to their husbands or fathers. They tend to vote in accordance with their socioeconomic or professional group, whether or not this coincides with the way their husbands vote.[6]

The working woman has less time, less need, and less inclination for religion and religious observance. She does not feel herself to be the plaything of destiny, nor is she cowed by the petty threats with which the *ulama* (religious scholars) maintain their hold on peasant women or idle small-town women. Such acts as going out without the husband's permission or speaking to men, which are punishable by damnation according to village and small-town ulama, cease to have any bearing upon reality in an urban context.

Although men have accepted the fact that women must work and appreciate an additional contribution to the family budget, they do not help with the children or the housework, and neither are they expected to by their wives. As a result, small children are left in charge of some relative—many families usually have an old mother or aunt living with them for economic reasons—or in the hands of paid help which is usually an illiterate peasant immigrant or a neighbor. In the higher income groups, more adequate maid and nurse services are available. This problem preoccupies most working mothers in the West and is, for the moment, more satisfactorily dealt with in developing societies where the nuclear family most often includes a female relative.

Women in large urban centers work as unskilled and skilled industrial workers, in the services, as clerks and secretaries in private businesses and government offices, as saleswomen in shops, maids in hotels and homes, as workers in banks, tourist firms, and travel agencies, and as college-trained professionals in the government, the universities, the hospitals, and in law, architecture, and engineering firms. It is also out of the urban environment that musicians, painters, ballerinas, and writers have emerged. Although the number of women relative to men is still low, the few studies made in this area show that the proportion of women has increased rapidly in the last fifteen years, a period that coincided with a rise in the standard of living, an extension in the urban middle class, and a rise in prices.

The incidence of women in the professions is worthy of some consideration. Turkey has a very large public sector which includes most heavy industry and most hospitals, clinics, and schools. As a result, government employment conditions were the first to be properly regulated, with pay scales and benefits guaranteed, as against the private sector where salaries are still largely subjected to supply and demand and where social benefits are a recent development. Since the majority of women work primarily out of economic necessity, government employment has always attracted them. It is a sector where 25 percent of the personnel is female. Most of this personnel is, however, employed at lower levels—women with decision-making powers number less than 1 percent—and occupies posts in ministries that deal with the so-called "social functions": education and health, tourism and information, and labor. The "technical" ministries, such as public works and agriculture, and the "traditional" ministries, such as interior, justice, finance, and foreign affairs, contain the lowest proportion of women at all levels. The universities, which were the obvious instruments of Westernization, have accepted women readily enough: the percentage of Turkish female academics comes third after the United States and Canada (not counting Communist countries). Medicine was one of the professions that attracted women first, and it was accepted by men as a legitimate province of women because of the "sacred" character of healing. This phenomenon is frequent in developing countries. In addition, the profession of doctor is a rewarding one in a society where men would rather have their women looked after by women doctors.

The fact that women work for the most part because they have to is not without some negative results: women feel a conflict between their duties as mothers and homemakers and their work outside the home. Since the great majority of Turkish women, like women elsewhere, think of themselves primarily as mothers and homemakers, the conflict is resolved to the detriment of their careers. Women are less ambitious, less interested, and less involved in their work than men are. There is a high rate of absenteeism for health reasons. In such cases men supervisors will be more lenient toward a working mother than toward a man, but, on the other hand, given equal qualifications, male personnel managers prefer a man for middle and higher level vacancies. These attitudes, both male and female, result in the fact that many women, especially in the government and private business sector, are overqualified for the posts they occupy, a phenomenon also noted in some Western countries.

These points show a general lack of integration of the female position-holder and the post. However, it has also been shown that in the case of professional women who come from relatively well-to-do homes and educated backgrounds, this is not so. These women display drive and ambition, are readily obeyed by male subordinates, and are often chosen by fair standards when competing for a post with male candidates.

The social life of the woman working in a large urban center depends upon the socioeconomic level of her group, the length of time the group has been established in the city, and the age of the woman. Men and women of the younger generation meet fairly freely and spend most of their leisure time together, with the tacit, overt, or grudging approval of their parents. Lower-middle-class women go to the cinema or on Sunday outings with their husbands, but otherwise lead fairly segregated neighborhood social lives. It is rare to see women and men dancing or dining together except in the more expensive restaurants of the larger cities, but not rare at all to see youngsters of both sexes and practically all higher socioeconomic levels enjoying themselves together. In the case of professional women, they will associate freely with their male colleagues, if all are unmarried, only if they come from a fairly sophisticated home background. Free university education has trained many a small-town girl as a doctor or a lawyer. These girls tend to return home to work and fit into the traditional patterns of their untrained relatives outside working hours.

In conclusion, some factors retard the emancipation of women from their positions as biological role-players subservient to men, and others favor their emergence as multifunctional members of society acting in their own right. Among the former are the Islamic tradition (which puts male honor and female chastity at a premium and considers women incapable of looking after themselves), the largely agricultural nature of the country, and the slowness of socioeconomic development. Allowing more traditionalist attitudes room for action are the end of revolutionary fervor and the creation of a more reactionary climate of opinion by the advent of the multiparty system. The emergence of a middle and lower-middle class has brought with it a return of the "Victorian" mentality which is at odds with the more radical mentality of the first years of the republic. As history has shown elsewhere, women's emancipation has always been championed by movements on the Left rather than the Right. A further retarding factor is that the imperial tradition of central administration and the paternalistic state discourage an interest and participation in voluntary public work. Although this is also displayed by men in Turkish society, women are thus deprived of a valuable instrument for social role-playing.

Factors that favor emancipation, on the other hand, have been, first and foremost, the modern legal system established by the republic, Ataturk's constant reminders of the necessity of giving women full citizen status, socioeconomic development, a falling birth rate, new inheritance laws, the transformation of the extended family into a nuclear family, compulsory and free education, urbanization, and the extension of communication networks.

Can it be assumed that the rate of female emancipation will follow the rate of social development and economic advance? The answer seems to be in the affirmative, provided that the social and economic policies chosen by succeeding governments favor the more progressive, as against the more traditionalist, methods. It can also be proposed that the sudden changes in direction that were thrust upon Turkish society in the early 1920s were made bearable and did not dislocate the social structure because, in the final analysis, only a very small number of women were able to use the rights granted to them by Ataturk. The vast majority of women are still tied to the land and under the social control of men. Such phenomena as elopement, migration and emigration, and demand for unskilled female labor provide a certain amount of release through safety valves in unbearable situations, while the general rate of emancipation remains slow, if constant. As elsewhere in developing countries, the social group most needed for the production of food and children is still relegated to an inferior status.

In the industrialized West we find no counterpart of the Turkish peasant woman, with her enormous work burden, or the small-town woman, who is almost completely segregated within her biological function, or the woman in the larger cities, who is partially segregated. When we consider women who are professionals and who belong to the middle and upper ranges of the social strata, we find similarities.

More conscious motherhood, which reflects itself in planned childbearing, brings with it the yet to be resolved conflict between home and career. Here also women have to gain acceptance by men in careers hitherto considered unfit or unsuited for women. Social and physical mobility, by taking professional, unmarried women away from their home backgrounds, has diminished their emotional security and created loneliness in exchange for economic independence. The Turkish woman here is at a disadvantage relative to her Western sister because of the social taboos still alive in Turkish society. These taboos, or residues from the Islamic culture, prevent the Turkish emancipated woman from playing as active a social and political role as her Western counterpart does. At the same time it is thought that she is less religious in thought and behavior.

It has often been said that women are an underprivileged minority and have to suffer accordingly. But this is false. It is minorities who are haunted by the fear of being submerged or assimilated out of recognition. Women are almost everywhere a *majority* fighting *for* assimilation, that is, for the anonymity afforded by civilized society to all its members equally. In this respect the Turkish professional woman who is at the vanguard of Turkish female society does not enjoy quite the same rights and is not accepted quite as readily by her male colleagues as her Western counterparts. As long as the concept of the family as it is understood today prevails or endures, these women, in the West and the East alike, will experience the deep emotional and intellectual conflict between their roles as mothers and as full-fledged members of society. Also, no amount of social engineering such as the provision of day and/or night nurseries, boarding schools, or suchlike home substitutes can help a conflict which is built-in biologically and has been reinforced by perennial custom.

Notes

1. Groups excluded from this study are upper-class women who make up "society" and politically militant students on the Left and the Right. It can be said that the functions and motivations of these very small groups are identical to those of their Western sisters and that their attitudes toward men and men's attitudes toward them come very near what is witnessed in the West today. Such women and girls feel free to make what decisions they please, and they do. An exception is found among industrial workers who economically feel and are treated as equals, and who take their stand in picket lines during a strike, but whose social life is still ruled by the mores of their recent past, which is village or small-town life. At the other end of the spectrum there are the women of the nomad tribes of the east and the southeast which represent a declining culture and are in the relative minority. These are also excluded.

2. The usual socioeconomic indicators—birth rates, schooling, income, exposure to media, and so on—favor the western part of the country as against the eastern part. Cultural and ethnic groups are made up of admixtures of population spills that occurred with the ebb and flow of the boundaries of the empire through the centuries. These groups have different customs, dress, and eating habits but the same Islamic and imperial culture.

3. In 1974, for the first time, the share of industry was larger, but this may have been accidental since indicators for 1975 suggest a reversal.

4. On the other hand, the republican ethos compensated for this by making divorce extremely easy when both parties agreed.

5. This may not hold for the younger generation owing to the very recent but intensive polarization between Left and Right among student and militant trade unionists.

6. Turkish law still requires written permission from a husband before a married woman is employed or is given a passport for foreign travel. Both requirements have ceased to be applied in practice for a number of years.

Bibliography

Abadan-Onat, Nerim. "Turkey." In *Women in the Modern World,* ed. Raphael Patai. Glencoe, Ill., 1967.

Benedict, Peter. *Ula: An Anatolian Town.* Leiden, 1974.

Çinar, Seniye. Unpublished. Istanbul, 1975.

Mansur (Coşar), Fatma. *Bodrum: A Town in the Aegean.* Leiden, 1972.

6 Women's Emancipation in Tunisia

Mark A. Tessler with Janet Rogers and Daniel Schneider

Background: Social Change in Tunisia

During its first decade of independence, Tunisia had a particularly coherent and explicit program of planned social transformation.[1] In 1956, following independence, a Personal Status Code replacing Quranic law in the areas of marriage, divorce, and children's rights was enacted. In 1958 a new educational program was instituted. It offered a bilingual and bicultural curriculum and laid the basis for gradual Arabization. In 1960 the country's president, Habib Bourguiba, denounced the traditional observance of Ramadan, arguing that the customary fasting decreased productivity and increased national economic woes. This desire to sweep away cultural barriers to progress, which Bourguiba once referred to as "outmoded beliefs," was reflected in countless speeches by the president and other officials. In one address, Bourguiba stated that "a large majority of our people are still entangled in a mass of prejudices and so-called religious beliefs."[2] In another, he said, "Faith and spiritual values are only effective to the extent they are based on reason."[3]

The object of the government was not to erode all aspects of traditional life. As the president stated in a 1965 speech, the country's "modern civilization" would be faithful, dynamic, and open: "faithful because it respects permanent moral and spiritual values, dynamic because it is capable of evolving on an intellectual and scientific plane, and open to a constructive dialogue between civilizations and cultures."[4] On another occasion he asserted that development would be accomplished "in accordance with the teachings of the Holy Book."[5] A determination to incorporate traditional elements into the social order under construction was noticeable in several domains. For example, Arabic was to be made the principal language of public life. Plans were laid for the gradual Arabization of many government ministries. Arabic textbooks were prepared and institutes were established to train teachers to instruct in Arabic. Tunisia also asserted its Muslim identity. Islam became the official religion, and Islamic symbols were incorporated into the national ideology. Nevertheless, the dominant emphasis was on change, not on continuity with the past, and this was especially so with respect to the status of women, the rights of youth, and other attributes of personal status.

The 1956 Personal Status Code was a particularly sweeping attack on the traditional status of Tunisian women, replacing segments of Quranic law with new statutes and thereby repudiating the religious[6] and legal foundation on which the status of women in part rested.[7] The code specifically forbade polygamy, making Tunisia the first, and so far the only, Arab country to prohibit the practice explicitly. More generally, the code made marriage and divorce civil matters. Unilateral repudiation by the husband was outlawed and religious prohibitions against women's marrying outside the faith were repealed. The Personal Status Code also modified relations between parents and children. The establishment of a minimum age for marriage, fifteen for girls and eighteen for boys, discouraged the practice whereby families arranged the marriage of a very young child. It also gave children, once they attain the legal age for marriage, a voice in the selection of their spouses largely denied them in traditional society.

Like Bourguiba's campaign against the traditional observance of Ramadan and other reformist programs, the Personal Status Code met with strong opposition from conservatives and those with a vested interest in the traditional system. In 1956, for example, a group of justices from the religious courts sponsored a petition against the code. And even judges on the government's civil courts were sometimes unwilling to apply it in the intended fashion. Nevertheless, the government was firm in its resolve to see the code enforced. *Sharia* judges were transferred, co-opted, or otherwise pressured into accepting the new laws. And, on at least one occasion, Bourguiba personally intervened in the proceedings of a civil court when he felt a woman had been judged unfairly. Discussing the matter later before an assembly of jurists, the president stated emphatically: "In this country we intend to behave like civilized men. As a citizen, a wife, and a mother, a woman has rights which no one is going to take away from her. Our judges are here to see that she is treated fairly."[8]

Official attempts to promote social change were also reflected in many other policies and programs. Overall, the most important instrument of planned social transformation was the Neo-Destour Party, Tunisia's single mass party which became the Destourian Socialist Party (PSD) in 1964. The party undertook an extensive resocialization effort, and its more than 1,200 territorial and professional cells met regularly to discuss national problems and acquaint the population with the need for change. As a leading student of Tunisia observed a few years ago, Tunisia, more than any other Arab state, developed a durable political organization that articulated and implemented its ideology.[9] Programs and institutions specifically designed to meet the needs of women were also established. For example, the National Union of Tunisian Women (UNFT) was created to promote a new understanding of the problems of women and to stimulate women's participation in national life. The UNFT held numerous meetings on the national and the local level in order to discuss problems of health, child care, birth control, professional opportunities for women, and other similar concerns.

Other programs designed to change the traditional status of women include official efforts to promote political participation among women and programs aimed at giving women professional training. The PSD included women on its electoral slates at various levels and strongly encouraged women to vote. In 1959, for instance, UNFT President Radhia Haddad was elected to the National Assembly. In the 1966 municipal elections, forty-four women were elected as councillors in eleven different urban centers. With regard to professional advancement, a series of programs run through the Ministry of Social Affairs was set up to help women adapt to modern life. One project involved the creation of regional training centers to teach reading and writing to illiterate women and to offer training in home economics. Another project established both centers of professional training where girls were prepared for work in hotels, offices, and medical establishments and centers of preprofessional training where girls with insufficient schooling were given remedial instruction.

As important as official pressures for change during this period was the intensifying impact of unplanned agents of social transformation. One of the most important of these was urbanization. The proportion of the population living in cities rose dramatically after independence. Estimates placed it as low as 15 percent in 1956 and as high as 45 percent fifteen years later. People moving to the cities were exposed to new ideas and required to develop new lifestyles, both of which called traditional values into question. Residence patterns changed and nuclear family arrangements became more common. New professional opportunities also developed, bringing with them new conceptions of time, money, social relations, and much more. All this, of course, affected women greatly. Many women found employment and acquired a measure of financial independence previously unknown. In the teaching profession, to cite one illustration, the proportion of women primary school teachers jumped from 8 percent to 13 percent between 1963 and 1968, with steady increments each year.[10]

The radio has been another important agent of unplanned social change, increasing exposure to nonindigenous ideas and producing psychological mobility even where there was no physical movement. Some studies suggest that in urban areas as much as three-fourths of the population listens to the radio every day. In the rural areas, though fewer people own radios and listen to them regularly, the overall impact may be even more intense. In one small village, for example, a team of sociologists from the University of Tunis reported that because of the radio people are no longer oriented exclusively toward local affairs. "Their personal center of gravity is shifted to Tunis, the bright center of national life."[11] Moreover, control of the radios existing in the village and the ability to interpret the radio's message were highly valued and were threatening the traditional system of social status.[12] Other agents of change have also been transforming life in the rural areas. Families were divided and many women were left alone for considerable periods of time as their husbands went off to the city in search of temporary employment. And in one study, sociologists found that traditional rhythms were broken by so simple a thing as the availability of canned goods and a few manufactured products. Women acquired more leisure time and men were required to earn money to purchase the goods that previously had been made at home.[13]

Perhaps the greatest stimulus for change was education. In the decade following independence, literacy climbed from 15 percent to over 30 percent, the proportion of children attending primary school grew from 25 percent to 70–80 percent, and the proportion of students completing high school increased from 3 percent to almost 30 percent. Further, the proportion of women in the school population grew steadily during this period. At the primary level for instance, women were 31 percent of the school population in 1958. A decade later they were 39 percent. Like other agents of unplanned social change, the expansion of education introduced new patterns of thought and behavior and added to the pressure for women's emancipation.

By the mid-1960s, official and unplanned pressures for social transformation had set in motion a psychological and cultural revolution. Studies show that exposure to these agents of change was associated with increased willingness to reexamine traditional values and to adopt nonindigenous social codes, including ones pertaining to women.[14] Especially among the growing professional and white collar middle class, but to some extent among the expanding proletariat too, support for the reform of traditional society and the construction of a social order blending new and old elements was rapidly increasing. So far as women are concerned, this meant that educational and professional opportunities were expanding, that substantial numbers of well-dressed, unveiled Tunisian women could be seen on the streets of major cities, that men and women could regularly be seen working together in business establishments and sitting together in coffee houses, and that public acceptance of all these phenomena was growing.

Because of these changes, Tunisia acquired a reputation as the Arab state in which women were making the most progress. As previously noted, it is still the only Arab state to have formally outlawed polygamy, and Bourguiba's many speeches about women's rights received considerable international publicity. Tunisia's reputation should not be permitted to give the impression that no significant obstacles or opposition to the emancipation of women remained. Moreover, it is not clear that women in Tunisia were significantly more advanced than women in some other progressive Arab countries. Nevertheless, the favorable position that women in Tunisia came to enjoy during the 1960s is quite apparent. To cite but one illustration, that of education, Tunisia had a higher proportion of women enrolled in primary school than any other Arab country except Lebanon. Further, Tunisia had a higher proportion of students enrolled generally than any other country except Lebanon. This indicates that high enrollment ratios for women were not within the context of an elitest system. Rather, the gains of women in Tunisia were particularly broadly based.

In the last seven or eight years, Tunisia's commitment to planned change has diminished considerably. Initially this was due to disorientation resulting from a number of political crises, most notably Bourguiba's recurring illnesses during the late 1960s, the ensuing struggle for power among his subordinates, the Ben Salah affair, and the struggle for control of the PSD as the president regained his health. For several years prior to 1969, Bourguiba had been sick and was frequently out of the country for reasons of health; and, as the president's political future was uncertain, there developed a struggle for power among would-be successors. The man who emerged as the dominant political figure during this period was Ahmed Ben Salah, the dynamic minister of plan and finance and architect of the socialist orientation that had characterized Tunisia since 1964. Ben Salah aggressively consolidated his personal position and used his power to intensify implementation of a sweeping cooperative program enacted in 1964. Others, however, resented Ben Salah's personal ambition and/or opposed his socialist programs. Thus in 1969, in the wake of several peasant demonstrations in opposition to the cooperatives and growing economic difficulties (attributed by some to Ben Salah's programs), the liberal faction of the PSD forced a showdown. It had been commonly assumed that Bourguiba supported the cooperative program, but the president sided with the liberals and repudiated his minister of plan and finance. Ben Salah was first removed from office, then ousted from the party, and finally tried and convicted of treason.[15]

Between 1969 and 1972, the PSD became more independent and, dominated by its liberal wing, talked increasingly about party democracy. But as the president's health steadily improved, a second confrontation took shape, this time between Bourguiba and the liberals. The issue was control of the PSD and it was resolved in favor of Bourguiba at the 1974 National Party Congress held in Monastir, the president's birthplace. Liberals who had dominated the 1971 Party Congress insisted that the 1974 summit had been convened illegally. But the delegates supported the president's position and later made Bourguiba president-for-life. With Bourguiba's return to a position of dominance in national affairs, more than five years of political competition came to an end. Politicians not supporting Bourquiba, including those instrumental in ousting Ben Salah, were gradually removed from positions of influence.

The regime that came to power following this period of confusion had conservative domestic economic policies and far less concern for planned social change. Bourguiba and Prime Minister Hedi Nouira, former director of the National Bank, have been comparatively uninterested in restructuring traditional society. Apparently, they do not believe such reforms are a necessary ingredient for social and economic progress. Thus, the reemergence of Habib Bourguiba has not meant a return to the kinds of cultural reforms that characterized Tunisia during the first decade of independence.

One result of these developments was a change in Tunisian

political processes and political culture. Popular political participation has diminished considerably. Party cells meet less often than before and party machinery has begun to decay. There has also been a decline in political trust[16] and the emergence of an "ideological counterculture."[17] As one Tunisian social scientist put the matter, "The Tunisian elite is in the process of losing its dynamizing and liberating powers . . . the political system has lost its equilibrium."[18] Another result of these developments has been a reduction in programs of resocialization and social engineering. The revolutionary elan that characterized the country earlier dissipated rapidly and indeed, as a respected Tunisian sociologist observed in 1972, the country began experiencing a "reactivation of tradition."[19] In 1969 Bourguiba gave a talk that signaled the change in his outlook. He discussed the need to put modernization "in perspective"; and referring to women's emancipation, formerly one of his most cherished goals, he warned that too much reform will lead to "a loosening of our morals." Freedom, he said, "must be coupled with religious and moral education in order to produce the respect for virtue that was formerly assured by long robes and heavy veils."[20] The ruling elite has also abandoned many of its earlier programs of religious reform and generally become more tolerant of traditional Islamic values and institutions.[21] Thus, in sum, the net effect of changes in political organization, ideology, and leadership is that Tunisia has lost much of the revolutionary momentum that had been generated by the mid-1960s.

If planned programs of resocialization and social transformation have diminished, the situation with respect to unplanned agents of modernization is less clear. The government today places less emphasis on education than in the past. Its high cost, the inability to provide appropriate jobs for all graduates, and the decline in standards accompanying mass enrollment are the major reasons for this. Thus, school enrollments leveled off after 1970 and have declined slightly since 1972, and the proportion of women attending primary school has not risen since 1970. Nevertheless, the country still maintains an impressive educational system and there is no question of going back to the preindependence situation. Indeed, with respect to both the proportion of total students enrolled and the proportion of women attending school, ratios in Tunisia remain among the highest in the Arab world. Therefore, though its relative impact has declined slightly, education remains a major force for social change in contemporary Tunisia.

Other agents of unplanned change have also remained important, and the impact of some has even intensified. Urbanization continues at a rapid pace, for example, and according to some criteria the country is today over 50 percent urban. Media participation is also growing, with the radio's dominant position increasingly shared by television. Finally, there has been an intensification of pressures for change in other areas. The economy has performed well in recent years, owing to several good harvests and increasing revenue from petroleum and tourism. Also, growing numbers of Tunisians are employed in Europe. Thus, on balance, unplanned pressures for social structural and economic transformation have remained intense since the late 1960s, despite the reduction in official programs of development. The question with which this situation confronts students of women in Tunisia is whether economic development and unplanned social change have continued to promote women's emancipation in the absence of a strong official ideological commitment and in view of the significant reduction in government programs of cultural reform and resocialization.

Changing Attitudes about Women

How have popular attitudes about women changed in Tunisia in recent years? How has the struggle for women's emancipation fared during a period characterized by high levels of unplanned social transformation and low levels of planned cultural change? These questions are important not only to those interested in women's emancipation in Tunisia but also to those seeking to evaluate the practical significance of the presence or absence of an official commitment to women's emancipation and other reforms in the Middle East generally. To shed light on this issue, the remainder of this essay presents and compares the results of surveys conducted in Tunisia in 1967 and 1973. (Details about the collection and analysis of the survey data are presented in the appendix.) Briefly, men and women in Tunis and men in several smaller towns were asked a series of questions about women's emancipation in 1967 and the survey was replicated in 1973. Respondents were drawn from a wide range of social categories and are generally representative of the middle and working classes.

In presenting the results of the surveys, conclusions may be reported about the extent and nature of changing attitudes toward women and also about resultant shifts in the distribution of support and opposition to women's emancipation. With respect to the first consideration, three observations are relevant. First, total support for women's emancipation declined markedly between 1967 and 1973. The proportion of persons believing education to be equally important for girls and boys decreased from 65 percent to

51 percent, for example. Similarly, the proportions considering it acceptable for a woman to exercise authority over a man at work and believing Muslim women should have the right to marry non-Muslim men declined from 46 percent to 32 percent and from 39 percent to 27 percent respectively.[22] Finally, diminished support for women's emancipation was found among both female and male respondents and among residents of Tunis and smaller towns. The latter finding demonstrates that the decline in support for women's liberation is not limited to a few categories of the population but rather is very broadly based.

A second observation is that support for women's emancipation did not decline to the same extent among all categories of the population. Support generally declined most among men in smaller towns and least among women in Tunis. There are a few exceptions to this generalization, but overall the pattern obtains whether comparisons are based on totals or on comparably educated subsets of respondents who differ on residence and sex. Thus, both sex and residence are significant specification variables, male gender and town residence being associated with increasing opposition to women's rights. Education is also associated with variations in attitude change between 1967 and 1973, though the nature of this association is not the same among men in Tunis, women in Tunis, and men in smaller towns. Among men in Tunis, the biggest decline in support for women's emancipation was among poorly educated respondents. Among women in Tunis, the biggest decline was among well-educated respondents. Among men in smaller towns, differences associated with education were negligible for most of the items considered. Thus, education is a significant specification variable among residents of Tunis, negatively associated with a decline in support for women's emancipation among men and positively associated with it among women.

A third survey finding is that support for women's emancipation did not decline to the same extent on the three substantive issues examined. The total decline was about the same for all three, but subsets of respondents did not change to the same degree in each instance. Among both men and women in Tunis, support declined most in the area of professional advancement for women and it declined only a bit less in the area of education for women. Among men in smaller towns, by contrast, acceptance of women marrying outside the faith declined most. Thus, though developments between 1967 and 1973 have increased conservative tendencies both in the capital and in smaller towns, so far as attitudes toward women are concerned the same issues are not most salient in each locale.

As a result of these attitudinal shifts, the nature and distribution of popular support for women's emancipation is not the same in 1973 as it was in 1967. First, though women were more in favor of it than men in 1967, the difference between the sexes is much greater in 1973 because opposition to women's liberation increased so much more among men. This conclusion obtains whether aggregate comparisons between the sexes are made or whether comparably educated men and women from Tunis are contrasted. Thus, though support for women's emancipation has declined among women in absolute terms, their levels of support relative to men have increased.

Second, while in 1967 there was generally more support for women's emancipation among men in smaller towns than among men in Tunis, the tendency was in the opposite direction in 1973 because opposition increased so much more outside the capital. Since respondents from Tunis and smaller towns are not comparable with respect to education, it is important to note that the observed tendencies hold when comparisons are based on comparably educated subsets of respondents as well as on all men residing in different places. In sum, while conservatism has increased overall in both city and town, the difference between the two is qualitatively different in 1967 and 1973 and, in the latter year, residents of smaller towns stand out as particularly opposed to changes in the status of women.

Third, there has been a change in the degree of support for women's emancipation in certain educational categories, modifying the relationship between education and support for women's liberation. This is particularly evident in the cities. In 1967 education was fairly strongly associated with support for women's liberation and high school and university educated respondents were almost always more in favor than other respondents. Among women, differences between respondents with an intermediate and a primary school education were also notable. In 1973 the relationship between education and support for women's emancipation remained among men in Tunis, and, in fact, became somewhat more pronounced since support declined more among poorly educated respondents than others between 1967 and 1973. Among women, on the other hand, attitudinal differences associated with education greatly diminished owing to the fact that support for change declined considerably among better educated women but not among others. Thus, the diversity of opinion among men was greater in 1973 than in 1967, whereas attitudinal differences among women were smaller in the latter year.

Implications and Conclusions

One should not fail to distinguish between findings derived from the surveys and more general conclusions based on those findings. If our methodology is sound, the former are accurate. But the latter remain propositions, open to discussion and in need of additional, independent empirical confirmation. Nevertheless, it is important to consider the broader implications of our data; and, based on the observed nature of attitude change between 1967 and 1973, some conclusions about three interrelated issues may be drawn. These issues are the comparative impact of planned and unplanned agents of change on attitudes toward women, the degree of social consensus and discord that is evolving with regard to women's emancipation, and the likely future of the struggle for women's rights in Tunisia.

Implications about the impact of planned and unplanned change are fairly clear. Since support for women's emancipation declined significantly between 1967 and 1973, it is reasonable to conclude that, in general, official efforts to promote cultural change are necessary if popular support for changes in the status of women is to be generated. Overall, in the period under consideration forces of unplanned change by themselves were not sufficient to increase support for women's liberation and were in fact associated with a decline in support.

The preceding applies with special force to people from smaller towns and to poorly educated men from Tunis. Two possible explanations for this suggest themselves. First, these people live in comparatively conservative milieus, where the impact of unplanned change is less intense than elsewhere and where traditional opposition to women's emancipation is greatest. Thus, in the absence of official programs of reform and resocialization, they are simply not exposed to sufficient stimuli to produce more favorable attitudes toward women. Second, since their limited educational and professional experiences orient them toward the developing sectors of society but do not enable them to play more than marginal roles in those sectors, their social position is precarious and their levels of frustration are high; and they thus reject women's emancipation both because it is a symbol of the forces responsible for their alienation and because it would increase the number of persons competing for jobs and status.[23] It follows from the latter explanation that opposition to changes in the status of women would remain high or even increase among these categories of the population if unplanned change were accompanied by planned programs of social transformation. The validity of these competing explanations cannot be tested without further study, but it is probable that the latter is most relevant in Tunis, where the relative social position of the poorly educated is less satisfactory and where opposition to women's emancipation increased most in the areas of educational and professional advancement, and that the former is most relevant in smaller towns, where the total social environment is more conservative and where opposition to women's marrying outside the faith increased the most.

On the issue of social consensus and discord, the data suggest that there is more of the latter concerning questions of women's emancipation. Between 1967 and 1973 total variance on attitudes toward women increased. More specifically, differences between men and women, between residents of Tunis and smaller towns, and, among men in Tunis, between well-educated and poorly educated persons increased during this period. Thus, overall, there is less agreement on issues pertaining to women than in the past and, other things being equal, the potential for discord is greater.[24] Perhaps the most important of these normative cleavages is the one between men and women. Agreement among women is greater than in the past. Feminist attitudes have moderated somewhat among well-educated women, and, more important, support for women's emancipation has remained constant or even increased among poorly educated women. Thus, women both disagree with men more than in the past and are more united in support of their demands for equal opportunity, and this could mean increased social tension between the sexes. The growing normative cleavage between city and town could also be significant. Cultural differences between comparable social categories in Tunis and smaller towns were limited in 1967, but this situation has changed and, if it continues, there could be unfortunate consequences for nation-building and efforts to construct an integrated national cultural system. At the very least, it appears that for the foreseeable future the disparities between opportunities for women in Tunis and elsewhere will grow and that any progress made in this area will be quite uneven.

In spite of these considerations, there are also factors militating against increased social tension surrounding questions of women's emancipation. For one thing, it appears that at least some women are less concerned about change than in the past, and thus they may be less disturbed by the demise of official programs of change or increased conservatism among men. Second and more important, the attitudes of men and women are not as different in comparable educational categories as they are in the aggregate. Among men, support for women's emancipation declined least among the well-educated, while among women it declined most among the well-educated. Thus, the attitudinal differences between well-educated men and women are only slightly greater than in the past. Further, in 1967 poorly educated men were generally more supportive of women's emancipation than were poorly educated women. Thus, among these respondents attitudinal change during the period under consideration did not always increase the normative differences between men and women. In conclusion, then, while attitudinal differences about the status of women have increased overall, there are cross-cutting cleavages that may reduce at least some of the social tension that could result from this situation.

The future for women's liberation in Tunisia is not encouraging. Popular support for women's emancipation has declined markedly in recent years and this decline has occurred in almost all social categories examined. Men in particular are more opposed to women's emancipation, and highly educated women, those who at popular levels must lead the fight for change, are also less in favor than in the past. Looking at absolute rather than relative levels of support also produces disheartening conclusions for those seeking changes in the status of women. On two of the three issues examined, less than one-third of the 1973 respondents, all of whom are literate and regularly employed, have views supporting women's emancipation. And in an area as basic as education, only slightly over half favor equal opportunity for women. Even among highly educated Tunisians, levels of support are not much higher. Only one-third of the men with a high school or university education believe women should be permitted to have authority over men in the professional world. Only a little over half believe schooling is as important for women as it is for men.

The forces producing this situation continue to operate in Tunisia and this indicates that, at least for the immediate future, popular support for women's emancipation is likely to remain low or perhaps decline even further. First, in some sectors of society programs of planned change appear to be necessary to generate popular acceptance of women's liberation. Yet there is no evidence that the kinds of reform and resocialization programs that characterized Tunisia during its first decade of independence are about to be reinstituted: the government seems to be encouraging instead a resurgence of traditional values. Second, the low social status and high levels of frustration and insecurity among men marginally integrated into the modern sectors of society appear to stimulate opposition to women's emancipation; and in the wake of the government's renunciation of socialist principles and growing economic disparities within the modern sectors, these stimuli are likely to intensify rather than diminish in the years ahead. Continued economic growth and a more egalitarian distribution of social and economic benefits could do much to reduce opposition to women's liberation, especially in the areas of educational and professional advancement. But the likelihood that this will occur is not great. Thus, if present economic and cultural policies continue, little additional support for women's emancipation can be expected.

Tunisia remains one of the Arab countries where women have made the greatest advances. But the situation of women in Tunisia has begun to deteriorate in recent years and the country is resting on its reputation so far as official policies toward women are concerned. The situation of women will have to deteriorate much more before it approaches that of women in conservative Arab countries, and this is not likely to happen for quite some time, despite the strides being made in some of these states. Nevertheless, Tunisia is no longer the radical and daring innovator it once was and, if present trends continue, in a few years it may not even be among the group of progressive Arab states where women have relatively, if not absolutely, high levels of freedom and opportunity for personal development.

Appendix

In 1967 a stratified quota sample of literate and regularly employed adults was drawn in Tunis and three smaller towns. Variables of sample stratification were education, income, and place of residence; quotas were established to assure that all empirically existing combinations of these variables were included in the sample. A total of 283 persons were interviewed. In 1973 a similar sample was selected, using education and place of residence as variables of sample stratification and substituting occupation for income to control for inflation between 1967 and 1973. A total of 349 persons were interviewed, using the same survey instrument employed in 1967. Respondents in each year were drawn from a wide range of social categories and collectively reflect much of the diversity of the Tunisian middle and working classes.

Strictly speaking, the samples are analytic rather than representative. Sampling quotas were established with a view toward maximizing variance and independence on relevant demographic variables and toward assuring that as many relevant subsets of the population as possible would be surveyed. Although the samples were not randomly selected, their diversity is probably sufficient to make them indicative of trends generally operative. Nevertheless, it should always be acknowledged, even when random sampling procedures are employed, that evidence presented by a single investigator must be considered tentative until confirmed by additional research.

To assess change over time, individuals from the 1967 survey were matched to those from the 1973 survey. To constitute a match, respondents from the two samples had to be of the same sex and highly similar with respect to age, educational level, income category, and place of residence. In cases where a respondent from one year could be matched with equal accuracy to two or more respondents from the other year, selections were made on a random basis. A total of 211 matched pairs were formed. They include respondents from almost all sample categories, and comparisons between subsets and the larger samples for each year show that the former are highly representative of the latter.

The dependent variables in this analysis are three survey items dealing with the status of women. Information on procedures used to design and administer the 1967 survey instrument has been presented elsewhere and testifies to item validity and reliability and the absence of interview bias and other forms of response set.[25] These procedures were generally used again in 1973, the only important difference being that a questionnaire rather than an interview methodology was favored. The interview schedule contained a large number of items dealing with women's emancipation; in selecting items to be analyzed for the present study the number was limited for the sake of parsimony and an attempt was made to maximize clarity and to represent all major tendencies discernible in the data. The three items selected as dependent variables, and the response to each indicating support for women's emancipation, are:

> Do you think it is more important for a boy to go to school than it is for a girl? (No)
>
> Is it acceptable for a woman to direct a professional enterprise employing many men? (Yes)
>
> Muslim women should have the same rights as Muslim men to marry foreigners. (Agree)

Variations over time in national political and ideological currents constitute the independent variable in this study. But it is unlikely that these currents have the same effect on attitudes among all categories of the Tunisian population. For this reason, data were analyzed according to a multivariate factorial research design. Education, sex, and place of residence were the parameters of this design and served as specification variables in our analysis of the relationship between political currents and changing attitudes toward women. These variables were selected, first, because many studies have shown them to be strongly related to cultural attitudes, including those pertaining to women; second, because they correlate with other potentially relevant specification variables—such as income, media consumption, professional status, and foreign travel—and thus may suggest how additional personal attributes affect the relationship between cultural preferences and social and political forces; and third, because they divide respondents into sufficiently diverse and important social categories to permit meaningful observations about the distribution of attitudes and attitude change throughout the sectors of society encompassed by the samples.

In analyzing the data, respondents were first grouped into three categories based on residence and sex: men from Tunis, women from Tunis, and men from smaller towns. Owing to problems of access, only a few women from smaller towns were surveyed. Then, each category was subdivided on the basis of education. Finally, for each of the categories formed by this concatenation of specification variables, the percentage of persons favoring women's emancipation in 1967, the percentage favoring it in 1973, and the difference between the two percentages were determined for the three items. Two points about the utility of this design should be noted. First, it enabled us to assess the specification effects of any single variable with the others held constant. For example, to determine whether place of residence affects the way that attitudes changed between 1967 and 1973, the nature of attitude change among residents of Tunis and smaller towns who were comparable with respect to education and sex was contrasted. Second, the combined as well as independent effects of specification variables could be considered. To assess the joint impact of education and place of residence, for example, the relationship between education and attitude change in each milieu was determined and the observed relationships were then compared.

Notes

1. See also Charles A. Micaud, *Tunisia: Politics of Modernization* (New York, 1964), and "Leadership and Development: The Case of

Tunisia," *Comparative Politics,* 1 (July 1969) :468–484. See also Mark A. Tessler, William M. O'Barr, and David H. Spain, *Tradition and Identity in Changing Africa* (New York, 1973), pp. 193–303, on which part of this account is based. For additional discussion of Tunisian political life during the first decade of independence, see Clement H. Moore, *Tunisia Since Independence* (Berkeley, 1965); Douglas Ashford, *National Development and Local Reform: Political Participation in Morocco, Tunisia and Pakistan* (Princeton, 1967); and Lars Rudebeck, *Party and People: A Survey of Political Change in Tunisia* (New York, 1969).

2. Habib Bourguiba, "L'enseignement: fonction sociale," Speech, 1965.

3. Habib Bourguiba, "Dimensions du sousdeveloppement," Speech, 1963.

4. Bourguiba, "L'enseignement," 1965.

5. Habib Bourguiba, "Discours prononcé à l'occasion du mouled," Speech, 1966.

6. As in other Islamic countries, defenders of the religion assert that Islam is not responsible for the traditionally inferior position of women, pointing out that the Quran improved the status of women at the time of its revelation. For example, a man could take more than one wife only if he could treat them all equally—a prohibition some Islamicists contend actually prohibits polygamy. Also, the Prophet reportedly urged that women be educated. In Tunisia, these arguments are to be found in Salaheddine Kechrid, *Le vrai visage de l'Islam* (Tunis, 1971). For a more general discussion, see also Germaine Tillion, *Le harem et les cousins* (Paris, 1966). Tillion believes that the traditionally inferior status of women must be seen as a Mediterranean phenomenon.

7. For a discussion of the Personal Status Code, see Jean Magnin, "Autour du code de statue personnel tunisien," in *Normes et valeurs dans l'Islam contemporain,* ed. Jacques Berque and Jean-Paul Charnay (Paris, 1966).

8. Habib Bourguiba, "Edifier une société saine et equilibrée," Speech, 1966.

9. Clement H. Moore, "On Theory and Practice among Arabs," *World Politics,* 24 (1971) :106.

10. *Annuaire statistique de la Tunisie* (Tunis, 1969), p. 100.

11. Jean Duvignaud, *Change at Shebika* (New York, 1970), p. 233.

12. Ibid., pp. 232–233.

13. André Louis, "Greniers fortifiés et maisons troglodytes: Ksar Djouama," *Institut des belles lettres arabes* 28 (1965) :373–400.

14. For a summary see Mark A. Tessler, "Cultural Modernity: Evidence from Tunisia," *Social Science Quarterly,* 52 (1971) :290–308. For a fuller discussion, including a summary of findings from other research conducted in Tunisia and elsewhere, see Tessler, O'Barr, and Spain, *Tradition and Identity.*

15. For more detailed accounts of these events, see Stuart Schaar, "A New Look at Tunisia," *Mid East* (February 1970): 43–46; and John Simmons, "Agricultural Cooperatives and Tunisian Development," *Middle East Journal,* 25 (1971) :45–57.

16. See Mark A. Tessler, Janet M. Rogers, and Daniel R. Schneider, "A Longitudinal Analysis of Political Attitude Change in Tunisia between 1967 and 1973." Paper presented to African Studies Association, Milwaukee, 1975.

17. See John Entelis, "Ideological Change and an Emerging Counter-Culture in Tunisian Politics," *Journal of Modern African Studies,* 12 (1974) : 543–568.

18. Elbaki Hermassi, *Leadership and National Development in North Africa* (Berkeley, 1972), p. 215.

19. Abdelkader Zghal, "The Reactivation of Tradition in a Post-Traditional Society," in *Post Traditional Society,* ed. S. N. Eisenstadt (New York, 1972), pp. 225–237, presents an excellent discussion contrasting social and cultural policies of the Tunisian elite in the years immediately following independence and in the last few years. For a more recent discussion of these changes, see Mark A. Tessler, "Single-Party Rule in Tunisia," *Common Ground,* 2 (1976) :55–64.

20. Habib Bourguiba, "Problèmes de la jeunesse dans leur vraie perspective," Speech, 1969.

21. See Sami Hanna, "Changing Trends in Tunisian Socialism," *Muslim World,* 62 (July 1972) :230–240; and John P. Entelis, "Reformist Ideology in the Arab World: The Cases of Tunisia and Lebanon," *Review of Politics,* 37 (October 1975) :513–546.

22. For more information about the traditional status of women in North Africa, focusing on Tunisia, see Tessler, O'Barr, and Spain, *Tradition and Identity,* pp. 242–247; and, *La femme tunisienne* (Tunis, 1960, gov't. publication). For more complete accounts, based on Algeria, see David Gordon, *Women of Algeria* (Cambridge, Mass., 1968) ; and Fadela M'Rabet, *La femme algérienne* (Paris, 1965).

23. This thesis is considered at greater length and additional data are presented in Mark A. Tessler and Mary E. Keppel, "Political Generations," in *Change in Tunisia: Essays in the Social Sciences,* ed. Russell Stone and John Simmons (Albany, N.Y., 1976).

24. It should not be assumed that variance on attitudes toward other cultural issues also increased during this period. With respect to at least one other issue, childrearing, the opposite was the case. See Mark A. Tessler, Janet M. Rogers, and Daniel R. Schneider, "Tunisian Attitudes toward Women and Childrearing," in *Family Life, Women's Status and Fertility: Middle East and North African Perspectives,* ed. James Allman (New York, 1978).

25. See Mark A. Tessler, "Problems of Measurement in Comparative Research: Perspectives from an African Survey," *Social Science Information,* 12 (1973) :29–43, and "Response Set and Interview Bias," in *Survey Research in Africa: Its Applications and Limits,* ed. William M. O'Barr, David H. Spain, and Mark A. Tessler (Evanston, Ill., 1973).

7 Women in Algeria

Juliette Minces

Translated from the French by Nikki Keddie

In *A Dying Colonialism* Frantz Fanon affirmed that through violence and armed struggle, the condition of women in Algeria, like that of young people, was undergoing a revolutionary mutation. He was referring to the struggle that the Algerian people were then conducting against French colonization, a struggle that lasted from 1954 to 1962. The very fact of taking up arms, of participating in a violent action, he argued, would lead women to realize their own alienation and, consequently, would lead them to emancipate themselves. As for men, finally convinced, probably, of the injustice of the condition in which they had until then kept women, they would support women's claims in greater and greater numbers. In other words, according to Fanon, armed struggle with no other purpose than national independence should by itself modify mentalities in an irreversible fashion and, in consequence, change the status of women.

Let us see what in fact happened.

Fanon's view did not take into account the motivation and the modalities of women's participation in the Algerian struggle. It also neglected the prevailing ideology of the Algerian national movement and instead granted too much to spontaneity and to redemptive violence. It may be affirmed, in general, that traditional mentalities, which are the most difficult to modify, are changed by armed struggle only to the extent that that struggle is supported by a modernizing and revolutionary ideology that, while exalting self-identification, is also capable of slicing off from tradition all its social and cultural conservatism in order to preserve only what can be liberating and adapted to the goals of a new society. The majority of Algerian militants, however, had no goal other than independence and were extremely vague when it came to envisaging the transformation of society, that is, to planning the society they wished to create.

This outlook was rooted in the nature of colonial Algeria as well as in the nature of the nationalist movement. The movement was organized as a front, bringing together diverse nationalist tendencies that were far from unified on the ideological level. In addition, colonial Algeria had a departmental organization which made of Algerian society one of the most politically, economically, and culturally dispossessed societies in the world. The Muslim population clung to rigid traditional values (which, nevertheless, they understood badly) out of rejection of colonization, and also to differentiate themselves from the "pieds-noirs," the European population. Administratively, Algeria was France, but it was a France populated by a majority of second-class citizens who had, on the morrow of World War II and the eve of the insurrection, less political weight than the 10 percent of the population who represented the European colonizers.

Denied identity and representation, the approximately 10,000,000 Algerians—who were called the "Muslims"—found themselves forbidden by law to study their language, Arabic, in the public schools. The teaching dispensed in these schools was addressed only to the students of European origin (history of France, geography of France, and so on). In addition, many Algerian children, especially in the countryside, did not attend school. In the 1920s indigenous schools declined both in quality and in quantity. As for French colonial schools, it was generally the middle classes who utilized them, as the rural population was too poor or too distant from urban centers to send their children there. When a family had to choose which children to send to school, boys had priority. Between 1959 and the year of independence (1962), however, the number of Muslim pupils rose from 600,000 to 1,000,000 in primary schools, and from 10,000 to 21,000 in secondary schools.[1] Families sometimes had recourse to Quranic schools, whose teachers confined themselves mostly to making pupils repeat mechanically the verses of the Quran. Aside from the schools, it was mostly the women who were charged with transmitting knowledge, as well as they could, and especially traditions, often reduced to magico-religious precepts in which superstition played a large role.

In the economic sphere there was a similar dispossession. The "Europeans" (the colonialists or colons) had monopolized 3,000,000 hectares of the best land and had cultivated certain crops that the Algerian population, although it constituted their labor force, did not consume (vineyards for making wine, for example). In town, Europeans held many positions, notably as public functionaries, that the Muslims could not bargain for. On the eve of the insurrection, the agricultural income of the 20,000 colons was 930,000,000 francs, while that of over 1,000,000 Algerian peasants and their families was scarcely 1,070,000 francs. The rural unemployed could not find work in the nonagricultural sectors: barely 30 percent of economically active Algerians were in these sectors. All the higher administrative posts and all positions in the tertiary sector were occupied by pieds-noirs, as were the overwhelming majority of subordinate posts.[2] As a result, unemployment was severe and pushed many Algerian family heads to emigrate to France in search of work.

All this weighed heavily in the formation and characteristics of the Algerian national movement, and consequently on women. Born in the proletarianized milieus of emigration, the national movement was to hesitate a long time between the demand for independence and the demand for a substantial amelioration of the colonial status. It was in the face of the failure of all the "reformist" attempts that, on November 1, 1954, a handful of little-known men—some of whom had lived clandestinely for years—who were solidly based in their home regions, launched the insurrection. The peasant population, profoundly affected by the colonial situation and penetrated by nationalist slogans that had circulated for a dozen years, quickly lent their support, and the National Liberation Front (FLN) was born. This insurrection was not, however, the expression of a homogeneous political organization, nor was it supported by a revolutionary theory. Not even the slogan of agrarian reform was put forth. It was an act of rejection toward the colonial system.

The FLN, which at first included only activist elements of a very modest status, a fact that stamped the initial underground forces with a populist tinge, came to include, from 1956 on, the cadres of all the diverse nationalist organizations that wanted to participate in a fight that now seemed possible. This admixture was to reinforce considerably the petit bourgeois and socially conservative character of the front. In 1957 the repression in urban centers—

notably during the "Battle of Algiers"—led large numbers of the militants to take refuge in the countryside, while the leadership managed to escape abroad. The blows inflicted by the French army became more and more severe from 1957–58 on. The core of the peasant cadre of the front, and hence of the movement, was annihilated in 1959. About 2,000,000 persons were "regrouped" in camps, out of a total Muslim population of 10,000,000, and hundreds of thousands more took refuge in Morocco and Tunisia. From 1957 until 1960 it was the peasantry who alone had carried the burden of the war. It was only when the countryside, exhausted by "pacification" and the regroupment of populations, stopped being active that the movement was again taken over by the cities.

Women during the Resistance

In the milieu of Algerian society and traditions, women, as such, hardly had a word of their own to say. In any case, of all traditions, those that concern women—and with them the family—are always the slowest to change. As a result, the participation of women in public life and the various political movements of the period was minute, and limited essentially to a small number of women whose more enlightened families had allowed them an education, often in France. There they could mix with French society and become more open to new ideas. As for the other women, the weight of tradition and their way of life did not allow them even to imagine that they could act politically as autonomous persons within an organization. That was for men.

When French repression became more severe and more effective and the men had to go underground or flee the country, they then turned over to women tasks that they themselves could no longer carry out. That is to say, in the majority of cases, women were *utilized,* entirely willingly moreover, as auxiliaries and adjuncts. It appears that there were relatively few women who entered the battle on their own initiative. The number of active women became notable in the cities only when it became too dangerous for the men to move.

As we have seen, from 1957 on the French army successfully launched search and destroy operations against villagers suspected of aiding the FLN. In fact, every man became suspect either of belonging to the secret organization or of aiding it with provisions or information. When one or several of the men of a family had been touched by repression or had had to flee, the women carried on in their place, serving especially as intermediaries, as informants, as relays, or as liaison agents. They also nursed wounded resistance fighters, taking enormous risks in both cities and villages. What was especially expected of them, however, was to bring pressure on the administration and the prison bureau to find out where their men were and to be able to help them as much as possible in the camps and prisons, as is so well depicted in the Algerian film, "The Wind of the Aurès" ("Le vent des Aurès") .

In town, the utilization of women became even more evident, especially when the FLN began to make bombing attempts. Protected by the veil and considered by the authorities to be too bound by tradition to participate in such activities, they were able to penetrate into places where men could no longer go. (In the beginning they were, in fact, rarely searched, unlike men.) For this reason they were used especially as bomb carriers. Their involvement, which was sincere and courageous, occurred here also, essentially, on the basis of replacement. That is, it was chiefly in the capacity of wife, sister, or daughter of this or that man that they became involved, especially among the lower classes. (In any case, female students did not exist in large numbers.) Women became truly active only when the FLN had a vital need for their participation. In the earlier stages, they were not even kept informed of what was being done; the clandestine meetings, the secret councils, only involved men, who made the decisions.

However, many of these female militants were arrested, imprisoned, and tortured. For propaganda reasons they were sometimes even made into "national heroines." The FLN wanted to prove to international, and especially French, opinion that the struggle they were carrying on was "progressive" even regarding women, since it needed the support of anticolonialist elements in France, that is, the Left.

Accomplishing these acts of bravery and taking such risks could have led the militant Algerian woman to become conscious of her own value and of her possible role as an autonomous person in society. But because it was implicitly understood that it was only for lack of men and under abnormal conditions that men turned to women, there was rarely any connection made between women's actions and their value.

Perhaps even more important in retarding the growth of consciousness was the objective of the struggle. As we have seen, the Algerian people battled for national independence, not especially to create a different Algerian society. Certainly, there was often discussion of "socialism," especially in what has been called the Federation of France of the FLN (that is, the immigrants who led the fight in France), but the word had no real content beyond an aspiration for a more just and egalitarian society. Such problems as agrarian reform or social class inequalities were not even broached among the masses. Those who had more precise ideas about the social and economic changes desirable or necessary for the construction of an independent Algeria had been, in many cases, physically liquidated by their comrades, in the underground especially, or had disqualified themselves at the beginning of the insurrection by refusing to accord it their support or participation. Such was the case of the militants of the Algerian Communist party (PCA), for example, who (even if they changed afterward) were at first too tied to the French Communist party to support an armed movement directed against the French. In addition, they could not detach themselves from the line of the French party, which did not admit that a nationalist demand in a colonial context could be "progressive." The French party still believed in the "True French Union," according to which the colonies would be truly liberated only when the working classes of the mother country were freed of exploitation. After all, for a great number of militants of the French Communist party, Algeria was still France.

This is precisely what the militants of the FLN no longer wanted. They wanted to be independent, at last, to direct their lives, their country, and their society. But that meant, in the minds of many, returning to the norms and way of life that colonization had devalued if not destroyed. Algerian-ness could not renounce being Arabo-Islamic. They wanted, that is, to recapture an organization of society that had never been challenged, despite the historical upheavals provoked in particular by colonization. The example given by the European society to Algeria was to be rejected. (Their women were not truly "respectable," despite the numerous points in common observable in the moral codes, for example, between pieds-noirs and Algerians.) Although they were envied by many young Algerian women for their freedom of movement, Western women in general were considered too different to be really imitated. The participation of Algerian women in the fight, according to the women, should aid in accelerating the process of decolonization, after which they could again take their place in the home, which they should never have been forced to leave. Unprepared for the profound changes that the construction of a new society implies, in large majority illiterate and without a paying job, maladapted by their upbringing to act independently, to take over, they were incapable of imagining another way of life than the traditional one they knew.

Women in Traditional Society

Traditional Algerian society was a world ruled by Islam, at once law and religion, which regulated social and personal life in all its details. It was a world of rural values; the exodus to the cities or abroad had not yet broken the structure of the extended family or of the village, with their networks of mutual aid and taboos. It was a world where men assumed all responsibilities, and where the eldest made the decisions for all the family, especially in the agricultural areas where property was undivided. This traditional world had its own equilibrium, its coherence, its cohesion, and its security.

In traditional society a woman had an inferior status from birth to death. Her arrival was not, like that of a boy, the occasion of unmixed rejoicing. All her upbringing led her to be the timid and docile servant of the male, whatever his age, who was brought up to be a despot by all the women of the house. A girl passed from submission to her father or her elder brother to that of her husband and her mother-in-law without ever becoming an independent being. Made for obeying, keeping house, and procreating (preferably males), she could be repudiated if she did not satisfy these demands. Among the very poor, nothing belonged to her, outside of the jewelry given her at the time of her marriage, not even her children. She took on an independent personality only when age desexualized her. Then, if she had brought boys into the world, it was often she who arranged their marriages, choosing her daughters-in-law whom she governed with the same nagging strictness that she herself underwent when young, regarding all that concerns keeping the house and bringing up the children. The "couple," as it is known in Europe and elsewhere, did not exist. Only the family group counted and the individual was submerged. A man, however, was subject to infinitely fewer prohibitions than a woman, since the honor of the whole family rested on her—her comportment, her "modesty," her "docility." Thus, except in the country, to go to the well or to the fields (when it is indispensable for lack of male hands), and, in the city, to the bath or the doctor, the woman was confined to the house. She did not even go out to make the purchases needed by the family. It was the head of the family who was in charge of this. All this limited considerably her contacts with the outside world and, consequently, the consciousness she had of her situation. It is not by chance that the most important stirrings occurred among high school or university women who had caught a glimpse of another possible way of life and who found themselves abruptly deprived of it by the will of a parent who decided that it was time for them to marry. Women did play a relatively important role within the family, but this role was restricted by the very fact that they did not play any role at all in the wider society.

In recent times, however, an exodus from rural areas has occurred because land was insufficient to support everyone and because repression in the countryside was particularly heavy. With the exodus accelerated first by colonialism, then by war, and finally by independence, traditional society was disrupted, especially in the cities.

Women since Independence

Despite the slight tendency of the first president of independent Algeria, Ahmed Ben Bella, to have women participate to a greater extent in public life (motivated in large part by concern with increasing his popularity), there had been scarcely any change in the role and status of women. No profound campaign of liberation has been undertaken among women, much less among men; the speeches made in public places in favor of the "sisters" who constitute half the population have little effect. Both the FLN (the single governing party, in perpetual "restructuring" since independence) and the state have deprived themselves of the means necessary to implement a policy of women's emancipation and a change of mentalities. It has been, in fact, a taboo subject. After the coup d'etat of June 18, 1965, which brought to power Ouari Boumedienne, there was even a certain step backward in relation to the preceding period—though only on the level of proclamations.

Legislation has scarcely been modified. The family code remains almost the same except for the prohibition of forced marriage and child marriage. Reform of the family code is repeatedly discussed both within and outside the government, but this remains only a prospect whose realization appears difficult. The repudiated wife is still unprotected against destitution. The right to work is, to be sure, recognized for women, and numerous women are now employed, but with rare exceptions they occupy only subordinate and menial posts, such as maids and hospital attendants, and such higher posts as secretaries in administrative offices.

According to the most recent census (1967), out of an active population (ages 15–65) of 5,580,000 persons, 45 percent of the men were unemployed while 97.5 percent of the women were without remunerated work. The total population had risen to about 12,000,000 and was growing each year by 350,000 persons. The employment problem remains very serious; it is indicative that in the six years between 1966 and 1972 only about 100,000 jobs were created in industry (which is predominantly capital intensive rather than labor intensive), while the economically active population grew by about 175,000 persons a year. In 1972 there were 400,000 Algerian emigrants working in France, accompanied by large numbers of dependents.[3] It should be noted that in the Algerian census the majority of working women, notably the large numbers who live and work in rural areas and the many domestic servants, are not counted. It may be estimated, however, that about 100,000 women are employed outside agriculture. The percentage of working women in "revolutionary" Algeria is well below that in Morocco or Tunisia: urban employed women may be estimated at 5 percent of the total employed in Algeria versus 15 percent in Morocco and 20 percent in Tunisia.[4] In Algeria as elsewhere it is sometimes affirmed that it is partly by work that women become liberated. Given the high rate of unemployment and underemployment in Algeria, however, it is felt that men must be given priority when a new job opens up. On the economic level, Algerian society as it is now constituted thus needs women to stay at home.

On the political level, the traditionalist groups of oppressors remain extremely strong, and have set the tone since independence. In the power struggle that broke out among diverse but not profoundly different factions at that time, the party leaders resorted to an appeal to the most backward traditions to squelch any attempt by such groups as the trade unionists to modify the social structure or to put into practice the oft-repeated slogan "by the people, for the people." The "blackmail" of nationalism, imposed by the brutality of informers, forced the masses into observing certain Quranic provisions (respect for fasting in the month of Ramadan, readoption of certain alimentary prohibitions) which had tended to be neglected during contact with European society because of the demands of industrial life, particularly for emigrants, or simply because of the difficulties created by the war. Those who did not observe these provisions were labeled "bad Algerians," even if their feats of resistance proved the contrary. From the point of view both of way of life and attitudes, it was a step backward provoked artificially for political reasons. It was for the ruling circles a means to regain power over the "nonconformists," and at the same time one means among others to reinforce their fragile base among the masses. That is, they could give satisfaction cheaply to the rural masses to whom the purpose of independence was to restore their "Algerian and Muslim" way of life.

Women had also to submit to these pressures, especially in the countryside and in small towns, if they wished to be respected. Those who refused to wear the veil or to be confined, those who wished to find salaried work, unless they belonged to the nascent administrative bourgeoisie, were rapidly labeled and often rejected. This contributed to the readoption of veiling among married women in the cities. In addition, the pressure on city women to veil was reinforced by a rural exodus that brought to the cities numerous traditionalist peasants who were shocked by the opulence and relative freedom of the bourgeois way of life. An unveiled and hence "immodest" young woman became the object of continual verbal and other attacks, especially in the capital city, and many preferred to return to traditional dress and appearances to avoid being molested in the streets. The model of the Western woman, who was the ideal of these young bourgeois women, was categorically refused by other classes of women; the Algerian woman was considered incapable of behaving "decently" if she became "liberated."[5]

The Algerian woman continues to be seen as a minor, needing permanent guardianship, unless she is constrained to work as the supporter of the family. No institution exists to which a woman or girl in difficulty could have recourse for assistance or advice. The great majority of lawyers are men; social workers are tiny in number, found only in cities, and have extremely limited power. There does exist in the framework of the FLN an organization of women, directed by "lady-patronesses" who know little of the real problems faced by their less fortunate sisters. Its role is more to temporize than to mobilize under feminist slogans. For it to be a more effective organization it would be necessary, among other things, that men not be an obstacle to the participation of women in this National Union of Algerian Women. This is not always the case now, especially in the countryside. In reality, the organization is essentially a point of contact between the power structure and the female population when the need is felt. The fact that the right of organization is not even tolerated except under the government's aegis hardly facilitates the task of young women sensitized to the injustices of which they are daily victims and desiring to create a movement for change. These young women, either because of their studies (this sensitivity is clearly strongest among women students) or because their activities in town or their contacts abroad have made them envisage possibilities in life that are refused to them, end up by regarding this situation as intolerable.[6] But only an individual solution can be envisaged, often in the most absolute solitude.

A National Charter was adopted on June 27, 1976, after widespread discussion throughout the country, which for the first time provided an ideological framework for the socialism desired in Algeria. The chapter in the charter devoted to women (whose problems were treated in a single page) emphasizes: "To improve the state of women actions must be taken which aim above all at transforming a negative mental and juridical environment that may be prejudicial to her recognized rights as wife and mother and to her material and moral security." Another passage of a single page deals with the National Union of Algerian Women (UNFA): "The UNFA must adapt its activity to the specific problems posed by the integration of women into modern life. It must realize that the emancipation of women does not mean the abandonment of the ethical code deeply held by the people."[7] Here again can be seen the recurring contradiction in the regime between modernism and tradition. Women should become emancipated without abandoning the ethical code, which is overwhelmingly traditionalist with regard to women and deeply held by the people. This is almost the squaring of the circle.

In the juridical and legal sphere, however, outside of family law, women since independence have had approximately the same rights as men, especially with regard to political rights. Thus they exercise the right to vote with some pride. Nevertheless in the elections to the National Assembly in February 1977, only 39 women presented themselves as candidates and only 9 were elected (4 from Algiers) out of a total of 261 deputies. This suggests that Algerian women, like women elsewhere, do not have a great deal of confidence in themselves or in their sisters.

For some years a special effort has been made to spread education. In 1971–72 close to 60 percent of children were going to school (with great regional disparities). Girls, however, attended less than boys, although the Algerian ratio was more nearly equal than the Middle East average. Girls constituted 32 percent of the primary school population, 27 percent of the secondary, and 13 percent of the population in higher education.[8] By current law education is supposed to be compulsory until age fourteen, but as in many countries this requirement is not yet fulfilled. In higher education it is encouraging to see a relatively large number of women in disciplines like medicine. These, however, are young bourgeois women for whom the problem of emancipation is not posed in the same terms or to the same degree as in the less privileged classes. Among the lower classes girls are generally withdrawn from school as soon as possible and married. Diplomas have frequently become guarantees of a better marriage, and a girl having one has acquired an additional value that permits the whole family to acquire a higher status.

Through the compulsory education of boys and girls, the political leaders hope to "modernize" mentalities, which, in their eyes, will then permit the "liberation" of women, at last to become "ripe," without shocks. We know from the example of Western societies what such a liberation is worth when social structures do not allow it. In fact, the refusal to Westernize the ways of Algerian society (in contrast to Tunisia or Egypt) outside of the administrative bourgeoisie, along with the refusal to transform social structures in a radical way (as has occurred in Cuba or in China) has retarded considerably the solution of the problem of the Algerian woman. Besides, considering the choice of a developmental model made by Algeria's rulers (creation of ultramodern factories, creating a very small number of new jobs), the woman wishing to work constitutes a burden, since there are already in Algeria 1,500,000 unemployed men. Women are superfluous as producers and neglected as citizens, arousing only defiance or irritation when they try to make themselves heard. They are too little conscious of themselves as a group. It is thus improbable that an effective feminist movement can be born in the near future. On the governmental and party level the situation of women does not yet constitute a problem; they count on girls' education eventually to resolve it, without, however, having transformed in this direction the content of education itself.[9]

Notes

1. Bruno Etienne, *L'Algérie: cultures et révolution* (Paris, 1977), p. 172.

2. Gérard Chaliand and Juliette Minces, *L'Algérie independante* (Paris, 1972), pp. 7–8.

3. For these and other details, see the relevant sections of Juliette Minces, *Les travailleurs étrangers en France* (Paris, 1973).

4. Ibid., p. 142. This book also contains general employment and unemployment statistics, mostly from official sources cited therein. Only urban workers can be estimated with reasonable accuracy.

5. The director of a major school in Algiers in 1971 demanded and obtained from nine female students, suspected of "misconduct," a certificate of virginity.

6. Hence the high number of suicide attempts and runaways among high school and university students. On this and other problems of Algerian women, see Fadela M'Rabet, *La femme algérienne* (Paris, 1964), and *Les Algériennes* (Paris, 1976).

7. The National Charter, with an introduction by Robert Lombotte, is in *Algérie: naissance d'une société nouvelle* (Paris, 1976).

8. Chaliand and Minces, *L'Algérie,* p. 148, based on official sources. There are indications that women's higher education has since risen.

9. There exists no recent (post-1970) general book or monograph on the situation of Algerian women, although there are unpublished theses. Slightly earlier books with important information include David C. Gordon, *Women of Algeria: An Essay on Change* (Cambridge, Mass., 1968) ; Farouk Benatia, *Le travail féminin en Algérie* (Algiers, 1970) ; and the important theoretical work of Germaine Tillion, *Le harem et les cousins* (Paris, 1966) .

Bibliography

Arnaud, Georges, and Jacques Verges. *Pour Djamila Bouhired.* Paris, 1957.

Benatia, Farouk. *Le travail féminin en Algérie.* Algiers, 1970.

Boudjedra, Rachid. *La répudiation.* Paris, 1970.

———. *La vie quotidienne en Algérie en 1970.* Paris, 1970.

Chaliand, Gérard. *L'Algérie est-elle socialiste?* Paris, 1964.

Chaliand, Gérard, and Juliette Minces. *L'Algérie indépendante: bilan d'une révolution nationale.* Paris, 1972.

Etienne, Bruno. *L'Algérie: cultures et révolution.* Paris, 1977.

Fanon, Frantz. *The Wretched of the Earth.* New York, 1961.

———. *A Dying Colonialism.* New York, 1967.

Gordon, David C. *Women of Algeria: An Essay on Change.* Cambridge, Mass., 1968.

Harbi, Mohammed. *Aux origines du FLN: le populisme révolutionnaire en Algérie.* Paris, 1975.

Lacheraf, Mostefa. *Algérie: nation et société.* Paris, 1965.

Lombotte, Robert, intro. to "The National Charter." In *Algérie: naissance d'une société nouvelle.* Paris, 1976.

M'Rabet, Fadela. *La femme algérienne.* Paris, 1964.

———. *Les Algériennes.* Paris, 1967.

Minces, Juliette. *Les travailleurs étrangers en France.* Paris, 1973.

Tillion, Germaine. *Le harem et les cousins.* Paris, 1966.

Zerdoumi, Nefissa. *Enfants d'Hier.* Paris, 1969.

8 Education and Employment among Kuwaiti Women

Kamla Nath

The relationship among economic development, modernization, and participation of women in economic activity has been the subject of a number of studies in recent years. These studies focus on the decline in the work participation of women in the early stages of economic development, which appears to be caused by a progressive lowering of their work participation in the traditional sectors (agriculture, cottage industries, petty trade). This change is compensated for only partly by increases in the participation of

---

This study of work participation and related changes among Kuwaiti career women is focused on 246 university graduates who have been leaders and pacesetters of the change among women. The survey on which this study is based was conducted during early 1970, with the active cooperation of Ms. Najat H. Sultan, a young Kuwaiti professional employed with the Ministry of Education. It was conducted in three stages. First was the collection of background information from published and unpublished official sources and discussions with prominent career women preliminary to the framing of a questionnaire, followed by distribution of the questionnaire to all the 219 (out of a total of 244) graduate Kuwaiti women in government service who were in Kuwait at the time of the study. The statistical analysis relates to the 77 questionnaires returned. The third stage was personal interviews with 18 women graduates (including some who had not returned the questionnaire) and 13 other key respondents. These included such leaders of change as the first Kuwaiti women teachers, the first women graduates, some mothers of graduates, women from one of the former slave families, an Arab sociologist (Fadil al Abbar from Riyadh, Saudi Arabia), and two British women who had lived in Kuwait for a long time and had seen and experienced the process of change from the beginning of the oil era (Violet Dickson, author of *Forty Years in Kuwait* [1970], and her daughter Zahra Freeth, author of *Kuwait Was My Home* [1956]).

women in the expanding modern sectors such as manufacturing and services. Boserup (1970), while analyzing these trends and the contributory factors, has argued forcefully for changes in the attitude of governments of the developing countries toward employment of women in the modern sectors of the economies and adoption of policies and programs aimed at increasing it. She argues that higher levels of work participation of women will not only contribute to accelerating economic development but will also relieve social and economic problems such as those created by accelerated migration from the rural areas to the cities. Although the trend can be noticed in a large number of the developing countries, in some of the Arab Middle Eastern countries the work participation rate of women has gone up in the process of economic development and modernization owing to the efforts of governments to encourage work by women.

The change from women working in traditional, family-centered work places—farms, cottage industries, and shops—to modern factories, offices, and schools located away from the home means not merely change in the location or type of work; it is a symbol of a broad-ranging process of social change that affects the whole spectrum of social attitudes, values, and institutions: the organization of the home and the family, and indeed the entire life-style of individuals and families. These social aspects of the change appear to be dominant in the Arab Middle East, where because of the strong socio-cultural and religious traditions, the participation of women in economic activity had been exceptionally low and the segregation of men and women and the cloistered, home-bound patterns of women's life had been the strongest.

The process of the change is brought out vividly in Kuwait, a small Middle Eastern state (area about 5,800 square miles) situated between Saudi Arabia and Iraq. In 1970 it had a population of 738,662 of which fewer than half were Kuwaitis. The rest were immigrants, mostly Arabs, from the Middle East countries who were attracted to Kuwait by the opportunities afforded by the oil boom that began in the 1950s. Until the oil boom began, Kuwait had been a poor and technologically undeveloped sheikhdom of about a hundred thousand people, who eked out a living as fishermen, pearl divers, animal herders, and carrier-traders; the last carried goods among the Arabian Gulf, India, and East Africa. Because of its location at the head of the gulf and an excellent natural harbor, Kuwait town was an important market and an entrepot for trade with the interior of Arabia. The carrier trade had also led to growth of a boat-building industry. But there was hardly any agriculture and all food had to be imported. Even water was brought by boats from southern Iraq because local water was too salty.

The socioeconomic hierarchy of Kuwait consisted of the sheikhs or members of the ruling family and the relatively rich merchants at the top; the bedouins, fishermen, and pearl divers in the middle; and the slaves at the bottom. Average family earnings were extremely low (see Shehab 1964:463). Members of an extended family generally lived together, in houses built around a common courtyard. There was strict seclusion of women of the families of the well-to-do. These women stayed within the *harem* (women's quarters) and met other women of the extended family, who were also their neighbors. They never did any nondomestic work, and most domestic work was done for them by slave women. Arabs have for many centuries run the slave trade from Africa. Seclusion of women was much less strict among the poor—fishermen, artisans, and bedouins. Their women often helped the men in their work. Many sold vegetables, eggs, clothes, or trinkets in the *suq* (market). Women of the merchants' families also earned a little, while staying within the harem. They made dresses or skull caps worn by the men or sold to their neighbors and relatives cloth, perfume, mascara, and so forth, brought by their men from India or other countries. A modified form of this practice was continued by women of these families, who would bring bundles of dresses and other articles to sell among friends and relatives when they went to Western countries on vacation. Other than the Quranic schools, where a few girls learned to read and recite from the Quran, there were no schools for girls (Calverley 1958:100). Religion and custom demanded that women be covered from head to foot in black. A girl was veiled at puberty and was married soon after. Marriages were usually with cousins. Polygamy was common. Besides the four wives that a man could have under Islamic law, he could keep slave women. Women grew up, got married, and died in the harem.

During the first fifteen years of the oil era, from 1950 to 1965, Kuwait was transformed from a small, traditional Arab sheikhdom of carrier-traders, fishermen, pearl divers, and bedouins into a modern city-state with large commercial and financial institutions. The Kuwaitis modernized their life-styles with astonishing speed and vigor. They filled the new schools and offices opened by the government in the thousands, and crammed their new modern houses with consumer goods of every description.

The change relating to Kuwaiti women, symbolized by the change from veiled women living within the four walls of the harem to young women moving about freely in the streets dressed in the latest Western styles, working in offices and schools, and driving their own cars, was not merely the most striking indicator of social change but also the best evidence that it was neither transitory nor superficial. Pre-oil era Kuwait had exhibited the patterns characteristic of other countries of the Arabian peninsula. "The loss of women power in conspicuous leisure activities, unproductive household tasks or various forms of disguised unemployment, which can be seen in every society, was more evident in the underdeveloped cities of the Middle East with Kuwait as an extreme example of having 0.4 percent crude female work participation rate in 1961. The pattern of the society can be described as, 'early marriage and female seclusion' " (Collver and Langlois 1962:368).

By 1970 the work participation rate of women had gone up to 5.2 percent, among the highest in the Arab Middle East. Behind this statistical change lay a massive increase in the education of women, their participation in modern service occupations in increasing numbers, and a growing trend toward adoption by the Kuwaitis of the life-styles characteristic of the cities of the western Arab countries, such as Lebanon and Egypt. In 1965–66 nearly 67 percent of the girls in the 5–9 age group were attending government schools, where they constituted 41.5 percent of the total student body. In 1968–69, 43 percent of all school students were female. About a thousand girls were attending the University of Kuwait which had been established in 1966. Education also became popular with older women who pressed forward into the adult education centers established by the government under advice from UNESCO. Female attendance at these centers was 5,215 in 1969 (Ministry of Education 1969).

An important result of the modernization of the community and the education of women had been the entry of women into government service in increasing numbers as civil servants, social welfare workers, and teachers. Hundreds of Kuwaiti women were working in schools and offices alongside men. The leaders of this change had been young women from the families of leading merchants, who were the richest in Kuwait and who also enjoyed considerable social prestige and political power. Acceptance of the changes by the young women of these families ensured their rapid spread throughout the community.

By early 1970 the veil had disappeared among the younger women. A number of the older women also had discarded the veil or had dispensed with the face covering, the *boshia,* while keeping the outer garment, the *abaya*. Education, travel abroad, and contact within Kuwait with the highly Westernized veilless women from western Arab countries (Lebanon, Egypt, Jordan) were the most powerful influences in inducing the changes. The movement to discard the veil seems to have begun in 1956, although Zahra Freeth, who had grown up in Kuwait, wrote in 1956: "There is no movement for emancipation amongst the women of Kuwait and I have never heard an Arab woman express the wish that she might one day walk abroad unveiled. The new interest which education has given them has not yet extended to matters of politics or social reform" (1956:85). However, it was reported to the author that in 1956 some girls of a higher secondary school burned their boshias as a protest against the veil. They were told by their parents, "keep the boshias or no school for you." The girls submitted and went to school with the boshias. But two years later the same girls, who were by then students at a university in Cairo and were home on vacation, tried again and succeeded. By 1970, the dress and living patterns of the young women had changed enough to be similar to those of their Western counterparts. Many of the young women even drove their cars to work. The fact that the changes were made so rapidly by the young women and were accepted by the middle-aged and older women shows that the community was ready for them and that the younger women had only to give the lead. One of the young leaders of the change told me, "At that time, there was so much excitement about the new wealth that the older generation could not decide which of the changes to accept and which to reject. New values were accepted along with the new wealth."

Marriage customs, however, still bore the strong imprint of tradition. Most marriages of Kuwaiti girls were with cousins, but they now chose their partners from among cousins. Polygamy had disappeared among the educated young, although it was still prevalent among the old. One heard now and again of an old man bringing another young wife from a neighboring Arab country.

Joint living of members of the extended family had gone, but one could often see a row of identical houses constructed by a father for the families of his sons; these had taken the place of rooms around a common courtyard. Moreover, most other rules of the extended family organization, such as accepting the decision of the oldest male in all matters of importance and various obligations of the members to one another, were still being observed.

That the speed or patterns of change witnessed among Kuwaiti women were neither automatic nor inevitable but were conscious choices by men and women, especially those whose decisions influenced the rest of the community, is clear from the fact that in neighboring Saudi Arabia, which had experienced similar superaffluence from oil revenues, the society is still holding onto traditional attitudes toward women. The Saudis believe that any mixing of the sexes is morally wrong and not in accordance with the teachings of the Quran. Girls have to wear the veil from the age of eleven or twelve and are educated in separate schools from the age of six. At university, female students are completely segregated from the male students and the professors. They watch lectures on closed circuit television and ask questions of the professor by the telephones installed in their classrooms. They are given one day in the week to utilize the library when male students are barred. There are no cinemas, theaters, or dance halls in Saudi Arabia, and women are not allowed to drive automobiles. Marriages are arranged by parents. It is felt improper for men and women to work together in the same location (Fletcher 1974).

A detailed enquiry by a social scientist could explain the reasons for such rapid changes in Kuwait, when other neighboring Arab countries are holding onto traditional attitudes. However, some of the more obvious influences for change in the case of Kuwait can be mentioned here. First, there is the maritime trading tradition of the dominant group in the Kuwaiti community. The traders have been the leaders and pacesetters of the community. They were the most affluent group before the oil era and after. The ruling family—the sheikh—has very close relations (including frequent marriage) with them. Before the oil era the customs duty on imports was the main source of income for the rulers. In contrast, the religious class is small and appears to have very little influence. The carrier-traders had seen cultural norms and patterns of social organization very different from their own in India and East Africa. In many a trading family, a branch had been settled in Bombay or other parts of the west coast of India. And it is well known that maritime trading communities accept changes more rapidly than the agricultural or pastoral communities which are not similarly exposed to foreign cultural patterns.

Second, Kuwait was a British protectorate until it became independent in 1961. During the colonial era, British patterns of living had been looked up to with awe and admiration, but adoption was slow partly because of the hesitation to adopt the patterns of the rulers. Lack of means may have been another inhibiting factor. But after the oil wealth started pouring in and particularly after independence, the floodgates of modernization were opened.[1] According to the mother of a university graduate, "We envied the daughters of the Britishers in Kuwait and wanted to give our daughters also the same kind of education and training but we couldn't do it then.

The moment we could we did." According to one of the leaders of social change, "Acceptance of Western patterns of living (which were always considered superior and the thing to achieve) came immediately as we achieved Western standards of income."

Third, Kuwait is a city-state. Social changes are generally more rapid in cities than in the rural areas because the friction of distance, which is a major inhibiting factor in the diffusion of new practices, is so much less in the cities. In the case of Kuwait the influence is further accentuated by the influx of very large numbers of Westernized women who come to work as teachers, nurses, secretaries, saleswomen, and so on. But it is noteworthy that they are allowed to live in Kuwait the way they like, whereas in neighboring Saudi Arabia they are expected to adhere to the traditional Arab Muslim cultural norms.

The fourth factor is the immense size of oil revenues in relation to the population. This has led to a high concentration of investment in economic and social services, including the building of a new modern city. And fifth, the distribution of oil wealth among all Kuwaitis by a deliberate policy of the Kuwaiti government has enabled them to buy consumer goods of every description and to adopt modern patterns of living. At a time (the 1950s and the early 1960s) when oil revenues in adjoining countries were being appropriated by the monarch (Saudi Arabia) or by the ruling elites (Iran and Iraq), the Kuwaiti government adopted a policy of distributing them among all citizens, through land acquisition payments, investment in education, medical care, social welfare, free housing, and provision of a job to every Kuwaiti man or woman who sought one. Land acquisition payments, which originated in the need to compensate the owners of lands and houses that had to be acquired for building the new planned city, were soon turned into a wealth distribution mechanism. Besides founding multimillion-dollar fortunes, they enabled a large number of Kuwaitis to make the change from mud houses, traditional living patterns, and poverty to modern villas, Western life styles, and superaffluence in one giant stride. The total land acquisition payments had amounted by March 1970 to $1,788.8 million—an average of $7,400 per capita.

As a result, a number of Kuwaiti women became university graduates. The first Kuwaiti women to receive university educations were those who went out of the country on government scholarships. The first group of six got their degrees from Cairo University in 1960. Thereafter, an increasing number went to universities in Cairo, Alexandria, or Beirut until the University of Kuwait was established in 1966. Few went to universities in Europe or the United States. Apart from the difficulty of learning a foreign language, sending females to Western universities was not favored by parents. The first woman to get a degree from an American university had returned to Kuwait, with a Master's degree in nuclear physics, only in 1970. However, the large majority of the graduates had visited Great Britain and Western Europe on vacation and a few had visited the United States. Kuwaiti males preferred to go to British or American universities, since their degrees had much higher prestige than those from Arab universities. The degrees of the female graduates were all in liberal arts with one exception. The number of women graduates had increased from 38 in 1966 to 155 in 1968 and 246 in 1970. The increase in numbers will be much greater in the future because of the large enrollment at the University of Kuwait (Central Statistics Office 1968, 1969–70).

One-third of the graduates provided information on the educational levels of members of their families, and of these the majority reported their parents to be either illiterate or barely literate. In only one case did the father have a college degree, and in another the mother was educated up to the primary level. However, most of their brothers and sisters were studying in schools and colleges. Of those who were married, all husbands had university degrees, and several had postgraduate qualifications. Thus, education was very much a first-generation experience.

Most of the graduates considered in this study were either unmarried or were young women who had just started raising families; nineteen of the twenty-six who were married had children (eleven had one child each, six had two children each, and only two had three children each). All except one were under thirty-five years of age.

Education at all levels was completely free for Kuwaiti men and women, and since 1966 it was made compulsory for the age group of 6–14 years. Education of girls up to secondary school level was the accepted norm. Most felt that women ought to acquire postgraduate degrees, while some considered one degree adequate. Half the reasons given for the education of women were economic or career-oriented in nature (to acquire a career, to establish economic independence), while the rest were "social" (social necessity, social prestige, training for homemaking). Some felt that special training (interior decoration, cooking, flower arrangement) was necessary to make good housewives, while others felt that general education was sufficient and that girls received adequate training by observing other women in their homes.

Coeducation had not been introduced in Kuwait at any level at the time of the study. Few graduates supported the introduction of coeducation in primary and secondary schools, but almost all favored it at the university level, since it was felt that it develops talent, creates confidence and academic competition, promotes understanding between the sexes, and removes the danger of sudden mixing at later stages in life. The few who felt that coeducation should begin earlier gave the reason that without it, people develop inhibitions.

At the time of the study 244 women graduates were in government service and only two were outside it. One had been in government service earlier but was at the time of the study a free-lance producer of the women's program for Kuwait television, and the other was an honorary social worker. Thus, Kuwaiti women graduates had a very high work participation rate (more than 99 percent), with the Kuwait government as almost the sole employer. The high participation rate appears truly remarkable when viewed against the low work participation rate of 2.3 percent for all Kuwaiti women in the working-age group.[2] More than half the women graduates were working in the Ministry of Education—as teachers in girls' schools or in various branches of the ministry's office. Nearly one-fourth of the total were listed as employed at the University of Kuwait as demonstrators and teaching assistants. The large majority of the women graduates were young, having received their university degrees between 1965 and 1970, and three-fourths (171 out of 244) of them were unmarried (Central Statistics Office 1969–70). This concentration of graduates in the educational service had arisen partly from the need of the government to find Kuwaiti teachers in place of expatriates for the girls' schools, and partly because teaching was considered to be the most suitable profession for women.

Educated career women were regarded as a symbol of modernization of the community. The first women graduates who came out to work were treated as celebrities. They were interviewed by journalists, and the Ministry of Information and Broadcasting prepared brochures on them to show visitors to Kuwait how Kuwaiti women were participating in and contributing to the progress of the country. The first graduates who started to work were all from the families of leading merchants, who had positions of prestige and power within the Kuwaiti community. As a result, work by educated women came to be associated with modernization and wealth—the thing to do, and not as an indicator of economic need. The economic rewards for working were substantial, nevertheless; the minimum salary for a graduate was 180 Kuwaiti dinars (KD) per month.[3] There was no difficulty in obtaining a job, since the government was committed to providing jobs for all Kuwaitis, men and women. It was reported by an interviewee that if a suitable job did not exist when a particular Kuwaiti woman applied for employment, an entire new section was created in a department to provide one for her.

Most of the graduates were working in the education sector—at the University of Kuwait, in girls' schools, or in the office of the Ministry of Education. They were primarily teachers, social workers, and researchers. All graduates were placed on entry in grade IV of the government service, in which the starting salary was KD 180, and moved to higher points within the same grade or to the next higher grade (III) as they gained seniority and extra qualifications.

Most of the graduates were in their first job, some in their second, and a few in their third. The primary reason for changing jobs was the vertical shift from teachers in schools to demonstrators or teaching assistants at the University of Kuwait. These women, who had already been appointed to their teaching positions, were not qualified to teach at the university, and were waiting to get scholarships from the government to study for postgraduate degrees at foreign universities which would enable them to teach. Promotion in the same job or shift to a different section of the same ministry or to a similar job in another ministry were other reasons for change. Among those who had entered government service in or after 1969, some had changed jobs within a year because of the desire to acquire a job suitable to their qualifications and preferences as soon as was possible.

Most graduates liked their jobs, mainly giving reasons of intellectual satisfaction, personal fulfillment, escape from boredom at home, and the filling of time. Economic reward was not a major consideration in liking a job. A few did not like their jobs because of the lack of cooperation from male colleagues, the lack of appreciation from their bosses, the tiring and time-consuming nature of jobs, involvement with difficult human relation problems, and the lack of discipline in the place of work. One worker reported that she had no work to do in her job.

It was common knowledge that most Kuwaiti civil servants did practically no work in their jobs. This situation created a difficult disciplinary problem in offices where both Kuwaiti and non-Kuwaiti women were working in similar positions. A male Kuwaiti working in the private sector said, "I will never employ a Kuwaiti woman in my firm. Who can pay her KD 200 every month for doing 'no work' except the Kuwait government!" Having no work to do or doing no work had arisen mainly because there were too many workers. The oversupply resulted from the commitment of the government to give employment to all Kuwaitis, irrespective of the need for their services. The jobs for women were also very largely sinecures, created by an immensely wealthy government.

Most graduates wanted women to become teachers, social workers, and doctors. Few desired for women such jobs as personal secretary, bank clerk, and television artist. Some were currently working as librarians and administrators but only a few mentioned these as job preferences. The only legal barriers against work by women related to their joining the armed forces and becoming members of the National Assembly.[4] Kuwaiti women did not have the right to vote. As a matter of convention, women were not sent abroad as members of the Kuwaiti diplomatic service and were not encouraged to take up employment in foreign countries.

The prejudices against jobs such as personal secretary, saleswoman, telephone operator, or television artist arose mainly from social inhibitions. In these jobs women either had to work closely with men or had to appear before the general public. One of the earliest graduates appeared for several years on the Kuwait television as director of the weekly women's program, but had resigned her post to become a free-lance producer of the program. Work by Kuwaiti women on television was not liked by the older members of the society, male or female. One of the first Kuwaiti women to become a schoolteacher expressed herself vehemently against the appearance of Kuwaiti women on television. She stated that she would not allow her daughter to appear on television even if she were paid KD 1,000 for each appearance. One person remarked that besides the girls' schools, the office of the Ministry of Education was the only place where husbands and other male members of the family liked women to work, mainly because men and women worked in separate wings of the office building. Kuwaiti women did not like the jobs of doctor or nurse because they required long training and hard work, and the additional income from them was not a sufficient incentive for going through the hardships of strenuous studies and training and long hours of work. In the case of other jobs such as lawyer, beautician, and shop manager, there was no precedent, and it was believed that once the initial barrier was broken by one woman, others were likely to join. This was corroborated by the fact that my co-worker in the study was managing an art gallery (as a second job), and one of the first Kuwaiti graduates had opened a hairdressing salon while another had started a women's dress shop.

Older male and female members of the graduates' families were generally favorable toward their kinswomen's working; the graduates reported that their families felt proud and considered work the most logical and natural thing for an educated woman to do. Encouragement for women to start working generally came from an older male member of the family, such as father or grandfather. Once the oldest male member in a Kuwaiti family had allowed or encouraged work by women, none dared oppose him because he was generally the decision-maker. It is of interest to mention, however, that the first Kuwaiti women to get into government offices in 1961 were not allowed by the senior male officials to go to work without a veil. These women, who as students had been leaders in discarding the veil, refused to accept the veil again and declined their job offers. Thereupon, the then minister of foreign affairs, Sheikh Sabah Al Sabah—who is now the ruler of Kuwait—allowed the women to work without the veil in his ministry. Other ministries soon followed suit in giving permission.

According to the graduates, the Kuwaiti community viewed work by women in a different fashion. Many felt that men had better opportunities for work and promotions than women. The inequality of opportunity of getting a job or pay was not noticeable at the time of entry into the service, but became apparent later when men went up the ladder much faster than women, and women never reached the top. Some women who had been in government service for several years expressed discontent with the fact that their bosses were junior to them and did not have higher qualifications. They said that these men were in the top decision-making positions only because they were men. They complained that they were dominated by men in the home as well as in the office and that men would not allow the participation of women at the crucial policy- and decision-making levels. A few of them even said that men considered women in offices to be just a decoration and a sign of modernization of the Kuwaiti community. Some women complained that men did not attach much importance to women's work. They were keen to change this attitude. The graduates wanted women to go to the National Assembly and get laws passed that would set women free from male domination. But the more tolerant ones said: "It is a man's world. Men have better opportunities for work and promotions. This will have to change, but the change will take time."

Combining work and family did not appear to create difficulties for the graduates, mainly because of the existence of domestic servants, including nannies and drivers, in most homes. The morning working hours of the Kuwait government (7:00 A.M. to 1:00 P.M. during summer and 7:30 A.M. to 1:30 P.M. during winter) were also very convenient in combining homemaking and work. Moreover, commuting between home and the place of work did not present problems. A majority of the workers either had their own cars or could make use of one of the cars of the family, and distances were not long. Most of those who did not drive wanted to learn. A few said that their families did not like women to drive cars.

The effect of women's work on the size of the family could not be ascertained, because most were unmarried or were married but had not completed childbearing. Most expressed a desire for three to four children, a few for two, and only one for one child. However, two wanted six children each. A number of the graduates expressed a desire for a small family, not because it helped combining work with homemaking, but because it was a sign of modernization.

Customs regarding marriage have undergone a major change during the last generation. Girls are no longer married at a very young age. The traditional arranged marriage, without the consent of the girl, is also not frequent. After discarding the veil women have much greater opportunity for meeting men, especially their various cousins and other relatives. Most women mentioned that the most common current practice is that several young men propose to a woman, who then indicates her choice to her parents. If the choice is from among the first cousins, the parents readily agree because it is in accord with the traditional practice. On the other hand, a choice involving an intertribal union among the Kuwaitis is not encouraged, and one in which the young man is either a non-Kuwaiti Arab or a non-Arab is strongly opposed. In such cases the female and the male have to go through a long struggle to obtain the permission of the family. There was no such case among the interviewees but references were made to two such cases in Kuwaiti merchant families. They mentioned also that instances of Kuwaiti women having married non-Kuwaiti Arabs were rare and there was no case of a Kuwaiti woman graduate having married a non-Arab. Many interviewees said that marriages for Kuwaiti women would always be arranged within the extended family circle and the choice would always remain limited to the various cousins because the older people wanted the family property to stay within the family. A number of Kuwaiti young men who had gone to Western countries to study had brought home Western (American, British, and

European) wives. They had been readily accepted by the men's families, because there was a tradition of men bringing wives from outside Kuwait. Attitudes allowing educated young Kuwaiti men to marry non-Kuwaiti women but forbidding young Kuwaiti women to marry non-Kuwaiti men have created a social problem, in that a number of educated Kuwaiti women have remained unmarried up to their thirties. Concern with this situation was being felt and expressed: "Confronted with such blockade around the majority of the Kuwaiti girls [not being allowed to date them and know them well] the eligible Kuwaiti young man rechannels his interest and looks for a wife from outside Kuwait. As a consequence many Kuwaiti men are now married to non-Kuwaiti girls. Statistically speaking, this leaves a surplus of Kuwaiti girls unmarried" (Rehman 1970:5).

Joint living of members of the extended family had almost disappeared in the graduates' families, and most graduates vehemently opposed it. Only two of the married women were living in joint families and they too explained that they were waiting for construction of their own separate houses to be completed. In several cases parents were postponing the approval of their daughter's marriage to the young man of her choice until he could afford to set up a separate home. Reasons for preferring independent living included avoiding family friction, having independence and peace, and being masters of their own domains.

The availability of domestic help, clustering of houses of the members of the extended family, and marriages among cousins (which resulted in the wife's and husband's families living in the same neighborhood) made looking after the home and supervision of the children of the working graduates, who were living in separate homes, quite easy. In the case of teachers, the government was particular that they be posted in girls' schools located as close to their homes as possible. Finally, the financial constraint, experienced by young couples in most countries in setting up a separate home, did not exist among Kuwaiti couples because of the very high income levels.

Mass education of women and their working in the modern service sector in large numbers constitute an advanced stage of modernization for the male-dominated society of the Arab Gulf states. When the educated career woman becomes the norm, practices such as polygamy, arranged marriage, and living of women in a harem become untenable, because the social practices and patterns of living induced by these changes are so radically different.

While the speed of change in Kuwait makes one wonder about the strength of the traditional patterns, it is clear also that many inhibitions and previous practices are still in existence. The coexistence of the traditional and modern in some aspects of living patterns and attitudes is a hindrance to the complete social and political emancipation of women as well as their wider participation in the whole range of economic activities. Kuwaiti women are choosing their own husbands but the choice is limited to cousins and young men belonging to the same tribe. Joint living has gone, but living in adjacent houses, if possible, and observance of most of the obligations of the joint family have remained. Kuwaiti men and women travel frequently to Western countries but there is a strong prejudice against sending women to universities in Western countries. Within Kuwait there is social and residential segregation between the Kuwaitis and the non-Kuwaitis. Kuwaiti women are getting university education in increasing numbers and are entering the modern service sector, but they have reservations both about taking courses like medicine that require long, hard work and taking up jobs in which women have to appear before the public. Most of them are graduates in arts or social sciences, and have taken up jobs as teachers, social workers, administrators, and research workers. And the women workers in the ministries are denied the opportunity of reaching the top.

These attitudes and practices will change. In the presence of overstaffing in the government service, on the one hand, and dominance of the technical and commercial services by non-Kuwaitis, on the other, the attitudes of the Kuwaitis (including women) toward technical and vocational education and toward various kinds of jobs will undoubtedly change, because the alternatives of educated women's remaining unemployed or returning to their traditional role in the home appear highly unlikely. Educated women will be coming out of the secondary schools and the University of Kuwait in the thousands and will want to enter the nontechnical jobs in government service. Moati's study (1969) on attitudes toward technical and vocational education among Kuwaiti and non-Kuwaiti students of government intermediate and secondary girls' schools concluded that the large majority of the Kuwaiti respondents (83 percent) wanted to have university-level education; 62 percent wanted to study subjects like liberal arts, social service, domestic science, teachers' training, and so on; and 86 percent wanted to take up employment. However, 72 percent felt that women should have government jobs and not work with companies or run businesses of their own. Ninety percent of the Kuwaiti respondents expected that the society would provide them with suitable jobs after finishing their studies. But even the superaffluent government of Kuwait will not be able to employ them as supernumeraries. Nor would it want to, because more and more of these women will be from the families of middle- and lower-income groups and not from the privileged leading merchant families. The government would have less incentive to give them highly paid government jobs, and the women themselves would have fewer inhibitions regarding working as saleswomen, secretaries, telephone operators, nurses, and the rest. Thus, a pattern of work participation similar to that of the western Arab countries would emerge.

In view of the commitment of the government to economic and social planning, the changes would be induced through changes in the secondary school and university curricula, which should emphasize technical and vocational education, and through changes in the salary structure that should provide adequate incentives for technical work. Some social attitudes, such as those relating to marriages of Kuwaiti women with non-Kuwaitis, to political participation of women, and to sex discrimination in promotion, will also change.

The nature and rate of changes will remain areas of interest to social scientists, because, while many of the present inhibitions are not expected to survive, it is equally unlikely that Kuwaiti society will adopt completely Western patterns. It has undoubtedly exhibited a remarkable capacity for change, but it must be emphasized that in the case of the changes relating to women, the patterns adopted already existed in the cities of the western Arab countries. Future progress will depend on the interaction of the modernizing pressures coming both from internal sources and from Western countries and the resistance to modernization coming from conservatives and from neighboring Saudi Arabia, which despite superaffluence is still maintaining a feudal attitude toward women.

Notes

1. I had observed a similar phenomenon of hesitation in adopting British patterns of living until independence, but far more rapid adoption afterward, in my native Punjab, India.

2. According to the Population Census of 1965, the number of Kuwaiti female workers was 1,092, constituting 2.5 percent of the Kuwaiti work force and 2.3 percent of the Kuwaiti female population aged 15–55. Of the 1,092, 911 were salaried employees and 668 worked for the Kuwaiti government. Kuwaiti women workers formed only one-eighth of all female workers in 1965, and their proportions were extremely small in all categories except for clerks (Central Statistics Office 1965).

3. In 1970 one KD was equivalent to $2.80.

4. However, in one of the personal interviews, a Kuwaiti man exclaimed, "Inshah Allah [if God wills], one day our women will reach the National Assembly!"

Bibliography

Boserup, Ester. *Women's Role in Economic Development.* London and New York, 1970.

Calverley, Eleanor T. *My Arabian Days and Nights.* New York, 1958.

Collver, A., and E. Langlois. "The Female Labour Force in Metropolitan Areas: An International Comparison." *Economic Development and Cultural Change,* 10, no. 4 (1962) :367–386.

Central Statistics Office, Government of Kuwait. *Census of Population.* Kuwait, 1965.

———. *Statistical Results of Survey of Government Officials.* Kuwait, 1966.

———. *Statistical Abstract.* Kuwait, 1968.

———. *Appointment of Kuwaiti Women Graduates in the Financial Year.* Kuwait, 1969–1970.

Dickson, Violet. *Forty Years in Kuwait.* London, 1970.

Fletcher, David. "Drawing a Veil on Classroom Life." *London Sunday Telegraph,* July 14, 1974.

Freeth, Zahra. *Kuwait Was My Home.* London, 1956.

Ministry of Education, Government of Kuwait. *Access of Young Girls and Women to Technical and Vocational Education in Kuwait.* Kuwait, 1969.

Moati, Yousef A. "The Access of Girls and Women to Technical and Vocational Education in Kuwait." Unpublished. Kuwait, 1969.

Rehman, Najjar Abdul. "The Neglected Girls of Kuwait." *Daily News,* (Kuwait), February 6, 1970, p. 5.

Shehab, Fakhri. "Kuwait: A Superaffluent Society." *Foreign Affairs,* 42, no. 3 (1964) :461–474.

9 On Changing the Concept and Position of Persian Women

Michael M. J. Fischer

Changing the roles of women and attitudes about them is not easy—it proceeds with the pace of larger social changes. There are two sets of logical distinctions to be made. First, equality, identity, and complementarity are three separate things. Men and women cannot be identical (a biological impossibility); to demand equality in some spheres does not imply that men and women may not be complementary in others. Second, honor and dignity are two separate things, as are liberation and emancipation. Honor and liberation have to do with that part of personal identity linked to institutional roles; dignity and emancipation have to do with that part of personal identity independent of institutional roles.

Women of the Harem . . . Women Voters

The older Persian (and European) view of women stressed notions of honor, complementarity, and harmony. Demands for equality usually were seen as destructive, rather than enriching, of these values. On the other hand, it has been suggested that professional Middle Eastern women (or at least Turkish women) are more independent and confident than their European counterparts be-

The heading derives from Simone de Beauvoir's query and discussion (1952: xxxiii). I owe much to the constructive criticism of earlier versions of this paper by Catherine Bateson, Lois Beck, Mangol Bayat-Philipp, Lina Fruzzetti, Byron Good, Mary-Jo Good, Mayling Hebert, Nikki Keddie, Steven Kemper, Mary (Farvar) Martin, Michael Meeker, Howard Rotblat-Walker, David M. Schneider, Mehdi Soraya, Jo-Ann Soraya, and Brian Spooner. I am indebted to John Perry for help with transliteration.

cause the greater separation of male and female worlds both socializes them to be independent and treats women in the "male world" as sexually neutral (Fallers and Fallers 1976). Much more research needs to be done in these areas of socialization and everyday male-female interaction, but what is clear is that modern demands for equality and liberation, for the educated and professional young woman,[1] are very often perceived by women as well as men as contradictory to the older demands for complementarity and harmony.

This perceived contradiction stems in part from and provides one of the intense moral conflicts between the emerging industrial-technocratic class system and the decaying patrimonial-agricultural class system.[2] Two historical acts may serve as an illustrative contrast. Upon the death in 922 A.D. of the famed mystic Mansur Hallaj, his sister appeared in public unveiled, and to shocked criticism responded, "Yesterday there was at least half a man in the world, today there is no man; for whom should I veil?" This ringing condemnation and challenge arise out of a very different vision of woman from that presented by Tahiri, Qurratu'l 'Ayn, in 1849 when she removed her veil to signal the equality of women with men as a basic principle of the new Babi religion. Among Muslims the argument for the liberation of women was made already in the twelfth century, but without much success, by Ibn Rushd (Averroes), following Plato: that to consign women to merely bearing children was to deny society half its labor power, to assure it a lower standard of living, and "because women in these states are not being fitted for any of the human virtues it often happens that they resemble plants" (Rosenthal 1971:65). In contemporary Persian terms the perceived contradiction in the values urged on women is most clearly articulated as a confrontation between conservative Muslim leaders and an aggressive modernizing state. Because the contradictory positions are grounded in social processes (changing class systems, antagonistic authority figures), they impose on young women (and men) psychological pressures in a way Ibn Rushd's speculations could not.

The changing position of Persian women can be seen in dual terms as, on the one hand, the erosion of an ideology that justifies the roles of men and women on the basis of communal and psychological harmony rather than individual achievement; and on the other hand, as a change in the means of enforcing male-female roles from small-scale peasant and merchant communities where a mixture of violence, pollution rules, and state legal facilities could be called on, to a fully bureaucratized modern state where violence (except by the state) is regarded as an infraction against social continuity, where pollution rules are redundant and regarded as silly, and where individuals rather than groups are held culpable. Two reasons for stressing these more general terms are, first, that while Iran is culturally dominated by Shiite Islam, other religious groups in Iran are undergoing similar changes, if more rapidly and less painfully; and second, that the changes in Iran have parallels with changes in the West.

Most of the ethnographic data comes from my experiences in Yazd (1970–71) and in Qum (1975). Yazd, a textile town of some hundred thousand people, has some four hundred Jews, four thousand Zoroastrians (counting villagers), and a considerable number of Bahais; the vast majority are Twelver Shiite Muslims. Qum is the major religious education center and the second major shrine town of Iran; it has no minority communities.

Indexes of Change

Despite lack of comprehensive statistics in Iran, the admission of women to education, public employment, suffrage, and legal responsibility is dramatic enough to be easily sketched. One need only compare Clara Colliver Rice's outrage in 1923 with Ruth Woodsmall's optimistic survey in 1960 and then look at the figures and legal changes since. Today, there are few areas excluded to women: aside from an activist queen, there have been two women cabinet ministers, a number of senators and Majlis representatives,[3] mayors, city councillors, writers, architects, lawyers, doctors, senior civil servants, journalists, and university professors. The statistics, of course, demonstrate vividly that only a beginning has been made. Iran still strains to catch up with Turkey, although it is decades ahead of Afghanistan and Saudi Arabia.[4] In the *1974 Iran Who's Who* (a rough index at best) only 272 or 7.5 percent of the entries are women. If one breaks the figures down by age group some improvement is seen. Figures on the relative increase of women university students are much more impressive,[5] although getting equal degrees does not yet mean obtaining equally good jobs.

The government claims to be, and is, among the major forces promoting change. There has been increasing public education for girls since the 1920s.[6] In 1935–36 Reza Shah attempted to unveil women by force. In 1940 the University of Tehran became coeducational. Since 1958 the current shah's sister, Princess Ashraf, has united the various women's groups into a High Council of Women's Organizations and has presented herself as patron and active promoter of women's emancipation.[7] Since 1963 women have been fully enfranchised, and female high school graduates have been inducted into the several national service corps (literacy, health), both to spread education, sanitation, and modern values, and to reinforce the respectability of unveiled women (corpswomen are supposed to wear uniforms). Schoolgirls also have uniforms, although some follow their elders—teachers, nurses, clerks—in provincial towns, putting on *chador*s (veils) after school or work to walk home. Finally, since 1967 women's legal rights have been slightly expanded to allow them greater freedom to initiate divorce suits and to make polygamy possible grounds for divorce.[8]

On the local level attitudes and practices lag behind the government push. Conservatives resist modern education for girls because, as an Isfahani craftsman put it: "*Chadori hastim* [we observe purdah]. I sent my daughter to school for six years but not longer. It is not good to send a girl to school 'naked'. I am teaching her to be a miniaturist at home and when she has fully mastered the skill, I will find her a husband. Why not let her choose a husband herself? Because youth chooses for immediate pleasure; older people consider more carefully what makes for a good, stable marriage." Similar feelings are widely expressed in Qum and are directly reflected in school attendance: in 1975 the ratio of boys to girls in elementary school was about two to one and in secondary school more than three to one. Change, however, is occurring even in the most conservative circles: two of the religious *madrasa*s (schools training religious leaders) in Qum have initiated parallel separate classes for girls. In one there are only female teachers; the other uses males who conduct classes from behind a curtain, directing questions by a seating chart. In other towns there are semireligious schools that allow girls to come in chadors and provide some general religious training (such as the Maktab Zarah in Shiraz, the Esmatiya in Yazd). These schools are staffed exclusively by females; in normal secular high schools the increasing use of male teachers for girls has caused many families to withdraw their daughters.

In the economic sphere, women have always been an important labor force in cottage industry—spinning, weaving, or even miniature painting as the above Isfahani girl—and agriculture. Today, they are gradually being drawn into the industrial labor force, as in the West earlier, as a separate cheap labor pool. Yazd textile mills hire women for unskilled tasks, physically separated from male workers, at the rate of the lowest paid unskilled men ($0.75 per day in 1970). Professional women are beginning to make some advances. In Yazd in 1970 they were restricted to teaching and nursing and one (Jewish) bank clerk; in 1975 a woman lawyer ran a close second in the three-way election for Parliament.

Erosion of an Ideology

In the last century an almost formulaic genre of Islamic apologia on the place of women has grown up (in Persian, Nuri 1343, Motaheri 1353, Tabatabai 1338, Voshnui 1392 [A.H.] and in English the Sunni work of the Pakistani Maududi 1972[9]). The formula has three parts of which the third is the most important. First comes a history of veiling (*hejab, pushesh*) and of the place of women in different societies. Here it is argued that Islam did not invent the veil and that the status of woman was elevated by Islam from that of chattel to that of a full person with legal rights: she may work, demand wages, get inheritance, control property, choose her spouse, and initiate divorce. The demand for women's liberation is depicted as rooted in the European experience of the industrial revolution (atomization of social relations, breakdown of family and village cooperation, increased sexual opportunities, and less need to marry in cities) and World War I (oversupply of women, widows and unmarried women forced to work, and work for low pay). It is argued that Iranian women do not have these experiences and problems, that their demands for liberation are misplaced imitations of the West, or even that sexual freedom and the consequent increased fixation on the battle of the sexes is an imperialist trick to keep Third World minds from thinking about true freedom (Sheriati n.d.: 26) and to sell European cosmetics and other sex-linked goods.

Second comes an analysis of the nature of men and women. Here it is argued that there are biological differences: men cannot bear children; menstruation is debilitating (pain, inability to concentrate); women are more emotional, men more rational; men are attracted to women, women need to be loved. Islam is defended as being natural, its regulations working with and not against the grain of nature. Third and most important are the moral arguments: sexual dynamics need to be regulated for social and psychological harmony; women have legal rights and are not prevented from fully participating in society; equality and justice are two different things.

Sexual dynamics in part belong to the analysis of nature; social regulation (Islam) must harmonize with this nature (God, nature, and Islam are one). Men and women, in Rumi's image, are like water and fire. If water is separated over a fire, it heats until it boils and steams; if there is no separation the water extinguishes the fire (Motaheri 1353:51). Open display of female beauty leads men to mental illness (desiring more than they are allowed or able to have; alleged ill effects of masturbation aggravated by explicit films, books, magazines). Free sex is empty sex destroying both love and marriage as a family bond: where sex is limited to husband and wife, marriage is the arena of sexual freedom; where sex is not so limited, marriage becomes a restriction, a prison. Love is a volatile natural force. It comes in many varieties (*shaghaf* or penetrating infatuation, *khilaba* or deceptive loss of one's sense through love, *hawa* or blameworthy lust, *'eshq* or laudatory love) and intensities and produces at least as much misery as joy. The suffering, violence, madness, and even death love can cause may be seen as tragic or evil, depending how voluntary the affliction. Never is the disease totally involuntary. Ibn al-Qayyim (1292–1350) uses the intoxication of drink as an analogy: the intoxication is involuntary for it is the effect of the alcohol on the body, but taking the first drink is voluntary (Giffen 1971: 128–129, passim). The intoxication of love leads to the overpowering of the rational soul by baser nature; the ensuing madness can lead to sins of incest, murder, and suicide, and to the enslavement of the self to another rather than reserving the only submission for God.

As men are enjoined to refrain from a second glance (*cheshmat darvish kon*), women are asked to refrain from being *zabandar* (flirtatious). This does not mean they should not take part in public life. A woman is required to behave and dress modestly, but she is not required to cover face or hands,[10] and she may engage in any activity and go any place a man may to the point of disturbing society by arousing desires.

What this means in practice is a division of labor incorporating separation of the sexes, justified by the contradistinction of equality and justice, and complementarity of natural differences. The arguments now become more tendentious. To require of women both female-specific roles (motherhood) and other roles (economic) is unfair (Maududi 1972:118). To insist that men and women should fill the same roles is like a parliamentary decree that all plants should flower in one season (Makarem, cited in Davani 1341:92). The philosophy of Islam is that one should keep management in the hands of the partner with more reason and keep spending in the hands of the partner with more emotion (Tabatabai 1338:25). Both men and women may choose their spouses and initiate divorce, but to give fully equal divorce rights to women only drives up the divorce rate, an antisocial result. A woman may not marry more than one man at a time so that paternity be known; a man may marry more than one woman but only if he can treat them equally. A daughter receives half a son's share of inheritance, but as a wife she is entitled to full support, a fact that Tabatabai calculates so as to make it appear that women in fact get twice as much as men: a man must give one of his two shares as support for his wife who already has a share, thus yielding two for her and one for him (Tabatabai 1338:25). Such abstractions, of course, are doubly false: a woman may inherit as much or more than a man;[11] a man does not support his wife merely on his inheritance.

It is good for women to study, and Goldziher is able to cite women in the medieval period who were important as links in the *isnad* (chains) of *hadith* (traditions), and women empowered to confer permission to perform various teaching and judicial roles on men as well as on other women (1971:366–368). If one asks casually whether there are any female Shiite *mojtaheds* (leaders who can make interpretations of the law for others to follow), one name will be forthcoming, that of Banu Amin Isfahani (d. 1977), author of a respected *tafsir* (commentary on the Quran). Possibly with qualification a learned woman of the past such as Amaneh Begum will also be named.[12] But upon reflection Muslim divines will deny to women the possibility of becoming a mojtahed, of becoming a leader of the Muslim community of men and women, of becoming more than a lecturer, teacher, or prayer leader of other women and of children, or of assisting their fathers and brothers as did Amaneh Begum. (Women played an important role as teachers in elementary religious schools for boys until the lads came of age.) For to be a religious leader and a model for others to follow, one must not be incapacitated religiously, intellectually, or biologically; and women are incapacitated in all three, say the most firm of the conservatives invoking a famous sermon of Ali. Religiously, women may not fulfill the fundamental duties of prayer, fasting, or pilgrimage when they are menstruating; "this abstention from worship is a proof of their deficiency in faith" (Qibla 1972:177). Intellectually, women are not able to learn from their five senses as are men partly because they are veiled and partly because they have less capacity, and so in law "the evidence of two women is equal to that of one man" (Qibla 1972:116). Biologically, women are less strong (in size, musculature, even eyesight and brainpower) and less sensitive (witness their ability to bear the pain of childbirth). Maududi goes so far as to insist that it is impossible for geniuses like Aristotle, Ibn Sina, Kant, or Hegel to come forth among women as it is for men to bear children (1972:120). Nuri, as if he were still in the nineteenth century, demonstrates this fact of nature by saying women statistically have smaller brains, hence less reason. Disregarding the contradiction between veiling here and the more liberal view cited above, the reasoning depends essentially on the assignment of reason to men. It is better for society if women do not participate in government, administration of justice, and war, for these areas relate to reason (Tabatabai 1338:29; Nuri 1343:268–270 cites hadith to this effect). Some women were given permission by the Prophet to fight, but when Ayesha, his widow, led an army against Ali, the first imam, she provoked his disparagements, cited above, of women and warnings against following their fickle lead; and she herself is said to have repented. The Quran assigns women a role obedient to men and the collected legal opinions of recent mojtaheds make being a male a requirement of being a mojtahed (see, for example, Shariatmadari 1353:9).[13]

When apologists assert that Islam raised the status of women beyond not only ancient savagery but also beyond that of the modern Frenchwoman, they refer not only to legal disabilities of women in the West, but primarily to the argument that because the Muslim woman is veiled, she can be treated as a person and not merely as a sex object; her person nonetheless is that of a female which differs from that of a male. However much Westerners may find these arguments open to charges of male chauvinism (there are female authors who argue the same line), the apologists' central point, however badly they make it, is a sincere moral vision. The key terms include *akhlaq* (morality), *estizan* (not invading others' privacy without permission or warning), *haya* (modesty), *namus* (honor), and *ensan* (the moral person). The key role model, which can have clearly liberal as well as conservative interpretations, is Zeinab who played a critical part in preserving Shiism by leading and speaking for the community while the fourth imam recovered from his wounds, but whose primary service was taking charge of domestic affairs at Karbala and on the trek to Damascus.[14]

Many of the contradictions felt today in the conservative Muslim vision derive from the changing social structure. The Muslim authors cited above are not far wrong in their analyses of the sources of demand for women's liberation in the West, nor in their perception of difference and a good deal of imitation in Iran. Things in Iran however have changed. The important "informal" female role in community religion is becoming attenuated as they themselves, at least in part, recognize when they say that Zeinab was a role model in the past and that today there is no model. The quasi-medical and pollution idioms that played a large part in women's lives (clean and unclean, hot and cold foods and illnesses, winds and physical loci of fears, evil eye and charms) are being devalued. Marriage as a web of legal and economic exchanges increasingly must fulfill the demands of individuals and nuclear families rather than extended families and whole villages, guilds or religious *mellets*. The initial stage of these changes is one in which men are given more positive replacements than women: it is men who are first educated and first drawn into the new economic roles, and who also are shouldered with greater burdens of paying for marriage and knowing what to do (illness, insurance, investment, and so on).

It was asserted that these changes do not only affect the Muslim community. The following sections will stress this by describing parallels in the marriage systems and community religious usages. The former have distinctly legal-economic rationales, the latter emotional support and manipulation.

Marriage and Inheritance

The changes in Iran can be thrown into sharper relief if a contrast is initially drawn with the Arab tribal stereotype. That stereotype—often confused with the situation in the Middle East at large—is constructed from three sources: partly from a logic of how to keep social order in the absence of a state, partly from Sunni jurisprudence, and partly from customs in certain Arab areas, such as a man's presumptive right to marry his father's brother's daughter (FBD), which he must waive if she is to marry someone else, and the obligation of men within five degrees of blood relation to answer affronts to the sexual honor and bodily integrity of the family. The stereotype stresses arranged marriages with explicit preference for the patrilateral parallel cousin, concern with namus (that honor which men lose through the misbehavior of their women), feuding over women as a constant expression of political and economic competition, patriarchal organization symbolized by bridewealth, and a lesser (if any) share of inheritance for daughters.[15]

While there are cultural continuities, the case on the Iranian Plateau differs markedly. Although there is a pervasive consciousness of namus, concern is less formalized, there is less use of named patrilineal groups, and a bilateral rather than a patrilineal ideology.[16] This is reflected in the legal system: the outstanding characteristic of the Shiite law of inheritance in contrast to the Sunni schools is its refusal to accord any special place to agnates (Coulson 1971:108ff). And third, the existence of a state places constraints on local communities: feuds and raiding will not be allowed to get out of control; joint tax and criminal liability of villages, guilds, or religious communities will force a degree of social cohesion; and indeed the state may promote an ideology of endogamy as a means of maintaining the functional units of society.[17] The Sassanian high priest Tansar argued for endogamy of the four strata of society on these grounds; and while the Islamic principle of marrying equals is opposed to this, in some areas it is interpreted to support similar medieval theories of stratification.[18] With the expansion of a salary and wage market as the way of organizing the labor of society, the ideology of the state has changed to promote individual mobility, both of men and women.

The transition between these two ideological stances of the state can be seen in Yazdi marriage behavior and rationales. The general rate of endogamous marriage is about one in three. The rate of landholding gentry can rise to above one in two, and that for upwardly mobile merchant families can be even higher. Similar patterns hold for Muslims, Zoroastrians, and Jews.[19] An obvious suggestion of these figures is that cousin marriage can be used as a strategy to concentrate and conserve wealth either in agricultural land or mercantile capital. But these are not necessarily the first rationales invoked by Yazdis.

Marrying with kin (*khish o qom*) or with strangers (*ghair*) is conceived as a dilemma of choosing between two desirable goals: for the health of the children, marriage with strangers is better; for marital harmony and stability, kin marriage is better. There are two traditional sayings frequently cited in support of endogamy: "trade out, marry in" and "father's brother's daughter marriages were/are sealed in heaven." The latter, however, is explained away as a divine sanction for one of several divinely acceptable marriages,[20] and hadith and *sunna* (precedents) exist opposing as well as supporting cousin marriage.[21] Ali (the first imam) married his father's brother's son's daughter but for his second marriage demanded a healthy and unrelated girl. The Prophet Muhammad is said to have urged marriage with strangers as a means of spreading Islam, setting the pattern himself,[22] a strategy now supported by Bahais. In Yazdi folk theory this often becomes the observation that if you marry out, you increase your kin networks: marrying in is redundant and you gain no new contacts. That in-marrying tightens family relations is a reason cited against it by modernist young people who want to assert their independence. Young men say that a girl from outside the family will be shy and obedient whereas a girl from the family will nag, complain that she does not have as many nice things as others, and so on. This is an obvious function of her knowledge of the strength of her structural position: if you beat or divorce a stranger girl, you only make her kin angry at you; but if you do the same to a relative, you cut yourself off from your own kin as well and so isolate yourself. On the other hand, to marry out is to marry a relatively unknown quality both in terms of moral behavior and again in terms of a structural leverage over her behavior.

No data are available to evaluate to what extent people are forced to marry against their will in the service of familial goals. Threats of suicide (both male and female) and postmarriage complaints are not infrequent. On the other hand, in a village community there is less pressure on the nuclear family: one's spouse need not be one's only confidant or even best friend. Extended kin and same-sex cohorts can be relied on for companionship and support. Conflicts perhaps arise in severe form when communities become smaller and status differentials increase (either the case of minorities in the process of withdrawal such as the Jews of Yazd, or the case of upwardly mobile status groups and individuals). These examples from my field research happen to be Zoroastrian; similar ones could be cited from other communities.

> A village boy became a white collar administrator. He wished to marry a girl from a large semiurban family. It was a good match for the latter, and to consummate the deal, he was able to arrange that one of her brothers take his sister. The second youngest of four sons did so and is unhappy about it, but finds it tolerable.

> Two families of equal status had complementary pairs of children. When the elder daughter of one was engaged to the elder son of the other, it was tentatively agreed that when the younger brother of the girl was of age, he should reinforce the bonds by taking the younger girl as his wife. When the time came, he had become an educated man with good future prospects. His intended father-in-law, however, had fallen to near the bottom of the village hierarchy. The young man reluctantly honored the family agreement.

> Another marriage between a well-educated man, a physician, and a peasant girl illustrated how status differentials can increase to the point of intolerability. As long as the doctor lived in Iran, the marriage was tolerable, but when he emigrated to America, where he had been trained, the differential was too much and he left the wife.

In a village community, just as one need not depend exclusively on one's spouse, so material support for the family is more dispersed than in the bourgeois isolated nuclear family. Division of inheritance after the father's death can have the effect of tying children to an undivided estate until fairly late in life, and in villages practicing preferential endogamy, legal division of estates can be put off for quite some time. At the time of a new marriage, support comes from both sides. The Muslims are the most explicit: *sedagh, mahr,* or *mahriya* is from the groom's side; *jehaziya* (dowry) is from the bride's. The mahr is an amount of money contracted by the groom at the time of marriage as payable to the bride on demand but primarily should he divorce her. Usually only a fraction is paid at the time of marriage. It is said that it is to the bride's advantage that it not be paid until divorce becomes a real possibility, since then payment can serve as a deterrent. The portion paid at the time of marriage is sometimes called *shir baha* (milk price) and theoretically is to pay the mother of the bride for bringing up the girl. In practice the milk price should be a nest egg for the bride or for use in providing the dowry brought by the bride, usually consisting of the furnishings for the house: cooking utensils, carpets, and so on. The house is provided by the groom.

The Zoroastrian pattern is similar. While there is today no formal mahr—which they relate to the fact that, unlike the easy divorce procedure of Islam, Zoroastrianism did not allow divorce; divorce is a twentieth-century innovation[23]—informally a similar division of responsibility is recognized: house from the groom, furnishings from the bride. Ideal ratios of the value contributed by each family differ: Zoroastrians, since they recognize no mahr, perceive a greater financial burden on the bride's family, perhaps as much as three to one, whereas Muslims usually place the burden inversely at one to two or more, except where patrilocal marriage is common and the burden is seen as greater on the bride's family.[24] In practice, of course, the ratio is determined by bargaining based on the circumstances of the families.[25] In the past Zoroastrians did recognize a formal mahr: the medieval *rivayat*s (answers to queries from the Indian community by the priests in Iran) not only recognize a mahr but specify a ceremonial amount—2,000 dirhams of pure white silver and two dinars of red gold of the Nishapur currency—although it is noted that this is only a formula and should be adjusted to the circumstances of the parties (Dhabhar 1932:197). Should the husband die intestate, the mahr is settled along with other debts before the inheritance is divided.

Again, Zoroastrians like to claim that "traditionally," brothers and sisters received equal shares of inheritance, and this may at times have been the case, but the rivayats recognize a division similar to the Islamic rule of two parts for a son and one part for a daughter. In the last century in Yazd (but not Kerman) daughters received no inheritance share; during the great migrations of males to Bombay (late nineteenth, early twentieth centuries) wives left behind applied to be placed under Islamic law to receive a share of inheritance as a source of income while their husbands were away.[26] Similar ebbs and flows in Muslim inheritance patterns occur: whether or not it can be maintained according to Islamic law, people will agree to the suggestion that the mahriya and jehaziya compensate a woman for only half a male portion of patrimony; and often jehaziya is considered to be that share of patrimony.

The Jewish pattern is similar: although like Zoroastrians they claim in casual conversation to have no mahriya, as a way of dissociating themselves from Muslims, they do have one: the *ketubah* or *mohar habbtulot.* Loeb reports that in Shiraz the ketubah price has been rising to make it more effective against divorce. The ratio in the past has been three to one, ketubah to dowry. Again, daughters receive no inheritance on the grounds that they have received their share in the dowry, and an attempt by the chief rabbi of Israel to introduce the Quranic inheritance rule of half a share for daughters failed for this reason (Loeb 1970:184–186). Like the Muslim case, the stress among the Jews is on payment to the bride rather than to her father: a fixed sum in case of divorce or widowhood, a pledge of support through widowhood, a pledge that male children will inherit the ketubah if she dies while married to the husband, and that female children will be raised by the husband until they marry.

The pattern of marriage exchanges, thus, is similar for all three groups—Muslim, Zoroastrian, Jew—and apparently stems from quite ancient times since similar terms can be found in the cuneiform texts of Mesopotamia (Levine 1968). It is not as rigid as the Arab tribal stereotype, but marriage bargaining involves attention to status and wealth. A Muslim wife had legal grounds against her husband if he did not support her according to her status; he had legal grounds against her if she tainted his status either sexually (through immodesty, adultery) or by taking a job he deemed improper. If the traditional patterns are similar, so are the effects of the modern economy. When young men get independent sources of income in the form of salaries or by setting up shops, it is usual for them to supply both house and furnishings as well as mahr and a nest egg. This expectation may mean a significant postponement of marriage as compared to peasants. Among Westernized Muslims who find the legal requirement of mahr tainted with the hint of bride purchase, a symbolic payment, a gold Pahlavi coin or a Quran, may be given instead of real wealth.

Community Religion

If marriage is one mechanism of locking men and women into social position and redistributing wealth from generation to generation, community rituals are another set of mechanisms of social cohesion and community mental health that are now being loosened. Women and female symbolism played a prominent role. Somewhat parallel to the Jewish notion that the active presence of God is feminine (the *Shekhhineh*) is the Islamic Sufi notion that God's mystery is a veiled bride. One's identity for purposes of fortune telling and curing was always determined by one's mother's name. Legendary women were central to the focus of popular Shiite worship—Fatimeh, Zeinab, Bibi Shahrbanu, Hazrat-e Masumeh, the Chehel Dokhtaran shrines[27]—and similar female saints are housed in four of the five major shrines of Yazdi Zoroastrians. Women ran certain ritual feasts and practiced evil eye projection techniques. With two exceptions (the shrine of Bibi Shahrbanu; the feast of Bibi Sehshambeh) these rituals were not exclusively female, but their strong female character conforms to the traditional assignment of regulation of emotional and psychological health to women.

For Zoroastrian women there is a monthly pilgrimage cycle: on the second day of the month (Bahman Day) there is a visit to the shrine of Pir-e Vameru, on the sixteenth (Mehr Day) to the fire temple, on the twentieth (Bahram Day) to the shrine of Shah Bahram Izet, and on the twenty-sixth (Ashtad Day) to the shrine of Seti Pir.[28] At these shrines one prays, and prepares a kind of *sofreh* (tablecloth set with food offerings), and often cleans the chaff off roasted chick-peas. The procedure at Pir-e Vameru will illustrate:

> The shrine room contains five oil lamps, four of which are set on white bricks at the four corners of the sofreh (tablecloth). On the sofreh are donations of roasted chick-peas, sugar ball sweets, dried fruits and nuts, fresh fruit, sugar cones, myrtle, cypress twigs, and an incense holder. On the walls are hung dolls of men and women, called Bibi Kuk, which are placed there by childless women in hopes of conceiving. Tea and oil bread are made by people who have vowed to do some act of charity, and stew is cooked for lunch. As at any shrine the form of worship is individual prayer, reciting favorite sections of the Avesta such as the Bahram Yasht, the appropriate Yasht for the day, and so on. But in mid-morning everyone attempts to squeeze into the room to listen to

> the recitation of the story done by an old lady. The fresh fruit on the sofreh is quartered, one piece placed in each corner. The reciter then tells the story in flat somber tones while gazing into a mirror. A second woman beats a slow rhythm with a spoon on a bowl of water and punctuates the recitation with soft *baleh*s ("yes . . . yes"). When the recitation is finished, the mirror is passed around and people line their eyes with the ash of pistachio or walnut which is supposed to give energy and general health. The bowl of water is passed around and the water is poured into one's hand. Sweets are passed around. People then break up into more informal groups outside the room. Some clean roasted chick-peas; others serve stew; others just chat, read palms, and relax.

Other sofrehs and the recitation of their stories are prepared on various occasions (see Fischer 1973:223–228). The themes of the legends are that while human beings are limited in knowledge and ability to control events, difficulties and the drudgery of work can at times be facilitated miraculously, and that the giving of help to others is a prerequisite for good fortune. The active supernatural agents in all these legends are female. A work story, named *Moshkel* (difficulty) *gosha* (from *goshadan,* to open, to solve), is told in longer or shorter versions while cleaning roasted chick-peas which then are also called "moshkel gosha." The chick-peas are for cooking, but some are taken whenever one visits shrines to be left there and to be handed out upon return as a kind of sharing with others the efficacy of the pilgrimage.

The pilgrimages (and others to more local shrines and to the major shrines visited in an annual cycle as well as for occasional vows) and sofrehs give women occasions to organize themselves, vary their routine, gossip and exchange information, arrange social affairs with women from other villages, and rejuvenate an idiom of health and good works for their families and menfolk as well as themselves. The rejuvenation and social relation building activity is done in a more specific way in evil eye procedures, for example, one called *chameru chachi:*

> A woman ties a cloth over her head with only two holes for the eyes and covers her hands so no one may recognize her; she takes a sack and goes to the fire temple and prays to God, stating that she is acting to help such and such a sick individual. She then goes into the alleys and knocks at every door but must not speak. People give crystalline sugar candy and grams for a soup and say a blessing, but at the same time they try to grab something out of the sack. Should they succeed it is auspicious for them, but usually the woman beats them off with a stick. The woman returns to the fire temple with the sack and prays. The collected food is shared between the poor and the ill person.

There are various other procedures such as writing names of suspected people with evil eye in charcoal on eggs at a trivium, and various prophylactic devices against illness and for good luck. But the point of the evil eye procedures of divination and dispersal are to alert the community to possible social sources of conflict and thereby to mobilize supportive feelings and action.

Muslim and Zoroastrian community rituals are variations on a pattern. Muslim women hold sofrehs in the name of Sekineh, Abul Fazl, Roqayeh, and Umm Kolsum,[29] either in private homes or at shrines. The Muslim sofreh usually involves inviting a preacher to read an appropriate preachment (*rauzeh*). One Muslim version of Moshkel gosha turns to the events of the Battle of Karbala at the end of each section of the story. The shrine of Sayyid Fathuddin Reza in Yazd currently has many sofrehs because several people experienced cures there. Special preachments for women are regular events; although normally males do the preaching, female preachers are appreciated. During Moharram in 1975 a large forum was filled by a female preacher from Tehran; males were rigorously excluded. *Charchin* is the Muslim variant of chameru chachi (a woman dresses up in clothes of indeterminate sex, with a cloak and a face veil, and collects items of food from each house). *Nazr gereftan* and *tir-e Hazrat-e ʿAbbas* are other techniques to determine the evil eye possessor who caused an illness and to find a thief. Shrine legends are transformations of the Zoroastrian shrine stories (see Fischer 1973).

Continuous with these rituals are ideas about purity and pollution, health and illness. Before one goes to a shrine or performs a ritual, one must be ritually pure. All three religious traditions—Zoroastrian, Muslim, Jewish—have codes of pollution and rules for purification, which include menstruation as one item of pollution. The Zoroastrian code requires the severest separation of a menstruating woman. According to the *Vendidad* (Fargard XVI) no one may approach her within three paces, food is handed her in metal vessels,[30] and she should not be given meat or other invigorating food that might strengthen the fiend of pollution and make her issue stronger. After the menstruation has ceased, she purifies herself with an ablution of two washings with consecrated bull's urine and one with water over three holes in the ground.[31] Menstrual blood for Zoroastrianism is one of the set of *nasu* (dead, decaying, polluting material) which includes corpses and tissues detached from a living body (cut hair, nail parings, spittle, semen). There is a major nine-day purification for more serious pollution (like bearing a still-born child) or simply for more thorough purification. This ritual (*bareshnum*) in recent years has ceased to be used by Yazdi women, and younger women have little patience for any of the menstrual segregation rules.

For Shiism, blood is one of the ten or twelve items of *najasat* (ritual uncleanness), a set including sexual sweat, feces, urine, and the touch of a non-Muslim. As in Judaism, the intent of purity rules (Arabic *taharat,* Hebrew *taharot*) has to do with cleanliness for prayer (see the explanations of Maimonides 1954, 1956). In both Islam and Judaism there are a series of graded forms of ablution and purification from the more serious and less frequent pollutions to the least serious and more frequent. Menstruation is a periodic pollution more serious than blood from a cut, and it involves a full ablution (Muslim *ghosl,* Jewish *miqvah*) before prayer or entering a holy place. Although in one sense Jewish women have the longest period of pollution (seven days of purification) of the three religions, unlike the complete separation of Zoroastrian women, Jewish and Muslim women are only enjoined against sexual intercourse and touching holy objects; daily life is not disturbed otherwise. Ghosl itself is not unduly burdensome and is enjoined on men after seminal emission, after touching a corpse on behalf of a deceased relative, and for certain vows; women should perform it after menstruation, intercourse, childbirth, touching a corpse, or abnormal bleeding.

The separation of menstruating women is a double-edged sword: it reinforces sex-role differences but it also allows women a sphere of manipulation—a ready excuse for refusing sexual intercourse or participating in rituals. Muslim women need not make up prayers missed during menstruation, and divorce proceedings initiated during a woman's menstruation are not valid (Milani n.d.:27–28).[32]

Honor, Dignity, Liberation, and Emancipation

The erosion of the conservative ideology is due both to the breakdown of its social basis in small-scale agricultural and urban communities and to the changes in the state ideology. The three major arenas of conflict with the emerging industrial ideology are notions of honor recognized by law, notions of veiling and modesty, and notions of appropriate division of labor.

Legally enforceable notions of honor, an important prop of the conservative ideology, no longer exist. A constant theme in popular Persian films is the duty of male relatives to revenge in blood the raping of heroines before the police and courts can intervene. No longer are there religious courts that could enforce the honor code of the law (*bab-e diasat*), impose blood price in cases of murder, or allow stoning in severe cases of adultery; therefore duties of revenge become issues of personal morality. In real life, as R. Antoun (1968) stresses for the Arab case, blood revenge is, and probably always has been, a last resort solution when other ways of protecting family and personal social standing have failed. The use of murder as a final admission of inability to resolve conflicts of honor is illustrated by an unusual case in Yazd:

> A married teacher fixed up a colleague with a bride. The colleague discovered she was not a virgin and refused to have her. The teacher offered him large sums of money not to say anything, for he had been her lover. After repeated refusals, the teacher enticed the colleague into a car and out into the desert where he was bludgeoned and then both body and car burned in a vain attempt to obliterate the affair.

On the other hand, in a well-known case of adultery, the woman was thrown out by her husband; murder by either husband or father or brother was not considered to be the only or necessary response. However, the woman now supports her father, a healer and opium addict, by prostitution. Muslim preachers, as Fallers and Fallers (1976) also note for Turkey, caution against jumping to conclusions about male-female indiscretions. Verbal insinuation (*ghaibat*) is a major sin. False accusation—were there Islamic courts—is punishable under the section of Islamic law protecting reputations.

The honor of one's women (namus) and one's reputation (*abru*) in contemporary Iran are flexible idioms of fallible personal morality rather than terms with legal import. Concern for the honor of another man is a valued quality called *ghairat* and an important part of the male code of conduct:

> Late one freezing cold night, I and three other males were stranded in the middle of the desert. After one of several cars which had vainly stopped to offer help in repairing our car had gone on, one of the young men through chattering teeth said he would have asked for a ride had the man's namus (honor) not been in the car.

A model is the oath of allegiance accepted by Ali from the women at the time of his appointment as successor to Muhammad: he did not take their hand as he would a man's, but put his hand in a bowl of water, and they without touching his, dipped in their hands one by one.

Rules of conduct, however, are complicated by conflicting notions of propriety and modernity. These come clearly to the fore over the issue of women's veils. In the 1930s Reza Shah, following Ataturk, attempted to abolish the veil as a major symbol of backwardness. Ayatullah Qumi and other Shiite leaders countered with a publicity campaign in defense of the conservative moral vision. Their temporary defeat is still symbolized in the folk memory by the Meshed riot of 1935 during a preachment by the popular Bahlul. When Reza Shah abdicated, women returned to a modified form of the veil without face masks. The veil thus no longer provides anonymity but is a complex moral device operated along at least three domains.

First there is the modesty component. In a chador (veil) a woman is theoretically free to use the public streets and to go to mosque and preachments, although the territorial and behavioral patterning is somewhat more subtle. M. C. Bateson and M. Good (personal communication) suggest:

> (a) Major streets and squares are primarily for men; women use back alleys; women may be bothered on one side of a main street but not the other; (b) women must always look as if they are busy, going somewhere; (c) women must not ignore males around them nor engage in sustained eye contact: there is a brief eye contact to acknowledge and convey disinterest.

One must add that a woman must look and respond modestly. In conservative areas a chador half-way back on the head, flashes of painted fingernails and toenails, and a jaunty walk are invitations for verbal propositioning and manhandling. Women may react to propositioning and manhandling with responses intended to shame or curse, but the range of repartee seems limited since response carries the danger of encouraging further exchanges. Appeal to third parties is more effective, either by screaming and cursing on the spot to mobilize other men against the offender, or by appealing to the manhood of a strong bystander, or in the case of a chronic offender by complaining to his family or superiors. The issues here are those already discussed: men keeping their gaze chaste, respecting other men's honor, and women not being flirtatious or immodest. Thus, under the pressure of the times, religious liberals can discern that what Islam requires is nonprovocative dress and a headscarf.[33] It is interesting that the headscarf remains so important, for it indicates that to many people the rules of hair covering are symbolically more deeply rooted than as mere rational signs of modesty.[34]

Second, there is a status manipulation component. Not only are veils rough markers of stratification, from villages (in the past and still today often headcloths without chadors) to lower-class urban (veils tied around the waist to allow free use of hands when working) to traditional upper class (full veiling whenever in public); but veils are also markers of intimacy from sons, brothers, husbands (no veils) to close friends and near kin (loose veiling) to the stranger (veiling to the point of covering all but one eye). Modern status, today, is marked by being without veil or with a pastel-colored or transparent veil, or by wearing the veil halfway back on the head so as not to cover all the hair.

Third, there is a religious-political component. In the past, non-Muslims, like the Jews, were forced to wear distinctively marked chadors, and in times of severe political confrontation (especially in western Iran) even to go unveiled ("naked," shameless and demonstrating their menfolk's impotence), thus inviting further abuse. Today Jewish women and Bahai women of Muslim origin in Yazd wear the Muslim chador; Zoroastrian women and Bahai women of Zoroastrian origin wear a headcloth. For modern-oriented Muslim women, the veil is merely a symbol of respect to be put on when entering a holy place. In shrine towns like Qum, women may even go so far as to put on headcloths under the chador and face veils.

Veils, thus, are flexible. They are as well practical equipment against dust, in place of having to dress up to go out, for napping blankets, privacy in nursing, and so on; and adjusting them judiciously can be an effective flirting technique. State pressure to unveil still exists, but through the schools, national service, and the open life-style of the elite and foreigners. This together with the push to achieve economic, educational, marital, and legal equality for women is the third arena of conflict between progressives and conservatives. In 1959 Ayatullah Borujerdi blocked the Women's Organization from staging the kind of public celebration it wished to mark the official day of emancipation of women by Reza Shah (Binder 1964:198, 251, 295, 297). In 1963 a concerted campaign was waged by the Shiite leadership against enfranchising women (Davani 1341). In 1970 a preacher was arrested for suggesting that the conscription of women into the national service corps was against Islam. In 1975 one of the issues dramatized by a demonstration in Qum was the "freedom" of women, that is, their falling into Western immorality and colonialism.

It is largely a symbolic battle. The old social patterns are changing. Women were not so restricted as either male ideology or Western feminists suppose. The battle is essentially one for domination between the old agro-mercantile-military gentry with its ideology of the genteel woman in purdah, and the new professional-bureaucratic-technocrats with their ideology of personal worth valued in individual achievement. Description is somewhat complicated because the personnel of the gentry are among the first to move into the professional classes. Aspects of the old ideology are preserved longer by the old dominated classes. What should be at issue are the meanings and goals of future social life. Liberation should not end with the victory over old patterns. Persian society, like European society, has a memory of a less atomized *Gemeinschaft* and a notion of human dignity (*ensan*), both of which should be trained upon the future to humanize industrial society—to seek emancipation in Simone de Beauvoir's sense of stimulating individuals to transcend given circumstances and actively work out rewarding projects. Neither the shah nor the religious conservatives seem much disposed toward this,[35] but social development with the help of sentient participants may be able to move beyond them both. The queen, for one, as befits her traditional female role (managing the emotional life), seems more receptive.

Notes

1. Young women, since older women have always been somewhat freer to participate in the "male sphere" and to ignore female etiquette.

2. On the notion of two class systems, see also Ahmad Ashraf (1971) and chapter 24 by Good.

3. Dr. Farokhru Parsay, an M.D. and the first woman Majlis representative, has served as minister of education, and in January 1976 Mahnaz Afkhami was made minister for women's affairs. The Twenty-Third Majlis contained fifteen women (of 268 seats); the Sixth Senate contained three women (of 30 seats), two elected, one appointed.

4. Istanbul University allowed women into a special section in 1915 and began full coeducation in 1921. Tehran University became coeducational in 1940. Saudi Arabian women were admitted to university in the 1960s but receive instruction from male teachers only through television.

5. In the decade 1962–63 to 1971–72, female enrollment in higher education increased sevenfold from 4,183 to 28,869; male enrollment increased threefold from 20,273 to 68,469. The eight major universities make up 45.5 percent of these figures (Institute for Research and Planning 1973a:15, 17). In 1971–72 women comprised more than a third of the total number of graduates in medicine and humanities; more than a fourth but less than a third in natural sciences and math; less than a fourth in law, social sciences, and education; and less than a tenth in agriculture and engineering (Institute for Research and Planning 1973b:7).

6. Rice says there were 1,200 girls in 10 free primary schools in 1923 (1923:154). Zaidi gives a figure of 21,389 girls in 190 girls' schools in 1930 (1937:37).

7. See Woodsmall (1960) for a list of women's organizations and mention

of a Federation of Women's Organizations which emerged in 1956 but was eclipsed for better or worse two years later by Ashraf's High Council. The current unified, government-supported Women's Organization is essentially a social-work operation providing literacy classes, vocational training, family planning advice, and so on.

8. A wife may apply for a certificate of nonreconciliation if her husband marries another woman, but the court can allow a second wife and refuse the first wife's request (Naqavi 1971:9, 69, 70), although according to the press this is rare. Other disabilities also still exist for women. A husband can bar a woman from an occupation that damages his or her family's position (Naqavi 1971:9, 34). At divorce, the father is normally given custody of the children: males under two and females under seven remain with the mother until they attain those ages (Naqavi 1971:44). Wives require notarized permission from their husbands to get exit visas to travel abroad. (Changes in the law in 1975 improved women's family position —*eds.*)

9. I am indebted to Mehdi Abedi for helping me translate the Persian texts cited in this section. Nuri and Motaheri are professors at the University of Tehran; Tabatabai, their teacher, is the dean of philosophy in Qum; Voshnui was tapped by the late Ayatullah Borujerdi to present an Islamic account of the place of women; Maududi is a leading Pakistani religious leader. Others to be cited below are Naser Makarem, a prominent mojtahed and teacher in Qum; Dr. Ali Sheriati (d. 1977), a French-trained Islamic reformist and hero of the religious youth; and Shariatmadari, one of the three major *marja' taqlid* (chief mojtahed) of Qum.

10. See the hadith of the Prophet, Imam Sadeq, and Imam Bagher cited by Motaheri 1353:122. The Quran used the word *hejab* (veiling, seclusion) only once (Surah Ahzab:54), to say that the women of the Prophet are different from other women. The injunctions for other women have to do with propriety and the morality of *estizan* (asking permission or giving warning of entering where there are women).

11. For instance, if a son dies, his father and mother get equal shares.

12. Daughter of Muhammad Taghi (Majlesi I), wife of Molla Saleh Mazandarani, and assistant in legal matters to her brother Muhammad Bagher (Majlesi II). She is acknowledged as a mojtahed by Ali Davani (1340:39–40).

13. Technically, a woman may become a mojtahed entitled to use her own *ijtihad* (interpretive reasoning), but not a mojtahed whom others may follow, making the appellation honorific but essentially meaningless. James Bill's sentence, "Iran has a colorful history of female mojtaheds" (1972:28), must thus be read as a loose usage of the word in the same sense as Ali Davani's description of Amaneh Begum as a mojtahed. Bill's cited source, however, gives no evidence of a colorful history of female mojtaheds.

14. Zeinab, Imam Hosein's sister, was the caravan leader of the survivors of Karbala. At their captor's court, she delivered a sermon on *shahadat*

(witnessing for God, being martyred), which brought many back to the Shiite cause. Her political role lasted until her nephew was recovered sufficiently to deliver a sermon that shamed the captors. She ruled the domestic scene at Karbala before the battle and her medical skills saved the life of her nephew. Her mother, Fatimeh, also played a public political role, giving two famous sermons on the inequity of those who seized the caliphate after the Prophet's death.

15. The stereotype is overdrawn. Rights to land and other resources and to personal protection and sustenance are vested to varying degrees in patrilineal groups named by tribal, clan, or lineage ancestors.

16. Not even Sayyids (descendants of the Prophet), despite their patrilineal genealogies, provide an exception.

17. A controversy exists as to whether next-of-kin marriage is advocated in the Zoroastrian sacred texts. While some orientalists (Boyce) and anthropologists (Slotkin, Spooner) choose to believe *qaetvadatha* in the Avesta and elsewhere has this meaning, others (Frye, Goodenough, myself) remain convinced by Sanjana's (1888) exhaustive refutation that this is etymological and contextual nonsense. It derives from charges by Greek authors against the Persians and parallels normal slander against almost any religious group in the Middle East, today most viciously whispered against the Bahais.

18. See especially the Yemen case where *kafa'a* (marrying equals) is interpreted as marrying within one's status group (Bujra 1971: chap. 4). See also Gibb 1961:7.

19. A sample of 381 Muslim marriages elicited from 126 respondents in a Yazd factory and in the Yazd bazaar on own, parental, sibling, and children's marriages yielded 109 or 29 percent as kin marriages (FBD-33, FZD-19, MBD-25, MZD-15, MFBD-2, FMBD-2, MMBD-1, MMZDD-1, FZSD-1, MZDD-2, FFBSD-1, far family-6, unknown-1). Of 56 marriages on a genealogy of the petty aristocracy of the hills to the south of Yazd, nearly half (27) were with kin. An even higher percentage was obtained from non-gentry in the isolated villages behind Bafq. For village Zoroastrians, of 539 marriages, 196 or 36 percent were with kin. A Yazd Zoroastrian merchant family genealogy yielded 53 marriages of which 19 were with kin, but of the 34 with non-kin at least ten were Bahais who have an ideology of marrying out. For comparison, among Parsis (Indian Zoroastrians) in rural Gujurat the one in three cousin-marriage figure is again approximated; and in a merchant family of Bombay, in the fifth descending generation from the founder, of 66 marriages, 39 were between kin and only 15 are definitely between non-kin. For Yazdi Jews 16 of 47 counted marriages were between kin.

The general range of these figures is confirmed by other studies such as the nutritional survey of villages in Fars run by Namazi Hospital (Livingston and Mahloudji 1970:38–39), and the Goods' study of Maragheh in Azarbaijan (personal communication). For Jews in Shiraz, Loeb gives a similar figure of 144 of 425 marriages between kin (1970:167–169).

20. Adam had two sons, Havil and Gavil (Cain and Abel). To Havil God gave a woman of the *mala'ek* (archangel), and to Gavel a woman of the *jinn*. Havil had a son, Gavil a daughter. They asked God what to do, and he approved their marriage. In other words, the first marriage problem happened to involve a father's brother's daughter marriage and God sanctioned it; it does not follow that everyone should try to marry a FBD, but if one does, the action is known to be acceptable to God.

21. See Falsafi (n.d. 11:275–282) for a discussion of hadith both pro and con, philosophical opinions on incest, and medical opinions on inbreeding. Falsafi draws the conclusion that if there were anything really wrong with endogamy, God knows all and would have made it *haram* (forbidden).

22. Twelve of his thirteen wives were older widows. Five were married to make their tribes sympathetic to Islam (Ayesha, Hafsa, Umma Habiba, Maymuna, Safiyya); two to demonstrate that war captives should be well-treated (Juwairiyya; the Jewish woman Safiyya); one to demonstrate that no stigma should attach to ex-slaves and that adopted sons are not to be counted as blood sons in incest regulations (Zeid, an ex-slave and Muhammad's adopted son, married and divorced Muhammad's cousin Zeinab, whom Muhammad then married); and two to prevent them from following their ex-husbands into Christian conversion (Sauda, Umma Habiba).

23. The medieval rivayats recognize two grounds for divorce: male impotence is not one; female sterility is ground for bigamy, not divorce. Apostasy and desertion are grounds for wives to remarry, but absentee husbands who return and find their wives remarried may reclaim them. Adultery by a wife is cause for death, but since Iran is ruled by Muslims, she may be punished by being abandoned without a guardian, or with her husband's consent she may remarry. The last and apostasy are the only recognized grounds for divorce.

24. See Kendall 1968:97. *Patrilocal* should be used with care. In the Yazd area, while there is a tendency to live near the husband's father, living with or near the wife's parents is not unusual. The same is true of the Kashan area (Rudolph-Touba and Beeman 1971:18).

25. The procedure is formalized among Muslims as it is not among Zoroastrians. The Muslim groom theoretically does not see the bride until the wedding night, although normally both bride and groom are given opportunities for at least seeing their intended *sub rosa*. In villages of Kerman, the bargaining may be done in a formal meeting of males at which the fathers of the bride and groom may sit next to each other, but remain silent throughout (R. Dillon, personal communication). Women are important initiators and brokers in the matchmaking.

26. Today Zoroastrians are under a uniform legal code, *Ain Nameh Zartoshtian*, adopted around 1935, which approximates Muslim codes except that a Muslim may freely bequeath only one-third of his property;

two-thirds must go by the Islamic formula, whereas a Zoroastrian may compose a will as he wishes.

27. Fatimeh, wife of Ali and daughter of the Prophet, not only is constantly invoked in prayer and parable, but her death is a major memorial, celebrated twice, for up to ten days each time, since the date of the death is disputed. Bibi Shahrbanu, legendary wife of Imam Hosein and daughter of the last Sassanian king, has a major shrine in Rey where only women are admitted. Fatimeh, Hazrat-e Masumeh, sister of Imam Reza, inhabits the shrine at Qum. The Forty Virgins (Chehel Dokhtaran) are said to have been miraculously taken into the earth to escape Zoroastrian armies; there are many so-named shrines.

28. I am indebted to the late Banu Luti Nasrabadi for initially taking me to these events.

29. The daughter, half-brother, daughter, and sister of Hosein, respectively. Sekineh was also a noted poet.

30. Metal does not conduct or absorb impurity and thus can be purified as porous materials cannot.

31. The number three has to do with the ethical dedication *goftarinik, pendarinik, kerdarinik* (good works, good thoughts, good deeds). *Gomez* (consecrated bull's urine) is a product of the bovine representation of Good.

32. The rule that divorce may not be initiated during menstruation has to do with a period of waiting: a full cycle from menstruation to menstruation without sexual intercourse must pass before divorce may be initiated, with a few exceptions. Further, since menstruation is regarded as a period of instability both for women and for the marriage relation, the rationale is that a serious step like divorce should be done deliberately when such disequilibrating factors are not present.

33. This is the solution for religious women traveling to Europe these days.

34. There is a stock comic scene (for instance, in the film *Droshky-chi*) of an unveiled woman, surprised by the entry of a man, so anxious to cover her head hair that she pulls her skirt over her head. Anthropologists have long speculated about symbolic connections between head hair and pubic hair. See Hershman (1974) for a recent review.

35. See the outbursts of the Shah in his now famous interview with Oriana Fallaci (1973).

Bibliography

Antoun, Richard T. "On the Modesty of Women in Arab Muslim Villages," *American Anthropologist*, 70 (1968) :67–97.

Ashraf, Ahmad. "Iran: Imperialism, Class and Modernization from Above," Ph.D. dissertation, New School for Social Research, New York, 1971.

Aswad, Barbara. "Key and Peripheral Roles of Noblewomen in a Middle Eastern Plains Village," *Anthropological Quarterly*, 40 (1967) :139–152.

Beauvoir, Simone de. *The Second Sex*. New York, 1952.
Bill, James A. *The Politics of Iran*. Columbus, Ohio, 1971.
Binder, Leonard. *Iran*. Berkeley, 1964.
Bujra, Abdulla. *The Politics of Stratification*. Oxford, 1971.
Coulson, Noel J. *Succession in the Muslim Family*. Cambridge, 1971.
Davani, Ali. *Nahziat do mah-e rohanian Iran*. Qum, 1341 Sh. [1962].
Dhabhar, Ervad Bamanji Nusserwanji. *The Persian Rivayats*. Bombay, 1932.
Echo of Iran. *1974 Iran Who's Who*. Tehran, 1974.
Fallaci, Oriana. "The Shah of Iran," *New Republic*, 1 (1 December 1973) : 12–16.
Fallers, Lloyd A., and Margaret C. Fallers. "Sex Roles in Edremit," In *Mediterranean Family Structures*, ed. J. Peristiany. Cambridge, 1976.
Falsafi, Mohammad Taqi. *Bozorg sal va javan az nazar-e afkar va tamayolat*. Tehran, n.d.
Fischer, Michael M. J. "Zoroastrian Iran Between Myth and Praxis," Ph.D. dissertation, University of Chicago, 1973.
Gibb, Hamilton. "Women and the Law," *Correspondence d'Orient*, 5 (1961) :1–16.
Giffen, Lois A. *Theory of Profane Love among the Arabs*. New York, 1971.
Goldziher, Ignaz. "Women in the Hadith Literature," *Muslim Studies*, vol. 2, London, 1971.
Hershman, P. "Hair, Sex and Dirt," *Man*, 9 (1974) :274–298.
Institute for Research and Planning in Higher Education, Ministry of Science and Higher Education. *The System of Higher Education in Iran*, Tehran, 1973a.
———. *Statistics of Higher Education in Iran*. Tehran, 1973b.
Kendall, Katherine W. "Personality Development in an Iranian Village," Ph.D. dissertation, University of Washington, Seattle, 1968.
Levine, Baruch. "Mulugu/Melug: The Origins of a Talmudic Legal Institution," *Journal of the American Oriental Society*, 88 (1968) :271–285.
Livingston, R. B., and M. Mahloudji. "Studies in Five Villages in the Province of Fars," *Pahlavi Medical Journal*, 1 (1970) :38–39.
Loeb, Laurence. "The Jews of Southwest Iran," Ph.D. dissertation, Columbia University, New York, 1970.
Maimonides, Moses. *The Book of Cleanness*. Princeton, 1954.
———. *The Guide for the Perplexed*. New York, 1956.
Maududi, S. Abul A'la. *Purdah and the Status of Women in Islam*. Lahore, 1972.
Milani, S. Mohammed Hadi Hussein. *General Aspects of Prayer* (E. T. Abul Qassim Taheri) . Unpublished. Meshed, Iran, n.d.
Motaheri, Morteza. *Masaleh hejab*. Tehran, 1353 Sh. [1974].
Naqavi, S. Ali Reza. *Family Laws of Iran*. Islamabad, 1971.
Nuri, Yahya. *Hoghugh-e zan dar Islam va jahan*. Tehran, 1343 Sh. [1964].
Qibla, Mufti Jafar Husain Sahib. *Nahjul balagha*. Karachi, 1972.

Rice, Clara Colliver. *Persian Women and Their Ways.* Philadelphia, 1923.

Rosenthal, Erwin I. J. "The Place of Politics in the Philosophy of Ibn Rushd," *Studia Semitica, vol. II, Islamic Themes.* Cambridge, 1971.

Rudolph-Touba, Jacqueline, and William Beeman. *Problems of Children and Youth in the Iranian Family: A Pilot Study in the Villages of the Kashan Desert Region.* Tehran, 1971.

Sanjana, Darab Dastur Peshotan. *Next-of-Kin Marriages in Old Iran.* London, 1888.

Shariatmadari, Mohammad Kazem. *Resaleh tozih al-masael.* Qum, 1353 Sh. [1974].

Sheriati, Ali. *Az koja aghaz konim?* Tehran, n.d.

Tabatabai, S. Mohammad Hussein. "Zan dar Islam," *Maktab tashayoh,* 3 (1338 Sh. [1959]) :7–30.

Woodsmall, Ruth Frances. *Women and the New East.* Washington, D.C., 1960.

Voshnui, Qavam. *Hejab dar Islam.* Qum, 1392 Q. [1973].

Zaidi, S. H. M. *The Muslim Womanhood in Revolution.* Calcutta, 1937.

10 Legal and Social Positions of Iranian Women

Behnaz Pakizegi

From the compulsory unveiling of women in 1936 to the present day, the legal and social positions of the Iranian woman have changed dramatically. Whereas only a few heavily veiled women could be seen on the streets before, now they walk openly and often without veils. Whereas publishers would not publish a book written by a woman in the past (Bagley 1971:49), today women are prolific writers and official members of the Iranian Parliament.

Although there are a few accounts of the history of Iranian women (for example, Salami 1971), less has been written about modern Iranian women. An attempt to understand the present-day Iranian woman may proceed through an examination of the formal laws pertaining to her, as well as through an exposition of the unwritten laws. The formal laws discussed here appear in Shafii-Sajadi's compilation of laws pertaining to the family (1974). Observations on social customs pertaining to the major events in a woman's life are based on the reported experience of many women, including myself. As often as possible empirical data have been sought. A word of caution is appropriate in studying the available statistics. Owing to difficulties in data collection and the training of researchers in Iran, the information is not always complete or reliable. However, it is the best available.

Iranian laws and social customs are intricately interwoven with the *sharia* or Islamic law (Arasteh 1964:190), so that any changes in the legal situation for women run the risk of offending some of the religious leaders. This means that changes have to be effected diplomatically and even, on occasion, covertly by the government.

Despite this, some major changes have come about in the legal status of Iranian women, particularly through the Family Protection Law (FPL) of 1967. The FPL did not formally repeal any of the previous civil code, and it thus left room for argument. However, in the revised version of the FPL passed in 1975 (article 28), prior laws conflicting with the latest laws were formally repealed. Although the legal position of women is changing quickly, their social position has been slower to change. It has often been observed that a country's legal system, especially if recent, can coexist quite peacefully with a contradictory social system; this is the case in Iran.

The first major event in a woman's life is, naturally, her birth. The legal system has little to say concerning the birth of a boy or a girl, but social customs abound. From the moment that friends and relatives find out that a woman is pregnant, particularly for the first time, prayers are said and pilgrimages made, in order that Allah may give a son to the family. Midwives are known to have left the mother in the midst of childbirth when they realized that the baby was a girl. Parties are given for the birth of a boy, and condolences for the birth of a girl. When villagers are asked how many children they have, they often report only the number of sons. This initial attitude is important because it is the foundation on which many later interactions rest.

Why are girls less valued? It is primarily because they entail more work and responsibility for the parents. As will become clear, girls are seen as requiring more protection, in order to develop "properly" and to be able to function in the society. They are also often more costly to maintain. A girl's appearance is very important, and a large expenditure is necessary to see that she is properly married. Also, upon marriage she brings more benefit to the husband's family than her own, and she is of little help to her parents in their old age.

The second major period in the life of the Iranian woman is her childhood and adolescence, the period of her socialization. Here, too, few laws and many social customs exist. This period is characterized by a gradual definition and limitation of her activities and position. From a young age her physical activity is limited. Jumping, climbing, and straying away from home are all discouraged (Touba 1974:136) in order to protect her virginity and safety. The boy, on the other hand, is gradually given greater responsibility and freedom. Brothers look after their sisters and tell them what to do and what not to do. In the cities parents often give spending money to the boy, and put him in charge of the financial needs of his sisters. Often, sensing their privileged position in the family, young sons even tyrannize over their mothers (Millward 1971:15).

Legally, elementary education is compulsory for all children, male and female. Many schools have been and are being built to actualize this law. In villages where schools and teachers are available, parents often prevent their girls from going to school. In a village near a small town in western Iran, about 14 percent of the girls seven to fourteen years of age went to school, while 46 percent of the boys did (Touba 1974:137). In the villages of the province of Fars in 1971, about 57 percent of the boys aged 6–19 years were educated as compared with about 19 percent of the girls of the same age (Jamshidi and Agha 1975, table 9). Reasons for preventing girls from going to school range from the unavailability of female teachers to the need for the girl's labor at home, and to the belief that girls do not need an education. The latter often stems from the belief that the main role of the girl is to become a wife and mother. This presumably requires knowledge only of domestic chores, and hence education for females is wasted time. In the cities and small towns girls and boys are treated in more similar ways than in the villages. If Fars is representative, it appears that almost equal numbers of girls (about 75 percent) and boys (about 84 percent) of the 6–19 age range are educated in the towns (Jamshidi and Agha 1975, table 9). Education up to a certain level (elementary for some and high school for others) is encouraged. But thereafter, the primary concern is finding a proper husband and "starting life." Often the aim of education is to place a girl in a position for a "better" husband.

The increasing numbers of educated women, on the whole, point to the increasing acceptance of education for girls. In 1956, 7.3 percent of the girls over ten years of age were educated, while in 1966 this figure increased to 16.5 percent (Rasekh 1974:155). One could assume that the figures are even higher at the present time. Education at the university level is also becoming increasingly popular for girls. The 1973–74 university census showed that about 30 percent of those attending universities all over the country were female. However, males and females enter rather different fields of study. For example, fields such as psychology, literature, history, and languages have more of the total female enrollment (34 percent) than that of the male (14 percent), while such fields as engineering, political science, and national development have more of the total male enrollment (48 percent) than that of the female (6 percent) (*Statistics of Higher Education in Iran* 1974: 34, 39).

The third and probably the most important event and period in the life of the Iranian woman is her marriage. Until very recently, the legal age of marriage was fifteen for girls and eighteen for boys. Under special circumstances, these requirements could be further lowered to thirteen and fifteen years respectively (Shafii-Sajadi 1974: 6). In 1975 the legal age for marriage was changed to eighteen for girls and twenty for boys, with exceptions granted to girls above fifteen years of age (FPL 1975, article 23). In reality, special circumstances occur much more frequently than evident in records, particularly in the rural areas, where marriages are not always registered. Economic needs and social obligations are probably the most common reasons for early marriages.

In the villages parents still have the greatest voice in the choice of spouse for a girl. In the cities the girl's wishes are considered although a great deal of social pressure is often used to influence her decision. Available figures from around 1965 suggest that about 80 percent of the marriages of industrial workers of Tehran relate to internal family ties or family business affairs, thus suggesting a direct influence of the family and relatives on marriages (Rasekh 1974:152). Although the figures are not the most recent ones, their being obtained in Tehran, which is probably one of the least tradition-oriented cities of Iran, is somewhat elucidating. However, things are changing quickly in this area, particularly for a small group of university educated people who have a way of meeting members of the opposite sex through means independent of their parents.

In both the village and the city, the primary considerations for the boy in choosing a girl are the girl's appearance and her social position, as exemplified by her family background; the girl has little control over either factor. The girl looks for a man with a better job and a higher social position than her own. A typical marriage advertisement by a woman in one of Iran's leading women's magazines illustrates this well:

> My characteristics: 23 years old, 165 cm tall, 53 kg, brown hair and eyes, fair skin, Muslim, high school graduate, nurse's aide, 20,000 Rls. income, well-dressed, cute and emotional, interested in fun and study; I want a husband who is Iranian, Shiite, 28–30 years old, unmarried, 175–185 cm tall, college graduate or higher, engineer, pilot, lieutenant, or high position office worker, 30,000 Rls. income, *mahriyeh* by agreement (*Zan-e Ruz,* May 3, 1975:61).

A typical marriage advertisement by a man in the same magazine is also revealing.

> My characteristics: 30 years old, never married, 170 cm tall, 70 kg, black hair and eyes, brown skin, Muslim, B.A., 25,000 Rls. income, intelligent, well-dressed, manly looks, emotional, enjoy music and picnics. I want a wife who is Iranian, Muslim, 24–28 years old, never married, 160–170 cm, high school graduate, housewife, place of residence after marriage, Tehran, mahriyeh by agreement (June 15, 1974:53).

Note that the man's and the woman's requests complement each other. A man wants the woman to be shorter than he is. The woman wants a man to be taller than she is. The woman wants a man with a higher education and better job than hers. The man wants a woman with a lower education and preferably no job.

A woman's legal rights in a marriage primarily involve the right to mahriyeh and the right to be economically supported. Mahriyeh is the sum of money or property that the groom promises the bride as "insurance" in case of divorce. In fact, the bride can legally refuse to sleep with the groom until the mahriyeh is paid. The amount depends on a variety of factors, such as the girl's beauty, her virginity, social class, education, and so on (Shafii-Sajadi 1974:2–3). In practice, however, few girls collect mahriyeh before divorce, and even then many are happy to forgo it in order to get their husband's consent to divorce (Bagley 1971:57). The custom of deciding on a costly mahriyeh is gradually changing among the more educated, as the possibilities of financial independence for the woman are becoming greater and the importance of factors other than economic support, such as psychological compatibility, is being recognized. In these cases, the woman agrees to receive a Quran or a piece of rock candy (as a symbol of sweetness in life), in place of the costly mahriyeh.

The husband, by law, is responsible for supporting his wife and children. This involves food, clothing, shelter, and any comforts (such as servants) to which the wife has been accustomed in her father's home. In turn, the husband is by law the boss (Shafii-Sajadi 1974:10). A study of women, who had gone to the Women's Organization's family services branch because of family problems, reveals that the majority of their problems concerned finances, primarily in the form of the husband not supporting the family (33.9 percent). Other complaints concerned children (7.1 percent), divorce (22.5 percent), and problems such as incompatibility of character, wife-beating, or wife-desertion (36.5 percent). This study dealt primarily with lower- and lower-middle-class men and women from all over the country, who would have more financial difficulties than those of the other classes. The higher classes might have fewer of these problems and/or would refer less frequently to the Women's Organization. In any case, the study reveals rather common problems concerning many people (*Analysis of the Family's Problems and Difficulties* 1973:29).

The duties of a wife are to bring a dowry and to provide services such as sexual availability, cooking, sewing, and cleaning. The lack of sexual relations is grounds for divorce. The dowry is not a legal requirement, but almost all families feel obligated to supply it. The bride's family is socially responsible to supply much of the furnishings of the house as dowry, and it is partly this that makes daughters so expensive. Although it often seems as if the mahriyeh is a greater obligation than the dowry, in effect the opposite is frequently true. As mentioned before, the mahriyeh is either never paid or, by the time of divorce, the money agreed upon has been devalued.

Before the FPL of 1967, men were legally permitted several wives, although the number of men who took advantage of this was few. For example, the number of co-wives in Iran in 1964 was given as 74,000, compared with a total population of about 25,000,000 (Bagley 1971:55). The FPL of 1967 held that if a man desires a second wife, he has to obtain permission from the court, which in turn, *when possible,* has to consult the first wife for evidence of the man's financial capacity and his ability to do justice to his consorts (article 14). In addition to the above stipulation, the most recent law (1975) requires that the man who wants to take a second wife has to have the consent of the first wife, unless she cannot fulfill wifely duties, such as having sexual relations and bearing children. In any case, the first wife has the right to ask for divorce if her husband takes a second wife (FPL 1975, articles 16, 17). This is an improvement over the past, although it is not as effective as it could be. Owing primarily to financial and social dependency, the first wife often feels that she has no choice but to consent. Through various threats and pressures, the husband often gets his way. The worst threat is often that he will divorce her to marry the other, and few women want to be divorced, left unsupported, and suffer the resulting social stigma.

Many more women face the possibility of divorce than the prospect of a second wife. Before the FPL of 1967, article 1133 of the civil code gave the man permission to divorce his wife at any time he wished. The woman had the right to ask for divorce only under certain limited conditions. The new law gives the woman the right to ask for divorce under more conditions and restricts the man's previously unlimited freedom. This has done much to make women feel more secure. Whereas many women's requests were ignored by the courts before, more prompt attention is given to them today.

Within marriage, roles are highly defined by custom. The man in the city works long hours during the day and hardly sees his wife and family. An informal survey of thirty men in Shiraz revealed that lower-class people worked an average of eleven hours a day (ranging from eight to fourteen hours) ; middle-class people, primarily shopkeepers, an average of fourteen hours a day (ranging from twelve to eighteen hours) ; and higher-class professional people an average of nine hours a day (ranging from five to twelve hours) , although many keep several jobs. Even when not at work, men spend most of their time in the company of other men, and women in the company of other women. In the villages and tribes, too, the jobs differ for men and women. The roles are not the same all over the country, but the differentiation is still found. What holds true in the city is observed in the countryside as well: there is very little mixing of men and women.

If a man sees his wife in a sexual relationship with another man, he has the legal right to kill her without being prosecuted for murder. In the case of his daughters and sisters, he can also kill them, but a punishment of a few months in prison is possible. The woman does not have this right (Shafii-Sajadi 1974:98) .

The fourth possible major sphere in the life of an Iranian woman is her job. The majority of the women in the country are villagers who work in the fields, tend the animals, and weave rugs and blankets. Few formal laws cover their jobs. In the cities, women are employed most frequently as teachers, servants, nurses, factory workers, and secretaries. Data for 1971 in Fars showed that only about 9 percent of the women aged 15–65, as compared with 75 percent of the men, were economically active in the cities (Jamshidi and Agha 1975, table 13) . The national figures for the number of economically active women in the cities is somewhat lower than that of Fars.

Until recently, a man could ask the court to stop his wife from working on the basis that it was detrimental for the family, for him, or for her. The reverse was not true (Shafii-Sajadi 1974:23) . The most recent revision of the FPL grants equal privileges to the woman, but adds that the court will grant the woman's request only if it decides that the man's cessation of work will not interfere with the income and affairs of the family (article 18) . The added clause, making the court's attention to the woman's request conditional, makes it unlikely that women will actually have the same rights as men as long as men remain legally the primary financial support of the family.

Socially and psychologically, too, many men do not like their wives to have jobs outside the homes, as it is often seen as an insult to men's abilities. An example of this attitude was seen in the man's marriage advertisement cited earlier. Also, women often take pride in not having to work. However, it is becoming more socially acceptable for women to have jobs outside the home.

Some of the job laws apply equally to men and women, such as the laws covering injuries at work. However, several important laws are applied differentially. Women (except nurses) are forbidden to work between 10:00 P.M. and 6:00 A.M., and they are not required to do "heavy and harmful" work. Both of these also apply to children, but not to men (Shafii-Sajadi 1974:60–61). Occasionally, organizations put those who cannot work the night shift into a separate category, which often means less pay. The purpose of these laws is to uphold family structure and keep women available for their families at night. It is not thought necessary for the father to be available at night. Also, since it is thought that women are physically weaker than men, it is believed that they should be protected from doing heavy physical work.

Women working in various organizations, such as educational institutions and factories, and wives of male workers are entitled by law to have their childbirth expenses paid for by the organizations' insurance. Women are forbidden to work for six weeks before and for four weeks after childbirth, during which time the employer has to hold the job for them and pay the salary. Legally, every woman who nurses must be allowed to feed her baby every three hours, and if in an organization more than ten women have infants, a baby nursery must be provided by the organization (Shafii-Sajadi 1974:60). Although in most cases a childbirth leave with pay is given to women employees, very few nurseries have been set up by the organizations, and women often have to leave their babies with older children, servants, or parents, without being able to feed them themselves.

The fifth major area of a woman's life is the remainder of her personal life. Legally, few laws cover this area, but again social customs are many. A woman's appearance is very important, so that in the cities particularly, women spend a great deal of time and effort on personal beauty. The latest fashions of Europe and America are quickly adopted and used to their best effect.

The view of woman as sex object can also be observed in the

streets. A woman walking alone in the streets of a city is touched, teased, made fun of, and harassed in a variety of ways (Millward 1971:19). Many women prefer remaining at home to going out alone and being bothered. This seems true of veiled women as well as of those wearing Western-styled clothes. A survey of twenty young women in Shiraz, half veiled and half unveiled, revealed that they all felt equally harassed on the streets by verbal and physical action, as well as by cars stopping to pick them up. In fact, since many prostitutes wear veils, veiled women may be stopped far more frequently than unveiled women. Several veiled women from cities and towns smaller than Shiraz mentioned that there is less harassment in smaller towns, but a more complete study has yet to be done. Even though men's bothering women on the streets is punishable by law, it is often observed by women that the police themselves enjoy the incidents and take the matter lightly. Thus, the mere physical movement of women in the city is highly restricted. Few women are seen in public places alone. Most women have to depend on others to go outside the house.

What can we conclude about the Iranian woman? Two main themes seem to run through the complex of laws and social customs. First, the woman is valued and values herself for her sexual appeal and the services that she can render to the family. In marriage advertisements the Iranian woman advertises her physical appeal and tries to live up to it in her everyday life. She considers her family her primary duty and derives satisfaction in life mainly through her children. Physical limitations on little girls are meant to guard their virginity, and village girls are prevented from going to school so that they can become good wives and mothers without unnecessary distractions. When seeking a spouse, men look primarily at a girl's appearance and her abilities as a wife and mother. Also, one basis for men's not wanting their wives to work is the fear that they will not be able to render family services as well as they would were they housewives only.

Second, the woman is seen, and often sees herself, as dependent, irrational, submissive, and in need of protection (Rasekh 1971:234–256). This is instanced by women's fear of being abandoned financially at divorce time, and, in a somewhat contradictory fashion, in the urban women's preferring not to work outside the house. If women do work, they prefer to be less educated and to earn less than their husbands. Women, even most university students, appear to agree wholeheartedly with the Islamic law that requires two women witnesses to every one man witness. Their argument is that women are naturally more emotional and are not to be trusted with rational judgments.

This view of women is also clear in the ambivalence with which Iranians regard the birth of a female child. It is one basis for the early care and protection given young girls. Mahriyeh and economic support reflect the financial dependence of women. Work laws concerning heavy work and night duties equate children and women and consider women in need of protection.

Much legislative progress has been made in Iran concerning women. Laws equalizing the status of women and men emerge frequently. However, many contradictions remain. Independence is encouraged at times and discouraged at others. For example, through a variety of laws applying to jobs (nurseries, equal pay for equal work, and so on), women are encouraged to become economically productive and independent. Despite this, other laws, such as, "the man is the boss of the family" and "the man is responsible for the support of the family," encourage dependence.

Even more blatant than the contradictions in the law is the large gap between the legal system and social customs. Both seem to reflect a system in a state of rapid change. More effort has to be expended in educating people and raising social awareness. Only in this way will any attempt in the direction of more enlightened legislation succeed. Better legislation might serve as a model for social change, but often it does not, especially if law enforcement is not carried out or is hindered at various points, as is the case in Iran. If more attention is not paid to educating people and raising awareness, particularly concerning sex roles, the gap between legislation and social customs will continue to grow. In fact, it is only when the awareness of the equality of the rights of the sexes has been assimilated that people will be ready to move beyond the veil, and into an era of higher awareness concerning human rights in general.

Bibliography

Analysis of the Family's Problems and Difficulties (in Persian). Tehran, 1973.

Arasteh, Reza. "The Struggle for Equality in Iran." *Middle East Journal,* 18 (1964):189–205.

Bagley, F. R. C. "The Iranian Family Protection Law of 1967: A Milestone in the Advance of Women's Rights." In *Iran and Islam,* ed. C. E. Bosworth. Edinburgh, 1971.

Civil Code of Iran (in Persian), Tehran, 1973.

Family Protection Law of 1967. Tehran, 1973.

Family Protection Law of 1975. Tehran, 1975.
Institute for Research and Planning in Science and Education. *Statistics of Higher Education in Iran* (in Persian). Tehran, 1974.
Jamshidi, Sadigheh, and Homa Agha. *A Look at the Education and Job Situation of Women in Fars Province* (in Persian). Shiraz, 1975.
Levy, Reuben. *The Social Structure of Islam*. Cambridge, 1957.
Millward, W. G. "Traditional Values and Social Change in Iran." *Iranian Studies*, 4 (1971):2–36.
Rasekh, Mehri. "Psychological Characteristics of the Iranian Women." In *The Role of the Woman in the Culture and Civilization of Iran* (in Persian). Tehran, 1971.
Rasekh, Shahpour. "The Influence of Economic and Industrial Development on the Change in the Form and Duties of the Iranian Family." In *Family and Culture* (in Persian). Tehran, 1974.
Shafii-Sajadi, Shahnaz, ed. *Compilation of the Laws Related to the Family in Iran* (in Persian). Shiraz, 1974.
Salami, Pourandokht. "The Rights of the Iranian Woman Through History." In *The Role of the Woman in the Culture and Civilization of Iran* (in Persian). Tehran, 1971.
Touba, Jacqueline. "Culture and the Relation between Patterns of Socialization in a Semi-Industrialized Area: Comparison between the Urban and Rural Areas of Arak." In *Family and Culture* (in Persian). Tehran, 1974.
Zan-e Ruz (in Persian). Tehran, periodical.

Part Two | Historical Perspectives

Handweaver in Birjand, Iran. Courtesy of Nikki Keddie.

Baluchi women and children in Iran. Courtesy of Dorothy Grant.

11 Turkish Women in the Ottoman Empire: The Classical Age

Ian C. Dengler

Questions concerning the specific positions of Turkish women in the Ottoman Empire are complex and are not amenable to immediate answers. The bulk of information must still be drawn from reports of travelers, with few good archival studies to supplement them. These various sources reveal that women in the Ottoman Empire lived in the same kinds of worlds separate from men that are found in most Islamic societies, worlds with their own rules, rewards, social hierarchies, and systems of status organization. It is not understood precisely how these worlds came into existence. In some part, they originated in the social organization of the Turkish nomadic peoples prior to their appearance in Asia Minor.[1] Sedentarization and Islamization then accentuated whatever social divisions already existed, so that by the end of the fifteenth century, when historical sources become more readily available, the organization of the world of women in Ottoman society appears to have been set very much in the pattern it was to keep until the reforms at the end of the nineteenth century.

Several elements must be taken into account in analyzing the organization of this world. Primary, of course, was the vertical division of the social order on the basis of sex. In effect, through legal and customary restrictions placed upon women as well as by means of a system of incentives encouraging marriage and childbearing, women were relegated to the confines of household and family. The restrictions placed upon women are what is most often described by our present sources. First, Turkish women were constrained in the manner of their public appearance. At least from the sixteenth century, and certainly by the end of the seventeenth, urban Turkish women had come to be veiled in public.[2] This custom was never absolute; it was most common among the upper classes,[3] and only laxly enforced among the lower orders and in the rural areas of the Ottoman Empire.[4] Yet, however irregularly observed in individual cases, veiling as a general rule did have the practical effect of helping to isolate women as a group from ordinary public contact with males.

Contact between women and men was further reduced by restrictions placed upon the physical movement of women in Ottoman society. Long-distance travel was discouraged, both by the general inadequacy of transport and by the necessity of providing separate accommodations for women. When not accompanied by their husbands or other family members, women appear seldom to have traveled, and then only for the specific occasion of a pilgrimage or family visit.[5] Even within their own communities women encountered restrictions on movement. At times, they were discouraged from or forbidden to move about certain parts of the city, in markets, places of amusement, certain kinds of shops, and religious establishments.[6]

These restrictions varied in effectiveness. Laws, in particular those of the seventeenth and eighteenth centuries, which sought to control the movement of women, appear to have been applied more to prostitutes than to women as a whole,[7] and seem not to have been systematically enforced.[8] Still, it cannot be doubted that the physical space alloted to women in the Ottoman Empire was narrower than that alloted to men and of a substantially different nature.

Perhaps the most effective way in which Ottoman society enforced the separation of the sexes was by depriving women of all but a few functions in the public sector of government. Women were virtually excluded from the governmental apparatus (the army, the court system, and thus most of the state administration). Indeed, the only visible sign of women's presence in the public sector comes from reports of women employed as teachers in girls' primary schools in sixteenth-century Anatolia.[9]

Women had little more place in commerce and industry. Certain kinds of work roles, most notably those linked to health care, such as nursing and midwifery,[10] were of necessity open to them, as well as a few others connected with textile manufacture, such as winding and weaving, cap-making, embroidery, stitching, and handkerchief-making.[11] Such work was a special labor role, however, traditionally that of women, and could be carried out in the home or in a work area separate from that of males. Moreover, the sale and distribution of the fabrics produced were handled not by the Turkish women themselves, but by various intermediaries, generally Jewish and Armenian women.[12]

Nor were Turkish women able to participate with males in other areas of social activity. Education and intellectual training were treated very differently between the sexes. Advanced training in Arabic and Persian, the languages essential in the cultured world of the intellectual elites, appears to have been unusual for women, and should be thought of perhaps as an occasional concession to a privileged daughter rather than as a customary expectation.[13] Consequently, women could very rarely make careers in the arts.[14] Only in music and dance does one find a certain number of women represented—though here by a reverse exclusion, for music and dance were areas of training left largely to women, and hence closed to males.[15]

Religious options for women were also more restricted than those for men. Religious instruction was not closed to women; countless young girls must have taken pride in learning the Quran by heart and thereby winning the coveted title of *hafiz*.[16] A few wealthy women were even able to acquire the status of *hoca, hacı*, or *molla*.[17] But there was no religious career for women. The *ulama* corps was closed to them and with it all appointments that might come from special religious training. Convents and similar religious institutions for women, not unusual during earlier periods of Islamic history, do not appear in the Ottoman records.[18] Turkish women most certainly had some role among the various heterodox Islamic groups, but never one comparable with that of males. Indeed, the women in these groups who gained importance did so because of the reputation and position of their husbands.[19]

Turkish women thus lived within a system of restrictions that made it improbable they would have either the need or the ability to interact with males outside the network of kin, family, and household unit. These restrictions were not, however, the only nor perhaps even the primary reason women came to accept their domestic role, for the Ottoman social system also provided women with a number of incentives for staying within the women's world.

These incentives were as various as the restrictions placed upon women in the Ottoman state. Most important was the increased sense of personal worth a woman acquired through marriage and the production of offspring. An unmarried woman had a very low status in Ottoman society. Her legal position was only a shade better than a chattel. Her social position was of an equally low order, for she was not covered by the regulations of Islamic society which both restricted and encumbered women, but which also defined them as women—especially those regulations concerned with veiling and social interaction with males.

The onset of puberty for women changed this. Veiling symbolized incorporation into the world of women, while marriage gave not only a formal position for women in the community at large but also legal control over their property.[20] The arrival of children, especially boys,[21] further enhanced their status and strengthened the ties between women, their kin, and their husband's kin, making divorce less likely. Furthermore, should a husband predecease a wife, she would acquire additional power and prestige as guardian of the family estate,[22] a position among the wealthy classes that could bring a woman considerable political power as well.[23]

Women in Ottoman society had, therefore, considerable reason for accepting the roles of wife and mother. They thereby insured their maintenance, obtained personal companionship, family, and community support, and, at times, considerable amounts of money which, it seems, they were free to spend in large measure as they saw fit. If excluded from the world of males, they were in no sense social outcasts, but respected members of the social order whose wishes and desires could have significant impact on the economic, social, and political life of the Ottoman state.

Of course, not all women were able to exploit to a like degree their position within the social structure. In reality, there were great differences in the interior structure of the women's world, not only with respect to wealth, companionship, family, and community support, but also to the effectiveness of the restrictions placed upon women. Present sources suggest that the world of women in Ottoman society had four separate levels: at bottom a servitor class made up largely of unmarried women defined by their labor role;[24] above them women of the artisan class, defined by their marital role; third, women connected with the households of urban notables and well-to-do merchants; and, finally, at the top of the social order, women who were part of the households of the beys, ulama, pashas, and senior government office holders who made up the ruling elite.

Of these four levels, the least information is found about the lowest, that of the servitor class. This class was apparently quite large in Ottoman society. Liebe-Harkort, in his study of the social organization of sixteenth-century Bursa, has suggested that this class as a whole, including both males and females, made up some 35 percent or more of the urban population.[25] Whether this was so in other cities we cannot at present say, but certainly the servitor class made up a significant portion of the social order within the Ottoman state. During the early centuries of Ottoman history, when conquests provided a steady source of slaves, the women of this class were largely of servile origin, though some free women were also employed as wage laborers.[26] Regardless of their origin, however, women of the servitor class were equally bound by the restrictions placed upon them as women. The work they performed was either household labor as cooks, housemaids, washerwomen, or domestic servants, or traditional female labor, such as work in the textile industry or as barbers and personal attendants in women's baths or hospitals.

Only in two work roles, those of entertainers and prostitutes, do women of the servitor class appear to have violated the rules of organization that separated the world of men and women. Even in these cases, however, Ottoman society managed to preserve at least the image of separation. Female entertainers were organized into corporate groups separate from those of men with their own rules of recruitment and training.[27] Furthermore, the Ottomans claimed that entertainers were not Muslims, but, variously, Jews, Armenians, other Christians, or gypsies, and thus not part of their own social order anyway. At all events, social contact between entertainers and the rest of Ottoman society was kept to a minimum.[28]

Prostitutes were treated in much the same fashion. They too were held to be non-Muslims, and thus outside the social order of Turkish women.[29] Where possible, the state attempted to confine the activities of prostitutes to certain parts of the cities, if not to suppress them altogether, though most likely with little success.[30] The most common way of dealing with prostitutes was to tolerate their existence but to deny them status and recognition as women workers. The Ottomans argued that prostitutes represented a category of errant married women whose husbands were either unwilling or unable to control them: the law code of Suleyman I (1520–1566) set out fines for prostitution under the section on adultery,[31] while prostitutes, as a category of laborers, were formally represented in the gilds and gild parades by their "husbands," not themselves.[32]

Restrictions Ottoman society placed upon women of the servitor class thus channelled them into household and domestic work at least in appearance if not in fact. But Ottoman society also provided these women with positive incentives for entering the domestic world as well. To begin with, Ottoman society did not as a rule consider the condition of servitor either as permanent or as especially demeaning. The majority of women of the servitor class remained in it only for a specific period, fulfilling what might be thought of as a service contract of between five and ten years, after which they could expect to be granted their freedom, some kind of settlement, or both.[33] They had, therefore, a stake in completing their term of service successfully. Diligence might lead to a higher position within the household hierarchy, or even open the way to rewards and social advancement through the generosity of their employers. Cases occur in which whole estates were left to servant girls, and while they were infrequent in the historical records,[34] they were most likely common in the imaginations of servant girls.

The simplest motivation for women in the servitor class, however, was the expectation that they would eventually achieve by marriage the benefits Ottoman society traditionally bestowed on married women. Marriages by women of the servitor class appear to have been common in Ottoman society. Liebe-Harkort found that over 50 percent of the women leaving wills in the Bursa records came originally from this class, a percentage which may well be in excess of the rate for society as a whole, but which at least suggests the rapidity and scale of upward assimilation for women of the servitor class.[35] Indeed, there is evidence of a well-organized network in Ottoman society that provided women of servile origin for marriages into families even at the top of the social order.[36] So well-known and accepted was this network that a special genre of upper-class literature apparently developed to comment upon the suitability of women of different nationalities for the future stability of the household. The poet Mishri (d. 1699), for example, presented his son a guide to the choice of a marriage partner that summarized what appear to have been the standard upper-class beliefs about the different kinds of women of the servitor class: Circassians are intractable and warlike; Russians hostile; French, German, and Hungarian women are cunning and lack respect for Islam; blacks lack any kind of physical appeal. Only Georgian women receive favorable comment; they are described by Mishri as engaging, honest, open, and undemanding—the ideal for a placid menage.[37]

To be sure, only a few women from the servitor class could expect to be assimilated into the upper levels of the social order. The majority of those who did marry, and who were not reabsorbed by minority communities, most likely did not rise beyond the artisan class, and then perhaps only its marginal elements. Even this transition enhanced their social position, however, for by it they would cease to be identified by their work roles and come to be measured by the socially more prestigious status of a married woman.

This does not mean that women in the artisan classes enjoyed a life free of the kinds of labor performed by women in the servitor class. In fact, their work, and indeed situation, was very similar, if not identical. The family was small,[38] servants were absent, the marriage unit was monogamous,[39] and extended and multiple kin groups were most likely rare.[40] Hence, women in the artisan class passed most of their lives within the household carrying out the necessary tasks of cooking, cleaning, and childrearing, or, when free of these, working to supplement the family income through the production of textiles and embroidered goods.

Some women no doubt found this style of life narrow and confining, but the evidence available suggests that women of the artisan class as a whole not only accepted their domestic role, but strongly identified with it. At Eskişehir, for instance, the effigies these women chose for their gravestones invariably show them in their preferred household roles—usually surrounded by their children or at work on their looms.[41] Wills deposited at Bursa show a similar identification with the household: an unwillingness to acquire advanced training in textile manufacture and a marked preference by women to divest themselves of property not related to the household.[42] This last point is even more succinctly put in the seventeenth-century judicial records of Kayseri, where women divest themselves of extrahousehold property three times more frequently than they acquire it.[43]

Thus, women in the Ottoman Empire from the artisan class and above show a marked tendency to eschew the outside world in favor of life within the world of women. It is, however, only among the households of the upper classes that this life became highly rewarding. Women in the families of the urban well-to-do mark a transition stage. They were, as a rule, freed from menial household tasks, but were expected in turn to supervise those women who did this work. Occasionally women of the urban well-to-do extended their interest in management beyond the household into the active world of commerce and trade, in partnership with their husbands, or as backers of commercial entrepreneurs.[44] At least one woman was both an active trader and a producer of goods: she was the owner of a good-sized silk atelier in sixteenth-century Bursa, with its own stocks of raw and finished goods, looms, and slave weaving women.[45]

Active participation in the outside world by women of the urban well-to-do was unusual, however, and merely serves to emphasize the degree to which such a life-style was possible in Ottoman society, where such women might choose to exercise it. Most did not so choose. Evidence from wills, *vakif,* and judicial records again indicates that the majority of women of this class only infrequently took an active interest in the organization of their capital, and then did so only insofar as it concerned the establishment of estates and trusts for the benefit of their heirs.[46]

Rather, well-to-do women appear instead to have used their wealth and position to become major consumers of luxury goods and leisure-time activities in the Ottoman economy. Certainly this was so in Bursa, where over 50 percent of their wills were made up of such items as clothing, jewelry, mirrors, and the like.[47] Indeed, a large domestic industry seems to have developed in Bursa to accommodate their needs.[48] Their reading habits suggest a similar predilection for amusement and diversion, although here our information is too meager to allow a firm statement.[49] But we do know that much of their free time was spent in idle consumption, on promenades, excursions, picnics in the countryside, and at the women's baths.[50]

Women among the ruling elites were even more favored, but on the whole similarly inclined. Throughout their lives they were surrounded by a vast hierarchy of governesses, teachers, bath attendants, personal servants, bed makers, scullery women, and pipe cleaners over whom they had or would eventually acquire command.[51] There was nothing material they lacked. They were spared all forms of household labor; even the role of manager could be delegated to others.

As a result, women of the ruling elites had a choice of activities even broader than that of women of the urban well-to-do. Some chose roles that touched very much on the border between the worlds of men and women. It is this class that provided the few women writers or poets on record,[52] as well as those women who chose some kind of religious career. The majority of women of the ruling elites, however, seem to have pursued the same kind of consumerist life-style adopted by the urban well-to-do, although on a much grander scale.

Yet women of the ruling elites had one role not open to other women in the social order: they could become political and social arbiters. For by the mere nature of the separation of men's and women's worlds in Ottoman society, each sex came to acquire a separate hierarchy with its own specific system of information exchange and decision-making. Women of the ruling elites, in part through personal ability, but primarily through linkage with their own friends, kin groups, and the army of subordinates placed under them, became heads of vast clientage and patronage networks that at times gave them direct control over the entire Ottoman state apparatus.[53]

So, for instance, the daughter of Suleyman I and the widow of the grand vizier Rustem are said to have been responsible for the decision of the Ottoman government to attempt the seizure of the island of Malta in 1565 and themselves paid for the outfitting of 400 warships.[54] Nurubanu, the mother of Murad III (1574–1595), sat regularly on his council of state and concerned herself with all the questions of government.[55] Safiye, the mother of Mehmed III (1595–1603), was given what Alderson calls "almost full power as regent" for the whole of the Ottoman Empire while her son was away on campaigns.[56] In the seventeenth century, with a succession of weak and underage sultans, the power of such women was to go even further. The most remarkable example is that of Kosem Mahpeyker who acted as regent for the empire in the name of her two sons Murad IV (1623–1640) and Ibrahim (1640–1648). When Ibrahim was deposed in 1648, her power was so great that she managed to continue her rule as regent for her grandson Mehmed IV, under the title of *Buyuk Valide* (Grandmother).[57]

Whatever the theoretical limitations, therefore, that were placed upon them by the customary divisions of men's and women's worlds in Ottoman society, women at the top of the social order had little to complain about. They had come to possess most of the advantages that Ottoman society could confer on individuals of *either* sex: wealth, power, and virtually unlimited control over self, property, and leisure time. It is this class of women that Lady Mary Montagu so enviously described at the beginning of the eighteenth century as the only free people of the empire, absolute queens of their harem and of the society they lived in, free to come or go anywhere, to move about undiscovered and unidentifiable, and free to spend their husbands' money as they might wish.[58]

Of course it is this last remark of Lady Mary Montagu's that puts the whole of her observation in its proper context. Women of the ruling elites enjoyed power and status only to the extent that they accepted the traditional division of the social order into a world of male and female. For the Ottoman system of restrictions and positive motivations was a conservative, self-fulfilling system that rewarded those who accepted its tenets and left little if any place for those who did not. As such, it was a system of social organization quite able to survive during the long period of political confusion and economic decline that marked the last two centuries of Ottoman history. Indeed, the disappearance of the few existing nondomestic work roles for women from the seventeenth century onward appears only to have accentuated the division of men's and women's worlds,[59] and to have heightened further the value Ottoman society placed upon the role of wife and mother.[60]

By the end of the nineteenth century, however, the whole of the Ottoman social system was in a process of slow mutation. Within the world of women the servitor class was now made up almost exclusively of free women drawn from the non-Islamic minority communities.[61] Slave markets were empty, soon to be closed, and the entire system of status mobility through marriage upward in the social order in a state of disarray.[62]

Women of the artisan class were experiencing similar shifts. Their identity with household and family had been dependent both on the absence of market labor roles and upon the high value society placed upon their domestic labor. The commercial and industrial expansion of the late nineteenth century forced a revaluation of these roles. Increasingly, women of the artisan class were offered employment outside the household and by the end of World War I they had become an important element in the general labor force. The traditional values of marriage and the home remained, but they no longer had the same power to isolate women from the world of men.[63]

Most significant, however, were the changes occurring among women of the upper classes—the urban well-to-do and the ruling elite. With the spread of literacy and especially the development of printing came new suggestions for ways in which these women could make use of their time and wealth. From the 1820s onward, women of the upper classes became sponsors and supporters of women's schools and other educational establishments.[64] At first these schools and the ideals surrounding them were traditional and religious in nature, but by the end of the century they had come increasingly under the influence of Western ideas of equality, providing a very different model for the place of women in the social order—a place the political and social reforms of the post-Ottoman period were, in part at least, to realize.

Notes

1. Evidence on this point is most incomplete, but it appears that strict separation of work roles as well as such customs as polygamy, limited female inheritance, and preferential treatment of males in matters of divorce, family, and community decision-making characterized the Central Asian pastoral nomads as far back as there are historical sources. For an excellent summary of materials available, see Lawrence Krader, *Social*

Organization of the Mongol-Turkic Pastoral Nomads (Bloomington, Ind., 1963); for more specific references, see William of Rubruck, *Travels,* ed. Bergeron (La Haye, 1735), p. 8; Plano Carpini, "Relation du voyage etc.," *ibid.,* pp. 28ff; Clavijo, *Embassy to Tamerlane, 1403–1406,* trans. G. le Strange (New York, 1928), pp. 242, 297ff; and 1640 Law Code of the Oirats or that of Chingis Khan, both to be found in V. A. Riasanovsky, *Fundamental Principles of Mongol Law* (Tientsin, 1937), pp. 97, 200.

2. Possibly, this was so at an even earlier date. However, prior to the sixteenth century we are without sources. P. Belon du Mans, *Observations de plusieurs singularitez . . . Trouvées en Grece, Asie, Judée Egypte, Arabie et autres pays* (Paris, 1553), II, xxxv, reports that women were generally veiled, at least in the cities, but that there were important exceptions, especially among minority groups. Seventeenth-century travelers report, however, that even these women had come to be veiled, and that the custom was enforced through a variety of coercive measures. See, for instance, *The Travels of Monsieur de Thevenot into the Levant* (London, 1686), p. 57; or Cornelius le Bruin, *Voyage au Levant* (Delft, 1700–1702), I, p. 453.

3. O. Ghiselin de Busbecq, *The Turkish Letters of Ogier Ghiselin de Busbecq,* ed. E. S. Forster (Oxford, 1927), p. 119. The observation has been made for other and more recent parts of the Islamic world as well. (See Reuben Levy, *The Social Structure of Islam* [Cambridge, 1957], p. 128.)

4. Domingo Badia y Leblich, *The Travels of Ali Bey* (London, 1816), II, pp. 105, 280; W. G. Browne, "Journey from Constantinople . . . in the Year 1802," in *Travels in Various Countries of the East,* ed. R. Walpole (London, 1820), p. 118; Bernhard Stern, *Medizin, Aberglaube und Geschlechtsleben in der Türkei* (Berlin, 1903), p. 186.

5. Belon, *Observations,* III, xvi; Gotthard Jaeschke, "Die Frauenfrage in der Türkei," *Saeculum* (1959):360.

6. Belon, *Observations,* III, xvi; N. Abadan, *Social Change and Turkish Women* (Ankara, 1963), p. 4; A. Afetinan, *The Emancipation of the Turkish Woman* (Paris, 1962), pp. 31–32.

7. This was especially true of laws directed at preventing women from entering the shops of sellers of fresh cream, who were apparently well known for their association with prostitutes (see Robert Mantran, *La vie quotidienne à Constantinople au temps de Soliman le Magnifique* [Paris, 1965], pp. 280ff). Amusement places ought to be considered in the same light.

8. Most of our information on the effectiveness of legal restrictions on movement comes from male travelers who never had much contact with Turkish women and thus were scarcely able to offer a very informed judgment. With the beginning of the eighteenth century, however, this began to change as a number of women not only were able to travel through the Ottoman Empire, but chose to write about their experiences as well. The most notable of these were Lady Elizabeth Craven, *A Journey through the Crimea to Constantinople* (Dublin, 1789); and Lady Mary Montagu,

whose *Letters* (L. Wharncliffe, ed., London, 1893) form one of our most important sources for the understanding of women's position in the Ottoman Empire. Both agree that in practice few if any restrictions were placed upon the movement of Turkish women, at least in the cities.

For earlier periods we are less sure. Two sixteenth-century artists, Hieronymous Beck and Nicolo de'Nicolai, portray considerable numbers of women moving with apparent freedom about the cities. Nicolai's works are to be found in his *Le navigatione et viaggi fatti nella turchia* (Venice, 1580), pp. 139ff. Beck's sketches have not been published yet; they are contained in the codex 8615 of the National Bibliothek in Vienna, and have been partially reproduced in H. Inalcik, *The Ottoman Empire: The Classical Age, 1300–1600* (New York, 1973). Note especially plates 27, 28, and 47.

9. Belon reports that no village in Turkey was so small that it did not have such a school (*Observations,* folio 180). For a general discussion of these schools, see Refia Ugurel, *Education de la femme en Turquie* (Lyon, 1936), p. 41.

10. It was a long-standing custom in Islamic countries that hospitals should have a women's section with women attendants, though as far as I am able to determine, there were never any women doctors. There were several foundations in Anatolia from the Seljuk period that we might expect to have women's sections, but this has not been established. In the sixteenth century Hurrem Sultan founded a hospital at the Mosque of the Hasseki for mad women. It must be assumed that women attendants were employed. Evliya Çelebi reports this to have been the case in the seventeenth century. (See Stern, *Medizin,* p. 102; for his remarks on midwifery, see p. 280.)

11. The most complete list of these different occupations is to be found in Evliya Çelebi's description of the twenty-sixth section of the Istanbul Tailors' Gild dating from the early seventeenth century (see his *Narrative of Travels in Europe, Asia and Africa,* trans. J. von Hammer [London, 1834], II, p. 202). For a more general discussion, see Inalcik, *The Ottoman Empire,* pp. 160ff; and Klaus Liebe-Harkort, *Beiträge zur sozialen und wirtschaftlichen Lage Bursas am Anfang des 16. Jahrhunderts* (Hamburg, 1970), pp. 90ff.

12. This is an observation made by a number of writers. Nicolai mentions it in connection with Armenian women working in the Istanbul market (*Le navigatione,* p. 139), as does also Belon (*Observations,* II, cii, folio 159; III, xiv, folio 182). The rule cannot, however, have been absolute, for Belon does mention occasionally encountering Turkish women in the market selling their own cloth goods. He adds that though these women wore a veil over their faces, one could easily see through it. Moreover, when they wished to speak, they lifted it up much as "the visor of a helm" (ibid., III, xiv, folio 182).

13. As with so much in Ottoman history, the sources only hint at what may have actually been the case. Information on women literati is itself

scarce enough, much less descriptions of their personal lives and training. Latifi, the biographer of the fifteenth-century poet Zeinab, mentions that her father chose to have her instructed after "he saw spark the rare jewels of her talent." (See Lucy Garnett, *The Women of Turkey and their Folklore* [New York, 1890–91], II, pp. 469, 532.) The same appears to have been the case for Sitki Umetullah (d. 1705) (ibid., p. 538).

14. At least there is no record of female artists among the court professionals. Belon, however, mentions that among the artisan classes, women who did embroidery work were skilled at drawing the picture of objects they wished to represent (*Observations,* III, xiv, folio 182).

15. There is considerable information about this kind of training, especially for the period after 1700. Garnett provides the most general description of the different classes of women affected, from gypsies to daughters of the well-to-do (*Women of Turkey,* II, pp. 469, 485). Mention may also be made of the autobiography of Halide Edib (Adivar), *Memoirs of Halide Edib* (London, 1926), pp. 355–359. Most striking surely are the portraits of dancing girls left by the early eighteenth-century court painter Levni (see E. Diez, *Türk Sanati* [Istanbul, n.d.], p. 278). Males were in no sense entirely excluded from this kind of training, but those who did receive it belonged to specific corporate groups associated with entertainers and, most likely, prostitutes (see Metin And, *A History of Theatre and Popular Entertainment in Turkey* [Ankara, 1963–64], p. 27).

16. Ugurel, *Education,* p. 47; Garnett, *Women of Turkey,* II, p. 502.

17. Ugurel, *Education,* p. 47; Garnett, *Women of Turkey,* II, pp. 390–393, 469. There remains much to be learned about the meaning of these terms to the women who used them. Among the well-to-do, such titles were surely a source of great personal pride and often appeared on public inscriptions ("Hoca Hafize Hatun Kiz Mektebi"). (See A. Afetinan, *Tarih boyunci Türk kadinin hak ve gorevleri* [Istanbul, 1968], pp. 75ff.) Among certain sectors of the population, however, such titles seem to have been synonymous with witches, divination, and, perhaps, fakery (See Emel Sonmez, *Turkish Women in Turkish Literature of the Nineteenth Century* [Leiden, 1969], p. 55).

18. Here again, one must argue from absence rather than on the basis of any specific policy of the Ottoman state acting to discourage such institutions. Even if they did exist, however, it seems clear that their role in public life must have been slight. For some discussion of the problem, see Margaret Smith, *Rabi'a the Mystic and her Fellow Saints in Islam* (Cambridge, 1928), pp. 173ff; and J. Spencer Trimingham, *The Sufi Orders in Islam* (Oxford, 1971), p. 18.

19. A characteristic example is the wife of Celalüddin, mentioned in the *Acts of the Adepts* of Eflaki (Garnett, *Women of Turkey,* II, p. 176; for later periods, see also p. 507). This does not mean that women had no part of consequence in religious movements. On an individual basis, some even raised to the status of a local saint, they were very much present. However, there existed few institutionalized mechanisms offering them a permanent life option in the religious world.

20. For a general discussion of this process of upward movement in the status hierarchy, see Mantran, *Vie,* pp. 195–197.

21. Ibid., p. 196. Much has been written about the theoretical preference for males in society, though little information exists to show how behavior was modified in practice. One exception is the series of wills studied by Liebe-Harkort. They show a clear preference for males in the birth order (*Beiträge,* p. 70).

22. Islamic law is not wholly clear on the question of guardianship. It recognizes three kinds: care for the upbringing of young children, care for choosing a spouse for the son, and management of property of minors. In the first case, Islamic law recognizes the right of women to act as guardians, whether widowed or divorced. No doubt this would have been so in the Ottoman Empire. The second case is less clear. Islamic law generally leaves the choice of a spouse to a male guardian, the *wali.* In the Ottoman state, however, the control over the selection of a spouse for a son appears to have been almost the exclusive right of the mother. There are numerous descriptions of this from the sixteenth century onward. (See Mantran, *Vie,* p. 197.) In the third case, only an extensive examination of wills and other documents will allow us to say whether women had much right of guardianship, since Islamic law has diverse traditions (see Levy, *Social Structure,* p. 142).

23. This was, of course, most clearly the case among the great households (see N. M. Penzer, *The Harem* [London, 1936], p. 177; and A. Alderson, *The Structure of the Ottoman Dynasty* [Oxford, 1956], pp. 80–81).

24. The question of marital status is at present beyond resolution. The servitor class was apparently made up of large numbers of slaves, who, at least initially, were not married. Occasionally, they married later without changing their status, especially in the case of black women. (See G. A. Olivier, *Voyage dans l'empire Ottoman, l'Egypte et la Perse* [Paris, 1801–1807], p. 179.)

25. Liebe-Harkort, *Beiträge,* p. 67.

26. Ibid., p. 41.

27. They were known as *çengi* and were often commented upon by travelers (see Belon, *Observations,* II, xxxviii, folio 110; Cornelis le Bruin, *Voyage,* I, pp. 436–438). A reasonably complete description of their social organization is to be found in Metin And, *A History of Theatre,* pp. 27ff.

28. Mantran, *Vie,* p. 281; Edib, *Memoirs,* p. 355.

29. P. A. Desjardin, *el Ktab* (Paris, 1893), p. 205; Stern, *Medizin,* pp. 189–190; Browne, *Journey,* p. 147; Nicolai, *Navigatione,* p. 157.

30. At times, at least in the imagination of some travelers, by truly draconian measures. Olivier reports that they were neither allowed nor tolerated, and where found to be Muslim, placed in a sack weighted with stones and drowned (*Voyage,* p. 161). More likely, the trade was regulated according to the elaborate procedures that we know about for other areas of the Islamic world of the period (see C. J. Wills, *Persia as It Is* [London,

1886], p. 40; and E. A. Duchesne, *De la prostitution dans la ville d'Alger* [Paris, 1853], pp. 53ff). For Ottoman laws on the subject, see J. von Hammer, *Des Osmanischen Reiches Staatsverfassung und Staatsverwaltung* (Hildesheim, 1963), I, p. 143.

31. Stern, *Medizin,* p. 184; von Hammer, *Staatsverfassung,* p. 143.

32. J. von Hammer, *Constantinopolis und der Bosporos* (Osnabruck, 1967), II, p. 402.

33. Garnett, *Women of Turkey,* I, p. 308; II, p. 412; George Young, *Corps de droit ottoman* (Oxford, 1906), II, p. 168; Montagu, *Letters,* p. 333.

34. Characteristic is a trust from the sixteenth-century Istanbul *vakif* records that a well-to-do woman named Ümmügülsüm Hatun established for her son, with the provision that it should pass to her two slave girls in the event of his death without issue. The provision was respected. (See M. Cunbur, "Ümmügülsüm Hatun vakfiyesi," *Vakiflar dergisi* [Istanbul, 1962], V, p. 94.)

35. Liebe-Harkort, *Beiträge,* pp. 66–67.

36. Garnett, *Women of Turkey,* II, pp. 190–206, 404–408. Ottoman women, often of high rank, were often central participants in the organization of this system. For a modern description of how such a system might have worked, see E. R. Leach's description of the custom of *kurdiya* in his *Social and Political Organization of the Ruwanduz Kurds* (London, 1940), p. 44.

37. A. A. Pallis, *In the Days of the Janissaries* (London, 1951), pp. 193–194. Similar attitudes toward the different nationalities can be found in the mid-nineteenth-century autobiography of Salmé, the daughter of the Sultan of Zanzibar. Her work is, incidentally, a defense of the harem style. (Emile Ruette, *Memoirs of an Arabian Princess* [New York, 1907].)

38. Liebe-Harkort, *Beiträge,* pp. 70–71.

39. Polygamy, when it existed, seems to have been confined to the families of the very rich. In the Bursa records, under 2 percent of the households had more than one wife. (Liebe-Harkort, *Beiträge,* p. 70.) This agrees with the views of numerous travelers. Typical is the remark of Jean Palerne: "There are few men who have more than one wife, if it is not the rich" (From his *Perigrinations* [Lyon, 1606], cited in Mantran, *Vie,* p. 193; see also Olivier, *Voyage,* p. 162; and Garnett, *Women of Turkey,* II, pp. 433–434).

40. This can be inferred from demographic materials as well as from travelers' descriptions (see especially Charles White, *Three Years in Constantinople or Domestic Manners of the Turks* [London, 1844], p. 296).

41. Süheyl Ünver, *Pierres tombales seldjoukides à effigie* (Jerusalem, 1960), pp. 10–12.

42. Liebe-Harkort, *Beiträge,* p. 90.

43. R. C. Jennings, "Women in Early 17th Century Ottoman Judicial Records: The Sharia Court of Anatolian Kayseri," *Journal of the Economic and Social History of the Orient,* 28 (1975):99–100.

44. Ibid., p. 65.
45. Liebe-Harkort, *Beiträge,* p. 90.
46. Jennings, "Judicial Records," p. 107; Liebe-Harkort, *Beiträge,* p. 80.
47. Ibid., pp. 241–242.
48. Ibid.
49. Ibid., p. 117.
50. Montagu, *Letters,* pp. 27–37; Lady Anne Blunt, *Twenty Years Residence among the People of Turkey* (New York, 1878), p. 16.
51. White, *Three Years in Constantinople,* II, p. 296.
52. Typical is the case of Ayşe Hubba Kadin (d. 1589), author of a long poem entitled "Jemshid and Hurşid," and who was linked to the court circles of Murad II and Selim I. Another, Tuti Hatun, wife of the poet Baki, was part of the court circle of Suleyman I. (See M. Uraz, *Kadin şair ve murarrirlerimiz* [Istanbul, 1941], pp. 25–28.)
53. A. Clot, *Aperçu général sur l'Egypte* (Brussels, 1840), I, p. 331; also, Olivier, *Voyage,* p. 169.
54. Stern, *Medizin,* p. 154.
55. N. Tomiche, "La femme en Islam," in *Histoire mondiale de la femme,* ed. P. Grimal (Paris, 1967), III, p. 138.
56. Alderson, *Ottoman Dynasty,* p. 23.
57. Ibid., p. 81.
58. Montagu, *Letters,* pp. 297–300, 338.
59. This was connected in large part with the decline of the textile and silk industries in the course of the seventeenth century (see White, *Domestic Manners,* II, p. 264). By the early nineteenth century, Turkish women still producing for market sales were to be found only in the inner regions of Anatolia or in the eastern provinces (see William Chesney, *The Expedition for the Survey of the Rivers Euphrates and Tigris* [London, 1850], I, p. 373; also Browne, *Journey,* p. 125).
60. Such, at least, is the image presented by travelers. There is also some confirmation in the style and subjects treated by Ottoman writers themselves, both male and female. See, for instance, the domestic poetry of Ani Fatima (d. 1710), as discussed in Garnett, *Women of Turkey,* II, pp. 538–540, or that of Nigar (d. 1916?) in Ugurel, *Education,* p. 55.
61. Garnett, *Women of Turkey,* I, p. 52.
62. Descriptions of slave markets from the early nineteenth century make it clear that slaves were no longer generally available. So, for instance, John Auldjo mentions finding only a few black women for sale in 1833, and scarcely anyone interested in purchasing. (J. Auldjo, *Journal of a Visit to Constantinople* [London, 1835].) Trade in blacks was perhaps the last to cease.
63. Garnett, *Women of Turkey,* I, pp. 214–215; Desjardins, *el Ktab,* pp. 147–148.
64. A. Afetinan, *Tarih boyunca,* p. 76.

12 Women as Patrons of Architecture in Turkey

Ülkü Ü. Bates

Monumental architecture, because of its public nature, is everywhere a political statement about the society in which it occurs. When one considers the limited formal political status of women in an Islamic society, it is a surprise to find a considerable number of buildings dedicated to, or commissioned by, women in Seljuq and Ottoman Turkey. One might ask what types of buildings in the pre-Ottoman and Ottoman periods bear a woman's name. What was the nature of the patronage that brought these buildings into existence? What was the rank or status of women patrons in the social hierarchy, and how did they finance monumental architecture? What structural or ornamental peculiarities characterize the architecture of women?

Emerging from an overview of architectural patronage is the discovery that women of the elite classes were active in areas of the formal political system where it is unexpected. Moreover, the ways in which such women were active in public life, and also the limits to their participation, shed light on the overall social system. A study of architecture, from this point of view, can then offer a realistic way of looking at the public or political roles of women in Seljuq and Ottoman times.[1] First, the types of buildings dedicated to women appear to be restricted in their functions. In the pre-Ottoman period of Islamic Anatolia, mausoleums commemorating women make up the largest group. The Anatolian mausoleum is generally a compact, tower-like edifice best described as a tombstone of monumental dimensions. Approximately 20 percent of all funerary structures built before the Ottoman period, excluding, of course, simple burial sites with nonarchitectural commemorative devices, belong to women.[2] On the other hand, there is only one mosque in Seljuq Anatolia that can safely be attributed to a female patron and not one is dedicated to a woman. This is Mahperi Hatun, whose titles are given as "Princess of Princesses, Mother of the Sultan of Sultans." Her mosque is in Kayseri and is part of a larger complex containing her *medrese* (school) and tomb.

Of approximately one hundred medreses known to date from the twelfth to the fifteenth centuries, 5 bear the names of women, and 3 of these are mothers of Artukid and Seljuq sultans. According to one study of caravansarays, 6 such buildings out of a total of 119 are named after women.[3] Significantly, 5 of the 6 were erected by Mahperi Hatun, who here too describes herself as "The Mother of the Sultan of Sultans." This extraordinary lady emerges in the history of the Seljuqs of Rum as one of the most prolific builders.

One immediate conclusion from this is that the de facto social and political participation of women in Seljuq society was greater than their formal political status would suggest. Tomb towers, for example, are major undertakings, each involving a substantial commitment of resources and labor. Moreover, tomb structures represent the earliest architectural symbols of the dominance of Islam in this formerly Christian land as well as proclaiming the political significance of particular families or dynasties. It is therefore particularly interesting that women should be associated with a larger proportion of these edifices than with any type of building in subsequent periods.[4] The question this raises is, of course, how or in what capacity did they participate in public life.

The considerable wealth and power that the Ottoman Empire commanded from the fourteenth century brought forth an enormous number of architectural undertakings. Particularly, the sixteenth century witnessed a building boom throughout the empire. One of the greatest Ottoman architects, Sinan, belongs to this century. Women contributed to these building activities in a way that is symptomatic of their social and political roles in Ottoman society.

In the Ottoman period, unlike the Seljuq, mosque architecture surpasses the mausoleum in its association with female names. Ayvansaray's catalogue (updated by Tahsin Öz) of mosques in and around Istanbul lists 953 structures.[5] Of these, 68 (or 7 percent) were built by or for women. Some of these mosques are among the great monumental mosques of Istanbul. One means of surmounting the problem of incomplete data for buildings erected throughout the empire is to look at those built by one well-known architect, Sinan. Of the 448 buildings designed or renovated by Sinan, 39 (or

9 percent) were commissioned by or dedicated to women.[6] While this, and the other figures given, may seem small, they should be evaluated against what might be expected for a society in which women held no formal office and compared with similar data for contemporary periods in the West where men also dominate the political scene. The fact that from 5 to 20 percent of building activity was undertaken by women is particularly significant when one considers the resources and organization that are required to build a monumental structure in a preindustrial society. Further, these great edifices are clearly associated with events in the arena of politics. They advertise the power of individuals and institutions.

How did women achieve and exercise publicly recognized power? This is answered by briefly examining the organization of women at court and the lives of some of the women active in architecture for whom there is documentation. The evidence, although perhaps not what would be desired, does nevertheless contribute to a further understanding of Islamic society.

In general, Ottoman women founded religious institutions: mosques, schools, *zawiyas*, and mausoleums. Secular buildings (hans, bazaars, bridges, caravansarays) are far fewer in number, and they were erected to serve as sources of income for the maintenance of religious buildings. There are no records of independent residential structures. For example, palaces were never erected for women. This practice finds its parallel in Ottoman society. Only rarely does a woman become the formal head of a household or separate from her family to establish a dwelling on her own.[7] However, within the household, and certainly within the palace, women head up a clearly demarcated area of activities. This comes to extend, in many instances, to less formally recognized power and influence in public affairs.

This is seen in the social organization of the *harem* at the court, which was headed unquestionably by the *valide sultan* (mother of the sultan). She ruled the women's and her own servants' quarters with absolute authority. Her titles were fanciful, "Cradle of the Great," "Mother of the Pearl," or "Of the Pearl of the Caliphate."[8] She was instrumental in the choice of wives and concubines for her son. She extended her voice and power to the men's quarters directly through the black eunuch and indirectly through her son, the ruler. As the influence of the valide sultan increased in the court, so did that of the black eunuch who eventually came to be the most important officer in the palace.[9] With the institution of the *kafes* system (literally, the "cage"), starting around 1598, the princes, including the crown prince, were extremely restricted in their movements. They remained in the quarters assigned to them within the harem. The valide sultan undoubtedly had direct influence in the molding of the character of the future sultans.[10] At this time, the valide sultan became politically powerful enough to be instrumental in the making and unmaking of the viziers[11] and played a role in the destiny of the sultan.[12]

The valide sultan is the woman who, more than any other woman of rank, commissioned buildings. She, as the mother of the sultan, enjoyed freedom, power, and wealth. The honor paid to her during the Seljuq period in Anatolia is also evidenced in the inscriptions of various buildings of Mahperi Hatun. While she mentions the name of her son, she omits the name of her more illustrious husband, Alaeddin Kaykubad.

Generally, no wife of a sultan, including the *baş kadin* (mother of the crown prince), seems to have had the privilege of a building inscribed to her during the imperial tenure of her husband. The exception is Hurrem Sultan, wife of Sultan Suleyman. On the other hand, quite a few women whose husbands held a lesser rank in the Ottoman bureaucracy became patrons of buildings. Besides the daughters or sisters of sultans, there are those women, who, at the death of a sultan, were married off outside the palace if they were childless or the mothers of daughters by the deceased sultan. These women brought with them dowries of respectable amounts and spent part of their fortune in philanthropic activities. The names of their husbands are rarely included in the dedication inscriptions. Hudavend Hatun, who had a mausoleum built for herself during her lifetime at Nigde, includes the name of her father, a Seljuq sultan. She is believed to have been married to a Mongol official whose name is not known. A possible explanation for the omission of the husband's name is that the bond between husband and wife was regarded as too private to be publicly acknowledged. Another more sociological conclusion might be that a woman shares less in her husband's social and political position than in those of her father and sons. The tie of marriage does not seem to determine female social position to the degree that descent does. Nevertheless, wives, especially legal wives who were also daughters or sisters of princes, were quite regally treated by their husbands. For example, according to a Seljuq historian, Alaeddin Kaykubad II was chosen to rule jointly with his brothers, although he was the youngest, in deference to his mother who was of royal blood and the daughter of the Abkhazien ruler.[13] Canonical marriages, which were seldom contracted by the Ottoman sultans, occurred between the rulers and royal women, especially in the early period.[14]

Next to the valide sultan, the daughters of the sultans, particularly those who were full sisters to the crown prince, were among the most privileged in the women's quarters. Understandably, the Ottoman princess is second to the valide sultan as a donor of buildings. In dedication inscriptions, the name of her distinguished father is mentioned but not that of her husband. A large number of daughters and sisters were married to viziers or local governors of reputable standing with whom the ruler wanted to enter into strong alliances. They took with them dowries that seem to have remained their private possessions.

Prince Demetrius Cantemir wrote in the late seventeenth century describing the practice of an Ottoman royal marriage that was affected by political and economic considerations:

> The Turkish sultans are wont to marry their sisters and daughters to the pashas and vizirs, though not of fit age, nay sometimes whilst in their cradles, of whom as husbands they are to take care, and be at the charge of their education; nor can they espouse another wife, before their marriage with the Sultana is consummated. When the Sultana is of mature age, she is conducted with great pomp and magnificence from the Serai, with her portion to her husband's palace. But if, in the meantime, her husband happens to die, or lose his head by the sultan's command, she is instantly betrothed to another pasha, who succeeds to the right and charges of the former. Murad IV's sister had four husbands in one year, and not one of the marriages was celebrated according to the custom. They were accused of some crime, and put to death by the emperor, and their riches with all their effects assigned indeed to the Sultana as his law-wife, but in reality brought into the royal treasury.[15]

In the hierarchy of court women, the *daya* (wet nurse) of the Ottoman sultans emerges as a woman of high status, and one who donated buildings. The dayas of Sultans Selim I and II and of Suleyman established mosques inscribed with their names and titles. The daya is an obvious extension of the parent-child relationship, and this woman's status derives from the fact that she acted in the capacity of mother to the sultan.

There is one question concerning the nature of patronage that is difficult to answer: to what extent is the female patron actually responsible for the final shape of the building? Often a building bearing a woman's name was raised during her lifetime, out of money from her own endowments. But what is not clear is the amount of freedom of choice she exercised in selecting the site and architectural design. A related question concerns buildings built by men in honor of women. To what extent do such buildings architecturally reflect the sex or social status of their recipients? One way of evaluating the quality or substance of women's involvement in architecture is through stylistic analysis of the buildings associated with female names. The structural and ornamental peculiarities of these buildings are rather striking and indicate that, at the very least, women patrons interacted dynamically with architects and builders. Also, even when one considers buildings built by men for women together with these women patrons, it is clear that they share certain distinctive qualities.

In pre-Ottoman Anatolia, the largest group of buildings associated with women's names are mausoleums. Four examples are mentioned here. The mausoleum of Mama Hatun near Erzurum was built in the early thirteenth century. It is celebrated for its peculiar plan and astonishingly fine workmanship. The burial building is surrounded by a round enclosure with massive walls and deep rectangular niches on the inner side. In this case, the surrounding enclosure for a funerary monument is unique. The monument was visited and carefully described by Evliya Çelebi, the seventeenth-century traveler, who praised the now lost marble sarcophagus.[16]

The second mausoleum is the so-called Koşk Medrese, in Kayseri, whose plan follows that of Mama Hatun's. It was built in 1339 by Amir Aratna, and bears the inscription "the great Nuyan, the prince of Amirs of the world, Amir Aratna, for his spouse the deceased Suli Pasha."[17] In this later mausoleum, the traditional polygonal structure is surrounded by high walls with arcades facing the tomb inside. These two funerary monuments are the only two of this plan, and thus constitute a class of tomb structures by themselves.

The next two mausoleums from Seljuq Anatolia have the traditional form of this type of building, but they are distinguished by their lavish surface decoration carved in stone. These mausoleums surpass other tomb structures in Anatolia in their wealth and variety of ornamental decoration. The so-called Doner Kunbet at Kayseri, dated to late thirteenth century, exhibits animal heads, heraldic emblems, and equestrian figures. The last and most celebrated of all mausoleums is the one that belongs to Hudavend Hatun who was mentioned above. Her tomb at Nigde includes motifs that range from the purely ornamental to enigmatic masks, harpies, and human figures placed among interlacing geometric lines. It was built in 1312. In brief, tombs associated with women's names are clearly distinguished by their unusual plans and decorative motifs.

With respect to buildings other than mausoleums, one important building from the Ottoman period belongs to a rather unusual type, a zawiya, or a convent for dervishes. A zawiya was built in 1388 at Iznik by Sultan Murad I Hudavendigar, in memory of his mother Nilufer Hatun who must have been long dead by then. Nilufer Hatun was the daughter of a Greek lord and was abducted in 1299 by Osman Bey to become the wife of his then twelve-year-old son, Orhan Bey. The marriage also symbolized the annexation of her father's estates. Orhan Bey was particularly faithful to her and left her in charge of the state while he was on various campaigns. It could very well have been Nilufer Hatun whom Ibn Battuta visited and praised as the regent of Iznik and wife of Orhan Bey.[18]

Nilufer Hatun was not the only non-Muslim woman who married a sultan and became a most prominent figure in the early Ottoman period. In fact, most of the women who came to the court were of non-Muslim origin and were acquired by the palace as slaves. Many sultans' mothers belonged to this slave group.

One woman who came to the Ottoman palace as a slave but later contracted a legal marriage with Sultan Suleyman II was Hurrem Sultan (1504?–1558). She was probably of Slavic origin, hence the name Russo or Roxalana. When she became the favorite consort of the sultan, the valide sultan was still alive, and there was already a reigning "first woman" in the court who had given birth to the crown prince, the eldest son of Suleyman. The mother of Suleyman died in 1533, and the "first woman" who could no longer resist the unlimited influence of Hurrem on the sultan resigned from her position at the court and chose to live with her own son in a distant province. Hurrem, now married and a "sultan" herself, reigned without a rival. Soon, through her plotting, the eldest son of Suleyman was strangled, which left the promise of the future throne to the sons of Hurrem.

Her spiral to power apparently was so astonishing that Busbecq accuses her in his *Letters* of being a sorceress.[19] Her participation in politics became apparent particularly during the long absences of her husband. She, joining with her daughter Mihrimah and son-in-law Rustem Pasha, took part in the dismissal and execution of one grand vizier. In a letter to her husband Suleyman, after chastising him for not writing longer letters, Hurrem Sultan evasively mentions her grievances toward the grand vizier and promises explanations when the sultan returns.[20]

Sultan Suleyman granted many presents to his sole legal wife and enriched her charitable and educational foundations by donations of money, villages, and arable fields. She is the only regal wife to lend her name to buildings during the lifetime of her husband. Her most magnificent contribution to Ottoman architecture is a double bathhouse in the center of Istanbul, with separate but identical sections for men and women. She also sponsored caravansarays in western Turkey, shrines in Mecca and Medina, and the building and repair of bridges.[21]

Mihrimah Sultan (?–1578), daughter of Sultan Suleyman and Roxalana, is the most famous princess in Ottoman history. She was also the patron of extensive pious, educational, and charitable institutions. She was an ambitious woman with a strong personality, as demonstrated in her mother's letters, and in the accounts of her contemporaries whenever her name is mentioned. Mihrimah Sultan played a considerable role in political life during the reigns of her father Suleyman II and her brother Selim II.

Mihrimah Sultan was married by her father to Rustem Pasha, governor of distant Diyarbekir, who is described as "not too handsome, but capable and intelligent."[22] Her wedding took place on the same day as the circumcision celebrations of her brothers. Later, Rustem Pasha, through the plotting of his wife and mother-in-law, succeeded in becoming twice grand vizier to Sultan Suleyman. The ascent of Rustem to the post, the execution of the previous grand vizier, and the strangling of the crown prince (the half-brother of Mihrimah Sultan) are directly attributed to her and her mother by the Ottoman historian Muneccimbaşi.[23] Mihrimah Sultan notably encouraged her father to carry out the campaigns to Malta.[24] Busbecq mentions that Rustem Pasha managed his affairs quite well with the support and help of the two women; that is, his wife and his mother-in-law.[25] According to Ottoman historians, Mihrimah Sultan was preferred by her father to his sons and was regarded a wise woman and a philanthropist.[26] When Hurrem Sultan appealed to her sovereign husband, she pleaded discreetly, "for the sake of your daughter Mihrimah."[27] Through her own dowry, from the revenues of the structures she sponsored, and from the inheritance she secured from her husband, Mihrimah Sultan amassed a huge independent fortune. She willed her possessions to pious and charitable institutions, although her descendants must have profited from the revenues of her foundations. She was fond of her brother Selim II; she loaned him 50,000 gold ducats when he acceded to the throne.[28] And she was the first formally to recognize her brother upon his accession to the throne.[29]

Mihrimah Sultan holds a unique position in Ottoman architecture, with two major mosques that bear her name, both with extensive dependent (side) buildings, such as bathhouses and medreses. The architect Sinan was charged with the construction of both mosques and the surrounding buildings honoring this princess. The beach of Uskudar on the Asian shores of Istanbul was the site for the first mosque (the Mosque of Mihrimah). The available plot was narrow and leaned against a steep hill. To balance the mosque against the hill, the architect raised it on a platform on firm foundations above the sea level. The lack of space for the usual courtyard that precedes the mosque is compensated with a double porch and a rather impressive fountain. The interior of the mosque is light and airy; it is imposing from the exterior, and despite its cramped site and the odds against it due to its natural setting, it achieves a monumentality. The architect successfully challenged the problem of designing a conventional building in an unconventional location.

The second mosque dedicated to Mihrimah Sultan is equally successful in solving problems created by the location. This mosque, also designed by the architect Sinan, is located at Edirnekapi, immediately inside the city walls, in a rather remote locale. The structure lacks a date, but is probably later than the Uskudar edifice. Because it has only one minaret against the two of the earlier one, it is safe to say that Mihrimah Sultan herself ordered the construction. On the other hand, Sultan Suleyman may have been responsible for the mosque at Uskudar, since it has the royal two minarets. The mosques ordered by valide sultans, however, traditionally have two minarets, acquiring an equal status with those built by rulers.

The Edirnekapi mosque is also built on a high artificial platform. Thus, it is not overwhelmed by the Byzantine walls or the low ground level. The platform on which the mosque stands is approached on three sides by stairways. The approaches are constructed provocatively with the use of landings for viewing the city, small kiosks for resting, vaulted passages, and double gates. Once on the platform, the limited size of the courtyard is disguised by the unusual presence of trees and shrubbery. Behind the arcading around the garden courtyard are the seventeen-roomed medrese cells. Thus, not wishing to sacrifice the medrese, Sinan organized the courtyard to serve dual purposes, an arrangement quite unique in Ottoman architecture.

The interior of the mosque is perhaps the loftiest and brightest in Istanbul. By transferring the weight of the dome to the thick arches, the architect was able to reduce the walls merely to screens on which he could open multiple rectangular and round windows. As Evliya

Çelebi noted, the mosque recalls a festive place, more like a *qasr* or palace.[30] From outside, too, the plasticity of the cube, the bulk of the round dome, and the accentuated arches which frame the depressed curtain walls, give the building a sense of monumentality despite its modest dimensions. It has been called one of the revolutionary buildings of the Ottoman architecture.[31] The mosque and dependent buildings of Mihrimah Sultan are remarkable testimonials to the utilization of space and the creation of grandeur on a small and cramped site without the sacrifice of any of the essential parts of a royal edifice. Mihrimah Sultan was a woman who did not compromise easily, the historians of the Ottoman Empire report, and her monuments stand as evidence of her spirit.

The New Mosque, or, as it is more appropriately called, the New Mosque of the Valide Sultan, is the last mosque to be built in Istanbul in the classical manner. Its odd site on the low shores of the Golden Horn, rather than on a more commanding site, makes one wonder if women were not given choice land for their structures. The mosque had a long history of construction which involved the direct planning and supervising of three architects by three valide sultans.

The construction started in 1598 under the auspices of Safiye Sultan, during the reign of her son Mehmed III (1595–1603). Her given Christian name was recorded as Baffo, and she took pride in being from Venice. She became the favorite consort of Murad III (1572–1595). For a duration of five or six years, Sultan Murad was faithful to her, shunning other women. Later he diverted his attention to concubines. Safiye Sultan, being the mother of the oldest son, once again enjoyed power when her son Mehmed came to throne, and she ruled as valide sultan. With her rule the so-called Era of Women's Reign in Ottoman history began. She exerted an extraordinary power over her son and became his chief adviser. He granted his mother the possession of freeholdings in Egypt, which served as the financial resources for the mosque she was planning to have built. Mehmed III, remarkably, never built a royal mosque for himself. Safiye Sultan, even before the construction of her mosque, selected scholars to serve at her foundation. She did not remain long enough at the Topkapi Palace to enjoy the completion of the mosque. She was banished to the Old Palace by her grandson Ahmed I, who succeeded to the throne in 1603. The new ruler had plans for his own royal mosque and its adjoining buildings. Since the economic situation would not have permitted expenses for two monumental mosques, that of Safiye Sultan was abandoned. The construction of the New Mosque of the Valide Sultan had been interrupted with the death of the first architect until a new one was appointed. The second interruption occurred during Ahmed's reign. It was resumed after his death in 1617. The new patron was Kosem Mahpeyker Sultan.

If an Ottoman woman is to be chosen to represent the power of the valide in her full capacity, it should be Kosem Mahpeyker Sultan (1589–1631), wife of Sultan Ahmed I. She came to the harem of the Topkapi Palace as a slave but quickly distinguished herself not so much by her beauty as by her intelligence, attractiveness, vivaciousness, and tact.[32] She was at least a year older than Sultan Ahmed when she became a *haseki* (of the ruler's room). Sultan Ahmed died in 1617 at a young age, and she was forced to retire to the Old Palace for a short interval. During her banishment she still held considerable power, as indicated by the unusual three-day visit of her stepson, Osman II, to her dwelling.[33] She returned to the Topkapi Palace as her son Murad IV ascended the throne in 1623, and she remained there as a strong ruler during the reigns of two sons and one grandson, until she was strangled on the orders of her own daughter-in-law and rival Hadice Turhan Sultan in 1651. During her tenure in the palace as the valide and grand valide, a period which forms part of the Era of Women's Reign in Ottoman history, she was directly and unquestionably instrumental in governmental policies. She occasionally presided at meetings. When the janissaries staged an uprising, it was Valide Kosem Mahpeyker Sultan who made the decision to melt precious metals from the palace treasury to mint coins with which to bribe these elite corps. When her son Ibrahim (1640–1648) showed an interest in governmental affairs, instead of relinquishing her power to him, she replenished the number of concubines in his harem to keep Ibrahim occupied with debauchery. Kosem Sultan was thwarted only by another woman, the equally ambitious and politically motivated Valide Hadice Turhan Sultan.

Hadice Turhan Sultan's son, Mehmed IV, was more interested in hunting game than in governmental affairs. She assumed the seat vacated by the great valide sultan and became the power behind the government. She directly influenced her son's decisions in his selections of viziers, some among the ablest men at the time. Having replaced the old valide, Hadice Turhan had to be persuaded to resume the construction of the abandoned mosque. This she did, only after having built a pavilion next to it from which she could personally supervise the construction. Ottoman historians recorded her death (1683) thus: "the great pillar of the state has passed away."

The New Mosque of the Valide Sultan and its dependent buildings were completed in 1663. Among these buildings are mausoleums, fountains, bathhouses, and the famous Egyptian Bazaar. The latter was completed before the mosque; it is an L-shaped market with six gates and eighty-six shops and chambers over the major end gateways. The first architect entrusted with the construction was Davud Aga, successor to architect Sinan in competence and fame. In order to raise the mosque on the narrow and undesirable site on the seashore, he had to build a series of islets and bridges on sunken piers of stone reinforced with iron. The mosque itself is not in any way innovative. The dome comes to a sharp point, most probably having suffered from changes of design through long years. However, to achieve a harmonious and vast complex on an artificial land-fill is no small task in itself. The strong will and generosity of the three valide sultans made the enterprise possible. The significance of the ambitious undertaking is more apparent when one considers the dwindling power and wealth of the Ottoman Empire at that time, and particularly the fact that Mehmed IV, although the ruler, did not have a mosque to commemorate his own name.

The most engrossing and innovative part of this vast complex is the pavilion built over a deep and high arch abutting the mosque. The pavilion is approached from the east, separated from the mosque by a long ramp. The pavilion, with a view of the harbor, consists of two rooms, an L-shaped hall, and a corridor that connects the structure with the royal loggia in the mosque. The loggia inside the mosque is spacious and has gilded lattices. It is more enclosed compared with the open galleries and loggias of the earlier mosques. It was clearly meant to serve the valide sultan. The pavilion is one of the exquisite examples of secular architecture of the Ottomans. The walls and ceilings of the rooms are covered with the best tiles and paintings of the period.

The last mosque that was donated by a valide sultan to be mentioned here bears the name of Pertevniyal, wife of Sultan Mahmud II and mother of Sultan Abdulaziz. The mosque, which is in the Aksaray quarter of Istanbul, was completed in 1871. Attached to it are a tomb building, a fountain, and a splendid courtyard which is approached by wide marble staircases that lead to monumental and ornate gates. The mosque is small, single-domed, and has two minarets. Its originality lies in its daring surface decoration. The motifs that are carved on its marble facades include those recalling Seljuq period floral and geometric interlacings, as well as the Indian flower arrangements found on the Taj

Mahal, and fanciful Western neo-Gothic windows. It is the only religious building in Istanbul that attempted the fashionable eclectic style of this time.

Besides the small gem of a building Pertevniyal Sultan sponsored, a tragic episode in her life is among the few facts known about her life. Her son Abdulaziz was forced to abdicate his throne in favor of his brother. Later he took his own life with a pair of scissors that were handed to him by her.

The funding of architectural undertakings by palace women was a complicated issue with no one basic form. From various accounts of the expenditure of specific women, it seems clear that they had income from several sources and that they could act quite independently in terms of managing their own money. There is no reason to think that the process of building for women was basically different from that for men in Ottoman society. According to written sources, women went through similar steps in acquiring land and financing and establishing *waqf* foundations (religious endowments) to maintain the enterprise. The subtle differences between women's buildings and men's are in the choice of sites allowed to women, in the ornamentation of their architecture, and in the content of dedicatory inscriptions, which are far more modest and less informative than those belonging to men. Finally, a woman's construction is more likely to have been interrupted to make resources available for another structure, especially if it happened to be sponsored by the ruler.

The women in the palace harem were paid regular salaries in addition to allowances for clothing, and they could control their own "treasury." Women of high rank in the Ottoman court or those from wealthy families of the society were given rich dowries, some of which were in the form of money and jewelry. According to Busbecq, the dowry was the only thing that distinguished a lawful wife from a concubine, for a slave had no dowry. If a woman brought with her an unusually high dowry, the husband undertook on his part to avoid concubines and to be faithful to one wife.[34] Even if this information might be taken as exaggerated and simplified, it does show the basic link between the status and wealth of an individual.

Women who were immediate relations of the ruler were often helped financially by the state. Mihrimah Sultan, daughter of Suleyman II, who commanded great wealth of her own, was given money from the palace treasuries during the construction of her mosque at Edirnekapi in Istanbul.[35]

The land to be given for an architectural enterprise was usually under the direct control of the ruler. A woman, or a man, requested a royal grant of land and property rights in order to establish a foundation. If permission was granted, the endowments would often be supplemented with a gift of the freehold of a piece of land, sometimes containing several villages.[36] Such land would finance the maintenance of the foundation.

Buildings that were built by or dedicated to women generally served religious functions. Secular buildings are quite rare, and when they exist they usually form part of the dependencies of a mosque, or are sources of income for the maintenance of a mosque. There appears to be no residential structure built by or for a woman, complying with the tradition that a woman is not viewed as an independent family head. The valide sultan appears to be a woman with acknowledged and often formalized power. She undertakes construction of various mosques, mausoleums, and schools. Her mosque could have more than one minaret, a right otherwise reserved only for the ruling sultan. In the dedication inscriptions she signs herself as the mother of the reigning son, in deference to the ruler, rather than as the wife of the late sultan. Daughters of sultans, and women who upon the death of a sultan had left the privacy of the palace, were quite active in architectural enterprises, even when married to men of lower ranks. In such cases, though, they did not include the name of the husband.

When the imposing power enjoyed by valide sultans is reviewed, one suspects that this institution was encouraged by one other motivation. In a household like that of the Ottoman court where the sultan sired numerous sons by several women, it seems that sons wished to distinguish themselves from half-brothers, through maternal descent, by honoring their own mothers. The utmost respect and power granted to mothers, and the buildings dedicated to mothers by their sons, may be partly a result of this desire for differentiation. Sultan Murad I was one of the earliest rulers to erect a structure (a zawiya) in the memory of his mother, long after her death. Mehmed IV (1658–1687) and Ahmed III (1703–1730) did not commemorate themselves with their own royal mosques, but preferred to accept the building of a valide or mother's mosque as the major structure of their reign.

It is true that none of the women's buildings attain the grandiose dimensions of buildings that men had dedicated nor were they built in important sections of the city. Whether dating from Seljuq Anatolia, or from the richest era of the Ottoman Empire, buildings associated with women are significant in number and exhibit architectural peculiarities not generally found in the more monumental but conservative royal structures undertaken by men to commemorate themselves. The architects working on buildings bearing the names of women seem to have been challenged with unusual structural problems, such as raising a mosque directly on the shoreline or designing a unique plan for a tomb. In the ornamentation of buildings, too, the architects were less constrained in the choice of decorative motifs. Women's buildings in Turkish Anatolia are often innovative in structural aspects, rich in decorative details, and testimonials to the quiet but real power of women.

Notes

1. A study of this kind can be extended to the architectural record of other Islamic countries. Unfortunately, published material on the buildings, especially on the inscriptions and *waqf* documents, is scanty and uneven.

2. These mausoleums are described and analyzed in Ü. Bates, "Anatolian Mausoleums of the Twelfth, Thirteenth and Fourteenth Centuries," Ph.D. dissertation (Ann Arbor, Mich., 1970).

3. Kurt Erdmann, *Das Antolische Karavansaray des 13. Jahrhunderts*, part I (Berlin, 1961), p. 62.

4. Fewer tomb towers were built after approximately 1400. This decrease in erecting commemorative buildings honoring individuals can be attributed to the centralization movement in the Ottoman Empire, the suppression of heterodox orders in Anatolia, and the increasing power of the ulama who represented the "high Islam."

5. Tahsin Öz, *Istanbul camileri*, 2 vols. (Istanbul, 1962).

6. Dogan Kuban, "Sinan and the Classical Age of Turkish Architecture," *Mimarlik dergisi*, 1 (Istanbul, 1967), pp. 13–44.

7. In the Ottoman court, at the death of the reigning sultan, unmarried sisters and daughters were removed to the Old Palace in the center of Istanbul, where they would spend their life in seclusion. Only the mother of the succeeding sultan remained in the official Topkapi Palace to organize the new harem. (R. Mantran, *La vie quotidienne à Constantinople* [Paris, 1965], p. 195; A. D. Alderson, *The Structure of the Ottoman Dynasty* [Oxford, 1956], p. 81.)

8. Fanny Davis, *The Palace of Topkapi in Istanbul* (New York, 1970), p. 203.

9. Halil Inalcik, *The Ottoman Empire: The Classical Age, 1300–1600*, trans. N. Itzkowitz and C. Imber (New York and Washington, D.C., 1973), p. 86.

10. Mantran, *La vie quotidienne*, p. 194; N. M. Penzer, *The Harem: An Account of the Institution as it Existed in the Palace of the Turkish Sultans with a History of the Grand Seraglio from its Foundation to the Present Time* (London, 1966), p. 174.

11. Inalcik, *The Ottoman Empire,* p. 98.
12. Ibid., p. 60.
13. Karim al-Din Mahmud Aqsarayi, *Selçuki devletleri tarihi,* trans. (into Turkish) M. N. Gencosman (Ankara, 1943), p. 133.
14. Inalcik, *The Ottoman Empire,* p. 87.
15. Demetrius Cantemir, *The History of the Growth and Decay of the Ottoman Empire,* part I, 1300–1683, trans. N. Tindal (London, 1734), p. 179.
16. Evliya Çelebi, *Seyahatname,* II (Istanbul, 1896–1938), p. 202.
17. Albert Gabriel, *Les monuments turcs d'Anatolie,* I (Paris, 1931), p. 67.
18. Ibn Battutah, *Travels in Asia and Africa,* 1325–1354, trans. and selected H. A. R. Gibb (London, 1963), p. 136.
19. Ogier Ghiselin de Busbecq, *The Turkish Letters,* trans. from the Elzevir edition of 1633, E. S. Forster (Oxford, 1968), p. 32.
20. Inalcik, *The Ottoman Empire,* p. 87.
21. Ibrahim Peçevi, *A History of the Turkish Empire* [in Turkish] (Istanbul, 1866), I, pp. 426–427.
22. Peçevi, *A History of the Turkish Empire,* I, p. 21.
23. Müneccimbaşi Ahmed Dede, *Sahaif ul-ahbar fi vekayi ul-a'sar,* trans. (into Turkish) I. Erunsal (Istanbul, n.d.), II, p. 563.
24. M. Tayyib Gokbilgin, "Hurrem Sultan," in *Islam ansiklopedisi* (Istanbul, 1964), V, part 1, pp. 593–596; and M. C. Baysun, "Mihr-u-mah Sultan," *Islam ansiklopedisi* (Istanbul, 1970), VIII, pp. 307–308.
25. Busbecq, *Turkish Letters,* p. 87.
26. Müneccimbaşi, II, p. 593.
27. Baysun, "Mihr-u-mah Sultan," p. 307.
28. Ibid.
29. Alderson, *The Structure of the Ottoman Dynasty,* p. 40.
30. Kuban, "Sinan . . . ," p. 20.
31. Ibid.
32. M. C. Baysun, "Kosem Sultan," *Islam ansiklopedisi* (Istanbul, 1967), VI, pp. 915–923.
33. Ibid., p. 916.
34. Busbecq, *Turkish Letters,* pp. 117–119.
35. Çelebi, *Seyahatname,* I, p. 165.
36. Inalcik, *The Ottoman Empire,* p. 148.

13 The Revolutionary Gentlewomen in Egypt

Afaf Lutfi al-Sayyid Marsot

The history of the Middle East abounds in stereotypes and clichés, nowhere more abundantly than in the realm of women's studies. The position of women in the Middle East, the Arab world, or Islam is frequently described as though only one of these three nomenclatures formed homogeneous blocs that one could conveniently describe and summarize en masse. The truth is obviously quite different. For although one can talk theoretically, in the abstract, of *women in Islam* and refer to the passages in the Quran and in the *sharia* that spell out the rights and obligations of women in an Islamic society, the practice in one Muslim country differs from that in another, since local societies have chosen to accentuate that element of religion that was most congenial to their way of life. Hence social differences within the Islamic community have led to different developments in each Muslim country, in the same way that social differences have led to different practices in various segments of the same society. For example, the rural, working-class woman in Egypt never wore the veil, while the upper-class, urban woman did. For that reason I would like to limit this article to a small segment of Egyptian women and to a brief period of time in the history of that country, to this century.

Before embarking on the concrete subject of the women in question, one can, however, outline certain basic elements that are found in common among most of the women in Egypt. These elements have their origins in the ancient Egyptian customs that have lasted with some modifications, and in the sharia, as well as in the historical experiences of that country. And while some of these elements may be found in other societies, Muslim and non-Muslim, no generalizations will be attempted here except in local terms.

From time immemorial Egypt has been an agricultural society, depending on irrigation. The implications arising from such an experience are twofold. In the first place, the reliance of an agricultural society on irrigation has created the need for cooperation on a wider scale than that of the immediate family. Any hydraulic society is usually highly centralized. In Egypt is found an age-old reliance on the central authority which led to the development of a hierarchic society rather than an egalitarian one. In the second place, women as well as men in an agricultural society work in the fields. The men perform certain tasks such as plowing, hoeing, and irrigating, while the women perform others like harvesting, winnowing, and livestock-raising and all its connected tasks. Both men and women sell and barter in the marketplace. Thus the rural structure is based on a cooperative venture and a division of labor between the sexes. In Pharaonic times women were the "focus of the house,"[1] the house ruler or leader, rather than the male, as is more common in other societies. Heredity in the royal families went through the female line. The conquest of Egypt by Persians and Greeks modified that picture, and aristocratic Egyptian women were relegated to an inferior position like their counterparts in Hellenic society: they were introduced to the customs of seclusion and the veil around the third century B.C.

The advent of Islam added a further dimension to that picture. The sharia gave the Muslim woman the legal right of inheritance from parents, spouse, and offspring, and gave her the legal right to own property and to dispose of it without her spouse's consent. Or to put it in another way, in theory the Muslim woman did not need her husband's consent in order to manage her property; to the contrary her husband needed her legal consent before he could touch her property. The law likewise made the husband entirely responsible for the support of his wife and family. Since the woman inherited only half the amount of the male, the apparent discriminatory condition was mitigated by the fact that the prospective bridegroom paid the bride a sum of money (*mahr*), which was stipulated in the marriage contract and without which a contract would be invalid. The mahr constituted the wife's legal property. In general it defrayed the expenses of furnishing the conjugal house so that automatically the contents of a house belonged to the wife, unless the husband could legally prove the contrary. In case of a divorce, the wife was also entitled to a sum of money, the amount of which was also stipulated in the marriage contract. The divorcée was entitled to an alimony for a limited period of time until she was proven to be free of child. In case of children, the father was liable for child support, paid to the mother who retained custody of the children until the boy reached the age of nine and the girl the age of eleven, at which time the children reverted to the custody of their father, unless he had waived that right, in return for which he usually paid no child support.

Implicit in the law, therefore, was the fact that woman controlled her financial life, but shared in that of her husband, and that nonsupport constituted grounds for divorce. The law also implied that women were to be supported in the style to which they had been accustomed in their parents' house—hence the legal as distinguished from Quranic injunction that women marry only equals.[2] Early in the twentieth century a famous case centered around the daughter of Shaikh al-Sadat, a religious dignitary. The lady, being of age, had married a lesser shaikh, Ali Yusif, without her father's consent. Her father then went to court declaring the marriage to be invalid since his daughter had married a social inferior. While the case was motivated by political factors, and was only shelved through the intervention of the British consul-general, Lord Cromer, it was a clear example of such valid grounds for divorce as social inequality.

When a husband acquired more than one wife, he was expected to provide for each equally in terms of housing and expenditure. Should he fail to meet these commitments, that too constituted grounds for divorce, since the Quranic injunction stipulates that equity among wives is imperative upon the believer, and equally stipulates that should that be difficult for the husband then it is preferable that he limit himself to one wife. Modern reformers have interpreted that passage to mean a limitation of polygamy since it is impossible to treat several wives with any degree of material and emotional equity. It is on these grounds, for instance, that Tunisia had prohibited polygamy. In Egypt polygamy at present represents 0.05 percent of marriages, so the government has not been willing to defy religious fervour for such a minute percentage of the population. Economic realities have already limited polygamy.

Muslim legal rights, plus seclusion in the *harem* (which came into the Muslim world with the Abbasid dynasty, and was carried to a climax under the Ottomans), have given rise to the strange phenomenon of an upper-class woman who was secluded in the harem, but who nevertheless continued to manage her property, and who formed an active element in the economic life of her society, either directly or through her agents. Jabarti, the great chronicler of the late eighteenth and early ninteenth centuries, gives accounts of women who "bought, sold, traded, and made their husband's fortunes," like the wife of Shaikh al-Sharqawi who was rector of al-Azhar.[3] And while such cases are rare, nonetheless we learn from Jabarti that aside from the Mamluks and the *ulama,* who represented the alien and the native elites in the land, the women formed the chief groups of *multazims* (tax-farmers) of the agricultural land, one of the major sources of income of that period.[4]

Because Muslim women in Egypt have controlled their property, or rather because some of the wealthy women controlled their property, we find women as well as men setting up charitable endowments which are known as *awqaf.* A waqf is property held in perpetuity, a mortmain endowment either in favor of the members of a family, when it becomes known as a *waqf ahli,* or in favor of a charity, when it becomes known as *waqf khairi,* or a combination of both; that is, it is endowed for the family and some charitable works. Most social services in Islamic societies were thus dependent on charitable endowments which set up hospitals, schools, drinking fountains, libraries, funds to endow penniless orphans upon marriage, to bury the destitute, to feed the poor, to educate the poor, to help the blind, to recite prayers for the dead, and so on. Among the powerful and the rich it was a noblesse oblige sentiment throughout the ages that part of one's wealth be expended on charitable works, generally after one's death, but not exclusively so. Aside from specific property that was endowed, the wealthy were also expected to undertake a continuous stream of charities that formed their share of the *zakat,* the alms that every Muslim is enjoined to defray and is one of the five pillars of Islam. During festive days the rich were expected to hold an open table for the poor and to distribute articles of raiment to the needy. As landholders they exploited their peasantry to the hilt, but they were also expected to distribute largesse on feast days. Thus, there was a definite tradition of public service on the part of the rich, both men and women. Undoubtedly today, it would be called paternalism, but in the past ages that term would be anachronistic. In the twentieth century the tradition of helping the less fortunate members of society was to cause the affluent women to found the social services that are necessary to any modern society, as will be seen below.

A question that jumps to mind is: how did women who were secluded in a harem learn to run their property, and how did they learn to run such complex establishments as the hospitals and schools which they founded later on? The answer is to be found in the life of the harem, which is where these women learned to become managers.

Authors of books dealing with harem life have tended to describe the harem in terms of extremes. The harem was presented either as a lascivious place where odalisques reclined in voluptuous poses in expectation of their master's visit, or in tones of revulsion as a place of idleness and apathy. No doubt there was a partial truth in both extreme descriptions for some of the royal harems. Life in an average affluent harem, as described to me by the women who lived it, was a very busy and gregarious one. The lady or ladies of the household had to exercise a number of executive and managerial decisions to ensure the smooth running of the household. An "average" household, if such a thing existed, numbered indoor and outdoor servants of both sexes, some free, some slaves both black and white, some manumitted, wives, children, and "poor relations," plus a variety of aunts, perhaps a mother and a grandmother.[5]

Ultimate decisions rested with the first wife, who sometimes chose the other wives for her husband. Squabbles among wives and among their progeny were frequent, as one would expect in any large household, but these were not based on Western concepts of love and jealousy for the husband's attention, but rather on more concrete factors such as precedence, favors for their offspring, and material benefits. There was a rigid hierarchy within the harem and a strict protocol reigned. Freeborn women had precedence over Mamluk (white) slave women; Turco-Circassians, whether free or not, had precedence over freeborn Egyptians. Wives and established concubines addressed each other as "sister" or as *"hanim"* (lady). Each wife had separate quarters within the family residence, and had separate servants. Each child had its own personal servant, and each infant had a wet nurse. Every wife had her visiting day, when her friends flocked in to be treated to a day's festivities and entertainment which included music and dancing.

Harem life, however, was not entirely devoted to idleness and gossip; it also had to deal with the practical details of everyday living. Household kitchens had to be supervised, and three separate meals a day prepared. In most affluent households open house was held, and the master would bring friends in to meals and be sure that the food presented to them would do him honor. In all the households that have been described to me the amount of food that was prepared and consumed in one day sounded like the activities of a fair-sized hotel or restaurant. Food was bought in wholesale quantities. Meat came by the carcass, fruit and vegetables in cases, mostly from the master's estates. Aside from the sheer logistics involved in serving meals to each lady and her children in their quarters, serving the master and his guests in the *salamlik* (the guest quarters or the men's quarters), and feeding the family retainers (each chore being entrusted to a separate set of servants), there was also the daily distribution of food to the poor, for leftovers were an unknown factor in the lives of these families. After every meal the remains were distributed to the poor, and in some households separate meals were cooked specially for distribution to the poor.

The cleaning of these large establishments was likewise a daily chore, especially in Cairo where the dust is a constant presence unless assiduously whisked away. When the Khamsin winds blew, this task was performed several times a day. And while all these chores and many others were carried out by the servants, they were supervised and planned by the women themselves. Labor was divided among the women of the harem, but ultimate responsibility, the settlement of inevitable squabbles, the organization of special events, all these rested with the leading wife, who was the dynamo of the entire establishment.

The children of the household likewise received a great deal of attention. The boys lived in the harem until the age of seven, and had a resident shaikh teach them the rudiments of learning and religion. When they grew older they went to school or into the care of other tutors, and were guarded by special servants, each boy having his own. The girls were also taught religion by a resident shaikha, who also recited Quran to the ladies. Teachers of embroidery and music were brought to the house to instruct both young and old. Later in time these teachers were supplemented by teachers of foreign languages, in general French. It also became fashionable to acquire a governess for the children; English nannies and Swiss frauleins were the most popular.

The master of the house entered the harem at nightfall, and left it in the morning, unless he was addicted to night life, in which case he seldom showed up in the harem. The master's advent was a signal for every wife to scurry into her quarters and prepare herself for the husband's visit, social or otherwise, for the husband, if courteous, would pay a call to every wife and visit for a while, before choosing where to spend his night. In some households there was a regular routine in which it was known that on such nights the husband went to such a wife, so that each wife knew her appointed day for receiving her husband.

The ladies of the house left their establishments veiled and chaperoned, in closed coaches, so that no eye could penetrate the darkness of the carriage and inspect the beauties inside it. Nonetheless, the women did have numerous outside activities. They visited one another on visiting days, to console in case of a death (for three days and every subsequent Thursday for forty days), and to congratulate on a betrothal in the family. On the feast days the entire household moved to the cemetery. The family mausoleum was equipped with bedrooms, separate kitchens for the men and the women, and with bathrooms, which allowed the family to reside with their dead relatives for the feast period. Visits to the bathhouse were also allowed although most affluent ladies had their own baths at home.

The image of a harem was thus one of a very busy household, where people continually bustled around and where no one could remain idle on pain of being charged with a chore. Even the "*jeunes filles*" of the household had to be busy with some embroidery, music, or whatever, or else they were given something to do by their elders. Daily routine and the efficient management of the house were the women's first concerns. These women therefore grew up with the notion that they would in time have to plan and organize their own households on a similar scale. They were accustomed to giving orders and to making their own decisions, for the master seldom if ever interfered in their lives, so long as everything functioned smoothly and above all unobtrusively, with an apparent effortlessness that belied the hard work that went on behind the scenes and the degree of organization that ensured a contant flow of services. The household and its organization were the domain of the women, their testing ground so to speak. How they ran it was a test of their efficiency and initiative as compared with their friends and relations. To this day one of the worst things that can be said about a woman is that she is incapable of managing her house; behind this apparently innocent expression lie visions of generations of efficient housewives who had no trouble in managing their houses.

The above image of the harem presses upon the reader the concept of the gentlewoman as someone who was accustomed to organization and to planning, for that is what they had been trained to do in life. That quality was to stand them in good stead when they later on sat down in a committee to plan how to set up and run a hospital or a dispensary. They may never have learned to cook, but they knew how to run large kitchens and serve a variety of meals. Above all, they knew how to manipulate people and how to delegate authority. The first talent allowed them to raise funds to finance their projects and marshal support for them from among their vast circle of friends and relations, while the second helped them to find the necessary staff to run their outfits with success.

If one is therefore to understand how these women were able to succeed in public service after a cloistered life in a harem, one must perforce reject the stereotype of the harem as a warm cocoon and come to regard it simply as a microcosm of upper-class Egyptian society, a society in which women felt at ease, and which they controlled. The outside world was simply a larger arena in which the women exercised their talents, and one which did not differ save in magnitude.

Throughout the history of Egypt the chroniclers report that in times of hardship the whole populace demonstrated in public before the authorities. Very few women had public roles or developed a primary political role, save for cases like that of Nafissa Hanim (wife of Murad Bey, the Mamluk ruler of Egypt during the last two decades of the eighteenth century) who looked after her husband's interests during his exile. Nonetheless, women did play a secondary role in times of crisis when they sought the authorities to complain of some measure of injustice or of hardship.[6] Women became politically involved when their interests were at stake. This limited involvement was to become more extensive in this century, and was to allow them to partake in the political movement that followed Egypt's cry for independence from British rule in 1919. That is why this article is called the "revolutionary gentlewomen" for the women had become politically involved in the events of 1919, but had also started a social revolution on their own when they discarded both veil and harem and set about organizing the country's social services.

In November 1918 some Egyptian nationalists founded a group to determine Egypt's political future once the war was over. That group came to be known as the Wafd, a word that means delegation. Part of that group had gone as a delegation to meet the British high commissioner, Sir Reginald Wingate, to discuss with him the future of Egypt in light of allied declarations of self-determination. The three men who formed the delegation, headed by Sa'd Pasha Zaghlul, ended by demanding complete independence for Egypt. When their request for a hearing at the Paris Peace Conference was turned down by the British authorities, the Wafd turned to public demonstrations, of a peaceful nature, to show the British that they meant business. The British authorities sent the leaders of the Wafd into exile and met the demonstrations with gunfire, thereby triggering off the "revolution of 1919." The events of that year could be described as a national manifestation of solidarity for the Wafd and its demands. While the political elite of Egypt had joined the Wafd, their wives also became involved in the movement and created a women's committee. The veiled gentlewomen of Cairo paraded in the streets shouting slogans for independence and freedom from foreign occupation. They organized strikes and demonstrations, they organized boycotts of British goods, and they wrote petitions which they circulated to the foreign embassies protesting British actions in Egypt; in brief they agitated side by side with their men.[7]

The existence of a revolution brought the women out of their harems and into the public arena, with the approval of their husbands, who in normal times would not have tolerated such a public display on the part of their womenfolk. The emancipation of women, which had been an intellectual issue over the past two decades, from the time when Qasim Amin (1865–1908) had published *The Emancipation of Woman* and *The New Woman*, then became a nationalist issue, closely allied to the nationalist movement. Thus it was a radical shock, like a nationalist uprising, which catapulted harem ladies into public life. From that moment onward their emancipation became a reality, and when the revolution had come to an end, the women continued to exercise their talents in public life.

Thus it was that Huda Hanim Sha'rawi, wife of one of the Wafd's founders, and a few of her friends founded the League of Women in 1923. The history of their deeds is written elsewhere, and by now their story is fairly well-known.[8] However, there are unsung female activists in Egypt, women whose achievements rank equally with those of the Women's League, because they were directed toward benefiting the whole society, not only establishing women's rights, important enough though that was. There is something fine and inspiring about a group of women fighting the political establishment—which comprised their husbands and relatives—to gain recognition of their right to education and to political equality, to say nothing of their right to earn a living were they so inclined. A less glorified but more concrete contribution was that made by the women who set up so-called charitable organizations, which among them covered the large majority of social services that exist in Egypt today. There they did not have to fight any establishment, but were on the contrary encouraged by the establishment: they merely had to cope with ignorance, disease, poverty, and apathy—much tougher opponents than any establishment could muster. But in the local tradition of helping the less fortunate, endowing charitable institutions, educating and ministering to the sick, these women, whether Muslim, Coptic, or Jewish, all joined together to create monuments to the constructive and creative power of women.

Women came out into public life because of the 1919 revolution, but once the revolution was over, they channeled their talents in other necessary directions. Having tasted liberty, they had no intention of accepting seclusion again, especially when so much needed to be done in the way of social services. Implicit behind the actions of the women who set up philanthropic organizations, therefore, was a revolutionary social concept. For where in the past philanthropic deeds had been financed by the rich, they were never actively supervised by them. These revolutionary gentlewomen, therefore, became unpaid public servants through their organizations. While some of the members were undoubtedly of the "lady bountiful" variety, the majority of the members were social activists, who literally rolled up their sleeves and actively took a hand in their projects, thus proving by example the equality of the sexes. They shouldered tasks that had previously lain in the domain of the male sex, like setting up hospitals. And because they were not in competition with anyone, they met with cooperation rather than with opposition on the part of the government.

The government, which was impeded by limited budgets and unmotivated personnel, was delighted to see much-needed projects set up in the land. Husbands and fathers who would have objected violently had their wives and daughters taken a paid position as a hospital administrator were shamed into quiescence by the very fact that the position was unpaid, and was for a benevolent cause to which they themselves had been forced to subscribe funds. Mothers who would have been horrified had their daughters suggested that they train as nurses, accepted the fait accompli of their daughters' nursing the poor as an act of philanthropy, as a religious duty, and as a national duty.[9] Activist women belonged to the elite, for it was their class of women who needed emancipation the most. Working-class women, both urban and rural, toiled equally with their men, and did not have the luxury of seclusion. In a hierarchical society like Egypt, what the elite did was aped by the lower segments of society. When the aristocratic women dispensed with the veil, the rest of society followed suit a decade later, when time had made innovation acceptable. When the same women took on public functions, they made social work respectable. By extension and in time, all work, paid or unpaid, became respectable. By the time women received the vote after the 1952 revolution, they had become active in all the professions and at all levels of responsibility. Today, women are encouraged to work as a national duty.

Activist women set up a number of philanthropic organizations, but for the sake of brevity two sister organizations are described here. They included as a founding member Hidiya Hanim Barakat and her friends and colleagues, Amina Hanim Sidqi and Mlle. Mary Kahill. Much as I would like to write about each of these women in her own right I must limit myself to describing one of them only, but as an example of all these dedicated women.

Hidiya Afifi was born in 1898 and died in 1969.[10] Her father Ahmad Pasha Afifi had functions in the palace and had been a magistrate. Hidiya was educated in the French convent of Notre Dame de la Mère de Dieu until the age of thirteen. It was then customary to withdraw girls from the public eye when they reached puberty. A few years later she became engaged to Bahieddine Barakat, a professor at the Faculty of Law of the Cairo University.[11] The young bride saw her husband for the first time on her wedding night in May 1918. Bahieddine was the son of Fathallah Pasha Barakat, a senator and leading politician, who was also the nephew and lieutenant of Sa'd Pasha Zaghlul. Thus, from her marriage Hidiya found herself in the center of the political activity of the day. Her father-in-law, who admired Hidiya's organizing ability, soon saw her as the link between the Wafd and the rest of the Egyptian ladies.

Hidiya was gifted with indefatigable energy, a clever and quick mind, the power to manipulate people, often in a quite ruthless fashion, and was simply and completely fearless. When the British authorities made it a criminal offense to distribute nationalist pamphlets, and several nationalists had been sentenced to death (although their sentences were later commuted to imprisonment), Hidiya blithely tucked the pamphlets into her shopping baskets and took the train to Upper Egypt, where at every station female schoolteachers met her and received a basket with the pamphlets at the bottom. The British soldiers who searched every train never suspected that the diminutive gentlewoman, swathed in her veils, was distributing nationalist propaganda.[12] On another occasion, she was in a shop and happened to note an establishment across the street that sold British goods. When she saw two Egyptians walking into the establishment she scurried across the street and loudly berated the men for breaking the nationalist boycott, and shamed them into leaving the shop without buying any products. It was little wonder that Hidiya became affectionately known among her companions as the "little soldier."

Through her father's functions in the palace, Hidiya also became a link between the palace ladies and the rest of Egyptian society. Two princesses had organized a philanthropic group which in 1908 set up a small clinic in the Abdin quarter. Unfortunately, these women only met once a month and were not very effective, until Hidiya later in time joined the organization. She soon convinced a large number of her equally activist friends into joining as well and the association, which became known as Mabarrat Muhammad Ali al-Kabir, or the Muhammad Ali the Great Philanthropic Association,[13] developed into the largest and most active organization in the country. The small clinic in Abdin blossomed into a full-fledged hospital and outpatient clinic, and a network of similar installations was created. Hidiya, who was treasurer of the association, ran the Mabarra with the help of the women who were on the central committee. A wealthy and generous princess was chosen as a figurehead president, a title which later went to King Faruq's sister, Princess Fawzia. After the 1952 revolution Hidiya was elected president, and when she died her youngest daughter, Mme. Zaki al-Ibrashi, was chosen president.

The same group of ladies then set up a second organization to deal with a different set of problems. The Société de la Femme Nouvelle was created in 1919. Where the Mabarra was to deal mainly with clinics, dispensaries, hospitals, and problems of health, the Femme Nouvelle concentrated on aspects of social welfare like setting up schools where girls were taught a trade, child care centers, orphanages, and so forth.

Both these organizations were financed by donations from the members and their friends, by sweepstakes, bazaars, and dances. The members of the organization were the women of the elite, both urban and rural, from both the *dhawat* and the *ayan* groups; they came from all religious denominations; and they cut across party lines. Whether their menfolk were in power or in the opposition, the women cooperated and succeeded in always finding a member who was connected to the government of the day and who would thus help cut the red tape, or obtain government sanction for some project. Perhaps that is one reason these women were more successful in their projects than their husbands were in running the country. When the ladies had a project planned, they would talk a large landowner into donating a plot of land on which they wished to build a clinic or dispensary. Next they would seek the *umda* (village headman) and impress upon him the importance of the project to the village and to himself. And since the umda was dependent on the large landowner, when he was not actually a client of one of the members of the organization, he soon spread the good word among the village. The villagers, following the suggestions of their hierarchical superior, would cooperate in building the dispensary, which thus lost a little of its "charitable" aspect and became a cooperative village venture. In some cases villages sent delegations requesting that they too might have "their" clinic like the neighboring village.

By 1961 the Mabarra had created twelve hospitals in Egypt of which one-quarter of the beds were free of charge, and eighteen dispensaries and clinics where patients were treated free or for a nominal fee of something like $0.05, and supplied with medication. Over a twenty-year span the Mabarra institutions had treated over thirteen million patients,[14] and were frequently the only medical installations in some territories.

Disease and hygiene were, and still are, a major problem in Egypt, which was the reason why the Mabarra expended its energies in that direction. In times of epidemics the members of the Mabarra were among the first to volunteer their services and offer the government their facilities. When in 1944–45 a malaria epidemic swept Upper Egypt and wiped out whole villages (as a result of secondary infections like pneumonia), the "ladies in grey" worked with the government officials for months in the stricken areas. Amina Hanim Sidqi, for example, lived for months in the villages, going from house to house in search of the sick who were afraid to receive treatment and consequently died by the hundreds. Aside from giving of her services, Mary Kahill donated truckload after truckload of rice and cereals from her estates to feed the stricken areas, where the inhabitants were completely destitute and many were dying from malnutrition more than from malaria. The following year a recurrent fever epidemic hit Lower Egypt, especially the province of Sharqiyya, and once again the Mabarra ladies pitched in, and set up mobile units, each with a doctor, nurse, and a Mabarra member, who toured the devastated areas. Villagers who would have locked their doors against the doctor and the nurse, opened them to the ladies in grey—who in many cases had estates in the area and could therefore wield moral authority in talking the peasants into accepting treatment for their sick. Resistance to treatment in such events is so violent that in some areas the police had to be used to collect the sick before they died. A year later, in 1947, a cholera epidemic broke out, and again the mobile units went out, this time to vaccinate the public. Resistance to vaccination was always broken down by the Mabarra women who cleverly caused the umda and his family to be the first to receive vaccination and so reassure the rest of the village that they were not going to die from the vaccine. These women were on the road for some ten hours a day, often unable to eat or drink for fear of contamination in the worst areas. They wheedled the sick into accepting hospitalization, they vaccinated those who were well, they fed and clothed the families that had been left without any sustenance when the breadwinner fell ill, and they buried the dead.[15] It is no wonder that these women were welcomed wherever they went.

The Mabarra was successful as an organization because it was efficient. The members gave not only of their money, but also of their time. Every hospital and clinic was supervised by a committee of members who daily inspected the wards and the kitchen and heard any complaints from the patients. Yet these women were under no compulsion to volunteer their time, except an inner one. Perhaps they were sublimating their energies into constructive work when they were unable to join in other public activities; perhaps they had more of a social conscience and felt that it was not enough to give money; perhaps, like Hidiya, they were born organizers. Hidiya was a phenomenon; while her nimble fingers busied themselves with her ubiquitous petit point or knitting, her agile mind was equally busy drawing up schemes, creating projects, finding solutions to problems, thinking of ways to raise funds, who to tap for donations, who to call to cut red tape. Between one stitch and the next she had mapped out her strategy and would reach for the telephone, with every last detail worked out in her own mind.

The list of achievements that the women of these two organizations planned includes a series of "firsts"—a child care center, popular kitchens in working-class areas where the workers could have a proper, balanced meal for a nominal price, birth control clinics, a home for elderly women, a rehabilitation center for the disabled war veterans. All their projects were enthusiastically supported by the government, when they were not planned jointly, and then turned over to the government, like the rehabilitation center. In 1964 the major hospitals were nationalized and the Mabarra turned over all its institutions, then invested its funds in other fields like child care centers and orphanages. That is why Hidiya Barakat was awarded the highest decoration a grateful country can offer. She was due to receive it on the very day she died suddenly of a heart attack.

Hidiya Barakat, Amina Sidqi, and Mary Kahill were pioneers who set an example of achievement. Had they been told that they were activists they would have been horrified; they were simply doing what they thought was right for people who had been blessed with wealth to do. These indomitable women showed what their whole sex could achieve through determination and hard work. Instinctively, they realized that the only way for a poor country to better itself was through tapping that unlimited pool of human resources, and getting people to work together toward a concrete goal, a clinic or a school. Mme. Sadat gave Hidiya the accolade for her social work when she was inaugurating a project after Hidiya's death. She said that in the field of social work in Egypt "we are all pupils of Hidiya Barakat."[16]

Notes

1. Joachim Wach, *The Sociology of Religion* (Chicago, 1944), p. 62.
2. Most passages regarding women in the Quran are in Sura IV, *Al-Nisa'*; the doctrine of *kafa'a* (equality) was introduced later on in time (see Noel Coulson, *A History of Islamic Law* [Edinburgh, 1964], p. 49).
3. ʿAbd al-Rahman al-Jabarti, *ʿAja'ib al-athar fi-l tarajim wa-l akhbar* (Cairo, 1882), IV, p. 161.
4. Ibid., IV, p. 218.
5. My information concerning harem life was obtained from friends and relatives, my grandmother, elderly aunts, and my mother. The older women had been harem wives; the younger ones were brought up as children in a harem, although they themselves had never been veiled or secluded. I was given multiple examples of houses where three generations lived together and who with their servants and retainers came to well over sixty inmates—the women could not exactly remember the names of all the retainers so only accounted for the major ones.
6. Jabarti, *ʿAja'ib*, IV, p. 218 and passim in every volume.
7. ʿAbd al-Rahman al-Rafiʿi, *Thawrat 1919* (Cairo, 1955), I, pp. 185ff., gives the wording of the manifestos.
8. Bahiga Arafa, *The Social Activities of the Egyptian Feminist Union* (Cairo, 1973). There are at present two works in preparation on Mme. Shaʿrawi, one by Margot Badran whose Oxford University dissertation was completed in 1977, and one by Mme. Shaʿrawi's granddaughter in Cairo.
9. Mme. Barakat was herself shocked when I registered in premedicine, yet she had allowed her eldest daughter to serve as an army nurse during the 1948 war with Israel, and had encouraged her second daughter and myself to work as nurses in Port Said during the 1956 war. Her second daughter was also in charge of the dispensary/clinic that Barakat Pasha had built and staffed entirely at his expense on his estates.
10. Most of the information regarding Hidiya Hanim Barakat was derived either from talks with her during her lifetime, or from information

generously supplied to me by her daughters Mme. Mortagy, Mme. Hassuna Saba, and Mme. al-Ibrashi, and by Mlle. Mary Kahill. To all these ladies I extend my thanks.

11. Barakat Pasha eventually became a cabinet minister in several governments, was président de la cour des comptes, and was one of the three regents of Egypt after Faruq had been exiled in 1952.

12. The story was told me by Hidiya Hanim and was further corroborated by many others, including the ladies who were on the receiving end of the pamphlets.

13. After the 1952 revolution it became known as the Mabarra.

14. Information on the activities of both Mabarra and Femme Nouvelle is derived from a pamphlet written by Hidiya Hanim and entitled, *Nabdha ʿan al-ʿamal al-siyasi wa-l ijtimaʿi al-nisaʾi fi Misr* (Cairo, n.d.).

15. Ibid., p. 12. I also know much of the information from personal experience, having worked with these ladies and known them most of my life.

16. On Hidiya Hanim's death a number of institutions were named after her.

14 Feminism and Nationalist Politics in Egypt

Thomas Philipp

The movement for women's emancipation and the Egyptian nationalist movement came into their own at the end of the nineteenth century. They were different expressions of the same profound problem of contact and confrontation with modern civilization. Earlier than any other Arab country in the Middle East, Egypt had been exposed to the Western impact, and was the first to experience direct domination, when Britain occupied it in 1882. The overwhelming presence of Europe and the collapse of much of the traditional order led to a reconsideration of Egypt's own position and identity in relation to the West. National independence seemed to supply the answer to Western domination.

Yet, to achieve this aim, it was also necessary to reform and revitalize society. The improvement of the position of women was part of this reform. Superficially, it would seem reasonable to conclude that those who supported nationalist aims also promoted feminism. Indeed, since the end of the nineteenth century, Egyptian nationalists have claimed that "there can be no improvement of the state of the nation without improving the position of women."[1] Historians came to the conclusion that "feminism formed a part of the content of nationalist thought,"[2] and that "women showed that they did not hesitate to participate in political struggles."[3] The Egyptian revolution of 1919 is pointed out as the

I am indebted to Hollis Granoff for allowing me to read her unpublished paper, "Egyptian Women in the Nineteenth and Twentieth Century" (1975). The present paper undoubtedly has benefited from this reading. Thanks also go to Judith Gran for valuable criticism and some editorial comments.

occasion at which the feminist movement showed its first tangible results. For the first time in Egyptian history, women participated actively in political demonstrations.

In 1919 Egyptian feminists could look back already on more than thirty years of intensive debate of the issue. Yet the relationship between the nationalist movement and feminism was by no means as harmonious and positive as it may appear at first glance. After 1919, when nationalist pressures emerged in the wake of the promulgation of a constitution for Egypt, women's political rights were not mentioned. Their equality with men was not discussed.

The picture that presents itself at the end of the nineteenth century is indeed a confusing one. Every shade of opinion regarding the emancipation of women was represented, and nationalists themselves were far from agreeing on the matter. Only one fact can be established immediately: the issue was an essential one, directly touching the life of everyone. An unceasing flow of books and articles about the topic gives evidence of its importance.

The debate over the emancipation of women originated among Muslim reformists. It was their contention that an Islam correctly interpreted and set free of traditional ballast was able to provide a viable system of beliefs and values even under the changed circumstances of modern times. Thus, they felt that the position of women had suffered, not through the commands of the original Islam, but by a misinterpretation of the Quran and later un-Islamic additions. Polygamy, for instance, was considered a harmful distortion of original Islamic precepts. Muhammad ʿAbduh,[4] the intellectual leader of the reformist movement, provided the successful, if somewhat sophistic, argument that the oft-quoted verse in the Quran, "marry such women as seem good to you, two, three, four, but if you fear you will not be equitable, then only one,"[5] actually enjoined the believer to marry one wife only since equally just treatment of several wives was beyond human abilities.

The debate of the reformists widened to include education. An education toward reason and independent judgment was postulated for men as well as for women in order to bring about a better understanding of the true Islamic precepts and to create a more viable society. Monogamy and education were the first topics concerning woman's position in society. Qasim Amin, one of the disciples of Muhammad ʿAbduh, brought the discussion of emancipation to a new level of intensity and general interest when he published in 1899 his book, *Tahrir al-marʾa* (Woman's emancipation).[6] In it he demanded the abolishment of the veil and the social seclusion of women. He opposed polygamy and arranged marriages and condemned customary divorce practices. He insisted on education for women as the only means to enable them to fulfill properly their functions in society and family. Qasim Amin's book caused an immediate uproar and numerous refutations were written. He tried two years later in a second book, *al-Mar'a al-jadida* (The new woman), to answer his critics and detractors. Going over very much the same issues again, he did, however, make a perceptible shift in argument. In his first book, Qasim Amin had gone to great lengths to prove that the changes he demanded were well within the framework of Islam, and were, in fact, required by a correctly interpreted Islam. In the second book, the legitimacy of emancipation is frequently found in such secular concepts as "natural rights," "evolution of society," and "progress." The opposition to Qasim Amin's demands did not come only from conservative religious quarters, but also from some of the Egyptian nationalists, whose ideology began to crystallize at the same time.

One of the leaders of the opposition to Qasim Amin's profeminist stand was Tal'at Harb,[7] a nationalist whose concern with Egypt's economic independence was one of the factors that later led him to found Bank Misr. In *Fadl al-khitab fi-al-mar'a wa-al-hijab,* published in 1901, and *Tarbiyat al-mar'a wa-al-hijab,* published in 1905, Tal'at Harb argued that the emancipation of women was just another plot to weaken the Egyptian nation and disseminate immorality and decadence in its society. He criticized Egyptians who desired to ape the West and claimed that there was a European imperialist design to project a negative image of the position of Muslim women. Too many outsiders were trying to meddle in Egyptian affairs; and Tal'at Harb mentioned pointedly the non-Egyptian origin of Qasim Amin's family.[8]

This attitude toward emancipation was shared by Mustafa Kamil, the leader of those nationalists whose aim was the immediate evacuation of Egypt by the British.[9] Mustafa Kamil's brand of nationalism could perhaps be described by what has been called aptly "counternationalism,"[10] that is, a nationalism that is foremost a reaction against foreign domination or the threat thereof rather than a concern with the political and social structure of society itself. For Mustafa Kamil, national independence became the demand overriding all other issues. National unity and strength were more important than social change. Introduction of change smacked of foreign designs to corrupt and weaken the society. Mustafa Kamil opposed the emancipation of women. His newspaper *al-Liwa'*, which became the mouthpiece of his party founded in 1907, *al-Hizb al-watani*, frequently rejected social ideas identified with Western culture and society.

To the nationalists who believed that conservatism in social affairs would prevent any alien, unnational subversion of society, there appeared to be much evidence confirming their suspicion about the foreign origin of the feminist movement. A look at the contemporary press dealing with feminism may help to illustrate the point. Before World War I, there already appeared in Egypt fifteen magazines in Arabic that specialized in issues concerning women. With one exception, they were founded and edited by women. This indicates not only the amount of interest elicited by these issues but also shows that, at least in journalism, women had already established themselves professionally.

One of the major factors in the opposition of nationalists such as Mustafa Kamil and Tal'at Harb to the emancipatory movement

Table 14.1. Pre–World War I Egyptian women's magazines.

Year founded	Magazine	Founder	Religious background
1892	*al-Fatah*	Hind Nawfal	Syrian Christian
1898	*Anis al-jalis*	Alexandra Avierinoh	Syrian Christian
1901	*al-Mar'a fi-al-Islam*	Ibrahim Ramzi	?
1901	*al-Mar'a*	Anisa 'Ata Allah	Syrian
1901	*Shajarat ad-durr*	Sa'diya Sa'd ad-Din	?
1902	*az-Zahra*	Maryam Sa'd	Syrian
1902	*as-Sa'ada*	Rujina 'Awwad	Syrian Christian
1903	*Majallat as-sayyidat wa-al-banat*	Ruza Antun	Syrian Christian
1904	*al-'A'ila*	Esther Moyel	Syrian Jewish
1906	*Fatat ash-sharq*	Labiba Hashim	Syrian Christian
1908	*al-Jins al-latif*	Malaka Sa'd	Syrian Christian
1908	*Majallat tarqiyat al-mar'a*	Fatima Rashid	Egyptian Muslim
1909	*Murshid al-atfal*	Anjilina Abu Shi'r	Egyptian Copt
1912	*al-Jamila*	Fatima Tawfiq	Egyptian Muslim?
1913	*Fatat an-nil*	Sarah Mihiya	Egyptian Jewish?

Sources: Filib di Tirrazi, *Ta'rikh as-sahafa al-'arabiya* (Beirut, 1913–1930), part IV, and K. T. Khairallah, *La Syrie* (Paris, 1912), pp. 88, 113.

can be determined by scrutinizing the religious and community background of this very group of women journalists.[11] Of the fourteen women founders and editors, one was Copt, two were Jewish, six—probably eight—were Christian, and two were Muslim. The identity of one could not be established. Nine, perhaps ten, of the women were from Syria. Only three were definitely Egyptians. The predominance of members of religious minorities is, in any case, overwhelming. The large representation of Christians from Syria and Lebanon reflects the general situation of the press in Egypt at the time. It is exactly this element that Mustafa Kamil eyed with unveiled hostility. For him, the Egyptian nationalist, the Syrians were intruders, *dukhala'*, who supported the English cause and anything Western. The emancipation of women was just another plot to weaken the Egyptian nation and to disseminate immorality and decadence in its society.

Women of Syrian Christian origin not only played a significant role as owners and editors of women's magazines, but they also contributed to the press in general with articles concerning women's position and rights. Nadia Faraq has investigated the role of women journalists of Syrian Christian extraction in detail. She argues that the liberties and rights that were still denied to Egyptian women at the end of the nineteenth century had already been obtained by women in Christian communities in Syria and Lebanon a generation earlier. Nadia Faraq comes to the conclusion that the Syrian women who wrote, for instance, in the magazine *al-Muqtataf* and lived in Egypt were very little concerned with the contemporary situation of the Egyptian woman. Their own social position and freedom had been assured and they looked toward Europe and certainly not toward the surrounding Egyptian society for guidelines for their own life.[12]

Such an "un-Egyptian" attitude could not be approved of by the nationalists. But the suspicion that the liberation of women was an unpatriotic development, weakening the national identity, was fed not only by the part Syrian women played in it; Coptic women journalists, too, must have contributed to the growth of this suspicion.

Stimulated by Mustafa Kamil's example, many Egyptian nationalists made a genuine attempt to overcome the religious differences of Muslims and Copts in Egypt and to create one national identity unifying both elements. For them, the tone and the content of a magazine such as *al-Jins al-latif*, edited by the Christian woman, Malaka Sa'd, must have been suspicious. The magazine avoided any political involvement. But, significantly enough, the only time it reported a political event was the assassination of Butrus Ghali Pasha, the Coptic premier of Egypt. Though the magazine was usually not involved in daily politics, one repeatedly finds appeals to the Coptic national—the terms *qawma* and *umma* are used—and its glorious past.[13] Armanusa, for instance, was feted as a kind of Jeanne d'Arc who tried to defend her fatherland against the Muslim Arab invaders.[14] When women's position throughout history was discussed, the high position of women in Pharaonic times was pointed out. It was emphasized that even in Roman and Byzantine times, the position of the Egyptian woman was a high and free one. The time of Islam was not mentioned with a word, and it was only stated that the position of women was currently extremely low, and that therefore one had to return to the values of the ancients.[15] Implicitly, Islam was made responsible for the downfall of women in society. This line of thought was bound to alienate most Egyptian nationalists, who at the time had only rarely cut all strings of loyalty to the Islamic past and heritage of Egypt.

It would be difficult to determine whether Mustafa Kamil's attitude to the issue was guided by his own loyalties to traditional Islam, or by the politician's instinct not to antagonize popular religious feelings. Mustafa Kamil also attempted to cooperate with the Khedive ʿAbbas Hilmi. He was aware that the latter had a strong dislike for Qasim Amin and Muhammad ʿAbduh. It might therefore have been politically convenient for Mustafa Kamil to oppose them on this issue.[16] But it is also remarkable that Mustafa Kamil never expressed in his long correspondence with Juliette Adam any thought or wish that Egyptian women should obtain the education and freedom of action that his venerated French correspondent had.[17] By and large, Mustafa Kamil's preoccupation with national independence and, consequently, international politics made him regard social change as secondary in importance and possible only as a consequence of independence. As long as this goal was not obtained, social change was eyed suspiciously as a means to divide society and to weaken its moral fiber.

In order to obtain a clearer picture of the relations between the nationalist and the emancipatory movement, it is not enough to point out the opposition of some of the nationalist leaders. More essential factors are the character and the aims of the women's movement itself and such nationalists as supported it.

Until the 1930s all evidence points to an exclusive restriction of the movement to women of the middle and upper class.[18] That does not seem surprising, considering that a certain amount of education and exposure to Western features were needed to be able to question the traditional position of women. Such opportunities existed only in the middle and upper classes at the time.

A typical representative of this group of women was Malak Hifni Nasif,[19] probably the most outspoken woman writer on the subject of women's emancipation during this time. Under the pen name Bahithat al-Badiya, she wrote numerous articles which appeared in the contemporary press. She wrote about all the topics concerning the women of her time: marriage, divorce, the veil, seclusion, and education. Her own marriage took her away from Cairo to the fringes of the desert and she began to look at urban life critically. She found that ignorance and idleness prevailed among city women, and that their relations with their husbands were determined by seclusion, tensions, and male despotism. Her bitter attacks against polygamy were founded on personal experience, since her own husband took a second wife. Her argument and choice of issues were evidently influenced by Qasim Amin's writings. On the whole, her views were slightly more conservative. She defended veiling, and her educational ambitions for women were more limited than those of Qasim Amin.

The women protagonists of emancipation not only shared a common upper- or middle-class social background, but addressed themselves only to women of the same background. The topics dealt with are evidence of the exclusive concern with women of the upper classes. A popular subject, for instance, is breast-feeding. We are told it should be done by the mother herself, in spite of all possible inconvenience, rather than being left to wet nurses. Education of children should not be left to the servants because the children would imbue the lower-class values and attitudes. Other frequent topics are the management of large households and the supervision of servants.[20] In an article comparing Egyptian village life with life in the city, Malak Hifni Nasif surprises us at first because she idealizes village life as healthier, cleaner, and quieter for the woman. However, she is not comparing the life of the peasant woman with that of the city woman, but the life of an upper-class woman in the city with the life she could lead in the countryside. In the latter case, the woman has to take much more personal charge of the cleanliness of the house and the food, the education of the children, and so on, because peasant women are as servants much less sophisticated than servants in the city and therefore cannot be entrusted with such affairs.[21] Such tasks also keep the woman from idleness, which was to be condemned.[22] Idleness in the secluded quarters of the upper-class household seems to have been one of the problems of women. Acquiring an education, activities in welfare organizations, or even teaching are suggested. In some of the magazines, patterns for sewing dresses are included.

In brief, those who agitated for the improvement of the position of women were people from the upper and middle classes concerned with women from the same social environment. The emancipatory movement had no intention of being a mass movement addressing women from all classes of the nation. Contacts with the lower classes were restricted to women who were servants or, possibly, the objects of the activities of charitable societies.

Another striking feature of the women's movement before the revolution of 1919 is its total lack of political involvement and the almost complete absence of patriotic nationalist expression. The very first women's magazine published in 1892 in Alexandria already set the mood: "The *Young Woman* is a scientific, historical, literary magazine, relevant to her sex . . . it has no ambitions in political affairs."[23] Years later, Malak Hifni Nasif told her audience, in a presumed mood of generosity, "Let us leave to him [the male] politics, which he loves so much."[24] When she tried at the end of the war in Tripoli to rally women to help the wounded, she did not speak in nationalist or political terms, but appealed to women, whose natural inclination is to help the suffering.[25] Occasionally, she displayed a vague patriotism,[26] but it seems that she and other women developed serious patriotic feelings and loyalty only when marriage between Egyptians and foreign women was at issue. Such marriages were thoroughly condemned for various reasons. Marriages between people of the same people *(jins)* were more harmonious. Foreign women dominated their husbands. Children of mixed marriages were not reared as Egyptian patriots. But the patriotic arguments pale perhaps somewhat in comparison with a more personal concern. If, so went the argument, educated Egyptian men marry foreign women, then there would be no men available for the educated Egyptian women. Somewhat sneeringly, it was added that in the time of the Khedive Isma'il, it was Circassian slave girls, in more recent times, European dance girls, who snatched away suitable Egyptian husbands.[27] Particularly bitter was an article by Malak Hifni Nasif concerning the marriage of an Egyptian Muslim woman to an Englishman. Here, religious sentiments against such a union—illegal, according to Muslim law—became stronger than her patriotic concern.[28]

If political participation was consciously avoided and if the women's nationalist notions were rather limited, where at all, then, was there a nexus between the women's movement and the nationalists? The answer has to be looked for in a nationalism that differed from Mustafa Kamil's "counternationalism" in emphasizing the internal reform of society rather than the necessity for the immediate political independence of Egypt. The spokesman for this reformist nationalism was Ahmad Lutfi as-Sayyid.[29] He had belonged, like Qasim Amin, to the disciples of Muhammad 'Abduh. Through him, both men had been made aware of the profound necessity to reform society. But while Qasim Amin had only hesitatingly left the Islamic framework of reference, Ahmad Lutfi as-Sayyid had made a clear cut. The society he wanted to reform was not any more the Muslim community but the Egyptian nation. It was his belief that the nation would only be able to exist independently if all its members could participate actively in it. Freedom of the individual, constitutionalism, and education were essential to prepare the Egyptian nation for political independence. Together with some friends. Ahmad Lutfi as-Sayyid founded in 1907 a newspaper, *al-Jarida,* which reflected the preoccupation of its contributors with social reform of the nation. Malak Hifni Nasif's articles appeared frequently in *al-Jarida.* She, Qasim Amin, and Ahmad Lutfi as-Sayyid repeatedly discussed in their writings the problems of society and its need for reform.

The argument that evolved was that the basis of society was the family unit; within that unit the woman played the most important role as mother and wife. If society at large was to be regenerated, liberated, and made progressive, it was the woman's position that had to be improved first of all. Only if she were educated and liberated could she, in turn, educate her children to be members of a free and progressive society. Only if she were able to fulfill her "natural duties," that is, those of mother and wife, could there be hope for a general improvement of the national society. At the turn of the century, education for the enlightened reformer and nationalist frequently seemed to be the magic cure for the various social, economic, and political ills of society. The protagonists of women's emancipation never cease to insist on the need for women's education. This insistence led not only to a moderate development of female educational institutions, but also found its echo in the Egyptian Constitution of 1924, where it was explicitly stated that obligatory free elementary education extended also to girls.[30]

But the demand for education was not an unqualified one. Ahmad Lutfi as-Sayyid, for instance, claimed that education for women should be unlimited. But when, an instance later, he enumerated the specific fields of study he had in mind, they were home economics, literature, and needlework.[31] In 1911, Malak Hifni Nasif developed a famous speech giving a ten-point program for the improvement of women's position. Five points concerned education; four of them were: education should be religiously oriented; elementary schooling for all girls is demanded; special fields taught should be hygiene, childrearing, first aid, and household economics; and a limited number of girls should be trained in the medical and teaching profession to fulfill the educational and physical needs of women. These demands were all quite new and by all standards revolutionary. But a closer look shows us also that the educational demands were strictly oriented toward the better fulfillment of the "natural tasks" in house and family. There was no intention to lead the woman out of her traditional realm into a more public arena of positions and professions. Any such intention is explicitly denied. Perhaps the clearest proof of the absence of any such desire is the tenth point of Malak Hifni Nasif's program: "It is the duty of our brothers, the men, to implement this our program!"[32]

By and large, Qasim Amin's argument conformed with this position. He, too, usually argued that the woman was a functionally important part of society and that her capacities and skills must be improved—insofar as they would benefit society. But occasionally he went further, claiming that women had equal rights for the simple reason that they were human beings just as men were. Therefore, at least on one occasion, he pointed out that the education of women should lead to a profession. Only a profession would give the woman economic independence, and only economic independence would guarantee her equality. But such a radical position was not taken up by any other protagonist of women's rights, and Qasim Amin, on the whole, was convinced that the duties of the woman are in the house and family. Only those women who do not find a man should take up a profession.[33]

The woman was seen as a member of a social unit, the family, not as a human individual. Her right to education was based on the requirements of tasks within that social unit, not on her potential capacities and ambitions as an individual. Therefore, higher education and professional training were not really necessary. Although the right of women to elementary education had been made part of the constitution, the first entry of women students in the University of Cairo in 1928 created an internal political crisis.

Just as any professional intention of the liberated educated woman was denied, so were political ambitions repudiated. Reports of women in England demonstrating publicly for their voting rights not only confirmed the worst fears of the opponents of women's emancipation, but horrified the liberal progressive elements in

Egypt as well. Ahmad Lutfi as-Sayyid reassured his readers that they should not be worried about the events in Europe. There, women had satisfied their demands for individual rights and began now to compete with men in politics. "Our [the Egyptians'] issue is not that of equality of men and women with regard to voting and positions. Our women, God bless them, do not put up such demands, which would disturb the public peace . . . They only demand education and instruction."[34] Addressing the founding meeting of the Educational Union of Women in March 1914, Malak Hifni Nasif said: "We have not come together here to demand the right to vote . . . like other women do because they are so satiated with progress that they suffer now from indigestion."[35] Again, Qasim Amin was slightly more radical when he mentioned the example of voting rights for women as introduced in America. But he clearly excluded any such possibility for Egypt at the moment.[36]

The women themselves disclaimed any political or professional ambitions. They were content to enhance their own personal freedom without feeling the necessity to demand a legal basis for it. Such a step could have had an impact on women of all classes of society. Certainly, for women of the middle and upper classes, there was also no immediate economic reason to pursue a professional career. The social concepts of the reformers and nationalists who favored a limited improvement of women's position in society reinforced this attitude. The limits to any improvement were set by the concept that conceived of the woman as only a functional part of the whole society and not as a human individual with the same innate rights and capacities as the man. This nationalist interpretation, developed by such authors as Qasim Amin and Ahmad Lutfi as-Sayyid and pursued by such outspoken women writers as Malak Hifni Nasif, helped to boost the position of women in the middle and upper classes considerably in some respects—in particular, in education. But by means of the same ideology also, very clear limits to emancipation were set. Principally, women remained excluded from public life. These ideological limits probably help as much to explain the retardation of women's participation in politics and public life even after the 1919 revolution as the traditional religious and general male opposition to emancipation.

By the end of World War I, Britain had ruled over Egypt for more than a generation. Early submission to its rule had been followed at the turn of the century by increasing nationalist stirrings. The first decade of the twentieth century saw the occurrence of anti-British and antigovernment demonstrations in Cairo. Nationalist demands and programs were formulated. With World

War I, Egypt had been declared a British protectorate. Increased military rule of the country and the events of the war itself had subdued temporarily the nationalist voices of the new elites of landowners and educated people. If the British had believed that this calm indicated Egyptian consent to their rule, they soon learned differently.

Only three days after the end of World War I, an Egyptian delegation under the leadership of Saʿd Zaghlul Pasha[37] presented itself to the British Resident expressing its expectations for Egyptian independence and demanding a representation of the Egyptian views at the Paris peace talks. The British, caught unawares, believed they were able to counter this step by repression and repeated exiling of Saʿd Zaghlul Pasha and his colleagues. The reaction was unexpected: Egypt exploded into violent demonstrations throughout 1919, usually known as the 1919 revolution. Measured by its final political outcome, these demonstrations could hardly be called a revolution. Though Britain saw itself eventually forced to declare Egypt formally an independent kingdom, it remained in firm control of all military and foreign affairs of Egypt and kept the Suez Canal under direct supervision. Revolutionary, however, it was, in that for the first time in the modern history of Egypt people of all classes and in all parts of the country participated in political demonstrations. It is questionable that they were all imbued by the same nationalist spirit, but discontent had been accumulated during the war. In the cities inflation had hit the lower classes, and in the villages the peasants had suffered from such measures as mobilization of draft animals, forced labor, and confiscation of products. The tax burden had increased. The frustration and disaffection of the various classes found an outlet in the general demonstrations of 1919.

Almost all accounts of the Egyptian revolution of 1919 mention the participation of women. The appearance of women in public as demonstrators was a novelty worth mentioning. But the reports differ widely as to the degree of this participation. The special correspondent of the *London Times,* Sir V. Chirol, who apparently arrived in Egypt only toward October 1919 writes:

> In the stormy days of March and April 1919, they [the women] descended in large bodies into the streets, those of the more respectable classes still in veil and shrouded in their loose black coats, whilst the courtesans from the lowest quarters of the city, who had also caught the contagion [of political unrest], disported themselves unveiled and arrayed in less discreet garments. In every turbulent demonstration,

> women were well to front. They marched in procession—some on foot, some in carriages shouting for "Independence" and "Down with the English," and waving national banners.[38]

It remains curious, though, that the reports that appeared in the *Times* during the very time of the demonstrations—March and April—never mentioned women demonstrators. The Egyptian historian, ʿAbd ar-Rahman ar-Rafiʿi, indicates exactly four occasions on which women demonstrated.[39] The first demonstration occurred on March 16, 1919. Rafiʿi estimates the number of participants at about three hundred. The list of names of those participating reads like a page from the social register of Cairo at the time. Apparently, various wives of politicians arranged this demonstration. Huda Shaʿrawi,[40] the wife of ʿAli Shaʿrawi, one of the members of the original Wafd delegation to the British Resident, participated, against the wish of her husband.[41] A second demonstration, by the same group, followed a few days later. In December of the same year, Muslim and Coptic women met in a Coptic church to draw up a protest against the Milner Mission sent by the British government to investigate the crisis. There is evidence for more demonstrations by women, and a suggestion that women from the lower classes began to demonstrate.[42] But the claim that "in every turbulent demonstration, women were well to front" is simply not borne out by other reports and photographic evidence.[43] It seems in fact certain that demonstrations of women, where they occurred, were strictly segregated from male demonstrators. There is nowhere an indication that women did more than take part in the general excitement. Their political demands were the same as those of their male counterparts. The rights of women were never mentioned. "The women's demonstrations of 1919 and 1920 should be taken as a hint of the size of the upheaval rather than as a victory for feminism."[44]

A women's movement which still was very small numerically and restricted to the middle and upper classes and which, moreover, did not itself put up demands for political rights, cannot have been a very promising cause for any of the newly founded parties to take up. Even Saʿd Zaghlul Pasha, to whom Qasim Amin had dedicated his book, *Woman's Emancipation,* does not seem to have exerted himself with regard to the political rights of women. When a new constitution was promulgated, women's right to vote was not mentioned. There seems to have been a short-lived flicker of feminist opposition, when a few women demonstrated for the right to vote at the occasion of the opening of the first Parliament on March 15, 1924.

But as late as 1929, Huda Sha'rawi—by then the recognized leader of the feminist movement in Egypt—could explain serenely to her audience: "When the traces of the war and its harsh rule had been eliminated, the Egyptian woman deemed it appropriate to leave to the men the solution of the political problems."[45] This echoes the attitudes of Malak Hifni Nasif and others who had consistently denied that women had any interest or ambitions in the political arena.

The first steps toward emancipation had been made before World War I: the educated public had been made aware of the issue; the first feminist program had been formulated; the first schools for girls had been opened; and the first women's organizations were founded. The issues the feminists had dealt with showed a concern with the daily life of the women, not with abstract political rights which at the time had not been firmly established for any part of the Egyptian nation. Personal status and relations with the husband, children, and society at large were the topics of immediate importance and realistic concern to women. The feminist movement after the revolution could build upon these foundations.

But together with the achievements, it also had inherited the ideological limitations of the prewar feminists. Even the supporters of the feminist cause had not perceived women as individuals, but only as important functional parts of a society that had to be reformed. Any change in their position was legitimized by the needs of society, not by their rights as human individuals equal to men. The impact of this thinking is reflected in the course that feminism since has taken in Egypt. In 1923, Huda Sha'rawi founded *Jam'iyat al-ittihad an-nisa'i al-Misri,* the Egyptian Feminist Union, which became the leading women's organization in Egypt. The organizers and exponents of feminism continued to come—as Huda Sha'rawi herself—from the upper class. Typically, the first concerns of this organization were education, welfare activities, and demands for a new regulation of laws relating to marriage and divorce. The Egyptian lawmaker responded to some of these demands when raising the age of marriage, making elementary education obligatory for girls, and so forth. A law to give women the right to divorce and to limit arbitrary divorce by men has been repeatedly discussed since 1920, but has not yet passed. In 1928, the first women students entered the university—still causing a government crisis. Since then, the education of women has made great steps forward.

It would go beyond the framework of this essay to discuss in detail the development of emancipation in Egypt after the revolution of 1919. Emancipation occurred and still occurs in the face of strong—but not necessarily specifically Egyptian—traditional male and religious opposition. It was only in 1956 that women obtained the right to vote. But more significant in view of the prewar heritage is the fact that the Egyptian feminist movement itself expressed demands for political rights for women only in 1935, after considerable progress had been made to improve the personal status of women by legislation, education, and—to a certain degree—by entering professional life. By demanding for women the right to vote, the feminist movement in Egypt had overcome its earlier self-imposed ideological boundaries and began to participate actively in national politics.

Notes

1. Qasim Amin, *Tahrir al-mar'a* (Cairo, 1970), p. 137.
2. A. Hourani, *Arabic Thought in the Liberal Age* (London, 1962), p. 215.
3. Siham Badr, *Frauenbildung und Frauenbewegung in Agypten* (Wuppertal, 1968), p. 51.
4. 1849–1905. Born in a village in the Delta, he went in 1869 to Cairo to study at al-Azhar. There he was drawn to the circle around Jamal ad-Din al-Afghani, the pan-Islamist, and under his influence, studied philosophy and participated actively in politics. After the British occupation of Egypt, he was exiled and spent several years in Europe. Upon his return, he concentrated his energies upon the internal reform and reinterpretation of Islam. In his position as great mufti of Egypt, to which he was appointed in 1899, he was able to introduce various legal reforms. His thoughts and teachings influenced a whole generation of reformists, nationalists, and modernizers.
5. Quran, Sura IV, verse 3 (A. J. Arberry, trans., *The Koran Interpreted* [London, 1953]).
6. 1865–1908. Born in Egypt, his family was of Kurdish origin. He was a disciple of Muhammad ʿAbduh and a friend of Ahmad Lutfi as-Sayyid and Saʿd Zaghlul. He had a French education and worked in Egypt as a judge.
7. 1867–1941. Born in Cairo, his father was an employee of the railway company. He studied law and, after a short spell in juridical administration, worked for various companies, mainly in financial aspects. He began to write on a variety of issues concerning Islam and the Egyptian nation. In 1907, he was, together with Ahmad Lutfi as-Sayyid, one of the founding members of Hizb al-umma, the first nationalist party. (See A. Goldschmidt, "The Egyptian Nationalist Party," in *Political and Social Change in Modern Egypt*, ed. P. M. Holt [London, 1968], p. 321.) His major achievement was the founding of the Bank Misr in 1920. This bank became the

most important means for the creation of an indigenous Egyptian industry and an increasing national control over the Egyptian economy (see Fathi Ridwan, *Tal'at Harb* [Cairo, 1970]).

8. M. Tal'at Harb, *Fadl al-khitab fi-al-mar'a wa-al-hijab* (Cairo, 1901), p. 7, and *Tarbiyat al-mar'a wa-al-hijab* (Cairo, 1905), pp. 14–16.

9. 1874–1908. Born in Cairo, his father was an engineer. He studied law and visited France several times. As a student, he had already became known as a militant nationalist, leading student demonstrations against the British and pro-British newspapers. It was his intention to mobilize the support of France and to generate enough internal pressure to force Britain out of Egypt. When France concluded with England the Entente Cordial in 1904, Mustafa Kamil turned away from Europe and searched for greater solidarity of the whole East.

In 1907, several months after Hizb al-umma had been founded, Mustafa Kamil founded his own nationalist party, al-Hizb al-watani. Its program was in many points similar to the former, but less flexible in its demand for immediate and unconditional evacuation of the British. See F. Steppat, "Nationalismus und Islam bei Mustafa Kamil," *Welt des Islams,* 4 (1956).

10. C. J. H. Hayes, *The Historical Evolution of Modern Nationalism* (New York, 1950), quoted in Bassam Tibi, *Nationalismus in der Dritten Welt am arabischen Beispiel* (Frankfurt, 1971), p. 22.

11. The information concerning the religious background was gathered from bibliographical dictionaries, etc.

12. Nadia Faraq, *"al-Muqtataf, 1876–1900,"* Ph.D. dissertation (Oxford, 1969), pp. 173–196. Ms. Sarruf, wife of the editor of *al-Muqtataf* wrote: "Let us leave the writers of Egypt and India to investigate the state of the Eastern women and whether it is lawful for her to unveil her face or show her hands while talking to man . . . leave all this and follow me in my imagination to Europe and America," quoted ibid., from *al-Muqtataf,* XXIII (1899), p. 564.

13. *al-Jins al-latif,* IV (1912), pp. 40–41.

14. Ibid., I, p. 278.

15. Ibid., VI, pp. 256ff.

16. Steppat, "Mustafa Kamil," p. 280.

17. See Moustafa Kamel Pasha, *Lettres egyptiennes françaises adressées à Mme. Juliette Adam* (Cairo, 1909).

18. Duriya Shafiq and Ibrahim 'Abduh, *Tatawwur an-nahda an-nisa'iya fi Misr* (Cairo, 1945), p. 117, maintain that even in the 1940s, the movement was an affair of the upper classes.

19. 1886–1918. Born in Cairo, her father Hifni Nasif was another disciple of Muhammad 'Abduh. He occupied various high administrative positions and also was an Arabist, teaching Arabic literature at the Egyptian University. She was one of the first Egyptian women to obtain a teacher's primary certificate in 1900. She taught for many years and wrote a great number of articles concerning women. In 1911 she presented in a speech to the Egyptian Legislative Assembly a ten-point program for the improve-

ment of the position of women. (See C. C. Adams, *Islam and Modernism in Egypt* [London, 1933], pp. 235ff.)

20. See, for instance: *Majallat as-sayyidat wa-al-banat,* I (1903), pp. 232–234; *al-Jins al-latif,* I, (1908), p. 43.

21. Bahithat al-Badiya, *an-Nisa'iyat* (Cairo, 192?), pp. 93ff.

22. *al-Jins al-latif,* II (1909), p. 51.

23. *al-Fatah,* I, quoted in Anwar al-Jindi, *Adab al-mar'a al-'arabiya* (Cairo, n.d.), p. 35.

24. Bahithat al-Badiya, *an-Nisa'iyat,* part II, p. 22.

25. Muhammad ad-Din Hifni Nasif, ed., *Athar Bahithat al-Badiya* (Cairo, 1962), p. 121.

26. See, for instance, her article, "al-Mar'a al-'arabiya ams wa-al-yawm," in ibid., p. 288.

27. Bahithat al-Badiya, *an-Nisa'iyat,* part I, pp. 29–31. For a running debate among various writers, see *al-Jins al-latif,* II (1909), eight articles titled, "Tazawwuj al-misriyin bi-al-Urubiyat."

28. Muhammad al-Din Hifni Nasif, "al-Badiya," p. 293.

29. 1872–1963. Born in lower Egypt, his father was a landowner. He studied law in Cairo and belonged to the circle of Muhammad 'Abduh's disciples. For several years after conclusion of his studies, he worked in government service. But soon he retired from service to enter public life as one of the founders of Hizb al-umma and the editor of *al-Liwa'*. In 1919, he participated briefly in political activities, but withdrew soon from politics and became the rector of the Egyptian University. (See A. Hourani, *Arabic Thought in the Liberal Age* [Oxford, 1962], pp. 171ff; and A. Lutfi as-Sayyid, *Egypt and Cromer* [New York, 1968], pp. 148ff.)

30. 'Abd ar-Rahman ar-Rafi'i, *Fi A'qab al-thawra al-Misriya* (Cairo, 1969), part I, p. 93.

31. Ahmad Lutfi as-Sayyid, *al-Muntakhabat,* part I, p. 36.

32. Bahithat al-Badiya, *an-Nasa'iyat,* part I, pp. 123–124.

33. Qasim Amin, *al-Mar'a al-jadida* (Cairo, 1911), pp. 26, 90–98.

34. Ahmad Lutfi as-Sayyid, *al-Muntakhabat,* pp. 81–82.

35. Speech printed in *al-Jins al-latif,* VI (1914), p. 272.

36. Qasim Amin, *al-Mar'a,* pp. 1–16, 26.

37. 1860–1928. Born in the Delta, his father was a prosperous landowning village headman. He went to Cairo to study at al-Azhar, where he came into contact with Jamal ad-Din al-Afghani and Muhammad 'Abduh. Later, he studied law and served in the government's juridical branch. He belonged to the group of Hizb al-umma. In 1906, he was appointed minister of education, in which function he initiated considerable improvement in the educational system. When he was appointed to the Legislative Assembly in 1913, he established himself quickly as the opposition leader. In 1919 he succeeded in mobilizing wide public support for his demands for Egyptian independence. He founded the Wafd party, the first truly popular party in modern Egypt. Until his death, he remained the leading figure in Egyptian national politics.

38. Sir Valentine Chirol, *The Egyptian Problem* (London, 1920), pp. 167–168.

39. ʿAbd ar-Rahman ar-Rafiʿi, *Thawra 1919* (Cairo, 1968), part I, pp. 126–127, 141; part II, p. 75.

40. 1879–1947. Born in Central Egypt, she was the first president of the consultative assembly created by Ismaʿil Pasha in 1866. At home, she had been taught French, Turkish, and music. She was married at the age of thirteen to a cousin whose children from a former marriage were already older than she. They separated after seven years of marriage. She became involved in the feminist movement. She was one of the founders of the Mabarrat Muhammad ʿAli in 1909 and also of the second women's organization in Egypt, *al-Marʾa al-jadida*. She also was a member of the Women's Wafd Committee and founded, in 1923, the Egyptian Feminist Union, which remained, until her death, the most important feminist organization in Egypt. (Yusif Daghir, *Masadir ad-dirasat al-adabiya* [Beirut, 1972], III, part I, p. 637.)

41. Interview with Huda Shaʿrawi in *al-Hilal,* XXXV (1927), pp. 650–654.

42. M. Sabry, *La revolution Egyptienne,* part I (Paris, 1920), pp. 66–67.

43. See, for instance, the photos in Sabry's book.

44. J. Lacouture, *Egypt in Transition* (London, 1958), p. 90.

45. Huda Shaʿrawi, *Dawrat al-marʾa fi harakat at-tatawwur al-ʿalami* (Cairo, 1929), p. 20.

15 Women and Revolution in Iran, 1905-1911

Mangol Bayat-Philipp

The decades marking the end of the nineteenth and the beginning of the twentieth century in Iran witnessed the emergence of a new modern national consciousness. The inherited political principles and attitudes of past centuries were for the first time discarded. Religious leaders and secular intellectuals, merchants, and lay politicians, united by their need to break away from the previous practice of political nonparticipation, created a new mood that craved for activism, heroic vitalism, and integral nationalism. Secret societies were established in the large cities offering a variety of speech and debating programs to their members.[1] They were used as platforms by their founders to sound the alarm, and to call for revolt against the corrupt Qajar government, as well as classrooms for the dissemination of new concepts and ideas. Men, with minds thus inflamed, walked out into the streets demonstrating against the oppressor, and shouting the freshly coined slogan: *Zindibad millat-i Iran* (Long live the Iranian nation).[2]

Much has been written about the constitutional revolution of 1905–1911, and about the role played by the *ulama,* the merchants, and the intellectuals of the time, but relatively little has been written on the women's role. Except for a few isolated references here and there, most available sources hardly mention women. Thus, one basically tends to assume that the revolution was strictly a man's affair, expressing only men's nationalist aspiration for freedom and self-expression. It certainly was not. With the help of scarce but unquestionably indicative incidental reports in various political memoirs, eyewitness accounts, and newspaper clippings, it is possible to draw a rather general but accurate picture of women's activities during that time. This picture shows that in this ancient nation that was still upholding centuries-old traditions and social values, the sudden revelation of an individualized politicized self-awareness was by no means to be found among men only. The new mood of rebellion caught and met a corresponding and equally legitimate desire for change among a small but then growing number of Iranian women.

Already in the 1840s, Babism, the newly founded religious "heresy" that called for significant changes along with the emancipation of women, found an enthusiastic response from a minority of men and women. One of the earliest and most outstanding followers of this movement was a woman, best known through her title Qurrat ul ʿAyn (1815–1851). The daughter of a *mullah* of Qazvin, and the wife of a leading *mujtahid* of the time, she was apparently quite a remarkable, intelligent woman, well-versed in the religious sciences, studies usually restricted to men, and she astonished her entourage by boldly participating in learned discussions with the local notables and ulama. Her conversion to Babism was swift, thorough, and equally bold. Gobineau writes: "Not content with a mere passive sympathy, she publicly professed her master's faith. She turned against not only polygamy but also the veil, and she appeared face unveiled in public places, causing much fright and scandal amongst her kin and amongst pious Muslims. Her public preaching, however, was applauded by an already great number of persons who shared her enthusiasm, and [helped] widen the circle [of followers]."[3] Qurrat ul ʿAyn broke her ties with her Muslim relatives, left her husband, and devoted her life to missionary activism, not only converting but also assuming leading roles on the battlefield when the Babis revolted. She died a martyr to the cause, but her memory and especially the poems she wrote kept alive the Babi spirit of revolt.

Doubtless, many converts to Babism were specifically attracted by the "modern" aspects of the persecuted religion. The call for reform pertaining to women's social status, however, was not reserved for this revolutionary religion only. True, in the 1880s and 1890s, two noted Babis, Mirza Aqa Khan Kirmani and Shaykh Ahmad Ruhi, devoted their pen to, among other subjects, the cause of women.[4] However, their contemporary fellow intellectuals, namely Mirza Malkum Khan and Mirza Fathali Akhundzada, who also wrote extensively about the same problem, were non-Babis.[5] Regardless of their religious background (Kirmani and Ruhi were Azali Babi; Malkum was a Christian convert to Islam who later reconverted to Christianity; Akhundzada was a self-professed atheist), all four writers strongly championed women's right to education, and declared themselves against polygamy. Their primary concern seems to have been the necessity to breed a new generation of Iranian patriots, and they felt that only with a proper "healthy" family environment, where the mother is educated and given a prominent role as the first educator of the child, could this be achieved. The subject of *hijab* (veiling), interestingly enough, was not touched upon. Nor was there any talk of equality. Nevertheless, this new conception of the woman as a responsible member of society can be considered a significant step forward.

Long before the emancipation movement started, Muslim women could and did defend their interests. In fact, Iranian history, not to speak of Muslim world history in general, has witnessed through the centuries the rise to social prominence of many leading women. Their struggle for power and influence, however, was carried on mostly within the closed doors of the *harem* and with the usual means at the disposal of the "weaker sex." In the nineteenth century the story of Anis ud Daula, the third wife of Nasir ud Din Shah (d. 1896), as related by Lord Curzon, offers us a good example. "She was originally a *sigheh* [temporary wife], being a miller's daughter, of the Shemiran district, who lifted her veil to the Shah while out riding, and so fascinated the monarch that she was removed next day to the royal harem. She has had no children, but her influence over the Shah has procured her elevation to the rank of a lawful wife and of first favorite, and has secured lucrative positions for all her relations."[6]

In 1872, together with other royal women, she accompanied the shah in his first trip to Europe. She did not travel farther than Moscow however, for the whole female retinue was then sent back to Tehran. Upon her return to the capital, having decided that the then prime minister, Mirza Husayn Khan Mushir ud Daula Sipahsalar, was chiefly responsible for her "disgrace," Anis ud Daula became one of the leading architects of a joint court and ulama conspiracy that eventually brought about the minister's downfall. This opposition had also assumed a "nationalist" dimension since the Sipahsalar was accused of selling out the nation by granting economic concessions to a British national on terms disadvantageous to Iran. Thus as a result of a sense of resentment and vengeance, a member of the Qajar harem became involved in one of the first important nationalist political movements. In 1891–92, the royal women's boycott of tobacco in protest against the concession granted by the shah to an English company for the curing and sale of Iran's entire tobacco crop, is another case of the effectiveness of the harem's ("so shrouded in the mystery common to Muslim countries") [7] activities.[8]

The successful boycott was to be a prelude to the constitutional revolution which finally broke out in December 1905. It was then that large groups of women of different social standing joined the men in public action. At first, they seemed to have limited it to fomenting street riots, proving to be quite apt at it. As a Western eyewitness testified, "They have a saying in Teheran that when the women take part in a [riot] . . . the situation becomes serious."[9] They were definitely useful in encouraging their men to demand freedom by adding their own fiery passion to the latters' revolt, and by providing the whole movement with an unabating moral support. "It is not too much to say that without the powerful moral force of those so-called chattels of the oriental lords of creation . . . the revolutionary movement, however well conducted by the Persian men, would have early paled into a mere disorganized protest. The women did much to keep the spirit of liberty alive."[10]

Though most Iranian sources fail to show an enthusiastic appreciation of women's activities, they acknowledge the fact that, on many occasions, some at least did prove their "patriotic zeal" and dedication to the nation. On January 10, 1906, as the royal carriage was bringing the shah to the house of a grandee, masses of women demonstrating in the street headed toward it, encircled it, and forced it to stop. Shouting that they recognized only the ulama as their leaders, they chanted in chorus: "We want the masters and leaders of our religion! We are Muslims, and believe in obeying their command! The masters have taken care of our properties! All our affairs are in the masters' hands! How could we accept your banishing them to exile? O, King of the Muslims, respect the command of the Muslim leaders. O, King of the Muslims, do not hold in contempt the ulama of Islam! O, King of Islam, if Russia and England come to your support, upon the masters' command, millions of Iranians will declare *jihad*."[11] Then a woman handed in to the shah a threatening letter, "Fear the time when we shall finally take away the crown off your head and the royal cane off your hand."[12] The following July, when the lay constitutionalists took refuge on the grounds of the British Legation, "thousands of women" were also seriously thinking of joining them. But British officials prevented them from doing so.[13]

It is clear that, at least at that early stage of the revolution when it was mainly led by the ulama whose "function as the symbol and embodiment of national aspirations ensured them unconditional support,"[14] women were content with their role as supporters. Most probably they were acting upon the ulama's instructions.

With the granting of the constitution in August 1906, women began to organize themselves into separate parties or *anjumans*. Members of these societies were mostly women coming from the upper classes.[15] These parties continued to assume a supporting role to their male leaders. Iranian sources often refer to their "devotion," "self-sacrifice," "encouragement," and "patriotism" during this period when the first Majlis[16] had to cope with the serious new task of governing the nation. For instance, when it tried to found a national bank without reverting to the hated practice of borrowing from abroad, women generously contributed large sums of cash money and donated their own jewelry.[17] However, in addition to this support, the women's parties began to manifest a desire for independent action separate and, to a certain extent, different from that of their fellow revolutionaries. A careful study of their activities as reported in the available sources tends to indicate that once the revolution's immediate aim, namely the constitution, was achieved, the women's movement followed a new direction. Women organized their societies on lines similar to but independent from the men's parties. Shuster wrote, "It was well known in Tehran that there were dozens of more or less secret societies among the Persian women, with a central organization by which they were controlled."[18]

Other sources seem to substantiate his claim. In September 1908, the *London Times* published Sir Edward Grey's[19] reply to a telegram sent by the Committee of Persian Women asking for support against Russian intervention in Iran's domestic policy.[20] The same paper in December 1911 printed the text of another telegram sent by the Persian Women's Society to the women's suffragist committee of London: "The Russian government by an ultimatum demands us to surrender to her our independence; the ears of the men of Europe are deaf to our cries; could you women not come to our help?"[21] In 1910, one of these societies founded a weekly newspaper called *Danish* (knowledge) edited by the wife of a certain Doctor Husayn Kahhal. It was apparently the "only newspaper written exclusively for women and discussing topics of special interest to women."[22]

Perhaps the women's parties' most enduring effort was the promotion of women's education. They gave public speeches on the need for women to acquire knowledge, opened new schools for them, providing their own budget and staff themselves.[23] The American

Presbyterian Missionary Society had already established a school for girls in Tehran in 1874. In the beginning only Armenian Christians were enrolled. In 1891, however, 2 Muslim women (Maryam Ardalan and Mihrtaj Dirakhshan Badr ud Duja) graduated and by 1909, 120 Muslims were in attendance. In 1907 the first Iranian school for girls (Namus) was established in Tehran. In 1908 a French girls' school (Ecole Franco-Persane) was founded. In August 1910, a foreign correspondent reported that:

> During the last year or two, the Persians have become awake to the necessity of doing something themselves on similar lines. It is stated that there are now more than 50 girls' schools in Tehran. Several older girls at the American School are training to become teachers, and a few of them are already teaching in the Persian schools during part of the day. The movement is in its infancy, but the fact that last April for the first time Persian women held a large meeting in Tehran to discuss problems of education seems to suggest that the education of women will play an important part in the future evolution of Persia.[24]

However, women's efforts in this field encountered serious and sometimes humiliating obstacles. The sight of girls and women teachers walking to school aroused a hostile public male reaction, which daily expressed itself with gross insults, obscene gestures, and spitting. In fact, the mullahs, led by Shaykh Fazlullah Nuri, a constitutional sympathizer who then became one of the most powerful opponents of the revolution,[25] declared these schools, and women's education in general, contrary to the Islamic law, hence *haram,* and denounced the whole project as a Babi conspiracy.[26] Such intimidation bore no result. A Western eyewitness, who had ample opportunity to discover the role played by these "veiled women who overnight became teachers, newspaper writers, founders of women's clubs," eloquently testified that: "the Persian women have given to the world a notable example of the ability of unsullied minds to assimilate rapidly and absolutely new ideas, and with the *élan* of the crusader who has a vision, they early set to work to accomplish their ideals."[27]

The 1906 Constitution did not grant them the right to vote. From among the thousands of women who backed the revolution, there appears to have been an important number who, bitterly disappointed, decided to fight the issues. For in 1911 they succeeded in finding for themselves a champion in the person of a Majlis deputy who initiated a debate on the subject in the Majlis. The only available source for this historical event is the *London Times.* In the issue of August 22, 1911, the following article was published:

> Women's rights in Persia: Appeal for the suffrage in the Mejliss . . . a champion of the woman's cause has been found in the Persian Mejliss. This is none other than Hadji Vakil el Rooy, Deputy for Hamadan, who, on August 3, astonished the House by an impassioned defence of women's rights. The Mejliss was quietly discussing the Bill for the next election, which takes place in the autumn, and had reached the clause that no woman shall vote. Discussion on a proposition so obvious seemed unnecessary and the House shivered when the Vakil el Rooy mounted the tribune, and declared roundly that women possessed souls and rights, and should possess votes. Now Vakil el Rooy has hitherto been a serious politician, and the House listened to his harangue in dead silence, unable to decide whether it was an ill-timed joke or a serious statement. The orator called upon the *ulama* to support him, but support failed him. The *mujtahid,* whom he invoked by name, rose in his place, and solemnly declared that he had never in a life of misfortune had his ears assailed by such an impious utterance. Nervously and excitedly, he denied to women either souls or rights, and declared that such doctrine would mean the downfall of Islam. To hear it uttered in the Parliament of the nation had made his hair stand on end. The cleric sat down, and the Mejliss shifted uncomfortably in its seats. The President put the clause in its original form, and asked the official reporters to make no record in the journals of the House of this unfortunate incident. The Mejliss applauded his suggestion and turned with relief to the discussion of subjects less disturbing than the contemplation of the possibility that women had souls.[28]

A few days later the *Times* published a letter from an "authorized" source in Persia, giving a "correct" account of the incident:

> Hadji Vekil el Roaya: I beg leave to ask for what reason should women be deprived of votes; are they not human beings, and are they not entitled to have the same rights as we have? I beg the *ulama* for a reply. Sheikh Assadollah: we must not discuss this question, for it is contrary to the etiquette of Islamic Parliament. But the reason for excluding women is that God has not given them the capacity needed for taking part in politics and electing the representatives of the nation. They are the weaker sex, and have not the same power of judgment as men have. However, their rights must not be trampled upon, but must be safeguarded by men as ordained in the Koran by God Almighty.[29]

Women's attempt to gain their political rights thus ended up in failure. The social and political mood of the time was not ready for such radical changes. Similarly, when a group of women were seen in broad daylight marching in the most crowded streets of Tehran and taking off their veils while shouting, "Long live the Constitution. Long live freedom. The Constitution has given us freedom.

We must free ourselves from the religious obligations to live the way we want!,"[30] public opinion was so strongly aroused against them that even the lay constitutionalists saw fit to deny any connection with these "ill-famed" women. They conveniently claimed that this "ugly scene" was a plot arranged by the reactionaries who had bribed these "prostitutes" to discredit the revolution in the people's eyes.[31]

On the nationalist front, however, women were more successful at making their voices heard. The years 1908 and 1911 saw a considerable increase in their activities to defend the constitution against its enemies from within and from outside. In 1908, the reactionary Qajar ruler, Muhammad Ali Shah, with the help of the Russian-officered Cossack troops, organized a successful coup d'etat against the Majlis. Conservative anticonstitutional ulama campaigned heavily against the constitutionalists. The parties, both men's and women's, played a leading role in the national resistance which, in July 1909, culminated in the deposition of Muhammad Ali Shah and the restoration of the constitution. They intensified their philanthropic work, especially in night schools for the education of the masses in the duties of citizenship and patriotism.[32] During these days full of tension and despair, women once more "made proof of their patriotism and dedication to the constitution." They were seen demonstrating in the streets, giving refuge to Majlis deputies, and hiding volunteer soldiers of the revolution. Some even wished to play a more active part in the national uprising by joining the ranks of the *Fida'is* (volunteer soldiers).[33] It was actually reported that after one of the battles in Azerbaijan, twenty female bodies, clad in men's clothes, were found among the dead.[34] Political assassination was the order of the day. Records show that at least one attempt was made by a woman. Shortly before the fall of the Majlis, Tehran streets were crowded with Cossack troops arresting the leading constitutionalists and their sympathizers. Conservative ulama were publicly denouncing the whole revolutionary movement, inciting the populace not to support the "irreligious traitors." In Maydan-i Tupkhana, the city's central square, a mullah was delivering his speech when "suddenly, from among the group of women, a woman got up, took out a gun from under her *chador* [veil] and shot the mullah."[35] She was immediately arrested and put to death on the spot.

Most sources describe the "feverish and at times fierce light that has shone in the veiled eyes of Persia's women"[36] of these troubled times. Such fierceness must have caused tension in many Iranian households. Browne related the tragic incident that occurred in

Tehran on June 11, 1908, when, after a meeting of the Majlis deputies, it was decided that they would no longer resist the court's pressure. "The people departed, weeping and sorrowful, and one man killed himself, declaring that he could not go back and face his wife with the admission that, after all the brave show and brave talk of past days, the Assembly was to be abandoned without the National Volunteers striking a blow."[37] With the events of December 1911 which led to the second coup d'etat against the Majlis, women's nationalist zeal reached its height. The *Times* correspondent reported: "The patriotic demonstrations continue. A curious feature is the prominent part taken in them by women. At a large meeting of women held in the great mosque of Sipah Salar addresses were delivered by female orators; it is said that they were very eloquent. One lady announced that, although the law of Islam forbade it, the women would nevertheless take part in a holy war."[38]

Morgan Shuster, the American citizen made treasurer-general in Tehran, who supported and was supported by the Majlis, had ample "striking proofs of the courage and patriotism of Persian women, and the practical value of their support."[39] Great risks were taken by wives of prominent court officials to provide him with necessary, sometimes vital, documents that helped him to fight his case against his opponents. Women leaders visited him secretly to warn him against possible plots or unknown enemies. Finally, when it looked as if the deputies were losing the battle and were about to capitulate to the enemy's demands, the revolutionary women made one last desperate attempt to prevent the defeat.

> Out of their walled courtyards and harems marched 300 of that weak sex, with the flush of undying determination in their cheeks. They were clad in their plain black robes with white nets of their veils dropped over their faces. Many held pistols under their skirts or in the fold of their sleeves. Straight to the Majlis they went, and gathered there, demanded of the president that he admits them all . . . These cloistered Persian mothers, wives and daughters exhibited threateningly their revolvers, tore aside their veils, and confessed their decision to kill their own husbands and sons, and leave behind their own dead bodies, if the deputies wavered in their duties to uphold the liberty and dignity of the Persian people and nation.[40]

An Iranian source confirms the story of armed women marching to the Majlis, ordering the deputies to "prefer death in honour to life in slavery."[41] But the battle was already lost. By January 1912, the Majlis was closed down, and the parties, men's and women's, that had struggled through the years 1905–1911 to establish and preserve the constitution, totally disappeared from the political scene of Iran.

The women's struggle was not, however, in vain. For it was during and after this period that a literary campaign for the reconstruction of their public image was undertaken. On the whole, the classical poets of Iran have been derogatory in their opinions about women. When they did not refer to them as beautiful playthings for love games, they compared them to "dragons," "snakes," and "devils," pointing out that they were created out of the "left side" and hence unable to tell the truth.[42] This deprecating attitude toward the woman was greatly influenced by the traditional Islamic belief that God has created her inferior to man. One can therefore appreciate the tremendous novelty implied in modern verses such as: "If woman is an impure dragon in the world, then the male dragon is worse than the female one."[43] Or,

> Thy left hand is not inferior to the right;
> had it worked it would have been as strong as the right;
> if woman is not like man, the fault is yours;
> we should demand education and art for women.[44]

The postrevolutionary poets and writers of Iran, just like their predecessors, stressed the importance of women's education as a means of creating a new generation of patriots.

> O girl, the mother of the new race!
> O girl, the cause of the race to come!
> Take example from the past and be a representative of the future generation;
> be then a rose in the Garden of Knowledge and [Thy] sons warbling nightingales.[45]

Iraj Mirza, the Qajar prince-poet of the constitutional period, published, within a few years' time, five different poems on the "mother" theme, praising her for her "patience," "self-sacrifice," "hard work," and "love."[46] But the woman is also beginning to be appreciated as an individual worthy of personal consideration, "Are women not human amongst us, or is there in women no power of distinction between good and evil?"[47] and equal to men, "You and I are both human after all, equal in creation."[48] She is encouraged to pursue her education as a means of self-improvement. "O girl of the Golden Age! Hasten towards the school. In the need of learning, accomplishment and wisdom, there is no distinction between thee and men!"[49] Poets beg her to seek a new image of herself. As Lahuti put it so clearly, "I don't appreciate the beauty of one who is ignorant; fascinate me no more by beauty, rather show thy worth."[50] She is also depicted as helplessly captive of archaic traditions and erroneously interpreted religion: "Where in the Quran has the Prophet ordered that a woman should become like a monster? Which *hadith?* Which *khabar* (claim) that a woman should make herself look like a scarecrow?"[51] Polygamy was also condemned. But it was the issue of veiling that rallied the pens of most poets of the time, Iraj Mirza, Lahuti, 'Ishqi, 'Arif, Bahar, to name only a few, campaigned heavily for its removal.

> O lift thy veil, my beautiful sweetheart,
> so that thy countenance may increase my dignity. Wherever thy
> veil is mentioned the rival laughs,
> but sobs choke my throat. I long to see thee free in the community.
> Upon thy soul I have no other desire except this.[52]

They called for joint action against it.

> If two or three speakers join their voice with me,
> an agitation will gradually start in the country,
> and by this agitation the faces of the women will be unveiled.
> Pleasure will be derived from social life.
> Else, so long as the women hide their heads in this shroud,
> half of the Persian nation remains dead.[53]

However, neither women nor their intellectual spokesmen succeeded in influencing the religious or the state authorities to change the social condition of the so-called "weaker sex." Although a relatively small number of mainly upper-class girls did enjoy the benefit offered by the schools established for them, men's attitudes toward them remained basically untouched by the political events of the day. It had apparently never occurred to the ulama or the lay revolutionary leaders and Majlis deputies, who had obviously encouraged and taken advantage of the part played by their women during these turbulent years, that in return they might have to consider granting women public recognition. In fact, in most of the historical accounts of the revolution subsequently published, the women's role is either severely underestimated or overlooked altogether. The feminist movement, however, continued its activities in favor of women's rights to education and self-expression, and its struggle for social emancipation.[54] But it was not until 1936, when Riza Shah Pahlavi officially abolished the veil, that the Iranian woman at last received the long-delayed attention she had so painstakingly earned during the revolution. Parvin-i I'tisami (1907–1941), the best known woman poet, who lived long enough to see it happening, celebrated the occasion with the following poem, entitled "Zan dar Iran" (Woman in Iran).

> It is as if the woman in Iran was not an Iranian before.
> She had no pursuit other than misfortune and distraction.
> She lived and died in a solitary corner.
> What else was a woman in those days if not a prisoner?
> No one like a woman dwelt in darkness for centuries.
> No one like a woman was sacrificed in the temple of hypocrisy.[55]

In sum, Iranian women were not necessarily "prisoners" and they did not live and die in a "solitary corner." If they wished, they could assert their presence in a male-dominated society. Their participation in the 1905–1911 political events seems to have been a spontaneous, free move on their part. There was neither a historical precedent nor a social tradition for such organized, politicized women's action to inspire and guide them.[56] Seen in this context, the role of women clearly reveals not only a new nationalist feeling that suddenly overwhelmed them and spurred them to action, but also a nascent though strong desire for official recognition. The revolution therefore turned out to be a fertile ground for their experimental struggle for emancipation. It did not bear immediate fruit, but the seeds were planted.

Notes

1. See Isma'il Ra'in, *Anjumanha-yi sirri dar inqilab-i mashrutiyat-i Iran* (Tehran, 1345 [1966]); and Ann K. S. Lambton, "Secret Societies and the Persian Revolution of 1905–6," *St. Antony's Papers,* 4 (1958).

2. In the present essay, I shall make no attempt to discuss the revolution itself. My task is to study the role and aim of women during that period. I shall therefore refer only to those revolutionary aspects that helped bring about their active participation.

3. Comte de Gobineau, *Les religions et les philosophies dans l'Asie centrale* (Paris, 1866), p. 168; see also A. Khavari, ed., *Talkhis-i tarikh-i nabil* (Tehran, 1324 [1945]), p. 250; and, A. A. Mushir-Salimi, *Zanan-i sukhanvar* (Tehran, 1956), II, pp. 70–98.

4. See Mirza Aqa Khan Kirmani and Shaykh Ahmad Ruhi, *Hasht bihisht* (Tehran, n.d.), pp. 141–145; and Kirmani, *Sad khitaba* (Tehran, n.d.), letters no. 32 and 34.

5. See Mirza Malkum's article on women's education in *Qanun,* 7 (August 18, 1890); and Mirza Fathali Akhundzada's *Se maktub,* unpubl. ms., Melli Library, Tehran.

6. G. N. Curzon, *Persia and the Persian Question* (London, 1966),

p. 408. For more details on the intrigues of women in the royal harem, see Ra'in, *Anjumanha-yi sirri,* pp. 13–23.

7. Ibid.

8. Bastani Parizi, *Tarikh-i azadi: muhit-i siyasi va zindigani-yi Mushir ud Daula Pirniya* (Tehran, 1348 [1969]), pp. 33–34.

9. Morgan Shuster, *The Strangling of Persia* (New York, 1968), p. 195.

10. Ibid., p. 191.

11. Nazim ul Islam Kirmani, *Tarikh-i bidari-yi Iraniyan* (Tehran, 1346 [1967]), I, p. 121; see also Ahmad Kasravi, *Tarikh-i mashrutiyat* (Tehran, 1353 [1974]), pp. 471, 646.

12. Nazim ul Islam Kirmani, *Tarikh-i bidari,* p. 120.

13. Letter of the then British chargé d'affaires to the Ministry of Foreign Affairs in Tehran, quoted in Ra'in, *Anjumanha-yi sirri,* p. 99.

14. H. Algar, *Religion and State in Iran, 1785–1906: The Role of the Ulama in the Qajar Period* (Berkeley and Los Angeles, 1969), p. 241.

15. A few of the well-known are the following:

Muhtaram Iskandari, daughter of a Qajar prince, who was also involved in the activities of secret societies (see Pari Shaykhulislami, *Zanan-i ruznamehnigar va andishmand-i Iran* [Tehran, 1972], pp. 143–152).

Malikiya-yi Iran, daughter of Nasir ud Din Shah and wife of Zahir ud Daula, one of the constitutionalist leaders (ibid., p. 11). This woman's letters to her husband are published in J. Qa'im Maqami, ed., *Asnad-i tarikhi-yi vaqayi'-i mashruteh-yi Iran* (Tehran, 1967).

Taj as Saltana, another daughter of Nasir ud Din Shah.

Safiya Yazdi, wife of a mujtahid, Muhammad Husayn-i Yazdi, one of the five ulama members of the first Majlis.

Sadiqa Daulatabadi, daughter of the leading mujtahid of Isfahan.

Badri Tundari, niece of Sayyid Abdullah Bihbihani, the mujtahid constitutional leader.

Wives and daughters of lay constitutional leaders. For a list of (female) feminists, see Badr ul Muluk Bamdad, *Zan-i Iran az inqilab-i mashrutiyat ta inqilab-i safid* (Tehran, 1968), II.

16. National Assembly of Iran.

17. See Kasravi, *Tarikh-i mashrutiyat,* pp. 610–611; M. Malikzada, *Tarikh-i inqilab-i mashrutiyat* (Tehran, 1328 [1949]), II, p. 204; E. G. Browne, *The Press and Poetry of Modern Persia* (Cambridge, 1914), p. 323.

18. Shuster, *Strangling of Persia,* p. 193.

19. The then British foreign minister.

20. *London Times,* September 15, 1908.

21. *London Times,* December 7, 1911. It also printed the London reply which reflects the British suffragettes' own helplessness at the time: "Unhappily, we cannot make the British government give political freedom even to us, their countrywomen. We are equally powerless to influence their action towards Persia."

22. Browne, *Press and Poetry,* p. 85.

23. Malikzada, *Mashrutiyat,* III, p. 179.
24. *London Times,* August 3, 1910.
25. He was tried by the constitutionalists and sentenced to death in July 1909.
26. Malikzada, III, pp. 179–180.
27. Shuster, *Strangling of Persia,* p. 191.
28. *London Times,* August 22, 1911.
29. Ibid., August 28, 1911.
30. Malikzada, III, p. 62.
31. Ibid.
32. See E. G. Browne, *The Persian Revolution of 1905–1909* (London, 1966), p. 245; A. K. S. Lambton, "Persian Political Societies, 1906–11," *St. Antony's Papers,* 16 (1958).
33. Kasravi, *Mashrutiyat,* p. 698.
34. Pari Shaykhulislami, *Zanan-i ruznamehnigar,* p. 85.
35. Malikzada, *Mashrutiyat,* III, p. 145; and Badr ul Muluk Bamdad, *Zan-i Iran,* II, p. 23.
36. Shuster, *Strangling of Persia,* p. 192.
37. Browne, *Persian Revolution,* p. 204.
38. *London Times,* December 5, 1911.
39. Shuster, *Strangling of Persia,* p. 194.
40. Ibid., p. 198.
41. Malikzada, *Mashrutiyat,* VII, pp. 93–94; see also Badr ul Muluk Bamdad, *Zan-i Iran,* II, pp. 16–20.
42. See the verses of Firdausi, Jami, and Nizami quoted in M. Ishaque, *Modern Persian Poetry* (Calcutta, 1943), p. 161.
43. Hasan Khan Vahid (b. 1881) quoted in ibid., p. 164.
44. Muhammad Hashim Mirza Afsar (b. 1880), ibid.
45. Poem by Qulzum, ibid., p. 166.
46. See M. J. Mahjub, *Tahqiq dar ahval va athar va afkar va ash'ar-i Iraj Mirza* (Tehran, 1353 [1974]), pp. 167, 177, 187, 189, 191.
47. Ibid., p. 79.
48. Ibid., p. 80.
49. Yahya Daulatabadi, quoted in Ishaque, p. 166.
50. Ibid.
51. Mahjub, *Iraj Mirza,* p. 84.
52. Poem by Lahuti, quoted in M. Rahman, *Post Revolution Persian Verse* (Aligarh, 1955), p. 147.
53. Poem by 'Ishqi, quoted in ibid., p. 146.
54. For a detailed account of the postrevolution feminist movement, see Bamdad, *Zan-i Iran;* and Shaykhulislami, *Zanan-i Iran.*
55. Rahman, *Persian Verse,* p. 76.
56. Prior to 1906, there were sporadic instances of women rioting in the streets and demanding justice over particular issues, or complaining of the rising costs of food (such as the bread riot), but they were neither organized nor politicized.

Part Three Case Studies: Nomads, Villagers, Town and City Dwellers

Family in Khurasan, Iran. Courtesy of Nikki Keddie.

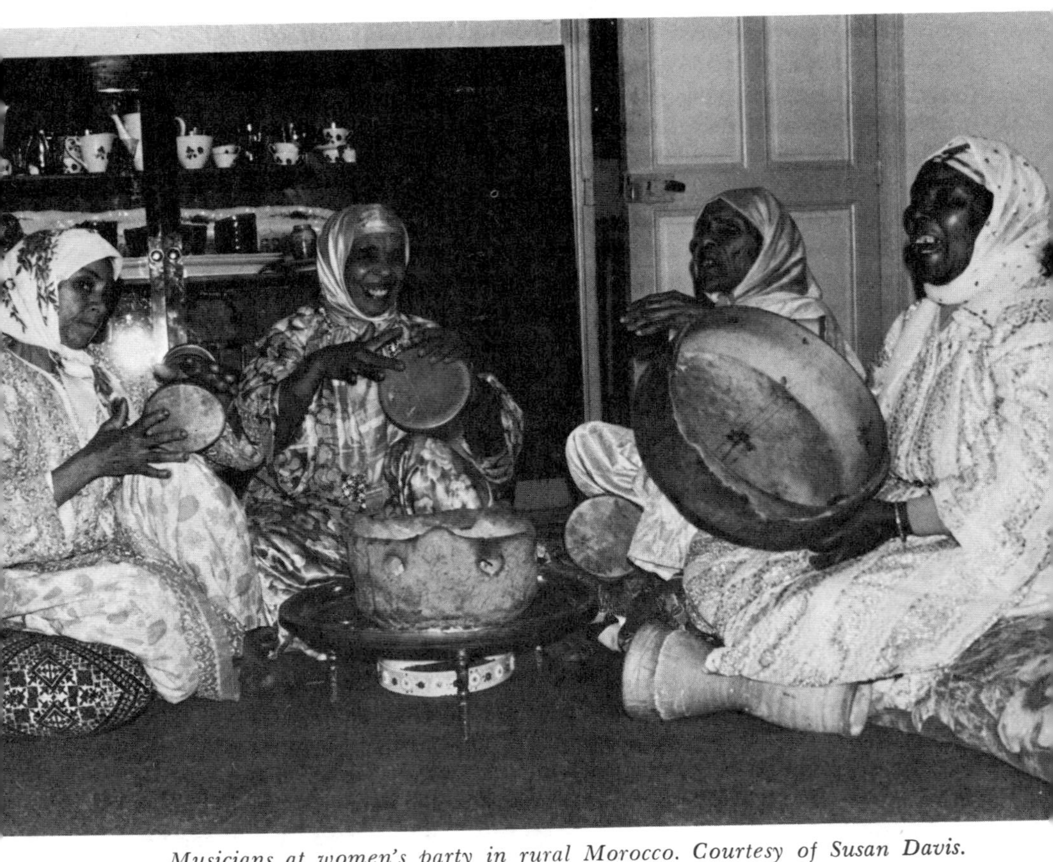

Musicians at women's party in rural Morocco. Courtesy of Susan Davis.

16 The Status of Women in Four Middle East Communities

Emrys L. Peters

In the four Arab communities of this study the position of women varies considerably, both with regard to their influence in domestic and political affairs and in their social relationships with men. Islamic laws and traditions are frequently evoked to account for behavior among Muslims, particularly behavior between the sexes, and, since much scholarship on Arabs has until recently been drawn from literary sources, the weight given to the determining influence of Islamic culture has been considerable.[1] Indeed, the uninformed impression in the West is still that all Arab women occupy a position of unmitigated servility: they are completely dominated by

---

I worked for twenty-seven months (between 1948 and 1950) among the bedouin. This research was made possible by an award made by the Emslie Horniman Trustees, and by a senior studentship from the Scarborough Committee for Studentships in Oriental Languages and Cultures. The same studentship enabled me to undertake my first research in south Lebanon in 1952-1953, when I was given an award by the University of Manchester. This university sponsored my research on the Tripolitanian olive plantation in 1964. The Social Science Research Council sponsored the eighteen months of research I have done thus far in the Lebanese Christian village, between 1969 and 1974. I wish to express my gratitude to all these bodies for making the research possible.

My wife and I worked together in both Cyrenaica and Lebanon. Much of the information I have used in this essay would have been inaccessible to me had I been working alone; she also helped me to correct the bias in statements made to me by males.

An early version of this essay was read as a paper at a conference in Athens in 1966 which was sponsored by the Wenner-Gren Foundation, and convened by Dr. J. Peristiany. I am grateful to Dr. R. P. Werbner for many profitable discussions concerning the issues raised in this article.

their men and kept out of sight most of the time, only to appear in public when they are completely veiled.

The four kinds of Arab communities examined here include the bedouin of Cyrenaica (Libya), where the people are Sunni Muslims; a horticultural community of Shiite Muslims in south Lebanon; olive farmers, Sunni Muslims, in a plantation area in Tripolitania (Libya); and a Maronite Christian village in central Lebanon.

Among the bedouin, women are excluded from inheritance, whether as wives or daughters. Their domestic status is high, and the veil is only situational, though women are excluded from the company of men in public. Politically, their status is high, and marriage alliances are crucial, although women have virtually no direct say in the choice of spouses. Women among the Lebanese horticulturalists inherit both as wives and daughters, and although marriage constitutes an alliance of sorts, its main effect is on the redistribution of plots of land rather than on political groupings. Domestically, women's rights over their husbands are fewer, but wives are more independent of their kinfolk. Women of the peasantry spend most of their time unveiled, but women of high status are heavily veiled (save for the few Christian Arab women, who are unveiled). In all cases, social access to women in their households is extremely difficult, even for male family friends, unless they are kin. On the Tripolitanian olive farms, women are for the most part isolated from other women, and their subservience to their husbands, even though they are involved in property matters, is conspicuous. Left alone on the farms by their husbands most of the time, this separation of women amounts to a segregation I have not witnessed elsewhere in the Middle East. Christians living in this plantation area observed limitations on the social behavior of women, particularly among the Sicilians, of whom there are many. They contrast markedly with their counterparts among Maronite Christian women in central Lebanon, whose freedom to mix publicly with men and whose social maturity is not only conspicuous in the Middle East context but is of an order that might be regarded as libertarian in many Western communities.

The concern here is with differences between communities, and it will be seen that an explanation of various forms of behavior is to be sought neither in Islamic culture nor in its adaptation to local needs. This is not to say, however, that Islamic culture is not a force in the behavior of people, no more than it would be profitable to argue that Christianity is inconsequential for studies of Christian communities. By the same token it would be as unrewarding to claim that social behavior in Muslim communities can only be understood in terms of the Quran and the traditions that have grown around it as it would be to say that behavior in European communities can only be understood by reference to the Bible and the vast body of interpretative literature accumulated over centuries. Two of the communities under discussion belong to different divisions of Islam: the bedouin are Sunni Muslims, and the south Lebanese are Shiites. Differences in law between Sunnis and Shiites are profound, particularly as the law affects the status of women as heirs. Yet any attempt to treat the differences described herein as resulting from these sects would be as barren as the attempt to interpret behavior in general Islamic terms. For, while Shiite law could be used to explain many details of behavior in the south Lebanese village, the bedouin neglect their Sunni law in many important respects. In Lebanese Shiite law, persons related through women are put on an equal footing with those related through men as far as the designation of heirs is concerned. Women can be sole heirs to property. Practice conforms closely to law; consequently, women regularly and legally come to hold proprietary rights in all forms of property. Sunni law is emphatically agnatically weighted for inheritance purposes, and women not only stand to receive less than men, but their designation as heirs is much more limited and tied to agnatic relationship. In practice, bedouin women do not inherit either as wives or daughters. Lebanese Shiite women are heirs, in accordance with law, but some other Shiite peoples do not observe the law: from an account of Iraqi marsh dwellers, who are Shiites (Salim 1962), it appears that their women are disinherited; and the details Barth (1964) offers of inheritance among the Shiite Basseri indicate that their practice is inconsistent with any school of Islamic law. Some Sunnis behave more in accordance with the law than do the bedouin, although showing inconsistency: the people of the Palestinian village of Artas provide an example (Granqvist 1931). The differences among these five peoples cannot be resolved in terms of their codes of law. It is of interest to note that a comparative review of Muslim communities shows that some Sunni communities are closer to some Shiite communities in their practices as regards inheritance of property than they are to other Sunnis, and vice versa.

Broad cultural traits, such as those embodied in the great traditions of Islamic religion, have, therefore, little explanatory value for the analysis of differences of behavior between peoples. Instead, the discussion becomes limited to general characterizations that rarely match actual behavior, save as they haphazardly correspond to disconnected acts of behavior in this or that community. It is for this reason, too, that discussions of sex differentiation are so often concerned with equality. Whether a woman's status in particular social relations is judged to be equal or unequal depends not only on the sex of the observer but also on the observer's cultural background—class, status, rural or urban origin, religious affiliation, and natal country.[2] Equality or lack of it will, therefore, not be assessed, since it is virtually impossible to evaluate. Even when both sexes hold the same right, this does not give equality, because the particular right is part of a cluster containing many others, and if the total clusters are not identical then there can be no equality of specific rights. For the significance of a particular right lies in its relation to others; detached, it is no more than a piece of information.[3]

The mode of investigation adopted here, therefore, aims to examine the rights of both sexes and seeks an explanation for the different ways in which rights cluster in one community compared with another, and of how these clusters are related to the social order. In doing this, the initial approach will be made through the life cycle, because the status of males and females, whatever other statuses may be available for capture, will inevitably vary with age. There is no such thing as *the* status of women—or of men for that matter—and to lose sight of this elementary fact leads to serious analytical distortion (see Fortes 1949, 1958). In what is to follow, the developmental cycle of the bedouin is given in detail, thereby facilitating comparison with the other communities.

Bedouin of Cyrenaica

Among the bedouin, there is little social differentiation among small children. The birth of a boy is the occasion for celebration and feasting. Any birth is a matter of joy because it establishes the fertility and sexual compatibility of a married pair, but when a daughter is born an animal is not usually slaughtered, as for a boy, and the expressed wish is that the next birth will be a male one. There are a number of reasons why sentiment should weigh heavily in favor of male children: there is an urgent need for the additional labor a man can command directly if he is to enlarge his economic assets; a daughter is excluded from succession; a mother has no guarantee of support in a son-in-law; and an aged man is unable to activate his agnatic rights fully except through a son (see E. Peters 1965). By comparison, a female child does not hold the same potential, although, as the bedouin are well aware, she holds other promises for them. Children of either sex, during the first seven years or so, spend most of their time in the female quarters of the tent under the mothers' control, playing in the camp together, running minor errands, or doing small chores. A father fondles both sexes of this age, but he is more lavish with his affection for his small son. He takes little part in the children's education, which is left to the mother, and disciplines the children only if they become obstreperous in or near the tent.

At about seven, the amulets (often a cowrie shell sewn onto a cap) worn by boys to avert evil or misfortune are removed from the clothing, and his clothing is now of a kind that makes him more distinctively male. In keeping with these changes, the young boy frequents the men's part of the tent more and more, and the young girl keeps more to the women's part. There is no exact age when these changes occur; nor do they come about overnight. The culmination does not occur until a boy has reached his teens and a girl has entered puberty. Meanwhile, both sexes continue to move between the male and female quarters of the tent, and even when a boy has passed the age of ten he is often seen sitting on the divide between the male and female quarters of the tent, intently absorbing all that goes on on both sides. Moreover, at this age the roles of the sexes are interchangeable with regard to their tasks. Thus, they may tend the fire together or herd a few goats or sheep on the edge of the camp, or they may go to a nearby shallow well to collect small quantities of water. Close as they may seem to each other, the small boy nevertheless begins to assume authority by instructing his younger sister, and she begins to obey.

From the age of about seven until manhood, the transition for a boy is gradual and unmarked by any divisive event. In his middle teens a boy may handle a rifle and is encouraged to do so; unless his father is very poor he wears a toga and a red felt cap; he keeps to the male part of the tent; and goat herding now becomes an allotted regular task. He is still not involved in the main herding activities; the number of animals in his charge are few and he remains within sight of the camp. When he reaches the age of seventeen or eighteen, he is given a small flock of sheep to herd, wandering with them away from the camp and remaining with them during the night. After this training with goats and sheep he moves on to camel herding. Success as a camel herder is one of the chief qualifications for the beginning of manhood proper, and it is often marked by a present of a rifle and sometimes, within a year or so, a horse. By this time the youth has matured into an agnate in a corporation of agnates, responsible enough to sit with his seniors when they discuss matters of plowing and watering rights, and to dispute with other people, to add corroborative weight to the decisions they reach.

A young girl when she reaches puberty passes much more abruptly from one status to another than her male agnate does. Henceforth, she lets her hair grow, she has to wear a head covering, and as she moves from tent to tent she draws her silk head shawl across the side of her face at the approach of males, except her closest kinsmen. Her movements are now much more restricted. She is no longer permitted to play freely with boys. Increasingly, she participates in activities of the tent, learning its intricate details; she has to spin wool, grind flour and cook, milk animals, and help to weave tent tops and carpets—all tasks that require skill and a long training period. Collecting brushwood for fire is an arduous task and carrying it back to camp is back-breaking; the unmarried daughter is usually responsible for this.

Most noticeable in a young girl, from an age soon after puberty until marriage, is her partial retirement from the general social life of the camp, lasting until she begins a new participation after the birth of children. Girls are not married until their late teens or later, and, since a young girl just past puberty is not looked upon as immediately marriageable, the restrictions placed upon her, her use of a head scarf to hide her face, and her contribution to tent duties, are all part of a growing process by way of induction into womanhood, rather than an abrupt alteration of status that accompanies a *rite de passage*. Entering into the age of puberty is a kind of acquisition for a girl since she has become capable of producing offspring. In bedouin culture this acquisition remains potential only, until she reaches the age of about fifteen or sixteen, by which time she is kept under close surveillance. A sexual relationship between a man and an unmarried girl carries with it severe penalty, and a rupture between the male kin of the lover and those of his accomplice; but if a man seduces a girl who has only recently entered puberty, his act is regarded as heinous, while the girl can be partly excused on the grounds of ignorance.[4]

Nubility in bedouin Cyrenaica begins from about fifteen years and after. During this period the greatest threat to a girl's chastity exists. A maiden, since precedence is accorded premarital chastity, possesses the honor of her male kinsmen. If she conceives out of wedlock or is seen having sexual intercourse, she suffers, it is true, but it is her brothers, and to a lesser extent her father and her first parallel cousins, who shoulder the main burden of disgrace. Nubile women are subject to restrictions because they possess what can be regarded as a kind of commodity: the ability to bear children. Like other commodities, it is owned by males, and its transfer from one set of males to another is a contractual arrangement. Until a contract has been concluded, a male who has exclusive usufructuary rights to a woman's reproductive capabilities has not been designated, and it follows that a woman's issue lacks designation also. Despite the public virginity test, an essential part of the marriage ceremony for all young girls which must act as a restraint on premarital intercourse, the circumstantial evidence is that premarital intercourse does occur, on however small a scale. Bedouin, although they would not give specific evidence, admitted the possibility when explaining that if a man had enjoyed sex relations with his bride before his nuptials he would draw blood from his nose or otherwise stain his toga to conceal from the public the failure of the virginity test. Indeed, I was present at a wedding when the virginity test was a complete failure in that the groom failed to produce a bloodstained cloth by any means; the festivities turned into a fiasco of bickering on the first of the seven days of celebrations, and although the groom suffered the opprobrium of his age mates, a year later when I visited the camp, the matter was not mentioned and the couple had remained wedded. Clearly, despite the emphasis on female chastity, the concern is not so much with the act of sexual relations but with its results. Hence, the overwhelming importance attached to the designation of an individual as possessor of a woman's procreative facilities. Young men cannot act independently toward women because they lack control over property and cannot, therefore, meet the cost of their amours.

One of the effects of puberty is that female social maturity is accelerated, compared with the progress of a boy of the same age. The onset of puberty is the beginning of womanhood, with the prospect of marriage and a wholly new status only five years or so ahead. A male child remains a boy and by the time his sister has entered full womanhood in marriage, he has only reached the stage of being a youth with little prospect of marriage for three years or more. Moreover, how soon a man leaves his youth behind depends very much on his sister's development, because his marriage is delayed until a partner has been found for her. Obviously, the details of marriages depend largely on order of birth and on age differences between children, but save for the chance of children of one sex, it is true to say that the marriage of at least one male is directly affected by his sister's marriage, and others are indirectly affected also. Thus, it is common for an eldest son's marriage to be delayed until suitable arrangements have been made for his eldest sister; and once this hurdle has been successfully surmounted, the next sister will soon be married off, to be followed quickly by the next son. A father, in other words, plans his children's marriages, and the first move is critical for the success of the others. For these reasons, the age of marriage is not the same for males and females; women have several years' start over men in the race for adult status. Paradoxically, women, derisively referred to by men as irresponsible, are quickened into the responsibility of control of a domain of their own while males still suffer the status of irresponsible youths, lacking authority.

The years before marriage are a training period for assuming authority. In early life the contribution of both sexes is peripheral, in the sense that their tasks could be done by adults without seriously dislocating their main productive activities. I do not wish to diminish the significance of the contribution of child labor to a production unit; the regret voiced about a childless couple is that they have no one to fetch and carry for them. A man without sons may "borrow" one of his brother's or sister's small sons, rewarding him later in life with a gift of animals or by making him his heir. Nevertheless, the main productive tasks do not become the responsibility of children until they reach their teens. Strikingly, the separation of the sexes now becomes pronounced. Previously, interchangeability characterized the relations of boys and girls, both often working together at their small tasks, sitting together in the tent, and even sleeping together. Puberty parts them. Henceforth, they are separately inducted, not merely into different pursuits, but into the fields of authority to which they will ultimately succeed. As if to clarify the distinction, the separation of the sexes is at its maximum during this premarital period. Women are not, however, completely secluded and wholly bereft of male company. Men see their sisters with their faces uncovered, converse with them in the female part of the tent, confiding secrets that they could not broach even with the confidante of all men, the mother. Men of this age discuss their love yearnings and marriage hopes among themselves; such discussions, whatever their emotional value, do not bring marriage a day nearer. The subject of marriage between proximate generations is disallowed. Between father and son, avoidance of anything relating to sex or marriage is strictly observed. Only one male, the mother's brother, is free to discuss these matters and present a case for marriage to a father on behalf of a son. Men also have access to their fathers through their sisters, who are free to discuss any matters relating to male-female relationships with their mothers, and the latter, in turn, press fathers to marry off their sons.[5] While men at this age are cut off from their senior agnates in this important field of relations, young women of the same age enter fully into these relations with their seniors.

Neither young men nor young women have any authority to dispose of or manage property. Ultimately, both sexes are under the authority of the head of a tent, a male, although a young woman is effectively under her mother's authority. Lacking any control over property, they also lack the means to make claims for themselves. Both are key helpers in production. Men herd the animals, plow, reap, store the grain, and transport it to the tent as and when it is needed; it is they who water the animals during the dry months and bring water to the camp for domestic use and consumption. Women spin and weave the tent strips, together with all the carpets and bags that are found inside. Anything that needs to be done to a tent—adjustments for wind changes, repair of ropes, pitching and dismantling—is done by women exclusively. Cooking is entirely their concern. They also do all the milking.

At this age, more than at any other time, interchangeability of roles or cooperation in joint activities is reduced to a minimum. This is not just a matter of convenience. Men are not permitted to interfere in women's work, any more than are women permitted to encroach on male tasks. The effect of this clear cleavage in the division of labor, as Durkheim long ago taught us to appreciate, is to create a solidarity stemming from the symbiotic relationships of men to women, and both to the land and the animals it supports. It also means that in every camp, whether small or large, a minimum number of men and women of this age will be present. Division of tasks between the sexes of about this age is the most important single element in determining the demographic constitution of local settlements, and this in turn is critical in marking out the pattern of social relationships in the universe of each group (see E. Peters 1965).

The consequences do not end here. A dependence is created in the division of labor between the proximate generations of both sexes. Young women are as valuable to their seniors in domestic work as males are to theirs in herding. Throughout the developmental cycle in production units, the period during which a male and female can perform all the necessary activities, without aid, is of very short duration. The arbitrariness of the authority vested in the senior generation is constrained by demands they have to make on the younger generation for labor. Tasks performed by young men and young women entitle them to food, clothing, and shelter, and, as long as they make their appropriate contributions, their fathers must yield to their marriage demands sooner or later. If need be, the pressure built up by son and daughter can be staved off temporarily with gifts—silver bracelets or earrings in the case of women, and a horse in the case of men. It was not without point that an elder, when I urged him to consider his son's desire for marriage, replied that he had already bought him a horse and the elaborate accoutrement that went with it. Nor is it fortuitous that gifts of this sort are made to sons and daughters whose marriages have been delayed considerably due to the father's holding out for a high bridewealth. Beyond a certain period, dutiful sons and daughters are considered to have done more than earn their keep; either marriage must be arranged or some of the paternal wealth must be distributed to them, although neither son nor daughter is free to dispose of these gifts by selling them to begin gathering a flock.

Prior to marriage, therefore, both sexes are held to be responsible beings, and through responsibility they acquire a limited measure of control. They fulfill their responsibilities, however, under direction. They have yet to accede to managerial status and the prospect of capturing proprietary rights is still more remote. Late adolescence to early adulthood is the most difficult period in the life cycle of the bedouin. Physically they have matured into adulthood and their activities compel them to carry the heavy responsibility of adulthood, but the legal right to assume the status is denied them. I wish to stress that these disabilities are suffered by both sexes, because it is at this time of their lives that women are said to "suffer" most. I hope the details given here suffice to show that the restrictions are not reserved for women only and that they share a developmental status with their brothers of similar age. There is no question of subjugating women as a category. Both sexes come under the same authority, and although sex necessarily determines many of the specifics of behavior, the constraints placed on both are concerned with moving them forward from one status into another—a kind of long, drawn out *rite de passage*.

Granted this high degree of premarital constraint in sexual, productive, and authority relations, a constraint not limited to single areas of social life but pervading a whole range of relationships, it follows that the changes brought about by marriage must be most profound if the long and careful preliminary discipline that both sexes perforce undergo is to make sense. What is at stake in marriage to make the training period for it so protracted, so constricting socially, and so heavy an emotional burden to bear? I suggest that the clue lies in the fact that a multiplicity of social relationships are absorbed by persons of both sexes as they grow, and that these rapidly coalesce at a point in time, coincident with marriageable age, to make marriage a momentous moment in change of status. It is because premarital control covers so many sets of relationships and is so strictly applied that the marriage ceremony has to comprehend a wide range of issues, and is a major event in bedouin life. This can be documented by considering some aspects of marriage, beginning with the marriage ceremony itself.

Nuptials, and the seven festive days that accompany them, are preceded by weeks, sometimes months, of negotiations. The bare formalities are the same whether the bride is a kinswoman from within the lineage or an unrelated person of another corporation. Over these weeks of negotiations gifts are passed to mark the beginning of the new relationship that entry into marriage involves. Bridewealth itself varies conspicuously from about two camels to twenty.[6] When marriage occurs within a corporation the bridewealth is small, and when an exchange marriage is arranged, the difference between the amounts promised may be as little as one sheep, although it is important to realize that both parties to the exchange promise more than this amount.[7] Some internal marriages carry a small amount of bridewealth, but external marriages command large amounts. This variation in amount is not a reflection on the bride or her kin. A parallel cousin marriage contracted with an agreement to pay two camels is not less important, as a marriage per se, than a marriage that has twenty camels attached to it. Stability of the union is not affected by the amount of bridewealth promised: a parallel cousin marriage, especially to a first cousin, leads to serious difficulties if it is broken, and although the bridewealth is small these marriages are as stable as those where the bridewealth is twice as much or more (see Evans-Pritchard 1951).

Bridewealth is concerned with social relations, and if this variation in amount is to be understood it must be viewed in terms of the nature of the relations that are initiated through marriage, whether these are new, with previously unrelated people; or are old ones being revived; or new ones being perpetuated. Thus, where strong links are already available—as with agnates within a corporation—the relatively small bridewealth documents the desire to add to relationships that already exist by transmuting some of them into affinity. A bridewealth of two camels is a measure of the value of affinity added to agnation. Where there is an absence of a marriage link between two corporations and an alliance is sought, then the bridewealth is likely to be massive—twenty camels if the bride's group is politically powerful. What this indicates is that a corporation wishes to build up relations of this magnitude. The exact number promised, whether it is eight, ten, fourteen, or twenty, depends on the value the suitor's group attaches to the alliance. An initial link of this sort commands a large bridewealth; in a succeeding link, say a marriage to the sister of the first spouse, or, in a succeeding generation, to a cross cousin such as a mother's brother's daughter, the bridewealth is of a considerably reduced amount—perhaps four camels. But this second bridewealth is earnest that the now established relationships are desirable and that the intention is to consolidate and perpetuate them. The amount of bridewealth is a most valuable indication of the change expected in a set of relationships. Further evidence in support of this view is given by the status conferred on women who carry a high bridewealth. A high bridewealth endows a woman with high status, enabling her to become a kind of chief woman of a camp; she occupies this role because the responsibility of mediating a major political connection has been allocated to her.[8] Women are not merely links, providing the cross-cutting ties that bind men together. Their positions constitute the reference points on the map of any corporate group's political relationships.

After the successful conclusion of bridewealth negotiations the nuptials take place as soon as the groom has been able to collect a number of articles, together forming a separate part of the bridewealth, which, unlike the promised camels, must be given at the time of the marriage ceremonies. These articles consist of a complete outfit of clothes for the bride, a carpet and a straw mat (the "bed"), a length of cloth to divide off the female quarters from the rest of a tent, cooking utensils, and a pair of heavy silver armlets. For the first time in her life a woman now has property over which she has proprietary rights. As long as she remains married, the consumable items in this part of the bridewealth must be renewed by her husband. Wives do not own their own tents,[9] but, save for the help they may be given on marriage, they weave them from wool provided by husbands. A tent means security of shelter for a woman, and it is interesting to note that at any time during her life a woman can demand shelter, whereas a male may be unable to make this demand for certain limited periods of his life. A bachelor is not always able to find tent accommodation, and perforce sleeps against the side of a tent to gain some shelter from the elements. This arises out of the fact that in a tent a woman is provided with her own private domain—the female third of a tent—but she also possesses access rights to the male quarters, since it is here that the "bed" of sexual intercourse is laid out. A wife is thus able to exclude her husband's brothers from nocturnal shelter, from a home in fact; but because female quarters are exclusively for use by women, women cannot be excluded by males.

During his lifetime a husband remains titular head of a tent as long as he has a wife in control of the female quarters. Without the services of a woman, a man surrenders his title to headship: there is point to the saying, "a woman is to a man as the tent pole is to the tent." Indeed, a woman can become head of a tent herself: if she is widowed, but still active, with a young child, she can recruit bachelors or widowers from among her kinsmen, give them shelter in her tent in exchange for their labor, and enjoy dominion over them until the unit is split on her son's marriage. Much attention is given in the literature to the care and protection provided for widows and old women; the provisions that have to be made for bachelors and aged widowers are more difficult to meet because the availability of a woman of the right age and status is a minimal essential in any domestic unit. A woman possesses both the right to a separate part of the tent and the right to control all the activities that go on there. The preparation and cooking of food, weaving, gathering tinder—all those activities without which the round of everyday living would come to a halt—are exclusively female tasks. Males are excluded from participation in these activities, and since they are barred from the female part of the tent, a woman must be present in all tents. A widower with or without young children, or a man who has hastily divorced his wife, is in a predicament that can only be resolved by the immediate recruitment of another woman, or else he must face the dispersal of the unit and the possibility of remaining homeless for a long period. Moreover, a widow, after her son has married and broken up her home, may go to live with her son, but she can also live in a tent on her own (see S. Peters 1952). A man cannot do this.

For a tent to be more than a dormitory, both sexes must be present. When, therefore, a bride is presented with domestic utensils and a tent at marriage, they are not for herself only: the husband gains possession of the domestic services of a woman. Part of his social life comes under his authority for the first time. Immediately after marriage, this authority is not effective if a man's mother is alive, because the latter anxiously awaits the arrival of a daughter-in-law to close the gap in domestic help created by the loss of her own daughter in marriage. Even in a case of first parallel cousin marriage, when the natal tents of both spouses are adjoining in a small camp, the new wife takes her place with her mother-in-law, and meticulously observes her new station. Until a child is born, then, a man shares his wife, domestically, with his mother, and only exerts effective authority over her sexually. Also, because the tent of a newlywed couple is used only for sleeping, the husband is still part of his father's domestic unit, and is, therefore, under his authority. It is not until the birth of a child—or the death of the parents—that the new couple are liberated to become tied to their own tent.

Thus far, of the changes precipitated by marriage, only those relating to limited aspects of bridewealth have been discussed. A full account of the marriage ceremony and its symbolic riches is out of place here (see E. Peters 1965). The discussion now turns to property and its distribution.

Males acquire their proprietary rights to animals and land by transmission through males. Women do not inherit. Bedouin are aware that in thus dispossessing women they are contravening the law, but to do otherwise would result in an uncontrolled alienation of property from the corporate group where ownership is vested. Bridewealth effects the transfer of property from one corporation to another, but the transfer is controlled. Since women are free to be married by men outside their natal corporations (nearly half their marriages are of this sort), female inheritance would mean an uncontrolled run on corporate resources. This would be serious enough if only mobile property were involved, but if land were threatened in this way also, the entire basis of corporate life would collapse. Therefore, the lack of status of women as heirs is, among the bedouin, related not only to the status of individuals as heirs, but to the nature of the property-owning group.

The property-owning group among the bedouin is a corporation of males clustered together on the basis of what is conceived of as agnation. Moreover, the relation of these groups of males to permanent property is a fixed one; the economy of mixed agriculture and pastoralism in Cyrenaica permits agnates to remain assembled on their homeland, absences for economic purposes occurring only two or three times a year for such short periods that it is unnecessary to move tent and family. This relationship to land persists from generation to generation, since the virilocal marriage arrangements, while they may not always be patrilocal, confine residence in the majority of cases to a homeland, the territory of a corporate group. By comparison, women are much more mobile. Marriage takes many women away from their natal homeland, and the mothers of women who marry within their corporation may well have been recruited from other corporations. If one views the matter in terms of one generation, some women, coincidentally as it were, remain attached to their homeland; this is too fortuitous to allow us to speak of a fixed relationship of women to land, and when successive generations are taken into account the relationship is seen to be even less permanent. Women are thus precluded from constituting permanent groups with enduring ties to parcels of land.

Mobile property in the form of animals is the other side of the coin: denied permanent rights to land and water, women (as a category) lack the basis to rear flocks and herds, since if they are to keep animals they can only do so through the good offices of men. Some women contrive to control a small flock of sheep or a few camels, but if they were allowed to inherit and to transmit freely, this, in effect, would be an invasion of the natural resources of a corporate group. Hence, proprietary control of both these major forms of property, and the transmission of this right, rests with males. In this respect women never reach full legal majority. On the other hand a man does not acquire proprietary rights until his father has died.[10] With regard to natural resources and mobile property, women of all ages and men—married and unmarried—who have yet to inherit, are together under the authority of senior males.[11] Marriage, retarded by senior males, as others in the community think, is a public challenge to this authority. The unendowed—males and females—combine at a wedding ceremony to announce that one of the bastions of authority is falling. Senior males stand apart from the festivities, overbearingly disregarding the warning there is in them. Inasmuch as rights to property are not and cannot be compromised, their disinterestedness is fitting; but since social relationships are not all subsumed under these rights, and because the authority, which stems from these rights, seeps its way into diverse fields of relationships, marriage leaves the rights intact but erodes the domain of authority. One aspect of marriage is the transacted transfer of property between two sets of senior males. It is the wedded couple who are instrumental to this transfer. Since they are implicated in this way, the interests of the senior males are delegated to them for fulfillment.

After marriage a son has a claim to his father's goods. The young man's wife and her children must be clothed and fed, and wool must be made available for weaving purposes. Claims to these goods are made by a wife on her husband, but he has to get them from his father, who is compelled to give. By this time a father will have probably retired from the arduous duties of herding, thus relinquishing effective managerial control of the animals to his married son, so that claims to goods are a recognition of rewards due for different services: at an earlier age, the son's labor was rewarded by his keep, but now his needs have expanded considerably, and his services have grown in status to match. A married couple, especially after they form a separate domestic unit, dismantle the authority of the family head and win a stake in his property, thus advancing toward greater independence. In this area of relationships, the couple act jointly to cream off as much as they can of the patriarchal wealth. Independent claims are also secured by the wife through bridewealth. In order to appreciate this, reference must be made to another aspect of bridewealth.

At the bridewealth negotiations, the details of the wealth to pass from the groom's kin to the bride's father and selected members of his kin are stated and witnessed. These negotiations are concluded by an advance "gift" of a few sheep,[12] which, assuming the marriage prospers, commences a series of gift exchanges that continues for years. The main part of the bridewealth payments are not given for about a year. Depending on the fertility or barrenness of the marriage, the first amount to pass will vary, but it will not amount to more than a small fraction of the amount promised, in either event. The remainder is left over as a debt, and may never be paid over to the bride's father, certainly not if relationships between the two sets of kin develop favorably. Against this remainder, the girl's father and brother can make claims on the services and good offices of the husband and his father. Also, a wife is enabled to extract wealth from her husband. The manner in which this is done follows a conventional pattern of behavior. A wife, as a result of a quarrel with her husband during which he insulted her, or particularly if he struck her, goes back to her father in anger. The word commonly used for the state to describe a woman who leaves her husband in these circumstances is *zaʿalana*.[13] She refuses to return until she is placated with a "gift." Sometimes this "gift" is a valuable pair of silver armlets, or one or more sheep. It always represents a redirection of property in favor of a wife. In later years, a wife no longer resorts to this ruse for extracting property from her husband, for the bridewealth debt has by now been buried beneath an accumulation of social relationships. The wife's father is well aware that further payments will not be forthcoming, and he formally renounces all claims by requesting that the bridewealth still outstanding is to be "put in front of her" (his daughter). It is not given to her outright, but she insists on marking an agreed number of sheep with her father's or brother's personal brand; she holds the right to nominate an heir, among her sons, to this property. A similar arrangement is practiced in a sororal and leviratic marriage; an amount of bridewealth is stated, but the woman's father agrees to leave it "in front of her." In some cases, women amass sufficient property in animals (their silver armlets and anklets they tend to sell for animals as they reach old age) to affect significantly the distribution of inherited wealth among a man's sons, and in doing so give one of them an advantageous start in the struggle for power.[14] These rights are not to be dismissed lightly as peripherally influential, but should be seen as rights that determine relations.

It is now necessary to clarify the relation of women to property. Both wives and daughters are disinherited, contrary to Islamic law, and they are well aware of this. But women do not meekly surrender such a prime right because they are submissive by nature, as some writers on Arabs seem to believe. They renounce rights—whether they are bedouin or of the other Arab communities discussed below—and in return they are able to make claims against the males who hold their property rights. This ability to press claims applies to heritable property and to bridewealth. These claims are neither "submerged" nor "shadowy," as Goody writes (1959). They are asserted by women unambiguously. Hence, when a man among the bedouin seeks access to plowland or water in his mother's brother's territory, or asks for a share of his animal products, the mother's brother must yield because his sister can make demands against him. Similarly, when a mother's brother assists his sister's son by making a significant contribution to his bridewealth, or to a blood-money payment, he does this not out of sentiment—which varies with the individual in any case—but in recognition of his sister's due share of his property. It is for this reason that the mother's brother, in Cyrenaica, is of such high import to the sister's son, not because he stands external to the affairs of the corporate group—often he is a member of the same group—but because the intricacies of property relationships compel him to participate in the affairs of the group into which his sister has married. Lest it be thought that a woman, as sister or mother in this context, merely acts as a channel along which relationships between mother's brother and sister's son flow, it must be made explicit that this is not so: a woman has her own defined position in relation to property. This is to be seen, also, in her diverting property from her natal home to her husband, according to her wishes, and if she is disinclined to effect this transfer, her husband will not receive the property.

Dispossessed of proprietary rights, women nevertheless help to shape things in all fields of behavior, and not only within the limits of small domestic groups. This women achieve without recourse to revolt, either of a ritual or a nonrational kind. What they do is force claims that they support with their rights. Their claims are not arbitrary; they are commensurable with their rights, otherwise they could not be sustained. For this reason unmarried women do not press claims, although during the years before marriage a woman is more restricted socially and has less status than at any subsequent time. If demands are to come from any females, if revolt is to appear among women, it is from this "deprived" group that either or both could be expected.[15] In fact, demands come from married women, and with good reason: the "deprived" group has not been deprived in the sense of being divested of rights; they have not acquired any yet. Women cannot rationally make demands against nothing. Backed by bridewealth and the rights with which they are thereby endowed, they have no need to make demands; they can force claims.

Bridewealth has further implications. Left largely as a debt it becomes almost a synonym for reciprocal obligations, for social relationships, that is to say. Indeed marriage is commonly referred to as "making relationships." What bridewealth and marriage do is to initiate a set of social relationships in which claims and counter-claims can be made against forms of property. Two parties of senior males assume the responsibility for initiating the relationships, which they have decided are in conformity with their interests, and thereafter they relinquish the future of these relationships to a pair of spouses, who, in some cases, have never met before.

It is necessary to interrupt the argument to point out that the question of social compatibility seldom arises as a serious issue (see Freedman 1967). The tent is divided into male and female parts, and for most of the daytime, at least, the sexes occupy their own areas of the tent. On the first day of the marriage ceremonies, sexual compatibility has already been tested, albeit in a preliminary manner. The virginity test is not only a witness to premarital chastity; it ensures also that the bride is not suffering some sort of sexual malformation. On the first night of the nuptials the marriage is consummated, and the following day the spouses are questioned about it by males and females respectively. The spouses continue to sleep together for the test period of seven days—the duration of the wedding festivities, in fact. Consummation reveals that the bride is sexually normal and that the groom is not impotent. If either defect is present, the arrangements are summarily terminated. Also, if these first seven days pass without impediment, it augers well for future sexual compatibility. It is indicative of the relatively minor importance attached to social compatibility that little provision is made for it before marriage or during the nuptials. A married pair is not compelled to remain in each other's company at any time during the day, not even for meals, which men always take separately and, if necessary, alone. They sleep together only for sexual intercourse. Social compatibility matures as time passes, and when the spouses associate socially to a greater extent. In the early years of marriage, at a time, that is, before companionship has had a chance to take a strong grip, and when divorce, for personal reasons, is most likely to occur, the need for continuous social relations does not exist. Social compatibility of the spouses is peripheral to the matter of marital stability. This point is stressed in order to throw the critical importance of the young spouses, particularly the wife, into relief. Whether the relationships initiated by marriage prosper is too important an issue to be left to the chance of two individuals of opposite sexes getting along together. In the final analysis, it is left to the considered adjudications they make, separately or jointly, on the relationships that they mediate.[16]

The priority given here to mediation, compared with linking and communication, arises from the consideration that while the latter are operative in marriages between corporations, they are largely irrelevant where the spouses are the children of a pair of full brothers or of close cousins resident in the same small camp of a few tents. The argument that a woman in marriage mediates relationships comprehends all marriage, whatever the particular form it takes or the territorial distance it covers. This becomes clear upon consideration of the interests served by marriage within corporations and between them.

Property rights within corporations entitle all agnates to an equal share of land and water resources. Inheritance rules make the male children of a man equal heirs to his property. If this equality were to be realized in practice, then it would mean an absence of social differentiation. It can be stated as a fact that while class does not exist, differentiation on the basis of wealth and status does. The main way in which this is brought about is by men struggling to break out of the treadmill of equal shares to capture more than their legal agnatic right. Part of the point of parallel cousin marriage is that it assists the unequal allocation of resources, because matrilateral and affinal connections among agnates can be used to make requests not permitted within agnation; and because agnates have the same rights to resources but not all of them have a sufficient number of animals to use their full share of water or the wealth (in the sense of money to buy seed and labor to plow) to grow a large crop, trading of resources between affinally and matrilaterally related agnates appears. An agnate cannot alienate his share to another agnate, since as agnates all men of a corporation have a legal claim to the surplus. Marriage thrusts a wedge of differentiation into agnation. A power seeker who marries one of his daughters to a poor agnate gains through her the unexpended surplus of a fellow agnate, thus enabling him to increase the size of his flocks and herds. With regard to animals, the distribution among heirs is rarely equal; the eldest son, for various reasons, is in a position to appropriate more than an equal share. In the succeeding generation, this unequal distribution can be partially corrected if an heir who loses property to his eldest brother marries his son to the eldest brother's daughter and defaults on the bridewealth; and this daughter has the ability to divert more of this wealth. The success of attempts to skim off surpluses from fellow agnates, and the readjustments in the distribution of inherited mobile property, hinge on the willingness of a wife to remain with her husband. A wife has the power to make or break a relationship.

The capture of unequal access to agnatic resources is the immediate aim of men. Assuming a man achieves this, he is then in a position to expand his animal wealth. Large flocks and herds, in a country where climatic vagaries lead to concentrations of surplus water here and deficiencies there, in any given year, can become a serious liability unless secure links to the resources of other corporations are available. For what such links mean is that local surpluses that accumulate in corporations can be redistributed by permitting affinal and matrilateral kinsmen to water their animals there when they are short of water in their homeland, or by granting them the use of plowland when they are experiencing a shortage of rainfall, or an unsuitable regime for raising a crop. It is partly for this reason that links leapfrog collateral sections (or neighboring corporations) where conditions are likely to be identical, and are dropped into selected sections at greater distances. Women residing in other corporations secure continued economic stability, where otherwise all corporate groups would be exposed to the persistent threat of local economic instability. Economic stability must be anchored in affinity and kinship. Contractual relations alone are too frail to provide the security required. In other areas of relationships, the ties of debt—essentially arrangements imposing obligations, but of a kind that can be summarily renounced—appear to be sufficiently strong to maintain them. They are, however, tenuous relationships, lacking the jural durability of those tied up in marriage.

Relationships do not, however, begin and end with the economic distribution of wealth. The member of a corporation who succeeds in capturing the equal shares to resources of fellow agnates also commands a following, since, in return for the shares, food and wool are given, creating dependency. First parallel cousin marriage, by converting an agnatic nephew into a dependent affine, can thwart the nephew's power ambitions, and leave the field clear for his wife's brother to conquer. Women positioned in other corporations also secure the political allegiance of a number of corporations: the extent of the spread of external marriages that a man of power possesses is an accurate measure of the span of his power. Whether one considers the case of a man who has succeeded only in dominating his brothers, or of one who has enlarged his field to the extent of a small camp, or another who can boast of the allegiance of several corporations, the domains of each are delineated by women.[17] If this view is valid, then women are not mere links, they are the points of articulation in combinations of corporate groups, which constitute the political structures and which form the basis of all political activities.

Finally, to complete the details of the developmental cycle for bedouin women, a few further remarks are needed. As women age, their daily relations with men of the camp are easier than before. They rarely cover their faces, they go into the male part of the tent more often, they are free to talk with men of all ages, and curtaining off the women's part of the tent is limited to the infrequent occasions when a gathering of strangers meets in the male part. Past childbearing age, a woman, who previously argued with males within the limits of her own domestic unit, now engages in public discussions, voicing opinions that may be backed by other women in the camp. It is wrong to suppose that because women are not among men during discussions they are no more than isolated units and wholly unrepresented. In most camps a leading woman is present, usually the wife of the camp sheikh, who greets guests on their arrival and entertains visitors in the absence of males. These female leaders rely on women for support; leadership among women is not given them *ex gratia* by males. Just as most men in most camps are agnatically related, so too, women, drawn from a wide range of groups, are also related consanguineously and affinally. Men are masters of the art of reckoning agnatic connections among males; women are equally adept at finding their way through a labyrinth of ties to establish links among themselves. Those women who rise to prominence in the camps are not isolated individuals who have been thrown into totally strange surroundings by marriage.[18] They lead connected groups of kinswomen. But they lead among men of a corporation other than their own natal one. Their presence there ensures that the interests of their natal corporations are respected and included in the deliberations of the corporations where they live as wives. They are mothers as well as wives, and guard the rights and well-being of their sons, as their participation in nuptials makes abundantly clear. They are included if inheritance disputes arise; and if, through her own efforts, a woman fails to gain her ends, she can call on her father or brother to assist her to deal, as an affine, with her husband or others of his close kin who threatened her son. If a man gives preferential treatment to one son in distributing his property, against the wishes of his wife, she is able to adjust the balance by giving her property to another son; or, if she wishes, she can tip the balance still further by giving it to her husband's preferred heir. Therefore, women are not intrusive to agnation. They do not constitute a category in opposition to males. They insist that their claims are met; so do men; neither forces claims in the absence of rights. The male-female dichotomy is false when applied to bedouin life (see Evans-Pritchard 1965). There are not two worlds, one for men and one for women. The sexes combine to form a single community, where women do not consistently press female rights, any more than men consistently press male rights, but where both sexes—amid the uproar of disputes and the calm of reconciliations, the growth of new relations and the breach of others—recognize a convergence of interests and attain a tolerable social life.

Shiite Villagers of Lebanon

The Shiite Muslim village of south Lebanon has a multicrop economy, with a variety of over twenty fruits and vegetables.[19] The population is divided into three ranks, distinguished by dress, occupation, and style of living: the Learned Families (as they like to speak of themselves), who live a leisured life, comprising roughly 20 percent of the population, owning roughly half the cultivable land and deriving additional income, in various ways, from the religious status accorded them in the village; the petty traders, who own the fourteen shops, and who, as a group, are better off than those whose income is derived almost solely from cultivation; and the peasants or laborers, who constitute the vast majority of the local population, who work their own land and that of wealthier people and are engaged as casual laborers in the coastal towns during the agriculturally slack period in midwinter, and among whom there are considerable differences of wealth. The discussion begins with the peasant group.

Until they reach the age of about seven years, boys and girls are treated in similar fashion to their desert cousins. From the age of about ten and onward, children of both sexes run errands about the village, or carry parcels for unrelated people and shopkeepers. In summer, when people from the coast flock into the hills and rent houses, or live with kinsfolk for two to three months until the worst of the heat and humidity on the coast has passed, children, especially boys, are kept busy daily. They are paid for their services. The payments are trivial for each task, but it is possible for boys to accumulate the equivalent of several shillings in a day. For this is a cash economy, and one of its features is that trivial payments can be made for trivial tasks. Among the bedouin, children are fortunate if they are rewarded at all, and what they receive can only be a piece of bread or meat, or the rare luxury of a sweet after a father has made one of his infrequent visits to market; the reward is eaten immediately. Among the Lebanese children the small coins they are given can be saved and later used to buy an article of their own choosing. From an early age these children learn to use wealth independently, and to gauge the value of their labor and the goods they see. This interest in evaluation is implanted at a young age, in a multicrop economy, when the value of one product has to be assessed against that of another, for exchange purposes; the absorbing interest in money and prices, which both sexes of all ages show, is a noticeable feature, and the inquiries they make are not moderated by considerations of privacy. This early training makes them well fitted for the kind of property relations they enter into a few years later.

Children who have reached their teens follow their fathers and mothers to the gardens and begin to learn methods of cultivation. At the same time boys continue to earn their small amounts, but girls of this age do not frequent the marketplace. Instead, they learn to sew, to make preserves, and other household skills; they also act as domestic servants for other people.

All these are spare-time activities until the age of twelve, since both sexes attend school compulsorily. Thereafter, the tasks they perform become differentiated, except that at this age all garden tasks are interchangeable. Where the differentiation is apparent, however, is in the household. Young girls assist their mothers with the cooking and bread-making, and they help keep the house clean. But it is not wrong for a boy to join them, particularly when the house has to be swept. Among the bedouin the differentiation between the sexes is clear-cut by this age, whereas, in Lebanon, interchangeability continues to characterize the relationship between the sexes in the growing and harvesting of crops. When they enter their late teens, sons and daughters are full-time members of a production team and spend long hours in the gardens working together. A full discussion of the multitude of tasks required in any economy, of the horticultural richness of this village, is outside the scope of this study: suffice it to say that harvests run in an uninterrupted sequence for nine months of the year, and even during the slack winter months vegetables are being picked. There are some tasks, however, that are exclusively the work of males; there are others that are allotted to women, but men are not barred from any of these.

An examination of these points of departure between the sexes leads to interesting results when compared with the bedouin. Lebanese males plow the land; in this women have no part. Many of the terrace walls on the steep slopes collapse in winter. If only a few stones have tumbled, women may assist men. Major repairs to large gaps in the walls are carried out by men only. Plots that have fallen into disuse are broken up laboriously with an adze by men, although it must be added that an adze is not a peculiarly male instrument, and is used by women for a number of purposes, such as splitting firewood. Much of the land has to be watered at regular intervals. Men do this work, sometimes having to rise in the middle of the night if the time allotted happens to fall at that inconvenient hour. The tasks listed are done mainly by males and are referred to as men's work; it is not wrong for women to help, and no evil will befall people or crops if they do. The same remark applies to women's work. Distinctively, this is weeding, but men can weed with women, or without their help for that matter. Add to this interchangeability between the sexes the fact that there is no differentiation of garden work according to age, and it can readily be appreciated that a small family is a highly efficient productive unit, maximizing its labor potential, and at the same time creating a high degree of cooperative dependency among its members. Nevertheless, there are three tasks that women do not undertake on their own—plowing, terrace repairs, and irrigating the plots. In these specific relations to property, women must depend on men.

Domestically, also, the cleavage between the sexes is far from being as sharp as in Cyrenaica. The Lebanese housework is mainly woman's work. Yet men are not removed from the preparation of food in the sense that any help or interference would bring bad luck. The separation of the sexes in this context is most at the meal, when, as in Cyrenaica, they eat separately even within the intimacy and privacy of an elementary family: the women sit in the center of the room and the father sits in the right hand corner facing the door, his two shoulders resting against two walls, and his sons beside him. Women control the kitchen, but because men are not wholly excluded from the preparation of food, they are not compelled to reside with women, as in Cyrenaica. A bachelor can live on his own. Life is not intolerably difficult for a man who wishes to remain a widower or unmarried. But if men can live alone, so can women. They do not plow but they can hire labor, in the same way as men can employ girls as domestic servants, there being a sufficient labor surplus to provide for the needs of both. Both sexes can live apart, many of them remaining unmarried because such a conspicuously high degree of interchangeability between the sexes exists with regard to productive activities and domestic tasks. This raises the question: why should the interchangeability of these roles be maximized in this south Lebanese village, and reduced to a minimum among the bedouin?

The critical productive activities in the Cyrenaican economy are plowing, herding, watering animals, and, to a lesser extent, gathering the harvest. Plowing, assuming favorable conditions, must be completed in a fortnight or three weeks, and during this time men work hard from early morning to sunset. Herding animals causes men to be absent from camp for several successive days, and when the pastures dry up as summer approaches, they are away for longer periods, dropping in at the camps for short respites only. Watering a flock of a hundred sheep takes several hours, and watering a herd of twenty camels is long and exacting. Barley is gathered as it begins to ripen, but when the whole crop is ready, it is work for several men for several days or weeks, depending on its size. To characterize the effort required briefly: concentrated and intense labor is needed urgently twice during the year, and if this kind of labor is not available, the crop is lost; regular labor must be at hand to give constant attention to the animals and to wander with them in search of pastures. Women cannot provide this kind of labor. They milk the animals, a relatively easy task for which substitution is possible. They can also tend a small herd of young goats with the help of young children. But the main tasks of production are beyond their capabilities, if they are to bear children as well. The nature of production shuts women out of a major role as producers. The economy also lacks diversification. Composed of only one crop and of animal herding, it is too concentrated to offer any alternatives for women: they, therefore, only process the products.

In the Lebanese village, there is a wide range of crops. Temporary incapacity is not catastrophic. If a woman has to hire labor for one harvest because she is incapacitated by childbirth, she is often fit enough to deal with the next. Infants add a burden to labor but they do not prevent it. A family of children is an asset, because even young boys and girls can pick fruit, assist with grape packing, and the like. Women's childbearing role does not preclude them from sustaining production. In an economy as diversified as this, the range of opportunities available to women is wide enough to minimize the dislocative effect of their biological role. And to make their participation effective they engage in the full range of tasks save for those that require immediate and continued attention for limited but critical periods. Therefore, in Cyrenaica, little economic diversity, coupled with the concentrated effort required for two short periods of the year, are important factors in the marked sex differentiation and the little interchangeability of roles; in Lebanon, conspicuous economic diversity promotes interchangeability of roles and minimizes sex-differentiation.

Neither the bedouin nor south Lebanese peasant women cover their faces, except in limited situations: since they both engage in tasks publicly, a veil would be an intolerable encumbrance. Nevertheless, bedouin girls during the period of nubility are restricted in their movements and draw the head scarf across their faces at the approach of all males save for those of their immediate family, while south Lebanese peasant girls during the same period are no more restricted in their movements nor do they cover their faces more than at any other time in their lives. Why this difference between the two? Bedouin marriages are arranged by the parental generation, for the reasons already given. There is urgent need, therefore, for them to control their nubile daughters. Covering the face is an essential part of this control. The marriages of peasant girls in the south Lebanese village are not strictly arranged; many of them follow premarital pregnancies, and, in cases where the parents take an initiative in arranging a match, the daughter must concur in their choice. But these Lebanese girls are to be distinguished from bedouin girls in two important respects. They inherit as wives and daughters, and they receive a settlement on marriage. They also contribute significantly to productive labor. Bedouin girls do not inherit, they are not given their bridewealth, and they only process the products of male labor. In all these respects, Lebanese girls achieve an independence of status not granted to their bedouin cousins.

Young women of the Learned Families in the south Lebanese village behave quite differently. Like their menfolk, women of the Learned Families do not work on the land at all. In public they are permanently veiled. They are distinguishable from other women by the black garments they wear, and the veil shows that they do not engage in agricultural activities: more important, the veil is meant to ward off the attentions of men. Women of the Learned Families remain indoors most of the time, and when they go out to visit, they go in small groups or with a male escort. Any women who brazenly frequent the village center would be suspected of concupiscence, but peasant women move freely out of doors: they must do so since almost daily they go to and from the gardens—some of them distant—and during these excursions they converse with men, call out greetings to them, and avert their gaze or draw their headcovering across the side of their face only when they pass adult male strangers. Women of the Learned Families are much more secluded, and they are brought up to regard unveiled female faces and the appearance of women in public places as vulgarity. Ascent in status places greater restrictions on the behavior of women.

In both classes, women inherit as wives, mothers, daughters, and sisters. The discussion of the division of labor shows the vital role peasant women play in relation to property. It is suggested that the rights held by women in property are derived from the contributions they make to production, for, unlike bedouin women, their activities are not confined to processing products handed over to them by men. Learned Families' women do not produce; neither do the men. Both absorb the surplus of male and female peasant labor, and both inherit. Therefore, the two distinct patterns of differentiation in this Lebanese village cannot be a matter of inheritance alone, even though a comparison between peasant and bedouin women suggests this as an immediate possibility. Since inheritance is not the only critical variable, why is it that control is exercised over the general behavior and marriages of women of the Learned Families, while women of the peasantry are allowed a considerable measure of freedom in both these areas of their lives? Part of the explanation of these differences is in the nature of the property groups to be found among the Learned Families and the peasants, respectively.

The rank of the Learned Families is founded in property ownership. Their disproportionate share of property in land allows them to hire labor and detach themselves from agricultural work. But the balance between them and the peasants, who get for their work half the products of the land, is a delicate one. Alienation of land is a threat to their rank. This threat occurs in two ways: men can sell land, and women transfer it through marriage. It is met by tying land to an association of males, with the authority to threaten disciplinary action against those who are tempted by rising prices to sell and, also, by controlling marriages. Because women must be prevented from dismembering the estate of the Learned Families they are denied free choice in marriage. The same applies to men. It is in the interests of both sexes to marry within their land association, for the threat comes as much from a man's marrying a peasant as it does from a woman's marrying a peasant—and this needs to be emphasized, since in most anthropological works, particularly those on Arabs, marriage arrangements are seen in terms of male interests, rarely female. The population of the Learned Families is, however, only about two hundred twenty.[20] Therefore, the high marriage rate within the group in the village—over 60 percent for males and over 80 percent for females—can only be achieved with an accompanying high spinster and bachelor rate, for demographic reasons. The precedence given to the maintenance of the total land holdings of the Learned Families is evidenced by the large number of unmarried people of both sexes, and this in turn shows the control of marriages of both sexes.

Among the bedouin, only one spinster was encountered during a stay of over two years—she was found to be sexually deformed on the first day of her nuptials. Lacking any property rights, she was forced to rely on the compassion of her kinsmen, for the claims that other women enforce accrue to them from marital status. Spinsters of the Learned Families are not doomed to commiseration. They become leaders of congregations of women that meet to mourn the death of one of the early heroes of Islam. They have the wealth to pay for a pilgrimage to Mecca or to other shrines venerated by Shiites. A spinster is also a benefactor for many men and women of her class; they vie for her favors. She becomes a sort of revered aunt credited with neutrality because, without husband or children, she stands in the same relationship to a number of people; she is endowed with neutrality, also, because the competition among her potential heirs, particularly those who are unlikely to receive much if she dies intestate, tends to inhibit her from decisively discriminatory decisions. Hence, spinsters act as foci for small groups within the Learned Families, consulted on important matters and serving as the repositories of troubles for their kinsfolk. Where women inherit and wealth is available for transmission, spinsters are likely to hold high status.

Comparatively, the differences between the Sunni bedouin and the Shiite Lebanese can be summarized as follows. Among the bedouin there is little separation of the sexes until girls become nubile, but from then until they marry the behavior of young women is strictly controlled. Marriages are arranged for both sexes by senior males. After marriage the formality in male-female relationships decreases. As men mature into managerial responsibility for flocks and herds, plowing and harvesting, women increasingly take over the management of the domestic unit, including the children, especially sons. Women agree to renounce their inheritance and assent to the transfer of their bridewealth to their nearest kinsmen. Both these rights to property they compound for claims against their kinsmen and their husbands. At marriage, women assume a political status, and some of them rise to positions of leadership.

In the south Lebanese village, women of high status wear the veil from infancy for their whole lives, their movements are restricted, and they do not associate with men. Peasant women wear a head scarf which they draw across their faces in certain circumstances only; they are much freer to move in and around the village, they work alongside men, and they engage in brief conversations, publicly, with virtually any village men. The majority of men and women of the Learned Families marry within their rank. Peasants have a much wider range of choice in marriage, and their marriages are often love matches. Although neither sex among the Learned Families engages in productive activities, there is interchangeability between them regarding domestic tasks, sufficient, at least, to allow some men to live alone. The peasants show great interchangeability between the sexes regarding production activities, and on a reduced scale regarding domestic tasks. Women among both the Learned Families and the peasants inherit, and they are accorded the same precedence as males in reckoning heirship. Sometimes women relinquish their property to a brother, and this is reported in the literature as a denial of inheritance—as if they would simply give away their most valuable material assets due to meekness, submissiveness, or some other quality peculiar to them. My evidence is that women who do this reside in coastal towns and are unable to manage their plots of land in the village. The kinsmen who receive benefices of this kind are obliged to maintain their sisters and their families for three months during the summer months, when there is a general exodus of people from the heat of the towns to the cool of the hills. These sisters, when they return to the coast, take with them enough fruit, nuts, and preserves to last for months. In return for the land they "give" to their brothers, they receive annually some 30 percent of their subsistence needs.

The control of marriage exercised by the Learned Families is to be seen in terms of the threat of alienation of property that the free choice of partner would pose. For the Learned Families the threat is immediate since both sexes inherit. Moreover, the threat is all around them, since they are a small minority of the village population, and, demographically, it is hard for them to maintain the integrity of their group. The fact that there are only two extant marriages for men and one for women outside their group is ample evidence of the success of the socialization they receive from childhood. The bedouin do not have to concern themselves about the alienation of natural resources because they are of a kind that makes individual inheritance impossible. Animal property, together with cereals, is the basis of bedouin subsistence, and if either of these forms of wealth is to be distributed outside the corporate group, this must be done in a planned way, such is their importance. Moreover, as I have stressed, their women have claims on men, and, given the scarcities of the semidesert, it is of critical importance that these claims be controlled also. By contrast with both the bedouin and the Learned Families, the peasants are not constrained within the boundaries of large groups; instead, they are fractionized into the small groups of individual families. Since both sexes inherit, each marriage effects a rearrangement of plots, and, as either spouse views the matter, one adds to the holdings of the other. In these circumstances, the control of marriage can safely be reduced to a minimum. Therefore, when property is held by a collectivity, whether it is individually transmitted or corporately owned, the premarital behavior of women is restricted and marriages are arranged. When property is individually transmitted and individuals do not constitute a collectivity, premarital control is lax and the choice of partner is permitted.

In this comparison the issue of political status remains. A paradox of combinations can be expressed: low jural standing but high political status for bedouin women, and the appearance of leadership among them; high jural standing but low political status for women of the Learned Families and the peasants, and an absence of political leadership. Clearly, the resolution of the apparent paradox is to be sought in the power of women to bring groups of people together. In this respect the women of the south Lebanese village are at a disadvantage, compared with bedouin women, because their jural status is so sharply defined in law and practice. This defines their social domain as well. They represent a known quantity, so to speak, and when they enter marriage their contribution is individual and measurable—as, indeed, it is for males. The status of bedouin women in relation to property is characterized by ambiguity. Moreover, they are born into corporate groups. When they marry they bring together two groups, or if they marry within their natal corporate group they knit together people whose interests coincide, in one way or another. Inheritance is not the only relevant factor here, however: transfers of wealth at marriage are also significant, and serve to demonstrate the differences between women in the two communities with greater clarity.

In the south Lebanese village, the property transferred at marriage is land. It is given to the bride as a marriage settlement (*mahr*), and it is registered in her name. The plot is provided by the groom himself, and, almost invariably, it represents an advance of part of the inheritance he is to receive from his parents. This marriage settlement is enlarged by a grant of land to the bride by her parents, and this, also, is given as an advance of part of her inheritance. Further, it is an accepted arrangement that both spouses, when they become heirs to their parental property, will have preferential claims to the land lying adjacent to the plots brought together by their marriage. In this way, they come to own a small joint estate when they begin their married life, which they work for themselves, thus achieving a measure of economic independence. They remain heirs to parental property after marriage, but the grants of land made to them at marriage considerably lessen their dependence on their kin; and, since these grants are part of their rights as legal heirs, they do not create a tangle of obligations. Marriage brings together two individuals, and the redistribution of property it occasions does not have the effect of uniting large numbers of people. A marriage settlement has the inherent tendency of isolating spouses from their kin.

Bedouin women are not given a marriage settlement. The bride's father is promised a bridewealth (*ṣāḥiba*), but he receives only about a quarter of it, after the lapse of about a year. The remainder is left as debt between the parties. These parties, however, are not two individuals, but two groups of people. The total number of people directly involved in contributing to bridewealth and receiving it varies, but can be as high as fifty and is rarely below twenty. This does not take account of the people involved indirectly through their gifts during the nuptial festivities; these usually number not less than a hundred and often very many more. Bridewealth, in contrast to marriage settlement, creates a structure of social relationships, or adds to one already in existence. It is in this context that a woman is placed on marriage; she not only serves as a means of conjunction between groups, she also mediates the relationships between them. In saying this, it must be stressed that these wives are not merely "women in between" (Strathern 1972), conveyances of sorts. A mediatory position is one that possesses an integrity of its own. In this sense, all bedouin women achieve political status, whether they marry within their natal corporate group—for a man, if he is to dominate his corporate group, must command the affinal alliances within it—or into another. The mediatory role is the foundation on which the power of women is built. The ambiguous position they occupy in relation to property, coupled with the demands they are able to make on their own and their husbands' kin, permit them to elaborate this structure, and reach political prominence. Clarity in the definition of their legal status, and the isolating effect of marriage settlements, rob the south Lebanese women of this kind of political opportunity. Spinsters sometimes achieve political importance, but the span of their effectiveness is limited to competing heirs.

Olive Farmers in Tripolitania

Olive farms in Tripolitania (Libya) were owned until 1959 exclusively by Italians. Thereafter, the Italians began to sell their farms until only about a quarter of the 186 farms remained in their possession by 1964. They were bought by bedouin with the financial contributions of men and women,[21] for the latter, in the pastoral areas of Tripolitania, inherit and transmit rights in animals and landed property.

Olive growing requires little labor, especially now that tractors can plow the strips of land between the lines of trees. Plowing is carried out about six times a year by those who are conscientious about it. The labor of one man for eighteen days, at most, is needed to complete the annual plowing required for a farm of medium size. Harvesting takes a little less time. Groundsheets are spread out under the trees, which are then thoroughly shaken. On a few of the farms, the fruit that falls outside the groundsheet is gathered by women. The only other labor is loading the fruit onto hired trucks, which transport it to olive presses on the plantation. Apart from olives and a few almonds, Arabs cultivate no other crops. Italians cultivate vines and press them for wine on the farms; they also have kitchen gardens, near the farmhouse, in which they grow vegetables and flowers. Arabs have pulled up their vines and do not keep kitchen gardens. Both Italians and Arabs keep a few sheep, but the number in a flock does not exceed twenty, so they can be left in the care of young boys without worry.

The participation of women in production is largely a function of economic differentiation. Arabs have essentially reduced the economic diversification introduced by the Italians to one crop.

Consequently, Arab women are unnecessary for production purposes on the farms. The only tasks required of them are those that have to be done within the house. Further, the amount of time men devote to farming each year is about a month. The astonishing amount of time in which men are free from farming duties is used to visit the pastoral areas to the south, to attend markets, and to sojourn in Tripoli, where many men have erected tin shacks in the shantytowns on the periphery of the capital. As a result, most men spend very little time on their farms. The prolonged absence of men—and even young boys—from the home heightens the isolation that women on the plantation suffer, and the vicious pye-dogs, which lurk near farmhouses, discourage all but the most resolute callers.

As explained earlier, in the camp life of the semidesert, women are tolerably free socially and go about unveiled. When they travel from camp to camp, however, they travel with male escort and cover their faces. The norms of behavior for women among the Arab farmers are similar to those of the semidesert. That is to say, the change is in the situation, not in the norms. For women who have migrated to the plantation, the camp has shrunk to a single household and freedom is enjoyed only within its confines. In some parts of the plantation, the farmhouses are clustered in fours, although most occur in pairs. There are a few instances of a small group of kin owning a pair or a cluster of farms. Mostly, neighbors are strangers, of tribally heterogeneous origin; and often Italian families are interspersed among them. Only occasionally, therefore, are women permitted to move among the farms in one cluster, and they can rarely move from farm to farm along the roads. Segregation for most women is complete. The retention of norms of behavior befitting camp life, in conditions that do not require the participation of women in production and where the population is heterogeneous in origin, diminishes the status of women to the point of degradation.

Italian women are much more favorably placed. Their relationships with Arabs of both sexes are either minimal or nil. But they perform diverse tasks, helping their husbands with the hoeing, pruning, and scything the grass that grows between the olive trees (the Italians tend their farms meticulously), pressing grapes, and growing garden produce. They also sew and embroider—household skills the Arab women still have to learn. In family groups they frequently visit their compatriots in the area. They often accompany their husbands to the capital, where they sell their wine, vegetables, meat, and flowers to relatives in business there. On Sundays almost all the Italians go to church, and gather together after the service.

Cultural differences between Arabs and Italians are so obvious that, it might be argued, there is no need to seek further explanations of the difference in status between their women. The importance of culture here is not being minimized: it certainly keeps Arabs and Italians apart socially. But there are differences other than cultural ones, and these have been shown to bear directly on the issue. Indeed, if the beliefs about differences among Italian women are true, they are to be understood not in terms of general Italian Christian culture, but whether women came as immigrants from industrial families in Milan, or from vine-growing villages in Tuscany, or from peasant homes in Sicily, and so on.

Maronite Christian Villagers in Lebanon

The impact of emigration on women is another variable that can be introduced in this discussion. The Maronite Christian village of central Lebanon is situated in an area from which people leave for the United States, Brazil, West Africa, Kuwait, Saudi Arabia, Australia, and other countries. Only in exceptional cases have women emigrated alone. When they emigrate they leave with a family. Many men, however, emigrate alone, some for short periods, some for twenty years or more. There are numerous instances of men marrying locally, begetting children, then leaving them and their wives to go to work in a foreign country, and returning to the village after an absence of one or two decades. Other men find work in countries nearer to Lebanon, and visit their homes for short periods once or twice annually.

Ecologically, this area is broadly similar to the area around the south Lebanese village. There is almost as wide a range of altitude, and the range of crops that can be grown is as great as in the south. Horticulture, however, is no longer the basis of the economy. People still grow vegetables and fruit near their houses, and some of them press their own olive oil and enjoy the freshness and quality of home produce. The worth of land is now in its value as real estate. In the village itself house building sites are very costly. Also, the village is only about eighteen kilometers from the center of Beirut, and its lands stretch as far west as the suburbs of the city. Recent industrial and other developments on the western boundaries of the village have meant that previously low-priced land now fetches astonishingly high prices, and many people who until the late 1960s enjoyed no more than a tolerable rural standard of living have become wealthy: about half a dozen are said to be dollar millionaires. Differentiation had been present before the boom conditions of recent years, but the general social conviviality among the people did much to obscure marked differences in wealth. Contemporarily, differentiation is hardening into stratification, and the social ease in relationships between rich and poor, which gave an added pleasure to life for everyone, is becoming increasingly impeded by class differences. This tendency is exacerbated by occupational differentiation—the village is near enough to Beirut for people to commute to work and, if the number of men and women working there continues to rise, it is possible that the village life will degenerate—it will become more and more like a dormitory. Higher education is accelerating these processes. The educational facilities available locally have long been of an unusually high standard, and a large percentage of the population has benefited from them. In recent years the number of youths entering university, either in Lebanon or the West, has risen sharply, and they are joined now by young women. During the past decade women have found employment in Beirut mainly as shop assistants and as secretaries. Higher education is professionalizing them, and providing them with a greater diversity of occupational choice.

Males assert that women were not heirs to property, and males of peasant origin insist that the position is still unchanged. They point out that, until the end of the First World War, they had been under Turkish rule, and that the Turks applied Sunni law in matters of inheritance, which, as they misunderstand it, denies women inheritance. The fiction of the transmission of property in the patriline is founded on the superior managerial status of males, not on proprietary rights. The facts are that abundant evidence shows that women did inherit in the past; many current disputes over inheritance originate in the property holdings of aging women or of recently deceased women, and the contemporary status of women, as heirs, is remarkably high. There is no reason for inheritance practices' excluding women: they cultivated the plots of land alongside their men, and some older women, at an age when few people of either sex bother to work the land, find it hard to abandon the habit.

In the ordinary course of events, the status of women would have been high. The frequent, and sometimes prolonged, absences of men from their homes makes it higher. While a wife is still young, her husband might emigrate for a few months, a few years, or for a decade or more, and these forms of emigration affect families irrespective of wealth. Women are left at home to manage the affairs of the family entirely on their own, not merely in that they rear the children, prepare food for them, and attend to household chores, but that they budget the family needs, employ men to keep the house in repair, and deal with business matters that arise. The wives of men who do not emigrate are familiar with the same kind of responsibility, because men's occupations take them away from their homes for most of the day, but they require that someone be available there to answer queries. This is particularly necessary for men who work in the building trade, in transport, as taxi drivers, or as masons. Effectively, these wives act as secretaries, and since literacy is almost universal in the population by now, they are highly efficient in performing these duties.

A priori reasoning suggests that, in these circumstances, all women are potentially significant in politics. In fact this is so, and the fact is given public recognition. Several women who for various reasons command a bundle of kinship and affinal connections are acknowledged by both sexes to be of critical importance in configuring political alliances, and to be among the leaders of local political parties. They enter the fray of argument with as much gusto as men. This status is achieved, moreover, without bridewealth or dowry. To assist a young woman to find a suitable partner, her parents register a valuable piece of land in her name, making her more attractive—it is true—to men who weigh such considerations heavily, but also providing her with an additional asset with which to make a choice. Young women are as analytically perceptive in estimating the worth and the consequences of a match as are young men. At least until 1974 the weaving of the threads of affinity to create the affinal sets was done by both sexes (see E. Peters 1976), but the pattern of the alliances conformed to male business interests. As yet, women are not sufficiently professionalized to determine the pattern of these affinal sets, but many of them represent the knots in the strands, which hold men and women in a set and which give it its durability.

Politically, the status of Christian Lebanese women resembles most that of the bedouin women, but the political contexts are widely disparate: among the bedouin, politics is within and between corporate groups, founded on collective ownership of natural resources; among the Christian Lebanese, politics is chiefly the creation of groups, and individual inheritance prevails. Otherwise, they present a contrasting pair: among the bedouin, marriages are arranged for both spouses, without consulting them, and, once the negotiations have ended, they are summarily instructed to proceed with the nuptials; among the Christian Lebanese young people are permitted a considerable latitude of choice in marriage, and marriage is preceded by courtship, sometimes for a period of years—but, then, unlike the bedouin, social compatibility is a grave consideration for them.

Concerning choice in marriage and the courtship that precedes it, Muslim Lebanese peasants are akin to the Christians. They differ with regard to political status. Here the Christians are unencumbered by rank, which, until recently, in the Muslim village strongly militated against the peasants' advancing politically. Some Muslim peasants of the south Lebanese village emigrate, but emigration is on a much smaller scale compared with the Christian village, and its rewards in most cases are almost inconsequential. There is far less occupational differentiation in the south Lebanese village than in the Christian one, and consequently women there are not drawn into the same diversity of activities. Finally, although basic literacy was widespread among these Muslim women, the education they received was—until a few years ago—vastly inferior to that provided for the Christian women, and a university education has been beyond their reach. The Muslim women of the Learned Families are taught basic literacy and they are given a Quranic education privately. Privacy characterizes their style of living. Like the Sunni Muslims on the olive farms, their labor for horticultural purposes is not required, and in both cases seclusion of women is practiced, but with a difference: the Lebanese Muslim women live in a nucleated village, where it is easy for them to meet amongst themselves, and to join congregations of women for ritual purposes; the Muslim women on the olive farms live in an area of dispersed habitations, where most of the inhabitants are immigrant strangers, and where the conditions convert the tolerable seclusion of the Muslim Lebanese women into commiserable segregation.

The styles of life in the four communities are markedly unlike. The nearest in this regard are the two Lebanese communities, but the sophistication of the Christian women gives their lives a qualitatively different texture. In this discussion attention has been drawn to a limited range of problems. Cultural nuances, as seen in the behavior of women in these four localities, have scarcely been touched upon. The appeal to general cultural traits was discounted at the outset on the grounds that they fail to account for obvious differences. But certain similarities of behavior exist in all three Muslim communities, which, perhaps, defy sociological analysis. Thus, in each, males and females take their meals separately, households have a male part and a female part, and mothers sleep with daughters and fathers with sons. Perhaps the similarity is only in the form of behavior and analysis would reveal sociological differences of content, but it is not possible to pursue this major issue here. The subject of differences in the social positions of males and females is a field of study, not a problem. The inclusion of issues raised in this discussion is a matter of personal choice, and is intended mainly to clear the ground for further investigation.

Notes

1. See Antoun (1968). His analysis is based partly on citations from the Quran, and partly on observations. As he views the matter, the problem is one of accommodating the great tradition to various localities in the Muslim world.

2. Both Evans-Pritchard (1965) and Gluckman (1954) have stressed this defect in discussions of the position of women.

3. Benedict (1967) takes equality to mean an equivalence of rights and duties. Thus, chastity, because it applies to women but not to men, implies inequality to him. Chastity, however, implies a number of things, including the right of a woman to withhold herself sexually from males until she has been married by a man who, thereafter, has strict obligations toward her.

4. When I related that an elderly townsman had married a girl barely thirteen years of age, the bedouin were disgusted and disinclined to accept the information. One of them claimed that a Muslim would not do this—he knew nothing of infant betrothal, nor of early marriage, in other parts of the Muslim Middle East.

5. It is interesting to note, in this context, that unmarried men discussed matters of sex and their marriage aspirations with my wife because they were too "shy" to discuss them with me.

6. To give some idea of the amount involved, the cost of a camel varied from about £18 to £25. Nowadays, they cost more than £150.

7. Exchange marriage, the bedouin know, is illegal. They circumvent the law by giving a promise of bridewealth for both marriages, and by making one of the promises marginally more than the other.

8. Other women may succeed in becoming prominent among women in camp life, but if they achieve political significance recognized by both sexes, it is usually a result of their husbands' rise to power.

9. When a tent is pitched in a camp for the first time, the young men course their horses and fire their rifles over the tent as they gallop past. This they do in honor of the woman of the tent, even though she is not its owner.

10. The bedouin relate a tale of a man, who, returning to his camp after a long absence, is told of the deaths of various types of kinsmen. He expresses condolences in each case, consistent with the commonly held sentiments about the different types. Finally he is told that his father has died, to which he replies, "Praise be to God, my property is free."

11. See Rosenfeld (1960). He attaches great significance to property as a determinant of male-female relations; indeed his argument is almost reductive. I, too, attach significance to property, but, whereas Rosenfeld considers its legal aspect, I view it as a bundle of social relationships caught in a matrix of many others, and, therefore, not meriting the analytical precedence Rosenfeld gives it.

12. This part of the bridewealth is known as *siaq*—the animals that are driven, on the hoof, to the meeting. The number given is usually about four to five.

13. See Rosenfeld (1960). He discusses this as a condition peculiar to women. The word has a number of meanings: annoyed, angry, vexed, put out, sad. It is applied to men and women, but not with the meaning of spirit possession of any kind.

14. I was present at the witnessing of a will when a woman stated she wished her youngest son to inherit her five camels, and all present rèpeated her statement.

15. See Lewis (1966). In his argument on spirit possession he attaches importance to the fact that when migrants return from towns, they bring back baubles for themselves, while women are deprived of the soap and scent they so desire. They are not "deprived" of town goods: they have not acquired rights to them, either directly or through claims on men.

16. Marx (1966, 1967) has emphasized the importance of marriage in linking interests, and how it serves as a channel of communication between groups. I agree with him on both counts, but I prefer to give precedence to the mediatory significance it gives to women.

17. See E. Peters (1967), where I discuss the political role of women in relation to the feud.

18. Several authors have referred to people's "marrying enemies." But marriages are made with chosen partners. Except in special circumstances, why choose enemies? People, for the most part, marry others with whom they wish to further existing social relationships.

19. See E. Peters (1963), where I give additional information on this village.

20. The population for this group and for the village as a whole varied between summer and winter.

21. Only one man signs the document of sale. Later, when inheritance issues arise, this is bound to cause serious trouble among the contributors to the cost and their heirs.

Bibliography

Antoun, Richard T. "On the Modesty of Women in Arab Muslim Villages." *American Anthropologist,* 70 (1968) :671–697.

Barth, Fredrik. *Nomads of South Persia.* London, 1964.

Benedict, Burton. "The Equality of the Sexes in the Seychelles." In *Social Organization, Essays Presented to R. Firth,* ed. M. Freedman. London, 1967.

Evans-Pritchard, E. E. *Kinship and Marriage Among the Nuer.* Oxford, 1951.

———. "Social Character of Bride-wealth, with Special Reference to the Azande." In *The Position of Women in Primitive Societies and Other Essays,* ed. E. E. Evans-Pritchard. London, 1965.

Fortes, Meyer. *The Web of Kinship Among the Tallensi.* London, 1949.

———. "Introduction." In *The Developmental Cycle in Domestic Groups,* Cambridge Papers in Social Anthropology, 1, ed. Meyer Fortes. London, 1958.

Freedman, Maurice. *Rites and Duties of Chinese Marriage.* Inaugural Lecture, London School of Economics and Political Science. London, 1967.

Gluckman, H. M. "The Nature of African Marriage." *The Anti-Slavery Reporter and Aborigines Friend* (May 1954).

Goody, Jack. "The Mother's Brother and the Sister's Son in West Africa." *Journal of the Royal Anthropological Institute,* 89 (1959).

Granqvist, Hilma. *Marriage Conditions in a Palestinian Village.* Helsingfors, 1931.

Lewis, I. M. "Spirit Possession and Deprivation Cults." *Man,* 1, no. 3 (1966):307–327.

Marx, E. E. "The Division of Domestic Tasks between Spouses among the Negev Bedouins." Unpublished. Tel Aviv, 1966.

———. *Bedouin of the Negev.* Manchester, 1967.

Peters, E. L. "Aspects of Status and Rank among Muslims in a Lebanese Village." In *Mediterranean Countrymen,* ed. J. Pitt-Rivers. Paris, 1963.

———. "Aspects of the Family among the Bedouin of Cyrenaica." In *Comparative Family Systems,* ed. M. J. Nimkoff. Boston, 1965.

———. "Some Structural Aspects of the Feud among the Camel-Herding Bedouin of Cyrenaica." *Africa,* 37 (1967):261–282.

———. "Aspects of Affinity." In *Mediterranean Family Structures,* ed. J. G. Peristiany. London, 1976.

Peters, S. M. "A Study of the Bedouin (Cyrenaican) Bait." B. Litt. thesis. University of Oxford, 1952.

Rosenfeld, Henry. "On Determinants of the Status of Arab Village Women." *Man,* 60 (1960):66–70.

Salim, S. M. *Marsh Dwellers of the Euphrates Delta.* London, 1962.

Strathern, Marilyn. *Women in Between: Female Roles in a Male World.* London, 1972.

17 Women among Qashqa'i Nomadic Pastoralists in Iran

Lois Beck

In an area of the world in which the roles and positions of women and men are presumed to be different and unequal, the case of the pastoral nomadic Qashqa'i of Iran presents a surprising degree of symmetry and equality between the sexes. There appears to be a correlation between a means of production that involves an integrated domestic unit and a balanced relationship between women and men. Where no clearly defined separation of women's and men's domains is found and where women's and men's activities are integrated, especially with reference to subsistence tasks, women and men tend to share in the decision-making and play active economic and political roles. The issue here is not the existence or nonexistence of private and public domains but the extent to which female and male activities are separate, overlapping, or united, and why.

The Qashqa'i of Iran

The Qashqa'i are Turkic-speaking, nomadic pastoralists whose ancestors originated in Central Asia and settled in the mountains of

---

The field research on which this essay is based was conducted over an eighteen-month period in 1970–71 and was supported by a Fulbright-Hays grant. The material of the essay derives primarily from residence in one Qashqa'i sub-tribe having nomadic and sedentarized components. This essay does not discuss the women of the Qashqa'i tribal elite, whose life styles, work patterns, and social contacts are greatly different from those described here (for an account of tribal elite women, see Beck 1975).

This essay has benefited from the comments and suggestions of Nikki Keddie, Michael Fischer, and Philip Salzman. Thanks also go to Suad Joseph, who discussed with me some of the ideas in this essay before it was written.

southwest Iran by the fifteenth century. Herders of sheep and goats, they migrate long distances between winter and summer pasture areas, located in the lowlands and highlands of the Zagros Mountains. Numbering well over a quarter of a million individuals, they are divided into five large tribes, each headed by a family of khans. The tribes were united in a political confederacy until 1954, when the central government of Iran removed its leader (*ilkhani*) from office. In 1962 the formal authority of the khans of each of the tribes was also removed, but the tribespeople still consider themselves defined by political affiliation to them, as well as by territorial, cultural, and linguistic criteria. At the local level, individuals are united by notions of patrilineal descent, the exchange of women in marriage, co-residence, and collective utilization and defense of resources. With the exception of the khans and some wealthy headmen, the Qashqa'i have not been characterized by much socioeconomic differentiation until very recently. Economic leveling mechanisms,. such as early inheritance, animal contracts, and sedentarization, contribute to the homogeneous nature of local groups.

The Means of Subsistence

The integration of female and male spheres among the Qashqa'i is related to the means of subsistence. Pastoral nomadism entails the periodic movement of animals and their owners according to external pressures and the availability of pastoral resources. Effective herd maintenance is best done in small units, and pastoral nomads divide ownership and control of herds among household units. The small nuclear or extended family household is the basic economic unit among the Qashqa'i, and all its members are of necessity drawn into the many tasks and responsibilities that sustain it: tending the different species of animals, preparing pastoral products, migrating, securing water and firewood, and so forth.

The role of the female in these household activities can by no means be considered here as subordinate, for she is an integral member of the household in its division of labor during the different stages of her life cycle. Learning tasks begins at a very young age (and earlier than for the male). Her work is respected and regarded as vital to the economic unit; no household can exist without her labor.

Economics and Politics

Some areas of women's and men's lives do not completely overlap, particularly with regard to economic and political ties with the wider society. Pastoral nomadism is a subsistence system dependent on the products and services of sedentary communities. Grain or other agricultural produce is usually the staple food; it may not be produced (or produced in sufficient quantity) by the household and has to be acquired externally, along with other foodstuffs (tea, sugar, vegetables, salt), metal and leather goods, and clothes. The pastoralist's economy centers on the periodic exchange of animals and animal products for these goods. Pastoral nomads are also brought into political articulation with others. Each household needs to arrange its land-use and migration patterns with tribal leaders. There is competition with agriculturalists and other nomads over territory and resources, which needs mediation. The central government exerts its force over the nomads in a variety of ways (land-use rights, migration routes and schedules, taxation, animal sale, army conscription, education).

Each household, to handle these affairs, has regular contacts with the elders, headmen, and khans of the tribe; merchants and money-lenders of the towns and cities; tribesmen and villagers with whom there is both competition over resources and exchange of goods; and government officials of various kinds (gendarmes, regional officials, agency and army personnel, court authorities).

These economic and political interactions are not seen as the joint sphere of the female and male but are regarded as the exclusive concern of the male. Activities away from the residence require that some persons stay home: it is women and not men who remain behind. Part of this is due to the demands of child care; part also rests on an ideology that limits the access of females to external contacts, out of concern for their safety and modesty, the legitimacy of their husband's children, and the honor of the family and lineage. The ideology also includes the notion that females are unable to conduct economic and political transactions adequately, since they are believed to lack the necessary knowledge in these realms. There is also a practical restriction on women's contacts outside the tribe: their ability to speak Persian is not as developed as men's, and most are unable to conduct complex transactions in Persian.

There are, however, many qualifications to these patterns of restriction. It is not unheard of for women to represent themselves or family members to a khan or government official if there is no male available or willing to speak on their behalf.[1] They are not condemned for such action. Instead, people feel pity for the lack of a male to aid them: if there is such a male it is *he* who loses honor, for he is seen as negligent in his responsibilities to them.

Women also enter domains external to the camp to make pilgrimages to shrines and to seek medical attention. Those women who are camped close to town have greater opportunities to travel there than women whose camps are distant. Women with frequent access to towns develop patterns of trading there, involving pastoral products, small woven goods, eggs, and chickens. Women from poor families can be seen begging in the towns and cities.[2]

A further point is that women *are* aware of the external contacts of men and of the subtleties of male transactions, and they show remarkable ability when required to act during their husband's or son's frequent absences. They may deliberately utilize their supposed ignorance in interacting with outsiders. Women are expected by outsiders to be unknowledgeable in pastoral, economic, and political affairs (probably because many town and city women lack access to these areas), and when they are asked questions relating to husband's or son's whereabouts, herd sizes, plans for migration, or illegal charcoal production, women feign ignorance and stupidity. Often they "divulge" information that is seen as useful by outsiders but is grossly and intentionally false. Women can thus manipulate contacts with others to protect their households and for their own ends, and they can selectively disseminate the information acquired to members of their unit, according to their own interests. Even in the husband's presence, when he is entertaining guests or discussing tribal affairs, they can influence events through subtle means, in the quality of hospitality offered (they do all the behind-the-scenes activity), in the moments they select to present themselves, and by supplying information or disagreement, sometimes from behind or outside the tent (often in the form of exclamations or clucking noises). But perhaps their strongest impact comes when the domestic scene is quiet and they present points to males who happen to be present. Sons are particularly vulnerable to their words, and so are brothers. Husbands appear to be more cautious, even suspicious, especially when a possible conflict of interest is apparent.

Where the political realm of a community is separated from the domestic realm, men's political struggles may have little effect on women's lives. The particular outcome of any conflict or decision-making process may leave women's activities relatively untouched. For the Qashqa'i, however, this is not the case. External economic and political relations have direct bearing on the economy, mobility, and resource utilization of the household, immediately affecting women's lives, and women play significant roles when they are given access to decision-making domains. Most decisions concerning the household are made in camps and tents, of which women are an integral part. They also help form the opinions that are later implemented in external domains.

When traveling peddlers come to the nomadic household, women and not men are the main mediators, because men are often away from the tent and because peddlers carry what the men feel are unneeded and overly expensive goods. Also, peddlers are low in status, and the nomad men either ignore or make fun of them. These persons carry an assortment of town goods, for which they accept in trade skins, wool, dried curds, and even the precious tea and sugar expensively procured in town by the men of the tent. Women are unhappy if peddlers' visits coincide with the husband's presence, for economic transactions are then limited or curtailed. A second kind of visitor to the tent is the religious specialist who is given pastoral or town products in exchange for religious and ritual services. This too is limited when men are present.

Both sets of relations are enjoyed by women. As low-status individuals, these men can be treated by the women with familiarity, to the extent that they joke about sexual matters. Also, the visitors are useful sources of information for women on the activity of other encampments and on sedentary kin; this information is of a detailed and personal nature rarely provided by the men of the tent.

When raiding, seizure of land, and defense of resources used to be more prevalent than they are today, women often took offensive and defensive action themselves. Although these were largely seen as male affairs, women appeared not to hesitate to enter engagements that were threatening to them or to their households. Also, they played active paramilitary roles: guarding camps and moving along with men engaged in hostile or protective activity. Women were not immune to capture or harm. Disputes still occur over resource utilization and stolen animals, in which women hurl epithets and enter into the frays. During the time of field research, one of the more serious casualties in fights between groups over land use was a woman who had been attacked by a man wielding a tent pole, which he had supposedly jerked out from beneath her tent in the midst of an encounter between two groups. (She claims that she was about to hit *him* with it when he took it from her.) That this occurred to a woman was not seen as particularly unusual by the people who were present at the time.

Women used to give loud and shrill cries in support of their men going off for raids or defense. Women continue to use this cry to express their support of political actions. It is also used by women at weddings, to signal the arrival of guests, particularly those from other tribes or groups, and to signify the transfer of the bride from her father's tent to that of her husband (all of which have political implications).

The Encampment

A distinction between private and public domains corresponding to female and male is not clearly demarcated for the Qashqa'i. There is a domain external to the camp (khans' camp or house, bazaar, gendarmerie post, government office) that periodically necessitates the presence of one household representative; this is almost always an older adult male. But it has been seen that women also represent their interests in this external domain, without being stigmatized, and there are many additional areas where they do have effective economic and political impact.

The domain in which women and men live their daily lives is that of the encampment, and a private-public distinction is even less relevant here. Three factors appear to create an integration of female and male domains: the encampment is small, it is isolated territorially from other such units and from sedentary settlements, and its specific functions involve cooperative member households. Although the Qashqa'i household generally herds its own animals (contrary to the patterns found among almost all nomadic pastoralists), few households camp alone. Instead, they form alliances for the purposes of defense of pastoral resources, mutual assistance in times of need, and protection of property and women in the absence of adult males. The encampment contains, on the average, three to five tents, depending on the seasons, resource availability, and other factors. Membership in specific encampments varies as individuals adjust themselves and their herds to the changing circumstances of the physical and social environment.

Although flexibility is fundamental in encampment composition, there are rules of conduct for interaction within the unit that further explain this as a social domain. The principal code of conduct is respect for the individual household unit, which is seen as self-contained and self-sufficient. Each household has sufficient labor to sustain itself and its tasks and sufficient equipment for the performance of all chores; no demands are expected from it and no goods need to be borrowed by or from it. Privacy is another rule. The physical arrangement of the encampment affords no one a view of life in another tent. Whenever camp is made, each tent is erected in a northeasterly direction, and hence no tent faces the entrance of any other tent. Life in and around each tent is directed forward; little if any activity occurs behind the tent. Approach to a tent is made in a large circle, so that entry is from the front, and arriving visitors are expected to make sounds so as not to disturb the possibly unprepared occupants. Dogs, guarding each tent, provide a defense screen and ensure that surprise appearances rarely happen.

The space of the encampment is defined somewhat differently by women and by men. While males tend to view the encampment as a number of individual households, females are more inclined to view it as a single community and to stress the points of connection between households. Adult males in the encampment remain by or in their own tents and do not approach those of others. Formality between them is prescribed, either in their offers of hospitality or in decision-making. If a decision concerning the encampment is needed, one man climbs a hillock and surveys the scene. Others see this and join him there.

When men are absent from the encampment, women treat the entire domain as their own. There is free visiting back and forth that is not structured by the relations among men. There is frequent gift exchange, often like item for like item, sent by child couriers. One tent undoubtedly has a water pipe and women get it out to smoke (which males consider a privilege of males). By the age of eight or nine, girls and boys form separate activity groups and use the encampment in different ways, boys being more likely than girls to travel a distance away to talk and play. At younger ages, children's play groups are not sex-divided, partly because girls have charge of the care of younger brothers and sisters, and it is these slightly older girls who channel activities within the encampment.

When adult males are present in the encampment, the women of the unit perform their tasks diligently and quietly, and the warm contact and noisy conversation that characterize women's interactions in the absence of males are gone. Men seem unaware of what goes on in their absence, but they cannot have forgotten the character of camp life experienced in their childhood. While male activities seem always to be handled with a degree of formality, women's behavior appears more changeable and adaptable: one set of behaviors, involving other women, is gregarious, warm, and loosely structured; another is warm but more closed and involves only immediate family members; and the third is respectful and restrained behavior when senior kinsmen and high status strangers are present.

Women's interaction allows an intimate exchange of information, and this is utilized by males in their own plans and activities. Men are dependent on the daily details of life that only women are able to supply, and women are aware of the utility of these units of information. They are not beyond exaggeration or even creation of news to fit their own perspectives on persons or events. Clearly, there is power in all this for women.

Under certain circumstances, women use the encampment in a markedly political fashion. In times of dispute, when face-to-face discussion is impossible, women shout to someone in close proximity, perhaps a youngster. The message is intended for others in the encampment, and the technique focuses group attention on critical events (see Collier 1974:94). Altercations between wife and husband become public in this way too; the man is ashamed of things his wife can introduce loudly to the community and guards his behavior accordingly. He does not resort to the same technique for fear of losing the respect of the community.

The Tent

The tent, woven by women out of black goat hair, is small and is not structurally divided into female and male sections as is common with the tents of many Middle Eastern nomadic peoples. However, women tend to perform their activities and store their goods on one side, while men sit by their fires on the other. The tent is the center of daily activities for both female and male, and here their domains of activity are most integrated. Within the household, neither the wife nor the husband is subject to the control of others, which furthers the autonomy of each; there is no chance for the development of female or male hierarchies here (see Lamphere 1974:105–108).

The household is the stock-owning and -herding unit and is economically self-sufficient. It is formed with the separation of a newly married son from the father, the father providing for his son a share of the household's property in proportion to the number of sons. This share includes sheep and goats, a camel or two, donkeys, and perhaps a horse, in addition to household goods of various kinds. At the time of the son's marriage, many relatives offer gifts of animals in the name of the new bride. These animals are not strictly owned by her, for if she is divorced or leaves, most of them remain with her husband. Giving them to her is a mechanism by which animals that are gifts for the new couple are distinguished from those of the groom's father, since both are herded together for several years. The groom's mother and the bride anticipate the separation of households and prepare to weave the new tent and construct its furnishings. The Qashqa'i woman does not own the tent, as is common elsewhere in the Middle East, and it is not a dowry item that is brought into and taken away from marriage.

A man herds his father's animals until he forms his own household. Then he herds his own and becomes economically responsible for the welfare of the new household. The bride assists in tasks of the father-in-law's tent until she has her own household. The products of the animals given at the time of marriage are by right hers to prepare. Men sometimes blame the separation of son from father on the quarrels of mother and daughter-in-law, but this does not seem to reflect reality. The bride has her own tasks and is not subordinate in work to her mother-in-law. She even acquires the help of her sisters-in-law and brothers-in-law.

A man and his sons are responsible for herding, caring for nonherd animals, supplemental animal feeding, shearing, branding, collection of heavy firewood, agriculture (if it is performed), and the wider economic and political tasks mentioned above. A woman and her daughters are responsible for milking, milk processing (yogurt, butter, cheese, oil, and so on), preparation of animal derivatives (skins, hair, wool), weaving, care of animals close to the tent, light firewood collection, bringing of water, gathering of wild plants, bread-baking, cooking, and child care. The tasks of each sex are mutually dependent, and each on occasion helps with those of the other.

Women prepare the goods taken to town by men for trade (wool, oil, butter, dried curds, skins), but women do not personally receive any payment. Men entrust the care of household supplies and town-acquired goods to women, who notify them when a particular product is in short supply. In the absence of men and without their knowledge, women frequently give small gifts of household supplies to relatives; trade them with peddlers for herbs, sewing notions, and dried fruit; and give them as alms to darvishes. Women also exercise control of goods when guests are present; men choose the animal to sacrifice if one is to be sacrificed, but women determine if there is rice for the guests, how much to prepare, and in what fashion to prepare it. One man said, "if my wife says there is no rice, my guests eat no rice."

Qashqa'i women are weavers of fine carpets, blankets, and bags (for which the Qashqa'i are internationally famous), all of which literally provide the substance of the home (the tent, too, is woven by them). They prepare the wool, card and spin it into yarn, collect natural substances for dyes, dye the yarn, prepare the loom, and weave. They plan the items to be woven, even their designs and colors, many years in advance, since major works can only be done once or twice a year, in the more sedentary periods of late winter (after the rains) and summer. They also plan the ultimate destinations of their woven goods. Almost all weaving is done for internal use: the household is outfitted, worn things are replaced, and daughters' dowries are assembled. Some weaving is done in the fulfillment of vows (a woman whose shrine attendance or prayers have been answered repays with the major valued good produced by her). Little weaving is done for the express purpose of sale, at least from the perspective of the weavers.[3] In times of need, the man of the tent may trade a piece of woven goods in town or use an item to discharge a debt to the moneylender. Among wealthy nomads, woven goods are given as gifts to special guests. Although men on occasion utilize woven goods to fulfill or enhance their external relationships, weaving is a valued woman's activity and women acquire prestige and status from their skills.

Although a considerable portion of the household's animals are brought to the unit by marriage gifts to the bride, the husband controls the economic transactions concerning them. Often, he utilizes those animals that were her gifts first, before those received from his father, to discharge debts, to sacrifice for guests, or to give as gifts, and all in his own name.[4] He does not do this unnoticed, and she may make difficulties for him as a result. Such actions on the part of the husband may jeopardize his relations with her father and brothers, whose proximity and interests are impediments to his selfish actions.

Male rather than female control of stock is typical of herders, primarily because stock are mobile and require attention away from the home and because they are raised for an external or market economy. Both tend to preclude female participation. The Qashqa'i pose no exception, but a detailed discussion would indicate that the situation of ownership and control does involve considerable female input.

The Migration

The process of making and breaking camp and migrating is shared by women and men, without clear distinctions between "women's" and "men's" work. One major task is sex-linked, however: herd animals leave camp before daybreak, in the company of adolescent and adult males. Since the Qashqa'i migrate through alien territory and the threat of conflict over trespass and stolen animals is omnipresent, herding during the migration is done by males.

In breaking camp, men tend to handle heavy items (tent pieces, tent poles, large storage bags), while women pack and load all other household items. Women are more likely to pack donkeys and mules than camels, although women adorn the camels and mules with tassels and woven goods. Young boys help their fathers, young girls their mothers, though adolescent girls often perform independent tasks.

But in seeing a camp in the process of dismantlement, these distinctions are scarcely apparent. The camp site is disordered and possessions are everywhere; all household members are busy with both individual and cooperative tasks. No one gives instructions to another (unless to a small child to get out of the way). Tying ropes around the loaded goods requires the attention of any two people who are handy. The camels, once loaded, often leave by themselves, with young males rushing off to accompany them, followed by the mules, horses, and loaded donkeys. The last flurry of activity is grabbing the few items that never seem to get packed, and, for the women, dressing in the best skirts (women wear their best clothes on the migration, for this is the only time of the year, other than at weddings, when they are seen by many others). The women are the last to leave the camp. The pack animals of the camp migrate together, but each family is responsible for its own animals.

Setting up camp is similar, though without the haste of breaking camp. Both processes take several hours. On reaching the new site, all animals are quickly unloaded and left to graze. Young girls and boys are sent after water; girls go after kindling. Women and men share in setting up the tent; it is usually a male who wields the club in pounding in the tent stakes. The baggage is piled on a line of stones in the tent, and the male (and only the male) digs the fire hole (the main symbol of home and family) in front of the tent and makes a fire for tea. Then he goes off to wait for the herds to appear and to meet with other men. The women do not have this respite, but continue to reassemble the camp. During the spring migration this process is hastened, for milking and milk preparation are the next immediate chores.

While it is apparent that there are jobs that either sex tends to do, there is considerable cooperation between them and an overlapping of activites. The female easily does those tasks a male usually does; the reverse is not as common but most aspects of women's work are not tainted. The bases of symmetry of work and cooperation between the sexes are the small size and independence of the household and the stake of each sex in the work of the other and in the household's welfare.

Decisions concerning migration and choice of campsite are made by men in groups. Some aspects of the decision-making process used to be referred to the khans of the tribe, and men of individual tribal sections gathered at the headmen's tents to discuss with them the khans' plans. Now migration is in the hands of gendarmerie colonels, from whom the headmen receive permission for their groups to migrate. But once the decision to begin migration is made, the men of the tribal sections decide when and where to go and how long to stay at each point. Women have little role in this process, except that they pressure their husbands into migration routes that include close proximity with kin, including those settled in villages. The separation of camps in winter and summer precludes much visiting among women in these seasons.

Marriage

The system of marriage for the Qashqa'i is relevant to a discussion of the domains of female and male. That Middle Eastern marriage systems are often endogamous certainly has an impact on the position of women. Women, as symbols of purity for the family, lineage, and tribe and as representatives of honor, are protected and guarded by men. A major way to effect this protection is to retain women within the group after marriage. In addition, an endogamously married woman is more likely to be better treated than a woman who is married outside the group. For the Qashqa'i, close kin, who have exchanged women in marriage, camp and migrate together, which means that women are often not separated from their natal families on marriage. They remain in close proximity to their fathers and brothers, who represent their interests, are concerned with their behavior and treatment, and intercede for them in case of maltreatment. Still, men's interests, particularly the ones that originally motivated the marriage alliances, are primary, and only unusual circumstances would allow these interests to be set aside. Whether women are married inside or outside the group, the women being exchanged are exchanged according to group-oriented strategy and have little say in the proceedings. Women do, however, have a great deal to say about the marriages of others, and usually initiate marriage proceedings and prepare the groundwork for the formal arrangements among men. In the case of infant betrothal, which is common, women and not men are the decision-makers.

The continuing relation of women and their natal kin after marriage enhances the integrated nature of the community and lessens the chances for separate domains for female and male to exist, since female and male are allowed access to kin of both sexes. An important culturally prescribed and sociologically significant kinship relation between a woman's brother and her daughters and sons means that women are continually provided access to their natal groups, which is especially significant for women who have been separated spacially from parents and siblings after marriage.

Women in their frequent contacts with kin serve as mediators between residence and kin groups. Information is gathered and exchanged, and through these linkages both female and male are better able to assess current situations with regard to resource utilization, co-residence, marriage, and conflict.[5] Women are not simply conduits of information, for they take active roles in seeking and giving information and disseminating it during encounters with others. This role, too, is a political one. Women play important political roles when they are related by marriage or descent to powerful men, such as in the case of the wives and sisters of headmen.

Religion

Religion is another area in which the concerns of the female and male are integrated. No sharp distinctions between "informal" and "formal" aspects of religion, as associated with the beliefs and practices of females and males, can be made for the Qashqa'i.

The Qashqa'i identify themselves as Shiite Muslims. Males have contact with conservative bazaaris and liberal government officials and access to mosques and religious specialists on their trips away from camp. They are skeptical about Islam as practiced by shopkeepers and moneylenders, and they remark cynically about the conspicuous use of Islamic symbols and sayings in exploitative economic transactions. A moneylender who makes the pilgrimage to Mecca (on his clients' money) is able to charge higher interest rates and pay lower prices for pastoral products than one who does not have the title of *hajji*. A few of the older Qashqa'i males perform some of the daily prayers. No one fasts. Alms are given in the context of local groups and not in the spirit of a specifically Muslim obligation. The services of Islam are sought, however, in life crisis events, and these are largely in the hands of women, because of women's concern with and responsibilities for children and homes. Males depend on these services and tolerate women's wishes with reference to pilgrimage, vow payment, and alms to itinerant darvishes. Women protect their pregnancies, families, and homes with prayers and amulets derived from religious specialists who travel from camp to camp. Amulets, carved from wood by Qashqa'i men, are placed on animals susceptible to the evil eye.

Every subtribe has one or two adult males who are literate in

Persian and who have some religious expertise and a rudimentary knowledge of Arabic: they write marriage contracts, recite Quranic passages at funerals, and provide general information at rites of passage. (Such literacy is primarily used in external economic and political affairs.) There are few female religious specialists among the Qashqa'i. Every woman possesses a special saddlebag containing dozens of small units of herbs, spices, dyes, and folk medicines. Some women have large collections and are sought out for particular items; they may also have detailed knowledge of folk medicines and cures. There is considerable reliance on outside and itinerant specialists, and women more than men establish and utilize these contacts.

Neither sex has exclusive access to or control over the supernatural. In societies where females are more subject to the demands and restrictions of patriarchy than Qashqa'i women, they often seek recourse in supernatural powers or conditions to mitigate their positions, posing a threat to men's more secular powers. (Men in subordinate positions find such recourse, too.) But as has been seen for the Qashqa'i, there is no marked asymmetrical relation between the sexes nor much mutual opposition or antagonism, and neither sex uses the offices or powers of "religion" to effect force over or instill fear in the other.

Islamic law (*sharia*) is almost totally irrelevant to the position of Qashqa'i women, since tribal custom governs women's legal rights and responsibilities. Women inherit no property (in this they are similar to many Middle Eastern women, particularly in villages and tribes), although the dowry that accompanies women on marriage is in some cases a substantial amount and could be seen as functionally equivalent to the inheritance shares of their brothers. However, not all women receive large dowries and most dowries are simply the conversion by the bride's father of bridewealth payments into household goods. Polygyny is rare, though the Qashqa'i are aware that plural marriage is the right of males by religious law. Marriage and divorce procedures follow tribal custom, though Islamic practices are increasingly added to them; marriage contracts are signed by a sheikh in town after the marriage consummation, so that the virginity of the bride may first be tested. Islamic ideology concerning women's relations with men is not readily apparent in Qashqa'i statements, and the Qashqa'i always seem to be comparing their own, what they regard as enlightened, attitudes toward women with those of the surrounding Persian-speaking population.[6] The lack of dependence on sharia law and Islamic ideology appears to raise the position of Qashqa'i women in relation to their sedentary neighbors.[7]

The Absence of Female and Male Solidarity Groups

Another factor that contributes to the relative symmetry of female and male positions among the Qashqa'i is the absence of sex-exclusive solidarity groups. In societies where males form and interact in exclusive political, economic, religious, or social groups, the status of men in relation to women rises, because activities are drawn away from the domestic scene and into a realm that excludes women and children. The formation of female solidarity groups is not as common a crosscultural phenomenon as male groups, largely because settlement patterns and social organization may be such as to preclude women's gatherings; child care, domestic responsibilities, and general subsistence activities are often incompatible with female groupings; and male-controlled institutions and value systems often inhibit or prohibit the formation of female groups. Where female groups do occur, ways to represent the interests of women, to influence decisions made in the extradomestic domain, and to mitigate the effects of male domination and patriarchy are found. Female solidarity groups have the ability to undermine male control of society's institutions and are a threat, and such groups are often carried on in secret or with care so as to avoid male discovery or displeasure.

Fundamental to the absence of female and male solidarity groups among the Qashqa'i is the mode of subsistence, in which female and male are partners in the operation of an economically independent unit. Men in nomadic groups usually have central gathering places, such as the guest tent of the most influential member of the camp or a central spot in camp, but the Qashqa'i do not. Business is conducted in the tent of the headman, but usually on an individual basis. Men do not gather in large groups in camp or in town. Wedding celebrations provide large groups, but the interaction of men there is often characterized by conflict and fights. (A primary activity of men at weddings is stick fighting, aggressive encounters set to the beat of a gypsy's drum.)

That females have no groupings either is somewhat more explicable, owing to the combined effects of household and encampment separation and mobility, the absence of issues that would draw them together, and an ideology involving female purity and honor that keeps them close to the campsite. A practical reason for this restriction is that women's labors are always needed; the small and independent household demands their continual presence. Also, men say they cannot entertain guests without the assistance of women. Women do not leave their encampments unless visiting kin or assisting in health care or childbirth, occasions that are also sought for their social and emotional content. The encampment does provide contact between and among women but the group's membership is small and variable. It is important to stress household self-sufficiency here: no woman assists another in the encampment in her chores (except in dire need). Women generally do their tasks alone. Even milking, which could be greatly facilitated by the mutual assistance of women, is done by each household's members. Water and wood are gathered in groups, but by preadolescent and adolescent girls. Just as sons free fathers from the main tasks of herding, so do daughters free mothers from certain household chores, especially those that draw them away from the tent. Hence, as a woman matures, she is increasingly isolated from other women.

Women interact in groups at weddings but these are infrequent occasions (only in the summer) and in different locales (which is restrictive since only women in the vicinity can attend). The group of women that does gather is characterized by intense and tearful greetings and exchanges of information. The months of migration also provide some interaction, as women whose tents are close visit. The migration itself affords little conversation because of the fast pace and the often difficult terrain.

The absence of female groups is also explained by the lack of issues that might draw women together. Qashqa'i women have few economic issues to unite them. Their subsistence tasks are not communal projects. They prepare goods for trade but are not allowed the actual transactions nor do they acquire payment for them. (Women traders elsewhere have the natural means for collective interests and action.) Men and not women control many of the political processes relating to tribal affairs, land-use, and sedentary contacts. Religion is a private matter and relates primarily to rites of passage and maternal functions. Religion might provide an arena for female groupings for the Qashqa'i, as it does in many Middle Eastern contexts, if settlement patterns were different or if women were able to leave their encampments more frequently. Formalized or regularized visiting patterns are not present.[8]

A further reason for the absence of female groupings is that Qashqa'i women seem not to be alienated by the operation and built-in constraints of the social system. They are integrated workers of the household, unequivocally in charge of the home, its activities, and many crucial pastoral functions. They achieve prestige through their weaving activities. They remain in contact with their natal families throughout their lives. Their husband's family is usually kin to them, and the concern of the affinal and natal families in their welfare is often parallel; they are guaranteed a place in the households of either of these groups all their lives. The marriage bond is stable and divorce is rarely a threat. Polygyny is not an issue for most (unless barrenness occurs). Finally, they play active roles and occupy important interstitial positions in the kinship and marriage system.

The Changing Contexts of Female and Male Domains in Pastoral Nomadic Society

The conditions of life for nomads in the Middle East are rapidly changing, and most of the changes seem to result in increasingly asymmetrical relations between the sexes. The increasing strength of the nation state and the growing importance of market and monetary economies mean that nomads are drawn closer to the powers and influences of the wider society. The state controls tribal movements and land-use, often greatly restricting migrations and encouraging settlement, and it hampers or oversees tribal leadership. Males are initially affected more than females by these changes, as activities external to the camp and tribe gain greater significance than they had before and demand the increasing attentions of the males of each household. The integration of nomads into state systems and market economies tends to erode women's status, because the very bases of status shift from the domestic and camp arena to a wider arena (see Kandiyoti 1977:61).

Pastoralism becomes less self-sustaining for individual households than before, with decreasing availability of land and pastoral resources and with inflation of necessary town products. The economic system of the household is forced to become more specialized and to emphasize products that will bring cash rewards, to the detriment of a diversified economy in which women are equal producers with men. The need for cash, rather than goods to barter, draws males into income-producing activities such as short-term shepherding contracts, sharecropping in agricultural settlements, and wage labor in towns. As grain and other externally produced goods rise in price, households increasingly turn their efforts to agriculture. Such activities remove men from many pastoral tasks, which women assume in their absence.[9] This does not necessarily enhance the status of women, for ownership and control of animals remain with men. Also, the absence of men usually means that flocks are few in number, and hence there are limited quantities of animal products for women's productive activities. Migration may continue, in which case all its difficulties are women's to handle. More frequently, women are settled in villages with relatives when men take jobs away from the camp. As men turn away from full-time herding, the location of women, and the tents or houses they maintain, are symbolic of the retention or nonretention of the nomadic (and sometimes tribal) identity.[10]

As extratribal forces intrude on the local economy, economic leveling mechanisms that used to contribute to the homogeneous nature of local groups do not function as before. The result is increasing socioeconomic differentiation, which places increasing numbers of men (and, therefore, their wives and children) in economic positions subordinate to others.[11] As households become less self-sufficient and more dependent on the income men acquire from shepherding, animal contracts, agricultural work, and wage labor, the economic bases contributing to complementarity of work between the sexes are undercut.

Another recent change is the adoption of mechanized transport; the migration can now be done in hours or days instead of weeks or months. While this eases the rigors of the trek, it cuts out many of the advantages of a slow move between pastures. For women, it ends the gathering of dozens of kinds of herbs, fruits, vegetables, medicines, and dyes, on which they and their productive activities had depended. It also restricts their patterns of interaction with kin, both female and male. Because the vehicle is associated with the male, it enhances the male role and gives him greater access to the outside world ("where the action is") and the technological wonders found there. In chapter 19 Chatty writes of bedouin men taking frequent trips to the nation's cities, often on motorcycle, while women are left at home with decreasing pastoral functions and fewer social interactions.

Education, too, is selectively drawing males into the cities, giving them a new commodity to "market" and a new element of status and success that further differentiates them from females.[12] Conscription into the army gives advantages (as well as disadvantages) to males: education, trained skills, and better knowledge of the nation's culture and language.

Sedentarization is occurring among all nomadic pastoralists in the Middle East as the life styles and economies become less viable in contemporary conditions. Other than perhaps bringing them closer to medical facilities, settled life does little for women but restrict their activities and productivity.[13] Through new patterns of forced immobility, women become home- and child-oriented, lacking the multifarious responsibilities, opportunities, and resources that pastoralism and nomadism once provided. Sedentarized women do not usually engage in field labor, and the main item of production (usually grain) is market-oriented, not home-oriented, and is male-controlled.[14] Increasingly, household products need to be purchased from outside. Land ownership is more difficult to obtain than animal ownership, and sedentarizing men often find that they end up owning little or nothing.

Sedentarized women may be able to weave more and do it on larger and indoor looms, but the products, like men's now, are market-aimed, and much of the joy of production for home and family is gone. Men borrow money on carpets yet to be woven, putting pressure on women to produce according to the tastes of the buyer and to produce quickly.

Nomads are often quick to emulate the patterns of female seclusion and restriction found in the milieus into which they settle, including that of veiling, in efforts to assimilate.[15] Men are sensitive to remarks about the "looseness" of their women, which refers to freedom of movement and general gregariousness, and they sacrifice this for a newly defined sense of propriety. Women and men alike are now subject to the incursions of outsiders, and this furthers men's attempts to restrict the interactions and movements of their women. When nomads were isolated in their mountain camps, strangers rarely came, and those who did were carefully watched by group members. In villages, men have decreasing control over their social environment; the seclusion and restriction of women by men is one means of regaining control.[16]

One possible advantage for women in these patterns of state control, market production, and sedentarization is that the household may become a more important unit for adult males than wider kin and political groups. Government control of raiding and land usurpation, along with confiscation of firearms, serve to deglorify the male role, for performing these activities well and with courage used to be a significant part of being a man. As political functions relating to the tribe are curtailed, men focus more of their attentions on the nuclear family and the bilateral kin group than on the large corporate group.[17] This seems to draw the male closer to his wife and family, but, as accounted above, other pressures arise to draw his attentions in an opposite direction.

Conclusion

The relative symmetry of female and male in a pastoral nomadic society in Iran is at risk of being unsettled in the future. While it is apparent that a differentiation of female and male can be found among nomads, primarily in male ownership and control of animal stock (which in turn involve a patri-orientation in residence and descent) and at the level of ideology (discriminatory parts of which appear to stem, in part, from the nomads' association with the surrounding Muslim population), it remains true that a socio-economic system that utilizes females and males in cooperative efforts for the family unit places them in complementary and mutually beneficial relationships.

Notes

1. The wife of the khan, given the title of *bibi,* often mediates the contact between tribespeople (female and male) and the khan.

2. Qashqa'i women sometimes wear veils when they visit towns and cities to conform to practices there. Otherwise, these cloths are kept tucked away in the baggage. The garb, the all-covering *chador* of sedentary Persian women, is worn loosely over the shoulders and is often tucked under the arms. It is worn by the Qashqa'i over traditional tribal dress and is often drab and dark, contrasting vividly with the brilliantly colored, gold-threaded, and sequined skirts and tunics underneath. Some Qashqa'i women are adopting light colored and flowered chadors to be worn in urban areas; a few do not bother with them at all. The only person to "wear" the chador in camp is the male, who sometimes calls out for it as he begins his nap, to place over his face and torso to keep away annoying flies.

3. Qashqa'i groups vary in the degree to which they are dependent on economic transactions in towns and cities. Those with greater contacts tend to produce woven goods for bazaar sale to a greater degree than those with fewer contacts. Also, some Qashqa'i tribes have special expertise in weaving and are more commercially oriented than others (Kashkuli, for example).

4. Kababish nomadic women resent the fact that their men "devour" the animals belonging to them (Asad 1970:90).

5. Other studies of pastoral nomads have noted the importance of affinal ties and the ties between women in the formation and maintenance of camp groups (Peters 1965, Salzman 1975, Nelson 1973:53). A similar analysis, for Navaho society, is provided by Lamphere (1974).

6. A (woman) *kalantar* (leader) of the Qora'i tribe of southwest Iran said: "Discrimination against women is largely an urban malady and a sign of social decline in the bigger towns. In the countryside and the tribes, women have always been treated as equals of men. The chador is an urban invention. In the tribe both sexes have to work together in order

to allow their society to function. Furthermore, people of good breeding, men who have been brought up in an atmosphere of freedom, would never deny the women what they themselves cherish most" (*Kayhan*, July 27, 1969).

7. A personal communication from Reinhold Loeffler on the differences in the position of Qashqa'i women and women of the neighboring Boir Ahmad tribes draws attention to the consideration of the role of ideology as an important factor in the degree of sexual asymmetry. The Qashqa'i possess an egalitarian ideology that is conducive to egalitarian patterns of work distribution and behavior; the Boir Ahmad, perhaps partly because they are more influenced by Islam, regard women and men quite differently (see chapter 32 by Friedl).

Martin and Voorhies, in attempting to account for the position of women in pastoral societies, found it "difficult to point to any single pattern of economic adaptation or social juxtaposition of the sexes among pastoralists as a whole" (1975:351). They did find correlations between the role of women in production and the degree to which the society is dependent on cultigens. They stress the importance of taking into consideration three factors, which in interaction produce particular patterns of female-male activities, roles, and attitudes: the specific ecological adaptation, the culture history of the society, and the prevalent "idea system" (e.g., Islam) (1975:365).

8. A woman's subsociety similar to that found among the Shahsevan nomads of north Iran (see chapter 18 by Tapper) is lacking for the Qashqa'i. Tapper's three conditions for its occurrence are absent.

9. Marx reports that bedouin men of the Negev can easily take on seasonal employment since their flocks are small and can be tended by women and children (1967:47). Cole writes of a change of subsistence-oriented camel herding to market-oriented sheep- and goatherding among bedouin in Saudi Arabia; in this case the relative position of the female is enhanced, for more time is available for her own pursuits, and sheep- and goatherding involves her help and provides products for her to prepare (while camel herding was a male task and the necessary migrations very time-consuming) (1975:161–162). In general, increasing productive activity on the part of women *along with* control over the products of production enhance female status (Sanday 1974).

10. Cole writes of bedouin men who are still considered tribal members although they have worked in towns for up to twenty years, as long as their wives remain in tents with the tribe (1975:70). Chatty, in chapter 19, shows a continuation of nomadism even though males and now adolescent females are increasingly involved in wage labor and nonpastoral work.

11. For an account of this process among Lurs in Iran, see Black (1972). Men with too few sheep to provide for household needs arrange shepherding contracts with wealthy herdowners. Their wives, daughters, and sons are then required to perform many duties connected with the herdowner's household.

12. The migratory, tribal tent schools of Muhammad Bahmanbegi in Iran bring education to youngsters of both sexes, but it is still relatively rare for females to pursue further education in the cities, with three exceptions. Young tribal women in increasing numbers enter his tribal high school, teachers' training school, and weaving school in Shiraz. The aim of the weaving school is to conserve weaving skills in the young generation; the students return to their tribes with their acquired knowledge.

13. This is in opposition to the few tentative remarks by Nelson on the advantageousness of sedentarization for women (1973:53–55). However, essential to this argument are the following: the degree to which males are drawn into new productive activities, the degree to which females retain productive activities and adopt new ones, and the degree to which females retain control over the products of this activity.

14. Patricia Draper has found similar changes among !Kung gatherers and hunters, as they leave a nomadic way of life and enter a sedentary one, where men assume control of "productive" activity (1975).

15. Amal Rassam Vinogradov notes the adoption of veiling by women of upwardly mobile segments of Berber tribal populations in Morocco (1974:103).

16. Carroll Pastner provides a similar but more extended discussion of the recent adoption of purdah by Baluchi villagers in Pakistan (1971:192–200).

17. Chatty, in chapter 19, demonstrates how bedouin redefine the functions of the corporate group as the tribe incorporates modern techniques of transportation; see also Cohen (1965).

Bibliography

Asad, Talal. *The Kababish Arabs.* London, 1970.

Beck, Lois Grant. "Women of a Tribal Aristocracy in Iran." Paper presented to the Middle East Studies Association, Louisville, Kentucky, 1975.

Black, Jacob. "Tyranny as a Strategy for Survival in an 'Egalitarian' Society: Luri Facts versus an Anthropological Mystique." *Man,* 7 (1972): 614–634.

Cohen, Abner. *Arab Border Villages in Israel: A Study of Continuity and Change in Social Organization.* Manchester, 1965.

Cole, Donald. *Nomads of the Nomads.* Chicago, 1975.

Collier, Jane. "Women in Politics." In *Woman, Culture, and Society,* ed. Michelle Rosaldo and Louise Lamphere. Stanford, Calif., 1974.

Draper, Patricia. "!Kung Women: Contrasts in Sexual Egalitarianism in Foraging and Sedentary Contexts." In *Toward an Anthropology of Women,* ed. Rayna Reiter. New York, 1975.

Kandiyoti, Deniz. "Sex Roles and Social Change: A Comparative Appraisal of Turkey's Women." *SIGNS,* 3 (1977): 57–73.

Kayhan International, Tehran, Iran (July 27, 1969).

Lamphere, Louise. "Strategies, Cooperation, and Conflict among Women in Domestic Groups." In *Woman, Culture, and Society,* ed. Michelle Rosaldo and Louise Lamphere. Stanford, Calif., 1974.

Martin, M. Kay, and Barbara Voorhies. *Female of the Species.* New York, 1975.

Marx, Emanuel. *Bedouin of the Negev.* New York, 1967.

Nelson, Cynthia. "Women and Power in Nomadic Societies in the Middle East." In *The Desert and the Sown,* ed. Cynthia Nelson. Berkeley, 1973.

Pastner, Carroll McC. "Sexual Dichotomization in Society and Culture: The Women of Panjgur, Baluchistan." Ph.D. dissertation. Brandeis University, Waltham, Mass., 1971.

Peters, Emrys. "Aspects of the Family among the Bedouin of Cyrenaica." In *Comparative Family Systems,* ed. M. Nimkoff. Boston, 1965.

Salzman, Philip. "Kin and Contract in Baluchi Herding Camps." Unpublished. Montreal, 1975.

Sanday, Peggy. "Female Status in the Public Domain." In *Woman, Culture, and Society,* ed. Michelle Rosaldo and Louise Lamphere. Stanford, Calif., 1974.

Vinogradov, Amal Rassam. *The Ait Ndhir of Morocco: A Study of the Social Transformation of a Berber Tribe.* Anthropological Papers, no. 55. Ann Arbor, Mich., 1974.

18 The Women's Subsociety among the Shahsevan Nomads of Iran

Nancy Tapper

Social activities and relationships among the women of the Shahsevan of Azerbaijan constitute a subsociety, an analysis of whose nature and functions can suggest conditions under which similar women's subsocieties may be found elsewhere. Shahsevan women take part in two definite spheres of social activity. One is based on camps, separate localized groups of households, and the other is based on the *kheyr-u-sharr* relations which bring together women from different localized camps for feasts. Separate camp communities of women do not build up into a larger structure, but the kheyr-u-sharr relations form a network that probably extends throughout the society. Moreover, in both camp activities and feasts women are able to maintain and manipulate ascribed and achieved statuses so that similar ranking systems based on a common system of values are assumed to be found among all Shahsevan women; these systems form a structure, and the women of the Shahsevan form a society of their own. Because these values and ranked positions are exclusive to women and yet dependent on and to some extent complementary to certain features of organization among

---

An earlier version of this essay was written in 1969 for a symposium. It is drawn largely from N. S. S. Tapper (1968) and based on field work among the Shahsevan women between July and October 1966. I wish to record my gratitude to Professor A. C. Mayer, who supervised my work on the Shahsevan and has made many helpful suggestions. Earlier drafts of this article received useful comments from Professors P. C. Salzman, N. Keddie, and L. Beck. The field work would not have been possible without the support and cooperation of my husband, with whom I have discussed the material throughout the preparation of the text.

men, and because this is a male-dominated society (see Lewis 1966:321), this structure is designated a substructure, and the women's society can be termed a subsociety.

The Shahsevan are pastoral nomads and seminomads inhabiting the region of northeast Azerbaijan, Iran. They migrate between winter pastures on the Moghan Plain and summer pastures on the Savalan Massif one hundred miles to the south. In the mid-1960s they numbered around fifty thousand people and occupied about seven thousand tents; traditionally, they formed a confederation of some thirty to forty tribes, each headed by a chief. Tribes vary greatly in size, from fifty to more than a thousand families, and are subdivided into between two and twenty-five localized sections (*tireh*). Typically the core of a tireh is a group of twenty to thirty agnatically related families (that is, tents) tracing descent from an ancestor three to seven generations back, after whom the tireh is commonly named. The leader or *aq saqal* (grey-beard) usually succeeds his father; he mediates relations between his tireh and others and with the chief and government officials, and he deals with disputes inside the tireh. In many of the larger tribes the chief and his relatives form a wealthy class distinct from the ordinary, "commoner" tribespeople.

Members of the tireh migrate together and own and occupy defined stretches of winter and summer pastures. They form smaller groups, however, for camping and herding purposes: in summer, herding units of about five tents camp separately, with flocks numbering three to five hundred sheep, while two or three of these units combine to form winter camps of ten to fifteen tents. Each herding unit and winter camp is led by a senior member, also called *aq saqal*.

Apart from the agnatic tireh members who hold pasture rights, other tents may join a camp for other reasons. Affines short of land may come for a season or more and may or may not pay for pasturage. Sometimes they may have the status of unofficial "retainers," which means that they make themselves available for menial services in return for pasturage for their animals. Others will be officially hired herdsmen who tend an employer's herd on a renewable six-month contract for a fee plus free pasturage. These "camp followers" may not be affinally or matrilaterally related to their hosts, especially if the latter are important men such as tireh leaders. Local grouping thus depends on patrilineal descent, affinity and matrilateral kinship, and economic contracts.

In each tent lives a household of, on the average, seven or eight people. The Shahsevan prefer large households, and often brothers and their wives and children or an old couple and their married sons stay together. There are no internal partitions in the tent, except in the first year of a son's marriage, when he and his bride sleep behind a curtain. The hearth, focus of all domestic life, lies between the door and the central peg of the large, circular, yurt-type tent. The staple food is bread. To obtain wheat flour and other supplies, the nomads sell milk, wool, and surplus animals. Herding, milking, shearing, and the marketing of produce are the work of men, who also see to the erection and maintenance of the tents. The male household head is rarely at home during the day unless he has guests. Younger men and boys help with the herding and fetch fuel.

Women and girls may fetch water, but normally they stay in camp to run the household. Their most regular chore, at least once a day, is baking bread over the hearth. For home consumption they also turn milk into cheese, yogurt, and butter, spin wool, and weave various colorful storage bags and rugs, given in a girl's trousseau on marriage. Shahsevan women do not wear veils, but cover the lower part of the face in the presence of unrelated men. This rule is strictly observed by newly married women; young girls and old women are more casual.

One further institution should be described. Kheyr-u-sharr (literally, "good and evil") is a concept denoting relationships of reciprocal attendance at life-cycle feasts. It also refers to the personal networks so formed. "My kheyr-u-sharr" means all those people whose feasts I attend and who attend mine. Feasts include weddings and circumcisions, betrothals and mourning gatherings. To initiate a relationship with B, A must just send B an invitation; if B attends the feast the relationship commences; otherwise it does not. Similarly, the sanctions on participation are automatic; if one partner defaults, the relationship may well be terminated by the other. The more powerful and influential a man or woman, the wider the circle of their kheyr-u-sharr, on which indeed their power and influence depend. The rules for kheyr-u-sharr participation are the same for both men and women, and the gatherings so formed are similar insofar as the focus of any kheyr-u-sharr is the individual (man or woman) who calls it into being. Implicit in this statement is the notion that no two individuals have exactly the same range of kheyr-u-sharr.[1]

Ascribed Status

Women participate in social activities based on the camp and household; here, relationships among women are based primarily on a system of ascriptive status which is determined in the larger society. The ascriptive position of women can be considered under two headings: the ideal status of women and a woman's status at various points in the life cycle.

When asked what the position of women in their society is and ought to be, Shahsevan of both sexes refer to two main principles: the segregation of the sexes and male domination. With regard to the segregation of the sexes, a woman's social contacts among men fall into three categories: (1) men who are *mahram*, within the forbidden degrees, that is, not marriageable, with whom women can be unrestrained; (2) *qohum*—all recognized male kin and affines outside the forbidden degrees, that is, men of a woman's tireh of origin and tireh of marriage, and any other men who might be neighbors in her camp. Conversation with such men is possible and may be inevitable in the course of running the household, but relations are much more restrained than those with men of the first category; and (3) *yad adam* or strangers, that is, all the men not included in the above two categories. No contact with strangers is normally permissible.[2]

These three categories have direct relevance for the women's subsociety, for at all formal gatherings such as feasts and religious ceremonies, where from the point of view of a woman guest, men of all categories will be present, men and women guests will be completely separated into different tents. Women's noninvolvement in the affairs of men and avoidance of strangers are referred to the ideal of shame and women's consequent embarrassment.

The second point the Shahsevan make with regard to the position of women is that of male domination. A woman should obey her husband at all times and have his permission for any activity outside the home. A Shahsevan husband said, "They [the women] belong to us and we are free and can do anything," and women concur. Women control the daily affairs of the household and men willingly accept their judgment in this sphere, but leadership in all relations outside and inside the family is held to be a male prerogative; for women, leadership is only possible after menopause, when their status approximates that of men. This happens both because of the old woman's presumed loss of sexuality and because of her freedom from many of her former domestic responsibilities, including childrearing.

As in most societies, ascribed status among the Shahsevan derives from age, birth, and usually marriage. There are five stages in a woman's life cycle, each clearly defined with regard to expected behavior and relative status. The style of headdress a woman wears is a signal indicating which stage she has reached. These stages are *ushaq* (child); *qiz* (marriageable but as yet unmarried girl); *gelin* (bride or daughter-in-law); *arvad* (wife, essentially an "established married woman," a stage reached after two or three years of marriage or the birth and survival of a son); and *qoja arvad* or *qoja nana* (old woman, a stage reached around menopause). Periods of greatest freedom are extreme youth and extreme age; greatest restrictions on behavior occur during the stages immediately before and after marriage. This is reasonable in view of the fact that at this time a woman is likely to be uncommitted to the welfare of either her natal or her marital family and is thus seen by both as a threat to their honor.[3] A girl before puberty or a woman with children of her own obviously has vested interests in the family with which she is living, and as a consequence there are fewer restrictions on her behavior. Only women who have reached the last two stages have influence in the subsociety.

Marriage is the ideal state, reached by virtually all women; therefore, and because the choice of a marriage partner is largely in the hands of the girl's father, marital status may be seen as ascribed rather than achieved. To the extent that the girl preserves her good reputation and is attractive and dutiful, an element of achievement is relevant. However, too much emphasis should not be placed on this last point, since a girl's family will demand she behave in a way that ensures her general suitability. There is a generalized preference for marriage within the tireh, which occurs about 40 percent of the time, but marriage with neighboring tirehs of the same tribe accounts for up to a further 50 percent. Families of equal status tend to intermarry; a woman's marital status is thus determined largely by her birth status since her husband's father and her own father will be men of equal substance. It is important to note that marriages outside the tireh include not only political unions between aq saqal families, but also marriages of poorer men who cannot find suitable mates within the tireh. These patterns of marriage choice have one important reflection in the women's subsociety: the girl who comes as a bride in an extratireh marriage has one potential advantage over the girl who has made a close kin marriage. The former will commonly have a larger and certainly more heterogeneous kheyr-u-sharr, and this very institution will allow her to maintain these wider contacts throughout her life.

Divorce and separation are virtually nonexistent among the Shahsevan. The only stated ground for divorce is the supposed infertility of the wife, but in practice even this is not considered an adequate reason.[4] No cases of separation or divorce were found in the "commoner" tribal groups studied, though a few were heard of elsewhere. Polygyny is rare and limited to those men who can maintain an extra wife or wives. Since ideally, virgins marry virgins, and a man should not take a second virgin wife unless the first has died, wives after the first in a polygynous household are almost always widows. The husband usually tries to treat co-wives equally; this is done without reference to the Islamic precept, but is seen as a purely Shahsevan value.

The stability of marriage among the Shahsevan is the product of a number of forces acting both at the inception of the marriage and in its later years. Marriage ceremonies and transactions are protracted and complex and involve considerable financial investment on both sides; they are designed to produce a permanent contract. Moreover, they are begun when the girl at least is so young that she has little opportunity to conceive of the idea that it may be annulled. An explicit discouragement to divorce is provided by the *kabin,*[5] a contract witnessed by a religious authority involving an agreement by the husband to pay a considerable amount of property to his wife if he should divorce her. Customary behavior by and toward a young bride emphasizes that she has not fulfilled her part of the marriage contract until she has produced at least one child, preferably a son; until that time she remains closely veiled, may not speak to her in-laws in public, and obeys the orders of everyone in the household. A main function of the marriage ceremonies is to emphasize the change of legal affiliation of the bride, from her father's to her husband's group; but until the ceremonies are completed by the birth of her son, her father's group is intimately involved in her honor. Both sides are interested in only one thing, that the bride should bear sons. Under such pressure divorce or separation could not be contemplated; in rare cases where a young bride manages to run away to her father's home, a delegation from her husband will be sure to bring her back soon with her father's sanction, if the latter has not sent her back himself.

A further factor supports these forces which act early in a marriage. Marriages between first patrilateral parallel cousins were rare in the groups studied, and those that occurred were mainly in response to particular conditions, such as the death of the young man's or the girl's father. Thus, a new bride rarely moves into a herding unit where her own close agnates are present. This means that she has no support on which she can call in the camp to pressure her in-laws in her favor. Once again, she is constrained to act strictly according to expectations. Once the bride has borne children, the pressure relents. At last she is considered to be incorporated into the tireh of her husband, which is that of her children who form her prime interest. Different forces are now adequate to forestall any thoughts of divorce or separation. Indeed, the Shahsevan material supports Lewis' argument that "where the wife relinquishes her premarital status and is incorporated in her husband's group, men and women here being subject to dissimilar agnatic loyalties, marriage is stable" (1962:43).

The fact of stability of marriage leads to perhaps the most important conclusion concerning the ascribed status of women. Given the absence of divorce, the congruence of economic and social standing between a man and his wife is likely to persist throughout their married lives. As a result, one possible way of ranking women in the subsociety is by the status of their husbands in the wider society.

An illustration of how much the identification of a man and his wife in terms of status is recognized and used by the women, is found in the way in which wives in a herding unit cooperate over domestic chores. Observation of a number of herding units showed that a man's position determines to a large extent the relationships his wife will have with other camp women and the kinds of economic cooperation she will give or receive.

On the one hand, the wives of the agnatic core of the camp very rarely cooperate in domestic chores. They seem to regard themselves as equals, and they manage their households independently. Though agnates are ideally good friends, and in fact there is rarely overt conflict among them, the difficulties that underlie the relationship, particularly questions of inheritance and leadership, are brought into relief by the relations among their wives. It is always said by the Shahsevan that women are responsible for a household's partition, and in fact their quarrels would seem to be the efficient, but only the efficient, cause of partition.[6] Basically, this is because a woman identifies with her own children, and her main aim is to guarantee the recognition of their rights over those of their cousins.

However, unrelated men and their families may join a herding unit as hired herdsmen or retainers. Wives of herdsmen, who receive a fee as well as free pasturage from the employer, are obligated to work with the women of the employer. Wives of retainers, who receive no fee but only free pasturage, are not required to work in the employer's tent; rather, the extent of their help and friendship is determined by the degree to which their family is dependent on that of the employer, the equivalence of the exchange of pasturage for services rendered, and the permanence of the retainer's position. For example, a herdsman's wife may help with bread-making in the employer's tent, though she is not paid nor in any direct way compensated for her time and effort. She does not take a share of the bread and will probably have to do this chore again that day to provide for her own family. Wives of both herdsmen and retainers may also help incidentally in processing milk, setting up a loom, or cooking for guests in the employer's tent, whereas it seems to be only the retainer's wife who cards or spins her own wool, washes clothes, or fetches water in the company of the employer's wife. A retainer's wife is likely to become a confidante of the family and may well accompany the wife to feasts.

The system of ascriptive status among women arises in the first place from what Barth once termed the "impediment of female sex" (1953:120) and from the segregation of the sexes. It produces, in turn, two ranking systems, one based on age and the other on the status of a woman's husband. These two systems are among those used by women to organize themselves at feasts and elsewhere.

Achieved Status

Achieved status can derive from two sources: the full exploitation of ascribed statuses, and the acquisition of special attributes in three areas of social action. These specialities lie in the magico-medical, domestic, and religious spheres and are really extensions of qualities required of all women.

The first speciality concerns the realm of magic, medicine, and midwifery. In fact, each woman has a modicum of knowledge and skill in each of these areas, but emergencies arise in which ordinary skills are felt to be inadequate. In every few tirehs there will be found a professional midwife (*mama*) who is also an expert on herbal and magical cures for those diseases or spirits that attack women and children. The skills involved are not unique to the midwife, and most mature women will have acquired experience of the way she works.[7] Her uniqueness lies in the fact that she specializes in these activities and hence has gained a certain aura of expertise and efficacy. For her services a midwife is paid in kind, or up to twenty tomans in cash.[8]

The job of the midwife is regarded as a necessary and not an honorary one. Since she appears at times of crisis as the only available expert, the family that is dependent on her tends to regard her with some distrust and skepticism, for needless to say her cures are not always successful. Among formal positions for women, that of the midwife is by far the most anomalous, but it is important to realize that this is not associated with any ideas of supernatural power for working either good or evil. She is not felt to be blessed with any kind of mystic benevolent power, nor can she threaten to use bad magic against others. Nonetheless, insofar as many of the illnesses that the midwife is called to treat concern beliefs and spirits that are only partly assimilated into the Shahsevan/Islamic cosmology as *jinn,* the lack of orthodoxy makes her position an anomalous one, and she is the object of both derision and awed respect.

Achievement in the domestic sphere presents a very different picture from that of the midwife. At life-cycle feasts and other ceremonies the host's wife is commonly aided by a female specialist cook who directs the preparation and serving of the food. A woman holds this position for reasons other than her ability to cook; the recipes for the dishes served at these feasts are identical to those normally served to guests. Moreover, few Shahsevan women would be daunted by the task of organizing a large meal. A cook (*ashpaz*) must be intelligent, strong-willed, efficient, and more independent than most Shahsevan women. She also needs a good sense of humor. As the position of cook is not hereditary, a woman who aspires to it must make herself known and available. The cook demands a fee of about forty tomans for most functions at which she presides. At certain times of the year she is much in demand, and her presence adds to the prestige of the host family, who may even send a horse for her to ride to the camp where the feast is to be held.

In the tireh there are one or two women held to be knowledgeable on religious matters. Commonly, they are women who with a male relative have made the pilgrimage to the shrine of Imam Reza at Mashhad, and are thereafter referred to by the title of *Mashhadi.* In effect, the position of Mashhadi among women is comparable to that of a *hajji* among men.[9] The Mashhadis are among the few women who pray regularly; their position is a highly conservative one, and they firmly support traditional Shahsevan customs and moral attitudes, sometimes by reference to imaginary Quranic injunctions. The opinions of such a woman in matters of family law and custom are sought by both men and women, and her advice is given equal weight with that of men.[10] In one case a betrothed girl was said to have been suckled by her fiancé's mother, but no one could remember or would admit the extent to which this took place. It was therefore uncertain whether the engaged couple were foster siblings according to Islamic law and hence forbidden to marry. A Mashhadi gave her opinion—that there was no bar to marriage—and there was general agreement that her decision must be right.

The marriage ceremonies were completed two years later in the usual manner.

Women Leaders

These kinds of specialization differ in the opportunities they offer for aspiring women leaders. The magico-medical specialist differs from the other two in that her relations with her clients are dyadic and private rather than public in nature. Her reputation is diffuse, and it would be difficult for her to exploit it for political ends. Ceremonial cooks and Mashhadis, on the other hand, are essentially public figures, and it is through such specializations that a woman may achieve a position of leadership. The life histories of three women illustrate these points. They are taken from my own field notes.

> Simi is mama [midwife] for at least four or five tirehs of Geyiklu tribe; the outer limits of her practice were not ascertained, but do not include her tireh of birth. She is now an old woman and herself the mother of four married children; her husband is still alive. She has been practicing her skills for fifteen or twenty years. Simi is always accompanied on her rounds by her son's daughter, a girl of the age of ten or eleven, who seems destined eventually to follow Simi's profession, though not for many years and probably not until after her menopause. In fact, Simi's eldest son's wife has been suggested as the likely successor to Simi's position after the latter's death.
>
> Simi has a number of personal characteristics that suit her for the job. Like a ceremonial cook she travels alone extensively throughout the pastures; this in itself indicates that she is more "shameless" than the ideal or average Shahsevan woman. Though in outward appearance Simi seems to be a typical Shahsevan woman—and in fact she has a normal marital career—she behaves quite unlike any other woman of the group of her clients. She takes great liberties in conversation with both men and women; she will roughhouse with young men, and she feels quite free to visit in any tent. Curiously, she punctuates her sentences with prayers and pious phrases. Though she is an old woman she does not appear to be senile or in any way deranged. Unfortunately, it was not clear whether Simi always behaved in an unusual fashion or whether this strange behavior, which is accepted by both men and women, evolved after she became a midwife.

Simi shamelessly oversteps the limits of conduct appropriate to her sex, placing herself in an anomalous and hence potentially powerful position. At the same time she engages in unorthodox magic and charms. Though she has considerable power within the area of her speciality, she does not seem to be able to transpose her influence to other spheres. She is an important individual in the limited area of midwifery and magic, but she is in no sense a women's leader. In this way the midwife's position differs greatly from that of the other two kinds of specialists who concern themselves with matters that are both morally correct and appropriate to the female sex. It is the lack of orthodoxy inherent in the midwife's speciality that prevents Simi from becoming a woman's leader, rather than anything in her idiosyncratic behavior. Though she deviates from the norms of modesty, this alone is inadequate to place her outside competitions for leadership positions; the latter themselves imply a lack of conformity, though less blatant than that of Simi, to the ideals of shame. Women occasionally referred to Simi as a bad, or indeed a mad, woman, but when questioned they carefully distinguished her from her medicines and magic, and it became clear that it was the latter, rather than any personal traits, that were extraordinary. Nonetheless, like the real leaders Simi has a large and heterogeneous kheyr-u-sharr. She is automatically invited to all feasts given by past or future clients, who make certain that she attends by sending a horse for her; on one occasion when a double betrothal feast was being held, both of the young men's fathers sent a horse for Simi.

Leadership is regarded as a male prerogative among the Shahsevan; to a certain extent positions of leadership in the women's subsociety echo those in the male sphere. Formerly, a tireh aq saqal was commonly one of the old men of the group. Nowadays, the old men of the tireh are still respected as such, but they are called *aq birchek* (grey hair), and the exacting position of tireh aq saqal is ideally filled by a younger man at the height of his influence and power. On the other hand, aq birchek when used as a woman's title implies not so much that she is old and past menopause but that she is a leader in the women's subsociety.

An aq birchek is a powerful woman; her influence is based on her position in the women's subsociety but is also significant in the male sphere. Men often comment about a woman who holds this title, "She is *our* aq birchek," and they may add by way of explanation that "she is the women's aq saqal." Typically, an aq birchek arrives at her leadership position after going to Mashhad as a pilgrim or having established herself as a ceremonial cook. Either of these specialist positions validates a woman's claims to leadership from an ascribed base. An aq birchek is always an old woman; this title is never applied to women who are capable of bearing children. The next two short histories illustrate the pattern of leadership represented by the aq birchek.

Fatima was born into the chiefly family of Kalash tribe, a small group attached to the large Geyiklu tribe. She was married to a reasonably well-to-do Geyiklu commoner by whom she had two children, a son and a daughter. Her husband died when her children were very young, and she was taken as a second wife by her late husband's leader, an aq saqal of another Geyiklu tireh who rivalled the Geyiklu chief for leadership of the tribe. She had three sons by him. As the wife of such a prominent man and the mother of four sons, her position as it related to that of her husband and her family was very secure.

Twenty years ago she was taken to Mashhad by her husband, who died a few years later. Her stepson lived in a separate tent, had a wife (Mashhadi Fatima's daughter by her first marriage) and several children, and then became the tireh aq saqal. From this time on, Mashhadi Fatima's influence in the tireh and domination of her own family were great.

She was an intelligent woman of strong character, and very fat, a characteristic much admired by the Shahsevan. Until her death at the age of sixty or sixty-five, she was a respected aq birchek of the tireh. Naturally presiding at all the feasts of the tireh, Mashhadi Fatima had kheyr-u-sharr relations with women of both the Marallu and the Davalu chiefly families, as well as with women in villages of the area. She was honored by all who knew her, and her wishes were respected even in matters that typically concern only men. For example, a superb bull camel owned by her sons was dying, and the men wanted to slaughter it in the prescribed manner for meat—to the Shahsevan, camel meat is a rare delicacy. Mashhadi Fatima intervened, declaring that this camel was too noble a beast to be eaten. The camel died naturally and was buried near the camp.

Durna is from a family of average wealth belonging to the same tireh of Geyiklu tribe. She is married to a patrilateral cousin; though she has been married for some twenty-five years, she has borne no children and is thought to be infertile. She accepts this fact as God's will; her husband never made any motion to divorce her nor has he taken a second wife.

Durna is a quick-witted, intelligent woman who because of her directness, commanding bearing, and excellent sense of humor is a popular and respected personality in the tireh. These traits are in no way compatible with the stigma that childlessness carries, and she seems to have acted consistently and consciously to improve her personal standing. She has made herself known and available as a ceremonial cook of the tireh. As such, she takes the most prominent role in the women's tent at tireh feasts.

Some years ago she and her husband went to Mashhad specifically to ask help from Imam Reza for their childless condition. But the effect, probably calculated, was to augment her already important position and to counteract further the stigma of her barrenness. A further area in which Mashhadi Durna went out of her way to gain specialist knowledge was that of the preparation of female corpses for burial. Having learned from a *mullah,* she is the only woman of the tireh who can direct this job according to the proper Islamic routine.

For all these reasons, Mashhadi Durna has a wide range of contacts as well as a very large kheyr-u-sharr. Though she is no more than forty years old, because she is barren she is classified as an old woman; thus, the very fact of her childlessness helped her to acquire the title of aq birchek when she was still comparatively young.

Mashhadi Durna and her husband are a family of average circumstances—not wealthy enough to employ a herdsman, which means that the husband has to share menial herding duties with others of their herding group. On the other hand, they have adopted Durna's brother's daughter to help her in the house. In return, they are responsible for the girl's trousseau. This is the only recorded case of adoption of a child with both parents living, and it can be explained by its context: the sole object was to provide Mashhadi Durna with help in her tent and hence more free time to fulfill her duties as a women's leader.

From these examples several points emerge. Though an aq birchek is usually associated with a tireh, and her relations with the tireh women correspond to those of the aq saqal with the tireh men, both Mashhadi Fatima and Mashhadi Durna lived in the same tireh and both were recognized as aq bircheks for many years. There seems to have been no competition between them, a fact that points to one of the most striking features of the position of aq birchek. While both women had in common certain personality traits and the intelligence to qualify them for leadership, Mashhadi Fatima seems simply to have consolidated her secure and powerful ascribed position without needing to emphasize her unique personal qualities per se. Her pilgrimage to Mashhad at a strategic time in life seems to have served this purpose very well. By contrast, Mashhadi Durna acquired specialist knowledge and skills and actively promoted herself by performing special tasks; in other words, the main basis of her influence was achieved status. Her trip to Mashhad confirmed the position she otherwise achieved through purely secular means. Thus, aq birchek can be either an ascribed title or an achieved position, and the role and its duties can be played more or less passively or actively. The common denominator seems to be simply a strong, assertive character; the position can be tailored by the woman herself. Moreover, the roles and rewards associated with women's leadership positions are not exclusive, and leadership positions are of a kind that makes competition simply irrelevant.

In the women's sphere the position of aq birchek itself does not bring many formal duties, but where an aq birchek achieves her position by the performance of certain specialist functions, she does not abandon them. For example, Mashhadi Durna is increasingly in demand as a ceremonial cook and body washer. Such duties as do exist are consultative and ceremonial. Aq bircheks' opinions are respected in all matters that touch on the female sphere. They have no sanction to ensure acceptance of their advice other than their ability to direct public opinion, but their advice is regarded as sensible and pragmatic (they are always among the most well-informed women) and in accordance with traditional values. In other words, their advice *is* a valuable guide to acceptable behavior. In addition, they represent women when ceremonial delegations are sent between camps. Thus, they are included in the small party that goes to fetch a bride in marriages both inside and outside the tireh, and they preside in the women's guest tent at all weddings of the tireh. On one occasion Mashhadi Durna was asked to take the mother of a betrothed man to the camp of his fiancée to seek the girl's mother's permission to hold the wedding feast.

The rewards of leadership are several. An aq birchek has a wide range of contacts and kheyr-u-sharr involving continual invitations to feasts. All Shahsevan women are full of anticipation for weeks before a feast, and an aq birchek who is invited to many such feasts is in an enviable position. Just how enviable becomes clear when it is realized that the average Shahsevan woman goes to about ten feasts a year, while an aq birchek, a midwife, and possibly a cook may attend thirty or more such functions.

Another reward involves the cooperation of women of the herding unit. Though her husband has no herdsmen or retainers, Mashhadi Durna can expect neighbor women to help her with household tasks, particularly weaving, without reciprocity on her part. This unusual situation is partly the result of Durna's personality, for quite simply she is good company. But more than this, she has recruited for herself a number of female retainers, perhaps to replace the daughter-in-law she does not have.

Further, the Shahsevan have an extraordinary propensity for ordering people, and animals, around. No comment that can be in any way turned into a command will ever be made as a statement. Some less important individuals may get a sense of power from ordering others to perform acts in which they are already engaged, but generally the degree to which a person is obeyed is a good indication of his or her status. The aq birchek as a recognized leader takes a big part in these battles of will in the women's sphere. She is rarely disobeyed, and though the issues are usually petty, the number of her successes seems to be a great satisfaction to her.

Finally, an old woman has some freedom in conversation with men, but more than this she gains quasi equality with men only in proportion to her own strong character. The aq birchek, as an old woman who has the approval of all the women behind her, has even more right to transgress from the female to the male sphere. The relative ease with which an aq birchek converses with men and expresses her unsolicited opinions on numerous topics indicates that, of all the women, she conforms least to the ideal of modesty. The women leaders join men in conversations on all subjects on more or less equal terms. For example, during the migration when men repair to a hillside and consider plans for the following moves, an aq birchek may well be among them discussing freely the problems of the migration that are largely of an economic or political nature.

A leader's freedom from those constraints that are the basis of the social segregation of the sexes, her willingness to take advantage of this freedom, and the men's acceptance that she does so, provide an important articulation point between the women's subsociety and the larger society. Nevertheless, it should be made clear that though the aq birchek can easily talk with men both on her own initiative and at their request, there are no *formal* channels for this kind of communication between the women (through their leaders) and the men.

Feasts

A woman's contacts with nonkin are few and infrequent in daily life. It is the institution of the kheyr-u-sharr feasting ties that allows for the development and expression of women's relations with other women, thus forming the women's subsociety, and it is during the feasts attended by kheyr-u-sharr that leaders arise and their influence can be extended to distant women who are otherwise unrelated. At feasts the interaction of the various factors discussed above can be seen: a woman's age, the corresponding statuses of husband and wife, and the special skills learned by some women. One such gathering—a betrothal feast, which seems to embody the most typical and representative elements of the kheyr-u-sharr gatherings—is described in some detail. This account also serves to give some idea of the range of women who may attend any given feast.

The idea of having more than a simple family gathering to signify the betrothal of a girl is a recent innovation. The kheyr-u-sharr invited to a betrothal feast is still smaller than that involved at the proper wedding feast, but perhaps because of this it is somewhat easier to unravel the patterns of interaction. In this account, women are listed according to the tireh into which they have married; boys up to the age of four or five and unmarried girls who attended the feast with their mothers or other female relatives are not mentioned. The term *notable* applies to aq bircheks, Mashhadis, and the wives of hajjis and of tireh aq saqals, and does not include any other elderly women. The following description is taken from my research.

The betrothal feast (*nishan*) was given for Khanom Gul, a spirited, good-looking girl from Hajji Salimlu tireh (Geyiklu tribe), by her father's brother, a man of modest circumstances who was her guardian, her father having died long ago. On this day she was betrothed to a man of average wealth and position from Qoyunlu tireh (Geyiklu tribe). Thirty-six women were present at this feast, in two parties (part of the kheyr-u-sharr of the betrothed girl's mother and part of the kheyr-u-sharr of the mother of the young man).

Not counting the girl's mother, sixteen women were from the betrothed girl's tireh, Hajji Salimlu. Every herding unit of the tireh was represented. Of the six notables of the tireh, three were present: the senior wife of the tireh aq saqal; Mashhadi Durna, the aq birchek and cook who was responsible for the cooking of the feast; and Simi, the midwife. The junior wife of the tireh aq saqal was rarely able to attend feasts where her co-wife was also present, while the two other notable women absent from the feast, co-wives of a hajji, were themselves unconnected with the principals. One of the women from the tireh, married to a retainer, whose brother was the young man to be engaged, attended as a member of the kheyr-u-sharr of his mother.

Not counting the young man's mother, nine women were present from his tireh, Qoyunlu. Among them was the wife of the tireh aq saqal, a hajji; in her own right this woman was an aq birchek and Mashhadi.

The remaining nine women were married into four other tirehs of Geyiklu tribe; these four tirehs were the nearest neighbors of Hajji Salimlu tireh. From the tireh of the betrothed girl's mother's father five women were present. The sister of the betrothed girl came in the company of her husband's brother's wife, who represented a lineage branch of the tireh, while the contingent was led by the wife of the tireh aq saqal, a hajji; in her own right the latter woman was an aq birchek. Two other women of this group were by origin from Qoyunlu tireh, and they belonged to the kheyr-u-sharr of the young man's mother. A first cousin (father's sister's daughter) and childhood friend of the betrothed girl came from another tireh. A third tireh was represented by two women: the wife of the tireh aq saqal and the oldest woman of the other branch of the same tireh. The fourth tireh was represented by the senior wife of the tireh aq saqal, a hajji.

Significantly, two women who were part of the girl's mother's kheyr-u-sharr and who lived in the same herding unit as the latter refrained from coming to the feast as a protest; they had hoped that a young man of their own family would win permission to marry Khanom Gul, his cousin. For a number of reasons the decision had gone against him in favor of a stranger from another tireh. The absence of these women was noticed by everyone present. They were said to be sulking.

As the women arrived they were ushered to the guest tent. Important women were greeted in chorus by the others, and four of the senior women from the young man's mother's contingent arranged themselves in the back of the tent (a place of honor) with their counterparts from the girl's side. The conversation of these women was followed by all the other guests in the tent. As other women joined the group there was much scrambling to find them places in the tent appropriate to their status. News and gossip were brought up and discussed, and the most lively conversations concerned marriage arrangements and the several important weddings that were due to occur before the autumn migration. Preparations for these weddings were discussed in great detail, for the women arrange loans of their household goods (utensils, carpets, etc.) to help the host family. There was much speculation about the women who would be present. At this point Simi the midwife appeared, and she greeted the other women in turn, kissing each of the children at whose birth she had assisted. Her contribution to the discussion was small; rather, she concerned herself with individual problems.

At mid-morning Mashhadi Durna arrived, and after stopping briefly at the guest tent, she went to the cooking tent and began preparations for the repast. There were ninety to one hundred men and women to feed that day. Soon eleven of the most important, though not necessarily the oldest, woman joined Mashhadi Durna in the tiny cooking tent. These included five wives of tireh aq saqals, two of whom were themselves aq bircheks; Simi; and four other women who were closely associated with the principals: the girl's father's sister and her father's brother's wife, the co-wife of the girl's mother, and the brother's wife of the young man. His mother was also present, though the girl's mother remained with her daughter in a separate tent. Older women with few other claims to importance remained to preside in the guest tent after the exodus of the notables; twenty-four women stayed in the guest tent eating melon, drinking tea, and chatting casually.

The conversation in the cooking tent which was directed by Mashhadi Durna was considerably more pointed. For example, the absence of the two women mentioned above was discussed only after Mashhadi Durna introduced the topic. Everyone was agitated, for the problem of Khanom Gul's engagement had been hotly debated for over a year. Every woman had her say, and then Durna commented that the two women were foolish to keep up the grudge and miss the feast, for the decision had been made and would not be reversed; grievances should now be forgotten, for the issue was closed. The women in the cooking tent concurred, and in fact what had been a burning issue seemed to have burnt itself out. After giving her final opinion, Mashhadi Durna quickly turned the conversation to arrangements for a large wedding to be held in several weeks' time. Other controversial topics were dealt with in a similar fashion.

Mashadi Durna was helped in the preparation and serving of the food by three other women: the girl's father's sister and father's brother's wife and the co-wife of her mother. The food was served first to the men and then to the women in two lots, first to the guest tent and then to those in the cooking tent itself.

It is interesting to note that the comparatively rigid seating arrangements of the guest tent are determined largely by factors of ascribed status, while personal factors and achieved status tend to disrupt any such formal ranking system. This is demonstrated when the notables following the ceremonial cook into the kitchen tent make no effort to order their places there. The equality pervading relations in the kitchen tent is striking; indeed, each woman represents a combination of achieved and ascribed status that renders her a leader in her own right. An aq birchek leads the discussion of controversial subjects, but in this select group she is no more than prima inter pares.

Major quarrels are aired and to some extent arbitrated by the women in the kitchen tent at each feast. Decisions reached here can with some ease be relayed to both those women not present in the kitchen tent and those who have not attended the feast at all. This is so primarily because the notables are important figures in day-to-day camp activities and discussions. Further, when a number of women from one camp or tireh want to attend a feast, the group journeys together in a party typically led by an aq birchek or other notable. Finally, it is frequently the case that an important woman of a tireh some distance from the feast alone represents the women of that tireh; on her return she is expected to pass on the news of the feast.

Other than the obvious part the kitchen tent gatherings play in social control, several important points emerge from the detailed attendance records collected at five feasts during a six-week period, which I attended as the guest of the senior wife of a tireh leader. Because of her husband's position she was considered an important woman, though she was in no sense a woman's leader. Her range of contacts was extensive but not so great as that of, for example, an aq birchek. One hundred and two women attended these feasts from nine tirehs of Geyiklu tribe and several villages of the area. They represent perhaps only three-quarters of the total number of women my hostess met in the six-week period, for she went to four other feasts as well. Thus, during only a short period of time her range of contacts was considerable; in the course of a year the number of women she would meet could be doubled and possibly tripled. Moreover, the size and heterogeneity of the group of women gathered together at each feast are very significant. These women can be seen as points in an "unbounded" social field. The opinions they each form as members of an action set (see Mayer 1966:108–110) at any one feast can be spread through other comparable contacts to innumerable women.

The women's subsociety in many ways acts as an information service. This can be inferred from domestic conversation as much as from discussion at the feasts themselves. Much of the news passed on at feasts concerns marriage, the main topic in which women's opinions are sought after and respected by men. At feasts the women have a chance to assess the suitability and beauty of the young girls who attend the gatherings with their elders, and since they are likely to have contacts with a large number of geographically dispersed, unrelated families, the intelligence system they develop becomes a most significant aid to a potential suitor from their own family.

Furthermore, at feasts women discover information about men who have gone on sheep-selling expeditions or who intend to make pilgrimages, and they get details of the presents a man has brought home for his family, camps that have moved to new pasturage, and so on. Naturally, much of this kind of information, unlike that about marriageable girls, is repeated in the men's guest tents as well, but it affords women chances to learn about the changing economic position of others and the reasons for the changes. Armed with such information, a woman can keep her husband up to the mark and secure her own and her children's position. Similarly, the information a man has collected and that gathered by his womenfolk make cross-checking possible and reduce the possibility of erring in an economic decision. The more well-adjusted and happily married a couple is (frequently a man and wife are very fond of each other, and there is great respect between them), the more likely it is to pool information acquired independently for the common benefit.

In view of the information service it should be noted that the recognized leaders, Mashhadis and aq bircheks, like the wives of hajjis, stand in a conservative and high orthodox position vis-à-vis the society as a whole, and it is these women whose beliefs and opinions are accepted and spread. This is supported by the attendance data for the five feasts mentioned above. Without counting the women whom my hostess met several times who were resident in her tireh of marriage, she met ten women from other tirehs at least twice in the course of these five feasts. Of these ten women, six in fact can be designated as leaders. This high proportion of distinguished women indicates the existence of an effective network[11] among important women. The actual mechanics of leadership can in part be explained through this concept. The effective network of a woman leader includes a number of other leaders and important women like herself. Especially in kitchen tent situations, the conversation of these women clearly is an important factor in determining values and regulating women's behavior. Decisions made at feasts and elsewhere are relayed, through the wide-ranging extended networks of each of these women, throughout the subsociety as a whole. For this reason it is possible to see how the women's subsociety among the Shahsevan acts as a pool of traditional ideas and concepts of correct behavior. The problem this fact poses for social change among the tribespeople is significant and probably typical of many societies.

Conclusion

The subsociety can be analyzed at three different levels: eligibility for membership, content of relationships, and structure. First it must be repeated that it is the characteristic of male-domination that prompts the use of *sub* as a descriptive prefix. In that the women do not overtly take part in the political and economic concerns of the larger society, their activities are of secondary importance in understanding the latter.

A woman becomes eligible to participate in the activities of the subsociety when she acquires through marriage full membership in the larger society. Actual involvement in women's activities depends on the institution of kheyr-u-sharr, which has two main principles: that every married woman is the focus of a kheyr-u-sharr circle peculiar to herself, and that she is also a member of the circles of all those women who belong to hers. In other words, there is a series of overlapping circles, each centered on a woman, that extends throughout the entire community. The ideology of kheyr-u-sharr is the basis of a network; every woman is linked with other women, each of whom has kheyr-u-sharr ties with yet others. This network is bounded only by the fact that it is exclusive to women.

The picture so far described is not complete; the structured nature of the whole remains to be considered. Though there is no overall leadership or coordination, nonetheless a common system of ranking women, of positions and roles, is probably found among all the women of the Shahsevan. Features of the larger society and elements inherent in the women's activities per se cause this to be so.

Men of the Shahsevan are differentiated and ranked in a number of ways—particularly by birth order, by age, and by wealth—and a woman is greatly affected by this ranking system, for her ascribed status is directly linked with the position of her father and then her husband in the community. Being thus identified with her husband (principally because of the stability of marriage), a woman is involved, albeit indirectly, in her husband's concerns in all areas of social life. This identification is used to order the relations of camp women among themselves and provides the basis of seating arrangements in the guest tent at feasts.

On the other hand, the very nature of women's activities creates the need for them to rank themselves along different lines as well. In this second case, a system based only on ascribed status is inadequate, for, needless to say, high ascriptive status is not necessarily related to qualifications for leadership. Other than the fission of whole groups, there is no mechanism in the larger society for resolving quarrels between women, even though the roots of such disputes are often to be found there. Opportunities exist at feast gatherings to settle just such problems; from among the women who engineer settlements, leaders emerge, and they and the other women are ranked in terms of achievement.

The structured authority positions that characterize the subsociety find their most spectacular functions at feast gatherings, where they also receive constant renewal of strength and legitimacy. However, the main basis of women's authority and the most fundamental, if less spectacular, occasion for its exercise occur in the daily, face-to-face relations of camp life. If the day-to-day contacts of women were more restricted, then feast gatherings would be unlikely to be structured or purposive. Further, if positions of authority and the ranking system among women applied only at feasts, or if, conversely, they were relevant only outside the context of kheyr-u-sharr contacts, this would not constitute a women's subsociety; it is the combination of these two contexts that is important. Thus, the women's subsociety in the Shahsevan is built both on the opportunity for a number of women to be in fairly constant contact day by day *and* on the networks of dyadic relations through which recurring feast gatherings are organized.

To emphasize the independence of the internal organization of the subsociety, two further points should be noted. There can be a considerable discrepancy between the status of a man in the larger society and his wife's standing in the subsociety. In such situations no attempt is made to reconcile the difference, for three reasons. First, the social segregation of the sexes prevents men and women from knowing well more than a few members of the opposite sex—hence, few men would be able to interpret another man's actions in terms of his wife's character. Second, the kheyr-u-sharr connections of a man and his wife need not be similar. Thus, an important woman's "public personality" at feasts is not necessarily associated with her husband, who may not be included in the host's kheyr-u-sharr and who may even be unknown to many of the guests, both male and female. And third, men, unlike women, tend to evaluate women less in terms of personal achievement or personality than in terms of ascribed status and the position of their menfolk.

Finally, on rare occasions the subsociety may act independently as a "subculture" concerned with innovation and the development of new ideas. For example, most magic and medicine are regarded by men and women as a female concern. Recently, the women learned, presumably from radio broadcasts, that cigarettes are a cause of cancer, a disease with which they are familiar, and mounted a campaign against excessive smoking. This preoccupation not only had noticeable effects on the women's smoking habits, but on the men's as well, since many women keep the keys to the trunks where their husbands' cigarette supplies are stored.

In a society characterized by strict sexual segregation, a consideration of activities exclusive to women can be important to an understanding of all social relations in the community. Certainly, the Shahsevan women's subsociety functions as an information service and as a means of social control. It is also possible that it acts as a psychological outlet for women in a situation of male domination. These functions may be fulfilled by various other forms of social organization, some of which have been described in the literature on the Middle East; however, subsocieties structured like that of the Shahsevan have not previously been noted.

As a working hypothesis, it could be suggested that forms of social organization among women similar to the one described here may be found elsewhere in the Middle East. However, they probably occur only where three conditions are fulfilled: some degree of separation of women's activities from men's (among the Shahsevan it would seem that this is due to the sexual segregation that characterizes all social activities, both day-to-day and ceremonial), opportunity for interaction (for Shahsevan women, social interaction is made possible not only because of the fairly large residential group of the tireh but also because they are free to travel, sometimes alone, considerable distances to attend feast gatherings), and a medium of interaction (this last condition is fulfilled in the Shahsevan case by dyadic kheyr-u-sharr ties, with their implicit reciprocity and obligation of mutual attendance at feasts). Each of these conditions can be met in ways very different from the Shahsevan solution, but only where they are met will there be a subsociety comparable with that of the Shahsevan.

Notes

1. On kheyr-u-sharr among Shahsevan men, see R. L. Tapper (1971: 236ff). It should be noted that a major aspect of the institution among the men is the collection of money contributions from guests at each feast. This element is also present among the women, but only to a nominal extent.

2. As elsewhere in this part of the world (cf. Peristiany 1965), the shame of a woman among the Shahsevan is essentially a group matter. *Namus* refers specifically to the sexual shame of a woman, but in that it concerns a larger number of people it might also be translated as "honor," the meaning being restricted to matters concerning women and sex; namus is quite different from *aberu,* a term meaning "face," dignity, or reputation in matters other than women or sex, though again, this is a group concern.

Though a woman's honor is the direct concern of her father and brother, and after marriage of her husband as well, the whole tirehs of all these people, and (according to informants) the tirehs of their mother's brothers and perhaps other affines, are interested in the preservation of the woman's namus which is their own as well.

Consistent with this, Shahsevan men often maintain that all the daughters and wives of their tireh are *mahram* to them, by which they refer to their freedom to converse with all these women. However, of course, marriages with such women are frequent, if not preferred, so that to call them *mahram* in the proper sense can be thought a misusage. The three categories of relationships with males are thus defined partly by kinship and affinal relations and partly by residence.

3. An unmarried girl will devote much time to her grooming and will wear more ostentatious clothing at this than at any other time during her

life. However, the fashions she adopts are designed to make her attractive from a distance. Romance is associated with feasts, when contacts between families of different tirehs are most likely to occur. Though unmarried men and women are not allowed to meet on these occasions, they will watch each other from afar; when romantic considerations are allowed to influence marriage choices, then commonly the spouses are from different tirehs.

4. The punishment for illicit sexual affairs and even for an innocent association was always affirmed to be death for the female, if not for both parties, and exposure without burial. However, no first-hand evidence of any such affairs was obtained.

5. The importance of the kabin, the equivalent of the Islamic "deferred dower," is that no sexual relations can take place until it has been arranged; it is the signing of this contract which "makes" the marriage. The kabin is a contract between individuals, whereas bridewealth and dowry exchanges represent the "contract" between social groups (cf. Lewis 1962:23). The kabin is the only required prestation when a widow remarries.

6. The composition of households (i.e., the population of a tent) varies widely. One basic principle is common to all—each tent almost always has one (and no more than one) group of unmarried siblings three or more years old. It is where this is exceeded that the household is most likely to split, since potential marriage partners (first cousins) should not grow up in the same tent.

7. Other medical specialists—both men and old women—do exist, but the clientele of the latter are both different and very much smaller than that of the midwife, and they do not seem to clash with her professionally. However, such an old woman with suitable character, stamina, and inclination might succeed a midwife when the latter dies, though the specialized knowledge of the midwife is said to be passed on from maternal aunt to niece.

8. Twenty tomans was worth about $3.00 at the time of field work. Then, a laborer's wage in the area was about 5 tomans a day; a mature sheep was worth about 150 tomans.

9. To my knowledge, no Shahsevan women have yet made the hajj, the pilgrimage to Mecca, though village women of the area are reported to have done so.

10. Apart from this consultative role, Shahsevan Mashhadi women have no special duties and certainly no special education or knowledge, unlike women religious leaders in many settled communities (cf., e.g., Fernea and Fernea 1972:399).

11. Epstein describes an effective network as those people with whom ego interacts most intensely and regularly and who are therefore also likely to come to know one another. In other words, it is that part of the total network that shows a degree of connectedness. The extended network is simply all of ego's dyadic ties that are not considered part of the close-linked effective network (Epstein 1961:57).

Bibliography

Barth, Fredrik. *Principles of Social Organization in Southern Kurdistan.* Oslo, 1953.

Epstein, Arnold L. "The Network and Urban Social Organization." *Rhodes-Livingstone Institute Journal,* 29 (1961) :29–62.

Fernea, Robert A., and Elizabeth Warnock Fernea. "Variation in Religious Observance among Islamic Women." In *Scholars, Saints and Sufis,* ed. N. R. Keddie. Berkeley, 1972.

Lewis, Ioan M. *Marriage and the Family in Northern Somaliland.* East African Studies, no. 15. Kampala, 1962.

———. "Spirit Possession and Deprivation Cults." *Man,* N.S. 1 (1966) : 307–329.

Mayer, Adrian C. "The Significance of Quasi-Groups in the Study of Complex Societies." In *The Social Anthropology of Complex Societies,* ed. M. Banton. London, 1966.

Peristiany, John G., ed. *Honour and Shame.* London, 1965.

Tapper, Nancy S. S. "The Role of Women in Selected Pastoral Islamic Societies." M.Phil. dissertation. University of London, 1968.

Tapper, Richard L. "The Shahsavan of Azarbaijan: A Study of Political and Economic Change in a Middle Eastern Tribal Society." Ph.D. dissertation. University of London, 1971.

19 Changing Sex Roles in Bedouin Society in Syria and Lebanon

Dawn Chatty

Numerous sheep-raising tribes migrate in the region along the Syria-Lebanon border, including the al-Fadl and the al-Hassanna bedouin tribes. Changes are occurring in their nomadic pastoral way of life, some as the result of modernization. A technological shift has occurred in the last twenty years: the camel, traditionally the tribal beast of burden, is being rapidly replaced by the truck. As a secondary or supportive technological device, the truck has been a positive force in the development of pastoralism. It has, however, generated changes within the pastoral family. Men's and women's roles, which were once directed toward traditional subsistence output, are now changing to accommodate market-oriented production demands.

The discussion of this essay is particularly relevant to current discussions of the "universal subordination of women" (Rosaldo and Lamphere 1974). One increasingly accepted framework for the analysis of "women's subordination" is the private-public dichotomy (Rosaldo and Lamphere 1974:24). Here, the "private," "domestic," or "informal" universe of women is regarded as generally subordinate to the "public," "extradomestic," or "formal" universe of men. That something resembling such a dichotomy does exist in many cultures studied by Western anthropologists cannot be denied. However, in a number of cultures, such as those studied by Thomas (1958), Mead (1935), and Turnbull (1962), the distinctions or boundaries between the private and public spheres are difficult to ascertain. It may well be that this dichotomy, far from being a

The field research on which this study is based was conducted during 1972–73 and was made possible by a grant from the National Science Foundation.

universal condition, is mainly a Western distinction and that it may not always be a relevant indicator of women's subordination. Such is the case among the al-Fadl and al-Hassanna bedouin tribes, where distinctions between traditional "domestic" subsistence production and the recently developed "public" market production are not clearly defined, and neither is the particular province of one sex or the other. Also, although male and female roles are different, they are complementary, and women's activities are not viewed here as subordinate to men's but as complementary to them.

Social Organization

Bedouin, or bedu, inhabit the desert and semiarid lands (*badia*) of the Middle East. These Arabic-speaking people regard themselves as members of tribes that are descendant from two ancestral branches: Adnan and Kahtan (sometimes called Qais and Yemen). Members of the al-Fadl and al-Hassanna tribes consider themselves part of the bedouin confederation of tribes of the Syrian Desert. As such, these two tribes were intimately involved in the massive population shifts that characterized the north Arabian peninsula during the seventeenth and eighteenth centuries. During this period, the movements of large tribal confederations in the Nejd northwards into the badia and the marginal cultivated land of the Syria-Lebanon region took place.[1] Only in the late nineteenth and early twentieth century was this process checked and a reverse movement begun. As the frontiers of tribal territory gave way to newly expanding agricultural frontiers, some tribal groups, including the al-Fadl and the al-Hassanna, found themselves encapsulated in marginal areas within well-populated agricultural regions. By the mid–twentieth century, tribal grazing land of the al-Fadl and al-Hassanna extended roughly in a band from Palmyra (Tudmor) in the Syrian Desert to the southwestern slopes of the Anti-Lebanon Mountains in the Beqaa Valley (including the slopes of Mount Hermon, Lake Huleh, and the Golan).

The al-Fadl and al-Hassanna, like other bedouin tribespeople, describe their social organization in the kinship idiom. In other words, "real" and "fictive" genealogical descent, which is traced through the male line, determines tribal composition and structure. A genealogical model of descent is common knowledge among older men (not women) and appears to be accepted and manipulated as circumstances dictate. The structure of the tribe resembles a pyramid composed of increasing numbers of descending units. The term *qabila* is used by the al-Fadl and the al-Hassanna to distinguish themselves from each other and from other structurally similar bedouin units. The qabila is subdivided into several main sections called *ashiira* (subtribe) or sometimes *fakhad*. The fakhad is a descent group whose common ancestor is said to have been many generations removed from the living. Each fakhad is further subdivided into units called *Beits*. The Beit is a group of agnates whose common ancestor is said to have been four to six generations removed from the living. Within the Beit, the only divisions named are extended families of one, two, or three generations. While the qabila, ashiira, and fakhad are traditionally organized to serve the tribal community's interests of mutual self-defense, the Beit is the basic economic unit. Today, with the greatly reduced political power and authority of secondary and higher tribal segments, the Beits tend to operate as semiautonomous economic and political units, each linked directly with the qabila head or *sheikh*.

The physical residences of the al-Fadl and the al-Hassanna are called *beits*.[2] They speak of either *beit sha'ir* (house of hair) or *beit hajjar* (house of stone). Both types of residence are found among the al-Fadl and al-Hassanna today. It seems that as early as 1920 both types of residences were not unusual (see Montagne 1947:244). Structurally, the beit sha'ir and beit hajjar are similar. Both are rectangular in shape and generally consist of two sections. One section is the women's domain. Food supplies and equipment, bedding, and household utensils are stored along the rim of this section. Here, women prepare food, care for the children, and carry out their daily household chores alone or in the company of other women. Only men of the immediate family are permitted to enter this section. The other section is almost exclusively the domain of men. Women, frequently found in this section, will withdraw from the beit or move to the women's section when nonkinsmen or strangers enter it. The household head spends much of his time here. The focal point of this section is the coffee *mangal* (brazier), and he is constantly roasting, boiling, and warming the bitter coffee to serve to the seemingly never-ending stream of visitors.

Meals, prepared in the women's section, are served to the men and guests around the mangal on large aluminum trays. Three or four men eat at a time, relinquishing their places to other men when they have eaten what they want. Women remove the trays when all the men have eaten. The remaining food is then distributed to the rest of the family in the women's section. On the rare occasion when there are no visitors, the whole family eats in the women's section. Occasionally, older women, especially when beyond childbearing age, will eat with the men and guests around the mangal.

There are several variations in beit structure. At times, beits include a third section where sick or young animals are cared for by the women and young children. In addition, during the summer a few chickens are sometimes kept here. During the winter, families using the beit sha'ir change from the long, light, cloth tent to the black, compact, goat hair tent. The light-colored tent permits a good flow of air. Thus, it is more suited to the hot, dry summer, while the compact goat hair tent gives better protection against the cold, wet winter.

The beit is rarely found in isolation.[3] Rather, two or more beits commonly form a residence or camping unit. These units of either beit sha'ir or beit hajjar are almost exclusively kin-based, utilizing patrilineal ties and/or marriage ties. Often the camping or residence unit represents only a portion of a family group.

The term *beit,* besides describing the residence, is also used by the al-Fadl and al-Hassanna to refer to the kin group sharing the same residence. In general, the agnatic joint family of one, two, or three generations comprises the beit. On the average, the beit consists of ten or eleven individuals, although fifteen is not unusual. Among the al-Hassanna, for example, beit Abu Muhammad consisted of ten people: husband and wife, four unmarried sons, and four unmarried daughters. The only change in the composition of beit Abu Muhammad occurred when a married daughter, repudiated by her husband, returned to the beit with her three infants. Another example, among the al-Fadl, is beit Abu Ali which consisted of fifteen people: husband and wife and oldest son, with the son's first wife and three children as well as his second wife and eight children.

In general, al-Fadl and al-Hassanna tribal members are distinguished from the agricultural population in adjacent areas by a particular type of clothing. In fact, as in many other cultures, dress is a "badge" identifying a man or woman as belonging to a particular community. Men wear a traditional long dress and a white or patterned head cloth held in place by a double braided band. At times a "Western" jacket is worn over the dress, particularly when trips are taken to the city. The women, without exception, always wear traditional bedouin dress. This consists of a long dress that sweeps the ground, generally in solid brown, dark blue, or black, and one or two black scarfs. Younger girls generally wear more colorful dresses, and their head coverings are generally only one black scarf loosely covering the hair and neck. In contrast, married women wear two black scarfs, thus entirely covering the hair, neck, and upper chest. A solid or decorated black scarf secures the first solid black scarf in place. Differences in the cut of the dress, the way the scarf is tied, and the patterns of facial tattoos identify women as members of various tribal and subtribal units.

The veil does not appear in the description of women's dress. The term *veil* has unfortunately been loosely defined in the literature, and it encompasses a wide range of outer coverings: from the complete body covering of some Afghani women and the facial mask of Omani and Arabian Gulf women to the simple sheer cloth drawn across the bridge of the nose among some Egyptian women. In village and urban settings, these types of covering, as well as the closely associated practice of seclusion, increase in frequency as women rise in class. Women of bedouin groups who emigrate to towns or cities frequently adopt the local form of the veil. Often they look forward to wearing a veil as the mark of achieving higher social status as urbanites.

Underlying ideological principles concerning women's dress in the Middle East play a vital role in social control. Women (be they city, village, or nomadic women) are regarded by their societies as major repositories of the honor of the family or basic social unit. They are regarded as something sacred, to be protected from desecration, and a modesty code can be said to operate (see Antoun 1968). Modesty as defined in the Quran refers not to the veil but to outer clothing and demeanor. When not within her circle of kinsmen, a woman's outer covering serves as a form or symbol of her social distance and protection (see Murphy 1964). The extent to which distance and protection are required depends largely upon the particular social and physical environment. In heavily populated, ethnically heterogeneous areas where strangers are common, the outer covering of women may be elaborate and involve a full covering of the hair, face, and body. In sparsely populated, ethnically homogeneous areas or areas where strangers are rarely present, the outer covering may be quite simple. Among the bedouin women, the outer covering consists of two scarfs which cover the hair, neck, and jewelry worn on the upper chest. The face is not covered.

Traditional Economy and Way of Life

The life mode of the al-Fadl and the al-Hassanna is pastoralism, a mode ecologically adjusted to the utilization of agriculturally marginal resources that would otherwise be neglected. The very nature of pastoralism is such that no pastoral group is ever entirely self-sufficient. Rather, it is always tied in relations of interdependence and reciprocity to adjacent sedentary communities. In that manner, pastoralists are able to exchange their animal and dairy products with agriculturalists and urbanites for grains and other metal and leather specialized goods. In the Middle East this adaptation and symbiosis among nomadic tribespeople, villagers, and urbanites is frequently called the ecological trilogy (English 1966).

Too often the term *pastoralism* is interchanged or confused with the term *nomadism*. The latter, a definition of a type of spatial organization, needs to be distinguished from the first, a definition of a type of economic organization or mode of life. Although the two terms are often interrelated, their interrelationship is not absolute. For example, nomadism without pastoralism characterizes the spatial arrangements of the gypsies or *nawar* of the Mediterranean. Pastoralism without nomadism occurs when a sedentary population utilizes local pastures and subsists in a suitable habitat on the products of the domesticated animals as long as techniques for storage of fodder are developed. The definition of pastoralism used here is animal husbandry by natural graze with some access to crop cultivation (see Chatty 1973a, 1973b).

The stability of any pastoral population depends upon maintaining a balance among three phenomena: pasture carrying capacity, herd size, and human population. Various mechanisms operate to ensure that the size of the human population is responsive to the population pressure of the animals on the pasture. Surplus human population (and by association, animal population) is continuously drained off through sedentarization and emigration. The viability of a pastoral society depends to a great extent upon the full labor participation of all members (men and women) in animal husbandry subsistence.

The annual pastoral cycle of the al-Fadl and the al-Hassanna was, and to an extent still is, shaped by ecological factors. The 75-mile-long and 5- to 8-mile-wide Beqaa Valley is the major setting of their pastoral cycle. The year is divided into two basic seasons: a long, hot, dry summer and a cold, wet winter. Pastoral movements are largely characterized by adjustments to these seasons and the associated grass cover of grazing areas. At the close of the rainy season (April–early May), al-Fadl and al-Hassanna camping units gradually migrate into the Beqaa steppe along the Anti-Lebanon Mountains from the north and east. The women of each household dismantle and pack the tents on the backs of the household camels. Three, four, and sometimes as many as fifteen households move as a unit. The camels, carrying the household baggage, small children, and sometimes the women, are gradually moved south, along with the herds of sheep and goats.[4] The men and young boys graze the herds on the pasture lands along the base and slopes of the mountain range for one or two months. After the grain harvest in June, the al-Fadl and the al-Hassanna break up into smaller residence units rarely larger than three households. These smaller units maintain particular relationships with landowners in the Beqaa Valley. Each household head arranges with a landowner the rights to graze sheep on the stubble of harvested fields. This grazing pattern continues throughout the hot summer months. By late September or early October, the al-Fadl and al-Hassanna begin to return north, and most of the camping units are in the northern part of the Beqaa Valley by November. If the winter rains have commenced, the pastoralists move north and east to their traditional winter grazing land east of Homs (in the direction of Tudmor). These traditional pastures in the badia between Homs and Tudmor are in bloom during January, February, and March. Once there, camping units disperse, and, according to most informants, a relatively inactive period of pastoral activity sets in until the lambing of the flock in February and March.

Before the advent of the truck, the al-Fadl and al-Hassanna conducted their major trade and transactions during the summer months. The slow-moving baggage camels in large measure delimited the range of movement. Consequently, the buying and selling of critical items was conducted through middlemen and brokers along their migration routes, rather than at market centers. Three major activities were undertaken by the al-Fadl and al-Hassanna to generate adequate capital with which to meet their expenditures. These activities included selling sheep's milk and butter, selling sheep's wool and meat, and camel service.

During late winter, women collectively made butter from sheep's milk and sold it to the various middlemen they encountered as the camping units migrated southward down the Beqaa Valley. The proceeds from butter sales, though small, were considered the exclusive property of the women and were used to purchase either personal or family luxuries.

During the early part of May, men clipped the sheep. Wool merchants and livestock middlemen came to the al-Fadl and al-Hassanna camping units and entered into agreements with individual household heads to buy wool and animals, at a set price per animal regardless of weight. Credit was established upon which the individual households could draw later in the season to purchase winter provisions.

Another traditional activity among the al-Fadl and the al-Hassanna was camel service. Once the agricultural summer harvest began, each household was able to use its three or four baggage camels to generate income. A common labor rate enabled one man with one camel to earn the equivalent of $6.00 per day for transporting agricultural harvest.[5] Often the men of the household preferred to make such work arrangements with landowners with whom they already had grazing arrangements. Such employment generally lasted three months, with payments made to the men or older boys in either cash or crops. This payment, together with the credit arrangement from the sale of wool and meat, did not always meet household expenditure requirements. In such cases, debts would be carried over from one year to the next.

Thus, in the traditional economy, all members of the pastoral household were actively involved in animal husbandry subsistence. Women and young girls cared for young and sick animals, milked the camels, sheep, and goats daily, and turned whatever surplus there was into butter to sell to middlemen. In addition, they regularly set up and dismantled camps when the household moved to follow optimal grazing conditions. Men and young boys herded the sheep and goats, clipped the wool, and entered into grazing and camel service agreements with local farmers and landowners. Very often during periods of heavy activity, the younger children and infants were left under the supervision of the oldest male or female of the household. In this traditional economy emphasis was placed on the active participation of all members of the household to maintain rather than increase production.

The Truck Replaces the Camel

In the mid-1960s (1963–1965) a change occurred within the Beits of these sheep-raising tribal units. Decisions were reached by the heads of extended families (tribal elders) to improve upon their mode of transportation and their beasts of burden. The camels, on which these units relied, were sold, and trucks were bought to replace them.[6] Within a two-year span, these decisions were so widespread that camels, which only recently were counted in the several thousands, virtually disappeared from the Beqaa Valley.

Male and Female Attitudes toward the Camel and the Truck

Camels were no longer found among the al-Fadl and the al-Hassanna in 1972. Whenever a discussion turned to the subject of the beast of burden, a pronounced difference of opinion inevitably arose between men and women. Men in general expressed their satisfaction with the shift from camel to truck and manifested an attachment to the truck which they had not held for the camel.

Women in general expressed a satisfaction with the economic benefits that the truck made possible. However, when men depreciated the camel as having been an economic handicap, women quickly defended the camel as something of a symbol of the "good old times" and extolled its virtues.

For example, during a discussion with a married couple, Ibrahim and Khadra', Ibrahim explained that the camels had been replaced by trucks because they were too difficult to care for. They needed constant supervision during herding because of their highly scattered grazing formation (a tendency to move about widely, sampling shrubs and grasses). Their tendency to break formation and disperse during migration used to cause considerable delay. Ibrahim also complained of the trouble that had come as a result of the agricultural development of the area. As more and more orchards were cultivated, closer supervision of camels was needed to avoid crop damage. Finally, Ibrahim complained about the feet of the camels. Their flat, padded feet had little traction on slippery surfaces, and as more roads were being paved, camel transport came to be extremely hazardous. The combination of paved roads and cars, according to Ibrahim, finally turned the camels into a burden. Clearly, men's attachment to the camel, in the past, was based primarily on economics.

Khadra', on the other hand, claimed that in the old times, when they had camels, they used to have a good and easy life. Her comments were not a defense of the past economic benefit of the camel, but rather reflected an emotional association of the past with the camel. "What a difference between the comfortable and easy life we used to have and the hard one now." When I asked Khadra' what was easy about the old life, she explained that when they had camels, women always worked together, and work was like entertainment. For example, milking a camel required at least two women, one woman to hobble the animal and keep other camels away and another to collect the milk.[7] She added that not only milking but also cheese-making and rug-weaving were once pleasurable cooperative tasks for women. And, as a final point, she added that packing and unpacking camp was always entertaining, for one never knew how many times the women, who always rode on the camels, would fall off during the journey. These reminiscences of Khadra' reveal the emotional attachment and nostalgia which women generally feel about previous times. But more than that they indicate a very real spiritual loss. Women regret the loss of certain elements of female communal solidarity and cooperation which, to them, were associated with the camel.

The truck, as a "beast of burden," was not frequently discussed by women. Although they did not criticize the vehicle, they did not praise it in the same manner as they praised the camel. Their remarks were generally confined to the sphere of market production. The women expressed satisfaction with the daily pickup of milk by the dairy companies and the great increase in capital they were accumulating. However, women had little, if any, contact with the household truck. They took no part in the decorating, cleaning, or mechanical repair and upkeep of the vehicles, whereas they had themselves once decorated the camels with handwoven tassels and ropes.

Men, on the other hand, were continuously occupied and concerned with the truck. Anecdotes about recent adventures, mishaps, and accidents with motor vehicles were prominent in their daily conversation. The men were physically involved with the truck. During the dry summer season, there was not one day in which a truck, parked by a home, was not cleaned and dusted by the men and boys. Unlike other mechanical instruments (tape recorders, radios), these vehicles were constantly cared for. Scratches were covered, engines were kept in tune, dents were removed, and the body of the vehicle was always gaily decorated. Talismans and proverbs to ward off the evil eye were always found somewhere on the vehicle as were tassels, photographs, and mementos.

Settlement and Work Patterns

With the shift from camel transport to truck transport, a striking physical change in living arrangements took place, affecting men's and women's roles. Before the advent of the truck, camping units, usually of two, three, or four households, had a migratory range of over two hundred kilometers through populated areas. Labor requirements included two or three young boys to take care of goats and sheep and at least two young men to tend the camels when they were used for harvest transport. Camel transport required numerous stops along the traditional migration routes from summer to winter pasture. These camps, set up and dismantled by women, were generally in remote areas along the Anti-Lebanon Mountains. The sheep and goats were then taken daily by the young boys to graze on natural pastures adjacent to the camps.

Today, in using the truck, camping or residence units are no longer found scattered in remote or distant areas. Rather, they are generally found by the side of secondary roads accessible by truck. Very little attention is now given to the distance between the herds and the residences. At times, the household's sheep are ten to fifteen kilometers from the settlement. Given the greater distance now found between herds and residences, young boys are no longer permitted to act as shepherds; older boys or hired men are preferred. Furthermore, although the truck restricts camping grounds to areas reached by roads, its use releases the household from the necessity of migrations that once took several weeks. With the truck, the same journey is now possible in as little as a half a day.

The truck was also instrumental in changing other work patterns of the members of the pastoral household. Traditionally, work patterns had been almost exclusively cooperative efforts to maintain the pastoral family's viability in subsistence activities. With the truck, work patterns in the household shifted their orientation, and many time-consuming traditional activities were modified or discarded.

The shift to truck transport not only reduced the time needed for actual migrations, but it also reduced the frequency of moving camp. At the present time, a camping unit rarely moves more than two or three times during the same season (in contrast with the seven or eight moves made previously). Fewer migrations has meant less work for the men. At the same time, the traditional method for earning a secondary income by hiring out camels is no longer available to a number of men. Today one truck can operate for the benefit of several households.[8] However, one truck used by one individual now can complete the same amount of work that previously had required about fifteen camels and as many men. Thus, the shift from camel to truck transport has removed a large number of men from active participation in the use of this valuable tool. Many men once involved in camel service now work seasonally in a variety of occupations. Roughly one-fourth of these men work in the newly developed sugar beet factories in the region.

Those men who use the truck most frequently have become the entrepreneurs of the pastoral community. Their economic and recreational activities, often conducted in the company of male kinsmen of their Beits,[9] are no longer confined to areas adjacent to the community settlement. Such activities, involving travel over long distances, now require personal initiative and financial and personal risk and can produce great profits.

Among the women many time-consuming activities have been replaced. For example, food preparation, especially cheese and butter production, is no longer undertaken in the household. Instead, cheese and butter are bought from adjacent markets, and more practical and less time-consuming food preparations are undertaken (that is, a shift from preserved to fresh food preparation). Furthermore, since the number of migrations has greatly decreased, the women's responsibility for setting up and dismantling camp has declined. For the married women, in particular, this has created a greater amount of free time. Traditionally a large amount of women's time had been devoted to rug-making and weaving in general. These rugs often had been given as wedding presents from mother to daughter. Today, the traditional handicraft of rug-making is no longer practiced, as the camel's hair necessary for this craft can no longer be obtained.

Unmarried young girls traditionally assisted married women in their tasks. Today, however, they collectively engage in seasonal labor in adjacent areas. This development is a direct result of the reduction in frequency of camp moves. As households tended to become relatively stable in an area, they began to conclude agreements of longer duration with farmers and large landowners. At first these work agreements involved only older boys, but by 1972 agreements were made whereby young girls, in groups, were also collected by trucks of landowners, taken to work in the fields, and returned to the residence units. Thus, reduced camp movements meant less work for the women, and the younger girls were freed to earn extra income along with the older boys to support the household.

In sum, then, work patterns among the al-Fadl and al-Hassanna have shifted from traditional cooperative activities for maintaining household viability to work patterns that include the incorporation of new cooperative activities for market-oriented production. This shift has strengthened the solidarity of the Beit not only among men and boys, but also among the women and young girls.

The coexistence of traditional as well as new cooperative patterns of activity is seen in the description of one day's events for six members of the domestic unit of beit Abu Ali. The head of this unit, Abu Ali, is perhaps the least physically active member. He is, however, continuously involved in sedentary activities that regulate and promote the well-being of the unit. For example, greeting visitors is one of his duties. In the past most visitors were tribesmen, but today they are usually villagers, military personnel, or business associates from distant cities. Any situation or problem involving a member of the Beit is brought to his attention, and he frequently acts as mediator or arbitrator in disputes. Today, between visits from other household heads or locally prominent villagers, Abu Ali devotes his time to teaching young boys to read. Education traditionally is regarded as vital to the bedouin, since it is believed that only by being able to read the Quran can one fulfill one's religious duties. Formerly a religious man was contracted to spend a season with a Beit teaching the children—a practice that has declined during the last twenty years. Today, it is the tribal elders who devote much of their time to the education of children.

The son of Abu Ali, Abu Malik, is frequently absent from the physical residence, attending to the household's herds and other holdings. He, too, is concerned about the formal education of the children. Many of his business and entrepreneurial efforts are directed toward creating profits that will enhance the children's educational opportunities. Although unable to read, Abu Malik is preparing to sell a hundred head of sheep to build a school house, if a government teacher can be found to teach in the community during the spring. However, as the al-Fadl and al-Hassanna are not considered Lebanese citizens, such an arrangement will be difficult.

Rifaa'i, the nephew of Abu Ali, is perhaps the most conspicuously absent member. Much of his time is spent driving a truck to take care of herd management and commerce. His activities are generally conducted together with his close male kinsmen. Under the supervision of Abu Ali and Abu Malik, Rifaa'i is a major contributor to the economic productivity of this unit.

Umm Ali is Abu Ali's wife and, as *ahl-il-beit,* is in charge of many aspects of the domestic unit. Although not the most physically active woman, she is continuously occupied overseeing the smooth functioning of the domestic unit. She holds the purse-strings of the beit. Small purchases are made by her whenever itinerant merchants come to the residence. The major purchases for winter provisions made at the close of the summer season are generally requisitioned by her and brought by the men. While she spends a good part of the morning smoking a water pipe in the women's section, she also greets her husband's guests and looks after their comfort. She supervises the preparation of meals and personally carries food to Abu Ali and his guests at the *majlis* (salon). In addition, she cares for the young children and infants during the mornings and afternoons when their mothers are busy with household or pastoral chores.

Umm Malik, the wife of Abu Malik, is perhaps the most physically active individual within the confines of the residence unit. Only when she visits her family for a day or when she goes to market in nearby towns is she ever absent from the residence. Her day is almost completely devoted to household chores (bread-baking, milking, food preparation, sewing, washing clothes, washing children, sweeping, and so on) and the supervision of the daily sale of milk to the dairy. Although Umm Malik has eight children, child-rearing as an activity is not separated from the general work in the beit. All women as well as older children cooperatively tend to infants and younger children. Nursing an infant is not considered as an exclusive category, but can and does overlap with numerous work and leisure-time activities.

Zeina, the daughter of Abu Malik, is frequently absent from the residence unit. She contributes to the household primarily through her work on an adjacent farm. This is especially during the summer, when she donates her daily labor earnings to her grandmother, Umm Ali. Her activities within the household are relatively light, consisting of simple chores or taking charge of young children and infants. Nonetheless, her support of the domestic unit is significant.

Leisure-Time Activities

The shift from camel to truck was a key factor in not only creating new cooperative work patterns within the household, but also in increasing periods of leisure time. Among the married and unmarried men, the increase in free time is frequently used to pursue new economic activities. Moreover, with the increased mobility that the truck offers, groups of young men frequently travel great distances in just one day. Visiting is no longer restricted to adjacent communities, but once or twice a week includes trips to friends and distant kinsmen in Beirut. Thus, men and young boys are able to pursue not only individual activities removed from the sphere of the pastoral economy, but are also able to develop social networks far exceeding tribal bonds.

Furthermore, young boys reaching the traditional *khayal* stage (19–20 years) are beginning to work seasonally on farms. Part of their income is set aside for future marriage expenses. The remainder of their income is occasionally used to purchase motorcycles.[10] This vehicle has become an object of prestige in much the same manner as the horse traditionally was. It is being used by the khayal for racing as well as games and exhibition riding at feasts or festivals.[11]

Among the married women and young girls, leisure activities follow traditional patterns, as they have little access to the trucks and public transportation is not yet well developed. Perhaps young girls have the least leisure time; after working from sunrise to mid-afternoon in agricultural fields, they generally must carry out light housekeeping tasks, such as bringing water, sweeping out the tent, washing pots, or tending to their younger siblings.

Older married women appear to have relatively more leisure time. Although the English expression "a woman's work is never done" holds true for the women of the al-Fadl and al-Hassanna, two or three hours of each day are spent sitting together with close kinswomen, smoking a water-pipe, drinking sweet tea, and discussing subjects of mutual interest and expertise: betrothals, forthcoming marriages, and imminent repudiations and divorces. Since the truck has reduced the number of migration stops per year, women's traditional opportunities for visiting during migrations have been greatly reduced. And as women are kept somewhat removed from the truck, long-distance visiting is almost nil.

While traditional visiting patterns have been restricted, women's traditional solidarity within the Beit has not declined. Residence patterns in bedouin society are patrilocal, and the strong preference for endogamous or, more specifically, parallel cousin marriage, serves to keep kinswomen close together. At marriage, the bride joins a unit of people who are blood relatives, rather than a group of strangers.

Conclusion

The shift from camel transport to truck transport among the al-Fadl and the al-Hassanna has directly and indirectly generated widespread changes in their total organization. Within the pastoral family, these changes are characterized by a shift from basically subsistence orientation to market orientation.

Traditionally, both men and women in the household were actively involved in subsistence production and contributed on a fairly equal basis to the labor demands of the pastoral household. Today, new patterns of work, cooperation, and enterprise are developing within the household. These new patterns, entailing the utilization of truck transport to manage the circulation and distribution of livestock produce, call for the contribution of men and women alike. Market-oriented production involves not only men and young boys, but also women and young girls. It is the women, today, who manage and sell the daily surplus of milk to dairy companies. Even the young girls actively contribute to the market economy through their seasonal agricultural labor.

This new orientation toward large-scale market production is not a step in the direction of settlement (a shift from nomadic pastoralism to settled agriculture). On the contrary, it is a "modernizing" of the pastoral way of life. As such, it seems unlikely that the men and women in bedouin pastoral society will be forced to give up their particular customs and values and adopt those of the settled agricultural communities (such as the veil and seclusion of women).

The shift from camel to truck transport has been a positive factor in the pastoral way of life, in general, and in the maintenance of family and lineage solidarity, in particular. The truck's use, however, has affected men and women differently. The emotional attachment women once felt for the camel has not been transferred to the truck. Though women now have increased interaction with nontribesmen, their access to tribal nonkinswomen has declined. Men, who did not appear to have an emotional attachment to the camel, now place a high value on the truck. This value is not simply based on economics; it also relates to the fact that the truck has become a focal point of male solidarity.

Among the al-Fadl and the al-Hassanna, men's and women's roles are being modified to accommodate changes in their total environment. Men, having access to the truck, exhibit mobility and enhanced individualism. Women, initially less mobile and somewhat tied to the household, have, nonetheless, rights over certain newly developed resources. One can foresee that later, as these changes grow more radical, women will further develop their opportunities.

Notes

1. *Syria* as a geographical expression has been variously defined. The term *Greater Syria,* no longer a political entity, is perhaps more appropriate for defining the region under consideration. The present definition of the frontiers of Syria is principally a legacy of the Inter-War Mandate. The French subdivided "Syria" into two political entities. One, Lebanon, was made into a larger territory than its old name implied. The other, Syria, became unrecognizably smaller. The Beqaa Valley, politically part of present-day Lebanon, is a natural continuation of the plain of Homs in Syria.

2. The term *beit* is used here to describe the physical structure, as well as the kin group sharing the structure. The term *Beit* is used to describe the minimal lineage.

3. A tent count in the Beqaa Valley indicated a pastoral community of approximately two hundred households. My sample consisted of thirty-one households.

4. A household needed a minimum of three camels to transport tents and supplies, as well as family members. Before 1963, 135 sheep and goats were necessary for a viable household, according to al-Fadl informants.

5. Fifteen Lebanese pounds; $1.00 equaled 2.5 Lebanese pounds in 1973.

6. Of the eight vehicles in my sample of thirty-one households, there were four Chevrolet and Honda half-ton trucks, two International Harvester tractors and bale wagons, and one stake truck.

7. In contrast, the milking of sheep does not require cooperative effort. It can be done by one woman. After tying the sheep in a double row head to head, one woman alone can easily milk thirty to forty sheep at a sitting.

8. The replacement of camels with trucks required a group effort within the Beit: several households had to participate in order to purchase a truck.

9. This association of male kinsmen is structurally identical to the traditional *khamsa* unit of the Beit. This unit traditionally operated for the defense of the Beit and its honor and prestige, but ceased to function effectively with the advent of the French military control in the region after the 1920s.

10. In one Beit, three of the fourteen unmarried young men owned motorcycles.

11. The similarity in social value of the truck and motorcycle is most apparent during festivals. For example, during three weddings in 1973, the bride was taken from her father's household and placed on the back of a truck with her possessions. The bride's brothers and cousins (khayal) joined the head of the procession on motorcycles. Traditionally, the khayal would have been mounted on horses, and the bride would have been seated on a camel.

Bibliography

Antoun, Richard. "On the Modesty of Women in Arab Muslim Villages: A Study in the Accommodation of Traditions." *American Anthropologist,* 70 (1968) :671–697.

Chatty, Dawn. "Pastoralism: Adaptation and Optimization." *Folk* (1973a) : 27–38.

———. "Structuring Forces of Pastoral Nomadism in Southwest Asia." *Development and Change* (1973b) :51–73.

English, Paul. *City and Village in Iran: Settlement and Economy in the Kerman Basin.* Madison, Wisc., 1966.

Montagne, Robert. *La civilisation du désert.* Paris, 1947.

Mead, Margaret. *Sex and Temperament in Three Primitive Societies.* New York, 1935.

Murphy, Robert. "Social Distance and the Veil (Tuareg) ." *American Anthropologist,* 66 (1964) :1257–1274.

Rosaldo, Michelle, and Louise Lamphere, eds. *Woman, Culture, and Society.* Stanford, Calif., 1974.

Thomas, Elizabeth Marshall. *The Harmless People.* New York, 1958.

Turnbull, Colin. *The Forest People.* New York, 1962.

20 Working Women in a Moroccan Village

Susan Schaefer Davis

While several studies have dealt with women's economic roles and related statuses in a generalized and multicultural manner,[1] more detailed data on the problem of women's economic roles in specific societies are rarer. This essay examines the economic roles available to Muslim women in one large Moroccan village and assesses the effects that playing these roles have on their status in Moroccan society.[2] A few sociological rather than ethnographic studies have discussed the relationship between women's economic roles and their status in Morocco. Forget, in a study of attitudes toward work, concluded that the majority (60 percent) of her urban sample favored female employment (1962). Nouacer suggested that factors entering into the evaluation of different women's jobs include whether they were traditional or modern and if they required contact with men (1962). In a 1966 survey of Rabat University students (a very different and select sample, presenting the views of the most educated part of the population), Martensson found that approximately 61 percent of the males and 73 percent of the females had favorable attitudes toward women's working professionally outside the home. If these favorable attitudes translate into a positive status for the working woman in Morocco, and if urbanites and villagers have the same attitudes, similar results should be found in the data presented in this essay.

The Village

The data for this essay come from a large Arabic-speaking village (population about ten thousand) in Morocco (a Muslim Arab and Berber country), located on the inland edge of a fertile agricultural area that had much French colonial contact.[3] While much of the population is involved in agriculture, it is employed mostly as wage laborers or sharecroppers on large and often modern farms, not on personal or tribal plots as was traditionally the case. The main crops grown today are wheat, oranges, olives, chickpeas, and sugar beets. Persons are also engaged in commerce (local shops), transport, and a few in industry in the nearby town's oil refinery. Because the larger town is only three kilometers away, there is a great deal of contact with current events and modernization; in fact, in 1972 there were perhaps fifty television sets in prosperous village homes. Yet the village has no running water and no paved roads or civic services such as a post office or police station; the nearby larger town seems to have a monopoly on these amenities. However, the village under study does have a primary school, a women's center (also used for civic celebrations), and a mosque and a saint's tomb that are the centers for a religious brotherhood having branches in several of the larger cities. Because this village has nearly ten thousand inhabitants, it offers a wider range of activities by which a woman can support herself than would a smaller village, but this range does not include options found *only* in larger villages; all would be found, some in one village, others in another. So while the village is less than strictly traditional, it does offer an almost complete array of the activities open to rural women today. Some of these activities are traditional, while others are of more recent origin.

Economic Activities of Village Women

If a Moroccan woman wants to support herself, what are her options? Strictly speaking, the fact that she is in the position to support herself implies a limitation of options. In a traditional village a woman does not usually *choose* to take on an activity to earn additional income or enrich her life as a Westerner might; rather, she does it out of necessity.[4] This necessity usually arises because her husband divorces or repudiates her and for some reason she cannot fall back on her family, or because the husband cannot or will not support her and the children even though they are still married. There is no tradition of professional single women in this area; women expect to be supported first by their families and later by their husband. Marriage is the norm for women in Morocco and virtually *every* woman marries; those who are single are temporarily divorcées. A recent study found that divorce is very common in Morocco, with 55 percent of the marriages of rural women in the sample ending in divorce (Maher 1974:194). If a woman bears no children she will almost certainly be divorced, and if she bears only daughters the husband may divorce her or marry a second wife simultaneously in order to produce male heirs. Incompatibility and the family's financial status are also factors in divorce. Laws exist providing for the payment of alimony or part of the bridewealth to the woman upon divorce, but they are infrequently enforced. There are also occasional cases of widows and a few spinsters who have no family to support them; how do these women manage to survive economically?

The women discussed here fall outside the ideal norm.[5] In distress, there *are* certain alternatives available to females, however, and these are described along with their implications for women's status.[6] There are only a few ways in which a village woman can support herself and increase her status simultaneously. The traditional public baths have men's and women's hours, and a woman who is often the wife, widow, or mother of the owner controls them during the women's hours. The small amount ($0.15) that each woman pays for admission is hers (even if she does have a husband), and she is responsible for managing the help, keeping the fires going to heat the water, and breaking up the inevitable fights over pails for water. This is one of the most profitable of the available activities, but is only open to those who already have some capital. This implies that a bath mistress does not always work from necessity, and this is indeed the case. In the two village baths, one woman was a member of an important family and worked there partly to earn her own spending money (to spend on things like a $1,000 gold belt) and partly to help maintain her important status in the village. In an area where women are still generally secluded, the bath is one of the main places where women of all families and social classes meet and gossip; most go once every week or two. Although clanging pails, splashing water, and crying children all conspire against it, the bath is one of the main centers of communication. The other bath mistress in the village used to run her family's bath for her son on women's day, keeping something less than the total earnings for herself. However, her husband recently died and with her share of the estate she purchased full rights to the bath, which she now runs as a means of livelihood. While her family-based social status is below that of the other bath mistress because her male relatives hold no important positions, she is still an important personage in the village because she is the hub of the women's communication network. This role has traditionally been available to women in villages large enough to support a public bath, but may decrease in the future when most homes have private baths.

Table 20.1. Effects of wage-earning activities on women's status and subsistence level.

EFFECT ON STATUS	INCOME-EARNING ACTIVITIES	ADEQUATE SUPPORT[a]	MINIMAL SUPPORT[b]	INSUFFICIENT SUPPORT[c]
INCREASE				
	Bath mistress	x		
	Seamstress-teacher	x		
	Seamstress	x		
	Holy woman			x
	Musician			x
	Midwife			x
NEUTRAL				
	Clothes washing			x
	Cooking (celebrations)			x
	Spinning, weaving			x
	Raising small animals			x
	Broom making		x	
	Clay brazier making		x	
	Live-in household helper		x	
SMALL DECREASE[d]				
	Water fetching			x
	Grain gleaning			x
	Bath masseuse		x	
	Bread baking and selling		x	
AMBIVALENT				
	Witch/magician			x
	Fortune-teller/seer			x
	Teacher	x		
SIGNIFICANT DECREASE				
	Field laborer	x		
	Prostitute	x		

a. Woman can support herself and family adequately.

b. Woman can earn enough money to barely subsist.

c. Woman cannot earn enough to subsist; several are frequently combined to earn a living.

d. These lower women's status since they cause a woman to be seen in public.

Since no one in the village has running water yet, the extinction of the bath mistress does not seem imminent.

Another way to support oneself and raise one's status is to be either a seamstress or a seamstress-teacher. The former sews clothing on her own machine, usually for children and women who bring her their cloth. In a large village, a seamstress with a reputation for good work can usually accumulate enough cash-paying customers to make a living. Traditionally, she sewed by hand, but now virtually all seamstresses have manual, treadle, or electric sewing machines. A new source of income, owing to the nearness of the larger town, is sewing ready-made clothing to be sold by shop owners there. A seamstress will ask shop owners if they have any work, and, after doing a few test-garments to demonstrate her skill, will make garments from the shop owner's cloth in her home, receiving a set fee for each garment completed. While exact figures are unavailable, approximately thirty local women worked as seamstresses. A seamstress-teacher may sew garments for money, but her main job is to teach young adolescent girls the skills of cutting out and sewing traditional women's clothing and more modern styles for children. Much more than the ordinary seamstress, a "good character" is a necessary attribute for a woman in this role. Her home, in addition to being a classroom for the teaching of sewing skills, serves as a young ladies' finishing school. The novel *Confidences d'une fille de la nuit* (Bonjean 1968) describes a more elaborate form of this in the home of a *sherifa* (woman of a saintly lineage) in Fez, where the girls sew, embroider, sing, pray, cook, clean . . . and learn to be all-around gentlewomen. The village equivalent is not nearly so thorough as its counterpart in urban areas; there is no praying, and any singing just accompanies the work. But in turn for being accepted as students, the girls agree to clean house, occasionally cook, and do errands for their teacher, in addition to paying a fee in kind (sugar, tea, or oil) or in cash. They thus learn to fulfill their teacher's high standards in these areas, and to sit politely and quietly while learning their sewing—or risk being expelled. Visiting the seamstress or seamstress-teacher is another of the few chances adolescent girls and women have to meet women outside the family and neighborhood group with which they usually interact, and the seamstress' house, and the woman herself, are centers of communication for women of the village.

To become a seamstress one does not need much capital; the skill is the most necessary aspect. Many girls receive this training (in preference to public schooling) and acquire machines as adolescents, so some divorcées will be able to earn money this way. However, those without the training will seldom seek it after a divorce; rather they will turn to another alternative. The seamstress-teacher does not in theory need more capital than the seamstress, but in fact she often has more. This is because she conducts classes in her home, implying she has a home large enough for this. More importantly, her main asset is a good reputation, something which she has built for years. It cannot be suddenly achieved if she should need it to start a school. Since they must know and teach the ways of a gentlewoman, one frequently finds seamstress-teachers coming from better families, where they have received such training. This does not mean that the poorer women cannot hold this role, assuming that they possess the requisite good reputation, but rather indicates that in fact these women are often better off to begin with than their counterparts who are seamstresses only.

For the above occupations there have been certain prerequisites: capital, previous training, or a virtuous reputation. Most women who need to support themselves are lacking in these, so that these status-raising remunerative activities are actually available to very few women. There are other activities available to women that can also be remunerative and raise one's status, but they serve both these functions to a lesser degree than those described above. These include the roles of holy woman, musician, and midwife, all of which also require a special talent.

The village is the home of a brotherhood, the members of which trace their origins back to the Prophet Muhammad.[7] In 1971 there were 324 living members of this saintly lineage, presumably about 160 of them females of various ages. In addition there are present women from other saintly lineages, imported to marry the local *shorfa* (saintly endogamy is preferred) or who have come to the area for other reasons. A woman of a holy lineage, a sherifa, is a unique type of specialist. Although other women's status derives from their own and/or their husband's activities, a sherifa has an inherited rank as a member of a saintly lineage. While she can raise or lower her status by her own behavior, inherited rank places her above other women from birth, so that ordinary women in need can never become sherifat. She has contact with the supernatural because of her descent rather than her current activities, as do some of the women described below. She may be sought out for advice by other women *if* she is highly respected (as only a handful of the plentiful local sherifat are), but she does not play a formal religious role. She is not usually paid directly, but if she is poor people may give her gifts of food and clothing. This is not a role that any woman can choose to support herself, but one that can be parlayed into income for a woman who has the correct genealogy and is in need.

Another type of female specialist is the musician. While certain types of prostitutes also sing and dance, there are a few women who are musicians only and play drums and sing in small groups at respectable women's parties such as birth celebrations, circumcisions, or weddings. While the men's half (the sexes do not mix at such parties) of these family celebrations will often engage singers who are also prostitutes, it is not considered proper for the women to do so (though they love to peek at them dancing for the men). Instead, they have a female musician's group that just plays while individual women at the party dance for each other. The musicians usually play popular folk tunes, but sometimes have contact with the spirit world when certain guests dance into trances. This is characteristic of only a few women, who have a particular tune (belonging to a particular spirit) that will possess them, and they dance until they collapse.[8] The musicians must play this tune when necessary, but not so long as to exhaust or harm the dancer. In general, the musicians are not seen as working with the supernatural as are the fortune-teller/seer and the witch/magician, and they are well-accepted members of the community. They can earn up to twenty-five dirhams[9] each at a "fancy" party, and while this is a good supplement, even in this large village where they are the only group, there are not enough celebrations for one to live entirely by this means. This activity is again of limited access; it requires training or talent, and local celebrations can only support four women in this way.

A third specialized role is that of the midwife. Since until recently there were no medical facilities locally available (and even currently these are seldom used), nearly all births occur at home. There are several midwives in the village, and a family usually chooses one as one elsewhere would choose a doctor to assist at the birth of all the children. The midwife is paid in cash at the time of the birth (as little as one dirham, a bargain compared with the twenty dirhams fee the hospital charges) and is also remembered with gifts of food and clothing on subsequent holidays. Her contact with the supernatural, like that of the musicians, is limited, hers to a few propitiations to ward off evil spirits during the birth. She, too, is an accepted member of the community, and falls into an affectionate and loose kinship-type role with the children she has delivered. As with the two previous roles, however, one needs training or talent to become a midwife, and a woman will not become rich doing any of the three.

The majority of the options available to village women for self-support have little effect on their status, aside from the fact that the necessity to work at all will lower it somewhat. These are termed *neutral* activities. It should be noted that the activities that require a woman to appear in public, thus displaying her lack of a male supporter, do lower her status a bit more than other neutral activities that occur within a house. It is also apparent that most of these activities provide very little income, so that a woman must combine several of them to support herself.

Most of the neutral activities are traditional household tasks of females and have only recently become locally available as "jobs" because of the increasing prosperity of some village families. While wealthy city families may have employed women in these capacities for centuries, it is only recently that a substantial number of rural women have filled these jobs. A rough estimate would be that 30 percent of village women engage at some time in one of these occupations. This is not to imply that these women support themselves in this way; many married women may occasionally do one of the jobs discussed below for extra pocket money. A much smaller number combine the jobs into a means of self-support.

A woman may help another (who is not a relative—one would help a relative without charge) with washing clothes, an exhausting job, given large families and no running water. The water is brought from the river by a boy on donkeyback, and washing is done in metal tubs made from the bottom quarter of an oil drum. Women living near the river often do all their wash there, saving the cost of water ($0.08 for twenty gallons) and getting a chance to gossip.

Other activities require *some* specialization, but a degree that many women have or can easily achieve. These include cooking for celebrations and spinning and weaving wool. While most women cook the food for family celebrations themselves, an especially large or extravagant one will require extra help. The women who are called in have a reputation for being good cooks and knowing special dishes and are also known to need money. (Many women of the best local families have all the requisite skills, but would only be asked for advice, never to contribute labor.) Similarly, some women cannot spin and weave all the wool to make blankets and men's *djellabas* or outer robes for their families, so they pay someone they know who is particularly skilled at these tasks to do it for them. There is some competition from men in weaving, and men actually have shops and support themselves in this way, while the women work at home part-time and charge less. There is also a market for spun wool at the weekly local *suq;* a woman may spin wool, either loosely (to be used for weft threads) or very tightly (for warp threads) and take it to the suq to sell.

Women also raise rabbits and chickens to sell at the suq. This is one of the few of these activities that well-off women as well as women needing money may engage in for remuneration with no social stigma attached. Whatever the case, the money earned this way belongs only to the woman, not to the husband or the whole family, and is hers to do with as she likes. In the case of better-off women, this may be the only personal money they have, the rest being wheedled from the husband. Ironically, the poorer women have more personal control of money since they earn it themselves.

A few of the neutral activities may provide enough income to barely support a woman without combining jobs. Two other jobs in which women may make enough cash to scrape by involve manufacture in the home, for sale, of clay braziers and palmetto-leaf brooms. The raw materials can be gathered free, and although both items often need replacement, one needs many clients to make even a meager income, and usually old women without families to support engage in these activities. Sometimes women do supplement this with another activity, like one of those described below. It is interesting to note that the braziers are made of clay from the river bank, as are the large jars used for carrying and storing water. However, the jars are more nearly perfect in form because they are made on a wheel at the pottery works—which employs only men. Although these women are not especially respected by the community, they are not censured either; since they *do* work inside their homes, they are usually considered "nice ladies."

Unsupported women can sometimes subsist by living with another family, usually one related to them. In the case of a divorced woman who returns to her parents' home, she is supported as she was before marriage, although perhaps with some reluctance because she was not expected to return. She is not actually employed in this case, yet acts as a general helper, readily doing tasks no one else wants to do to justify her presence. However, she earns no actual cash and is closely controlled by her family, so she usually does not enjoy this type of support.

The neutral activities that somewhat lower a woman's status because they involve her appearance in public include the jobs of water carrier, grain gleaner, masseuse in the public baths, and bread seller. Women fetch all the water for drinking, cooking, and utensil-washing from the well. With only two wells in the village to serve ten thousand people, one can wait several hours for a turn. Because of this young girls are often sent; an older woman needs to be home to manage the house. Like the public bath, the well is a center for communications, so that the women who do have to go do not resent it as much as they might. However, those who can afford it pay a woman about five dirhams a month to bring them one or two jugs of drinking water every morning, usually before dawn as the well is least crowded then.

Another activity is one that all families probably engaged in when they had their own land: gleaning the grain left on the ground after the harvest. Now that most families do not live directly off the land and most farms are large and not self-owned, only some women still do this. The landowners regard allowing this as a form of charity, and poor women do it, sometimes accumulating one or two sacks of wheat if especially industrious. Since it is after the harvest, this occurs in June or July when the sun is very hot, and one must remain bent double looking for the fallen heads of grain. It is excruciating work, and obviously only those who are really poor engage in it.

While the bath mistress collects the admission fee, she usually has two or three women working for her inside the bath. These women, the "scrubbers," work all day in the hot steam, filling and carrying pails of water for the bathers and rubbing them down with a coarse string sponge to remove dirt and dry layers of skin. One can do all these chores oneself, but higher-status women usually have the scrubber do them and pay her around one dirham. She is also paid a daily wage by the bath mistress, and combining the two she can usually manage to survive. This is a low-status job, more because of the strenuous work than because of the public appearance. Because there are only two baths in town, there are just a few openings.

Another limited-opportunity, lower-status neutral job is the baking and selling of bread. Bread is the staple of the Moroccan diet, and every household makes bread once or twice daily and sends it to the public oven to be baked. Bread is only *bought* by bachelors or families with unexpected guests, and because the village is large, enough bread can be sold daily for two or three women to earn money in this way. These are older women past childbearing age and the only females to be seen as vendors in all the shops along the main street. Although this job is of rather recent origin because of the increased population and especially work-seeking bachelors in the village, it is threatened by the commercial bakeries in the nearby town.

A few of the ways in which women can earn income have an ambivalent effect on their status; that is, women in these jobs are both respected *and* feared, and sometimes even despised. This is at least partially due to the fact that these women deal with the supernatural in their roles as fortune-teller/seer or witch/magician.

The fortune-teller or seer and the witch/magician may be one woman or two separate ones. The fortune-teller/seer often uses Tarot-like cards to tell fortunes and may also discover the reason for an illness or the whereabouts of a missing person. The witch/magician is more active in such matters; rather than discovering things, she prepares potions and spells to deal with certain problems such as an unamorous husband or the cure or cause of illness. She deals mainly in what is often called "black magic"; "white magic" is done by men, either religious teachers who know Arabic and the Quran and can use them to advantage in their craft or by male magicians without religious training. Female magicians have no ties to formal Islam; in fact, there are no formal religious roles for village women. It has been observed that while men's magic deals more with incantations, formulas, and writing, women's is more straightforward and generally involves poisoning, usually of husbands. These women, both the fortune-teller/seers and the witch/magicians, are usually old and are viewed with apprehension, especially by men. Women cannot easily enter these occupations at any stage of their lives; rather they are socialized into them, often by their mothers. They also are not very financially rewarding; one is paid a consultant's fee of approximately one to five dirhams for each case.

Another job that appears to have an ambivalent effect on a woman's status is that of schoolteacher, but not because of contact with the supernatural. In fact, the sampling is very small (two primary school teachers, one high school teacher, and two women's center teachers) and differences in personal style make it difficult to generalize about the reasons for the ambivalent effect teaching has on status. It has a positive effect because of the pay; it is a civil service job and pays well (about 350 dirhams per month).[10] Yet these teachers are not universally highly regarded. This may be partly due to the fact that teaching (except in the women's center) puts them in contact with men (other teachers, janitors, and administrators) and this has a negative effect on their status. One can see that this is not the only negative aspect, however, from the case of the teachers at the women's center who deal only with women. Even these are not totally positively regarded. Judging from the comments of local women, this is due to their habit of frequently "putting on airs" or acting superior, a behavior one is tempted to assume when one holds one of the few well-paying professional jobs for women. As time passes and people learn that teachers can maintain their moral standards, and teachers learn to have more respect for their clients and neighbors, one would expect teaching to have a more totally positive effect upon a woman's status.

One of the last two means of self-support available to these village women, the job of field laborer, substantially lowers their status. Yet in terms of job availability and income provided, this is one of the two "best" local jobs. Because this fertile part of Morocco was heavily colonized by the French, there have been large mechanized farms for decades. As a result of the introduction of sugar beets as a crop in 1956, population was affected. Migrants settled to work on the farms and doubled the population of the village. The village also grew because partible inheritance decreased the land available for farming and men left the land of their families. Migrants, including women, entered the agricultural labor pool. Girls from nine to ten years of age as well as old women are accepted, as long as they are able to work from sunrise to sunset. Although these jobs are open to both men and women, women are somewhat preferred because they are cheaper to hire. Overall, wages have recently increased from four dirhams a day for men and three dirhams for women to five dirhams and four dirhams, respectively, but women still work for less money. Because this village is in a rich agricultural area, although each crop is seasonal, a woman can work nearly all year around on one crop or another. There are olives to harvest in the fall, oranges in the winter, and sugar beets, wheat, and chickpeas to be weeded and then harvested in the spring and early summer. Although tractors are used when possible, much of this work must be done by hand. The supervisors in the fields are always men, though some do the same field labor as women. There are several men in the village who have teams of workers, and when the owner of a large farm needs labor he contacts one of these, who tells his workers when and where to be ready to be picked up by the trucks that usually transport them to the field, sometimes up to twenty kilometers away. In some areas the team organizers charge the laborers for a place in the group, but in this village they do not, probably because field workers are much in demand and could easily find a job with another team.

Being a field laborer is the most common way for a woman to support herself and her family; an estimated 8 percent of the village girls and women are thus employed. It is open to anyone; no capital or prior training is necessary, only good health. Only women (and also men) who really *need* the money work in the fields, however, since it is a very low-status and physically exhausting job. Especially for women, the fact that they are out in the open all day unveiled (a veil is a hindrance in collecting olives or weeding chickpeas, not to mention the problem it causes in breathing), and may be available for a quick trip to the other side of the orchard with one of the young men, makes this a very low-status activity. An unmarried girl who works in the fields lowers her potential bridewealth. Perhaps it was not very high in the first place because her family is poor, but by doing field labor she loses the opportunity to claim a sterling reputation as one of her assets. She may in fact be just as chaste as if she had remained at home, but no one will believe that, because of all the opportunities she has obviously had, and everyone presumes that women are weak and cannot resist (see Vinogradov 1974). Such women are therefore forced by circumstances into a position of susceptibility to social criticism, although their efforts on behalf of their families may win grudging admiration. They do not relish the idea of working in the fields, but acknowledge that eating is more important than their preferences or than social criticism. Working on the same principle, their better-off relations are somewhat embarrassed to have female kin out in the fields—but not enough to keep them honorably in the home by supporting them. An example is a local woman of good family who had once been married to an important city judge. She had two children and was divorced, and she supported her family by field labor. Her respectable relatives (two brothers and a sister and family; her parents were dead) wished she would stay respectably at home, but they did not take on the obligation of supporting her.

The final alternative in supporting oneself comfortably—the second best of the two local jobs mentioned above—is less frequently chosen than field labor, and somehow both more and less prestigious. This is prostitution, which is in theory abhorred by the society. Yet prostitutes are thought to lead a rather glamorous, if sinful, life; they pamper themselves, buy beautiful clothing and jewelry, have money to give to relatives as gifts, and receive much attention from men. Women are ambivalent in talking about people they know who are prostitutes. They would *certainly* never want to be one, would be truly horrified at the thought of their daughters' doing this, and they look down on the girls who are prostitutes. Yet they discuss these girls at length, what a prostitute really does, the clothing and jewelry they buy, and how they help support their families. There is some feeling that these girls are forced into such a job (one girl known to the author in fact chose it over field labor when her family threatened to force her into the latter), so they are often pitied rather than blamed for their occupation. In fact, even some respectable women interact socially with prostitutes, for example when both are guests at a wedding or circumcision celebration. Since many prostitutes live together in a house in a larger town instead of locally, there is little opportunity for social interaction with village women, but when prostitutes visit the village they are not shunned socially. There is some verbal censure behind the prostitutes' backs and less often to their faces. Moroccan Arabic is a perfect medium for double entrendres, so it is up to the girl to decide how to interpret the comment, and she seldom challenges it.

There are two types of prostitutes, the ordinary prostitute and the one who also sings and dances for men (*shikha*). All shikhat are prostitutes, but not all prostitutes are shikhat. Because they dance, sing, and play instruments and therefore get higher prices for their work, shikhat are more glamorous. But again this usually presupposes some training, which most women who turn to prostitution lack. Rather, they are most likely to be just prostitutes, and living usually in an area well away from their families. If such ordinary prostitutes have children, they are often left with relatives. (By contrast, in the larger cities there has developed a maid-prostitute combination: the job seekers sit on a particular corner near the old city wall, and are hired for one task or the other. In that case, they can probably maintain their children in rented rooms and say they work as a maid, while a regular prostitute who lived in a "house" would have nowhere to lodge the children. The fiction of being a maid is also used by wayward village girls whose parents are curious about their jobs in the city.) Since fewer women go into prostitution than field labor, even though it is more glamorous and certainly better paying, one concludes that prostitution is the lowest-status way to support oneself reasonably well. The lower status derives in part because a woman damages her own reputation but also because her family's reputation is injured.

Conclusion

All the activities described allow a woman to support herself, to a greater or lesser degree. Their effect on her status in the community, with a few exceptions, is deprecatory because the ideal woman is a virtuous wife and a good mother and remains in her home and out of the public eye. The jobs that may enhance a woman's status are also those that can be done inside, out of the male public's eye, those of bath mistress and seamstress-teacher. They also involve their holder as the center of a communication network, which enhances status; information is one of the few commodities to which women have free access in this society, and these women are rich in it. Information about others is power and can be used to raise or lower their status and thus control them. Unfortunately, because of the need for capital or prior training and the relative scarcity of such jobs, few women earn a living in these ways.

Most of the other activities do not have a significant effect (positive or negative) on one's status, except that working in them at all indicates a lower status. Excepted, however, are activities that expose women to men, like field labor and prostitution, which are the least desirable to participate in.[11] Interestingly, more women can support themselves in these status-lowering activities without having training or capital than in the neutral ones, which pay less well. Thus, "independent" women, whose status is already threatened by their repudiation or other lack of support, are further threatened in that the most profitable opportunities easily available are also those that will greatly lower their status. Such a woman thus has a double burden, that of supporting herself and her family, and that of trying to guard her reputation, and often achievement of one precludes the other.

These conclusions are in general agreement with those of Nouacer (1962) who states that woman's work was valued when it was deemed traditional and did not involve contact with males; the activities that increase status all fit these conditions. Agreement is not total, however, in that the seer and magician also fit these conditions, yet are not unambiguously regarded as high-status occupations. Forget (1962), too, wanted to discover the criteria used for ranking jobs as "very approved," "very disapproved," or "above criticism"; again, we would expect high approval to coincide with high status. Forget's urban sample includes some jobs unavailable in rural areas, such as factory worker, secretary, and waitress, but there is also some overlap with occupations available in rural areas. She found that approval of a job depended upon whether it fit in with the local ideal of femininity; approval was not contingent upon whether a job was considered traditional or modern, or whether it required much education or paid well. The results here generally agree with hers in areas of overlap (seamstress-teachers are approved, bath masseuses disapproved), with one notable exception. She finds teachers are beyond criticism, while in this study they are perceived ambivalently. This may be an example of how the perception of teachers will change with time, as suggested earlier. Forget's urban sample had had longer contact with teachers.

In general, however, the results of this study do not support those of Forget, Martensson, and Nouacer, all of whom found the majority of their samples in favor of women's working. For most of the women considered here, working lowers their status. There are two main possibilities as sources for this disagreement. First, the earlier studies were of attitudes toward women's working, while this one assesses the effect of working on status. Thus, the earlier studies may have elicited an idealized response; perhaps these writers would not be so positive if they were evaluating the status of actual women already in the labor market. A second possibility is that the diverse origins of the samples may have caused the difference; urban groups may in fact feel differently about working than rural people do, and perhaps with time and more exposure to modern, better-paying jobs, the rural group will come into agreement with the urbanites. Presently, however, having a job is usually a liability for these village women.

Notes

1. See Boserup (1970), Hammond and Jablow (1973), and Sacks (1974). Although Youssef (1972) focuses on Latin American and Middle Eastern countries, her perspective is still quite broad. In a multicultural survey, Sanday examines women's status and finds that "female productive activities may be a *necessary* but not a *sufficient* precondition for the development of female power" (1973:1697), and that other factors such as female control over the products of their labor and/or the presence of female solidarity groups are necessary for women to wield economic and political power in a society.

2. The most commonly used definitions of status and role are those set forth by Ralph Linton. In this schema, a status is a position (specifically, a collection of rights and duties) in a particular pattern of reciprocal behavior among individuals or groups of individuals. A role is the dynamic aspect of a status, that is, the actions involved in fulfilling a status, and the two are inseparable (Linton 1961). Authors who have focused their research on women have found that the definition of status needed to be further refined. Thus, Sanday writes: "Female status is generally defined in terms of (1) the degree to which females have authority and/or power in the domestic and/or public domains; and (2) the degree to which females are accorded deferential treatment and are respected and revered in the domestic and/or public domains" (1974:191). The second definition is the one used in this essay; a woman's status in the village refers to the deference and respect accorded her by local males and females. Males and females in the village are basically in agreement on the status which working confers on a woman in either the public or private domain.

3. Field work was conducted in the village in 1970–1972. This settlement of 10,000 people is called a "village" because of its physical character and its lack of conveniences.

4. Although the sample population was urban rather than rural, Forget also notes that many women in Morocco work out of necessity; one of her

informants said a woman works "in order to clothe and feed herself and buy soap" (1962:115).

5. For the ideal woman in traditional Moroccan society, the focus of life is the home. She is an excellent housekeeper, a virtuous wife, and a devoted mother. While her activity is in the home, her father or husband deals with the world outside the home. He supports and protects his women, and they run the household.

6. A preliminary examination of Morocco's 1971 census results found that only 8 percent of the total female population was economically active (Castadot and Laraqui 1973:3). Since it also notes that 46 percent of the total population was under fifteen years of age, it can be assumed that approximately 17 percent of adult females were economically active. This is less than one-fifth of the adult female population; it is apparent, if census data are accurate, that working, in an economic sense, is not very common for Moroccan women.

7. Lineages in Morocco that can trace their origins back to Muhammad are considered holy and their members, living and dead, are shorfa (saints).

8. The women who are put into a trance by a special "tune" are members of a religious brotherhood.

9. In 1970, five dirhams was the equivalent of $1.00.

10. In 1970 per capita annual income was 1,015 dirhams, or about 84.6 dirhams per month, in Morocco (Department of State, "World Data Handbook," 1972).

11. Being a fortune-teller/seer or witch/magician is also frowned upon, even though done in the home, but comparison is difficult because these activities are subject to special rules.

Bibliography

Bonjean, Françoise. *Confidences d'une fille de la nuit.* Tangiers, 1968.

Boserup, Ester. *Women's Role in Economic Development.* New York, 1970.

Castadot, Robert, and Abdelkader Laraqui. *Morocco.* Country Profiles. New York, 1973.

Department of State. "World Data Handbook." In *Issues in United States Foreign Policy.* Washington, D.C., 1972 (August).

Forget, Nelly. "Attitudes Towards Work by Women in Morocco." *International Social Science Journal,* 14 (1962):92–124.

Hammond, Dorothy, and Alta Jablow. *Women: Their Economic Role in Traditional Societies.* Addison-Wesley Modules in Anthropology, no. 35, Reading, Mass., 1973.

Linton, Ralph. "Status and Role." In *Theories of Society,* ed. Talcott Parsons et al. New York, 1961.

Maher, Vanessa. *Women and Property in Morocco.* New York, 1974.

Martensson, Mona. "Attitudes vis-à-vis du travail professionnel de la femme marocaine." *Bulletin Economique et Social du Maroc,* 27, no. 100 (January-March 1966):133–146.

Nouacer, Khadija. "The Changing Status of Women and the Employment of Women in Morocco." *International Social Science Journal,* 14 (1962) :124–129.

Sacks, Karen. "Engels Revisited: Women, the Organization of Production, and Private Property." In *Woman, Culture, and Society.* ed. Michelle Rosaldo and Louise Lamphere. Stanford, Calif., 1974.

Sanday, Peggy. "Toward a Theory of the Status of Women." *American Anthropologist,* 75 (1973) :1682–1700.

———. "Female Status in the Public Domain." In *Woman, Culture, and Society,* ed. Michelle Rosaldo and Louise Lamphere. Stanford, Calif., 1974.

Vinogradov, Amal. "French Colonialism as Reflected in the Male-Female Interaction in Morocco." *Transactions of the New York Academy of Sciences,* series II, 36 (1974) :192–199.

Youssef, Nadia. "Differential Labor Participation of Women in Latin America and the Middle Eastern Countries: The Influence of Family Characteristics." *Social Forces,* 51 (1972) :135–153.

21 The Status of Women and Property on a Baluchistan Oasis in Pakistan

Carroll McC. Pastner

What is the exact relationship between the status of women and their access to property? The complexity of this question becomes very apparent if we look at Muslim societies, for unlike many of her non-Muslim sisters, the Muslim woman has always had very specific legal rights to property. But access to property need not imply actual control over property. While legally recognized as "economic persons" to whom property is transmitted, Muslim women are constrained from acting out economic roles because of other legal, as well as ideological, components of Muslim female status.

Putting aside for the moment the issue of actual control over property, there are two ways in which the topic of Muslim female access to property can be approached. One is on the level of law and involves the study of de jure rights accorded to women by Islam and its various modern civil counterparts. The second approach goes beyond the legalistic ideal and tries to establish the

Field work was conducted with Stephen Pastner on the oasis of Panjgur in 1968–69 and was funded by the National Institute of Mental Health. I am grateful to William E. Mitchell and Paul Magnarella for their comments on an earlier and quite different draft of this paper. It should be understood that the topic of property rights in Islam is vastly complex and that what is presented here is one briefly stated personal understanding of a large body of jurisprudent and related ethnographic materials.

circumstances under which women actually do or do not gain access to property. Differences in de facto property access by women in the Muslim world are wide-ranging; accordingly, the actual dispensation of rights must be documented rather than assumed. It is argued in this study that access or nonaccess to property by Muslim women must be empirically viewed in terms of social organizational factors and ideological concerns. What is of interest is not so much whether legal ideals are being locally met, but rather how accommodations are made to these ideals in pragmatic terms. In any given Muslim community, consistent means of dealing with the question of women and their rights to property are developed. That is, there are perfectly good analytical reasons for women in specific communities gaining or not gaining access to property that is accorded to them by divine law, and where relevant by secular counterparts of religious law. More generally speaking, to investigate empirical cases not only demonstrates variations among communities with regard to the degree to which legal ideals are met, but also provides a more accurate and sophisticated view of the status of women in Islam.

The Muslim example pursued in this study is a large oasis settlement in Pakistani Baluchistan. There are both similarities and differences in the status of women along the dimension of property access between this case study and other Muslim settings, several of which will be considered where appropriate.

Islam and Women's Property Rights

Islam is characterized by a vast body of revealed, codified law applicable to virtually every area of public and private social life. While there are variations in the legal schools of Islamic law, for the most part these are regional interpretations of a core of jurisprudence contained in the Quran and other holy writings. Such variations can be presently ignored in order to make several basic points about women's property access in Islam.

The most general observation is Islam's paternalistic concern for the moral and economic security of women. The creation of access to property for women in Islam is one means by which a protected female status is ideally achieved and maintained. Second, there is an emphasis in divine law on the status of women vis-à-vis men. It is through men that women become "protected persons," and it is through men that women are granted access to property. The economic status of women is dependent upon the economic status of appropriate males, and, accordingly, Islam stipulates specific property rights to women through marriage from their husbands and through patrimonial inheritance from their deceased fathers.

The property transmitted to women at marriage, which is similar to some non-Islamic forms of marital gifts, can be labeled an *indirect dowry*.[1] Known generally as *mahr* in Islam, this form of property allocation is very different from what anthropologists refer to as *bridewealth*. Bridewealth consists of goods transferred from a groom and his kin to the bride's father, which are subsequently used by her brothers to gain their own brides. This type of marital gift has sometimes been interpreted as the outright purchase of women, although, less simplistically speaking, the gifts are made in exchange for economic and procreative rights over women and play a complex role in specific kinds of economies. It is generally believed that in pre-Islamic times there was bridewealth as such. The Prophet Muhammad, however, transformed this marital custom into a socially and economically different type of transaction. As a form of indirect dowry, mahr consists of gifts from the groom to the bride with her marriage guardian (usually her father) as intermediary or middleman. Islamic law demands a bridal gift of this sort to legitimize marriage and insists as well that mahr is the inalienable property of the wife.

But there are several complications in the Quranic right of women to mahr. One is that the marriage guardian sometimes manages to alienate a part or even all of mahr to his personal economic advantage. Another is that husbands have legitimate managerial rights over their wives' property. Third, mahr can legally be paid in installments, with part transferred at the time of marriage and the remainder deferred until some later date. The prompt installment usually consists of clothing, jewelry, and household furnishings, while the deferred portion is a set amount of cash or property agreed upon in the marriage contract. In fact, wives can waive their right to the deferred portion, and in a well-established marriage it is ordinarily never paid. According to the general Islamic ideal, however, deferred mahr should be paid at the death of the husband or under certain conditions of divorce. Since the ethnographic case outlined below provides a specific example of the custom of deferred indirect dowry, further details about this form of property access can be postponed for the moment.

Islamic inheritance rules are extremely complicated since there are several categories of potential heirs, with virtually every contingency anticipated as to available near and distant relatives. Women are included in all categories of potential heirs, but their portions are never mathematically equal to those of men. Thus, a daughter receives a one-half share of her father's estate compared with her brother's full share. As in the case of mahr, a woman's hold on her patrimony is, technically speaking, inalienable, although the property can be rightfully managed by her brother or husband. It should be stressed that there are a number of ways Muslim women, from a legal point of view, can be wrongfully excluded from their inheritance, but also that women may willingly forfeit their right to patrimony in order to substantiate other rights contingent on kinship relationships.[2]

A third form of property access for Muslim women is not explicitly outlined in divine law but is nonetheless an established custom in many Islamic settings. In anthropological terms, this is "dowry," or gifts, from parents to their daughter at the time of her marriage which, in the Islamic case, usually consist of movable wealth in the form of clothing, jewelry, and household goods. The provision of a dowry is sometimes rationalized as a substitute for a daughter's inheritance of patrimony, particularly under circumstances in which it is practical to avoid the fragmentation of agricultural land. As with the two previously mentioned forms of property, dowry should remain the inalienable property of women and can constitute a by no means insignificant economic asset, particularly when it takes the form of jewelry. Sometimes dowries are matched up with indirect dowries in betrothal negotiations in order to bring about business and political alliances between well-to-do families. Under other conditions, part or all of dowry is paid for out of mahr, thereby representing an economically unimportant outlay by the bride's family. On the whole, there is a good deal of variation in the functional significance of Muslim dowry and the means by which it is provided.

In sum, Islamic law concerns itself explicitly with the economic rights of women, but in terms of the inheritance of patrimony does not regard women as the equals of men. There are as well empirical difficulties in the dispensation of female property rights. But there is also a strong deemphasis on conjugal property, or property jointly owned by husbands and wives in Islamic marriage, and despite the right of male management over women's property, it is still a fact that Muslim women (unlike many non-Muslim women) are accorded exclusive rights to several forms of property. The paradox is that while they are legally recognized as "economic persons" capable of receiving property, it is difficult for Muslim women to exercise full economic rights because of other aspects of their status that define them as "protected persons." Considerations of physical seclusion, better known as *purdah,* require that women in Muslim communities be severely constrained from economic (and other) activities taking place outside the home. The necessity for male spokesmen in the public sector of society, as well as other manifestations of female seclusion, affect the actual control women have over the management and disposal of property that is otherwise rightfully their own.

The Baluch of Panjgur

One of the largest settlements of the western part of Pakistani Baluchistan, Panjgur Oasis is situated in a district known as Makran, adjacent to the Iranian border and the Persian Gulf. The environment of Baluchistan is dry and inhospitable, but does permit habitation based on pastoral nomadism, irrigated forms of agriculture, and some limited dry-crop farming. Panjgur Oasis consists of a central bazaar, a district administrative headquarters, and a number of villages and hamlets supporting a population of about eleven thousand. Social structure on the oasis is best described as "feudal" and revolves around three major social strata: the *hakim,* a small traditional ruling elite; the *baluch* who make up a broad middle layer of cultivators and shopkeepers; and the *hizmatkar,* consisting of landless tenants, craftsmen, and ex-slaves. All units of stratification, however, are Baluch from a linguistic and cultural perspective, and all indigenous oasis dwellers identify themselves as Baluch in relation to other ethnic and cultural groups from outside Baluchistan.

The role of kinship is important to an overall understanding of social organization on the oasis. Kinship terminology is bilateral; that is, it does not differentiate grandparents, aunts, uncles, or cousins on the basis of paternal or maternal descent. Genealogies do not play the significant role in social organization that they do among tribal groups in other parts of Baluchistan and in the Middle East generally. Only the elite hakim maintain records of blood descent which are best described as pedigrees used to validate elite birth. Nonetheless, there are explicit ideals of blood or consanguineal kinship relevant to all three strata, with a strong bias toward the value of agnatic relationships. In other words, one's relatives on both the mother's and the father's sides are significant persons, but for men in particular relatives on the father's side share more rights and obligations than do those on the mother's side. Kinship also plays an important role in ideals about what are considered to be suitable marriages. Marriage between persons who are related is the preferred ideal, although the incidence of kin endogamy (in-marriage) is actually quite low. Status group endogamy, in contrast to kin endogamy, is both an ideal and a reality; baluch marry baluch and so forth, although a girl can marry into a higher status group but never into a lower one. Residence upon marriage is ideally patrivirilocal; that is, the couple lives in or near the husband's father's household.

The economy of Panjgur Oasis is based on the cultivation of dates made possible by the use of irrigation water from manmade underground channels. Social patterns relevant to this economy are based to some extent on cooperation among fathers and sons and among brothers, but even more significantly on patron-client relationships between nonrelated men of unequal social status. This stress on reciprocal relationships between nonkin has historically resulted in a good deal of fluidity in economic and political alignments on the oasis and also partly explains why, despite the presence of an ideal for kin endogamy, there is a statistical deemphasis on this kind of economic and political alliance formation between families.[3]

Taking these socioeconomic factors into account, what role do women play in Panjgur society? Muslim communities are to a greater or lesser extent characterized by sexual segregation and the subsequent division of social life into two domains—the private (household) and the public (nonhousehold). While men participate in both these sectors, women are severely limited in their participation in public social arenas and are thereby relegated to the private or domestic domain of society. Thus it is in Panjgur, where women are physically and morally sequestered by means of an institution fundamental to traditional Muslim life—purdah.[4]

One of the definitive features of Muslim purdah is that social intercourse between men and women is delimited by the criterion of kinship. That is, men and women have social access to one another only if they are related through blood or marriage. Nonkin and strangers are classified as inaccessible to the domain of the household and its women. Virtually every woman on the oasis practices purdah, although in varying degrees according to her age and social status. Young girls and postmenopausal women are less constrained by such aspects of purdah as the use of voluminous cloaks and veils. Women of the elite hakim status category are more effectively secluded than other women, if only because their families can afford houses with large enclosed courtyards as well as numerous servants to ensure that hakim ladies lead what can only be described as a rather leisurely life. Of great significance to the perpetuation of purdah on the oasis is that women do not participate in the labor involved in the date economy (including harvesting), apart from some gathering of "windfall" dates near the home and the household processing of dates. The income derived from such produce is contributed to the household economy, unlike that derived from embroidery and sewing done in the home, which is at the woman's own disposal. Women do not participate in any activity that could in any way be regarded as "public." Accordingly, they do not even go shopping in the bazaar; this is done instead by males of the household or servants. Being excluded from public social arenas, women center their social lives around extensive visiting in the household context.

A number of hizmatkar women, particularly those from the subcategory of ex-slaves, provide the exception to the nonemployment of women outside the home. Some are the domestic servants of baluch and hakim, yet others are midwives, and some are peddlers who provide shopping opportunities for other women and serve to sell embroidery done by women in purdah. A greater physical mobility, and even financial independence, sets these working women off from others, but it should be emphasized that their labors are relegated to the nonpublic, female sphere of social life.

It is not the purpose of this study to depict fully the social life of the women of Panjgur and the significant ways in which it differs from that of men. What should be stressed is that property transmission for women takes place in the internal domestic realm of the oasis society in which both women and men participate, and that in this context women receive property from men by virtue of their statuses as daughters and wives.

The Contraction of Marriage

The residents of Panjgur subscribe to the Hanafi school of the Sunni branch of Islam dominant in all of Pakistan. According to their Muslim beliefs and local Baluch custom, they regard marriage as a civil, not a religious, contract which should entail a material transaction. Instigated by the family of the groom, betrothal is marked by a number of ritualized exchanges of food and gifts between members of the two families and, more importantly, by the drawing up of a contractual agreement that an indirect dowry will be paid by the groom and his family to the bride. Dowry is also a consideration in betrothal negotiations, but need not necessarily be written into the marriage contract which is to be witnessed and signed at the wedding.

There are two components to indirect dowry on the oasis: *mal* and *lub,* which correspond to the prompt and deferred forms of what is Quranically defined as mahr. Mal consists of gifts transmitted with the aid of his kin from the groom to the bride, whose marriage guardian (usually her father) serves as an intermediary. These gifts are always in the form of movable goods, and include jewelry, embroidered dresses, other items of female clothing, household utensils, bedding, and a small sum of cash. While it is not unheard of for a father to withhold some or even a good deal of the mal from his daughter, social pressure is such that he hesitates to cheat his daughter. Mal is regarded as the exclusive property of the bride, although some of the items are for obvious general household use, and the husband will ordinarily retain managerial control over the cash and jewelry. The size of mal varies according to the status of the bride and the nature of the marital union being contracted. In terms of the latter criterion, mal is reduced for widows and divorcées, as well as for brides who are close kin of the groom. In terms of the status group affiliation of the bride, as of the time of research, hakim virgins received up to 5,000 Rupees (about $1,000), baluch about 300–500 Rupees, and hizmatkar as little as 20–50 Rupees. The number of dresses and other items vary accordingly: up to twenty dresses for hakim and often only one dress for hizmatkar brides. It is important to note that the entire mal ideally should be transferred in full prior to the wedding, often serving to delay betrothal for men of lesser economic means.

The second component of indirect dowry on the oasis is lub, a deferred portion agreed upon by the two families in the drawing up of the marriage contract. As a promise to transfer wealth under certain specific conditions of divorce, lub need not consist of existing property at the time of marriage, but, unlike the immediate outlay of property in mal, it represents a potential drain on either the existing or anticipated estate of the husband. The wealth involved in lub can consist of either, but usually both, movable and immovable property in the form of cash, date trees, and irrigated or nonirrigated land. The function of lub is to provide financial insurance to the wife when divorce is instigated by the husband for "unwarranted" reasons. That is, a woman can be divorced for her adulterous behavior or her sterility (real or assumed) and she will receive no lub, but if her husband repudiates her for what is judged insignificant reason, he must transfer lub to her as a condition of divorce. The stipulations under which lub is forthcoming in individual cases are defined either in a civil court or, more usually, in a religious court presided over by an Islamic judge.

What does the divorcée do with property transferred to her in the form of lub? While rightfully her own property, it is managed by her male kin—usually her father or her brothers—to whom she returns upon divorce. If she remarries, her right to lub is lost and it reverts to her ex-husband and his kin. If she does not remarry, lub is inherited at her death by the children she had with her ex-husband. Since the children of a divorced couple usually remain with the mother until the age of seven or eight, but then go to their father, this means that lub is never irrevocably transferred from one kin unit to another. Through either the remarriage or death of the divorcée, the property eventually returns to the kin unit from which it came. In the meantime, it is the divorcée and her own kin who have had to manage the property as well as enjoy its economic benefits.

That the property involved in lub is ordinarily set at quite high amounts makes it understandable that husbands are deterred from divorcing their wives for "unwarranted" reasons. In fact, the cash portion of lub can be set at twice that of mal. A local male adage has it that "this is why you try to remain at peace with your wife—for the sake of a hundred date trees." By the same token, women (who also have the right to divorce) are also deterred from instigating a divorce for "unwarranted" reasons. In truth, it is difficult for women to gain lub when they initiate separation for any reason, with a major exception being the husband's impotence or insanity. Even if a woman is willing to forgo lub, she is further dissuaded from initiating divorce by the fact that she can be made to return the mal.

What is the effectiveness of the institution of lub in the overall deterrence of divorce? According to official statistics and on the basis of observation, lub does indeed serve as a deterrent to divorce on the oasis, particularly among propertied families who potentially have the most to lose. Among landless tenants, on the other hand, material considerations are less relevant and the rate of divorce for them appears to be much higher.

Since mal and lub relate importantly to other points not yet covered about the transfer of women in marriage, more will be said about them below. Let us complete the enumeration of marital gifts by noting that, even though it need not be formally included in the marriage contract, a dowry is also transferred at marriage. Known as *waj,* dowry is given to the bride by her parents and close kin several days prior to the wedding. Waj never includes immovable property, such as land or trees, but is made up of jewelry, clothing, household effects, and a sum of cash. Compared with mal, the dowry is definitively smaller in terms of both goods and cash. Among the baluch, the usual amount of cash is about thirty Rupees, while hakim brides receive somewhat more, and hizmatkar, a good deal less. There are two important points about waj. One is that it remains the inalienable property of the wife, even under any circumstance of divorce. Second, the small size of dowry suggests that it cannot be an institutionalized substitute for patrimonial inheritance by daughters, nor can it be rationalized as such, as is done in a number of other Muslim settings.[5] Interestingly, in ascertaining the existence of waj after that of mal and lub, men and women were rather consistently defining marriage in terms that did not always include waj. As several persons stated, marriage "is" mal and lub.

One note of caution is that the significance of jewelry included in dowry cannot be entirely overlooked as an economic asset for women. This is especially so for daughters of wealthy families who receive gold jewelry instead of the less valuable items affordable by poor families. The potential security provided by jewelry for appropriate women is substantiated by the fact that both ideally and in reality, the control by women over their dowries is inalienable, even if divorce instigated by the wife should occur. But it is still true that dowry in Panjgur does not, equitably or otherwise, serve as a substitute for patrimonial inheritance by daughters, as evident from the fact that the women of the oasis do inherit patrimony.

Daughters as Heiresses

Three forms of property access for women on the oasis of Panjgur have thus far been outlined, all of which exist in the context of marriage. Two of these, mal and waj, consist of movable wealth and are forthcoming in the contraction of any marriage, although in varying amounts according to the status of the bride's family and other contingencies, such as the degree of kin relatedness between the bride and groom. The third form of property access, lub, is an eventuality only under specific conditions of divorce instigated by the husband.

The fourth category of female access to property is inheritance (*miras*), of which there are three potential sources. One is the inheritance by daughters of dowry items, particularly jewelry, from their mothers. Second, a widow can receive one-third of her husband's estate, unless he has brothers, in which case her allotment is one-sixth. She is less apt to receive this property if she remarries, since the other heirs will do all they can to prevent the alienation of a piece of the estate. The primary economic role of the widow who does not remarry is to act as the trustee of her husband's estate for their not yet adult children.

The third source of inheritance pertinent to women is patrimonial inheritance in which a daughter should receive a half share of the estate compared with the full share of her brother. Whether or not they themselves have any substantial property to pass on to their children, most men assert the righteousness of inheritance rights for women, but largely in terms of their being religiously defined. Women, on the other hand, seem more pragmatic and are differentially aware of the existence of patrimonial rights, with women from propertied families being more cognizant than others. What, however, are the empirical realities of patrimonial inheritance by women? Precise statistics from the oasis itself are not available, but official figures indicate that about one-quarter of the owners of irrigated and nonirrigated land in Makran are women.[6] While it might be that Panjgur proves an exception to the rest of the district, this is doubtful. Keeping in mind their one-half share, it can be assumed that many women are receiving what is rightfully theirs. Still, several women said they had forfeited their right to patrimony, and others said they were compensated in cash for their shares by their brothers. Nonetheless, the overall situation in Panjgur differs from other Muslim settings in which women are either much more consistently denied their inheritance (but sometimes compensated in dowry), or in which women themselves more consistently forfeit their inheritance.[7]

A woman in Panjgur invariably inherits immovable property in the form of patrimony under two major sets of sometimes related conditions. These are when she has no brothers, or when she is joined in a *sarmal* (mal-less) marriage. To inherit in the absence of male siblings ensures that an estate is not further subdivided among more distantly related potential heirs. A sarmal union is one in which the groom takes up residence with his father-in-law, and in return pays a smaller mal and is not bound by the stipulations of lub. While neither a predominant nor socially valued kind of marriage, sarmal can be very practical for both the husband and his father-in-law. The former gains the economic advantage of a smaller material outlay at marriage as well as incorporation into a propertied household; congruently, for a man to bring in a son-in-law can also be advantageous, particularly if he has no sons of his own.

Even aside from considerations of sarmal and the possible absence of male heirs, women on the oasis do receive their patrimony, although not altogether consistently. What, then, do they do with it? Because of the fundamental facts of sexual segregation and the nonparticipation of women in the public domain, it is difficult for women to control and dispose of their own property by the means available to men, this being a particularly cogent point if it is recalled that socioeconomic organization on the oasis is dominated by reciprocity between patrons and clients who are unrelated and of different social status. Women are not free to establish such dyadic relationships with men; the constraints of purdah and the regulations concerning proper modest female behavior vis-à-vis nonkin males prevent women's participation in the economy in this manner. Thereby, women's landed and watered property is managed by those men with whom they are allowed social intercourse—husbands, brothers, and other related men—who have a vested interest in such property and the women who own it.

Therefore, the women of Panjgur do not individually control the property to which they have access. This is not to say that they do not influence decision-making about the disposal of their property; to subvert a metaphor, women are not totally impotent in this regard. It is the older woman who is more capable of pursuing a somewhat more active economic role than is the young woman. First, old age in itself brings a larger measure of authority for both men and women. More pertinent, as noted above, menopause brings some relaxation of the constraints of purdah. A number of times widows were seen consulting about economic matters with nonrelated men in households in which they were visiting at the time. Nonetheless, women's economic activities are indirectly manifested, limited to consulting *with men* and maintaining and disposing of property *through male spokesmen*. Such an economic role is consistent with the nature of a social system based on a stringent division of economic tasks according to sex. Any economic "wheeling and dealing" engaged in by a woman who has access to property is limited to the "private," that is, domestic, sphere and her manipulation of decision-making by its economically active men. This should make clear the enormous difference between access and control with regard to Muslim women and their property.

To what extent are choices of marriage partners by men and their families influenced by hopes of gaining wealth through a wife's patrimonial inheritance? While such calculations are certainly not unheard of, particularly in the case of sarmal unions, there are other factors that suggest they are otherwise inappropriate. First, wedding a potential heiress is not an easy solution to a man's economic problems because of the deemphasis on conjugal property in Islamic marriage. A husband's managerial rights over his wife's patrimony must be shared with her male kinsmen who have also inherited portions of the estate. Second, only one-quarter of a wife's estate can be claimed by her widower, who may be bypassed in court in favor of their sons or even the wife's male kin, if there are no sons. Last, gaining property through one's wife is not culturally appropriate; as in another Muslim context,[8] it is considered "undignified" for men to gain property through women, this being one reason why sarmal marriages are not regarded as ideal unions.

The Function of Indirect Dowry

Now that the important question of female patrimonial inheritance has been examined, let us return to the marriage gifts of dowry (waj) and indirect dowry (mal and lub) to specify in more detail their role in the contraction of marriage. Of particular interest is the significance of lub which can result not only in the outlay of a good deal of cash, but also the (temporary) alienation of irrigated and nonirrigated property from one kin unit to another. The fact that the divorce rate on the oasis is low and that lub is thereby not an outstanding feature of social and economic life, should not dissuade us from investigating its ideological implications.

To summarize the economic characteristics of dowry and indirect dowry, mal is given to the wife by her husband at the time of marriage, while lub is paid to the wife only if she is divorced for what are Quranically and locally defined as "unwarranted" reasons. The economic feature distinguishing mal and lub is that the former never includes immovable property while the latter does, particularly if cash is not readily available. It should be restated that lub holds particular significance for propertied families and, accordingly, the divorce rate is lower among the well-to-do. Dowry (waj) consists of movable goods given to the bride by her own family and unlike mal, which is frequently returned when divorce is instigated by the wife, is the inalienable property of the woman under any circumstances. The most significant characteristic of waj is that it does not serve as an institutionalized substitute for female patrimonial inheritance since women *are* accorded rights to inheritance, albeit not altogether consistently. This partly brings about a clearer understanding of indirect dowry. First, dowry and indirect dowry on the oasis are not matched in order to create economic alliances between families, this being partly axiomatic since mal, in any given instance, is always considerably greater than waj. Second, aside from the fact that dowry does not substitute for female inheritance and, quite logically, is smaller than in other Muslim settings in which dowry does serve this function, there are additional reasons for mal's being larger than waj that have to do with ideological concerns relevant to the contraction of marriage.

Anthropologists frequently define marriage in terms of the exchange by men of women and goods. While one might conclude that this is a rather dehumanizing (or defeminizing) view, one appropriate component of this definition of marriage is the estimation of the social prestige that goes along with the exchange of women and goods. In terms of the relative prestige of those giving women in marriage ("wife-givers") and those receiving women in marriage ("wife-takers"), the usual understanding is that prestige goes to the party that transfers the least goods, or the least valuable goods, in the contraction of marriage. In this light, prestige in Panjgur goes to the wife-givers since, even aside from the consideration of lub, mal itself economically outweighs that which is given to the bride in dowry. A secondary marriage gift, no longer consistently practiced on the oasis, reinforces this inequality in prestige. This is *kaman bakha* (bow price), the gift of a gun, horse, or sword from the groom to the bride's brother or her paternally related male cousin.

Related to these economic factors are concerns about the honor of the bride and her family in the contraction of marriage. Considerations of honor mean that, for one, a woman can never "marry down" but can marry a man of higher social status than her own. In describing the haggling that invariably takes place when a betrothal is made, residents of the oasis stressed that in order to ensure the honor of the virgin bride and her kin, her family tries to set as high a mal and lub as possible. In related fashion, a central theme of female gossip is whether an honorable indirect dowry had been set for such and such a marriage. A similar topic is the timing of the payment of mal, with a good deal of censure generated by weddings taking place prior to its completed transfer.

Another way to approach the prestige functions of indirect dowry and its role in the validation of honor is to look again at marriages (applicable to all social strata) in which indirect dowry plays a less significant or essentially irrelevant economic role. Mal is reduced or made nominal in close kin endogamous unions and in "exchange marriages" in which two brides are simultaneously married into each other's families. Lub is invariably forfeited in either of these types of marriage. In addition, both mal and lub are lowered for divorcées and widows; that is, nonvirgins. Sarmal marriages also involve a reduced mal as well as a forfeited lub, and while highly pragmatic under certain conditions, such unions are thought to be distinctively less prestigious and less honorable than other types of marriage.

Particularly significant is the criterion of kin endogamy. It was noted above that despite its low statistical occurrence, in-marriage among kin, as in many other Muslim settings, is a highly preferred ideal.[9] As the residents of the oasis put it, "It is dishonorable to give your daughters away to strangers." Both men and women hold this view, although women also emphasize certain psychological benefits from not being married into a nonkin (strange) household.[10] Since mal and lub constitute significant economic considerations in kin exogamous unions, but not kin endogamous ones, indirect dowry can be viewed as a means of compensating for the loss of honor that otherwise accompanies kin exogamy.

The fact that kin exogamy statistically outweighs kin endogamy on the oasis makes the economic and ideological significance of indirect dowry more cogent. At the root of these ideological concerns about the contraction of marriage is the fact that a family does not lose interest in its daughter when she marries. In arranging marriages, the protection of daughters can be achieved in one of two ways. One alternative is kin endogamy, which represents a union between families who are already acquainted with each other and share previously established mutual rights and obligations. In the case of kin exogamy, the absence of familiarity and already established reciprocal rights and duties is compensated for economically, not only by the immediate payment of mal, but by an insurance policy in the form of lub. In either of these two ways, the honor of a daughter and her family is preserved and the protected status of the daughter is ideally guaranteed.

Conclusion

It is hoped that two points in particular have been elucidated in this study. One is that in their capacity as daughters and wives, Muslim women can and do have access to several kinds of property, including movable items such as jewelry and cash, and immovable wealth such as land and trees. The other point is that limitations on Muslim women's legal access to property and their actual control over property stem from other components of their female status. That is, Muslim women are "protected persons," constrained from engaging in activities taking place in the public domain of society and forced to play out their economic roles largely through men: men who are related to them through blood or marriage and who have rights and responsibilities to "protect" appropriate women and their property. Empirical differences among Muslim communities as to the degree to which women have economically meaningful control over their own property will depend in large part on the degree to which women participate in the institution of purdah. Panjgur happens to be a particularly conservative community in this regard but does not constitute an exceptional case. As far as their legally defined access to property is concerned, the women of Panjgur cannot easily be classified as "downtrodden" or "oppressed" persons. That various interpretations can be placed on their being "protected" is another matter altogether, but one which likewise deserves careful scrutiny and the avoidance of preconceptions about the status of Muslim women.

Notes

1. The terms *indirect dowry, dowry,* and *bridewealth* in this paper follow the usage of Goody and Tambiah (1973), who have put forth the latest general treatment of these important transactions.

2. For examples, see Mohsen (1967) and Rosenfeld (1960). The rights women substantiate by forfeiting inheritance include various kinds of material and nonmaterial aid from their families after marriage.

3. See Pastner and Pastner (1972) for a fuller treatment of these points.

4. I have dealt with the question of purdah on the oasis in several other papers. These include an historical treatment (Pastner 1972) and a discussion of female social structural and psychological adjustments to purdah (Pastner 1974). An excellent general theoretical treatment of purdah is found in Papanek (1973).

5. To take two geographically widely separated Muslim examples, Maher (1974) describes how in a Moroccan town women are given dowries (but no patrimonies), which are matched up with indirect dowries to bring about "business" alliances; while Eglar (1960) shows how brothers in Pakistani Punjab rationalize noninheritance by their sisters by trying to show that they had already received their "fair share" in the form of dowry. Examples from other Muslim areas also exist.

6. Representing the latest available statistics, this estimate is based on figures from the 1961 census for Makran. It is interesting to note that early in the century the British remarked that women in Makran were in a "stronger position" in terms of inheritance than women in other parts of Baluchistan (*Baluchistan District Gazetteer,* VII, p. 75).

7. For a general discussion of how Arab women, for example, are denied their inheritance, see Baer (1964).

8. Stirling (1965:123).

9. Indirect dowry is similarly lowered, made nominal, or eliminated in other Muslim settings too numerous to list here in which there is also a stress on preferred kin endogamy of either the bilateral or agnatic variety. The following remarks are hypothesized to apply generally to these other appropriate settings, whether or not the rate of kin endogamy is empirically high or low.

10. These benefits are largely conceived of in terms of a bride's relationship with her husband's mother in the context of the patrilocal extended family. It is felt that a mother-in-law who is a relative is less apt to mistreat and overwork her daughter-in-law.

Bibliography

Baer, Gabriel. *Population and Society in the Arab East.* London, 1964.

Baluchistan District Gazetteer, vol. VII, *Makran.* Gov't. publication. Bombay, 1907.

Eglar, Zekiye. *A Punjabi Village in Pakistan.* New York, 1960.

Goody, Jack, and S. J. Tambiah. *Bridewealth and Dowry.* Cambridge, 1973.

Maher, Vanessa. "Divorce and Property in the Middle Atlas of Morocco." *Man,* 9 (1974) :103–122.

Mohsen, Safia K. "The Legal Status of Women among Awlad ʿAli." *Anthropological Quarterly,* 40, no. 3 (1967) :156–166.

Papanek, Hanna. "Purdah: Separate Worlds and Symbolic Shelter." *Comparative Studies in Society and History,* 15, no. 3 (1973) :289–325.

Pastner, Carroll McC. "Accommodations to Purdah: The Female Perspective." *Journal of Marriage and the Family,* 36, no. 2 (1974) :408–414.

———. "A Social Structural and Historical Analysis of Honor, Shame and Purdah." *Anthropological Quarterly,* 45, no. 4 (1972) :248–261.

Pastner, Stephen, and Carroll McC. Pastner. "Agriculture, Kinship and Politics in Southern Baluchistan." *Man,* 7 (1972) :128–136.

Rosenfeld, Henry. "On the Determinants of the Status of Arab Village Women." *Man,* 60 (1960) :66–70.

Stirling, Paul. *Turkish Village.* New York, 1965.

22 Iranian Women in Family Alliance and Sexual Politics

Paul Vieille

Translated from the French by Nikki Keddie

Before the agrarian reforms of the 1960s, the Iranian peasant was generally a sharecropper whose relation to the land from which he drew his subsistence was not judicially fixed. This relation was mediated by a social tie to the landlord, involving immediate consequences that helped determine the status of women. The land cultivated and the future of the lineage, the family, and the children did not depend as much on man-resource equilibrium as on political equilibrium, and on the power relationship between the peasant and the proprietor. At the village level this was an equilibrium with three poles: the landlord facing two rival lineages or groups of lineages (unions of families). The equilibrium was, by its

---

The majority of the material in this paper is based on my observations and research in Iran from 1960 to 1968, and especially on research conducted in 1966 among the families of peasants and industrial workers, which focused on the problems of birth, death, and sexuality. Individuals of 150 households (100 peasant, 50 industrial worker) were interviewed, men and women separately, by men and women interviewers, respectively. Interviews were recorded on tape. For administrative reasons it was not possible to carry out the systematic analysis of data collected, and the study here is based on a first appreciation of the data. It presents some of the hypotheses elaborated on the basis of the quantitative analysis that was made. The research was partially financed by the Population Council of New York.

A more detailed discussion of some of the problems raised by this study may be found in some of my earlier publications: P. Vieille and M. Kotobi, "Familles et unions de familles en Iran," *Cahiers Internationaux de Sociologie,* December 1966; and P. Vieille, *La féodalité et l'état en Iran* (Paris, 1975). In the latter is found a discussion of interviewing in Iranian society.

nature, variable and unpredictable. It hid from the individual or from the lineages the relative stability of the collective man-resource equilibrium. In addition, the concept of equilibrium could not arise at the level of the village collectivity, since it was divided. Equilibrium, besides, was not in the interest of the landlord, who dominated through the division between the lineages that he maintained, and who profited from every growth in the number of workers for reasons at once economic (he took a fixed proportion of the production, whatever its volume and the condition of its increase might be) and political (the competition of individuals, families, and lineages for access to the available land increased his power) . Similarly, the peasants knew that their power in face of the landlord, and hence their fortune, was tied to the number and especially the cohesion of the groups they formed. The means to assure this cohesion are two: ties of filiation and matrimonial relations. First of all, each family, lineage, and union of families tried to multiply its descendants and gave considerable value to the fecundity of its women. The lineage was the real propagator of the model of high fecundity. Next came matrimonial relations: uniting families within a lineage, and trying to unite families among several lineages or segments of a lineage. The importance of matrimonial relations in ties between families was, let us note in passing, immediately tied to the valorization of fecundity.

The Devaluation of Women

Through the value given to fertility and the importance of marriages in alliances between families, lineages, and unions of families, social relations would seem to lead to the high valuation of women. However, what one observes is the opposite. From the earliest age, the devaluation of women is apparent. There is higher mortality among young girls than young boys, a difference that is opposed to the norms of physiology. Society thus makes a choice. It is certainly not avowed as such: the equality of children by sex is affirmed as is that by age rank. The differentiation appears constantly, however, in habitual practices and activities. People want more boys than girls and they want boys more; they want a boy as the first child. Beliefs regarding the prediction of unborn children show the representations attached to each of the sexes: the signs for a boy appear on the right side of the pregnant woman. This is the noble side, as opposed to the left side, that of servile tasks. (See the relation between the left hand and the right hand: the former is used for the inferior services of the body, the latter is turned toward the exterior, toward the other.) The signs for a boy appear also in the weight of the mother, her voracity, and her good character; the signs of the girl are the opposite. If a boy is born, people say "He was expected." If a girl is born, "She brings happiness." At birth, the little girl is "bitter" and her first smiles mean, "Do not throw me out, I will find my place." The little boy whose "mood is bad" is better cared for, better nourished, and better dressed; people are more attentive to his needs and they find that he is easier to bring up; they accept joyfully the trouble he provokes, but take badly that given by the little girl.

The girl is considered to be made for obedience, the boy for pride and independence. A popular saying gives the expected conduct: "Scold a girl and she lowers her head; scold a boy and he flees." It appears normal that the boy is authoritarian regarding his sister: "He is learning to be dominant!" Finally, if a child dies, a boy is mourned more than a girl.

How do we account for this inferiority in popular language? The little girl is not devalued because of what she is in childhood, but because of the status to which she is promised and the consequences of this status. When people complain of the trouble she gives, it is not so much because of this as it is because of the reflection in the present of expected cares. People emphasize first that the girl is going to enlarge another family, another lineage: "We bring them up and eventually give them to others." The boy, on the other hand, stays in the family and the lineage, supports his parents in their old age, and assures the strength and perpetuation of the lineage. The motif is symptomatic of the endogamous dream that families and lineages pursue in the power relationships of rural society. The arguments appealed to cannot, however, have a very great real value, since families and lineages exchange daughters and receive the equivalent of what they give. In the many endogamous marriages in the lineage, the departure of the girl is only such in a very narrow sense, at the level of the conjugal household, which is only one of the poles of the familial institution and is not the only group within which conduct regarding women is elaborated.

If the "departure" of the girl cannot be considered the true motive of her devaluation, it is in the examination of the problems that this departure poses for social relations, and of perceptions tied to these relations, that we will find the explanation. The problems are reduced to a single but considerable one: that of virginity. It is a social obligation that is absolute in the relations between the families and lineages that give and receive the young girl at the moment of marriage. The young girl must be a virgin on her wedding night; if she is not, she cannot be established in honorable conditions and her family will be covered with shame. Hence, virginity is the chief concern of parents in the course of bringing up their daughter. Father and mother are obsessed by rape and premarital sexual relations. Surveillance and protection are constantly undertaken by parents and brothers, with no circumspection, for the problem of her virginity is presented to the young girl in an open way. The haste to marry is tied to the fear of prenuptial relations, which are also severely prohibited. The fear of families is fed by the training they give their son: if he is designated the protector of his sister, who is ritually forbidden to him, he is at the same time a threat to other girls, regarding whom he is not at all held on his guard. The permanent fear in which people live regarding virginity explains their exaggeration of the material difficulties occasioned by bringing up a young girl. It is, however, not this fear that is the basis of the devaluation of girls. To explain that we must examine the significance of virginity.

The value of virginity does not originate either in a concern to be certain of paternity or in the fear of illegitimate births. To test paternity other traditional means exist, like the delay period of widows; and in many "traditional" societies, sexual relations before marriage are infertile although free. Iran does not seem to have been more ignorant of contraceptive techniques than these other societies.

The hymen of the girl is considered, and called, her "capital," and it is not rare when one questions peasants regarding the value of virginity to get this response: "He paid a lot to get a virgin." Are we, however, dealing with a true economic relationship or not? Does the price paid for the marriage buy a material good which is "virginity"? In reality, a great deal more is involved. This is shown clearly by the conduct followed (or that people declare they would follow) in the rare case that the girl is not (or would not be) a virgin on her wedding day. The family who gave her returns the bridewealth they received, but adds something to keep the family who received the young girl from making the matter public and dishonoring those who were incapable of protecting the virginity of the family member.

The idea of the honor of families and lineages is in fact central in the question of virginity: honor consists of giving and accepting only goods that are ritually pure. The loss of virginity is an offense against honor, an irreparable loss of honor. For peasants, the hymen is a sign placed by God of the prenuptial chastity of the woman, by which is indicated her value, extrinsic to the woman herself. The following dialogue between inquirer and peasant informant occurs frequently:

> "If, on the wedding night, it appears that the girl is not a virgin, what importance has it?"
> "That proves that she has fornicated, so she is denounced."
> "But, that is in the past!"
> "No, since she is not a virgin."

One could compare this view of the loss of virginity as an indelible sign of a transgression that cannot be erased (that is, of a physiological fact external to the affective and spiritual life of the woman, as a sign of a personal, permanent taint) with the refusal of Islam to pronounce on conscience, but to judge only by the accomplishment of rites and external signs. One would have to show how this representation of sin and transgression constitutes an ideological prolongation of effective social relations and of social organization. I cannot here proceed to this general demonstration, but shall only indicate the articulation of the value accorded to virginity in social relations.

Sexuality is not a personal adventure. As in all agrarian societies, the value of a woman comes first from her being a producer of male producers, who are the principal means of production. As such, she is an instrument of the politics of alliances between families and lineages (a reinforcement of the cohesion of a lineage and of the relations between two lineages). She is also, as I have said, an instrument of sexual politics. The contracts that involve her by virtue of the politics of alliances and sexual politics constitute the elements and the major events of the relations between social groups. In these relations, the woman is objectified and has no autonomous existence; she is a good, doubtless of value, but a good about whose nature there must not be any possible contest, whose value, more exactly, must be easily established and who must have the greatest possible symbolic value relative to the object for which it is destined: the alliance between two families. Thus, maximum symbolic value is that of the virgin girl who has been preserved in that state with a view to the alliance, who has not been, previously, the instrument of another alliance. In this regard it is symptomatic that for a second marriage the freedom of choice left to the woman is much greater than in the first, where she has none: she no longer represents the same interest for family alliances.

Thus, virginity is the sign of the honor of a family and of a lineage in its most profound, most essential, relations with another family and another lineage—those that deal with the exchange of women, the producers of producers. Virginity thus has meaning not in the perspective of the young girl but in that of her family and of the honor of her family in social relations; she is the sign of this honor. The control exercised to preserve this honor is, and can only be, strictly external; it cannot be moral. A moral control would signify the recognition in the girl of a free will that cannot be conceded to her. The girl, however, interiorizes the value of her virginity as an absolute rule of life, a postulate of her existence. She does not dispose of it and her offense would be precisely in transgressing the prohibition; an ethical significance is, however, added to and transforms the prohibition. Here it is symptomatic to note that, in the most disorganized urban milieus, where control over the young woman after marriage is no longer exercised by her family, by her husband's family, or by the group of the neighborhood, breaking the hymen in marriage tends, despite marriage, to lift the barrier to a free sexuality.

Thus is invalidated the explanation of the value of virginity by concern for the future marital fidelity of the woman. ("She will remain attached to her husband since she has not known another man and has no experience of a free relationship.") Marital fidelity, like virginity, just because of the apprenticeship which the mode of assuring virginity involves, can only be obtained by external controls.

Discussion of the problem of virginity has allowed us to grasp the origin of the differentiation of the value of girls and boys, of women and men. Woman, valued as an exchange good, as being a procreator and a means of sexual pleasure, in relations between families and lineages, is devalued as a person. Her status in the politics of lineages makes of her, besides, a subject of continual anxiety. The boy does not pose the same problems. He is both threat and protection; he is destined to head a family, to regulate the relations between this family and other families, notably through the politics of marriages. He is not imprisoned in the "natural" roles of sex and reproduction; he is politics and culture, and "on him rests the order of the world."

Fecundity

Raised for marriage and procreation, a woman acquires her own social status only by fecundity. Her prestige with her husband, family, and village is at its maximum with her first pregnancy and birth, especially if her first child is a boy, whose name, besides, is often made a part of hers. After marriage all those who surround a young wife await with anxiety the announcement of a pregnancy. The event releases an anxiety; thenceforth the young wife will be cherished by her husband and her in-laws. If, on the contrary, there is delay, anxiety grows on all sides. The father of the young girl has given a product for reproduction; he is discredited by his daughter who does not immediately promise a child. The husband's family, on its side, has acquired a young wife to increase its descendants; if her sterility continues, the husband loses interest in his wife and threatens to send her back or to take a second wife. The household is constituted to procreate; sterility is a broken contract. The young wife who is, habitually and without proof, taken to be responsible for the sterility of the couple, will do everything to change her state: pilgrimages, magic practices, potions, and so forth. If she does not succeed, she will have only a diminished status, and her family will feel dishonored by it.

Social incitements to childbirth continue after the first birth. There are, notably, the uncertainties of the position of the wife in the household; the marriage is easily broken by the will of the husband alone. Even if this does not happen in the countryside, the option left to the husband to send back his wife easily leads the latter to look for means to attach her to her home. Children are reputed to be "nails" that attach the wife to the home. After marriage, women hasten to multiply these ties which guarantee them against repudiation. In the effective multiplication of children, the absence of institutions allowing for their reduction plays as much of a role as do the incitations to their multiplication. The desire for limitation exists, more among women than men, because women are the chief victims of the increase in the number of children; the lack of discussion by the couple on such a subject creates an obstacle even when the spouses have the same desire. Within the village, between the group of men and that of women, the expression of values is likewise blocked by values tied to the politics of family unions. Let us consider, for example, the group of women: they actively surround the young wife, initiate her, guide her through the first pregnancies, welcome the newborn, and combat sterility. In them are transmitted ancient popular practices regarding magic, pharmacy, and medicine. They help the young wives and exert a considerable pressure in favor of fecundity.

Later, when all in the village consider that a woman has enough children, they do not speak openly of the limitation of births, nor act accordingly because impeding conception is traditionally "evil." The memory of contraceptive products, usually potions that allow the interruption of pregnancy, is maintained, but they are spoken of in an undertone and only used secretly. People prefer less certain methods, which, if they succeed, seem to leave the responsibility to nature, such as carrying heavy loads and running up stairs. Finally, a woman who has many children is blamed but rarely assisted; her too great fecundity becomes a defect. She suffers her trouble in silence, does not dare speak to her husband of the limitation of births, bursts out occasionally in recriminations addressed to her husband, and more to her children: "Papa sows you and leaves me your care," but without result. The tension between husband and wife is generally latent, sometimes open, never emerges into decisions capable of reducing it, and finally brings about in individuals a tension between the level of aspirations and that of practice.

Everything concerning the child from gestation to the end of childhood is in the woman's domain. The man cannot allow himself to be interested in things considered beneath him. He is turned toward the outside world, toward the political relations of the family and the lineage with other groups, and toward the complex demands of a traditional society. He is proud of sowing the land and impregnating his wife; he thereby affirms his right to participate in virile society. His status forbids him, however, to interest himself in a precise way in that nature that he claims to dominate; he must keep his distance as the master with regard to the servant. Between woman and young child, on the one hand—the pole of nature—and man on the other hand—the pole of politics and culture—exists a rupture. Wife and child represent for the latter potentialities subject to the hazards of chance in his domain. Pregnancies and births hence must be and are multiplied to the limits of nature, and political contingencies then allow the children to live or, very often, condemn them to death. The submission to nature affirmed in peasant culture thus signifies in reality submission of the woman to nature by a masculine culture that dominates her and, finally, the submission of woman-nature to masculine culture.

The wife, the mother, is clearly more occupied than the man with the problems of young children and their needs, and she is more concerned with lowering infant mortality, just as she was seen to be more concerned with limiting births. Here, also, feminine values do not achieve realization; masculine values are imposed on women by their prestige, by the fact that they come from the dominant group, that of men, and especially by the institutions they reproduce. The wife only succeeds in entering the lineage and the local group through her adolescent and grown-up children. Thus, it is not surprising that tension is not more frequent in households on the subject of infant mortality.

Women's Status

In the household, both the legal definition, until the reforms of the 1960s, and the reality for the wife was an inferior status. She had to be "obedient and submissive" to her husband, who had over her a right of correction and used it frequently. In speech she was called, with sexual overtones, "the incomplete one." No more than to a child, to whom she had an equivalent status, did a man have to tell her the truth; a precious object, she was for the man an inferior being toward whom sincerity is not considered necessary. She had no other rights than those the husband conferred on her in a paternalistic way according to the habits or injunctions of custom and religion; not to seek out useless quarrels; to be generous to her; not to repudiate her, for "the angels turn away from repudiation," and repudiation is "blameable." In reality, the pre-1967 rules of divorce, still widely followed among the popular classes, consecrate the absolute authority of the husband in the household. Until the recent reforms, only the husband had the right to repudiate at will—repudiation was done without formalities, without a motive, without indemnity (canonically, the husband should, however, help support the ex-wife for three months or if she is pregnant until the birth of the baby, and give her a "consolation gift"). Divorce could also be made under some circumstances on the demand of the wife, in which case the husband had the right to compensation. This unilateral means of disposing of the couple's fate was traditionally little used in the countryside since it implicated families as much as individuals. By contrast, in the urban milieu, on its way to disintegration and to individualization, it constitutes a real and constant threat for the wife who, when sent back, was generally separated from her children and "devalued" for a second marriage. The rights of the wife in the couple thus tended to be assured by financial means; in case of repudiation the husband must contract to pay a sum, generally high, to his wife.

The activities of the wife are, like herself, devalued. The value of her work seems unknown not only when she is occupied solely with domestic activities (household, preparation of meals, bringing up children and so on) but even when she has activities of agricultural production (rice and so on) or crafts (carpet-weaving and so on) equivalent to those of a man. Let us consider, for example, the activities of carpet-weaving; the status of the woman stands out in it in a very symptomatic way. The rug is the furniture of the house, the wealth of the interior; its design with multiple enclosures is the image of the secluded space of the woman. A peasant woman must know how to weave; it is a disgrace if she does not; however prestigious is the house where the blows of weavers resound, more prestigious still is that where they weave for family consumption and not for the market. Weaving, a woman's home activity, is, however, despised by men, who regain their rights when production is aimed for the market; then it enters into their domain of activity.

Civil and religious law accords some economic rights to women (notably the Islamic rules of inheritance). In fact, it is rare that these rights are respected, or they are only respected in principle and with bad grace. Thus, boys consider as a usurpation the part of the heritage that goes to girls. It is rare that the rights a woman holds on real property are respected, on a piece of land, for example. The brother, the husband, and other male relatives habitually take hold of the resources that, legally, should be hers. Even her income for work is ordinarily taken (as, for example, in carpet-weaving). Then, aside from daily transactions (purchase of food products), the woman in popular milieus, in town as in the country, has few relations with the market; the use of money is still a masculine privilege. The economic status of the woman is immediately tied to her practical and ideological inferiority. She is considered a subordinate being, not able or having to possess; besides, she has not in these conditions any recourse to defend her own rights. Thus, she is either robbed by the economic agent with whom she deals or despoiled by the protector she accepts or who is imposed on her: husband, parent, intermediary and so on.

Inferior in civil law, the woman is also inferior politically. In the traditional political life (alliances of families, of lineages and so on), she has no recognized role, although she intervenes in it in a roundabout way. In "modern" political institutions her rights were recognized with difficulties. The additional articles of the Constitution of 1906 stipulate that "all citizens are equal before the law," but that formulation was only agreed upon by modernists and traditionalists because of an ambiguity to which both finally agreed: for the former it meant the equality of men and women; for the latter it could not apply to women who, lacking reason, could not be considered citizens with full rights. Thus, the right to vote was not accorded them, and they had to await the royal edicts of 1963 in order for their political rights to be expressly affirmed.

This rapid review of the elements of women's status, to which one could add some others, such as the dimorphism of instruction (the young girl was not traditionally sent to school, even when her brother was), shows the subordinate position that women occupied in society. Essentially conceived as a being of nature, an instrument of reproduction and of sexuality, placed at the disposal of males who utilized her in the framework of the policy of alliances and in sexual politics, she was, in the same fashion, objectified and relegated to an inferior status, devoted to the servile work of the house. She was in no way the equal of the man, and no one believed in her capacity to rise to his level.

Sexuality

People have often stressed the opposition of East and West regarding problems of sexuality. As against the West, the East is said to admit sexuality fully and to bathe in a diffuse eroticism. Islam allows, indeed encourages, sexual activity, opening to sexual impulses numerous legal paths: multiple marriages, successive or simultaneous; concubinage; and, in Shiism, temporary marriage. The Quran itself incites men to marriage, treats sexual problems realistically, promises the elect a garden of paradise, where they will meet *huris*, creatures of another world "with modest glances, with large and beautiful eyes," "resembling the hidden pearl," "whom we have formed perfectly and whom we have kept virgin," and "whom neither man nor demon will have touched before them." Religious exegesis has long discussed the sense of this representation of the garden, without a purely spiritual interpretation having ever been admitted. In popular thought there is no question of metaphor: paradise is sex and the believer prays to God to reserve him the promised huris. In addition, ancient phallic cults continue in the countryside (notably in the region of Dezful) and even in Tehran, where not so long ago people once a year decorated the trunk of a tree that they called *nakhl* (palm tree) and came to attach ribbons and bits of string (while making vows for unborn children) to a cannon found in a central city square. Sex is also a constant subject of dreaming, of preoccupation, of conversation. In conversations among men, among women, and even between men and women, it is discussed without shame: jokes, sexual boasting, questioning others' sexuality, fears for one's own sexuality, erotic stimulation, utilization with the aim of seduction, and so forth.

If in other respects sex is subordinated to procreation, sexual pleasure is seen as the motivating force behind procreation: sensuality was created by God to incite men to reproduce and maintain the species. Thus, marriage is represented first as the opening of sensual pleasure. The phallus dominates daily life, and it would not be exaggerating to speak of Iranian peasant society as a society centered on sexuality. This valuing of sex is not, however, a simple transposition of an actual pansexualism. Let us begin here by indicating the division of roles in sexuality for the couple. Undoubtedly, it is not entirely unique to Iranian society: our object is not, however, intercultural comparisons but the comprehension of one social structure.

There is no physical contact during the course of the sexual act other than that of the genital organs; other erogenous zones are not excited and used by sexuality. The lower classes do not undress to make love; the bodies remain covered; it is believed that nudity can bring on male impotence. In addition, the caress is practically unknown; the sexual act begins with intromission and ends with ejaculation, so that man and woman are physically united only in coitus. However, no gesture of love is forbidden by any cultural, religious, or other canon. Doubtless, one could say that the conditions of sexual activity are unfavorable in the countryside because of poverty, living arrangements, and the presence of the family. These circumstances do not, however, solve the contradiction between the ideal representation of sexuality and its practice. Sexuality is physically isolated from the body as a whole and temporally isolated from daily life. It is still intellectually isolated from the conjugal union: there is no communication between spouses on the subject of pleasure, not only during the sexual act but even outside it. The avowal of pleasure is inconceivable from woman to man, and also from man to woman. Sexuality thus appears to limit itself quite rigorously to coitus.

If we examine roles in sexuality, three aspects come out with particular clarity. Only the man has the right to show his desire. He can show it whenever and wherever he wishes to his wife; besides, he can show it to whatever woman he wishes, except those who are religiously forbidden to him; no one will find fault with him for it. If someone is to be reproached, it is the woman who should not have put herself in a situation where she could provoke the desire of the man. The woman, for her part, must not in any case show that she has a desire. Even in married life it would be improper; she must affect as much indifference toward sexuality as she showed disinterest in her own marriage.

Yet the woman is conceived of as having much more desire than the man; people willingly enumerate the difference: nine times more. Finally, the woman must not remain insensible to the activity of the man in sexuality; her partner places his pride in his power to lead her to pleasure, to "make the woman move."

The roles can thus be defined in the following manner: the man conceives himself as revealer of the latent erotic powers of the woman. Only he arouses the desire of the woman and fulfills it. The woman before his intervention would not be able to desire; afterward she could not remain insensible without frustrating him in the result he expects from an act whose sole author he considers himself. In addition, if woman contains a great potential of desire, a man can use it when he wishes; he is only responding to what is awaited. He does not have to ask himself whether the woman desires that he approach her, since it is in her "nature" to desire much but to be unable to show it. In one sense, the man reveals the woman to herself in forcing her. These are the roles expected by the man; they dominate, as the man is superior to the woman. The system, however, does not function completely smoothly; the role of a woman appears in particular to be composed of two parts that are scarcely compatible, whose opposition is only the result of a more profound contradiction of culture and activity. In order to reveal it, let us remember first that the precoital role of the woman in sexuality is the prolongation of established aspects of her status in daily life and of a certain number of beliefs.

In the culture, reproduction, childbearing, and nursing are the feminine and uniquely feminine functions. By nature they belong to the domain of women, and men should not take any part in them through affection, through participation in the states and sentiments that they arouse, or through practical help in the tasks they engender. They represent one of the lowest forms of labor, carried out in the entrails, in blood, in this world of flesh with which the culture is obsessed. By contrast, sexuality and sexual enjoyment are masculine values; only a man has the right to want to make love, only he is the potentiality of sensual pleasure, and only he is promised its enjoyment.

The division of roles is apparent, besides, in many beliefs and practices regarding sexual life. Thus, sterility is always first attributed to the woman. Also, it is the woman who is declared responsible when a couple has only children of the same sex. A woman's sterility means that she cannot have a child; a man's sterility is only represented by impotence. The woman is not perceived as a being having a specific sexuality. Her internal organs are seen as like those of a man; she is seen as ejaculating, but she is not seen, as are boys, as having an autonomous sexual life.

But if a woman is not sex for herself, she is only sex for men. Thus, a woman is not perceived as capable of refusing if she happens to be alone with a man other than those who are ritually forbidden to her, just as a man alone with a woman not forbidden to him is not conceived as being able to resist desire and possession. Comradeship or friendship among men and women is inconceivable and cannot exist; all verbal communication and all physical approaches take on a sexual content and are suspect. For a woman to laugh, for example, is an amorous call; to look at a man is a solicitation, and so forth. It does not matter what meaning a woman gives to these acts, since for the man they have a sexual sense. Also, the fidelity of a wife is not seen by the man as flowing from a personal tie—a fidelity of love and virtue—but from a thorough physical control. Cloistering and the veil are the very means to fidelity: external means adapted to an object that is also external, to segregate, to avoid a contact that can only have a sexual content.

On the other side, the impersonalization of sex means that the "girlfriend" (if one may use a term whose transposition is quite misleading), a phenomenon traditionally limited to the aristocracy but now being extended, tends to be a sexual instrument only, regarding whom one nourishes no designs of appropriation, that is to say, of marriage. Thus, she is conceived of as indifferent to her partners and interchangeable among them. She tends to be the hetaera of ancient Greece, distinguished from the prostitute by her membership in the same social category as her partners, by a high intellectual level, and by the fact that she does not demand a salary for her services.

The traditional justification of polygamy is the sexual satisfaction of the man; the number of four wives authorized by Islam corresponds according to one author to the man's "four temperaments." Coitus interruptus is also seen as legitimate in exegesis when the consequences of pregnancy can endanger the pleasure of the husband or when the latter wishes to guard against a birth that might destroy his property rights over a slave concubine.

If in the traditional situation woman is a sexual good at the disposition of a man, in a period of social change like the present, positions can reverse without the value of sexuality being modified. In certain urban milieus in the course of intense acculturation, it is not rare that the "purchased" wife, especially when she is of a social origin superior to her husband's, comes to conceive that she can refuse the sexual services owed to her husband. She then tends to make them be paid for.

Because of the context here emphasized of the relationship between men and women, one might ask about the stimuli for bringing together the two sexes. No halo of personal relations, emotional or intellectual communication, exists. Besides, the coming together of man and woman seems shackled, in comparison with the conditions of sexuality in other societies, by the coolness that the woman must show in her precoital role and by her inferior status. Certainly, the very image of the woman is sex; she is in a way the absolute, unconditional stimulus. In fact, the preliminaries to the sex act are ordinarily extremely simple: a puerile game of verbal provocation (evocation of sex), touching, simple physical approach, and so on. Sexuality thus appears to be closed up upon impulse. It scarcely seems that the image of the woman as erotic object could be reconstituted and renewed in the couple.

One might wonder where sexual motivation is formed and maintained. Here one finds again the male and female groups already encountered in regard to fecundity. The apprenticeship of roles in sexuality and sexual stimulation have as chief origin these very groups, privileged places for communications regarding sex. These communications are much more active on the side of men than on that of women, who are more oriented toward fecundity. Besides, whereas the group of women is not divided by age categories and privileged communications take place there in a vertical fashion, among men, sexual communications take place between pairs or quasi pairs within age categories whose limits are not very precise. Between younger and elder males there is a certain shame; here sexuality is a taboo subject outside of rather formal communications (which is explained below by the position of women in the relations between older and younger men). What is important to note here, however, is that in male communications concerning fecundity, women appear rather like adversaries who should be subdued by sex. The opposition of the sexes, in sum, appears like the real stimulus to the union of the sexes. Sexual activity is, finally, a collective confrontation of men and women.

To recapitulate: woman is an inferior being, a sexual object with whom communication is not sought. The relation between men and women is the physiology of coitus. Woman in sexuality is not conceived as different from man; she does not exist as another. Her enjoyment is the achievement of the man, just as the field of wheat that ripens is the fruit of his labor. In addition, a sexuality that is not integrated with a more complete communication of a man to a woman is also without communication within the individual; sex for him is an activity detached from his other activities—one that finds in itself its own goal; the detachment of the orgasm from intellectual and emotional activity tends to make of it the very object of the intellectual and emotional activity.

These beliefs, these habitual modes of conduct, impose themselves with a considerable force on the individual; they are tied to the organization of society, to the place of the man as a political creature and the place of the woman as a creature of nature in this society. They do not seem to lead to a sexual awakening. The conditions of access to women do not lead there either.

Sexual Politics

Islam multiplies, as I have said, the legal facilities of access to women, and, on this level, Iranian institutions and social habits conform to religious dispositions. But what do these institutions signify in reality? Marriages are nearly always arranged. Marital constraint is probably exercised with a view to the good of the persons subjected to it, but, whatever the solicitude of the parents, they must be unaware of the reasons of love. Concubinage with slave women has passed, as has slavery (at least in Iran; it seems that it exists, hidden and on a small scale, in certain Arab states of the Persian Gulf). Temporary marriage hardly flourishes except around the great sanctuaries and places of pilgrimage, as brothels were formerly near the cathedrals of the West. There remains polygamy; like concubinage, it was and is only possible, because of the expense it involves, for the wealthier groups of the population. It is, besides, only in these groups that it once had, it seems, a real importance that is now in decline; and it is only among these groups that it had as its effective motive the satisfaction of "sexual vitality." In the other social categories it is rather the consequence of the sterility of a first marriage or of the economic advantage of the wife's work (carpet-weaving, for example), in which peasant polygamy in Iran is no different from that observed in Egypt or North Africa.

The legal facilities for access to women thus appear in reality to be little utilized. In addition, we must insist on the fact that these facilities have nothing to do with freedom of access. The recognized rights of individuals only take on meaning in the concrete conditions in which they are exercised. The fact that official institutions permit several concurrent or consecutive unions and unions of several kinds is superimposed on extremely strict social controls on access to women. A man, in reality, has no access to a woman, whatever tie he envisages with her, except through another man. A boy and a girl, a man and a woman, as long as they are not ritually forbidden to each other, never meet each other; at most they may sometimes catch a look at each other.

Every relationship must be mediated by an arrangement with the one or ones who, through one or another claim, dispose of the women: especially the "elders," father-heads of the family, and hierarchies of alliances of the families and groups of the locality. Marriage is a transaction; to the gift of the generating sex—woman—corresponds a countercurrent of countergifts or goods or money and political obligations. The one who cedes these cannot allow in such an important transaction that the ceded object could have been altered without his knowledge. His violence in case of alteration, the loss of virginity, has no other function than to regain his ridiculed prestige. The social rule that demands that access to the woman be mediated by the "guardian" of the woman also explains the violence that adultery entails.

Adulterous relationships are not allowed either, no more possible or frequent among the poor people of the country and towns than are relations before marriage. The legal difficulties of proving adultery, which might be taken as an institution favoring sexual freedom, can only be utilized by the upper classes whose power and arrogance defy popular judgment. The lower and middle classes condemn fornication very strongly and punish it with the most extreme rigor. The woman is considered chiefly responsible in it; she is stoned, sent to a house of prostitution, and so on. The popular verdict is less severe for the boy who, however, must in any case leave the village. It is only in Tehran, in acculturated milieus, that a certain liberalization has intervened in the course of recent decades. Among certain social categories, among officers notably, adultery is frequent.

We thus see that the juridical facilities for access to women only hide the nonexistence of free access, and the fact that most men can only have access in these conditions to a woman whom they have not personally chosen. The multiplication of legal forms of the sexual relationship is basically to be classified on the same level as the valorization of sex discussed above.

One might at this point ask oneself if the implicit criticism contained in the presentation given of the institutions that manage the relations between men and women is not subjective, oriented by a humanistic tropism, if in fact we are not faced by traditional institutions functioning within a society that entirely accepts them. It is worth insisting here on a major contradiction of fact: this society that gives so much value to sexual activity is sexually unhappy. The real frequency of female frigidity is not known; it is, besides, particularly difficult to know, for various reasons. First, no words exist for designating the special aspects of female sensuality. The fact that men estimate in general that 30–40 percent of women are frigid constitutes a disturbing index regarding men's own satisfaction, since the masculine code of sexual practice demands obtaining the participation of the women. We do not possess, besides, direct indexes or individual avowals of masculine dissatisfaction in heterosexual relations. Several aspects of culture and conduct reveal it: the lament of popular songs, the frequency of other forms of sexuality such as masturbation, homosexuality, and bestiality. We should note in passing that these practices, especially the last two, are strongly disapproved by Islam. It is, therefore, not due to respect for religious law that freedom in love does not exist, but because social institutions are an obstacle to it.

When one considers the social significance of the contradiction between the level of institutional values and that of the effective practice of sexuality, one is led to conclude that it conceals a sexual politics whose terms can be characterized in the following fashion:

> Sexuality is overevaluated; marriage is considered to be a superior state; great facilities are assured for the controlled union of the man and the woman. Society is bathed in a diffuse sexuality.
>
> Sexuality is, however, strictly controlled. Women, a sort of inferior caste, submit to their elders; free access to them is forbidden and impossible. The male candidate for marriage is forced to accept unconditional submission in the hierarchy of families and unions of families to satisfy the impulses exacerbated by culture. He must submit politically, in a relationship of personal dependence.
>
> The conditions of access for men and the status of women contribute to creating sexual dissatisfaction by their limitation on sexual activity and by the absence of personal communication between the sexes. This dissatisfaction tends to close the system in on itself; it contributes, in turn, in the existing cultural conditions, to the overevaluation of sex.

Sexual politics, an instrument of the power of the elder over the younger, is joined to matrimonial politics, an instrument of alliances between families and lineages. (Doubtless one would find in the relationship of the two politics the origin of the presentation noted above, of the relationship between fecundity and sexuality, supposed to have been instituted by God.) Both politics suppose the objectification of the woman and her reduction to the status of a good, a good for the reproduction of producers (to the profit of families, unions of families, and lineages) and an object of enjoyment (to the profit of individual males).

This reduction, however, does not proceed without difficulty because the concept of the woman as a being of nature is in contradiction with her consciousness and with the fact that she too is a being of culture. The valuation of procreation and sexuality and of the importance of women in intergroup relations reflects on her role. In addition, her husband, like her, feels a need for a personal relationship to prolong the status of the couple in society and of sexuality. The woman tends to conform to the role that the man expects of her and, at the same time, to overstep it in several ways. She thus introduces an unexpected element contradicting the application of masculine culture to relations between man and woman.

A first type of response by women to male conduct tends to define what one might call a culture of injury. The woman takes pride in her deprivation, she refuses to demand anything of her husband, and she considers it immodest to make a request of him. When she and her children lack necessities and her husband thinks only of prestige expenditures, she refuses to complain and opposes to circumstances the force of her soul.

The first lesson she learned from her mother was to mistrust men and to do without them; man is bad and unfaithful; the man is the stranger and his family the enemy; she must be proud and impassive; internal peace comes at this price. Woman imposes and affirms herself, by her silence, her reserve, her capacity to suffer, her disdain for goods, advantages, and prestige. She is not a thing that is taken but a being who gives herself, who sacrifices herself. She goes beyond ritual prohibitions by giving another value to prescribed gestures, that of her spiritual submission to a collective morality represented as God's will. She claims respect through renunciation itself, by spiritual authenticity. To the violence of masculine rapacity, she responds by no less a violence but a contrary one that denies the value of the man to whom she thus equates herself. This attitude, insofar as it is systematic, is aristocratic or, perhaps more exactly, belongs to certain lines of aristocratic women strongly marked by a certain sense of Islam. For the great majority of women, it is, however, one of the essential sources of the notion of conjugal fidelity. Whereas for the man the fidelity of the woman is only the fruit of the control exercised by measures of segregation and by the threats that men in general load upon her; for the woman, the barriers that separate her from the man take on an interior value—cloistering and the veil become the very symbols of her sacrifice, her renunciation. The power of the man is thus rendered useless.

A second means for woman to go beyond the role assigned to her, an attitude much more widespread in popular milieus and the source of numerous aspects of conduct, is duplicity, taking the word in its literal sense. This double attitude leads to an apparent hypocrisy, although it seems it is rarely experienced as such. Woman submits herself to marital and masculine authority and to the dominant values which are defined by men and, at the same time, plays her own role inside the institutions that deny power to her.

One example of this behavior is the game of the woman inside the family, particularly in relation to her sons. Man seeks in his children and his sons the reinforcement in number and prestige of the family and the lineage. On her side woman is socially recognized through her sons; it is due to them that she derives a respect denied to the wife, the daughter, or the sister. It is at this point that the specific game of the woman intervenes: she expects from her son an attachment with which she will counterbalance the superiority of her husband in the household. She makes of the son a rival of the father at the same time as she submits to him; she thus acquires, through mediation, but by her own activity, her own status and power in masculine society. The same evasive conduct is found on the economic level. The woman does not defend the rights that are refused to her but carries on hidden activities. To take hold of a few coins, to hide them away, is a widespread popular habit. This clandestine form of economic activity is found among women of comfortable milieus in the resort to usurious loans against property as security, which is an operation at once absolutely certain and hidden.

In sexuality more than elsewhere, this habit of deviation is widespread. The masculine catechism of the role of the woman says that she must not show her desire, but all women know and utilize methods to provoke the desire of the husband; they learn them in groups of women. They are not ignorant, either, of those that can turn him away, but their main concern is to catch and to keep their husbands. The primordial maxim, coming ahead of magic practices, is a rule of sexual conduct: to satisfy their husbands sexually. The woman is far from the sexual passivity into which the man wants to project her, but she provokes her husband only by circuitous maneuvers.

There is, finally, a third type of behavior by which the woman manifests her own existence: open violence, an exceptional conduct reserved for exceptional situations. For example, if a husband neglects his wife, it is easy for the latter to denounce him publicly, to tax him, rightly or wrongly, with impotence. This is a terrible accusation which, at one blow, destroys all the prestige of the man. Similarly, the polygamous home is habitually nothing but a hell of intrigues and violence. This behavior in polygamy, which is apparently normal in masculine ethics, becomes the source of a perpetual torment: calumny and disputes constantly appear to recall that the sexual morality of the man does not fit the aspirations of the woman, that Islam in particular, which legitimized polygamy and charged the man with maintaining concord among women, on this side has greatly overestimated the strength of the man, or has forgotten to formulate a feminine ethic of polygamy. In any case, the institution is foiled by reality; man, as orderer of society, is here seriously doubted, and his sexual activity, conceived as sovereignly independent, is especially conditioned by feminine conduct.

Whatever the conduct of the woman, the man understands that she is a being endowed with will, with a capacity for acquiescence or refusal; he is thus led to incline toward her, to deserve her, at least because the culture demands that he obtain her participation in the act of love, whose name in Persian is, curiously, the "prayer" of the man to the woman.

In fact it is not rare, especially in that period of sexual dazzlement that follows marriage, that a true amorous passion ties the couple. But how to conciliate the egalitarian and personal relationship of sentiment with the hierarchical and reified relationship of law? Their joining is impossible in principle and in fact; a greater or lesser tension always exists between them. The "official" model, weighing on the total organization of society beyond the couple, tends to crush the spontaneous model which scarcely finds any external support. At any rate, the relations of the husband and wife tend to contradict the model images of masculine culture. The contradiction has its origin in the conduct of the woman, who is not an object but an actor, participating or refusing, provoking or frustrating, in an indirect way the desire of the man. She is the conqueror at least as much as she is conquered by him, contesting his authority in the family and the lineage, intervening in "politics" through her sons, and so forth—all things through which she makes herself equal to him. Woman represents the eruption of spontaneity in the culture that comes from above. But she is unexplained and inexplicable in this culture; her direct or indirect conduct, which the man at any rate perceives, is in the domain of the incomprehensible. Hence the presence of masculine delusions that malign the image of the woman (is she a being by nature perverse and demonic?) and the resentment frequently felt toward her are explained. Islam finally rallies to this application of sufficient reason by avowing that it is impossible for the man to understand the woman. The undeceived statement attributed to the Prophet addressed to polygamists provides an example: "You will not succeed in making peace reign among your wives, whatever your good will."

Bibliography

Bousquet, Gaston H. *La morale de l'Islam et son éthique sexuelle.* Paris, 1953.

Hansen, Henny H. *The Kurdish Woman's Life.* Copenhagen, 1961.

Seklani, Mahmoud. "La fécondité dans les pays arabes." *Population,* 15 (1960) :831–856.

Tillion, Germaine. *Le harem et les cousins.* Paris, 1966.

23 Women, Class, and Power: Examples from the Hatay, Turkey

Barbara C. Aswad

Women in the Middle East, as in much of the world today, live in class-based societies where men hold the dominant positions of power and economic control. Men assumed the controlling positions in the agrarian empires of the past and remain in power in the neocolonial societies of today which have been imposed on the area from varying centers of capitalist accumulation. In only a few of the societies, such as South Yemen (Petran 1975), and in some sections of the Palestinian community—both societies in revolt against colonialism and neocolonialism—are we witnessing some concerted efforts toward actual power shifts and equalization of formal power positions between the sexes.

However, within the existing systems, the degree of power held by women in relation to one another and to men varies greatly depending upon such variables as class, the amount of stratification in the social unit as a whole, and conditions of political fluctuation such as protest and social revolution or rapid capitalization. The examples found in this paper are taken from the Hatay region of Turkey, a region that was part of Syria until 1939 when it became a pawn in pre–World War II politics and was transfered by France to Turkey. The rural example is drawn from Arabic-speaking villagers and the urban example from a primarily Turkified upper class with mixed ethnic backgrounds. The area has become one of increasing capitalist interests.

As an example of the class variable in women's power in this highly stratified region, it is quite obvious that a woman from a landed upper-class family has more power, authority, and status than a male sharecropper. This is due not only to her class but to the fact that the family is a political and economic unit among the ruling class, and she has a strong position in the family. Although much of her access to power is through her male kinsmen who are in primary positions of control, she does have direct access to them and influence over their decision-making. Her activities and kin connections form such an integral part of upper-class control that, in a comparative context, her degree of power is closer to that of her male kinsmen than it is to women and most men in other classes. Her position is more similar to women in other exploiting families in similar neocolonial societies around the world, such as Whitten describes in Ecuador (1969), than to other women in her own locale. In the Hatay, where the same families have had major control for almost a century, her position is primarily obtained through descent and marriage, and secondarily through her management of upper-class activities.

Numerous other social scientists have discussed the importance of family and extended kin ties in the Middle East. The Farsouns have analyzed the many functions of the family in Lebanon, a region of weak governmental control and strong nonstate and antistate organizations. They also link its strength in that area to the neocolonial situation of Lebanon and show that the family provides the many social services that are not forthcoming from the state or other organizations (Farsoun 1970, Farsoun and Farsoun 1974). Sweet, in discussing the complementary nature of women's activities within kin groups, provides some good examples of the sharing of power and decision-making. Commenting that this process is not usually observed by the outsider, she says: "When a decision is made in a traditional Middle Eastern social unit, the spokesman may be a most distinguished man in role and status but he is more apt than not to be voicing a consensus to which women have lent their weight. He would be a fool not to have listened to his mother, his aunt, his sister, or his wife, for it is they who know and manage the welfare of the internal or interior components of the social units (family, household, lineage, village) for which he is the minister of external affairs" (1974:391).

The nature of kin groups and correspondingly the position of women in those kin groups vary according to class position. I have previously discussed the ability of generally corporate patrilineages of an Arabic-speaking rich peasantry in a plains region to control and accumulate property and to commercialize their agriculture while forcing weaker kin units to lose their lands and become poor peasants, landless sharecroppers, and workers (1971). Thus, kin units as such have served as useful resources in the acquisition or maintenance of capital and power. Within the kin units, nonprofit principles of economic exchange have helped to spread the risks involved in dealings with external agents. It is difficult for many women in Western industrialized societies who are members of households with limited political and economic functions in the society to understand these principles fully. It is important to add, however, that the patrilineal bias of these rural, generally corporate kin groups places men in positions that have primary access to external power relationships.[1] These include access to patrons, markets, political party organizations, loans, and so on. Since these external agencies are almost exclusively headed by men, both in the centers of imperialist control such as New York or Moscow, and in metropolitan areas of the periphery such as Beirut, Istanbul, Antioch, or Riyadh, the networks act to reinforce local male dominance. Among various legal biases against women, perhaps one of the most threatening and often cruel is the right of the patrilineal segment to keep children from their mother in the case of divorce. The additional bias favoring men in the granting of divorce makes this a double threat.

Within the rural landowning patrilineages I have studied, women are also denied access to land through inheritance unless they are brotherless (1967, 1971). In the same village under conditions of rapid capitalization, the increased advantages that go to those who have external access to economic and political power have resulted in a reduction of control over resources for some men and most women of the lineage. That is, women as a group suffer in the process of rapid stratification. Thus, the investment and marketing processes become more concentrated in the hands of a few men as greater risks and more capital investment are required for cash cropping and the "green revolution." Inequality in opportunities for sons and daughters is another result. Sons are sent off to be educated and many marry educated urban girls, leaving a good number of lineage girls unmarried or late in marrying. Some lineage girls begin to pick cotton during harvest time for fear that they will not obtain security through bridewealth. Previously, women of landowning lineages had not engaged in this type of labor. Fathers will not allow their daughters to marry down in class; they are not educating them although they have the chance, and the girls show signs of stress such as ulcers, nervous disorders, and occasional violence. The "protection" of the lineage which had previously been to the economic advantage of the women is turning increasingly into dominance and exploitation.

Among landless sharecroppers and laborers, the most exploited in the class system of the area, there is no "estate" and men and women have only their labor and their children's labor to sell. The nuclear family is characteristic and bilateral kin relations are maintained primarily as intraclass networks for job related information. Patrilineal descent groups like those just described do not exist, and the most important networks involve interclass relations with employers. As in Western industrial working-class families where both partners work, women seem to enter freely into decision-making processes; however, they have double jobs, working along with men as well as raising children and performing important domestic functions. In this class, if there is a demand for cheap labor and children can participate (such as picking cotton), then the raising of large families is a necessary strategy for survival.[2] This adds to the difficulty of a woman's job but also increases her status within her class.

Thus, instead of making generalizations about women in any cultural area such as the Middle East, it is profitable to analyze comparatively the types of networks and political economic systems in which women are found. One would expect to find differences between women in neocolonial societies such as have been discussed here and those societies that have managed to exist outside of state or market control and that have some control over their resources, such as tribes or chiefdoms. Although these societies seem to be getting fewer and fewer, one would expect to find that dominance per se is less within these groups because the degree of monopoly of surpluses and ablity to exploit within the group is obstructed by patterns of economic exchange involving reciprocity, redistribution, and sharing. Tribes are generally more egalitarian than chiefdoms since patrilineal kin units compete for leadership positions, whereas among chiefdoms such as the bedouin, certain lineages have inherited priority in political and economic control. Thus, certain women in a chiefdom have significantly more power than other women. As to the male-female power relation, it appears that among the nomadic chiefdoms, women's role is quite secondary owing to the necessary mobility connected with raiding. Raiding is essential to their economy (Sweet 1970), and the best age for a raider or warrior corresponds to a woman's best reproductive years. Of course the political role of men as mediators with male-dominated state agencies and with markets and traders also adds to male dominance.

States and suprastate organizations have numerous patterns of dominance. Historically they have often exploited men as a group more extensively than women, in such organizations as armies, labor crews, and so on (Sacks 1974:221). Childbearing and the domestic functions of women generally meant that men were more available and dependable to exploit collectively at the period of their greatest strength than women. Many variables must be considered in the discussion of state and suprastate patterns of dominance. Capitalist and noncapitalist states have different patterns; geography and the degree of state centralization also play a role. Colonial and neocolonial patterns in highly centralized Egypt have been different from those in mountainous, decentralized Lebanon where kin groups can more easily gain economic and political control. Areas of direct colonial control, such as Algeria where colonial powers monopolized most positions of political and economic control, would differ from areas such as the Hatay, where local upper-class families were permitted to partake in colonial benefits. In the former, most local men were also deprived of some degree of power (Vinogradov 1974). These are among the complex of variables that must be considered in any particular case.

In a previous paper I discussed the landowning elite in the small provincial "agro-city"[3] of Antioch (population 65,000), which is located in the Hatay and beside the mountains bordering the northeast Mediterranean, and the women's role in maintaining the upper-class positions of economic and bureaucratic control (1974). Historically, this elite emerged as the new commercial landowning upper class during the last century. Under a form of French colonialism, less direct than that found in Algeria, they were allowed to evolve into a local branch of the national bourgeoisie. They controlled a significant portion of the lands of the area, and the same six families monopolized the most powerful political positions of the city for almost a century. Currently, their power is being challenged by other commercial and bureaucratic elites.

There is no doubt that men occupy the formal and more obvious public positions of power in this city. They have the important positions in the economy of exchange, and engage in strategies of vertical and horizontal mobility through political parties as they mediate between internal and external sources of power. However, one immediately notes that their political positions are also obtained and maintained largely by relations of consanguinity and affinity (descent and marriage). These relations necessarily involve upper-class women. In this case, rather than the domestic production role through which some peasant women gain power, these women operate in a semipublic role involving important communication networks of upper-class cohesion and boundary maintenance through their systematic visiting patterns, termed the *kabul* in Turkish or *istiqbal* in Arabic.

The kabul comprises much of the daily activity of the elite ladies. Each woman reserves a particular day of the month in which she receives anywhere from twenty to eighty women. Since there are several kabuls each day, any woman may attend as many as three or four a day; however, most seem to average four or five a week. The time is from 4:00 to 7:00 P.M., after the main meal of the day. The number and status of the visitors indicate the hostess' power. (For a discussion of the rules of etiquette at such meetings and of the occupational and ethnic composition of the groups, see Aswad 1974.)

There is much intermarriage among the dominant families (see Aswad 1974:11–12). The visiting patterns follow crucial intermarriages among the elite families. About half the marriages of these six families cross political factions. The overlapping horizontal networks thus form these ladies into a quasi group, counteracting the divisiveness of the male-dominated political arena. In addition to these intraclass strategies, the networks involve visiting between upper- and middle-class persons but they do not cross political factions. Rather, these are vertical networks within the same faction, involving patronage and upward mobility. Both processes, that of upper-class cohesion and definition and that of extension of power downward, are essential in the persistence of a local elite which is divided in its role as an intermediary for externally based powers.

The frequency of visiting is directly related to social distance, with visits occurring most frequently among those who are considered close relatives and less frequently among those who are considered distant relatives and among nonkin. The degree of actual relationship correlates to some extent with the social distinction owing to the frequency of intermarriage among the leading families, but it is interesting that it is a bilateral reckoning in a patrilineal society, and also that it is definitely a social calculation. For example, the following relationship was described as "close": a woman and her mother's mother's sister's son's son's daughter. This distant affinal link included important economic and political ties directly involving four of the six leading families (Aswad 1974:14).

The principle behind visiting in general is reciprocity, but for the kabul it is balanced reciprocity. The return should be equivalent and within an agreed-upon time limit. Not returning a similar visit within that time strains or breaks the relationship. As Sahlins shows, people deal as parties with separate economic and social interests (1968:82–83). Generalized exchange on the other hand implies that the expectation of reciprocity is left indefinite as to time, quantity, and quality. It occurs among members of a unit or close relatives, and failure to reciprocate does not break the relationship. Thus, the kabul is distinguished from visiting among members of the immediate family, and it is also separate from informal friendship groups.

The kabul is found only among the upper- and middle-class women.[4] It has a higher frequency among the upper class, and arrangements are made for its performance. Entry into this function can be accomplished successfully only by those women who can assign some domestic chores to maids. The importance of this is evidenced by their husbands' desires to provide such assistance. Women in these families have certain rights over land and other property, and they have influence over their male kinsmen, including their sons. They are active in arranging marriages, a political and economic function, and they may even be responsible for influencing their husbands to place certain men in political positions. They have public prestige and respect. They are also recognized as negotiators in factional disputes involving property, marriages, and other problems within and among the families. They serve in the informal establishment of the patron-client relations of their male kinsmen. Thus they have power and the society accords them high status; their actions and style of behavior reflect their position.

It has often been noted that part of women's power comes through what is often called negative power, that of cajoling, threatening humiliation, withholding favors, gossip, pressuring, and so on. To some extent the kabul is an example of institutionalized gossiping that takes on a public function. It is held in homes, but is an accepted and publicly acknowledged daily occurrence. It demonstrates the political apex in which kin relations meet with women's role in communication. The nature of information gathered and exchanged in these meetings was not indicated strongly enough in the earlier publication (Aswad 1974). The major source of "homework" for their participation in class cohesion or mobility seems to be in two areas. One involves the exchange of information of an economic nature, ranging from the agrarian conditions, prices, and marketing situations in the villages under their control, to the prices of latest Paris fashions. The second involves the exchange of information of a political and social nature regarding the villages. Since the women represent land-controlling families who have lands in differing regions, this information is often of a comparative nature. Information is exchanged on the activities of their families and other families. This relates to marriages, career plans of their children, who is in and out of what position, and the general behavior patterns of the men and women of their class and those who aspire to join their class. Most of these items are political in nature when they concern a family-based intermarrying elite.

This finding seems to add another dimension to the area of "domestic" versus "public" activity. Friedl distinguished public and nonpublic functions in Greek villages and showed that men received much of their status and respect by monopolizing public places (1967). Sanday distinguished domestic domain as "activities performed within the realm of the localized family unit, while the public domain includes political and economic activities that take place or have impact beyond the localized family unit and that relate to control of persons or control of things" (1974:190). In the study of upper-class women the power of the families is so extensive that much of the "domestic" becomes "public." A second aspect of the domestic-public division involves the importance of not confusing the physical structure of the home with "domestic" functions. Thus, women engage in visiting patterns important to class organization. These are not "domestic" functions just because they occur in the home. A Communist cell meeting that occurs in a living room would not be considered a domestic function if performed by men, and neither should these. They are publicly acknowledged and serve as institutionalized forms of the important "grapevine" component of power and decision-making.

In Antioch, the establishment of a competitive system, recently organized in the form of the Ladies Club, is primarily associated with the emerging elites, with those women excluded from the kabuls of the traditional elites, and with younger members of the traditional elite. Thus, new networks are provided in a changing economic and political structure.

Women's networks have been underplayed in Mediterranean and Middle Eastern literature, perhaps because they are less obvious than men's, but clearly they tell us much about the function and dynamics of class and power in society.

Notes

1. Beck also stresses the importance of external contacts (1974).
2. For a good discussion of this relationship, see White (1973).
3. The term *agro-city* was used by Van Dusen (1972) in his insightful analysis of Syria's current political situation. It is interesting to note that even though Syria has expelled most of its traditional leading families, there are now definite middle-class and military "big families" in these agro-cities (Van Dusen 1972). This kind of city is also briefly discussed in Hourani and Stern (1970:16ff).

4. When an elite kabul network was compared with a lower-middle-class visiting network, the latter contained only half the number of visits of the elite network. Also, while the elite woman divided her visits between upper and middle classes about evenly, the other visited mainly in her own class and saw more friends and neighbors and fewer relatives (Aswad 1974:18–19).

Bibliography

Aswad, Barbara C. "Key and Peripheral Roles of Noblewomen in a Middle Eastern Plains Village." *Anthropological Quarterly,* 40 (1967):139–152.

———. *Property Control and Social Strategies: Settlers on a Middle Eastern Plain.* Anthropological Papers no. 44. Ann Arbor, Mich., 1971.

———. "Visiting Patterns among Women of the Elite in a Small Turkish City." *Anthropological Quarterly,* 47 (1974):9-27.

Beck, Lois. "Theoretical Perspectives on the Position of Women in Iran." Unpublished. Boston, 1974.

Farsoun, S. K. "Family Structure and Society in Modern Lebanon." In *Peoples and Cultures of the Middle East,* vol. II, ed. L. Sweet. Garden City, N.Y., 1970.

Farsoun, Samih, and Karen Farsoun. "Class and Patterns of Association among Kinsmen in Contemporary Lebanon." *Anthropological Quarterly,* 47 (1974):93–111.

Friedl, Ernestine. "The Position of Women: Appearance and Reality." *Anthropological Quarterly,* 40 (1967):97–108.

Hourani, A. H., and S. M. Stern, eds. *The Islamic City.* Philadelphia, 1970.

Petran, Tabitha. "South Yemen Ahead on Women's Rights." *Middle East International,* 48 (June 1975):24–26.

Sacks, Karen. "Engels Revisited: Women, the Organization of Production and Private Property." In *Woman, Culture, and Society,* ed. M. Rosaldo and L. Lamphere. Stanford, Calif., 1974.

Sahlins, Marshall D. *Tribesmen.* Englewood Cliffs, N.J., 1968.

Sanday, Peggy. "Female Status in the Public Domain." In *Woman, Culture, and Society,* ed. M. Rosaldo and L. Lamphere. Stanford, Calif., 1974.

Sweet, Louise. "Camel Raiding of North Arabian Bedouin: A Mechanism of Ecological Adaptation." In *Peoples and Cultures of the Middle East,* vol. I, ed. L. Sweet. Garden City, N.Y., 1970.

———. "In Reality: Some Middle Eastern Women." In *Many Sisters,* ed. C. Matthaisson. New York, 1974.

Van Dusen, Michael. "Political Integration and Regionalism in Syria." *Middle East Journal,* 26 (1972):123–136.

Vinogradov, Amal. "French Colonialism as Reflected in the Male-Female Interaction in Morocco." *Transactions of the New York Academy of Sciences,* 36 (1974):192–199.

White, Benjamin. "Demand for Labor and Population Growth in Colonial Java." *Human Ecology,* 1 (1973):217–236.

Whitten, Norman. "Strategies of Adaptive Mobility in the Colombian-Ecuadorian Littoral." *American Anthropologist,* 71 (1969):228–242.

24 A Comparative Perspective on Women in Provincial Iran and Turkey

Mary-Jo DelVecchio Good

The status of women in Islamic societies has often been discussed with reference to women's roles, to the culturally derived restrictions such as honor and shame upon women's freedom, and to the "private world of women" and the "public world of men." This essay takes a somewhat different perspective and focuses on the position of women in stratification systems in Iran and Turkey.

Social scientists who have examined stratification systems in the Middle East have most often subsumed the female social hierarchy within the male social hierarchy. The validity of the approach that ties women's class and status positions to those of their fathers and husbands is not disputed here, for the family as well as individuals are units in a social hierarchy. Class position and certain aspects of life-style are determined for the entire family by the class and status positions of the household head who is most often a man—a husband or a father. However, more recent works on women in the

I would like to thank Byron Good, Michael Fischer, Vivian Blackford, and the editors of this volume, Lois Beck and Nikki Keddie, for their critical reading of and suggestions for earlier versions of this paper. Research in Iran in 1972–1974 was sponsored by grants from the Foreign Area Fellowship Program of the Social Science Research Council and the Pathfinder Fund of Boston. I was a Peace Corps volunteer in the Turkish cities of Elazig and Istanbul in 1964–1966 and did research in Turkey in 1969.

Middle East have begun to explore the variations in status hierarchies between male and female social worlds (Pastner 1974, Davis 1975, Good 1974).

A different perspective, which focuses primarily on variations in life-styles and on association patterns of women, is taken here and provides an understanding of the following: how a subsystem differs from a general stratification system in a community (that is, the difference between the female- and male-dominated systems); what the status of women is in a community, and how it is changing; and how the overall stratification system in a community has changed and is changing. A comparison of provincial Iran and Turkey should further an understanding of the bases of stratification in general, and among women in particular, in Middle Eastern societies. The variations between Iran and Turkey suggest that three factors are of particular importance in structuring patterns of hierarchy and association among women in provincial settings:

> The degree to which traditional patterns of social contact and social entertainment are maintained, and the degree to which new forms are introduced;
>
> The degree to which opportunities for women to participate in the public world of business, the professions, and the bureaucracy are limited or available; and
>
> The degree to which the national political ideology formulates new status roles and introduces changes in women's roles.

It appears that in Iranian provincial town society, the status-group hierarchy of women is differentiated to a lesser degree than that of men and that the hierarchy is flatter in the social world of women;[1] whereas in Turkish provincial society, the status-group hierarchy of women tends to be more sharply differentiated and more closely mirrors the patterns of male stratification. These differences between provincial Iran and Turkey, and between male and female spheres, are related, first, to the extent to which traditional patterns of association are maintained; second, to the degree and manner in which women participate in the public world; and third, to the politicization of status differences in national political ideologies and cleavages and its impact on women's roles. The contrast between Turkey and Iran in these three areas may be partially attributed to the time differential in the modernization processes in educational, religious, economic, and political spheres, which in turn affected the redefinition of women's roles in these two societies. Ataturk (1923–1938) was able to draw upon the ongoing processes of modernization begun by the Young Ottomans and continued by the Young Turks in the nineteenth and early twentieth centuries for his reform programs. In contrast, Reza Shah (1925–1941) had to introduce modernization processes into a society that was dominated to a greater extent by conservative religious and provincial elites.

The Iranian Case

Maragheh, once a Mongol capital (thirteenth century), is located in northwest Iran. Its population, predominantly Azerbaijani Turkish, numbers approximately sixty-three thousand. The town is a provincial capital and has long been an administrative and agricultural center. Although Maragheh is located in a geographic cul de sac, which has limited its industrial development and isolated it from some of the modern influences of the capital of Tehran and other metropolitan industrial centers, the patterns of social relations among women do not differ greatly from other provincial towns of similar size. However, when Maragheh is compared with more cosmopolitan centers such as Tabriz, Isfahan, and Shiraz, one is struck by the negligible role that its women play in the public sphere.

Hierarchy in Provincial Iran

During the day the streets of Maragheh are filled with men, young and old, going about their business, or loitering, gossiping, and taking in the scene. When women are present on the main streets or in the alleyways of the bazaar, they are almost always veiled and accompanied by children, other women, or a male member of the immediate family. Women rarely appear unveiled in public and those who do are clearly foreigners to the town. A few upper-class women from Maragheh do occasionally visit friends and family without a veil (*chador*) if they are accompanied by their husbands in the family car.

The town is considered by many Tabrizis to be religiously conservative, and many of its own inhabitants consider it a *Hoseinkhaneh* or a House of Hosein.[2] Significantly, of all social occasions that include persons other than members of an extended family, religious occasions appear to be the most frequent. Wedding celebrations are confined primarily to the months after the mourning months of Moharram and Safar and prior to Ramazan. But funerals, mourning anniversaries for the dead, "black *beirams*" (happy holidays devoted to commemoration of those who have recently died), and *mersiyehs* (*rowzehs*) (held in homes in fulfillment of vows) give the town's social life a definite religious tone. The most important public event in the town is the yearly series of Moharram dramas. People from all status groups participate in the religious life of the town, but participation varies by sex and status group in a highly structured way.

Status groups in Maragheh are fairly closely linked with the class structure of the town.[3] Each status group includes members of several classes and vice versa. For example, the traditional old elite is a status group of those families whose economic base was ownership of villages and now is ownership of large tracts of agricultural lands, vineyards, and gardens, as well as families whose primary income comes from wholesale trade. The professional-managerial group, or "new elite," includes those whose major source of income derives from the central government as well as those who have private practices. In addition, some members of this group are sons of merchants and landowners, and they continue to own land or shares in commercial enterprises. Among the third status group, that of white collar workers, middle-level bureaucrats, and teachers, income comes primarily from the state, but some members of this group also own gardens or other property inherited from their farmer fathers. Somewhat more marginal to this group in economic terms but one with similar aspirations are the lower-level civil servants. Among the fourth status group, which consists of the traditional *bazaaris*, shopkeepers, and craftsmen, there is wide variation of income and wealth. Although their relationship to the means of production is grossly similar, inequality in the marketplace is widespread. The fifth status group, that of lower craftspeople and unskilled laborers, is more homogeneous in terms of class, but there is inequality owing to variations in income.

Life-style distinctions in Maragheh tend to follow these broad status-group lines, especially for the men of the town, and express inequalities in wealth, power, influence, and prestige. The distinctions between the old and new status groups refer to differences in the cultural mode of these groups, in their use of status symbols.

Self-groupings for women follow these divisions when the system as a whole is examined and when families rather than individuals are considered.[4] And women do derive much of their status position from that of their fathers and husbands. However, by examining the association patterns and in particular the religious behavior of women as opposed to that of men, one discovers that certain status symbols, which maintain these distinctive groups for men, blur and are less precise for women. Thus the stratification system among women appears to be flatter or less differentiated. This perspective suggests that there is a subsystem within the stratification system that is primarily relevant to the social hierarchy among women. This flattened hierarchy is attributable to four factors:

> Women encounter cultural and social restrictions that prevent most of them from pursuing professional or other occupational roles that are in the public, male-dominated sector (particularly the new occupations); and those who are professionals have a restricted role in the public sector;
>
> Women rely on their extended family members for intimate friendships rather than on colleagues or co-workers;
>
> Women rely on neighborhood women for social contacts and social entertainment outside the family;
>
> Men do not expect their wives to conform to the patterns of behavior that are particular to their own status group (in contrast to class-related behavior).

Variations in religious behavior are among the most significant ways by which men symbolize the differences between themselves and other groups in the social hierarchy. Yet, when women's religious behavior in Maragheh is observed, not only do fewer modes of behavior symbolize status-group differences, but also women associate with women from a broader range of status groups than do men.[5]

Women's Association Patterns and Hierarchy

Mersiyehs (rowzehs), *sofreh*s, *taziyeh*s, and memorial ceremonies are given by women in their own homes to fulfill vows or to commemorate family members who have died. These religious gatherings always include performances by *mullah*s or *rowzehkhan*s (usually male but some females as well) who sing about the events of Karbala, the martyrdom of Imam Hosein and his followers, and the suffering of their women. Women respond to these performances through ritualized crying and mourning. These occasions vary in the elaborateness of the religious meal prepared and in the number of rowzehkhans who attend and sing. Funeral ceremonies are usually concluded with dinners for close friends and family members. Sofrehs may be extremely elaborate dinners in honor of Abu-Fazl Abbas or more simple fares in honor of Khanom Roqayeh, the daughter of Imam Hosein. However, at each mersiyeh or religious gathering (the simplest are held during the months of Moharram, Safar, and Ramazan) tea and cigarettes are served to all who attend. Women from a broad range of status groups were present at the many religious occasions I observed, and there was little difference in treatment of guests along status-group membership lines, in the behavior of the women present, or in their professed religious beliefs. Even in style of dress, the greatest differences were among age categories rather than among status groups or classes. The women who attended many of these mersiyehs were primarily from the two middle-level social status groups, the "newer" group of white collar and government employees and the "older" group of bazaaris. But several wives of professional-managerial husbands attended and there were always a few wives of laborers.

Family status differences were not totally disregarded in these contexts, but they were not emphasized. Women who were teachers were introduced as such, usually with some pride. And women whose husbands were professionals were always pointed out as welcome guests who honored the hostess with their presence.

Mersiyehs (religious gatherings) given by women of the new or old elite status groups were similarly eclectic affairs, with some women from the bazaari and bureaucratic classes present, as well as an occasional old woman from the working class. Many status differences between women of adjacent groups were blurred, although to a lesser degree than among the middle-level groups. One was always aware of the "important" women in the room, as women from the middle class shyly pointed out who was who in Maragheh society. Thus, the blurring of status differences occurs primarily between women of status groups that are horizontally adjacent and of similar class standing. The higher one moves in the social hierarchy, the more pronounced is the recognition of differences among members of classes in the vertical social order.

Class differences did structure some forms of religious behavior for women. Women from the old and new elite never attended the *shabihs*, the religious dramas, during Moharram.[6] Attendance was considered behavior unbecoming to the position of a member of the upper class. On the other hand, women from the middle and lower classes did attend the Moharram dramas whenever they had the opportunity. They participated in the only way that women were allowed to participate in these events—as rather unwelcome observers.

The similarity of religious behavior and association patterns among the various status groups of women is in striking contrast to the differences among these same status groups in the male hierarchy. Men in the bazaari status group associate with their neighbors from the bazaar, with men who are from their own status group, whereas teachers and bureaucrats find their social acquaintances among their own colleagues. The mixing of these groups seldom occurs except when the extended family members gather (a bazaari father with a teacher son is common) or when funeral ceremonies are held in large mosques (again extended family, friends, and acquaintances). Men pay short visits to show respect at these ceremonies, and there is less intensive social interaction than at the women's gatherings held in the homes. Similar to the middle-level groups, the old and new elite rarely associate with each other for social entertainment, unless they are from the same extended family.

Men in the bazaar gather for daily prayer in the mosques located in their section of the bazaar. They are sometimes members of religious circles (*sireh*) that meet every night during Ramazan. During Moharram, bazaaris are often direct participants in the religious dramas as members of the *Hoseiniyeh*s, the men's religious societies, that are responsible for the Moharram performances. All the men from the bazaar spend some time observing these performances during Moharram. Some workers partcipate in these Moharram religious activities, especially if they are attached to the bazaar crafts and shops. But many workers could not afford time away from work to join these religious activities.

Men from the white collar status group tend to shun the religious gatherings of bazaaris, regardless of their own religious beliefs. Few think of participating in the Moharram *dasteh*s, the chain and chest beating processions, and most believe that those who engage in ritualized self-mutilation such as slashing the tops of their heads are behaving in violation of true Islam. Those who do participate in a Moharram group attend one that advocates reason and rationalism in Islam. This group sings and chants poetic prayers during Moharram, but it does not dramatize the events at Karbala nor do its members indulge in self-flagellation. Most bureaucrats also avoid the services and gatherings in their neighborhood mosques.

Men from the old elite are patrons of many of the town's religious activities. They turn over their caravansaries to be used by the men's religious societies who perform the Moharram dramas, and some invite these groups to their home courtyards to perform there. Many have a joking attitude toward religion and religious functionaries, but they continue to participate as sponsors of these activities. Most men of the new elite, however, are adamantly opposed to the entire religious tone of the town, and they frown on the Moharram dramas. If they tolerate them, it is usually for political purposes. Otherwise, they view these activities as evidence of backwardness and superstition.

It is perhaps most important for men from the newer status groups, the white collar and new elite, to firmly differentiate themselves from the bazaari and old elite in their patterns of behavior and belief, because they are trying to be that which their fathers were not. (The professional-managerial group usually had fathers who were either landlords, merchants, or bazaaris, and the white collar group generally had fathers who were bazaaris.) These men differ from their fathers in occupation, education, and life-style. They are modern in a way that their fathers were not and cannot be.

On the other hand, women who are married to men from these new groups are often not very different from their mothers in the role they play in the home, in their lack of educational attainment, in their religious beliefs and practices, and in their patterns of association beyond the extended family. What happens to those women who do differ from their mothers, who do have a high school education, or who have a new career as a teacher, bureaucrat, or professional midwife? In general, they continue to attend the mersiyehs given by their neighbors, although less often than women who do not work. And those whose fathers are bazaaris still go to watch the Moharram dramas when they have the opportunity. Friends whom they invite to their homes for their own mersiyehs and religious gatherings or for casual socializing are still drawn from the extended family and neighborhood rather than from their colleagues in school or at the office. They continue to be integrated into the traditional social networks.

Yet the situation is fluid and changing. Younger women from the new elite are beginning to have additional social networks. Some, such as the young wives of a group of doctors and engineers, attend weekly card-playing or tea circles (*dowreh*) that include a few out-of-towners. Younger career women from the white collar group are less likely to belong to these exclusive, secular circles, but they have begun to differentiate themselves from their mothers and other traditional women in a variety of ways. Some symbolize and assert their differences by wearing flimsier veils to the mersiyehs; they show less reverence to the rowzehkhans (religious leaders), and they participate less intensely in the ritual crying. But the most elementary and striking means by which they can and do symbolize their new status position are in the way they decorate and furnish their homes, and in the place where they choose to give birth to their children (hospital versus home). These women as yet form a very small minority in Maragheh and in many other provincial towns. They must continue to rely on traditional social networks dominated by traditional women. The stratification pattern among women can be expected to begin to resemble that of the dominant male pattern only after a greater proportion of women enter "new" or "modern" roles in provincial Iranian society and seek to symbolize felt status-group differences through their behavior and in their patterns of association.

It has been shown that status-group differences are less important to the structuring of association patterns among women than among men in provincial Azerbaijan. The major focus has been on religious gatherings in delineating male-female differences because these are the most frequently held social occasions that include members beyond the extended family. It has been noted that nonfamilial, secular, and rather exclusive social gatherings are beginning to be of some importance to those few women who have a modern profession and/or who are married to men of the town's new upper class. Nevertheless, these secular gatherings do not preclude their participation in the less exclusive religious gatherings. Women from the middle and lower classes of both new and old status groups also associate with one another in casual, secular, neighborhood gatherings. Thus, status-group distinctions are not as important in structuring patterns of secular association for the majority of town women as they are for men. It has been noted that class distinctions are more significant in the structuring of association patterns than status distinctions. While there is a certain amount of mixing of classes in women's religious gatherings, there is always an awareness of grosser class differences. However, these are downplayed in religious and neighborhood gatherings as long as the boundaries of propriety are maintained.[7]

The Restricted Role of Professional Women

Women in provincial towns such as Maragheh are beginning to enter occupations that bring them into the "public sphere." Yet these new professional or occupational roles in the more conservative provincial towns are remarkable for their restricted nature. Women teachers, midwives, and bureaucrats operate in a world of children or a world of women. In 1975 education was still segregated by sex, and no women teachers taught in the boys' middle or high schools in Maragheh. Women who were bureaucrats in the

Ministry of Health (nurses, midwives, and clerks) worked in segregated offices and served almost exclusively other women and children. Women bureaucrats (the rare few) in other ministry offices were usually segregated by sex in their offices. Furthermore, no women worked in public places of business (banks, shops, and so on) as managers, secretaries, or clerks. The only women who consistently had encounters with adult males as part of their occupational roles were nurses and nurses' aides at the hospitals, and these occupations have very low prestige in provincial Iranian towns. Thus, even women who have modern occupational roles do not yet fully participate in the public sphere.

The Limited Role of Wives as Status Bearers

Wives of men in modern professions also play very limited roles as representatives of their husbands' status positions at public occasions in provincial society. Few women from the provincial upper or middle classes entertain mixed company beyond their own extended family groups. Close male associates may never encounter their colleagues' wives in mixed social situations. And the impetus for the rare mixed dinner party usually comes from young professional couples who are outsiders to the town.[8]

Both the restricted role of women in modern occupations and the limited role of wives as bearers or representatives of their husbands' status positions inhibit the development of status-group distinctions in the social hierarchies of women in provincial towns.

Metropolitan versus Provincial Patterns

Status-group distinctions are relatively more important in structuring association patterns among women in the larger urban centers such as Tabriz or Tehran than in provincial Iran. Large portions of the female population in both of these major cities continue to associate primarily with neighbors and family members in a style similar to that of traditional Maragheh. However, status-group differences do structure patterns of association for women whose social identity includes being modern or being a member of a professional group either as wives who have internalized their husbands' status or as professionals in their own right. Thus, the criteria for association within the modern upper and middle classes is status by occupation, status by husband's occupation, and status by family heritage.

In Tabriz, women married to young professional men (university professors in particular), upper-level bureaucrats, and business managers often gather at informal women's teas and intimate mixed dinner parties with a limited network of other women whose husbands are of similar rank. Although their own paternal family backgrounds range from traditional landlord families and merchants to upper-level bureaucrats and professionals, and their own educational attainments vary from middle school diplomas to university degrees, they associate together at various social occasions because of their husbands' status positions. In many cases, these women also maintain other social circles, including the more traditional and exclusive family circles. But few continue to associate with neighbors from a variety of class and status groups.

Formal teas hosted and attended by the wives of upper-level bureaucrats constitute another type of modern social gathering designed to fulfill the social obligations and duties of a woman's husband's "office." These differ from the more intimate social gatherings of the young professional wives in that the women attending need not be "friends." Indeed, both hostess and guest have roles defined by their husbands' positions, and their relative status is derived from and a direct reflection of their husbands' relative status.

Gatherings of female colleagues are less common in Tabriz than in Tehran, but some groups of professional women do hold social gatherings. In Tabriz, professional nurses, who attended university together and who often worked in the same hospitals, meet as friends and colleagues to celebrate weddings, births, and other events. These women associate with each other because of the similarity of their own professional status rather than that defined by their husbands' or fathers' positions.

These three forms of association among women are modern patterns that complement the status distinctions that have developed out of the modern occupational sector and the accompanying changes in life style. A comparison of women in modern occupational roles in metropolitan centers with those in provincial towns indicates that women in the metropolitan centers are less restricted in their occupational roles in the public sphere. Women professionals and bureaucrats in Tehran, and to a lesser extent in Tabriz, often work in the same offices as their male colleagues and deliver services to both the male and female public without a loss of "social honor." However, the restricted role for professional Iranian women is still dominant in the educational sector (excluding institutions of higher education) and in much of the public health sector. And as in less modern cities, few women are found in the sales sector, although one does encounter women in the more prestigious business offices of airlines and banks.

The Turkish Case

Among the most impressive contrasts between patterns of female hierarchy in provincial Iran and Turkey are the differences in behavior of women in modern occupations and in the extent to which status-group distinctions structure association patterns. The Iranian data indicate that professional and paraprofessional women have restricted roles in public life and that few hold jobs that bring them into continuous contact with adult males. In contrast, the professional and paraprofessional women in provincial Turkey participate to a greater extent in the public sphere.

The Neuter Role versus the Restricted Role

In Elazig, a provincial town in eastern Anatolia, a considerable number of women were working in public places in 1965. There were female bank clerks, secretaries, bureaucrats, and even doctors. As the majority of high schools and all the middle and primary schools were coeducational, women taught and administered these institutions alongside male teachers. In other Turkish towns, one finds women judges, pharmacists, and bank directors who operate in a public world that seems to be far less exclusively male than its Iranian counterpart. While women do not usually attend the provincial restaurants and bars (except the officers' clubs), they do promenade with their husbands or female friends in provincial towns. This practice is rare in Azerbaijan. Professional women also belong to clubs, such as teachers' clubs, and associate with colleagues at these places after work, whereas in Maragheh the attractive Women's Club building is seldom used for gatherings of women colleagues.

Lloyd and Margaret Fallers have suggested in a provocative essay that professional women in Turkey "act as 'professionals' . . . interacting with the public with the part of their person which is trained and skilled. They do not act as total personalities and certainly not as 'females' " (1976:254). This type of behavior in the public sphere may be considered a "neuter role,"[9] in which the sexual identity of professional women does not interfere with their professional identity or behavior. The Fallers suggest further that "these Turkish women who work in the public sphere bring with them from the traditional separated world of the women a sense of independence of men which makes them more able to concentrate on the tasks at hand" in the public world (1976:254).

While there is much merit to this suggestion, it does not account for the contrast between Turkey and Iran. In both societies women rely on the judgment and support of other women. The role of the professional woman is conceived of quite differently in provincial Iran than in provincial Turkey. This is due to the degree to which Turkish reformist ideology (which emphasizes the modernization of women's roles) has been institutionalized at the provincial level. As previously noted, Turkey has had the advantage of a longer era of purposive modernization.

Iran has made great gains in the last decade, particularly through the Revolutionary Corps, in introducing provincial women to public professional roles as teachers and health aides. And the Shah and Empress as well as Princess Ashraf have stressed women's rights. But as of 1975, there has been no major attempt in the provinces to alter radically the traditional attitudes and values that relegate women to positions away from the adult male public domain. Females continue to be educated separately from males until they attend universities, which have overwhelmingly male student bodies. Turkey, on the other hand, began to undergo an ideological revolution under Ataturk which has had far-reaching consequences for the roles women take in public life. The introduction of coeducational elementary and high schools seems to be particularly crucial to the acceptance of women in public roles as professionals, teachers, administrators, and clerks, even while the persistence of traditional patterns of separate private worlds of women and men enables Turkish women to play a neuter role in public occupations.

Association Patterns

Association patterns among women in provincial Turkish towns appear to reflect the status hierarchy of the male world to a greater extent than those in Iranian provincial towns. Women who are teachers, professionals, and bureaucrats gather as a status-conscious group at one another's homes as well as at local teachers' and ladies' clubs. Women who are married to men from more modern and secular status groups are called upon to represent their husbands at mixed social gatherings. Wives of army officers, in particular, and bureaucrats from other regions of the country (often metropolitan centers) give and attend mixed dances and dinner parties in conscious efforts to introduce "modern" styles of entertainment to the provincial scene. Women who represent the modern status groups by virtue of their own education and occupation as well as that of their husbands tend to shun social events that are dominated by traditional women who represent Islamic conservatism. And although *mevlud* gatherings of women for religious worship do occur in Turkish provincial towns, these religious occasions do not dominate the social life of Turkish provincial women as religious occasions do in Iran. They are much less frequent and socially central.

The reception day (*kabul gunu*) has been spread to many Turkish provincial towns by wives of bureaucrats from metropolitan areas (Benedict 1974). This indicates that the modern status group of women in these towns has had considerable influence on styles of entertainment and association among local provincial women. The discussions of Benedict (1974) and Aswad (1974) of the reception day in two provincial Turkish towns note that this form of entertainment is restricted to women from the middle and upper classes. In both cases the women who attend and give these receptions are representatives of their husbands' class and status positions in the community. Within the social hierarchy of these gatherings, most of which are among near social equals (Aswad 1974:13–14), the relative status of a woman "is fixed and changes only as the social position of her husband declines or ascends" (Benedict 1974:46).[10]

The Turkish reception day and the Iranian provincial dowreh differ in their status function in the community. Both Benedict and Aswad noted that the reception day networks range from twenty to seventy-five or eighty people. Visiting patterns are further complicated by competing days, thus attendance may vary. In Maragheh, the women's dowreh usually included about ten people. The circle of doctors' wives met weekly and serially at each member's home. Thus, each member entertained the other members of the dowreh every few months, rather than at a personally set reception day. Both the reception day and the dowreh are associations of status groups that emphasize the inequality of outsiders. Yet the larger network of the reception day suggests that the function of the association is more oriented to public display of status-group concerns and to establishing within the female network additional means of communication among segments of the provincial elite that include both local and nonlocal elements.

The dowreh, on the other hand, is often an extremely selective and tightly knit group of like-minded women. The more traditional circles carefully limit their membership to the landed and local elite, often including only members of an extended family (in contrast to the political dowrehs of Tehran society). The more modern group of doctors' wives who formed a dowreh are equally exclusive in their membership, and nonlocals from the same professional status group are often not invited to attend. Wives of high-level bureaucrats from other towns are often left out of the social life of Maragheh society in spite of their husbands' high status. Many of these women refuse to move from Tehran to take up residence with their husbands in the provincial areas. As a result, they have negligible impact on the association patterns and styles of entertainment in the provincial towns. Language differences between bureaucrats from Tehran and those from the local area symbolize the gap between locals and nonlocals in the female hierarchy and serve to exacerbate the communication gap between the local and nonlocal elite.

The Turkish reception days also differ from the religious rituals, the mersiyehs, which so dominate the Iranian provincial scene.[11] Mersiyehs draw in women from all status groups, whereas reception days exclude the wives of more traditional shop keepers and bazaaris. Social status is an important criterion for inclusion in the reception day network. It is not an important criterion for inclusion in the network of provincial Iranian religious rituals, although it does help to determine who will attend a hostess's mersiyeh.

Conclusion

Status-group differences are less important to the structuring of association patterns, first, among women than among men in provincial Iran, and second, among women in provincial Iran than in metropolitan Iran and provincial Turkey. The basic hypothesis has been that female hierarchies become sharper and more differentiated when more modern occupational and cultural systems develop and begin to affect women in their occupational roles, in their group associations, and in their social identity. This study is but a first step in an attempt to understand when, why, and how such changes begin to affect the hierarchy patterns among women.

The data suggest that the development of more differentiated hierarchical patterns and increased status distinctions are associated with three factors. The first is changes in patterns of association and representation of class and/or status positions. These changes occur when women become adjuncts to their husbands (and in a sense less independent) as representatives of their husbands' status positions; when "modern" forms of entertainment are considered essential to communicating and maintaining one's or one's husband's status position; and when women associate with female colleagues. The second factor is changes in the role of women in the occupational sector. These changes are effective when there is a critical mass of women in a community in public roles (dependent upon educational and occupational opportunities); when professional women take on roles that are less restricted, and perhaps neuter, in the public realm; and when there is a self-identification with modern values associated with new occupations, and thus the emergence of a new group consciousness based on similarity of status. The third factor in more differentiated hierarchial patterns and increased status distinctions is changes in the role national ideologies play in legitimizing efforts at modernization in general and in changing roles of women in particular. These changes are effective when modern values have filtered down from metropolitan regions to provincial towns and when modern ideological positions regarding women's roles are frameworks for concerted official action.

In Iran, changes in patterns of association and women's occupational roles have been closely associated with the degree of urbanization and modernization of the occupational structure. In Turkey, an additional factor, reformist ideology, has made women more conscious of their identity as status-group members than their counterparts in provincial Iran. Additional research into the role of ideology should be useful in clarifying this relationship.

Does modernization of women's roles lead to greater inequality in these societies? Although changes in objective inequality, that based on differences in income and wealth, have not been discussed here, modernization of the economic sector has led to increased differentiation in the class structure just as it has led to greater status differentiation of subjective inequality in both Iran and Turkey. Objective inequality may be increased as women assume income-producing occupational roles; however, patterns of ownership, income distribution mechanisms, and taxation policies are more powerful in structuring objective inequality. The contrast between Turkey and Iran suggests that while expansion of the modern economic sector does lead to increased class divisions, the degree of relative inequality of income and wealth is dependent upon government policies rather than solely on the level of modernization. As has been noted by many Iranian as well as Western economists (International Labor Organization 1972), the recent rapid expansion of the modern economic sector in Iran has led to increases in the relative inequality of income groups and thus to sharper class divisions. In Turkey, the relative inequality of income groups appears to be modified by a stiff graduated income tax and by a more evenly distributed modern industrial sector. Turkey has had neither the benefits nor the dislocating effects of an oil boom. In spite of the Turkish government's attempts to encourage industrial development throughout the country, the eastern provinces continue to lag behind the economic development of the western provinces, as have those groups in the traditional as compared with the modern economic sectors.

With regard to subjective inequality, increased status differentiation among women as well as men does lead to the introduction of diverse systems of prestige and to new cultural cleavages. The cultural cleavages introduced by modernizing trends in the social position of women are increasingly apparent in the major cities of Iran and Turkey. Women whose life-style is modern in manner of dress, entertainment, religious practice, and work seldom associate with women who are more traditional in their behavior, regardless of similar class positions. Yet, class and status have become increasingly coterminous in the more metropolitan and modern centers of Iran and Turkey. Nevertheless, cultural and economic cleavages appear to have different emphases in Iran and Turkey. In Iran, the most powerful social divisions appear to be played out in the economic sphere. In Turkey, the most powerful social divisions appear to be cultural cleavages which are played out in the political sphere of party politics. In both societies, women have begun to be public (in contrast to private) representatives of those social divisions as they take on more modern roles.[12] Thus, modernization of women's roles does lead to sharper economic and cultural distinctions within the social hierarchy of women just as modernization leads to increased stratification in the society at large. And as women are increasingly affected by these modernizing trends, they will continue to exchange associations based on female solidarity for those based on status.

Notes

1. Rosenfeld found that "non-hierarchical and egalitarian relations are shown to hold among women, while competitive, hierarchical relations hold among men" in an Arab village in Palestine (1974:139).

2. Hosein, the son of Ali and the grandson of the Prophet Muhammad, was martyred on the battlefield at Karbala in a dispute over succession to the caliphate. For Iranian Shiites the battle at Karbala symbolizes the struggle of the forces of innocence (Hosein) against the forces of tyranny and injustice (Omar and the Umayyid caliphs). A *Hoseinkhaneh* is a group of people who gather to mourn the martyrdom of Hosein and who dedicate their lives to his memory. Those inhabitants of the town who referred to Maragheh as a *Hoseinkhaneh* perceive the town as being such a group writ large.

3. The concepts *class* and *status group* require clarification before pro-

ceeding with the analysis. Traditionally, *class* refers to a social group's relationship to property and to the means of production, and to its control over what is produced. Thus, classes are differentiated in a hierarchial order according to relative inequality in the economic sector. *Status groups,* as discussed by Max Weber, are communities defined "above all else [by] a specific *style of life*" (1966:24) and by inequality of social honor or prestige. The concept *life-style* is central to the notion of status group. It indicates both the way in which one lives as well as one's world view, values, and aspirations. Thus, status groups are cultural groups. A modern-traditional continuum is useful for understanding one aspect of cultural variations in both Iranian and Turkish status distinctions. Status distinctions (as opposed to those of class) become more important in structuring association patterns among women and in altering the social hierarchy as a society modernizes.

4. There is a distinction between a woman's status as an individual in a particular social milieu and the status group or class to which she belongs (based on her husband's position or, if unmarried, her father's position). A woman's position may be enhanced by factors such as age, religious knowledge, and personal qualities, in addition to her class position.

5. I am not claiming that women in these gatherings do not vary in terms of relative prestige or rank; I am only claiming that social group differences do not preclude association of women from different status groups, and to some extent of different classes.

6. These religious rituals portraying the events of Karbala extend over a ten-day period, from the third to the twelfth of Moharram.

7. It is improper for lower-class women to petition *directly* women of higher rank for favors while attending religious gatherings. Lower-class women also know that they will be excluded from other neighborhood gatherings if they "embarrass" women of higher rank by directly asking for favors. An intermediary may be used at times to make a request. However, the practice of avoiding downwardly mobile family and friends to avoid "embarrassment" was widespread in Maragheh.

8. Bott noted that geographically mobile couples in London tended to rely more heavily on the conjugal relationship for emotional support and entertainment than couples who were less mobile (1957). This pattern appears in Iranian society as well.

9. The *neuter role* is one in which the sexual identity of the professional woman neither structures the style of her relationships with superior or subordinate co-workers nor limits her professional identity.

10. The kabul gunus in Elazig were similarly limited to women of the same status group. The wives of the top level bureaucrats and upper level army officers did not attend the reception days of the wives of local teachers, middle level bureaucrats, or middle-class merchants.

11. The rowzehs of Tehran's upper classes are elite affairs, however, that exclude those who do not belong to the appropriate class.

12. Women have always been representatives of particular social divisions in a society. But by participating in the public sector in new or modern roles, they present those divisions that are symbolic of their status in new ways and to a broader audience that includes men as well as other women.

Bibliography

Aswad, Barbara C. "Visiting Patterns among Women of the Elite in a Small Turkish City." *Anthropological Quarterly,* 47 (1974) :9–27.

Benedict, Peter. "The Kabul Gunu: Structured Visiting in an Anatolian Provincial Town." *Anthropological Quarterly,* 47 (1974) :28–47.

Bott, Elizabeth. *Family and Social Network: Roles, Norms, and External Relationships in Ordinary Urban Families.* London, 1957.

Davis, Susan. "The Determinants of Social Position among Rural Moroccan Women." Unpublished. Trenton, New Jersey, 1975.

Fallers, Lloyd A., and Margaret Fallers. "Sex Roles in Edremit." In *Mediterranean Family Structures,* ed. J. G. Peristiany. Cambridge, 1976.

Good, Mary-Jo DelVecchio. "Social Stratification and Women in Provincial Iran." Unpublished. Cambridge, Mass., 1974.

International Labor Organization. "Employment and Income Policies in Iran." Unpublished. Geneva, 1972.

Pastner, Carroll McC. "Accommodations to Purdah: The Female Perspective." *Journal of Marriage and the Family,* 36 (1974) :408–414.

Rosenfeld, Henry. "Non-Hierarchical, Hierarchical and Masked Reciprocity in an Arab Village." *Anthropological Quarterly,* 47 (1974) :139–148.

Weber, Max. "Class, Status, and Party." In *Class, Status, and Power,* ed. Reinhard Bendix and Seymour Lipset, 2nd ed. New York, 1966.

25 The Domestic Social Environment of Women and Girls in Isfahan, Iran

John Gulick
and Margaret E. Gulick

The lives of the women of this study in the Iranian city of Isfahan were for the most part secluded in and limited to the domestic environment. The domestic scene is woman-dominated, and infants and toddlers of both sexes begin their lives in this context. Girls, as they become older, become integrated into it, and the cycle is soon repeated with their early marriage and lack of opportunities for appropriate employment outside the home.

These general points are of course illustrations of the seclusion of women in the Middle East generally. This has always received great attention, but much of it has been superficial, partly because outside observers, frequently men, have had little access to Middle Eastern women. Consequently, there are generalizations about it that have many times been repeated and therefore perpetuated without sufficient examination of their accuracy. Among them are the ideas that: female seclusion is rapidly disappearing because of the modernization that is transforming the Middle East; since

---

The information in this essay comes from a study made in Isfahan, Iran, in 1970–71. We acknowledge the financial assistance of the National Science Foundation and the Carolina Population Center that made possible the research that produced the data presented in this paper. The field research was carried out under the auspices of the University of Isfahan's Center for Population

modernization is especially evident in cities, the disappearance of female seclusion there is especially rapid; and secluded women are either subdued and powerless or are domineering and powerful. This study tries to provide a more realistic view of the situation.

The intensely domestic environment of women persists in the city because most city dwellers do not have the opportunity to experience viable alternatives to it, and because the enculturation of children and the early marriage of girls tend to perpetuate it. However, the adaptations of individual women to these circumstances are not all the same. Some seem subdued, but in many there is strong self-assertiveness. There is also great awareness of the cultural changes taking place in the city and in Iranian society generally. Radical and massive change of the secluded domestic social system of women will require radical changes in external institutions and wider cultural patterns. However, such changes

---

Studies whose director was then Dr. Mahmoud Sarram. We are very grateful to Dr. Sarram for his many kinds of assistance. We also wish to thank Dr. Ghassem Motamedi, then the Chancellor of the University of Isfahan, for his support of our project.

We are most particularly grateful to those people without whose direct contribution this project would not have been carried out: Elaine Maleki, Farideh Bassiri Malek, Fereshteh Sarram, Farajollah Afrasiabi, Pauline Afrasiabi; and the field interviewers who were Naser Badami, Eshrat Darab, Mashid Emami, Ginous Hakimi, Sedigheh Karimpour, Asghar Kelishadi, Ali Langroudy, Mehdi Mansouri, Heshmatollah Nosrati, Parvaneh Rafe'i, Shaheen Shadzi, and Mahnaz Tashakkor.

The information presented here was obtained from a purposive sample of 174 women and their husbands. The original purpose of the research was to gain insights into the people's readiness, or lack of it, for family planning. We hoped that the study would be extended on a long-term, longitudinal basis, in which multiple feedback would develop between the families and public institutions concerned with the population problem. Consequently, more than half the women were obtained from the list of currently registered patients at a family planning clinic. The remainder were women in two residential clusters located in contrasting parts of the city, for in the longer-term research we hoped to study neighborhood networks. We were unable to establish the long-range extension of the project, but we did accomplish a sequence of interviews and observations that took place over about a year among a substantial number of the families. With some exceptions, as many as six visits were made to the husband and/or wife in each household. The interviewing was done by a team of women and men university students whom we trained and worked with very closely. The men interviewed the husbands, and the women interviewed the wives. An additional source of some of the information presented in this paper was a special study among 62 schoolgirls that was done by one of the women members of the research group who was a part-time teacher. This concerned the girls' attitudes toward wearing the enveloping head-to-heels veil (*chador*) worn in public by most of the women in Isfahan.

need not necessarily be wholly externally imposed, for they could receive positive responses from some of those who are currently immersed in the traditional system, thus stimulating further change. Though persistent, the secluded domestic social system of women is not a monolithic structure.

Although the sample included only married women and only wives of childbearing age, because of the researchers' primary interests in fertility behavior, the women appeared to be similar to the inhabitants of Isfahan in general in at least two respects. The educational attainments of the men and the women were similar to those of the comparable age cohorts in the 1966 census, as was the distribution of various household types. So, while generalizations from the sample to the population of the whole city cannot confidently be made, the researchers do believe that the sample is an aggregation of people who are not peculiar in any important aspect of their lives, except possibly in the prevalence among them of an interest in practicing contraception.

Most of the women of the study wanted to limit the number of children they have; the modal preference was for two sons and two daughters. Most of those who currently felt their families were incomplete wanted to delay the next pregnancy, often "until this baby is in school." However, success in spacing children was very unusual, and whether these women and their husbands will significantly limit their total number of children is problematic, even though some were frank in admitting having had, or having attempted, abortions. Nearly 80 percent of the women reported that they were, at the end of the year-long study, using some method of pregnancy prevention: pill (fifty women), coitus interruptus (thirty-one), intrauterine device (twenty-three), condom (seventeen), nursing babies and believing this to be adequate protection (fourteen), abstinence (three), and rhythm (one). However, this simple enumeration does not convey any idea of the great dissatisfaction expressed by most of the women with the ways (often several different ones) that they had tried to prevent pregnancy. One of them even said that she had tried every way and did not like any of them. The fears and problems connected with some of the methods (especially the modern clinical ones) and the ambivalence of the women about whether to have more children have been discussed elsewhere (Gulick and Gulick 1975).

The average age of the wives was 26.3 years (range 15–47 years), and their average age at first marriage had been about 15 years, ranging from 9 to 25 years. (The legal minimum is 15 years, but legal marriage at 13 and 14 can be arranged with special permission.) The husbands were, in the average, nine years older than their wives. Each couple had an average of 3.38 living children (ranging up to 9). A subsample, consisting of cases in which the wife was under the age of 35, had an average of three living children, a figure very similar to comparable figures derived from another study of the urban area of Isfahan province (Lieberman et al. 1973:83).

The sample included a very small number of educated women, and such women also constitute a small segment of the whole city's population. While there has been much publicity about educated, unveiled, unsegregated, "modern" women in Iran, they are exceptional people who are mostly from well-to-do families. Undoubtedly, the number of these women is growing, but it is not known whether the proportion of them in the total population is increasing. "Modern" women have status and provide models for possible emulation if educational opportunities can be enlarged relative to population increase. However, little-educated and illiterate women constituted the bulk of the sample and are far more typical of the population as a whole at the present time.

Nine of the 174 wives had nondomestic, institutional jobs (nurse, hospital servant, teacher, and university student); 13 of the husbands had white collar jobs (clerk, typist, primary school teacher), and 7 husbands had professional jobs (secondary school teacher and supervisor, medical student, physician, and engineer). All the rest of the wives were either housewives only or housewives who earned money in domestic ways such as carpet-weaving or sewing (plus 1 midwife). The great majority of the husbands were in skilled or semiskilled occupations. Construction, factory work, automobile or truck driving, and a variety of jobs in food, cloth, and other shops were the most common types of jobs.

The Domestic Environment

The household organization of the families in the sample was varied. Almost four-fifths of the couples lived in "simple households": nuclear families consisting of husband, wife, and their unmarried children. The remainder lived in "complex households": they lived and regularly ate together with one or more relatives or related nuclear families. However, this only hints at the extent of living association with relatives. More than 40 percent of those in simple households (all together, more than half the whole sample) lived in the same walled compound with relatives.[1] This compound was most often the traditional Isfahan house consisting of rooms arranged around a rectangular courtyard. Since most of the rooms are not specialized, the house is well suited to multiple occupancy by separate families, all sharing the courtyard, the water supply (if any), the toilet in its own cubicle, and the main door to the outside. The modern house is a one- or two-story building, with a walled yard attached to its south side. It is much less likely than the traditional to contain more than two separate households.

Of special interest was the presence of uxorilocal residence and matrilateral ties in a culture of presumed patricentric patterns. It is true that among the complex households the single relative most often eating with the nuclear family core was the husband's mother. It is also true that, considering the compound as a whole, an additional related family was most likely to be the husband's brother, his wife, and children. However, the links were uxorilocal in more than 10 percent of the complex households. For compounds as a whole, links were to the wife in about a quarter of the families. In at least some of these instances, such as married sisters and married female cousins, the fact that Iranian women can and do inherit property was undoubtedly one factor in these alternatives to virilocality. For 15 percent more of the families there were non-commensal relatives of the wife as well as of the husband in the compound.

Further complicating the picture were the consanguineal relationships reported by sixty-nine of the husbands and wives. Of thirty-seven couples in which the primary link to relatives in the compound was virilateral, one-third were related to each other. In other words, the wife's mother-in-law was also her consanguineal or affinal aunt; her sister-in-law was also her cousin. Within complex households, dual relationships of this sort were even more likely; for nearly half the couples commensal with a relative or relatives to whom the primary link of the couple was virilateral—such as husband's brother or husband's parents—there was a link with the wife as well. Furthermore, among most of these same couples, the relationship between husband and wife was matrilateral; that is, he was related to his wife through his mother. While unrelated couples were as likely to be sharing a compound with relatives as related couples, they were less likely to be commensal with those other relatives.

This frequent presence of relatives, and "dual" relatives, in the same compound may as often as not be the result of necessity rather than preference. About half the ninety-six women living in compounds with relatives said they did not have enough living space, but only a few indicated that they were planning to move. A similar proportion of those living in compounds with only *unrelated* persons or families indicated that they felt crowded. Since women spent a great deal of their time in the compound, it may be that the close quarters with any other persons felt to be incompatible generated feelings of crowdedness. More than half the women and men who were asked if they wanted their children to live with them after marriage said no, and the response of one man might be balanced against that of one woman (not his wife). He said he wanted his married childern to live not in his house, but close by so that he could see them daily. The woman, living in a situation of five related households (eighteen people) in the seven rooms of the compound, said, "The further away you are, the more friendly you are."[2]

Contact with a woman's relatives is, of course, not limited to those who may be living in the same compound with her. Often, relatives not in the compound are only a few doors away. Related or unrelated, migrant or native to Isfahan, living in a simple household compound or not—whatever the angle of analysis—at least 65 percent of the women reported very frequent, often daily, contact with their own consanguineal relatives. These were likely to be a woman's sister, her mother, the sister of one of her parents who was also mother-in-law, and her sister-in-law who was also her cousin.

A web of female relatives, consanguineal and affinal, plus unrelated neighbor women, and the children of all, is the usual daytime population of houses and courtyards—the ambience for tending and shaping little children and bigger girls, retailing gossip, working at household chores and money-making crafts such as carpet-weaving, influencing and interfering with each other. The interviewers were seldom able to talk with a woman completely alone, because there was usually no place to go where complete privacy was possible. There were obvious disadvantages to this, but there were advantages as well, since the flavor of a female subculture within a compound often is more apparent in the reported interactions among the women than in an individual woman's answers to specific questions. The desirability of intrasex companionship and support was occasionally verbalized. For instance, a set of two boys and two girls was often mentioned as a good number of children to have, because a boy should have a brother and a girl should have a sister. Questions about commensality in the compound brought a number of responses indicating that the women ate together when their husbands were not home, but separately when they were.

Some of the implications inherent in this domestic environment for desirable qualities in children are mentioned later. Another kind of implication, however, is inherent in combining a picture of the domestic environment with information about the pressures to marry a daughter by age 15–16 and with information about the seclusion of some of the women to the extent even of their husbands' doing the shopping. If the domestic environment is a woman's near-total environment, she cannot help but give early thought to what she wants in her daughter-in-law, and to what most congenial domestic environment she can give her daughter. Her daughter-in-law is very likely to become part of her household, especially at the beginning of the son's marriage. This is not the preferred arrangement of the majority of women, but it is a frequent economic necessity. A woman's son-in-law is less likely to be brought into her household, but this arrangement was found both among the women and among their married daughters. These instances run counter to the comments made by some of the women that girls will belong to other people. These comments were made at times in the context of saying that they expected their sons, when married, to live with them—but not their daughters; and at times in the context of saying their daughters need not have as much education as sons because the usefulness of that education would be to others rather than to their parents.

When women talked about the characteristics of a son's future wife, or of a daughter's future husband, the majority of them had definite ideas as to whether the marriage should be to a relative or not. Those who were related to their own husbands tended to favor relatives for their children's spouses, but a sizable proportion felt otherwise. Conversely, those who were unrelated to their own husbands leaned toward nonrelatives for their children's spouses, but again, quite a number wanted relatives. There were instances of infant betrothal, cases of early informal arrangements with relatives about which there were current doubts, cases in which nonrelatives were preferred for sons' spouses but relatives for daughters'—or vice versa, cases in which possible spouses among her own or her husband's relatives existed for some, but not all, of her children, and cases in which a woman preferred to choose partners for her children from among her own relatives but wanted none from among her husband's.

Often these preferences seemed to reflect satisfaction or dissatisfaction with a woman's (or man's) own marital situation. Certain themes repeated themselves. If a daughter is given in marriage to a relative, the familiarity provides promise of fewer unpleasant surprises after marriage, and the web of kinship provides greater protection against mistreatment and divorce because of pressures that can be brought to bear upon the husband. Possibly for these reasons, a somewhat larger proportion of women said they preferred relatives for their daughters' spouses than for their sons'. The disadvantage of marriage to a relative for either son or daughter, however, is the probable magnification of every little marital upset. As one person said in stating a preference for marriage to nonrelatives, "with relatives, there is such a lot of talking every day."

Overall, more people preferred choosing spouses for their children from among nonrelatives to choosing them from among relatives. There was little suggestion that choice of mates was in the children's hands, although more women indicated that these choices were for their sons to make than did so for their daughters.

Desire for harmony is one reason for early interest in the choice of a child's spouse, and this desire is probably intensified by the large amount of disharmony that seems to be experienced, particularly between women and their mothers-in-law and between the wives of brothers. In one compound, the resident wives of brothers indicated that they were getting along well together in the absence of their mother-in-law. She was on pilgrimage to Mashhad, and they anticipated that when she returned their relationships would become more difficult again because she was a troublemaker. This is an instance of the supposedly typical situation in which old or older women decidedly influence, if they do not dominate, the domestic scene. However, the influences can be exerted in the other direction. One woman (in another household) said that she expected help in her old age from her sons "if their wives allow it." Another woman said that she and her husband would like to live with their son when they grew old but wondered if his wife would agree. These are cases where younger women are perceived as having as much, if not more, power than older women in ways that affect men as well as other women.

Urbanization

The members of the sample were not selected on the basis of whether they were natives of the city or migrants born elsewhere. Forty-one percent of them turned out to be migrants, and while the presentation of data in the Isfahan census does not permit a comparison of this frequency with that of the migrants actually living in the whole city, it is very similar to the 43 percent of migrants discovered in a survey done in the Iranian city of Shiraz (Paydarfar 1974:511).

In general, the migrants had come from villages, most of which were in the same province as Isfahan, but nine women had come from other large cities including Tehran. The latter tended to have fewer children, be better educated, and have husbands in professional jobs—exceptional people as far as the sample is concerned. The comparisons here are based on the characteristics of the 102 native women and the 63 migrant women who had not come from other large cities.

The migrant and native women are essentially the same in average age and length of time married, and this fortunate circumstance facilitates further comparisons between them (see Gulick and Gulick 1976). About 79 percent of the migrant women moved to Isfahan either at the time of their marriage or (more frequently) after they were married. This is not an aggregation of people who first came to the city as single women seeking jobs and/or husbands. On the contrary, they came typically as married women, most of them already married several years. Their average age at marriage was slightly older than that of the natives (15.5 years versus 14.3). While it is not known how the migrant women may or may not differ from their fellow villagers who did not migrate, it is unlikely that they constitute that sort of special, self-selected group, distinctive in various ways from nonmigrants, that has been discovered by other studies in other cultures.

Median marriage ages of from 13 to 15 have been found in a study of four Iranian villages (Petrosian et al. 1964:64); one could guess that the great majority of the migrant women in the sample were typical village women, immersed in the secluded domestic environment, who moved to the city because their husbands did. Isfahan definitely has job attractions for professional, skilled, and semiskilled men; it has relatively few for women. In fact, 14.4 percent (13,006) of the women in the rural areas of the Isfahan subprovince were employed, as of the 1966 census, as opposed to only 9.2 percent (12,872) in the city of Isfahan. For *young* women these differences in employment were even greater: 24.1 percent of the 15- to 19-year-old rural women were employed, in contrast to only 7.9 percent in the city. Greater proportions of rural area women were employed than were Isfahan women until age 30. After that age, the percentage of employed rural women decreased and that of employed city women increased slightly, with a high of 11 percent for 40- to 44-year-olds. Among both rural and city women, these jobs consist largely of carpet-weaving in private homes, particularly among the young and the rural women. Women's rural employment includes some agricultural work, mostly on their own families' farms; city employment includes domestic service and work in textile factories. There are some economic opportunities for *educated* women in professional and in technical jobs, and slightly over 1 percent of Isfahan women (1,733) were in such occupations, mostly as governmental employees, in 1966 (1966 Census of Isfahan Shahrestan: 114, 130, 171, 187, 295, 299).

The educational facilities necessary for professional and technical jobs are available only in cities, but few city girls continue their educations far enough to prepare themselves for such jobs. In 1966, 60.1 percent of city girls aged 10–14 were in school, as opposed to 9.2 percent of the rural girls, and 23.9 percent of the city 15- to 19-year-olds as opposed to 1.0 percent of the rural. Although nearly a quarter of Isfahan girls aged 15–19 were still in school, only 8.5 percent of them had progressed beyond the ninth grade (1966 Census: 76, 114, 130). These students consisted almost entirely of daughters living with their families.

It is concluded that the urbanization of the migrant women has resulted in no immediate or discernible lessening of the domestic seclusion to which they were already accustomed in the villages and which is the characteristic environment of the native city women as well. Indeed, the seclusion may have been intensified because of the possibly greater threat posed by the large mass of urban strangers. Economically active females under age 30 are less frequent, relatively, in the city of Isfahan than in its rural surroundings. The ethos of female domestic seclusion, which keeps women from competing with men for scarce jobs, may perhaps keep younger, especially unmarried, women from competing with other women for jobs such as the sex-segregated ones in textile factories where they would be under the supervision of males. Greater *potential* for change does seem to be present in the city, but that potential has yet to be realized by the great majority of city natives, let alone the migrants. In fact, a phenomenon that has been observed by others in Asia generally is that industrialization may *decrease* employment opportunities for women (Boulding 1972:12).

The main way that poor, uninfluential people, city native or migrant, can increase their chances of getting better than menial or unskilled jobs is through education. This potential that the city offers is recognized, but in varying degrees, by the people. For instance, in one migrant household, the core nuclear family was augmented during most of the year by the presence of two boys. They were nephews of the wife, and their parents were still village dwellers. The boys were going to secondary school in the city, but they returned to their village during the summer. In another case, by contrast, the mother said she had no ambition to send her daughter to school at all. "Poor people cannot let their children study," she said. Her 5-year-old daughter was already carpet-weaving, as she herself had been at the same age. Though herself born in Isfahan, this woman's parents were village migrants, as was her husband.

Although most of the 7- to 12-year-old sons and daughters of the natives and migrants in the sample were in elementary school, the migrants seemed to be taking less advantage of this potential than the natives. While 93.6 percent of the natives' sons and 92.7 percent of their daughters were in elementary school, 81.4 percent and 59 percent of the migrants' sons and daughters were. The differences were made up for by the fact that more of the migrants' sons and daughters were working. The relative frequency of working sons and daughters increased among the 13- to 18-year-olds and more so among the migrants than among the natives. More of the natives' teenagers remained in school, whether still in primary or having progressed to secondary. However, only a minority of the boys and girls in both groups were in secondary school: migrant sons 19 percent, daughters 15.4 percent, native sons 35.7 percent, daughters 11.1 percent. The greater frequency among migrants of working children was not an indication of their greater success in improving their employment status. On the contrary, it was for the most part evidence of the poverty trap that can await the rural migrant to the city (Boulding 1972:13) . Most of these youngsters were working, or, in the case of the girls, getting married, instead of going to school, and their educations were minimal.

A quarter of the migrants' and half of the natives' 13- to 18-year-old daughters were already married. Those who were working, almost entirely in domestic crafts such as carpet-weaving and sewing under older women's supervision, were doing so on an interim basis preceding marriage, developing skills that might usefully augment family income later.

This is not to deny that urbanization provides greater opportunities for education, and for girls' education as well as boys'. Indeed, the native wives were definitely better educated than the migrant wives (54.5 percent as opposed to 31.8 percent having had some schooling) . However, realizing that potential is a slow, difficult, problematic, and uncertain process. One reason is poverty, and the other is that for girls, even in the city, there are few chances for enough education to achieve career rewards. More of the native than the migrant mothers expressed status-related career aspirations for their daughters (teacher, physician) , and more of them expressed the desire not to have a large number of children (more than four) , but these sentiments had not led to any marked differences in actual accomplishment.

As far as domestic social organization is concerned, there were no striking differences between migrant women and natives in the various arrangements that were discussed in the previous section. However, there were a few differences in degree that invite some comment. Among the migrants, a greater proportion of the nuclear families were living in compounds with no other relatives; they were more likely to be renting space in other people's houses. Though immersed in relatives outside the nuclear family (65 percent reporting very frequent, often daily, contact), migrants were less immersed than natives (76.5 percent), and even less immersed than the second-generation native women both of whose parents were also natives (79.7 percent). Not surprisingly, migrant women more frequently reported regular contacts with those of their relatives who did not live in Isfahan (35 percent as opposed to 16 percent). It is interesting that the frequency of husbands and wives related to each other was less among the natives than the migrants (35 percent versus 46). Most of the migrants were married in villages where, probably, the range of choice of spouse is even narrower than in the city. City living, far from bringing about less association with relatives, is compatible with it and may even reinforce and encourage it. Women migrants, for the most part, come with their families and pursue in the city the domestic lives in which they were enculturated.

Enculturation

The common generalization about a preference for sons is borne out to some extent by the findings of the study, but not dramatically. Stories were heard about the greater celebration of the birth of a son, and a number of women wanted more sons than daughters. However, most women (and men) wanted children of *both* sexes. These included a woman who felt burdened with five children—all sons—but was still hoping for a daughter.

What is life like for daughters after they are born? In order to have some systematic data on ideas about childrearing, a series of questions was asked of those sixty-two women who had children aged 5 and 6. The children were divided almost equally between boys and girls. Just over half these women said that they thought there was no difference between rearing girls and boys. This answer (in conjunction with others) may be indicative of the mothers' perceptions of themselves as treating both boys and girls similarly. Most of them had children of both sexes, and they tended to desire the same qualities in all children of that age: politeness and quietness. Keeping in mind the close living quarters of so many of the women, it is not difficult to understand why polite, quiet children who do not "bother" people would be defined as "good" children.

Among the women who thought there *were* differences in rearing boys and girls, a number mentioned the additional care needed by girls. This additional care seemed to be related to the perceived need for more protection of girls than of boys, and the need for more supervision and control even at age 5 or 6. Little boys more often than little girls were sent out of the compound on marketing errands. Despite the principle generally expressed by mothers of little boys as well as little girls that children of 5 or 6 years should be given certain household duties, a larger proportion of the mothers of sons indicated that, in fact, their children did not help out. Those boys who did help were most frequently sent outside on shopping errands. The mothers of little girls mentioned a variety of tasks, such as washing dishes, sweeping, looking after a younger child, and carpet-weaving. Many mothers were fearful of having their small children of either sex play outside the compound because of bad influences and dirt. Two fathers worried about the care daughters needed. One had two sons and wanted two daughters but said he was afraid to have them because of the difficulties involved in controlling and disciplining them. The other had two baby daughters and was already worrying about their going "ten steps away from the house" because "so many bad things" could happen to them, which would not matter if they were boys. A number of mothers of girls spoke of the need to keep them from playing with neighbor boys even inside the compound.

The seclusion-in-public of veil-wearing (the head-to-heels *chador*) begins early, as does male responsibility for enforcing that seclusion. A mother of 5- and 7-year-old girls mentioned that her 12-year-old son hit his sisters if they went out without chadors. Another woman said that while she agreed with her husband that their 6-year-old daughter should wear a chador outside, she did not agree with him that a head-scarf was necessary at home.

Of the second- to sixth-grade schoolgirls in the chador survey, most wore them regularly. The majority of these wore them willingly, and most gave religious reasons for doing so. Other reasons given were that their relatives wore them; that everyone in their neighborhood did; that their parents wanted them to; that their clothes should be covered because they weren't nice enough. One girl who gave the last reason said that if she had nicer clothes she would not wear a chador. Several girls seemed obviously to be repeating reasons they had been given: it is a sin not to; a father or grandfather was a prayer leader or *hajji* or *sayyid,* and his reputation was at stake; or their parents insisted. Among those whose parents insisted were a number of girls who wore chadors unwillingly and would have preferred not to wear them. One woman, who may have had to cope with similar unwillingness in her 5-year-old daughter, mentioned that it was better in her childhood when girls were ashamed not to wear chadors and would not have been tempted to go without. Another woman, mother of daughters aged 5 and 6, had the opposite opinion: she said that her mother had forced her to wear a chador but that she did not force her own little girls. In sum, little boys seem to be given more freedom to go outside the compound and more freedom from most household tasks than little girls of the same preschool age. In addition, many little girls must learn to wear chadors when they go outside. Even the most willing must find it difficult at first to keep the chador properly wrapped around them, although a tiny girl was seen with her family in the modern Farah Park, adroitly keeping her chador on while coming down the slide.

Some of the women in the subsample of those who were asked questions about childrearing reported that their husbands did the shopping, but apparently most of the women did the shopping themselves. A number of little girls saw their fathers work at some household tasks such as household repairs, or help out at home some of the time such as when there were guests, but most of the fathers were reported never to help with household tasks—often, but not always, because they were gone all day. Family decisions with regard to money, more than half the wives reported, were made by the husband. More than two-fifths of the women, however, said that they alone, or together with their husbands, made these decisions.

Fathers were described by their wives as being, on the whole, demonstrative of affection, especially with their daughters, especially when children are very small, and especially with whichever child is youngest. There were some women who seemed to think their husbands should be the disciplinarians, but there were more who felt they both shared in this. However, they seemed to think that because of the fathers' absence during the day, their admonitions might be heeded more, especially by the sons. Some women voiced concern over the severity of husbands' discipline, and others, with fears of "spoiling" the children, over the lack of it. Many women mentioned hitting or beating their children and quarreling with them. Some women also reported that their husbands were critical of them for being either too severe or not severe enough. The impression for the most part is *not* of men who were remote from or stern with their children.

When girls and boys reached school age, most of them were sent to school, although, as was shown in the preceding section, migrants' daughters were less likely to be sent than city natives' daughters. Illiterate women, both migrant and native, likened illiteracy to blindness. Reasons given why elementary school-age daughters were not in school usually had to do with poverty, or the lack of a girls' school near enough to be of use, or lack of space in school. In 1971 elementary school was reduced from six to five grades, probably in an attempt to provide schoolroom space and teachers immediately for all young children, while the slower process of building new schools and training additional teachers proceeded at the same time.

For *very* poor families, the small financial contribution that a 7- to 12-year-old daughter could make with her earnings from carpet-weaving *might* have been a factor in keeping her out of school, but it is more likely that the cost of shoes and clothes suitable for school, notebooks and pencils, and registration fees for several children were beyond their means. There were also hints here and there that the parents' unfamiliarity with procedures and powerlessness in negotiating for space in crowded schools might have kept some children from ever beginning school.

Some of the same causes were operating among children who dropped out before finishing elementary school. In addition, there were children who seemed to have dropped out because they did not like going and because keeping them in was not a top priority with their parents. Overwhelmingly, however, both men and women wanted their daughters to be literate. A number of migrant women in particular said they wished they had been able to go to school when they were young. One of these said she had been allowed to go to the only school available (boys and girls together) until the third grade when her father took her out because he did not want her in school with boys any longer.

The most commonly expressed educational aspiration of both fathers and mothers of school-age daughters was for their daughters to complete high school. However, fulfillment of these aspirations had already become impossible for most of the forty daughters aged 13–18. Of these, 15 percent were still in elementary school, including the only married daughter continuing her education; 20 percent were working (all in domestic crafts except one who was an employee in a girls' school) ; 40 percent were already married; and 12.5 percent were in secondary school. Only a couple of the daughters no longer in school had even entered secondary school. Many had not finished elementary school, and some had had no schooling at all.

The cost of secondary school was mentioned as prohibitive by a large number of women. But there were other factors involved, one of which was related to the small percentage of girls in secondary school and to a continuation of the secluded domestic environment. It is the composite of pressures for early marriage. To some extent, the cost of secondary school was one of the pressures, because if a daughter cannot be kept in school, one mother suggested, there was no alternative to staying home but marriage—in other words, no appropriately protected employment for a girl with only elementary school education. This mother thought neither staying home nor marriage was a good solution to the problem of keeping a young teenage girl safely occupied.

Concern over the chastity of pubescent girls—or over their reputation of being properly decorous—is a pervasive pressure for early marriage. It is involved in the talk about girls needing more "care" and in the statement by a girl who wore the chador occasionally that she would wear it more regularly when she went to secondary school. It is probably involved in the occasional refusal of a father to send his daughter to secondary school, not because of the cost, but because of the "bad influences" (in the sex-segregated school or on the way to and from it?). Insuring the chastity (and the pliability?) of one's son's bride may be a major reason for many women's explanation of why their own parents had given them in marriage at such young ages and why they had given their own daughters in marriage at ages younger than what they said they would have preferred: pressure from the families of prospective bridegrooms—often beginning when a girl was only 9 or 10.

Eagerness to discharge their responsibility for finding suitable brides for their sons may be another reason why women pressure other women to give their daughters at such young ages. The mother who thought that neither staying home nor marriage was the solution for her 13-year-old daughter indicated that she wanted her to go to secondary school but that the expense was beyond their means. At a later interview, the daughter's wedding to her maternal grandmother's sister's son was due to take place soon. The mother said that even if secondary school had been possible, she would have given her in marriage at this time anyway because "they have been asking for her since she was in the fourth grade." This was in spite of her earlier statement that she wanted her daughter to marry at the age of 16.

A number of parents indicated that people would talk if daughters were not married by the age of 15 or 16. Many mothers said they wanted their daughters to marry at the age of 20, but 56.4

percent of the seventy-eight women who answered by giving a specific age mentioned ages under 20, particularly the age of 15. An even larger percentage (69.5 percent) of the sixty-nine men answering specifically gave ages under 20, clustering on 16 and 18. Young as their hoped-for ages for marrying their daughters may seem, the majority of the twenty-nine already-married daughters aged 13 and over had been married at younger ages than their mothers had hoped for. One example of how this came about has been given. Another example was the case of a mother who said she wanted her 11-year-old daughter to marry at the age of 17 or 18, "or right now if she had a dowry."

Thus, the enculturation of girls seems to lead to early marriage and the repetition of the secluded domestic cycle for another generation. Another researcher describes female age at marriage as occupying a "pivotal role in the emergence of modernism" in women's attitudes and behavior: marrying early tends to preserve traditional patterns of male dominance and female seclusion because women, still in effect children, are placed in positions dependent upon and subordinate to their husbands, and very often, their mothers-in-law (Fox 1973:521–524). The evidence here is in accord with this assessment; the continuation of early marriage is the result of systemic pressures on individuals regardless of their personal choices.

Conclusion: Adaptations to Change

In a modernizing city like Isfahan—which has acquired some Western-type industries and businesses, a modified European-type school system with separate facilities for boys and girls, and Western-type vehicular traffic and mass communications—the secluded domestic environment continues to be the characteristic life-style of women living under the socioeconomic conditions of most of the women of the study. It is assumed that these conditions are not exceptional, but are, rather, typical of the majority of the city's inhabitants.

Urbanization, the process in which rural people move to the city and adapt themselves to living there, has not, for these women, meant any substantial change toward less emphasis on the secluded domestic environment. Given the first point, and assuming that it could be verified on a larger scale, there is no reason why urbanization in itself *should* effect such changes among such people, but the issue is raised because the assumption has so often been made that radical cultural change does follow quickly or automatically from urbanization.

Though systemic change in the female domestic environment has not occurred, some discernible changes have. The chief one is probably the increasing number of girls who go to elementary school. The effects the elementary school experience in itself may have on these girls are not known, but it is possible that it may have cumulative results in the widening of their horizons. Wider horizons and innovative ideas are not likely to be generated by the rote memorization that typifies the schools, but association with a larger number of peers may sometimes do so, as may the acquisition of literacy and the growing awareness of secondary school possibilities. However, a girl's going to elementary school does not prevent her from being married at 15, and this traditional, premodern practice is a key element in the secluded domestic environment of women and its perpetuation over time.

Though it is persisting, the domestic environment of women is not a monolithic structure typified solely by superordinate males and subdued, submissive females. There are variations in the individual adaptations and characteristics of members of both sexes. There are women as well as men who either prefer the traditional system or see no practicable or achievable alternative to it. There are also men, as well as women, who at least verbalize a positive attitude toward change. Particularly interesting is the substantial number of men who expressed educational and occupational aspirations for their daughters which, if realized, would remove those daughters, as grown women, from the traditional secluded domestic environment. It is not known if many of the men actually perceived this important implication or if many of them were voicing insincere, inflated aspirations in order to impress the university men interviewing them. However, a considerably larger proportion of the men than of the women expressed high occupational aspirations for their daughters. This may be due to the greater amount of education among the men and perhaps also to a greater awareness among them of "outside," nondomestic possibilities. Among both the men and the women in this study, the more schooling a person had, the more likely he or she was to express high status aspirations for children. These tendencies have been found in other studies, and so, contrary to what might well have been predicted, there may be a genuine sentiment among at least some of the men in favor of nondomestic occupations for their daughters. This is not true of all or most of the men, but the verbalization of the sentiment was made by forty-two of the eighty-seven men who expressed aspirations for their daughters' futures, including nondomestic occupations and marriage.

What, then, are the prospects for radical, systemic change of the secluded domestic environment of women on a large scale? It cannot be assumed that modernization and urbanization, at least in their present forms, will inevitably lead to such changes. It is quite possible that among many Iranians the secluded domestic system will continue for the foreseeable future. At the same time, it does seem inevitable that the small proportion of highly educated, professionally employed, and not domestically secluded women already in the population will increase, at least to some extent, because an increasing number of women are going on from secondary school to university education and technical and professional training. However, for members of individual families like those discussed in this study, to change radically their domestic life style will require many readjustments. Moreover, for such change to occur on a massive scale, radical and massive readjustments in the general social system would, it is assumed, be required.

What incentives are there for people such as those in this study to delay the marriage of girls from the typical 15 or 16? One could be the raising of the legally minimum marriage age to 18, provided the new regulations were enforced. The present 15-year minimum does not seem to have been enforced very well, and therefore it seems unlikely that the higher age could be either, except by a new system of effective penalties and by the provision of genuine alternatives to early marriage that would be accessible to large numbers of people like those discussed. The most likely such alternative is secondary schooling. In 1970–71, girls' secondary schools in Isfahan were considerably fewer than boys', and the expense of secondary education for both boys and girls was considered prohibitive by many parents. However, Iran has the financial resources for implementing its plans for large-scale school construction and teacher training programs, and for providing free secondary education. The provision of secondary school opportunities for more girls is, therefore, at least a realistic prospect.

Secondary education for girls does not in itself change the secluded domestic social system. It is likely to delay marriage till an older age and to provide greater awareness of, and opportunities for, occupations other than the domestic ones. Further delay in marriage and also practical experience outside the domestic environment are already being provided for female secondary school graduates when they are drafted into one of the Revolutionary Corps, of which the Health Corps and the Literacy Corps are perhaps the best known. A steadily increasing involvement of women in these innovative institutions may give great momentum to broadening the young women's horizons, giving them self-confidence in actual nondomestic work, and intensifying their interest and competence in competing for scarce jobs. However, unless opportunities for such jobs exist in some abundance, most female secondary school graduates and corps veterans are likely to have no choice but to marry and pursue a domestic existence that is more or less secluded depending on the preferences of themselves, their relatives, their husbands, and their husbands' relatives.

The further necessary step in changing female domestic seclusion is, therefore, making available large numbers of nondomestic occupations for women. This is a more problematic prospect than the provision of more secondary schools, for it involves either the creation of many new types of jobs for women or the greatly increased competition for the same jobs among men and women, or both. Unemployment and underemployment are already problems in a situation where the competition for jobs is almost entirely among men only. The extent to which the economic system can, in the foreseeable future, also accommodate the competition of substantial numbers of women is one problematic issue. Another is whether the extent of men's psychological dependence on female seclusion is great enough to constitute serious and extensive resistance to women's involvement in nondomestic employment even without the added stresses and strains of economic competition between men and women. If it is true in Iran, as Papanek (1973:316–317) says it is in Pakistan, that men are characteristically dependent for their own emotional security on the seclusion of women, then the difficulty of radical change is increased. Although what men may desire in and for their wives may be different from what they hope for their daughters, all that can be stated here and now is that among the men in the sample there were some who, by mentioning professional jobs for their daughters, *may* have indicated less emotional dependence on the seclusion of women than is often thought to be typical.

Notes

1. The varieties of relationships and arrangements have been detailed in Gulick and Gulick (1974).

2. Details on crowdedness and the mobility of people in and out of compounds are found in Gulick and Gulick (1974, 1975).

Bibliography

Boulding, Elise. "Women as Role Models in Industrializing Societies: A Macro-System Model of Socialization for Civic Competence." In *Cross-*

National Family Research, ed. Marvin B. Sussman and Betty E. Cogswell. Leiden, 1972.

Fox, Greer Litton. "Some Determinants of Modernism among Women in Ankara, Turkey." *Journal of Marriage and the Family,* 35 (1973) :520–529.

Gulick, John, and Margaret E. Gulick. "Varieties of Domestic Social Organization in the Iranian City of Isfahan." In *City and Peasant: A Study in Sociocultural Dynamics,* ed. A. L. LaRuffa et al. New York, 1974.

———. "Kinship, Contraception and Family Planning in the Iranian City of Isfahan." In *Population and Social Organization,* ed. Moni Nag. The Hague, 1975.

———. "Migrant and Native Married Women in the Iranian City of Isfahan." *Anthropological Quarterly,* 49 (1976) :53–61.

Lieberman, S. S., Robert Gillespie, and M. Loghmani. "The Isfahan Communications Project." *Studies in Family Planning,* 4 (1973) :73–100.

Papanek, Hanna. "Purdah: Separate Worlds and Symbolic Shelter." *Comparative Studies in Society and History,* 15 (1973) :289–325.

Paydarfar, Ali A. "Differential Life-Styles between Migrants and Non-Migrants: A Case Study of the City of Shiraz, Iran." *Demography,* 11 (1974) :509–520.

Petrosian, Angela, Shayan Kazem, K. W. Bash, and Bruce Jessup. "The Health and Related Characteristics of Four Selected Villages and Tribal Communities in Fars Ostan, Iran." Unpublished. Shiraz, 1964.

Plan Organization, Iran Statistical Centre. *National Census of Population and Housing, January 1966,* vol. XXIV, *Esfahan Shahrestan.* 1968.

26 Self-Images of Traditional Urban Women in Cairo

Sawsan el-Messiri

Traditional urban women of Cairo are called *banat al-balad,* which means "daughters of the country" and usually refers to a certain type and class of women. Egyptians commonly describe the *bint al-balad* (sing.) as one who wears the *milaya-laff,*[1] a square of black material which is wrapped sari-like around the body and which is the dress of the illiterate lower and lower-middle classes. Bint al-balad is thought of as a preserver of local tradition and values. Egyptians often identify her as a *baladi* (folk) woman who still practices folk remedies, believes in *jinns* and saints' miracles, and who attends *zars.*[2] In this, she differs from Cairene women who are

---

Data for this paper resulted from field research carried out at two different intervals. Some of the data comes from a study of the concept of *ibn al-balad* (son of the country) (el-Messiri 1969), while the rest was gathered in 1971 specifically for the present study. Since ibn al-balad is usually the husband, father, or son of bint al-balad, the former research was directly relevant to this study.

To understand the life patterns of banat al-balad, the author participated in daily routine activities and in special events such as visiting saints and tombs; attending *mulids* (festivals to celebrate the birthday of a saint), marriage ceremonies, and funerals; and going to public baths and fortune-tellers. Intensive interviewing of thirty women was used to determine details and particulars of their self-images. The thirty women were selected to represent two age groups: half were married women in the 40–60 age group; the other half were in the 16–25 age group, only five of whom were not married. Part of the participant observation and interviewing was done in group situations, since it was extremely difficult to engage anyone in solitary conversation, given the close residence patterns and the many people living in single apartments. Gatherings of up to fifteen persons would occur, with many neighbors, friends, and relatives coming and going, including children. Sometimes men were present.

educated and who occupy a higher status in the social stratification of Cairene society. The focus of this paper is the self-image of banat al-balad. It is concerned with how such women conceive themselves in relation to other groups or types of women and how they view their relations with men in general and with their husbands in particular. Individuals interact by typification, interpreting their own and one another's behavior according to a process of abstraction based on experience of social reality.

The Traditional Urban Community

As a group, banat al-balad dwell in certain Cairene quarters known as al-Darb al-Ahmar, al-Jamaliya, Bab al-Sha'riya, Bulaq, and Masr al-Qadima. The history of these quarters is as old as Cairo. The community of banat al-balad, as popularly described, is the kind Janet Abu Lughod calls "traditional urban." Abu Lughod categorizes the Cairene population according to three main types or models: the rural, the traditional urban, and the modern or industrial urban. "Traditionalism refers primarily to the persistence of economic activities, forms of social relationships, and systems of values which were once typical within the Cairo of a hundred years ago but which, since the advent of the twentieth century at least, have been increasingly challenged by several ways of organizing production and sale, regulating identity and behavior, setting definitions for the good life" (Abu Lughod 1971:219). According to Abu Lughod the heart of Cairo's traditional urbanism lies in those districts that have been settled the longest, that is, the medieval city. However, not all residents of these communities have a lineage from the Middle Ages or even from a century ago. The communities are changing constantly; while a sizeable number of rural migrants settle in, at the same time many of the old residents leave their quarters for modern communities. But despite this mobility, whatever traditional activities still survive in Cairo are to be found chiefly in these old quarters. Therefore, the traditional model, with its cultural and physical boundaries, corresponds to the community of banat al-balad as it is commonly understood.

The community of the banat al-balad, while having the longest history of settlement, is not far from the new and modern zones of the city. Hence, a common physical feature of this community is the coexistence of the old and new. Medieval mosques stand side by side with twentieth-century mosques, large paved streets with alleys, and new buildings with old ones. Old Cairene quarters are divided now into districts which emerged from and supplemented the original divisions of the community into *harat*.[3] Some of these harat are small, deadend lanes or backyards in which children play and women meet and chat. In the past the buildings of each small lane belonged to one family, but now they are occupied by different families. Some of the larger flats are now divided into three or four apartments and each apartment is shared by two or three families. The division within the apartment is sometimes made by a wooden partition. In one of these buildings there are more than two hundred and fifty people altogether, with about twenty-five sharing one apartment. This pattern of housing is common in these quarters. For example, the number of families who share flats in al-Darb al-Ahmar represents about 30 percent of the district's total number of families (Egyptian Association 1970:83).

The original harah in medieval Cairo was not only a geographical and administrative unit but also a social unit. Its people were unified by ethnic, religious, and/or occupational characteristics that segregated them physically and socially from other subgroups of the city. Now the harah is no longer unified on the basis of ethnicity, religion, or occupation, but more on the basis that the same lane is shared by neighbors. However, the inhabitants are predominantly Muslim, and there are very few foreigners.

Another distinctive feature of this community is that its population shares certain demographic characteristics that set them apart from other parts of Cairo. Cairo as a whole is one of the most densely populated cities in the world. It is estimated that in 1977 it had a population of more than eight million. According to the sample survey of 1966 it had a population of 4,964,004 with a density of 19,594 people per square kilometer. The Old Cairene quarters are the major pockets of population density in the city. The medieval section has a population of 277,577 and a density of 77,857 people per square kilometer. In spite of this density the area is full of ruined and demolished buildings which are often used as refuse dumps. Much of the housing in the area is in a state of extreme deterioration. Forty-five percent of the buildings are in bad condition and 37 percent of them are substandard. Fifteen percent of these buildings have neither water nor electricity. The region is also deficient in medical and recreational services. Furthermore, these quarters receive many if not most of the rural migrants to Cairo. The population of these quarters in 1947 represented 37 percent of the total population of the city, and in 1960, despite their decline, they still accounted for 30 percent (Abu Lughod 1971:219).

The level of education in these areas is low and the rate of illiteracy is high compared with those of Cairo in general. At least

50 percent of the population of these areas is illiterate, but among its women alone illiteracy is over 60 percent. Of those who are literate only a very small portion have ever reached university level. The occupational distribution in these quarters is related to the standard of education. The percentage of those who work in professional occupations is much lower than the percentage of those who do manual work. The most common occupational categories, in which about half the working population fall, are craftspeople, laborers, factory workers, and sellers. This is a high percentage compared with the 32 percent who work in these occupations in Cairo as a whole. Owing to these factors, incomes are low (Egyptian Association 1970).

Characteristics and Roles of Traditional Urban Women

The bint al-balad identifies herself as *bint al-hitta* (daughter of the place). Hitta also connotes the concept of community; it has physical and social boundaries that may extend from a small alley to a whole quarter, depending on the number of people with whom the bint al-balad identifies herself. Within the hitta there is constant interaction between men and women. Women are not secluded from men. The contiguity of the houses and of the living units brings together people who are sometimes mere neighbors and have no kinship ties and gives rise to certain patterns of social interaction.

Gatherings are informal intermixings of age groups and sexes and demonstrate women's openness and talkativeness. Girls express an open and joking attitude toward elderly people of both sexes. For example, 18-year-old Fatima constantly teased the eldest man in the group (over 50) and joked that he was just the man she dreamed of since she felt young men were useless. Fatima used to shout at her mother and either contradicted her views openly or disregarded them completely. A 20-year-old girl publicly cursed her parents because they did not send her to school. The youngest girl (17 years) at one of the gatherings was generally outspoken and bold. When she was asked her opinion of the ideal husband, the men present pointed out that since her fiancé was there she could not speak out frankly. She, however, answered by addressing her fiancé: "I have chosen you and you appeal to me," thus implying that there was nothing to be ashamed of. The most striking elements in these gatherings are the openness and lack of inhibition regarding sexual issues, and the focus of married women in particular on sex in jokes and sarcasm.

Elderly banat al-balad are addressed by the title *umm,* which means mother of so-and-so, usually the eldest son. Another title of address is *hagga,* which is given both to those who have made the pilgrimage to Mecca and to elderly women. The title *mu'allima* (master or chief) is given to certain working women.

The bint al-balad in the quarter can be recongized not only by the milaya-laff but also by the very attractive way in which she wears it. Although it is black, the dress worn underneath it is bright and colorful and cut in an attractive, half-open, half-closed manner. It may have a low-cut decolleté but with ribbons that appear to close it or a line of buttons that are kept partly open. The milaya-laff is wrapped in such a way that the midriff and hips are particularly marked to show the beauty of the figure. It can also allow one naked arm to show while the other one is covered. Certain accessories go with the milaya-laff, such as a headkerchief, either of white or of some brilliant color, embroidered on the edges with large flowers that hang from it like a fringe. Although this headkerchief is supposed to cover the hair, it is usually left loose enough to slip continuously, just as does the milaya, so that the bint al-balad will have to stop in the middle of the street to take off her kerchief, retie it, and rewrap the milaya around her body, thus performing a series of alluring gestures that are sure to attract the attention of the passersby. Other accessories such as slippers and bracelets complete the picture of bint al-balad. She customarily wears high-heeled slippers or clogs so that her walk will be punctuated by attractive clicks, or she wears flat slippers but with an ankle bracelet that makes a tinkling sound. She wears gold bracelets on her arms, and the most important item in her makeup is the black *kuhl* (eyeliner). Thus arrayed, she walks coquettishly in a manner that makes her hips seem to roll and swing to the rhythm of her clicking slippers, tinkling bracelets, and the little bursting noises of chewing gum bubbles.

Many banat al-balad in the hitta have occupations outside the home. The roles they play reflect the coexistence of the old and new in their communities. While some women still hold certain traditional jobs (such as the *ballana,* a woman who bathes other women and does depilatory work), many others work in factories, in tailor shops, or as dressmakers, shop assistants, nurses, or government employees, depending on their education. Inside their homes many women take an active role in their husbands' work. In one harah there are many migrants from the oases who are wholesalers of cooked beans (*ful midammas*). Their women are occupied daily with cleaning and washing the tons of ful that will later be cooked in huge pots and circulated to individual sellers. Similarly, women whose husbands are merchants of other food products prepare and cook the food while the men do the marketing. Also, many craftsmen work in their flats, with the participation of the whole family. Some women in these quarters work as servants, but since this job is looked down upon, they try to conceal it by working in another quarter.

The banat al-balad of the study represent various typical roles that women play in these harat.[4] Some of these roles are closely associated with the popular image of banat al-balad. One example is the muʿallima (master or chief), a term referring to certain working women, mainly butchers, hashish merchants, coffeehouse keepers, or important merchants in the market. They are usually reputed to have powerful status in the hitta. They direct large and successful enterprises. Traditionally the muʿallima has in her shop a large special chair or sofa on which she sits and smokes a water pipe. She is coquettish, gives much care to her appearance, and adorns herself with expensive jewelry. Her dress, however, is a man's *galabiya* (long flowing gown) which is complemented by a mannish air and a look of seriousness and toughness. She participates in quarrels like a man and disciplines anyone she dislikes with a beating. The muʿallima is considered a local leader within the hitta. For example, if she notices that one of the men of the quarter is fond of a particular girl, she immediately interferes and acts as a mediator in their marriage. If two persons are on bad terms, she reconciles them. If she sees that a member of the hitta is going bankrupt, she will volunteer to enter as a partner with him in a project. She encourages those who have talents and no capital by personally financing certain projects for them.

Muʿallima ʿAziza is said to be a typical bint al-balad. She is about fifty years old and has been working as a butcher for the past twenty-five years in an old Cairene quarter. She works independently of her husband. She supervises all activities in her own butcher shop five days a week, from early morning to late at night. She tends to her customers, directs her apprentices, and helps them to cut up meat when the shop is crowded. Apparently she is quite wealthy, for she recently bought a new butcher shop for her son at the cost of several thousand pounds. She lives in one of the new buildings of this quarter, and thus her furniture and flat, which consists of two newly furnished rooms, differ from the older dwellings around. In her home Muʿallima ʿAziza wears a gaily-printed galabiya and a white kerchief. Although of huge build, she is extremely coquettish in manner. In her shop, however, she puts on a black dress, a black headkerchief, and a serious air.

Another typical bint al-balad is Umm ʿAli, a housewife, who had a son by her first husband before he left her to marry a friend of hers. Umm ʿAli sold her jewelry and set up a laundry shop. One of her customers, a tailor, showed great interest in her son. She accepted his offer of marriage "so that he might help her bring up the boy and help her tend the shop." She bore him a daughter and a son. This second husband then befriended a group of drug addicts, at which point he sold his business and left for Alexandria. Lately, Umm ʿAli has been practicing different forms of fortune-telling. At first she was shy: "This is a business for gypsies and not for respectable people, but I was forced into it by the jinn. They gave me their orders in a dream and threatened to drown me in boiling water if I did not comply." She does not tell fortunes as a means of earning her living but rather as a hobby for her neighbors. She takes a reward only if her prophecies come true. Umm ʿAli is a very social person, cheerful, and a first-rate conversationalist with very expressive features. Although over fifty, she is very coquettish and fond of frills and bright colors.

Another role associated with bint al-balad is that of the ballana. Umm Gaʿfar works in a baladi (folk) public bath and goes every month to women in their homes to bathe them and perform depilatory work. The process of bathing in a baladi bath usually takes at least two hours. Not only is the ballana's role changing but so too is the class of client. Fifty years ago the public baladi bath was an essential institution, since private houses had neither baths nor tubs. Only the elite could afford to have tubs similar to those of the public baths for their own personal use. Therefore, the ballana in the public bath used to attend to women of all classes (Amin 1953:95), but now only the lower classes go to the public baladi baths.

Another role associated with bint al-balad is that of the *dallala*. The dallala is usually a middle-aged woman who knows the merchants of various goods and who also has close personal contact with the women of the quarter. She is aware of their various needs and tastes and will buy from shops to sell to women who are confined to their homes. However, now she buys and sells all sorts of goods. Recently, dallalat have been buying products wholesale and selling them by installment to those who cannot afford to pay cash.

Women of Other Social Classes

The bint al-balad compares and contrasts herself with women of three other Cairene social classes: migrants from the countryside, upper-class women, and middle-class educated women. Each class is thought of in terms of character types.

Fallaha

In colloquial parlance *fallaha* (peasant) denotes the very opposite of bint al-balad, both in terms of residence and character traits. The fallaha is regarded as awkward, inept, stupid, and narrow-minded. Bint al-balad assigns herself to a higher status and shuns certain tasks which a fallaha would naturally perform, such as carrying on her head a load of pots to be washed in the river. The fallaha's "backwardness" is further apparent to bint al-balad in a crudeness of taste in furnishings, clothing, and hairstyle. The synonym for crude taste is, in fact, *fallahi.* (However, upper-class Egyptian women call things that are rustic or in poor taste *baladi.*)

An important point of contrast between bint al-balad and the fallaha concerns cleanliness. This is well illustrated by the remark of one bint al-balad, "The fallaha may become modernized and wear flowery and chic dresses, but underneath you will find complete filthiness, whereas bint al-balad is particularly clean both inside and outside." Bodily cleanliness for bint al-balad involves removing all bodily hair, a procedure called *al-hifuf,* performed either in a public bath or at home. Cleanliness is also manifested in the care given to the female organs: after intercourse bint al-balad will wash herself thoroughly with her fingers.

Cleanliness, however, is not related to hygiene alone but also to bint al-balad's concern with her glamorous image, which she consciously seeks. Her "sex appeal" lies in exaggeratedly large eyes, fine features, a round lively face, and a "chameleon" body that is well rounded and not fleshy or bony. The glamorous effect, however, must be maintained with a certain reserve and modesty. Both glamor and modesty are combined in bint al-balad's wearing apparel, the milaya-laff, which reveals the graceful bodily curves yet covers what should not be revealed or what is shameful.

Conservative modesty is an attribute that bint al-balad and fallaha share. But bint al-balad perceives her rural sister as more modest than herself because she is less modern. In turn, the fallaha refers to bint al-balad as *gaziya* (gypsy) because in the house she wears open and sleeveless dresses which the fallaha would not permit herself.

The bint al-balad regards the fallaha as bumbling, awkward, slow, unaware of facts, and inarticulate. In contrast, she sees herself as *hidi*', implying a rapid intuitive grasp of any situation or, as the common saying has it, "one who understands while still in the air." One can take advantage of the fallaha and can make a fool of her, but not so with bint al-balad, who is more likely to be the one fooling others. A popular description of bint al-balad is one who "is capable of playing with an egg and a stone at the same time"—and without breaking the egg. She sees herself as alert and inquiring—attributes emanating from a style of life that brings her into contact with a wide variety of people and situations. It was inconceivable to Muʿallima ʿAziza that one fallaha, a resident of the quarter for thirty years, did not know how to go alone to the next hitta. In comparison with the fallaha, bint al-balad is experienced, alert, and unable to be fooled and able to interact with anyone with quickness and confidence.

Upper-class women

Bint al-balad also contrasts herself to *bint al-zawat* (upper-class, "aristocratic" woman). Banat al-zawat are regarded as "the high gentry of Garden City and Zamalik," remote from and elevated above the banat al-balad. They act like Europeans and are ultra-modern in material possessions, attitudes, and customs. Basically, however, bint al-balad views her aristocratic counterpart as one who wears an elegant exterior to cloak an immoral self "of which only God is aware." Bint al-zawat is seen as spoiled and lazy, attending only to her personal appearance and shunning family duties and housework. Bint al-balad, on the other hand, would sacrifice all for her husband's and family's welfare and sees herself as superior as a wife and mother.

Bint al-zawat's aloofness and sophistication lead her to refrain from many activities and habits that bint al-balad would consider natural. For example, one bint al-balad said she "would not hesitate to scold and beat anyone who annoys me. I do not feel shy about sitting on the ground or in a baladi coffee-house if I am tired, whereas bint al-zawat would never have the guts to do so." The bint al-balad sees herself as courageous and outspoken in words and actions. As a baladi woman, it is natural to eat with one's hands, to wear the milaya-laff, and to use traditional utensils. Muʿallima Bahiya described one family as "high" because of "their adherence to a specified weekly menu and their use of knives and forks."

Intimate and personal ties are highly valued by the bint al-balad. The remoteness of the bint al-zawat makes her appear unsympathetic, impersonal, and selfish in her neighborly relations. Umm Fathi's experience of the hitta exemplifies this: "Garden City may give you peace and quiet but never the sociability and considerateness you find here, on all occasions, in joy or misfortune. If I say 'ah' in pain, everyone around rushes to help me; someone knowledgeable in baladi remedies prescribes one and another volunteers to fetch a doctor. Can you find this spirit in Garden City?"

Bint al-balad's sense of identity is more strongly linked to her quarter (hitta) than to members of the nuclear or extended family. Bint al-zawat, however, identifies herself with such-and-such bey or pasha[5]—the most prominent male member of her family. For bint al-balad, to leave her quarter is to negate her identity and her origin. For this, she would be mocked and accused of trying to put on the airs of an aristocratic lady.

Middle-class educated women

Bint al-balad not only differentiates herself from but considers herself equal in knowledge to the educated woman, since the "school of life" exceeds any formal training. In adhering to certain values and standards of behavior, bint al-balad is even superior. Mu'allima 'Aziza tells of an "educated" niece who had illicit relations with a man. "This girl cared for neither honor nor reputation; she is worthless. This is something a bint al-balad would never have allowed." Umm Bulbul cites the example of a famous doctor who married an educated woman, and regrets he had not married a bint al-balad who would have "comforted him and made him feel a man. His 'educated' wife criticizes his behavior and objects to his many personal demands."

To the banat al-balad, an educated woman becomes snobbish, looking down on the hitta and desiring to leave it at once. Umm Ga'far's brother married an educated woman who refused to receive his family at the wedding because they were baladi-dressed women. "This woman should realize that we, banat al-balad, brought up her husband, educated him, and made him a man." However, if an educated woman does not negate her identity as a bint al-balad, she is respected as genuine. As one bint al-balad observed: "My neighbor's mother works as a ward attendant in a hospital but she herself is university educated and works as an airline hostess. She married a doctor but still lives in the hitta. She loves baladi people, talks like them, and follows their style of life. Occasionally she holds a zar and invites us. She is a real bint al-balad."

Nevertheless, despite some feelings of superiority to the educated woman, the bint al-balad aspires to an education and regards it as an improvement on instinctive knowledge. She may feel inferior to her educated daughter, but she still wants her to have a school education. One often hears: "Learning is more than religion. However experienced I am, there will be things I do not know that an educated girl will know."

As a working woman, the bint al-balad is a *bint al-suq* (daughter of the market) which implies a character-type associated with the nature of the job—buying and selling fruits, vegetables, butter, fish, and so on. Muʿallima Zuhra, as a bint al-suq, is exposed to all kinds of people and experiences and observes many kinds of human problems. Such work requires foresight and intelligence; it is said, "one bint al-balad equals twenty men in trading." In contrast, a woman employee in the government is "bound to her desk and hence lacks experience and is unaware of the world about her." Thus, bint al-suq denotes cleverness and a certain worldly poise or ease in any economic or social situation. For example, women clients come to Muʿallima ʿAziza in her butcher shop with a variety of complaints: difficulty in finding servants, bad treatment from their husbands, financial problems, and so on. "The market is life and this is our school," ʿAziza remarked. The marketplace provides contact with a wide range of behavior and social problems, thereby enriching the bint al-suq's own experience in comparison with the woman confined to her home.

Several women of the hitta do governmental work. The bint al-balad regards the salaries they make as too low to make it worthwhile to neglect the home. Zaynab, for example, earns eighteen Egyptian pounds per month and her husband is in debt. But Zaynab neglects her husband and thinks only of her personal appearance and pleasures. The bint al-balad considers the government employee conceited, superficial, and neglectful of her wifely duties. This explains why she spends her salary only on selfish, superficial pleasures.

The Opposite Sex

Bint al-balad's relation to the opposite sex is governed by certain values that color her behavior and hence reflect her self-concept. She conceives of herself as honorable and modest. The milaya-laff is a suitable dress for her because it protects her modesty, just as a miniskirt would injure her modesty. One bint al-balad recounted the time a woman, not originally from the hitta, came wearing a miniskirt. "Everyone ridiculed her and one of the hitta grabbed her handbag and threw it on the ground. When she bent down to pick it up everything showed and everyone regarded her with contempt until the holy blessing of the saints rid the hitta of her." The emphasis on modesty is often due to the hitta's being considered a sacred place, owing to the location of tombs of saints in it. Indecency is therefore an offence. One bint al-balad observed that "the saints' tombs of the quarter protect us from immodest and dishonorable people and drive them away."

Concern for reputation is another aspect of this conservatism. Women of the hitta are known by all and their actions are closely observed. Their behavior must accord with the hitta's expectations of them. Even a youngster is allowed to reprimand immodest behavior. A woman's reputation can be ruined by the mere rumor of her going around with a man before marriage. This could stigmatize her, or "break her wings" as one phrased it, leaving her without pride. In such a state people regard her as corrupted (in the village she might be shot). Hence, the bint al-balad does not appear in the streets with a man who is not her father, brother, or uncle. Intimate gestures between unmarried couples are scorned. One bint al-balad recounted the following: "One day I met my nephew in the street. He lives in another area and is not known in our neighborhood. Because he is unable to speak, he has the habit of holding one's hand while communicating. While I was talking to him in this manner, a man from the hitta stopped me and took me home. His suspicion was not lifted until my mother confirmed my story."

Walking hand-in-hand with a man who is known to be the bint al-balad's fiancé is not proper as long as no official contract has been made between them. One bint al-balad who owns a shop in the neighborhood was complaining that her relative goes hand-in-hand with her fiancé (and they have been rumored to be lovers), although they have not even been formally engaged: "I have been in the hitta for twenty-five years and I have netted this shop one thousand pounds. Yet I am going to sell the shop and leave the hitta because of the disgraceful behavior of my relative."

Nor should a girl be photographed with a man who is not a close relative. A man from the hitta (and a university graduate) narrated this incident: "I wanted to propose to a neighbor of mine of whom I was very fond. But I changed my mind when I saw a photo of her and a male neighbor. I wouldn't permit my sister to do this, and I would expect my fiancée to be similarly conservative."

Receiving men at home in the absence of the father or husband is considered very improper, and numerous stories are cited to show how this behavior may have harmful consequences. An elderly bint al-balad used to leave her daughter with a male teacher in the house for private lessons. After a few months, he became fond of the girl and had sexual relations with her. "The greatest blame falls on the mother who allowed a stranger in the house and then left him alone with her daughter." The man was considered vile and low, but he was excused on the basis that "you cannot have petrol and matches near each other and at the same time not expect fire." The girl too was blamed, and it was felt she was not a real bint al-balad, or else she would have protected her honor. The main issue in this case was that the girl allowed premarital sexual relations—the most shameful and condemned act in these quarters—and the only thing that saved her from being completely ostracised was that the man proposed to her.

When a man proposes to a woman in such a situation, neither *mahr* (bridal payment) nor *shabka* (betrothal gift) are expected of him. This is very humiliating to the bride since the mahr and shabka are very important to banat al-balad. For banat al-balad not only boast of the amount paid to them, they also take great pride in the speed with which the money is paid. One well-to-do woman prided herself upon the fact that her daughter's suitor was ready to pay 300 pounds immediately and wanted to marry her within the month. Such an attitude on the part of the suitor reflects the girl's great desirability as well as the fact that he is well off and is ready to "buy" her. *Buy* in this context refers to nonmaterial aspects, since the amount of mahr symbolizes the girl's status in terms of family, personal reputation, and beauty. Banat al-balad are thus always urged to choose, as the common saying goes, "he who desires you, not the one whom you desire."

The bint al-balad is assumed to be honorable and capable of protecting herself. She is described as "one who can be trusted among a hundred men" and "she is a man among men and no one can fool her." When a young bint al-balad expressed her fear of men molesting her in the street, the immediate reaction of the men present was, "Do you really fear men in the street? I am sure that if any man dares to bother you, you would immediately take off your shoe and beat him."

Flirting is a frequent kind of interaction between sexes in the hitta. "A man keeps following bint al-balad, thinking he is cute. When he finds that she is not interested in him, he becomes irritated and insults her, saying, 'who do you think you are?' and he pretends that it is she who is accosting him." On the other hand, the bint al-balad who is careful about her reputation realizes that such talk could ruin her. If she is courageous and outspoken, she will finally beat him physically, since she knows that a strong reaction is expected of her to preserve her reputation. The following is an incident recounted by a twenty-year-old bint al-balad:

> A certain cowardly hashish merchant persisted in flirting with me several times. He even followed me to the movie and sent me tea with the waiter in the movie. The fact that I rejected his advances prodded him into saying dirty things about me in the quarter, like "loose woman" and "daughter of a whore." One day I became furious and followed him to the baladi coffeehouse, snatched off his glasses, and beat him with my shoe. He tried to insult me again, but I answered back with a flood of insults. He even took a chair and tried to hit me with it, but I ducked and he fell and I fell on him and beat him. On that day I shocked the market; everybody heard about this incident, particularly since this man was known and feared as a tough guy. Since that day he has lost the respect of others. Had I not done what I did, he would have kept on saying I am a loose woman.

By beating him she not only put a stop to his improper behavior and protected her reputation, but she also humiliated him so badly that he had to leave the neighborhood. He would never again be considered manly and would be constantly reminded, "You have been beaten by a female. You are not a man."

This does not mean that flirting is always rejected. On the contrary, it is often used as a means of getting acquainted. As one man pointed out, "Bint al-balad at first refuses flirtation and may hit the flirt with her slipper. But it may end with understanding and harmony between them." Since molesting may ruin a woman's reputation it must be done in a very subtle way if it is to achieve harmony. For example, the bint al-balad will walk with one of her friends and the would-be flirt will walk with one of his. The two men start talking in a voice loud enough for the courted girl to hear. The conversation seems to be taking place between the two men; however, their words are really addressed to the girl. She is made aware of this by the twofold implication in their choice of words. The girl answers by talking to her friend in similar terms. The conversation between the interested couple is far from obvious to the outsider. Such dialogue relies on puns, cleverly chosen words, and jokes in which the hero is the suitor.

The Husband

Bint al-balad's concept of her husband reflects her concept of herself as woman and wife. To bint al-balad, the support of the family (including her own support) is the full responsibility of the husband and is part of his identity as a man. A man should be capable of "feeding his wife." This expression is used symbolically to denote his ability to earn money to provide for his family. The husband who does not fulfill this role is described as "one who is fed by his wife." He is not a man and is often called a "female" (*mar*ʾ*a*), which is a most degrading status for a husband.

The ideal husband in the bint al-balad's eyes is a well-to-do man who enables his wife to be a "lady" (*sitt*), a nonworking woman who has the leisure to sleep as long as she likes, servants for the housework, and all the comforts and luxuries she desires. Thus, what is important is not only the fact that she does not have to work to earn her living, but also that her husband can afford the luxury of maintaining her in style. It is interesting to note that though bint al-balad claims to disdain certain attitudes of upper-class women, she still aspires to the same material comforts that those women enjoy, wishes that her husband might provide them, and to some degree idealizes that situation.

Bint al-balad expects men to prefer a housewife to a working woman. One educated man indicated that men are now seeking working women as wives in order to raise the family income, but a woman responded, "It might be true that men now desire working women as partners, because of the rise in the cost of living, but deep in their hearts they prefer a housewife if they are real men." It is expected that the husband of a bint al-balad who worked before marriage will demand that she leave her job, if he wishes to assert his identity as a man who does not need the financial help of his wife. An elderly bint al-balad pointed out that her two daughters, who were government employees when they got married, were asked by their husbands to resign. The girls did not object; "after all, their husbands are well off."

Husbands who insist that their wives work are looked down upon. One bint al-balad complained: "My husband, who is married to two other women, is treating me badly because I don't 'bring him money' as do the other two women." She was objecting because her salary would go into his personal pocket when he should be the one to provide for the whole family.

If she wishes to work, bint al-balad considers her income a supplement to her husband's, to be used as she wishes, with no obligation toward her husband or the household expenditures. But if her income should be needed for household provisions, she will be the first to sacrifice her personal desires. A man commented, "The income of the wife is for herself; it should not be spent on the husband. He is the one who should feed her." Men who have no occupation in these quarters are referred to disdainfully as "those who are fed by their mothers." If, on the other hand, the woman happens to spend her income on the family either because of some shortage in the husband's income or for some other reason, she thereby acquires a higher status. One bint al-balad remarked that "any woman who has authority over her husband is usually one who has an income and provides for her home."

Some banat al-balad (especially elderly ones) prefer a man of the quarter (*ibn al-balad*) to a government employee. "How could anyone prefer an effendi over an ibn al-balad, when the effendi's pocket is always empty and the ibn al-balad's is always full?" "The effendi will never be preferred to the ibn al-balad because his income is limited. Once he is done with the butcher and grocer, nothing is left of his salary."

But it is not wealth as much as the ability to earn one's own living that is at the core of bint al-balad's notion of masculinity. One young bint al-balad noted that some girls prefer hashish merchants (who are rich) as husbands. The common reaction of elderly women was: "Those who prefer hashish merchants are the ones who come from a similar environment." To banat al-balad a real ibn al-balad and an ideal husband is "a man who earns his living from the sweat of his brow."

As a "real man," the husband should know and fulfill his obligations. The husband's main duty is meeting the needs of his home. Many banat al-balad express their appreciation of their husbands in the following terms: "What a man! He fulfills my every wish, he keeps my home full of everything and showers me with jewels." The husband who can afford jewelry provides his wife with far more than her immediate needs. Jewelry, especially gold, is not so much an ornament as an investment and a sign of prestige. A woman with high prestige is said to be "dressed in jewelry up to her elbows." The value of gold is stable, and when a woman buys jewelry it is usually thought of as "an asset to help in time of crisis." Thus, while the ideal husband would add to her jewelry, a bad husband would force her to sell it. As they say, "he disarmed me of the jewelry that I was keeping for a time of need."

The husband should also control his home. For banat al-balad control of the home means that "he knows everything within it. For example, he knows the price of a cup of tea as well as the price of a meal, and he brings the provisions himself." If the husband neglects these activities and the wife takes over, he loses her respect. For example, Umm Fathi's husband used to work as a tailor but because of his hashish addiction he started to neglect his work and home responsibilities to the extent that she had to take over. "I had to buy even his galabiya for him because I had to make him appear respectable in front of people. But he became so irresponsible in his life and his home that we had to separate. He is not a 'homely man'; he is a hashish addict, mean and vile."

The husband is also expected to control his wife. To control her means being aware of all her activities, knowing when she goes out and comes back, where she goes, and whom she meets. He has to be tough, that is, "a lion"; otherwise his wife will have no regard for him. The relationship between the husband's masculinity and his control over his wife is made clear in the following: Muʿallima ʿAziza, the butcher, said, "My sister, who is a bint al-suq, married a man who is soft. She started to lead her own life and became a 'sport,' that is, she came and went at her leisure. Whenever her husband dared to object, she would kick him out of the house. Finally she had to leave him to marry a real man." Another working bint al-balad cited the incident of a woman married to a man who was weak but who provided her with a luxurious life. For a long time this woman carried on an affair with another man until it was discovered by chance, when she and the man were in a car accident. The bint al-balad commented on that incident: "As long as the husband is soft, the woman will do what she wants. Unless he is like a 'lion,' the woman will neither fear nor respect him. If the woman gets spoiled it is due to the man; if she stays pure it is also due to him."

The husband who does not control his home and wife is not respected; he is not considered a real man, for his wife overrules him. A real man may be so tough that he beats her, but banat al-balad are of the opinion that a beating is nothing but an expression of jealousy that springs from love, and they appear not to mind greatly their husbands' beatings. "Beating one's love is like eating 'dry raisins' (sweets)." Since it is also an expression of the masculinity and toughness that are expected of the husband, there is nothing really shameful in being beaten.

The emphasis of bint al-balad on the virility of her husband springs not only from the importance of intercourse to her but also from the status she derives from being the object of sexual attention. One elderly bint al-balad explained: "The woman who agrees to live with an impotent man deserves the consequences of this choice, because in this case she should become a servant. The free woman would ask for divorce." It is the duty of a virile husband to satisfy the woman in sexual relations by having frequent and lengthy intercourse.

Three banat al-balad debated the importance of a husband's virility. Umm Fardus was divorced from her husband for two years because he married a young girl. She and her husband agreed to remarry on condition that he keep his young wife. When they had remarried, he rented a separate apartment for her and agreed to provide fully for her and for his children. He visited her every now and then, but Umm Fardus complained that he did not sleep with her. The second woman said to her that as long as he looked after her and the children and fulfilled her needs, why the complaint? Umm Fardus' immediate reaction was: "How could you say that? This is not even accepted by the Islamic *sharia*. Life is not only food and drink; we are human beings who need other things too. The wife certainly needs a man who will sleep with her. What will she feel when she sees the husbands of her women neighbors coming back to them at the end of the day to sleep in their arms? Of course she will be jealous and boil with frustration." The third woman said, "Why have marriage then, if it were just a matter of food and drink or money? I had them in my father's home, anyway. What I need is a man in my lap."

Bint al-balad conceives of herself mainly as a housewife who has certain duties to fulfill toward her home, husband, and children. Her main duty toward her husband is to make life comfortable for him, that is, "prepare his bath, dress him, cook for him, clean and take care of the home, and please him." These duties are expected of her regardless of whether she is only a housewife or a working woman as well. A working bint al-balad said: "We banat al-suq have to free ourselves on certain days for our men. Otherwise, if I am busy all the time, he will wonder why he married me. I have to change dresses for him because if he always sees me working and busy and tired, he will say (and he would be right) 'why didn't you stay unmarried?' " She is careful to dress and to groom herself every night, to appear at her best when he comes home, as an expression of her interest in pleasing him, all of which are part of her conception of her role as a wife.

She also sees herself as an efficient housekeeper, capable of living on the smallest of incomes, which contributes to the establishment of her husband's career. It is often said about men who have accumulated wealth that it was due to the cleverness of their wives. Umm Hasan, who married a worker, uncomplainingly helped him by working from early morning till late at night to provide for her home, her husband, and her five children. She continued to do so until her children had grown up and her husband was able to buy his own shop. Everyone said she was an example of a real bint al-balad, the "one who lives," meaning that she tolerated any standard of living without complaining, for the sake of her husband, her children, and her home.

Conclusion

The self-images of traditional urban women in Cairo, although abstracted from a certain social reality, may nevertheless conform with or contradict actual behavior; the relation between self-images and actual behavior is one that has yet to be fully investigated. Another limitation to a study of images is that typification tends to eliminate nonhomogeneous elements, presenting a whole, where in the actual conditions of the city, behavior is rapidly changing within a complexity of conflicting social relations. Women of these urban quarters will have little choice in the future: poverty dictates that they must work, as well as to continue to look after their families. Their self-images and their images of others are undoubtedly changing, albeit slowly, and it remains to be seen how men, also, will adjust their lives and their attitudes to this situation.

Notes

1. Arabic terms are given in the colloquial dialect of Cairo.

2. The term *zar* refers both to a ceremony and a class of spirits. The purpose of a zar is to cure mental illness through contact with the possessing spirits which cause such maladies.

3. *Harah* is now used to denote a small lane with no political significance. During the Fatimid period the harah constituted a major subsection of the city. Cairo at that time was subdivided into ten to fifteen harat, and each harah represented a unit of administration and control. The city expanded, and by the time of the French expedition the city had fifty-three harat. The French combined them, creating eight large sections, each known as a *thumn* (the Arabic term for one-eighth). These basic divisions established more than a century and half ago have been retained with certain boundary modifications in the present administrative organization of the city (Abu Lughod 1971).

4. Only five out of the thirty informants were not working outside their homes.

5. *Bey* and *pasha* are Turkish titles that denote high status and prestige and are used to refer to the male members of wealthy families.

Bibliography

Abu Lughod, Janet. *Cairo: 1001 Years of the City Victorious.* Princeton, 1971.

Amin, Ahmed. *Qamus al-adat wa-al-taqalid wa-al-ta'abir al-Misriya.* Cairo, 1953.

Egyptian Association for Social Studies. "A Social Survey of al-Darb al-Ahmar." Unpublished. Cairo, 1970.

el-Messiri, Sawsan. "The Concept of Ibn al-Balad." Master's thesis, American University in Cairo, 1969.

27 Women and the Neighborhood Street in Borj Hammoud, Lebanon

Suad Joseph

Networks of neighboring women in Borj Hammoud, Lebanon, constitute critical units of the social order, shaping street life and assuming significant social functions in the context of Lebanese society. Much of Lebanese social organization is generated from networks of personal alliances and friendships. Women, because of their responsibilities and activities, are opportunely located to create such networks in the street which then become pivotal in the lives of men, women, and children.

Street life in urban lower-class neighborhoods is frequently a rich public sphere of social activity. Studies testify to the vitality and intensity of social relations that find their locus in the street. These studies show that street-based networks can produce long-lasting and politically significant relations (Whyte 1943) ; they can create a community of emotional and moral support for chronically unemployed men (Leibow 1967) ; they can have a pervading impact on the socialization of the young (Thomas 1967, Gans 1962) ; and in

I would like to thank Lucie Wood Saunders, Nikki Keddie, Lois Grant Beck, and Elizabeth Warnock Fernea for reading an earlier version of this paper and offering many helpful comments. This paper, written in 1975, is based on field work carried out from March 1971 to May 1973 under a National Institute of Mental Health Grant for doctoral work at Columbia University.

ethnically and racially mixed neighborhoods they can provide a basis for an internal ethnic or racial order (Thomas 1967, Suttles 1968).

Most of these studies, however, have concentrated on the street life of lower-class men. Only a few studies depict the street-based networks of lower-class women (De Jesus 1962, Moody 1968). For the Middle East, although few studies describe lower-class women, some studies analyze women's networks in different contexts. Elite women's visiting networks in Turkish towns have been found to cross political factions and to operate as cohesive mechanisms in opposition to the divisiveness of male political activity (Aswad 1974). They have also been found to create connections and information exchanges between town elites and nonlocal servants, thereby producing semipublic space for pulling together different cultural systems (Benedict 1974). Among Arab-Israeli villagers, women's relations, unlike men's, have been characterized as reciprocal and egalitarian (Rosenfeld 1974). Armenian women in Greater Beirut are reported to have credit associations that provide group therapy, mechanisms of social control, and independent incomes for the women (Hamalian 1974). In Iraqi villages, networks offer women moral and emotional support (Fernea 1965).

Two provocative descriptions of urban women's street life are given by Elizabeth Fernea (1975) and Naguib Mahfouz in his novel *Midaq Alley* (1966). Both Fernea and Mahfouz detail the rich and intricate web of social relations that give a village-like character to urban streets. My own field work in the municipality of Borj Hammoud, Lebanon, verified that the urban lower-class street can be a locus of profound outdoor sociability and as such produces critical units of the social order. The research also revealed that, as an institutional setting, the street was particularly the domain of women.

The Street as a Female Domain

The street became a female domain largely because the responsibilities and activities of women kept them at home. In the Camp Trad neighborhood of Borj Hammoud where intensive household studies were conducted, women spent about three-fourths of their waking time within their apartments and streets. This was as much a function of the roles they performed as it was of the attitudes that supported those roles.

Almost all the women were married and living with husbands and children, or, if unmarried, living with parents. Women in Camp Trad rarely worked for wages outside the home. In over one hundred households only eight women were employed outside their homes. In general, women stayed at home to bear and rear children and to do housework. Since large families (five or more children) were common, care of the young was a full-time occupation. Given the level of amenities, housework was time-consuming even with small families. Laundry was usually done by hand and those women with small children or large families often washed clothes three or four times a week. Shopping for food and cooking were daily tasks. Bread was purchased once or twice daily, meat an average of three times a week, vegetables three or four times a week, fruits about twice weekly. Eggs, milk, and yogurt were purchased as needed, while durable foodstuffs such as grains, rice, oil, olives were often purchased less frequently but in larger quantities. The fact that these goods were obtained from different places added to shopping time (bread from a baker, meat from a butcher, and so forth). However, almost all this shopping was done within three or four streets of the women's homes.

House-cleaning was also a daily task. Apartments usually had one to three rooms, housing an average of four to eight people per apartment. With windows and doors left open and dirt and pollution quite heavy, the apartments needed frequent cleaning to meet neighborhood standards. Most homes were meticulously clean and neat.

The time spent with children varied in the street. Most elementary school-age children were in school, although some worked or stayed at home to help. Mothers either kept their children indoors after school doing school work or playing or let them play outside. In most cases there was a high degree of verbal communication between mothers and children, much physical contact and comforting, and strong affection bonds established.

Outside of housework, visiting was the single most time-consuming activity of women in Camp Trad. Before housework, during, and after it, they visited. The only waking time considered inappropriate for visiting was the first hour following the return of the husband from work when it was assumed he would like privacy to rest and eat. Some women visited even then.

Because of their responsibilities and their poverty, women visited mainly in their own buildings or streets. About half the people they visited daily lived in their own building and more than two-thirds in their street. Visiting was so integral a part of women's lives in the street that it was assumed every woman would join a local network. Those who did not want to be involved with neighbors had to keep their doors closed, leave home, or rebuff them by not offering adequate hospitality or by not returning visits. Most women, though, kept up a brisk exchange of visits in the street. Even women with no children or with grown children stayed at or near home because of habit and because the attitudes that supported the roles of lower-class women in general called upon women to stay at home. Women who came and went too frequently were suspected of illicit or immoral behavior. Therefore, the attitudes that supported the childrearing women also functioned to keep the other women at home as well.

Men, on the other hand, because of their work conditions, spent most of their waking hours beyond the street. Most adult men, including out-of-school youths, were wage workers. Workdays averaged eight to fourteen hours, six days a week, with some men working seven days a week. Most men came directly home after work, relatively few being accustomed to coffeehouses or bars. But since their work kept them until late in the evening, many men came home exhausted, wanting only to eat, rest, and sleep. A number of men who had seasonal, contractual, or day-work spent much time at home at irregular intervals. In general, though, men were not a regular part of weekday street life. A poignant statement of men's working conditions is expressed in the fact that some women who knew one another well did not know or rarely saw one another's husbands. Given these conditions, the streets were particularly the domains of women in Borj Hammoud.

Emergence of the Street in the Social Order

The street was not only the domain of women, but was also a public domain;[1] that is, it was the locus of critical extradomestic, extrakin social functions. Significant units of the public social order emerged in the street because it produced conditions in which people could exert some control over their lives in an otherwise fluid, complex, and at times precarious urban and national life.

Borj Hammoud was characterized by great flux. It had witnessed rapid population increases—from 2,000 in 1920 to 20,000 in 1942 and to about 200,000 in 1973. The increases were accompanied by high population turnover. One Maronite priest reported a yearly 30 percent population turnover in his parish. The turnover had brought with it tremendous heterogeneity: Lebanese, Syrians, Palestinians, Armenians, Jordanians, Iraqis, Egyptians, Greeks, Italians, Kurds, Maronites, Roman Catholics, Latin (Catholics), Greek Orthodox, Greek Catholics, Syrian Orthodox, Syrian Catholics, Armenian Orthodox, Armenian Catholics, Armenian Protestants, Arab Protestants, Shiites, Sunnis, Druze, ʿAlawites.

The great flux in Borj Hammoud was an expression of the fluidity in Lebanese national life. The base of Lebanese polity has been deteriorating for some time (Joseph 1975a). Corruption has pervaded all government levels and, as recent fighting reveals, government institutions have been weak and little respected. Inflation has been rampant; unemployment and underemployment were already about 20 percent and increasing in 1964 (*Etude Mensuelle* quoted in Badre 1972:200); labor strikes were monthly and weekly occurrences during the research period; wealth differences were so great that in 1964, 14 percent of the population was receiving 46 percent of GNP and increasing its share.

In the context of rapid increases, turnover and heterogeneity of population, and instability of national life, the street allowed for bonds of familiarity and continuity. Outside the street, social networks were shaped by national, ethnic, religious, regional, village, and kinship bonds. Friendships in the street transcended these categories, particularly through the networks of women. Most streets had a stable core population; the women and children of these households tended to know all the residents of their street. Men might know most of the residents, but did not usually know as many neighbors or become as involved with them as did their wives, sisters, and children. The street, then, through the networks of women, created the village-like conditions of familiarity that in an earlier Borj Hammoud period (Joseph 1975a:243) and in other Middle Eastern cities (Lapidus 1969:49) were created through the quarter.

The street, or *zarub,* as used by residents of Borj Hammoud and discussed here, was a section of a larger street bounded by the intersections of other streets. Streets were small, usually not more than one hundred meters long and ten meters across. There were six to ten buildings on each side of the street, each ranging from one to six floors, with most having four floors or less. Most buildings had two apartments per floor, each with one to four rooms, although two was more common. Doors left open, as they often were even in winter, tended to encourage passers-by to drop in and visit. Privacy was also limited by the thin walls that allowed normal voice levels to be heard in adjacent apartments, including those across the street. These conditions increased the visibility and vulnerability of domestic affairs to public control—control exerted through the networks of women.

Given the accessibility of private life and the great intensity of social interaction, co-residence in a street became a basis for intimacy. Women tended to know everything happening in their street.

That knowledge and intimacy, channeled through their networks, gave them a control over local life. Therefore, women's networks became significant in control of local life, first, because street life was vulnerable to such control, second, because women's presence in the street opportunely located them to exert control, and third, because the local and national flux created a need for such control.

The control articulated through the networks shaped the street into an important social unit that carried out numerous social functions. The street became a boundary marker for placing people. It was a critical and bounded unit of the children's social order. It was a nexus of relationships and reciprocity. It was a unit of social control. It was a place for airing disputes and rendering customary justice. It provided a ready structure for integrating new residents.

The Street as a Boundary Marker

Although streets did not have formal names in Borj Hammoud, residents attributed personalities to them. Women of one street frequently spoke of *zarubna,* "our street," as being "friendly, pleasant, quiet, cooperative." Other streets were named after a relative, a friend, a well-known person or institution. For example, they would say, "my brother's street," "the street of Umm George," "the street of the Blind School." People meeting one another described their streets in this manner and thereby placed one another.

More than two-thirds of the daily visiting of women occurred between women in the same street. Women frequently stood at one another's windows or set up chairs to sit and visit in the street. Formal visits as well were concentrated within streets. Interviews with sixty-four women in different households on four different streets revealed that during the previous two years, approximately 50 percent of the people whom they had visited on occasions of death, 40 percent on holidays, and 50 percent on births were living in the same street (Joseph 1975a:319). Beyond the street, relations were based on kin, village, and other categories. The street, however, was shaped by these social networks; its integrity and character came from these relations. As the social network was bounded mainly within the street, the street became a boundary marker for people's location within or outside an intense social arena.

The street was a boundary marker of a social unit for men as well as women. This was expressed in the manner in which youths and adult men used the corners of the street. The corners, as boundaries at which other social units began, were used continually as meeting and socializing spots. One corner witnessed daily a succession of use by street residents. In the early morning small children played there. From midmorning to about noon, unemployed or underemployed men stood there alone or in groups, observing passers-by or chatting. The older school-age children would replace the men around noon, after their lunch and before their return to school. In the early afternoon the corner would be occupied again by little children or the unemployed men. Older male youths, aged fifteen to twenty, regularly gathered at the corner in the late afternoon and throughout the evening to be joined or displaced by men home from work. The corner was not continually occupied, and the groups that used it occasionally overlapped. The corner was the province of the street men; nonresidents stood there only if they had friends in the street. Men did not usually congregate in the middle of the street during the weekdays,[2] although they might on weekends. Women never stood at the corners and only small girls were allowed to play there. One twelve-year-old girl suffered beatings from her older brother because she lingered on the corner. It was considered vulgar and indecent for a woman to stand on the corner, although quite acceptable for her to linger and talk in the middle of the street.

During holidays and weekends the street throbbed with men, women, youths, and childern playing, visiting, parading, and exhibiting themselves to one another. In moments of local or national crises, people gathered in the street to talk, exchange information, and express opinions. On summer evenings, men and women often sat visiting in the street while their children played around them. The street then was an arena of intense social interaction for men and women.

The Street as a Unit of Social Order for Children

For the children the street was even more of a boundary marker than it was for adults. It became a unit of the social order. With the exception of time spent at school and on errands for parents and neighbors, children spent almost all their first ten to fourteen years within the street. When they were allowed to play outdoors, they had to play within the street. Mothers rarely allowed their children to stray beyond its boundaries. Outside their kin ties, the entire social network of children was usually coincident with the street. Their play friends were street friends and, even more narrowly, building friends. At the elementary school level, school acquaintances who were not a part of the street were not usually brought home and did not exchange visits, even if they lived in the same neighborhood a few streets away.

Teenage youths in school occasionally did bring friends home from school who were not street friends. These friends could even become primary friends. But since so many of the youths dropped out before or during high school, this meant that these friendships tended to end with school. Teenage working youths also brought home friends from work occasionally. Close friends, however, tended to be incorporated in the network of the family and tended to visit the family as a whole rather than just the friend.

Children of the street regarded adults of the street as having special prerogatives over them. These adults could ask children to run errands for them, mildly discipline them, and give them advice. Adults paid particular attention to their neighbors' children, protecting them in the street, often feeding them, straightening their clothes, and in general giving them more attention and care than children from other streets. In this manner the children usually came to have a special regard for their street.

The Street as a Nexus of Relationships and Reciprocity

Intense and deep relations developed among the street women. They relied on one another continually for services, using one another's children to run errands and do housework, borrowing money from one another, and depending on one another for emotional and moral support. There is a saying in Arabic, "The neighbor who is near is better than the brother who is far away." This saying was frequently repeated in the street when minor or major crises emerged and neighbors rushed to one another's aid. One Catholic Palestinian woman with a large family was willing to provide the services of her children when asked by her Shiite and Sunni neighbors, citing the saying. Her own family was in north Lebanon and could not help her. When her newly born child died, her neighbors stayed with her, and when she gave birth again, her neighbors cleaned and cooked for her.

For all intense relations the norm was one of total sharing. It was considered improper for a woman to keep to herself something that her close friend did not have. Those with television sets were expected to share them with their close friends. A television set became a drain on the house since visitors had to be admitted and to be served coffee and food. Some women complained about neighbors who stayed late every night watching television, even past the bedtime of their hosts. Tape recorders, radios, and cameras also had to be shared with friends, as did various food items. If a woman received a special sweet or delicacy, she was expected to give some to friends in the street. Likewise, if a woman cooked a special dish, especially a holiday dish, she would be expected to send some to her friends and even to immediate neighbors who were not necessarily good friends. If a woman cooked a meal that a friend was known to like, then again she would be expected to send some.

The effect of these intense reciprocal relations was to distribute goods in the street and to make it difficult for friends to outdo one another economically. Sharing did not equalize households in the manner described for Latin American peasantry (Foster 1961, 1962; Harris 1971), but it did mean that relations became fragile if one friend advanced economically and another did not. To the extent that reciprocity operated, it seemed to do so through women's networks.[3]

The relations emerging in the street were based on networks established by women.[4] The female network tended to become the household network. Working men could not contribute much to the creation of such friendships and family networks, other than kin networks, since they spent relatively little time at home and since their friends could not visit if they were not at home. Men's work friends, to the extent that they developed, did not tend to become household friends. They met during or after work. Because of this, men tended to be much more oriented toward kin or toward the networks created by women. In fact, men could be regarded as more kin-oriented than women. Street friends rather than kin were more critical in the daily lives of women. Men who lived alone had more time for friends because they often did not have nearby kin and because they were not effectively incorporated into the street networks. Since adult males were allowed to visit homes only in the presence of a household adult male and since street networks were created through females, then single men tended to remain peripheral to the street networks. This is further testimony to the fact that women created the household networks in the streets.

The content of communication received by men concerning local affairs was channeled through women, because women created the networks and were the more involved in street affairs. Women were the usual interpreters of local events, and households were influenced by women's perceptions of street life. In one case two women who had been extremely close got into a fight and stopped visiting and talking with one another. Their husbands, who also had been friendly, found it difficult to visit one another under these conditions. As the visits between the men stopped, they relied more on their wives for information concerning the other couple. The men soon became disaffected with one another and each took the part of his own wife in the dispute.

The Street as a Unit of Social Control

The networks in the street operated as mechanisms of social control, and behavior was contained within customary boundaries. Again, this was in the women's arena because women knew everyone in the street and everyone's activities. As in most situations lacking coercive instruments of control, gossip was an important mechanism. Houses were so close, walls so thin, indoor and outdoor activities so accessible to public viewing that very little could be kept secret. Women gossiped about everyone's activities, movements, social lives, and maternal and marital roles. No realm of behavior was invulnerable to scrutiny and censure.

Women not only observed one another's behavior, but actively intervened to stop unacceptable behavior. In one incident, two women fought so angrily that one pulled a knife on the other. Neighboring women rushed in, calmed and reconciled them, and reminded them that neighbors needed one another. The understood principle that neighbors could intervene in one another's lives allowed one woman, a Syrian Sunni, at times beaten by her husband, to rely on her female neighbors for protection. Since it was unusual for men to beat their wives in this manner, neighbors were upset. Four or five women would run to her and physically stop his abuse, then try to persuade him to be understanding of his wife. In accommodation to him, they told her to understand him.

The street women also maintained social control by communicating information through their networks. My neighbor, Umm Hanna, once told me that another neighbor, Umm Ahmed, was upset because I had not returned a visit. She offered to go with me to visit her. During the visit Umm Ahmed asked why I had not visited in so long. I tried to explain and Umm Hanna lied that I had on a number of occasions said that I wanted to visit and that I always asked about her. In this manner feelings were soothed. Such incidents were endlessly a part of street life.

The Street as a Forum for Customary Justice

The social control activities of women also involved at times an adjudication of customary justice. The street became a place for airing disputes and rallying support. In almost all major local and national crises, people gathered in the street to discuss events, evaluate sides, and take positions.

A dramatic example of the importance of the street for airing disputes and gaining support occurred in the case of an Armenian family. The daughter-in-law did not get along with her husband's female relatives, with whom she and her husband lived. The women frequently argued or did not speak at all. During arguments, they shouted at each other in Arabic so that neighbors could understand. As with most Armenians in the street, they spoke Armenian in their homes. (All other street residents spoke Arabic.) One summer evening the daughter-in-law stood at the street corner shouting abuses at her female in-laws, who, from their balcony, shouted back at her, detailing her previous bad behavior and reciting specific events in which she was shameless, abusive, or dishonorable. Neighbors stood on their balconies and in the streets to listen to the fight. No one intervened since the family was not very involved in street networks. However, people listened and talked about the fight and later a few women visited the family to express their opinions. The fact that the Armenian women, who always spoke in Armenian, would feel compelled to address each other in Arabic in a family crisis, reflects the importance of the street for airing disputes, making positions publicly known, and rallying support.

Street Networks as Integrating Mechanisms

Given the high population turnover, the visiting networks of women provided a ready mechanism for integrating new residents in local life. A new resident was usually visited on arrival by her neighbors and she would return the visits. In a few days the woman would learn from her neighbors about local shopkeepers, vendors, and doctors. She would be informed of those who sell on credit and those who demand cash, those who were trustworthy or disreputable. She would also be told about the backgrounds of her various neighbors. Through these networks, the women often adjusted much more quickly than the men to their new environments.

Unity and Dissension in the Street

The networks of women in the street, like all aspects of Lebanese society, were characterized by numerous lines of affiliation which had the potential of complementing or conflicting with one another. For example, one network of women consisted of two Palestinian Catholics, a Palestinian Greek Orthodox, a southern Lebanese Maronite, and a southern Lebanese Shiite. Two of the women were distantly related; one was from the same village as the husband of another; all were from the same general region. All had grown children who were close friends. The Lebanese Maronite and the daughter of one of the Palestinian Catholics had both been married and divorced from Lebanese Shiite men. All supported the Palestinian cause but for different reasons. All lived on the same street, except one who lived on the next street. The ties that bound them included proximity, religion, kinship, village, politics, nationality, and friendship. Usually these other ties supported the relationship; but these same ties could also wreck it. This particular network had been stable for years. Other networks, however, changed, their members leaving, separating, regrouping, and new ones joining. Since these complementary and conflicting affiliations characterize all social life in Lebanon, it is useful to observe that in times of crises, the same ties can unite people or wrench them apart, depending on the circumstances and political content of the crisis. Two crises occurred that demonstrate the alignments in one street. In one crisis, the street divided along religious-national-political lines; in the other the street responded as a unit.

In May 1973, the Lebanese government and Palestinian guerrillas engaged in a two-week war. Borj Hammoud was on the border between two Palestinian camps and a progovernment area dominated by the right-wing Kata'ib party. In this crisis the residents of the street divided into a number of mutually suspicious groups. The Armenians predominately supported the Kata'ib, some joining forces with them and positioning guards on building tops. The Shiites were warned by the Armenian and Kata'ib leadership not to support the Palestinians and they largely remained silent during the war. Most Maronites and some Greek Orthodox supported the government and the Kata'ib party. A number of these Christians who had not been on visiting relations prior to the war began visiting one another, exchanging newspapers, information, and support. The Syrians were subject to government persecution and about fifty thousand of them reportedly left Lebanon during the crisis. A few from the street did leave, and those who did not remained at home or visited only other Syrians. The Palestinians in the street felt isolated. A number who had been quite active in the street took on a low profile, remaining at home and becoming cautious with neighbors. The women reduced their visiting. This is partly explained by the fact that, given the curfews, men were at home, and street visiting was usually reduced when men were at home. However, the networks continued to exist and visiting resumed when the crisis was over. The crisis was a national and an international one. The lines of affiliation and the tensions in the street were responses to national and international political alliances and therefore were largely along national, religious, and party lines.

In the other incident, the alliances were quite different, and the residents of this same street acted in unison. A Syrian Sunni youth,

Adnan, who lived in another part of Borj Hammoud but who had an uncle living in this street, was courting a Palestinian Catholic girl of this street. On his regular visits, he drove his car recklessly down the street and past her house. His girlfriend's brother and brother's friend decided to put an end to Adnan's intrusions. One day they stopped him as he drove through the street, insisting that he was endangering the lives of the children. Words were exchanged and Adnan was hit. Adnan said he would return to take revenge. He gathered his Lebanese Shiite friends from the Nab'a area of Borj Hammoud and made a plan of return. In the meantime, people gathered in the street to ask the youths what had transpired. As they were explaining the event, two cars raced down the alley. People jumped into doorways, but the friend was hit and slightly hurt. When the cars left, several hundred people gathered in the street to discuss the event. The event was seen as an intrusion into "our street" by outsiders. They unanimously supported the defense of the street's integrity. Later in the evening some of the men saw the culprits, caught them, beat them, and turned them over to the police. They also accosted Adnan's uncle who lived in the street and berated him for his nephew's bad behavior. The uncle apologized and within a few days had arranged a reconciliation meeting between his nephew and a number of street people. The uncle explained that he would not ordinarily take responsibility for his rough nephew's actions, but that he had to make peace for the good of the street.

Implications and Conclusions

The street is a basic social unit, shaped by the internal networks of women, which carry out numerous important functions affecting men, women, and children. Other functions, such as the political and economic contacts made in the street, were not elaborated here. For example, women often convey information concerning jobs for their families. They also make contacts or convey information that is important for such things as political patronage. The study demonstrates the vitality of the street as a social arena. Two questions remain: why should people carry out such important social functions through units as potentially unstable and nonbinding as street networks; and why should the street have become a female arena?

To understand the significance of the street it is necessary to explore the structure of Lebanese society and its recent developments (Joseph 1974, 1975a, 1975c). As mentioned above, Lebanese governmental institutions are weak and little respected (Binder

1966). Public order and critical public issues are not managed and decided through the formal governmental institutions but rather through a welter of networks that weave together people on the basis of kin, sect, patronage-clientage, political party, village, region, and friendship. The mechanisms for determining courses of action are not the formally constituted laws established on the basis of universalistic principles such as are usually associated with the state, but rather particularistic mechanisms more common to intimate relations in small groups. In a society in which the public institutions are not the upholders of public order or justice, it is necessary for people to secure themselves through other means such as personal alliances. In Lebanon, a person's best investment against any future occurrences is a network of kin and friends. Social relations and commitments to these relations become critical elements in the social order.

This has been especially true with Lebanon's recent developments in urbanization. Sixty-five to 75 percent of Lebanon's population now lives in cities, 50 percent in Beirut alone. While this movement to the cities has been occurring for some time, the rate has rapidly increased in the post–World War II period. However, urbanization at the lower-class levels has not on the whole been accompanied by the kind of formal organization building that is prevalent in Western urban areas. Schools, clubs, unions, churches, and sports groups have not kept pace with urban growth. For example, Borj Hammoud had only one mosque for its approximately eighty thousand Shiite Muslims; it had only thirty-seven schools each enrolling an average of two to four hundred students for the over one hundred thousand school-age children; it had no hospital, no local courts, and only three small police stations. Again, lacking formal organizations to meet their needs, the people of Borj Hammoud had to rely on informal networks of kin and friends. This pattern was even more accentuated among the urban poor since the public institutions that did exist were less accessible to them than to the more advantaged classes. The informal networks that were most accessible to the urban poor were those within immediate proximity. But residents relied on street friends not simply because they were available, but also because other networks were not as employable. Constrained by their poverty, they maintained no extensive daily long-distance relations, and they found street friends an important channel for meeting daily needs.

That these networks became predominately female reflects the amount of time women spent in the street and the roles and responsibilities that required their presence in and near their homes. Few women in this neighborhood were gainfully employed. The overwhelming majority of men worked, although at times intermittently. While many urban lower-class Lebanese women did work outside their homes, there was often a preference and a need for women to remain at home. The desire for children, the tendency toward large families, and the centrality of kinship in their lives frequently encouraged and pressured families to opt for female domestic roles. Women in the homes carried out numerous functions, some of which have been discussed here. A variety of social, political, and economic activities critical to the position and development of the family came under the purview of such women. The networks described here are one expression of these activities. In other neighborhoods where more women were employed or more men unemployed, the character of the networks differed from those in this neighborhood.

The domestic role of women is therefore one of many strategies families can adopt periodically or continuously in their development. The basis on which strategies are adopted must be seen in the context of the social, political, and economic environment in which the family is located. It is not sufficient to argue that women are universally assigned to the private domain and men to the public (Rosaldo and Lamphere 1974). Such arguments ignore the historical specificity of the cultural and structural contexts in which men and women live their lives.

Among the conditions relevant to the position of men and women in complex societies that require fuller analysis are the character of production, the system of stratification, and the requirements of state-level political organization. The relationship between the emergence of public and private domains and the state as it impinges on the roles of men and women needs further investigation (Reiter 1975, Joseph 1975b). In terms of this discussion, it is clear that women in this sector of Lebanese society do operate in a domain that can be called "public" and that their activities are critical in the daily lives of the people in this neighborhood.

Postscript

The 1975–76 war in Lebanon undermined or destroyed some of the social fabric. At the same time certain kinds of social relations intensified or expanded. Among them were neighborhood committees and groups that took charge of maintaining law and order and cleanliness in the local streets. Some of these groups were promoted by political groups; others, however, were spontaneous developments precipitated by the crisis and created out of the friendships and acquaintances that already existed. Both males and females were in these groups, although reports from people in various districts indicate that women were more active than men.

In January 1976 I visited Beirut during a lull in the fighting. Because of the danger involved I did not visit Borj Hammoud, but I did speak to some residents by phone. They indicated that the neighborhood had remained relatively calm, with no actual fighting occurring in Camp Trad. Some questions now pose themselves, the most significant one in terms of this study being the relationships between the newly formed groups and the women's neighborhood networks. It seems reasonable to assume that women who already knew one another and had ongoing, effective relationships would be an important contributing element to the street-based groupings emerging in the crisis.

Notes

1. Here I take exception with the literature that equates women's activities with private, domestic domains, a theme often found in the Rosaldo and Lamphere reader (1974), a book which nonetheless makes many contributions to the study of women. The concluding section of this study develops this point further; see also Joseph (1975b).

2. There were a few exceptions to this. One was a single unemployed male incorporated in his sister's household next door. A second, a rather lazy vegetable vendor, and a third, a grocer whose store was in the middle of a street, were treated almost like women. That is, the women visited, bantered, and exchanged sexual abuses with them freely.

3. Unlike Rosenfeld (1974), I found that women's relations were hierarchical as well as egalitarian. Rosenfeld's study concerns villagers; the urban context of my research may partially explain the difference.

4. See Joseph (1977) for descriptions of one local woman's social relations.

Bibliography

Aswad, Barbara C. "Visiting Patterns among Women of the Elite in a Small Turkish City." *Anthropological Quarterly,* 47 (1974):9–27.

Badre, Albert. "Economic Development of Lebanon." In *Economic Development and Population Growth in the Middle East,* ed. Charles A. Cooper and Sidney S. Alexander. New York, 1972.

Benedict, Peter. "The Kabul Gunu: Structured Visiting in an Anatolian Provincial Town." *Anthropological Quarterly,* 47 (1974):28–47.

Binder, Leonard, ed. *Politics in Lebanon.* New York, 1966.

de Jesus, Carolina Maria. *Child of the Dark.* New York, 1962.

Fernea, Elizabeth Warnock. *Guests of the Sheik.* Garden City, N.Y., 1965.

———. *A Street in Marrakech.* Garden City, N.Y., 1975.

Foster, George M. "Interpersonal Relations in Peasant Society." *Human Organization,* 19 (1961) :174–183.

———. *Traditional Cultures, and the Impact of Technological Change.* New York, 1962.

Gans, Herbert J. *The Urban Villagers.* New York, 1962.

Hamalian, Arpi. "The Shirkets: Visiting Patterns of Armenians in Lebanon." *Anthropological Quarterly,* 47 (1974) :71–92.

Harris, Marvin. *Culture, Man and Nature.* New York, 1971.

Joseph, Suad. "Allah Kathir: Poly-theisms and Politics in the Emergence of the Lebanese State." Unpublished. New York, 1974.

———. "The Politicization of Religious Sects in Borj Hammoud, Lebanon." Ph.D. Dissertation, Columbia University, New York, 1975a.

———. "Urban Poor Women in Lebanon: Does Poverty Have Public and Private Domains?" Unpublished. New York, 1975b.

———. "The Production of Consciousness in a Plural Society: A Case Study in Lebanon." Unpublished. New York, 1975c.

———. Zaynab: An Urban Working-Class Lebanese Woman." In *Middle Eastern Muslim Women Speak,* ed. Elizabeth Warnock Fernea and Basima Bezirgan. Austin, Tex., 1977.

Lapidus, Ira M., ed. *Middle Eastern Cities.* Berkeley, 1969.

Liebow, Elliot. *Tally's Corner.* Boston, 1967.

Mahfouz, Naguib. *Midaq Alley.* Beirut, 1966.

Moody, Anne. *Coming of Age in Mississippi.* New York, 1968.

Reiter, Rayna. "Men and Women in the South of France: Public and Private Domains." In *Toward an Anthropology of Women,* ed. Rayna Reiter. New York, 1975.

Rosaldo, Michelle, and Louise Lamphere, eds. *Woman, Culture, and Society.* Stanford, Calif., 1974.

Rosenfeld, Henry. "Non-Hierarchical, Hierarchical and Masked Reciprocity in an Arab Village." *Anthropological Quarterly,* 47 (1974) :139–166.

Suttles, Gerald D. *The Social Order of the Slums.* Chicago, 1968.

Thomas, Piri. *Down These Mean Streets.* New York, 1967.

Whyte, William Foote. *Street Corner Society.* Chicago, 1943.

Part Four | Ideology, Religion, and Ritual

Mother preparing daughter for school; Qashqa'i nomadic tribe of Iran. Courtesy of Dorothy Grant.

Women washing clothes and dishes in Amirabad, Iran. Courtesy of Dorothy Grant.

28 The Negotiation of Reality: Male-Female Relations in Sefrou, Morocco

Lawrence Rosen

One of the most intriguing problems raised for anthropologists is how the members of a single society, though sharing in a broad set of cultural assumptions, may nevertheless possess diverse interpretations of reality. Central to the modern anthropological concept of culture is the notion that, within any society, certain propositions about the nature of the everyday world are so broadly shared, so much a part of common sense, that each individual can presume that everyone with whom he interacts readily understands the general import of his statements and the basic direction of his actions.

The materials on which this study is based were collected over a period of two years in and around the city of Sefrou, Morocco. I have also profited from discussions with several female anthropologists—some of whose writings are referred to in the text—who have done extensive investigations of the social life of women in Morocco. The research was supported by the National Institutes of Health and the University of Illinois Center for International Comparative Studies. Originally prepared during my tenure as a research associate of the University of Chicago's Committee for the Comparative Study of New Nations, the study was completed with the aid of grants from the Carnegie Corporation and Russell Sage Foundation while I was a member of The Institute for Advanced Study, Princeton, New Jersey. I wish to acknowledge this support with gratitude and to thank Clifford Geertz, Hildred Geertz, Margaret Fallers, and Mary Beth Rose for their invaluable comments on earlier drafts. For all the guidance he gave me, the late Lloyd Fallers deserves special acknowledgment.

At the same time, however, it may be true that, despite certain shared concepts and mutual understandings, people who are in constant and intimate contact with one another nevertheless entertain substantially different views of the nature of their social world and the kinds of persons who comprise it. How such separate yet coexistent interpretations of reality are made manifest and how they affect the relations between their respective adherents are questions of fundamental importance to the understanding of many societies.

There are few places where this issue is raised more dramatically than in the relations between men and women in the Middle East. In numerous studies of the region the relatively sharp separation of the social lives of men and women has been duly noted. As embodied in poems and proverbs, Quranic doctrine, and folk psychology, the distinctions between the sexes have been expressed as pervasive and immutable differences derived from and justified by the incontrovertible principles of nature and law alike. Although the nature, extent, and consequences of the actual separation of the sexes vary according to economic standing, familial relations, and local practice, this division is of basic significance to the social and cultural lives of most Muslims. However, except for those studies of the general patterns of social organization, the magico-religious practices of each group, and the modernization of Muslim women, surprisingly little work has been done on the ways in which men and women in these societies view each other and the ways in which these alternative orientations reflect fundamentally different views of reality.

The Structure of Male-Female Relations

For purposes of analyzing the relations of Middle Eastern men and women, the small city of Sefrou, Morocco, presents itself as an excellent touchstone. The city lies in an irrigated strip that runs along the western edge of the Middle Atlas Mountains some fifteen miles south of Fez. The 25,000 inhabitants are of rather diverse origins: quite a few are recent immigrants from the surrounding countryside, and many speak their native Berber dialect as well as colloquial Moroccan Arabic. Despite the diversity of urban and rural backgrounds, the literature affirms a high degree of similarity in the conceptions and relations of men and women throughout the country.

In many respects the men and women of Sefrou, like those of other areas in Morocco, live in separate worlds, their relationships more intensely cultivated within distinct realms of activity than in direct interchange with each other. But just as those two worlds meet and diverge at numerous points, and just as their conceptions of each other touch common themes in their different orientations, so, too, does each rely on principles of relatedness that share certain features.

It is often remarked that women's lives are largely restricted to the private realm of household, family, and kin group while men lead public lives in the workplace, the market, and the sphere of political relations. Women, as we shall see, are viewed by men as naturally weak and unreliable, and the differentiation of spheres is directly related to this view. As noted by Amal Vinogradov: "The inherent limitations in the character of women confine them to the sphere of 'nature,' whereas men are capable of operating in the sphere of 'culture.' These two worlds of 'nature' and 'culture' correlate with the private and public sectors of social life. A woman, therefore, is relegated to the 'natural' and private world of childrearing and general domesticity, while a man's life unfolds in the 'cultural' or public world of politics, trade, and religion" (1974:193).

From the studies of Moroccan women conducted by Vinogradov (1973, 1974), Maher (1974), H. Geertz (1978), and others, a picture of the separate social lives of women emerges with great consistency. Although young girls may attend Quranic school with boys, and some few—mainly in the larger cities—continue their segregated education beyond, once most Arab girls reach puberty they are kept very close to, if not actually confined within, the precincts of their homes. The household itself is often occupied by an extended family, with different nuclear families occupying separate rooms around a common courtyard. Although men and women of the extended family mix a good deal within the house complex, it is not uncommon, particularly among larger and wealthier groups, for men to eat and sleep in separate quarters from the women. Conversation between men and women within the house is common, but the topics and styles of communication differ in mixed and segregated company.

Once she is married, a woman's role changes significantly. In most cases a newly married couple resides in the home of the husband's parents. As a wife, a woman is subjected to substantial confinement within the house. Occasional visits to friends or relatives may be made in the company of other women of the house, and poorer women may do their own marketing. The young wife is, however, largely dominated by her mother-in-law. The latter, jealously guarding her role as manager of the household and common kitchen, asserts her control over the internal workings of the household in many ways. She will often claim the right to teach the new wife how to cook—even though the girl is perfectly competent in this respect—and she guards the young woman's seclusion at home and veiled appearances outside with great care. The young wife is drawn into the constant talk by the women of the household concerning their lives, their relationships with the men, and the faults each of the women sees in the others. Quarrels are frequent, and often spill over into public view, with neighbors and relatives called upon to notice, to support, or to mediate (H. Geertz 1978). Men are often caught up in the tensions that arise between their wives and mothers: a man who shows too much love for his wife will be thought by his mother to be in need of a magical remedy, which may be added surreptiously to his food (Vinogradov 1973; Maher 1974:100–103); a father whose wife and daughter-in-law are at odds will be badgered by each for favors or find his pronouncements purposely undermined as each of the disputants seeks to establish her own position.

In most instances, however, men seek to interpose themselves between the women as infrequently as possible. As young boys they will have spent most of their time in the company of women—witnessing their internal differences, being used by the women as vehicles for communication and spying between households, and observing the rituals and erotic dances engaged in by the women during festive periods of visiting. As they grow into young manhood their relationship to parents and different categories of women is an anomalous one. Sons should not engage their fathers in any discussion relating to sex, and since their decorum in front of their fathers should continue throughout life to be circumspect and reserved, it is not uncommon to see a grown man extinguish his cigarette or rise to leave a cafe when his father enters. His tie to his mother, if less clearly regulated by etiquette, is no less intense. It is she who may be instrumental in viewing prospective brides and it is she who may intercede with his father for favors. At the same time, she is a woman, a creature of less responsibility and self-regulation, and hence an individual to be honored as much in her person as she may be the object of anger for her weakness and petty manipulations.[1]

The separation of the domains of men and women is deeply affected by their differential access to resources and the general insecurity of married life. As Maher notes, Moroccan women are largely excluded from earning wages, and what properties they do possess tend to be dominated by their husbands or agnatic kin

(1974:121–131). To achieve some minimal security and companionship, they are forced to depend on other women. Their ties with one another, however, are necessarily strained. On the one hand, they depend on one another for mutual support and the sharing of everyday tasks; on the other hand, they are often in direct competition with one another for scarce resources and for influence over the men. Alliances are constantly shifted as individual women seek both security and relative advantage, and the full range of social ties is constantly employed and rearranged in the process.

The economic insecurity of women is intensified by the frequency of divorce. In any given year, between one-third and one-half as many divorces as marriages are recorded in Morocco. The proportions vary somewhat from city to countryside and from one region of the country to another, and there is reason to believe that many marriages and divorces are never registered. Although polygamy is lawful and not infrequent among certain sectors of society, the more common pattern is one of serial monogamy. Thus in his study of a shantytown of Casablanca, Adam found that the average number of marriages was 2.4 for men and 1.7 for women, and that 6.8 percent of the men had married more than five times (1949–50). Men possess the legal power to divorce their wives arbitrarily. However, this simple invocation of divorce is often blunted by the powers possessed by a woman and her kin.

Briefly, a Muslim marriage to be valid requires the payment of bridewealth. The sum varies from a mere token to several thousand dollars, and does not include accompanying gifts and wedding costs. To a certain extent the bridewealth paid—and, more particularly, the dowry purchased for the bride with an additional sum supplied by her marital guardian—constitute an index of social importance. Because a young man may be dependent on his kinsmen to gather the bridewealth and because certain powers may be accorded the bride by the terms of the marital contract, a husband may be economically dissuaded from the arbitrary use of his legal powers.[2] In maneuvering for relative security, therefore, women must constantly arrange and rearrange their ties with their kinsmen, the women of the household, and their husbands and sons accordingly.

As distinctive as the problem of security and relative advantage is to the women, their actions must be understood as part of a broader pattern of Moroccan social life. In Morocco, as H. Geertz states, "Personal ties carry a very heavy functional load in getting the work of society done" (1978). Although one is born into a particular kin group, one's inherent ties constitute a sociological resource to be drawn upon in the formation of a highly personal network of affiliations. In trade relations, political ventures, and familial life it has been repeatedly noted that the particular content of any affiliation is sufficiently open-ended to permit the development of a distinctive and highly ephemeral set of personal relationships. In this respect, the creation, servicing, and manipulation of personal ties are characteristic of both sexes, although each draws on different resources. As Vinogradov has written: "Moroccans tend to view the world as unstable and chaotic and people as unreliable and open to manipulation. An individual, therefore, has to bargain for his own security and protection by all the means at his disposal. Moroccan women may have an advantage: they have their sex, their magic, and their skills in the management of social relationships" (1974:196).

It would, however, be a mistake to view Moroccan society at large, or the women's world within it, as simply an arena of conflicting interests, one in which the sheer control of valuable resources is alone determinative. For there are distinct regularities to the ways in which Moroccans conceive of others and themselves as particular kinds of persons, and regularized ways in which alternative possibilities can be structured into a distinctive set of personal relationships (C. Geertz 1975:51–52; Rosen 1968a, 1972, 1973).

The Rope of Satan

As in any society there are in Sefrou certain individuals who are more capable than others of articulating their views about the nature of mankind and its various subdivisions. I was fortunate in having as one of my language teachers and initial informants a man, referred to here as Si Abdallah, who was particularly good at organizing his ideas and communicating them to a foreigner. From one of our earliest interviews Abdallah set forth a paradigm that must be regarded as central to the Moroccans' conception of the nature of the sexes.

"There are," said Abdallah, "three fundamental elements of which human nature is composed: *ruḥ, nefs,* and *'aqel.* Ruḥ refers to one's soul. It is that portion of one's nature that will continue to exist after one's death. It comes from God and will return to God. No one can understand God. If we did know our souls, we would lock them up in our bodies and never die."

"Now there are some," Abdallah continued, "who say that one's nefs and one's soul are really the same thing. But this is only partly true. Like the soul, nefs is life itself, hence all living creatures—angels, men, animals and the *jnun* [the invisible creatures of the netherworld]—all possess nefs. Nefs is really all the thoughts and attitudes we have that lead us to do bad things. Well, actually, it doesn't always lead to bad things, but it can. It is all the things we share in common with the animals, all the passions and lusts. Sometimes these desires are necessary for doing good things, but then only if they are guided by reason."

"And that is what ʿaqel means: reason, rationality, the ability to use our heads in order to keep our passions from getting hold of us and controlling us. God gave Adam reason so he would know good from bad. God gave man the freedom to act as he pleases, but he also gave us reason so we would not be completely at the mercy of our nefs. By studying the Quran and by following the advice of good teachers and good leaders we can develop our reasoning abilities so that we can use our passions as we want instead of being led around by them."

"So nefs," he continued, "really has two sides to it: We need desire, for example, in order to have children, but if it is not controlled by reason we would just be like animals. We need to think about ourselves in order to get money and provide for our families, but if we don't control it with our reason we would just be greedy. We say that when a man 'has nefs' he has 'self-respect,' but if he is 'in love with his nefs' he is just an 'egotist.' What you call psychology we call *ʿilm n-nefs,* 'the study of nefs.' Reason gives us the flexibility to handle our nefs and all the bad things it might lead us to do. Just as God put joints in our body so that we would be flexible enough to cope with a variety of physical situations, so too He gave us ʿaqel so we might also have flexibility of mind and know good from bad, right from wrong."

I then asked Abdallah whether nefs and ʿaqel were the same in all kinds of people—in children as opposed to adults, for example, or in women as opposed to men.

"Yes," he replied, "because we are all human beings we all have nefs and ʿaqel, but not all in the same amount or pattern. It is all a question of proportions. When children are born they are all nefs and only a little bit ʿaqel. Their minds are totally blank and their senses work like a camera taking a picture of this, an impression of that. Unlike the animals, though, we have the potential for developing our ʿaqel to a very high degree, but first, as the Commentaries say, our minds are like empty pieces of paper on which our fathers write. Only learning and discipline will develop a child's ʿaqel until he is old enough to control his own nefs. That is why you frequently have to punish a child even if he may not have done something bad, because unless you do his passions will later be his master."

"And what about women?" I asked.

"Ah," he said with a smile, "women are quite another matter. You see, women too have ʿaqel, but in their case it can't develop as much as in men. It's just in their nature. Women have very great sexual desires and that's why a man is always necessary to control them, to keep them from creating all sorts of disorder, to keep them from leading men astray. Why else do we call women *ḥbel shitan* (the Rope of Satan)?[3] That is why women must be cloaked when in public, live in houses with small windows placed so that others cannot see in, and married off before they can give their fathers any trouble. It's like the saying goes: 'A woman by herself is like a Turkish bath without water,' because she is always hot and without a man she has no way to slake the fire."

Abdallah was, of course, able to elaborate endlessly on the nature of women and the need for men to control them.[4] Like many others he assured me that the high incidence of adultery in Europe was due to the fact that uncircumcised husbands lack the strength to keep their women satisfied and that it was, therefore, only natural that these women would have to seek relations with a number of different men. The sexual potency of the Muslim man, I was nevertheless assured, was enough to handle several women at the same time; hence the feasibility of polygamy in their part of the world.

I remember, too, being shown a marriage manual by another of my informants. The book had been published in Egypt some fifteen years earlier and obviously had passed through a number of inquisitive hands since that time. It was a thick book, well-laden with illustrations intended to depict certain points about the nature of women and the relations between the sexes. There were pictures of men smoking hashish and drinking liquor while haunting visions of the malformed offspring they would produce hovered in the background. There were pictures of middle-aged matrons who were constantly thinking about men's bodies, and more provocatively posed young ladies displaying the irrepressible sexuality of the female. There was even one drawing purportedly representing a woman who failed to respond to her husband altogether. This, I was told, was due to the fact that a woman's sexual desires are inversely proportional to those of her father, so that if a man was himself consumed by his passions, he would deprive his daughters of even that degree of passion desirable for a proper marriage and legitimate procreation.

The pattern, then, is reasonably clear and straightforward. For Abdallah, as for his male compatriots, women are seen as possessing extremely intense sexual desires which, untempered by an equally well-developed reasoning ability, are capable of wreaking havoc on the established social order. Men, in turn, are extremely vulnerable to this feminine sexual onslaught, simply because the best among them still possess passions of their own. To place a man and a woman together in any situation in which this quintessential force would have the opportunity to take its "natural course" is considered both socially foolish and morally suspect. This is not to say that women are regarded as wholly lacking in intelligence or wit; but in the absence of great ability to develop their reasoning powers through Quranic study and regular prayer, they are more likely to have their intellectual powers turned to the formulation of devious plots or the practice of various magical arts. Thus, for all the variation from person to person that exists for each of the above features, it is, I shall argue, through this overall image of the *natural* differences between the sexes that Moroccan men conceive of their women. It is through this focus, this cultural screen, that Moroccan men comprehend their actual ties with women and define, in very concrete situations, the relevant features of those ties and the ways in which they ought to be handled.[5]

But what of the women's view of men? Do they too rely on an explanatory scheme which, perhaps with its own peculiar twist, defines the relation between the sexes in terms of an indigenous "natural science"? Since I was unable to carry out intensive interviews with many Moroccan women, the answer to this question must be based, in part, on somewhat more indirect and inferential data and in part on the findings of other anthropologists who have done careful studies of Moroccan women. From this evidence it may be argued that it is not primarily in terms of a set of concepts dealing with the nature of the sexes as such that women seek to understand their relations with men. Rather, the women focus on the specifically *social* as opposed to *natural* relations between the sexes, and their conceptual orientation is, therefore, substantially different from that of the men.[6] This argument requires some elaboration.

We have already seen that from the men's point of view the relationship with any particular woman, regardless of her role or status position, is not really a relationship of equals. In a sense, it is not even a relationship of two kinds of the same creature, for the nature of women is regarded as unalterably different from that of men. Whether as cause or effect, there are, as a simple matter of descriptive fact, a number of sociological repercussions attendant on this assertion. One of them is the fact that, broadly speaking, provided that women do not overstep the bounds of public decency and do not create unmanageable strains within the household, they are generally left to handle their own affairs and to pursue their own social lives in reasonable separation from those of men. In Sefrou, as in most parts of Morocco, this means that Moroccan women spend most of their time in the company of other women preparing meals, caring for children, celebrating various festivities, and establishing an internal pecking order through gossiping about others, berating the dependent members of their households, and displaying their relative powers and influence over men.

If the worlds of men and women are relatively separate, it is nonetheless quite obvious that the two frequently impinge on each other directly. In the distribution of household resources, for example, or in the quest for a relative's mediating influence, there are many social situations in which particular men and women must contend with the simple fact of each other's existence. Thus, in addition to ordering their own internal social hierarchy—and perhaps because of it—the women themselves must often bring whatever influence or power they possess to bear on those decisions that will directly affect the character and composition of their own social world. This is not the place to discuss the legal arrangements that may exist between a husband and wife: the financial burden a man might have to bear in case of divorce, or the partial safeguards a wife might possess by virtue of the terms of her marital contract or legal standing. Nor can we adequately relate the innumerable ways in which a Moroccan woman might make the life of her husband or certain other men an absolute hell of nagging and bickering, of recrimination and argument with other close relatives. The point to be stressed here is that insofar as questions arise for Moroccan women that bear directly on their own rather separate social world, primary attention is given by them to the various social relationships involved and to the ways in which these relationships can be manipulated to one's own particular advantage. Women may, on occasion, refer to men as intrinsically worthless or childish (see, for example, Vinogradov 1974:196), but they are more likely to give greatest emphasis to the ways in which men can be ignored, outflanked, or outwitted by the arrangement of various social pressures within the household or family.

This is not to say that men are totally unaware or unconcerned with the actual relations that exist between themselves and their women or that the women, on their side, may not refer to the relations between the sexes in terms of certain assumptions about basic human nature. Instead, it is to say that each possesses a different primary conceptual orientation, a different set of guiding ideas through which particular situations are defined and particular beliefs maintained. It is no simple perpetuation of the bias of Moroccan men, therefore, to argue that, by and large, women who are confronted with problems that involve men focus most of their attention on manipulating social relations in the family rather than on interpreting such relations in terms of a clearly defined stereotype of essential human nature. Being less capable than men of imposing decisions from on high, Moroccan women simply must work with the primary resource available to them—the relations among members of the family—in order to influence situations and decisions to their own benefit.

This orientation becomes most clear when the question arises as to the choice of mates for one's sons and daughters. From the women's point of view, a marriage changes not only the relationships of the dependent involved but the composition—and perhaps the internal order and hierarchy—of the women's social world. Particularly in the case of a son's marriage, each of the women will be affected by the arrival of a new bride in the house (assuming patrilocal residence) and the creation of new ties with the women of the bride's own family. Similarly, the marriage of a daughter establishes new social ties for all the women concerned as well as for the girl herself. Whether a particular marriage is in some degree endogamous or involves a family of outsiders, a whole new element is injected into the women's world by the formation of a marital bond. One can, therefore, study a series of marital negotiations and consequences with an eye to the structural arrangements that occur in the wake of such an event (H. Geertz 1978). Or, on the other hand, one can study the same situations from a primarily cultural perspective, in which closest consideration is given to the various ideas that the participants themselves employ in defining and guiding their own actions.

It is from this latter perspective that we shall look at a specific marriage negotiation that occurred in Sefrou and on the basis of which answers may be sought to the following questions: What really happens when the separate conceptual schemes of men and women—one stressing the perception of human nature, the other the structure of actual relationships—come into direct contact, and indeed conflict, with each other? What forces are at work in the definition and resolution of such a situation, and how do they relate to the conceptions held by the parties involved? The specific incident around which the answers to these questions will be built concerns a conversation I overheard during my last visit to Sefrou.

The Conversation

I stayed in Sefrou at the home of Haj Muhammad, a wonderful old man whose dignified carriage and rich raconteurial skills blended magnificently with his little-boy smiles and the insouciant tilt he gave to the favorite old *tarbush* on his head. One morning shortly after my arrival, the Haj suggested we go visit a friend of his. We wound our way down the hill from the Haj's house, past the crenelated walls of the Old City, to the door of the house of Si Abdelqader. A young girl opened the door, ushered us into the guest room, noted that her father had already left on his regular trip to the countryside, and fetched a pot of tea before hurrying off to tell her mother that there were guests in the house. A moment later Si Abdelqader's wife entered the room and greeted us. She was a stout woman, well into her middle years, and the Haj was such an old and dear friend of the family that there was no discomfort whatsoever in the quiet, intense conversation that ensued. I had visited in Si Abdelqader's home a few years earlier and was aware that several of his daughters were of marriageable age. It took me some time, however, to fit together enough pieces of the conversation between Si Abdelqader's wife and the Haj to realize that a marriage had been arranged for one of these daughters and that while the girl had no objection to an arranged marriage as such, she was adamantly opposed to this particular union since the man in question lived in a city that would place the girl far away from her own family and friends. As I later recollected, a portion of the conversation concerning the marriage went something like this:

Mother: Well, she comes to me and she cries and she says: "Mother, I don't want to marry him. He lives far away and is always moving and I won't have anyone from my own family nearby."

Haj: Why is she crying? Doesn't she have any sense ['aqel]? Doesn't her own family know what's best for her?

Mother: She goes to her sister and she says that in the house of this man she will have no one to talk to, none of her own relatives. And her sister comes to me and says that we won't be able to visit her in that man's house, and maybe if I were to talk to her father he would see how much his little baby is suffering.

Haj: Ach! That girl is crazy. Her head is spinning, that "daughter of sin" (*bint l-haram*). She has no self-respect (*qlil nefs-ha*). She has no respect for her father at all.

Mother: And then she says that she will wait until her brother comes home from Europe next month with his wife, that Frenchwoman. She says her brother's wife would never approve of such a marriage and that she, in turn, will get her husband to talk to Si Abdelqader and convince him that this is not a good marriage.

Haj: May Allah give her pain, that little bitch! She makes for such unrest! She is absolutely consumed with passions, like all girls. But we'll take care of everything.

Mother: Well, I don't know. Who knows what's what. I don't understand it. It's in God's hands.

Haj: Of course. And we'll fix everything as soon as Si Abdelqader gets back—and before his son comes home.

Mother: Well, it's up to God. I don't know.

Haj: It's all set. When Si Abdelqader returns we'll take the groom to my house, bring two notaries up from the court, make a *fetḥa,* and register the marriage. That will finish the matter once and for all. That will cool your daughter off.

Mother: Well, sir, I don't know. Maybe that's the way it is. I just don't know. Everything is in the hands of Allah!

Bargaining for Reality

There are a number of points that can be drawn from a study of this particular case. Although characterized by certain unusual features (such as the fact that the brother of the potential bride is married to a foreigner and only returns to Morocco occasionally), it does indeed exemplify some of the more important mechanisms of Moroccan marital politics. In terms of contemporary Moroccan law it is illegal for a marriage to be recorded if the bride has not appeared before the notaries to give her personal consent—a fact of which almost all women are aware. But if the registration of such a marriage without the bride's knowledge is irregular, it is not at all unusual for the bride to be constrained to accede to the wishes of her marital guardian, whatever her own feelings about the union may be.

But in order to understand the full implications of the conversation between the Haj and Si Abdelqader's wife, it is necessary to go beyond the strictly legal or sociological aspects of the case. It is necessary to consider this situation from another perspective and in terms of a very different theoretical scheme. For it is possible to look at this conversation as an example of an encounter between a man and a woman, each of whom maintains a rather different view about the nature of the sexes and their respective social roles, and who, when they are brought into direct confrontation, must now engage in what might be called a process of "bargaining for reality." As developed by psychologist Thomas J. Scheff (1968), this notion of reality-bargaining refers to the process by which several actors, each of whom possesses a different view of what is really true about the situation in which all are involved, attempt to make his or her definition of the situation prevail. Because these individuals are engaged in a common activity demanding both definition and resolution, their concepts of reality are subject to negotiation, which in turn is significantly affected by the relative power possessed by each of the participants in this particular situation. Scheff thus refers to psychiatric interviews in which a therapist may impose his version of reality on a patient as the price for his personal and professional aid, or a lawyer may suggest to his client a version of what "really happened" that will absolve the client of any legal responsibility. If, as Scheff implies, reality is not an objective fact to be recognized but a definition to be bargained over, it is necessary to ask how we are to determine when such a situation exists and what role the different powers of men and women play in its application.

In the sense in which the term *reality* is used here, it refers to an experience of the world in which one lives rather than to that world as a set of physical constructs neutrally defined and existentially given. Moreover, as an experience of that world, reality, in this highly expressive sense, is, for any man or woman, best regarded as an ongoing experience, an activity, a continuing realization rather than a product, a fact, or a truth. But to say that it is created and lives in the "mind" rather than in "nature" is by no means to say that any given view of reality is without its own distinct regularities. Quite the contrary, an image of reality must conform with certain facts external to itself (the brute facts of sexual dimorphism, for example) and certain forms of internal consistency and coherence. And of at least equal importance is the fact that such a conception of reality must be sufficiently comprehensible to and consonant with the views of others as to permit, and indeed vitalize, relations with those persons who form part of one's social and cultural environment.

In the case of the Moroccans' expressed views of the opposite sex, the canons of consistency and congruity are indeed discernible. In almost any situation in which the subject of women arises, one constantly hears men refer to the generic constitution of that gender: women, say men, do not possess "the wherewithal" to grasp fully the essential elements of pure religion; they are "naturally" prone to traffic with powerful forces of the netherworld; they are "by natural disposition" led to create problems in the family; and so on. For men, the experience of women is so constantly mediated by a set of terms and referents concerning the nature of the sexes as to constitute persuasive evidence that the view of women as naturally different from men is indeed a fundamental feature of the men's orientation to the real world. And, although less direct evidence can be cited, a similar degree of consistency and pervasiveness appears to inform the women's own more "sociological" orientation to their men. If the references by men to women or women to men were mere verbalization, post hoc rationales or "as if" propositions, a much less uniform, pervasive, and regular set of expressions might be employed. Accordingly, it can be argued, at least as a working hypothesis, that the "natural" and "social" orientations of each of the sexes do indeed constitute fundamental conceptual orientations which define and make meaningful each group's perception of reality.

Inasmuch as the concepts involved are capable of being used to define different situations—and capable, too, of being manipulated in this way for quite varied purposes—we can, building on the ideas of Scheff (1968) and Gallie (1968), refer to such concepts as "essentially negotiable."[7] That is, a certain degree of vagueness accompanies the use to which any of the terms referred to can be put: there is an element of uncertainty inherent in these terms, such that their application to any situation by one person may be contested by another. This uncertainty of application is so very much a part of the concept's own composition, and the resolution of any dispute so dependent on the ways they can be employed as to grant the concepts themselves an aspect of essential negotiability.

In the specific case of Si Abdelqader's daughter, the concepts employed by the Haj and the girl's mother clearly display this quality of essential negotiability. Each understands the meaning the other associates with such words as *passion, sense, respect, suffering,* and the more complex terms referring to familial dissension and relatedness. The question is whether these terms really define the present situation. The Haj, of course, thinks that his own conceptions should apply. He argues that this is a straightforward example of female sensuality's blinding a girl to her natural place within a set of socio-legal arrangements sanctioned by the traditions of religion, society, and ordinary common sense. For Si Abdelqader's wife the reality is quite different. She believes it is a question of the actual relations that exist, or would be brought into existence, by the formation of this particular union. And since each of the terms and concepts employed can apply to a variety of different situations—and since this vagueness, this differential utility, is an inherent characteristic of the careers of these terms—it can be argued that it is, in no small part, the essential negotiability of these terms that makes this discussion a true dialogue whose outcome is not prejudged by the terms used or the conceptions expressed.

The essential negotiability of the concepts makes bargaining over the definition of the situation capable of being articulated. In order to establish that the present case really does involve such a reality negotiation, we must read the text of the conversation between the Haj and the girl's mother in the light of certain additional information. That Si Abdelqader's wife and the Haj were bargaining for reality is indicated by several supplemental facts. For one, it must be understood that the dispute referred to had been going on for some time before the morning of the reported conversation, and that it continued for some time afterward. Si Abdelqader, as further questioning revealed, had arranged this marriage without very great care or conviction. Under the right circumstances he might very well have agreed to break the engagement. However, instead of engaging him in a subtle dialogue mediated by respected friends and relatives, Si Abdelqader's daughters openly declared their opposition to the marriage and attempted to forestall its enactment by constantly harassing their father and upsetting the order of the household. Accordingly, Si Abdelqader began to feel that, in part, his general position as the head of the household was being challenged. Although his right to choose his daughters' mates was never directly questioned, he was aware, on the one hand, that to give in to his daughters' tactics might have endangered his ability to make decisions for the women of his household on a wide range of issues.

On the other hand, Si Abdelqader was constantly reminded of the women's capacity to disrupt the order of the house, a situation he sought to prevent not only for the sake of familial tranquility, but because he sincerely wished to find a workable solution to the problem. Although he consistently seemed willing to seek some other husband for his daughter, no proper rationale or set of mediating persons had, as yet, come forward to save both Si Abdelqader's face and his regard for his daughter's happiness.

As a respected friend of the family the Haj was ideally placed to seek an appropriate solution. As a traditionalist, he could be counted on to express the male view of natural superiority. As a realist who had experienced many unsettling disputes within his own family, he could be relied on to listen to the mother's views and discern their strength and import. The sheer fact that the two came together for this conversation is of no small importance. They were indeed prepared to listen, to argue, and to negotiate their different views of the situation.

The actual course of their discussion further justifies the characterization of their engagement as a process of reality-bargaining. Throughout, each of the parties not only implied a particular course of action that could be taken but argued for a way to define the very situation in which they were involved. In trying to establish that her conception of reality was the crucial one, the mother kept referring to the actual relationships of the people involved. The Haj, in turn, saw the matter from the perspective of essential human nature and the implied need for men to act with reference to that fact above all others. The mother in particular seemed to be trying to suggest a basis for resolving the conflict if only the Haj would accept that this was a case of placing one's regard for the social well-being of one's dependent women over simple assertions of male dominance. The Haj, in turn, was suggesting the terms in which the mother ought to explain the situation to her daughter, thus acknowledging the issues of paternal decision-making. Each played the role assigned members of their sex with classic precision: the Haj acted the part of the forceful male while the mother played the role of the dependent and submissive woman. Many of the harsh things said by the Haj ("May Allah give her pain, that little bitch!") are not only common to the Haj's rather robust style but are also far less severe Arabic idioms than the translations indicate. Similarly, the mother showed no surprise when the Haj indicated the men's intention simply to marry the girl off regardless of the women's desires. Whether she regarded it as a bluff or a show of expectable male authoritarianism is unclear, but her response, from the look on her face to the gestures of her hand, was one of feminine confusion and uncertainty. Her overt assertions of divine omnipotence and personal obtuseness, however, were not simple assertions of weakness and fatalism. Quite the contrary, it may be argued that, by her expression and her utterance ("It's in the hands of Allah!"), she was, in fact, implying that the men might think that they have a grasp of the situation but that control over the matter is not theirs alone. This does not mean that it is in the hands of God either. For just as the Haj could acknowledge the total power of Allah and proceed to indicate what the men were going to do about the situation, so too the mother was able to imply that the women were also not without additional resources of their own. The reference to Allah, then, might be interpreted less as a literal statement of theology than as a cautionary phrase, a sort of conditional marker, an assertion that power is not always what or where it appears to be. The mother's statements in this regard also buy time, since the Haj might begin to wonder exactly what temporal possibilities, what potential actions by the women, are really implied in the utterance of this supernatural platitude.[8] The mother's statements were, therefore, revealing for their broader connotations and themselves a function of the relative powerlessness of either party to impose his or her own concept of reality in an arbitrary or unilateral fashion.

Nor is the conversation between the Haj and Si Abdelqader's wife a unique encounter or one limited solely to marital negotiations. For example, when a young clerk in Sefrou encountered difficulties with his wife, the legal aspects of which have been described elsewhere (Rosen 1970:36–37), he spoke to me and other men largely in terms of the irrepressible sexuality of women and the pressures he had initially encountered from his mother to continue residing with his bride in his parents' home. When his wife and mother began fighting, it was only by being transferred to Sefrou that he was able to extricate himself from his mother's desire to keep him and his wife within the mother's house. However, his difficulties with his wife continued despite the new residence. He wanted to ask his parents for help in paying the remainder of his wife's bridewealth that would be occasioned by a divorce, but his mother insisted that reintegration into the prior social arrangement was the proper solution to the situation. The young clerk, however, argued that only an appreciation of his wife's irrepressible passions could explain both his failure to control her and the need to isolate her from other women who would only exacerbate these tendencies. In the constant discussions between the actors, each held not simply to a preferred solution but to a solution that was consonant with, indeed dependent on, his or her different interpretations of what kind of problem they were, in fact, confronting.

Similar situations can be seen in Maher's discussion of a conversation with a man in the Middle Atlas Mountains (1974:180–184), in H. Geertz's appraisal of the marriage negotiations of a man from a wealthy Sefrou family who sought to marry an educated Berber girl (1978), and in the autobiographical account by Rachid Boujedra (1969) of his relationship with his divorced mother. Such negotiations of reality are found even more commonly when men, in dealings with one another, must, for example, decide whether a particular form of sacrifice does indeed require political support (Rosen 1972:22, Waterbury 1970:90–91), whether a given act creates an obligation or is merely a favor (Rosen 1968b:223–230), and whether two relatives are really close members of the same family or merely distant kinspeople of the same tribe from whom desired acts cannot be as easily demanded (Rosen 1968b:61–86).

In each of these situations it is clear that the kinds of resources on which each of the participants can draw is crucial to the outcome of the negotiation. But power—in the sense of control of critical resources through which one's will can be imposed—is terribly diffused in Moroccan society; it seldom cumulates in unambiguous fashion for most or all of the possible situations a person may encounter.

Moroccan women in general are, as I intimated earlier, not without certain powers in their own homes. An issue may, of course, be joined in such a way as to pose a direct challenge to a man, who then relies on all his legal and economic resources to enforce his own solution. In certain instances a woman may be able to prevent or frustrate such arbitrary action by the contractual and financial limits that have been built into her marriage. But it is much more often the case that women will—perhaps must—give primary consideration to the actual relations that exist among the various members of the women's own social network. The ability of the women to make the lives of all concerned quite miserable, the ability to publicize a family quarrel to the point of threatening a public scandal, and the ability to exact revenge at a later time are all forms of action that women can use to considerable effect. Each case is, in this respect, a special one; but in general it can be said that the capacity to make one's own view of a situation and its solution stick is, if not equally divided between the sexes, certainly not weighted in all cases to the side of the men. The fact that, as of a year and a half after the reported conversation, Si Abdelqader's daughter was still unmarried clearly indicates that the characteristic qualities of such disputes in Morocco—their length, their intensity, and their Byzantine complexities—are continuing to be very much in evidence.

In sum, it appears that the social separation of Moroccan men and women also corresponds to a certain conceptual differentiation. Like the dialects of a single language, though, these different sets of ideas and beliefs are not so distant from each other as to restrict communication altogether. But the separation is nonetheless great enough so that even, for example, in a marriage characterized by sincere and deep affection, there is on the man's part an assumption that this is not really a relation of equals, just as on the woman's side there is a constant emphasis on the malleability of internal family relationships. When conceptual disagreements do occur, the terms in which they are expressed allow for a significant degree of bargaining and an exercise of respective powers. Although it is indeed possible for Moroccan men to proclaim that their definition of a given situation is the valid one, women possess sufficient means for hedging against the sheer imposition of this male fiat to grant them the capability of disputing the interpretation to be applied in the first place. Despite the fact that the statements made may appear to be simple and unilateral declarations, such encounters as we have described here might better be seen as processes of bargaining over which a person's view will indeed be used to define a particular circumstance. What is negotiable, then, is less one's view of reality as such than its scope, its impact, and its differential importance.

The conversation between the Haj and Si Abdelqader's wife was one of those momentary and ephemeral encounters of everyday life that depend for their very existence and intelligibility on a set of conceptions about the real world and the kinds of persons who live in it. Their dialogue was not solely an expression of the given conceptions of the world in which its participants had been reared, nor were their actions an unthinking response to the prerequisites of their positions in society (although neither their utterances nor their behavior is to be understood without an appreciation of these factors). Of crucial importance to the course of their conversation was the fact that they could—indeed, were required to—negotiate through and about their views of what was really true about their common situation in order to be able to comprehend its nature and take some meaningful action. The fact that the fate of Si Abdelqader's daughter was not settled by this encounter or by those of subsequent months does not negate the lesson to be learned from the conversation of the old man and the girl's mother. For it was by this engagement, at once unique and characteristic, that each was able to seek a direct acceptance of his or her own view of the situation and to assess the other's mettle and adherence to that view.

The process of bargaining for reality has its distinctive features in the Moroccan context as in every society, but the dynamic quality of such transactions is not without common features in a wide range of social settings and situations.[9] Reality-negotiation may be seen as part of the necessary process by which individuals, utilizing the resources of their language, their culture, and their personal backgrounds, confront one another and seek to establish that degree of understanding, mutual comprehension, or individual clarification through which real communication, perhaps even real intersubjectivity, becomes both possible and manifest. "The heart of the sociological enterprise is the negotiation of meaning between the self and the other" (Brittan 1973:26). The result of this negotiation may be a deeply felt participation in the same system of meaning, that union of mutually understood situation and symbol-laden encounter which Walker Percy describes as "one man encountering another man, speaking a word, and through it and between them discovering the world and himself" (1961:52). In other instances, however, the parties may not come to a shared view of reality but continue to retain their separate orientations. Their negotiation does not result in a fusion of viewpoints, but it does clarify the world and sharpen, by direct experience and the probing of existing boundaries, the breadth and power of their individual orientations.

The close analysis of examples such as those cited here also demonstrates the independent aspect of language-use in the formation of social ties in societies of this kind. Because social bonds are not rigidly defined or sanctioned and because sociological resources are diffused, language becomes a critical vehicle for tapping what resources one does possess. A man can have all the money or property he might need to impose his will, yet if he cannot get others to accept his view of a situation as one in which those resources can be brought into play—a situation in which they are relevant—he may never have the opportunity to draw upon them. Another man—or woman—may be more forceful in dominating the terms of discourse, and unless the right key can be found to unlock the resources one has stored up, one will be blocked from invoking them. The great emphasis placed in Arab society on rhetoric and language is to be understood, in part, in terms of the need to dominate the concept of the situation in order to have the opportunity to utilize one's social and material capital. With so many socially recognized sources of power available and their distribution so widespread, language becomes a key to the definition of situations in which one's own resources can be useful and another's discounted.

The orderliness and accountability of everyday life is, as Garfinkel has argued, a "contingent, ongoing accomplishment," a kind of "work" or "project" (1967:1). This project is deeply affected by the context and the personalities of the people involved. But it is also a cultural process, a fundamental feature of social life conducted through and molded by those linguistic and cultural symbols by which differing conceptions and evaluations are expressed. It is through such minute encounters of ordinary existence and the close analysis of their texture and their place that both the anthropologist and the participants come to interpret their normal relationships and attribute meaning to their everyday activities.

Notes

1. See Boujedra (1969) and Amin (1968) for the views of two North African men toward various categories of women.

2. On the social and legal aspects of divorce in Morocco see Rosen (1970).

3. In a personal communication, Kenneth Brown notes that the term *ḥbel shitan* also has a second meaning. In addition to "rope" or "towline," *ḥbel* can refer to the string of beads which the members of a religious brotherhood use in the recitation of their prayers. The implication, then, is that women are associated with the "brotherhood of the Devil" and that close attachment to them is tantamount to paying homage to their spiritual leader, Satan himself. Or, it might be interpreted as meaning that women are in the hands of the Devil like prayer beads in the hands of the faithful. Vinogradov also notes: "It is no accident that women are referred to in Morocco as *Habl el-Shitan,* the Rope of Satan. For in addition to being Satan's towline, they are also capable of tying a man up, *rbt, thqef* a cultural euphemism for saying that he is rendered impotent" (1974:196).

4. For a similar account of a Moroccan man's view of woman see Bowles (1963). On the classical distinction among nefs, ruḥ, and ʿaqel see Calverley (1963) and Tritton (1971). For an investigation of the nefs-ʿaqel paradigm in the Indonesian setting, see Siegel (1969).

5. This view is consistent with the descriptions of numerous other scholars. See, for example, Amin (1968:36–39), H. Geertz (1978), Maher (1974:84–85), and Vinogradov (1974:193–196).

6. This interpretation is also supported by the evidence contained in the works cited in note 5.

7. Contrast my theory of *essentially negotiable concepts* with the theory of *essentially contested concepts* in Gallie (1968:158).

8. I am indebted to Clive Kessler for his comments on this aspect of the situation.

9. For other examples of this process, see Berger and Kellner (1964) and Emerson (1969).

Bibliography

Adam, André. "Le 'bidonville' de Ben M'sik à Casablanca." *Annales de l'institut d'études orientales,* 8 (1949–50):61–198.

Al Amin, Ahmed. "L'évolution de la femme et le problème du mariage au Maroc." *Présence africaine,* 68 (1968):32–51.

Berger, Peter, and Hansfried Kellner. "Marriage and the Construction of Reality." *Diogenes,* 46 (1964):1–24.

Boujedra, Rachid. *La Répudiation.* Paris, 1969.

Bowles, Paul. *Their Heads are Green and Their Hands are Blue.* New York, 1963.

Brittan, Arthur. *Meanings and Situations.* London, 1973.

Calverley, E. E. "Doctrines of the Soul (Nafs and Ruh) in Islam." *Moslem World,* 33 (1943):254–264.

Emerson, Joan. "Negotiating the Serious Import of Humor." *Sociometry,* 32 (1969):169–181.

Gallie, W. B. *Philosophy and the Historical Understanding,* 2nd ed. New York, 1968.

Garfinkel, Harold. *Studies in Ethnomethodology.* Englewood Cliffs, N.J., 1967.

Geertz, Clifford. "On the Nature of Anthropological Understanding." *American Scientist,* 63 (1975):47–53.

Geertz, Hildred. "Familial Relations." In *Meaning and Order in Moroccan Society: Three Essays in Cultural Analysis,* ed. Lawrence Rosen, Clifford Geertz, and Hildred Geetz. New York, 1978.

Maher, Vanessa. *Women and Property in Morocco.* Cambridge, 1974.

Percy, Walker. "The Symbolic Structure of Interpersonal Process." *Psychiatry,* 24 (1961):39–52.

Rosen, Lawrence. "A Moroccan Jewish Community during the Middle Eastern Crisis." *American Scholar,* 37 (1968a):435–451.

———. "The Structure of Social Groups in a Moroccan City." Ph.D dissertation. University of Chicago, 1968b.

———. "I Divorce Thee." *Transaction,* 7 (1970):34–37.

———. "Rural Political Process and National Political Structure in Morocco." In *Rural Politics and Social Change in the Middle East,* ed. Richard Antoun and Iliya Harik. Bloomington, Ind., 1972.

———. "The Social and Conceptual Framework of Arab-Berber Relations in Central Morocco." In *Arabs and Berbers,* ed. Ernest Gellner and Charles Micaud. London and Lexington, Mass., 1973.

Scheff, Thomas J. "Negotiating Reality: Notes on Power in the Assessment of Responsibility." *Social Problems,* 16 (1968) :3–17.

Siegel, James T. *The Rope of God.* Berkeley, 1969.

Tritton, A. S. "Man, *Nafs, Ruh, ʿAql.*" *Bulletin of the School of Oriental and African Studies,* 34 (1971) :491–495.

Vinogradov, Amal Rassam. "Man's World, Woman's Place: The Politics of Sex in North Africa." Unpublished. Ann Arbor, Mich., 1973.

———. "French Colonialism as Reflected in the Male-Female Interaction in Morocco." *Transactions of the New York Academy of Sciences,* 36 (1974) :192–199.

Waterbury, John. *The Commander of the Faithful: The Moroccan Political Elite—A Study in Segmented Politics.* New York, 1970.

29 Women, Sufism, and Decision-Making in Moroccan Islam

Daisy Hilse Dwyer

Islam, like most of the world's major religious traditions, has tended to present a strongly masculine image to the world, Men have provided Islam's great mystics, proselytizers, political leaders, and scholars. Because of religious restrictions preserved in Islamic law, men and men alone have served as *imams* in the mosques and *qadis* in the courts. In regions like the south of Morocco, communal prayers in the major mosque areas are conducted by and for men alone. Whether before outsiders or before local audiences, men have represented Islam to the world and have made and conveyed its particular public image.

That public image has been so compelling in the long and successful history of Islam that the impact of women upon Islam has been largely ignored. Women are hazily designated as the inculcators and defenders of Islam in the home without a careful appraisal of the particular kind of Islam that they inculcate or the manner in which they exert their influence. To correct this imbalance, this study focuses on women's impact upon religious decision-making as it occurs in the lives of both female and male Muslims.

Sufism in Morocco

The aspect of Islam on which women have the greatest impact in Morocco is the mystical or Sufi tradition, in which saintly personages are venerated and supplicated. Women, like men, partake of that tradition in numerous ways. At the behavioral level, adherents display their involvement through individual devotions to particular saints, or they show their allegiance by engaging in the communal practices of religious organizations, which are variously called Sufi orders, fraternities, or brotherhoods in the literature. These orders trace their ritual and dogma back to particular saintly founders (who can also be supplicated on a more individual basis). Although it has been continually attacked by proponents of a purer, more orthodox Islam as an unwarranted accretion, this mystical tradition, in both its individual and communal aspects, continues to be vital in Islamic ritual and belief.

Sufism forms a core religious phenomenon in all Islamic regions. In Morocco, however, it has attained a considerable complexity. Literally thousands of individual saints are venerated in Moroccan cities and villages, and numerous orders enjoy substantial memberships and command strong loyalties. In 1939, for example, nearly one-fifth of Morocco's adult male population was estimated to hold formal membership in the twenty-three leading Sufi orders (Geertz 1968:51). While that figure is somewhat misleading in the sense that Moroccans establish such allegiances with varying degrees of formality so that a boundary around formal members per se cannot meaningfully be drawn, it nonetheless begins to convey the importance of the phenomenon. A larger estimate is probably more representative of Moroccans' involvement in the highly diversified array of practices that characterize Moroccan Sufism, past and present. My own investigation in the south of Morocco in 1971, for example, shows that 92 percent of the population of two sample areas, containing a total population of 136, had been linked to Sufi orders and/or to the cults of individual saints at some time in their lives and continued to cite these loyalties as meaningful to them. Parents dedicate children to a saint through the fortieth-day haircutting ceremony that is associated with a particular saintly order. Individuals sacrifice to a saint during a crisis and may receive returns that are sufficiently favorable to evoke a feeling of continuing loyalty. In other cases adherents supply money necessary for an annual celebration dedicated to a neighborhood saint, or they give substantial gifts and time during the larger three-day celebrations. In still other cases, the recitations associated with the rosary of a particular order are done daily in adherents' homes; these rosaries may also be blessed in the order's lodge to symbolize a stronger personal commitment. Finally, certain individuals regularly congregate for weekly communal devotions at a *zawiya* or lodge. The last criterion was most likely the one employed in determining the 1939 membership estimate.

All the mechanisms for displaying allegiance continue to be utilized in the south of Morocco by both men and women, and their use points to the tradition's continuing viability. Another, more recent phenomenon is perhaps more reflective of the present importance of the mystical tradition in the Taroudannt region: far from falling into disuse, the lodges of the Sufi orders are now being rebuilt with substantial assistance from the local government, a sign that the orders are still playing a role in local social life and politics, although perhaps a different one than played in the past.

What is the place of women in this still vital organizational structure? First, it must be stressed that while many formal aspects of the mystical complex are associated with men, most of these elements have female correlates or are also associated with women. Thus, while *mwasim,* the major festivities in honor of saints, are generally organized by men, most *ma'arif,* the one-day local saintly festivities which far outnumber mwasim, are generally organized by women. The women of a neighborhood collect the money, prepare the food, invite the guests, and ultimately distribute the *baraka* or supernatural power. Similarly, while religious orders have formal male hierarchies, auxiliaries organized by and for women also occur (as discussed below). Again, while males constitute the most powerful and best-known of the saints in Morocco, female saints also exist and are venerated. Far fewer in number and less frequently anthropomorphized, these female saints are nonetheless credited with distinctive powers. Lalla Soliha, for example, is visited by girls who seek suitable mates; Lalla Mimuna, a date palm, is the meeting place for the *'abid* (black) order at their festivities and is additionally the site at which old women devotees predict the coming year's weather conditions; Lalla Mbaraka, a stone wrapped in cloth, is carried by believers to assure their personal health. And not least, a host of female functionaries, primary among them curers and *muqaddamat* (leaders and caretakers), exist (Fernea and Fernea 1972). These women hold religious positions that may be legitimized through election, through the ritual transmission of power, or through birth.

Women's Sufism thus exhibits its own organizational complexity, a reality that makes a simple association of "formal" religion with male and "informal" religion with female unwarranted. More important, however, women hold a functionally primary place in the mystical complex in general. They do this by holding a preeminent position in the determination of the affiliations of future adherents, male and female, within Sufi Islam.

In essence, the primary inculcator role rests with women. The importance of that role would be misinterpreted, however, if it were reduced in scope to its socializing aspect only. Rather, to assess its proper importance, we must recognize that affiliatory decisions are not merely passed down by women, nor are they made by women on the basis of male-oriented assumptions. Instead, affiliatory decisions are generally made by women in the light of a set of premises and priorities that are geared to the exigencies of *women's* daily life.

The Real and the Ideal in Decision-Making

To begin to understand women's impact upon the affiliatory process, Moroccans' statements concerning the process should be examined. What emerges at the superficial level is an apparently straightforward set of pronouncements. Most Taroudannt informants, male or female, state as a first premise that a child should follow the religious affiliation of his or her father and that a wife should take on, or at least promote, the affiliation of her spouse. In short, they state that affiliation should be patrilineal at birth and male-oriented at marriage.

Actual life histories, however, belie these ideal pronouncements, as do the more tempered verbal qualifiers of those informants. While still affirming the male-centered ideal, Moroccans often add that people actually do as they like in real life. In the end, they are impelled not by normative rules but by *khater* (personal inclination), which they say can lead individuals in many different directions. The notion of khater thus becomes important in explaining a host of real-life decisions that stand in opposition to the patrilineal or male-centered ideals. Far from being automatically provided with fathers' affiliations, for example, children in the Taroudannt area tend to be associated with mothers' groups quite as often. Changeovers to husbands' affiliations at marriage occurred in only 38 percent of the cases in which spouses were of different saintly persuasions. By contrast, 54 percent of the men changed over to women's affiliations when their affiliations differed from those of their spouses.

Given these tendencies, what premises seem to underlie the decisions that are actually made? The following concerns seem particularly to affect women's decisions. Mothers search out saints and Sufi orders when uncertainties occur or when crises arise, with the childbearing years defining a particularly precarious period. When children become ill or die, when daughters remain uncourted, or when a mother has not yet guided a sufficient number of offspring into the safer, later years of childhood, the founders of Sufi orders, like other saints, are called upon as protectors. Correspondingly, when women are ill or barren or when their marriages appear endangered, saints again are sought out for support. By contrast, if a woman bears many healthy children or when medical attention is available through a solicitous, concerned husband, she tends to visit saints more rarely. Indeed, she might even fail to affiliate her younger children or to maintain her own ties.

These pragmatic, short-term aims, geared as they are to crisis situations, are often carried through in ways that accord with the demands of a woman's particular situation. A woman might choose an individual saint or Sufi order because of its geographic accessibility, for she is often severely restricted in her mobility owing to general notions of propriety or to a husband's jealousy. This is particularly true during the early marital years. Other things being equal, Taroudannt women consistently choose the nearer saint among those provided by their own or their spouses' affiliations. Similarly, women seek out saints with whom intensive historical ties have already been established. Thus, in cases in which mothers and fathers were affiliated with easily accessible saints, mothers chose the more intensive tie in 75 percent of the cases. Moreover, when a family contained a saintly ancestor, whether on the mother's or the father's side, mothers always called upon this genealogical association.

What is important about these decisions, of course, is not that they are highly rational, but that they contradict the patrilineal, male-centered ideal. While men stress the patrilineal element (Crapanzano 1973:48), women give equal weight to their own saintly heritages when allegiances are formed. Saintly concern and aid are seen to be bilaterally accessible and women operate in these terms.

Bilaterality and the Selection of Female Functionaries

Women's belief that supernatural power is bilaterally accessible not only concerns the paths through which saintly aid can be gained, but it also concerns the transmission of genealogical baraka (power that is inherited from the founder of a Sufi order or some other saint and can be utilized by the holder vis-à-vis supplicants). In Taroudannt, women tend to see links through women, like those through men, as potential routes for such power. Indeed, female links are especially pertinent in the transmission of certain talents.

Most curers in Taroudannt, for example, are women. While some have gained their power through happenstance (a person born in a breech birth or with a caul, for example, is felt to have immediate curative power, albeit for only certain diseases), most curers state that they have gained their powers through inheritance. The term *warat* (to inherit) is sometimes specifically used in this sense.

Traditional methods for curing, such as the use of a burning skewer on the flesh, the laying on of a broom handle or shoe, or the curer's spitting on the wound, are believed to be passed down from generation to generation. Significantly, in most cases these powers are transmitted in the maternal line.

The inheritance of such power is not dependent upon the attainment of the status of saintly descendant in the formal sense. While the title of *murabta* (saintly descendant) is denied to those curers whose ties to their saintly forefathers are through female links, the power of those saints is believed to be viable within them. Thus, the curer Lalla Zahara, a direct descendant of the founder of the ben Nasriy order, passed her power to cure stomach ailments, as exhibited through the laying of a burning knife onto an abdomen coated with mud, to her daughter. The latter then passed it on to her own daughter. While Lalla Zahara's saintly descent was formally recognized (note the use of the religious honorific Lalla), the daughter and daughter's daughter used no such title in their highly successful curing, for neither's father was a saintly descendant or murabt.

Thus, while a patrilineal principle is at work in the use of the honorific, a matrilineal, or rather more broadly, a bilateral principle, is utilized with regard to the actual transmission of power. Such an extended principle is recognized as logical by Taroudannt women. Two entities, it is said, must be transmitted for curative powers to be effective: baraka and technical knowledge. Technical knowledge is learned through watching, and a girl child, by virtue of her spending many hours with her mother, has far more opportunity to watch her mother at work. Early on she displays both her interest and competence. This in turn predisposes the mother to pass on to her daughter her supernatural power. This is eventually done formally, through a verbal commission (*ukiltik,* I appoint you) or through another appointive act such as spitting into the initiate's hand.

While the curer is one kind of religious functionary whose power is primarily transmitted from woman to woman through institutionalized techniques, the muqaddama (or saintly representative) also has her power transmitted in similar fashion. While in some cases the muqaddama is merely a caretaker of a zawiya or saintly shrine (a male muqaddam can also serve in a purely caretaking role), on frequent occasions these women carry out religious functions. In many instances, they do the ritual shaving of infants on the fortieth day; they tell fortunes and cure illnesses, especially when the latter are caused by the evil eye or by evil underworld spirits; and they offer protection during perilous times (such as pregnancy). The muqaddama of the Taroudannt zawiya of the Jilaliy order, for example, performs all of these functions. By contrast, her husband, the muqaddam, fulfills far fewer religious duties in addition to his caretaking role.

While many muqaddamat are designated as murabtat because their descent from the saint is patrilineal, that heritage again seems not to be essential for the successful fulfillment of their religious functions. The former muqaddama of the Jilaliyya was a murabta and her husband was a murabt. That couple, however, had no daughters, and so the muqaddama called upon her daughter from a previous non-murabt marriage to succeed her. The successor's powers were not deemed to be weaker despite her nonsaintly descent.

Women's Approach toward Saintly Personality

As much as women interpret saintly descent in ways that are in keeping with their particular religious purposes, so too are the personalities of saints and the founders of religious orders evaluated according to criteria distinctive to women. While both sexes believe that saints have distinctive personalities with differential talents, interests, and involvements, women make choices about their saintly patrons with certain of these characteristics particularly in mind. As a consequence, saints are called upon differentially by men and women according to each sex's particular social requirements.

Particularly important in this regard are the kinds of protection sought from the saints. Moulay ʿAbdulqadr of the Jilaliy order supports children in cases of illness, Moulay Ibrahim promotes marriages, while Sidi Saʿid ʿAbdunnaʿim is visited by women whose babies are weak or unaccountably die. Mothers frequent these saints attendant upon their need for such talents.

Mothers also look for another trait that men almost never seek out: the opportunity that saints afford for switching saintly involvement. Again, saintly personality is felt to be reflected in this very important trait. Some saints are believed to be permissive, openhearted, and understanding while others are jealous, narrowminded, and irascible. The permissive and open-hearted saints like Moulay ʿAbdulqadr are quickly and enthusiastically invoked by women, for they can be rejected without recrimination if their help does not suffice. Irascible and jealous saints, to the contrary, are avoided because of the stiff penalties they impose in cases of lapsed or multiple allegiance. Si Ahmad Tijaniy, for example, is said to have told his believers that anyone who took another saint in his stead would die in a state of apostacy (Abun-Nasr 1965:39). Similarly, Sidi bu Nega is said to have forbidden his followers to affiliate themselves with any other saint; otherwise illness would strike. In part because of these stringent requirements, women avoid the Tijaniyya whenever possible and seldom solicit Sidi bu Nega even though that saint is known for his power to ward off the deaths of children. Sidi bu Nega is approached only as a final recourse when all other saintly aid has failed.

This preference for saints who are known to be understanding is quite marked among Moroccan women. Women more often than men visit saints in situations of uncertainty—in cases of illness, death, or psychological frustration. Faced with difficulties, women often feel themselves compelled to shift from saint to saint. Men, by contrast, are not as intimately involved in the highly precarious early years of their offsprings' childhoods. Moreover, by virtue of their financial independence, they have many more options available to them, such as doctors and hospitals, when illness strikes. To them, the possibility of switching allegiance is of secondary importance.

The emphasis on the attribute of flexibility necessarily leads to a skewing of children's affiliations away from orders like the Tijaniyya and toward those like the Jilaliyya and ben Nasriyya, away from those saints like Sidi bu Nega and toward those like Sidi Sa'id 'Abdunna'im. The trauma associated with Tijaniy membership in women's minds is relevant from this standpoint. Of six sample cases in which Tijaniy affiliation was predominant within a child's family, three mothers refused to affiliate their children with that order, citing the narrowness of the founder as the reason for their opposition. Moreover, two of the remaining three women voiced fears about the ultimate impact of Tijaniy support. Being recent immigrants to the city, however, they felt powerless to activate alternative involvements. The sixth mother gave concrete support for her reservations and fears. She looked back upon her life and affirmed that if Tijaniy affiliation had not prohibited her from seeking other saintly protection, three of her five children might not have died. Significantly, of the three women who rejected the Tijaniyya, two sought Jilaliy and one sought Derqawiy support.

Saintly Concerns in Women's Later Years

In the sense that mothers act as their children's representatives to the supernatural—giving gifts on their behalf, visiting saints with them, and changing children's allegiances when necessary—children's affiliations also become mother's affiliations. And in the sense that a woman's overall success depends in large part upon her success as a mother, affiliatory decision-making for children tends to define the affiliatory process for women during the maternal years. However, other important affiliatory decisions are made by women during other portions of their life cycle. The virgin who is not sought after as a bride, for example, is believed to be hampered by *jnun* (netherworld spirits). Saints alone can fight these negative powers. By climbing the tower of Moulay ʿAbdulqadr, for example, and by leaving her hairbrush, scarf, ribbons, or henna cup at the top, the virgin can obtain the protection she desires. Similarly, the older woman who senses that death is nearing may feel a strong compulsion to become aligned.

Interesting in terms of its implications for women's perceptions of saintliness and of their own religiosity are the decisions of old age. Again, certain personality characteristics are particularly valued. And as before, flexibility is sought, a trait that now does not refer to the ease with which the adherent can change allegiance but rather to the saints' flexibility concerning devotional requirements. For members of the Jilaliy order, for example, certain devotions and prayers need not be said exactly at the proper hour nor with undivided attention. Instead a Jilaliyya can gear her schedule more closely to household demands. Women who are interrupted by husbands, who are busy with grandchildren, or who are faced with household crises thereby can postpone their ritual observances without incurring saintly wrath. (This tendency toward favoring looseness in devotions stands in opposition to the perseverance of women in some other regions, such as Kurdish Muslim women [Hansen 1961:147].)

Other, more demanding orders, by contrast, are generally avoided by women, for women generally feel that they will be incapable of performing exacting religious observances. Formal membership, as exhibited in the taking of a rosary blessed in the order's lodge, for example, is particularly avoided, for formal membership not only implies greater rewards for perseverance, it also implies greater punishment if requirements are not met. These feelings serve to explain why most women carefully avoid membership in the Tijaniyya even into old age. Si Ahmad Tijaniy is known to be severe and uncompromising; he is believed to punish even unavoidable postponements in devotions and to require complete concentration when litany is said. Thus, only one woman performed the Tijaniy devotions among the seventeen old women in the sample areas. By contrast, four women performed the Jilaliy, three the ben Nasriy, and two the Derqawiy devotions. Significantly, even the one

Tijaniy woman refrained from taking a rosary that was formally blessed at the zawiya. She used beads that were bought in the marketplace instead.

Further evidence that the Jilaliy, ben Nasriy, and Derqawiy orders fit well with Moroccan women's demands is that some of their older female devotees are formally organized. There are Jilaliyyat and ben Nasriyyat in the city of Taroudannt, groups that consist of elderly women who congregate and worship at shrines that are specially designated for their use. There are also Derqawiyyat who meet in the regions outside the city to perform similar devotions. These groups have formally designated leaders who are chosen either by the women themselves, as is the case for the Jilaliyyat leader who is selected for her strength of character, or by the male hierarchy of the order, as is the case for certain rural Derqawiyyat. Moreover, all these groups have ongoing, formally initiated memberships. The new initiates bring gifts of sugar, tea, or other comestibles; then the group blesses them, invokes God's grace, and passes their rosaries through the hands of its members. Through the initiation, the women are believed to commit themselves to the order for life.

Although ignored and scorned by men, these female groups have numerous functions that are regarded by their members as essential to society. The Jilaliyyat meet each Friday and pray over a basketful of stones, called the stones of the ancestors. By so doing, they accord recognition to the ancestors, an Islamic obligation. Similarly, each year the Jilaliyyat move a sacred pile of rocks to see what is hidden within it. They predict the following year's weather from the creatures (snakes, scorpions) that emerge.

From a male perspective, these groups are peripheral. Indeed, when the organization of Sufi orders is discussed by their male members, these groups, which are formal and continuing, are seldom mentioned, a bias that reinforces the notion that men alone have formal religious organizations. In turn, because men tend to view these organizations with disdain, the female groups have faced numerous problems. The Taroudannt Jilaliyyat, for example, have recently been moved out of the saintly shrine that once housed them, the new (male) muqaddam of the shrine calling them an annoyance. Similarly, the pile of rocks that the Jilaliyyat transported in their yearly fertility ceremony was recently scattered, and the government told the women to establish a new pile in a less strategic location. Considerable debate ensued among the members as to whether a new pile would suffice.

The continued existence of female groups might be taken as

proof of their particular tenacity. Despite threats from outside and despite male disdain, the Jilaliyyat, ben Nasriyyat, and Derqawiyyat continue on. Gifts and dinner invitations continue to be provided to their members, and a piece of sugar or a blessing from the groups is still sought out by women in crisis. Indeed, the old devotees are respected for their religiosity by most younger women, who often state that they later intend to join the female auxiliaries' ranks.

Women and the Course of Male Development

Women, thus, make decisions for themselves and their children in the light of their own perceptions and needs, and they apply them within a unique organizational framework that is complex and ongoing. For daughters, mothers' interests are largely synonymous with their own later interests and so provide continuity and relevance for later life. In this sense women's influence is constant and continuing. For sons, however, the considerations that motivate mothers sometimes become palpably less relevant to men's later lives. Thus, we must ask what effects women's decisions have upon men's religious lives in adulthood. Are their effects short-lived or continuing?

It is clear from male life histories that grown sons sometimes find changes in saintly allegiance to be advantageous. Taroudannt men, more often than women, look to the Sufi orders as they establish social, economic, and political ties. In women's lives these economic and political considerations and, to a more limited extent, the social ones are of lesser importance. Understandably, men sometimes embrace the orders and cults that women typically reject for other reasons, to obtain the benefits accruing from the appropriate ties.

The major group profiting from such shifts is the group that women most shun, the Tijaniyya. Order of the rich and the powerful, the Tijaniyya has always permitted the amassing and display of wealth (Abun-Nasr 1965:47). In encouraging such behavior, the Tijaniyya draws most of its membership from among a community's wealthier inhabitants or from the economically and politically aspiring. Through it, its members can provide themselves with a flattering self-image and with strategic personal ties.

While the Tijaniyya attracts many of its members through its reputation as a haven for the wealthy, however, it also discourages the participation of others who are less powerful. Theoretically open to all men, the order is in fact actually closed to most men. The poor man, like the average woman, cannot cope with the rigidity of Tijaniy observance. The hired hand at harvest time or the vegetable seller in the market cannot easily leave his work to perform the exacting Tijaniy devotions. Workers of this sort require greater flexibility. The Jilaliy, ben Nasriy, and Derqawiy orders more readily meet these needs.

While shifts in allegiance do in fact occur, then, adequate reasons also exist for many men to maintain their childhood affiliations. The Jilaliyya, the ben Nasriyya, and the Derqawiyya, the orders that women most favor, provide opportunities for camaraderie and community which appeal to many men. Men generally continue to support and attend these orders to the extent they find their benefits to be satisfying.

The Interplay of Male and Female Systems: An Occasion for Conflict?

Divergent tendencies thus emerge for men and women with regard to the mystical complex. To what degree do conflicts arise as a result, particularly with regard to the crucial issue of childrearing? In answering this question, one does well to look at the religious life cycles of the two sexes, for men and women not only vary in their approaches to the saints and Sufi orders, they also differ with respect to the times during their lives when they develop intense saintly ties. Moreover, affiliation to different saintly orders and cults tends to be associated with different life stages for the two sexes. All these differences affect the influence that men and women ultimately have upon children's affiliatory ties.

The importance of life stage in women's decisions has already been demonstrated. Concerned with the welfare of their children and with their own security at home, something that again is directly related to childbearing, women show a deep concern in their children's affiliations during the childbearing years. By contrast, the religious concern of men tends to be less consistent during the early years of marriage and during the long years of parenthood. While men over fifty often become intensely involved in the Sufi orders as they change their work habits and as they become concerned with the afterlife, men in their twenties, thirties, and forties affiliate themselves less frequently. More nearly masters of their fates during these years (they hold the divorce right, they are typically not designated as the cause of a couple's childlessness, they have various options at their disposal regarding medical aid), men have less reason to deal with the crises of early adulthood by seeking supernatural protection.

This is not to say, however, that all younger men remain unaffiliated. Some do indeed work actively within the Sufi orders and cults. These younger men tend, however, to immerse themselves in the Sufi orders less as a response to crises than through a desire for a relatively unencumbered camaraderie. The Derqawiy and Jilaliy orders, for example, place relatively few limitations upon conviviality and are thereby somewhat appealing. In a rather different vein, the Hamadsha and ʿAissawa orders foster a mode of expression that is incorporated into daily life only with difficulty: that of possession. Younger men, like other men and women, tend to affiliate with these two orders if they discover a personal propensity toward trance. By providing these attractions, these orders become the primary recipients of a rather limited younger male membership. By contrast, the more staid and more demanding of the orders, like the Tijaniyya, draw relatively few young men to their organizations. The swell in Tijaniy membership awaits men's later years.

This skewing of affiliations, like the skewing that occurs among women, can be understood in terms of the concerns of young versus old. It should also be interpreted in terms of different life-cycle images. As much as older women look for ease in their saintly devotions, in part because they deem themselves to be incapable of performing rigorous observances, younger men generally regard themselves and others as wanting in religious steadfastness. Self-control and abnegation are associated with the old age of men in the Taroudannt world view. As a result, men in early adulthood strive less seriously in these directions.

Men's involvement in Sufism, particularly in the more rigorous orders, therefore, tends to occur much later in life, for it is only with maturity that Muslim men are believed to be equal to the rigors of such devotions. Interestingly, this later involvement on the part of men helps perpetuate women's influence. Women make decisions about sons in terms of their own priorities, causing certain orders to be favored and others ignored. Men might subsequently change affiliation to certain of the more neglected orders according to the benefits that they later seek. Their involvement in these groups generally occurs, however, late enough so as minimally to affect the affiliation of their own children. As a result, a new generation of children is again affiliated by women according to women's priorities, and women's influence is maintained.

Most men, then, tend to forfeit affiliatory decision-making willingly to women when children are still young, or they tend to be in accordance with women's decisions, for those decisions are often akin to their own. Given these tendencies, the tensions that could conceivably arise through a clash of male and female viewpoints do not typically occur. Instead, conflicts tend to be engendered only when fathers, by being older or by being religiously precocious, have made commitments to cults and orders that women find objectionable. In these cases, men more often apply pressure for allegiance to be determined according to their own priorities, whether for children or wives.

In the end, women are allowed relatively free rein with regard to affiliatory decision-making for themselves and their children. They work rationally according to certain premises that reflect women's concerns and priorities, and so tend to pass on their own religious allegiances. As a result, the affiliatory process is far from a male-dominated or patrilineal one. Instead, women emerge as the primary decision-makers with respect to the Moroccan mystical complex. They also emerge as the transmitters of a resilient and distinctive religious system that is largely of their own making.

Bibliography

Abun-Nasr, Jamil M. *The Tijaniyya: A Sufi Order in the Modern World.* London, 1965.

Crapanzano, Vincent. *The Hamadsha: A Study in Moroccan Ethnopsychiatry.* Berkeley, 1973.

Fernea, Robert A., and Elizabeth W. Fernea. "Variation in Religious Observance among Islamic Women." In *Scholars, Saints and Sufis: Muslim Religious Institutions in the Middle East since 1500,* ed. Nikki R. Keddie. Berkeley, 1972.

Geertz, Clifford. *Islam Observed.* New Haven, 1968.

Hansen, Henny Harald. *The Kurdish Woman's Life.* Ethnografiske Kaekke, no. 7. Copenhagen, 1961.

30 Sex Differences and Folk Illness in an Egyptian Village

Soheir A. Morsy

In the past few years new orientations in the study of women's roles in society have emerged. For the Middle East, more balanced accounts of sex roles are offering new bases for the evaluation of male and female relations. Reports based on actual observations are undermining the traditional ideological explanations that in the past provided convenient interpretations of sex roles in the absence of empirical data. This study explores the relation between sex roles and illness. Illness is utilized as a probe into social life and as an index of sex status. An examination of deviations from sex role expectations associated with the folk illness of *ʿuzr*[1] illuminates these role expectations.

ʿUzr in the Village of Fateha

Fateha is a peasant community of 3,200 people in the northwestern corner of the Egyptian Nile Delta, nearly midway between Cairo and Alexandria. The village partakes of the general organiza-

---

Field work was conducted in Fāteḥa over a period of a year between August 1974 and July 1975. Data for this essay are derived from the study of ethnomedicine in the village. The development of ideas presented in this paper derives from the cooperative efforts of the Anthropology Women's Collective at Michigan State University. My long associations with Linda Easley, Patricia Murphy, Barrie Thorne, and Soon Young Yoon have contributed greatly to my understanding of sex roles. Professors Brigitte Jordan and Arthur Rubel were helpful in providing critical comments on this and earlier versions of the study. I also wish to acknowledge the financial support for field work provided by the Wenner-Gren Foundation for Anthropological Research and the American Research Center in Egypt.

tion of Egyptian rural society and its articulation with an encompassing social structure and cultural tradition. Fateha villagers share with their urban counterparts various folk medical beliefs and practices. Beliefs in sorcery and witchcraft as causes of illness in the village are extensions of those of the dominant culture. Finally, the prevailing ideas and legal pronouncements concerning the status of women in the village are not unique to this locale. The prerogative of male dominance is yet another extension of the values and dictums of the larger society of which the village is part (Mohsen 1974, al-Sa'dawi 1972).

The condition that inhabitants of Fateha describe as 'uzr is clearly a variant of a worldwide phenomenon generally referred to as spirit possession. While the local form is interpreted and dealt with according to culturally specific assumptions, it partakes of the general pattern described in the literature on spirit possession (Lewis 1974, Oesterreich 1974, Walker 1974). As in other forms of possession states, 'uzr entails the invasion of a person's body by a spiritual agency. Disturbing emotional experiences are incriminated in the incidence of the ensuing illness. Both physical and behavioral symptoms are used as diagnostic indexes. Thus, in addition to correlating 'uzr with nonspecific bodily symptoms, informants regularly referred to impaired social behavior in terms of interpersonal relations and to deviations from culturally recognized role behavior.

The onset of the symptoms of 'uzr cannot be attributed to a single cause. Instead, informants' interpretations of the onslaught of the illness disclose more than one level of causation. Spirits are believed to be the agents of the illness. Their actions are usually explained in terms of their concern for the welfare of the persons whom they possess. Their seemingly contradictory conduct of inflicting illness upon such individuals is rationalized by both the *ma'zur* or *ma'zura* (possessed male or female) and members of his or her family. It is said that the spirits, by inflicting harm on humans, exert pressure on them and force them to evaluate their detrimental practices. The specific mechanism by which they force people's attention to self-inflicted harm is variable. Illness may be precipitated by the actual invasion of patients' bodies by the spirits. It may also be brought about simply by their touch or through their winds. The pains of illness are not allowed to subside until measures are taken to rectify the patients' situation of distress. Thus the ultimate cause of 'uzr is sought in affected persons' social relations. The affliction is known to be induced by a variety of negative emotional experiences, including sadness, quarrels, fright, and anger.

Apart from shamanistic diagnostic practices, the identification of ʿuzr seems to rest primarily on behavioral changes and on the changing loci of physical discomforts reported by the maʿzur. While there are definite signs of withdrawal from social life and deviations from social role behavior, the symptoms of ʿuzr are anything but specific. Behavioral correlates of the illness may include such contradictory conducts as excessive sleep or insomnia.[2] The most significant diagnostic symptom is mobile pain. Other physical indicators of ʿuzr are variable and may include any combination of a variety of symptoms.[3] This variability of symptoms militates against the isolation of a specific illness syndrome. Moreover, a valid explanation for the occurrence of ʿuzr is not always readily available at the time of adoption of the illness role. It is possible for a person to be labeled maʿzur by reference to a disturbing emotional experience that occurred several years prior to the manifestation of symptoms. Thus, the fluidity of the symptomatology of ʿuzr, and its causation, makes it a very convenient and readily available illness role.

The general course of ʿuzr therapy conforms to the procedures outlined in both contemporary and ancient accounts of therapeutic rituals of spirit possession (el-Shamy 1972, Lewis 1974, Oesterreich 1974). The basic objective of the shaman is to establish communication with the *asyad* (spirits).[4] In the context of a *zar* ceremony, the maʿzur is the vehicle of communication. Having reached an altered state of consciousness through the stimulations of a variety of musical instruments and through the rhythmic, exhausting swaying of dancing to a rapid beat, the afflicted person starts to speak in an unfamiliar tone of voice. The sound is immediately recognized as the asyad's response to the *sheikh*'s (shaman's) calling. Speaking through the mouth of the maʿzur, the asyad then proceed to explain the circumstances that led to their association with their host. They also set the conditions for reconciliation and for sparing their host from the ravages of illness. Many of their demands are directed to the patient's personal advantage.

Another ceremony, a *sulha* (reconciliation), may be performed and at this time the wishes of the asyad are granted. Sacrificial offerings may be made and expensive items of jewelry and/or clothing may be worn by the patient. The affected person may also be reminded to honor his or her promise to the asyad and is asked to reiterate a commitment to paying regular visits to the *hadra* (zar) and joining the *tariqa* (way) of the possessing spirit in the dance arena.

Once a sulha is performed, the asyad no longer cause physical discomforts to their host. They are said to make the affected person feel out of sorts only when he or she becomes sad. Thus the asyad never leave their host but the symptoms indicative of the association remain dormant and surface only when the person has another unpleasant emotional experience with which he or she cannot cope adequately. Hence, once a person has experienced ʿuzr, the other members of the household become particularly sensitive to his or her needs. Care is taken to avoid the precipitation of another illness crisis and, by extension, an economic crisis. Traditional practitioners note that efforts to control ʿuzr involve attempts at eliminating the symptoms of the illness, not its cause.[5]

From an analytical perspective, the folk illness ʿuzr may be attributed to stress factors impinging on the afflicted person. Stress implies a situation in which there exists a disjunction between the cultural canons according to which an individual has been socialized and his or her social actions. Deviation from culturally stipulated behavior may prove taxing to various degrees, depending on the nature and extent of departure from established norms. However, in certain cases, the contradiction between prescribed and actual behavior may be mediated by certain cultural mechanisms in the form of institutionalized means of deviance. The ʿuzr labeling may be considered one such mechanism. Thus women who are barren, for example, refer to their diagnosis as *maʿzurin* to justify their deviant situation of being childless in a society that places primary emphasis on female reproductive and maternal functions. Such women seek this label and try to have eyewitnesses present when a traditional diagnostician announces a verdict.

The compensatory value of spirit possession to persons who are particularly susceptible to social stresses and conflict has been demonstrated in cross-cultural studies of possession cults (Lewis 1970, 1971, 1974; Maher 1974:25, 97; Walker 1974). In Fateha, although the maʿzur does not belong to an established institution of the type associated with traditional cults, the illness role itself forces attention on personal grievances and distress and induces a temporary enhancement of social position. The mediating function of spirit intrusion in asymmetrical social relations is illustrated by the case of Zeinab:

According to established cultural norms, Zeinab is expected to be obedient to her mother-in-law. Like other daughters-in-law, she is held responsible for a variety of domestic chores which should be completed to the older woman's satisfaction. When Zeinab's husband was away from the village for a period of three months, she was expected to go on living in his extended family household. Under the labeling *maʿzura,* these cultural injunctions were temporarily suspended. Zeinab's neglect of her domestic duties, her disrespectful attitude toward her mother-in-law, her eventual abandonment of her husband's home, and her residence in her father's house were all considered legitimate forms of behavior. This shift from one category of socially sanctioned action to an opposite, but equally approved, form of behavior needed justification. In Zeinab's case, the vindication was epitomized in the tragedy of her child's death. This emotionally devastating experience explained her affliction and, by extension, her deviant behavior. Under ordinary conditions such behavior would have had some dire consequences, possibly her divorce.

The social significance of ʿuzr and its relevance to role behavior cannot be overemphasized. The onset of the illness is accompanied by a more marked departure from culturally stipulated role behavior than is the case with other folk illnesses. Thus, a woman who has been affected by the evil eye, for example, may feel headachy and drowsy, but she does not withdraw from social life and ordinarily goes about her business of fulfilling her maternal responsibilities. This is in sharp contrast to the condition of a female informant who suffers from ʿuzr. She refuses to nurse her child (a most abnormal form of behavior among village women), and her participation in neighborhood social intercourse is minimal. The social significance of ʿuzr is also marked when contrasted with another folk illness, *rabt* (tying, or rendering sexual impotence). In case of the latter, although the consequences of the state of illness involve a drastic deviation from expected role behavior, they are of a more private nature.

The strikingly more public or social nature of ʿuzr is also reflected in the therapeutic efforts to pacify the illness-causing spirits. Such rituals are often performed in a public arena, in full view of an audience of relatives and other fellow villagers. Moreover, the very term *ʿuzr* (excuse) provides the illness with a social definition. It offers the maʿzur (excused) a temporary dispensation from the requirements of social canons. The alternative term *malbus* (worn or possessed), which, more explicitly, refers to the pathology of the illness, is used more frequently by traditional medical practitioners but seldom by the majority of villagers.

Sex-Role Expectations and Differentiations

The differentiation and ascription of status on the basis of sex is basic to all societies. Cross-cultural studies point to a wide range of variation and demonstrate that sex-role differentiation varies from one society to another and does not follow a fixed pattern. This lack of definite ascription points to the absence of biological determinants, although biological differences may shape the roles of males and females. Sex-role differentiation is, to quote Ashley Montague, "a cultural expression of biological differences" (1975:15).

Ascribed relations between the sexes have their basis in the differential access of males and females to the major material and nonmaterial sources of prestige and power—such as material wealth, personal autonomy, culturally sanctioned decision-making power, and political and religious leadership (Friedl 1975:7). The following discussion does not proceed from an assumption of the universality of male dominance, neither does it focus on dispelling the characterization of women as powerless. Instead, it seeks to identify indexes of social dominance in the various domains of village culture without a prior assumption of the nature of male-female power relations. Attention is focused on patterned behavior. The primary emphasis is not on individual variation but on stable features and cultural constraints imposed on social actors.

As in other cultural contexts, sex is one of the principal bases for role differentiation in the village of Fateha. Minimal differentiation characterizes the first few years of life, but the stage just prior to adulthood is preparatory for adult sex roles. By the time a person in Fateha reaches adulthood, his or her behavior is guided by clearly defined sex-role expectations.

The husband, through his agricultural laboring, is expected to provide his wife and children with shelter, food, clothing, and medical care. Thus, the most significant role for an adult male is that of provider. Another equally valued attribute of the male role is sexual potency. Numerous linguistic expressions used by villagers symbolize positions and acts of dominance by reference to the male position of command during sexual intercourse. Much of this symbolism centers around mounting behavior which is considered an exclusively male prerogative. Henpecked husbands are said to be mounted by their wives. Older men, although authority figures in their families, are known to be guided by their wives. Such men are said to have "dried up," that is, lost their potency and by extension their power of command over their wives. The significance of virility transcends its value as indicator of male superiority in matrimonial relations. Males and their procreative functions are valued instruments of propagation of the male line in the village patrilineal kinship system. When a group of men was asked to describe the worst possible experience that a man can undergo, the majority responded by reference to sterility. One respondent noted, "who would ever know that a man had lived if he leaves no children to memorialize his life?"

In some cases, the ideal attributes of the male role may not be realized. The less than favorable economic conditions of the peasants may force some men to abandon their culturally stipulated responsibilities as breadwinners. Women with chronically ill husbands, for example, may find themselves the sole providers for their families, and widows who have no adult male offspring are known to take on exclusively male tasks. In cases where male economic responsibilities are curtailed, the illness role is a potential refuge. Thus, a male villager who lived in his wife's family's household and contributed minimally to her support derived justification for his departure from male role performance under the labeling *ma'zur*. Similarly, some men who suffered from temporary loss of sexual potency were identified as the victims of sorcery.

The adult female is defined primarily in terms of her domestic and maternal functions. The married woman, along with helping her husband in the fields or on occasion working as an agricultural laborer, is also responsible for all domestic work. In addition, all aspects of child care are within the female labor domain. While the peasants of Fateha associate their adult females with domestic duties, this facet of female role expectation is of only secondary significance relative to women's principal function of bearing children. Women who do not fulfill this function are seen as something less than normal. Although people may try to comfort them by telling them that barrenness is "from God," in reality they are despised. Childless women are considered "useless."

In the village all men, with very few exceptions, are involved in agricultural tasks. Women, in addition to their culturally stipulated maternal roles, contribute heavily to local subsistence activities, depending on their age, marital status, and the socioeconomic status of their kinship groups. In spite of this contribution, especially as it relates to tasks carried out within the household, women do not have control over the products of their labor. Neither do they have a corresponding share of socially sanctioned power. Their economic contributions are fragmented and diffuse, and always considered of a supplementary nature. They do not engage as a corporate group in any economic enterprise. Their cooperative efforts are confined to baking and to occasional labor exchanges during times of heavy agricultural work. Their work in the fields is viewed as complementary, and it is males' field labor that is considered prestigious and skillful. A woman's work in the home is seen to be easily done by any other female or even a male when necessary. Man's work in the fields, on the other hand, is considered more vital for the family livelihood, and informants readily assign to it a monetary value. Differential control of the products of agricultural work is also evident in the village. Males, who are usually the owners of agricultural land, are also regarded as the owners of its products, regardless of the amount of female labor invested in the production process. Men have full right to dispose of these products.[6]

Ownership and transfer of property are also subject to differentiation. Women inherit from their fathers half the shares of their male siblings. In some cases the Islamic *sharia* is completely ignored, and the father's land is registered in the names of male offspring only. Some women who inherit land from their fathers may turn over their shares to their brothers. They do so as a means of social insurance against their husbands' maltreatment, divorce, or old age. Unlike her husband, who is by definition the dominant party in the marriage, a woman, especially in the early years of marriage, is under threat of divorce. A woman who leaves her share of inherited land to her brothers knows that they are under obligation to reciprocate her generosity. She can exploit this situation in making demands on her husband and his family. After she has borne children and as her position in her husband's household becomes relatively more secure, she may justify the demand for her legal share of land from her brothers by reference to her children's numerous needs.

Some women who claim their share of inheritance may turn it over to their husbands. A minority of women insist on registering the land in their own names even under the threat of divorce. The more common situation of compromise involves the transfer of half the woman's land to her husband in return for his labor in planting it. By contrast, the husband is not expected to make his wife a co-owner of the family's residential property in which hours of female labor are invested for general cleaning, maintenance, and even repairing and building walls.

Control of material wealth in the village is recognized as the basis of social dominance. Men's privileged position is justified by reference to their status as breadwinners. In the few cases where women, rather than their husbands, own property, they are characterized by a marked degree of independence. Similarly, wealth in the form of land or jewelry entitles a son's wife to preferential treatment in her husband's extended family group.

The study of economic organization in the village leads to the hypothesis that in a cash-oriented economy where the sexual division of labor is such that males control goods and services that have exchange value (unlike use-value production characteristic of female labor, such as in child care and household work) and females have limited access to or are altogether denied such control, females are subservient to male authority.

The social prestige associated with males and their potential economic contributions is evident as early as the time of birth. Women who give birth to many daughters are scorned by their mothers-in-law. It is said that a girl belongs to her husband's household where she will eventually work and where her family will be cursed. A boy, by contrast, is recognized as the potential protector of family property and honor and as the propagator of the family line. The preference for male children is also reflected in the differential behavior of families on the happy occasion of the birth of a male which contrasts with the subdued reaction when a female child is delivered.[7] On the latter occasion, the maternal grandfather is not considered under obligation to provide his daughter with the traditional gift, and the paternal grandmother may sing: "Why did you come, O girl, when we wished for a boy? Take the *zalʿa* and fill it from the sea, may you fall into it and drown."

Family relations provide another important milieu for isolating indexes of social dominance. In nuclear families the husband is definitely the center of authority. While deference to males is the cultural ideal, women do not always comply with their husbands' wishes. However, those who transgress established norms risk the wrath of their spouses and public ridicule. Wife-beating is considered the legitimate right of husbands. A married woman is also expected to comply to any subtle or overt sexual gesture from her husband. She is expected to reply when he addresses her as *ya bet* (girl), but would never dream of reciprocating by referring to him as *wad* (boy).

As a married woman's children grow up and take on responsibilities for agricultural and domestic work, her own labor efforts gradually become confined to the domestic domain. She starts to enjoy a sense of security in her grown children, especially her male children. Sons, who by the age of fifteen take over the larger part of agricultural work, are known to exert a great influence over their fathers' actions. It is clearly at this point in the developmental cycle of the family that a woman's power in the household is on the rise, and it reaches a climax when she becomes a mother-in-law. At this stage, she is in a better position to wield power than at any previous period of her life. As an older woman, and especially as an older mother, her advice and wisdom are sought by females as well as males. Her modesty declines sharply for she is no longer identified with sexual activity and she is no longer subject to all the limitations imposed on younger cohorts. Moreover, older village women who are freed from commitments to field labor have greater control over subsistence products in the household. They have more time and resources to devote to the intricacies of nonformalized power relations within and among households.

In extended family households, the oldest male is the center of authority. Next in line comes the oldest woman. As long as the father is alive, his married male children and their wives are at the mercy of his wife, who is the actual primary locus of power. She is known to have great influence over her spouse and her sons. Her power over her children and her sons' wives receives cultural sanction. A wedding night ritual best symbolizes the superordinate position of the mother-in-law in relation to her sons' wives. The older woman stands by the door entrance and lifts up her leg, and the bride passes beneath.

In cases where fathers are deceased, some women take on the statuses of their husbands and become principal loci of authority in extended families. In cases where the oldest female lacks the necessary health and personality attributes of an authoritative figure, power and control of resources in the household rest with the oldest brother and his wife. In sum, the power of women in the household is a function of their age and the stage of the developmental cycle of the family.

While political participation outside the household is limited for both males and females, political leadership is confined to males. None of the ten members of the local chapter of the Arab Socialist Union is a woman. When elections were held in the village, women's votes were cast for men of their kinsmen's choice. Thus, men exploit their authority over women for political purposes and direct women's participation in political activities. Similarly, religious leadership for women is nonexistent, and their participation in public religious activities is minimal. No women are ever seen at the village mosque where men congregate for the Friday midday prayers. Another practice, approved for males but condemned for females, is the joining of *zikr* processions.[8] During the saint's day celebration a woman was severely criticized for having joined such a group. However, her behavior was seen as justifiable when her relatives spread the word among the audience that she was ma'zura.

Further assessment of sex status in the village may proceed by an examination of the differential degrees of autonomy and decision-making power. From her childhood, a female perceives males as her guardians and protectors. Indeed, some of the most crucial decisions related to women are delegated to their male kinsmen. Thus, unlike her male siblings who may actively participate in the choice of a marriage partner, a woman may be forced to marry a man for whom she harbors the greatest dislike. A woman who is being considered for marriage is not expected to have any say in the choice of her marriage partner. In reality, she may express her wishes indirectly through her mother or other older female relatives who are known to play a dominant role in match-making. However, the father, backed by the authority of other adult males in the family, has the final word and, for considerations of his own, may resist his wife's influence and neglect his daughter's wishes. Thus, although exceptions do exist, a daughter is expected to accept her father's choice of a marriage partner. Three women attributed their ʿuzr to their sadness when their parents announced the choice of husband-designates. One noted, "My father said, if I pick a dog for you to marry, you will marry him." Under the labeling *maʿzura,* two of these women did in fact refuse to marry the designated males.

Differential autonomy in decision-making is evident in a variety of situations. As mentioned earlier, a man's right to the sexual services of his wife is indisputable. The wife's claim to her husband's sexual services is also recognized. Failure of the husband to perform his sexual duties is sufficient grounds for a wife to seek divorce. However, a woman's impatience is translated into action only after her husband's repeated failures. In contrast, she risks the harm of his fury on her first refusal of his demands. Some women report that they are sometimes forced to engage in sexual intercourse with their husbands and on occasions have been hit for refusing to do so. Similarly, while a woman's right to divorce is recognized, she is bound by legal and social sanctions that undermine this prerogative (Mohsen 1974:38–42). Women are often under the threat of divorce, especially during the early years of marriage. When faced with the possibility of repudiation, a woman may mobilize the support of her relatives and seek the help of intermediaries. The conclusive decision rests with the husband, who has the final word over the termination of the matrimonial relation.

Further evidence of differential autonomy is detected in relation to freedom of movement within and outside the village. Men congregate on the village streets at night and spend hours joking, exchanging stories about their sexual experiences with their wives, and having a good time with their friends. Women do not leave their homes after sunset except to run necessary errands. They may also stop for visits at their neighbors and relatives after having asked permission of their husbands or mothers-in-law. In making their request they are expected to state and justify the purpose of the visit. Women complain that their husbands prevent them from going to visit their friends from premarriage days. The intention is to integrate the wife in the husband's family and to emphasize his control of her actions. Thus, unlike men, who maintain their childhood friendships, women may have to sever their ties to their premarriage friends. Restrictions are also imposed on women when they travel outside the village. On market days, women walk in groups or they may be escorted by their children. Unlike the case for men, it is considered shameful for a woman to travel unescorted outside the village. Except for older women, most adult females abide by this principle.

The pattern of sexual asymmetry which the foregoing discussion has brought into focus is clearly reflected in the ideological subsystem of the culture. One finds that differentiation extends to the evaluation of persons' physical and moral status. Women are generally believed to be incapable of rational decision-making. It is said that "a woman's opinion, if it is correct, causes a year's worth of destruction." As noted in other accounts of female status in the Middle East (Antoun 1968, Maher 1974:91), women are also believed to be "lacking in mind and religion." Their weakness is said to make them particularly susceptible to the temptations of the devil. Thus, although the cultural prohibition of premarital sex is not universally upheld, the nature and intensity of the penalty for such transgressions are clearly functions of the culprit's sex. A woman who does not remain a virgin until the time of marriage risks the loss of her life. A married woman may also anticipate a similar fate if her husband discovers her illicit relationship with another man. In a case of marital infidelity in the village, the wife was brutally beaten by her husband, while her lover, a married man, was only reprimanded by village elders and made to pay her husband compensation.

As in many parts of Egypt, women's sexual passions are curtailed by the practice of female circumcision, the ablation of the clitoris (Ammar 1966:121, Berque 1957:44). Although clitoridectomy predates Islam, and no Quranic reference to the practice can be found (Blackman 1927:280–316, Meinardus 1970:322–325), the residents of Fateha justify the custom by reference to the Islamic *sunna*. In this respect it is similar to male circumcision which is also explained in terms of Islamic teachings. However, in the latter case there is no conception of the procedure as a means of controlling sexual desire. Instead, the hygienic function of male circumcision is emphasized. It is important to note that clitoridectomy is primarily a practice to safeguard premarital chastity and virginity. Women's right to sexual gratification within marriage is recognized. Since the clitoris is identified as the locus of sexual excitement, the gypsy woman who performs the operation is always cautioned against its complete excision. It is said that women who have been subjected to the complete removal of the clitoris "drain their husbands of their strength." Informants note that for such women orgasm is delayed. Synchronization of male and female phases of heightened sexual excitement is often brought about by the use of hashish which prolongs sexual intercourse. Women generally report that they enjoy sex, and their conversation and joking often center around this topic.

Since men regulate agricultural activities and control exchange-value products, dominate political and religious activities, and enforce decisions affecting women, it is possible to characterize the village as male-dominated.[9] This is not to say that the power differential between individual males and females is fixed nor to deny the reality of women's covert power. Power relations are not static and are subject to patterned changes, and female power, like male authority, is indeed a social reality (Beck 1975, Morsy 1972, Sweet 1974). The point to be stressed is that when a woman in Fateha chooses to manipulate events to her personal advantage, her efforts are subject to cultural constraints compounded by the limitations of her specific situation. These boundary conditions define the extent of her accomplishments. Thus, choice may be curtailed by the lack of implementable alternatives (Angrist 1975:183).

Differential Incidence of ʿUzr

Power relations are intimately related to the onset of folk illness and to explanations of illness causation. Power relations within the family are by far the most significant precipitating factors associated with the folk illness ʿuzr.[10] During the course of the study, power differentials associated with forced marriage, the threat of divorce, and the domineering behavior of affines were isolated as the ultimate causes of the affliction. Under conditions of stress the sick role offers a temporary modification of status. The following brief accounts of ʿuzr cases illustrate this mediating function of spirit possession.

Fawzeya, a childless wife, had been diagnosed maʿzura many years ago. She said the asyad first came to her when her father hit her after she refused to marry a man he had chosen. The marriage plans were abandoned and the spirits were pacified. They did not bother

her again until two years after her marriage to her present husband. The sheikh diagnosed her condition as ʿuzr in her reproductive organs. In the last fifteen years the asyad were kept happy through her weekly visits to the hadra. She noted: "God did not bless me with children all this time and I always have to force myself not to be sad, but this is impossible. People never leave each other alone and they have to eat each other [gossip]. My husband's face turns yellow [pale] each time a child comes into our house. May God keep my brother; if it were not for him the man [her husband] would have thrown me out like a dog."

A few months later Fawzeya came down with another attack of ʿuzr which clearly coincided with her husband's arrangements to take another wife. The marriage arrangements were temporarily suspended. Her brother threatened the husband by hinting that he would throw him out of the barber shop (which the brother owned). Additional pressure was brought to bear on the husband by other villagers. An older woman said, "It would be truly shameful to find you in the midst of *tabl* [drumming during a wedding] when your cousin [his wife's brother] has a *ganaza* [mourning procession]."

Khadra's case also illustrates the social basis of ʿuzr:

> When my husband died he left me with three girls. They were all little. I took my share [of father's inheritance] and I brought my daughters up. I married them all. Two are outside [her household]. My second daughter's husband is very poor so he lives with me. I became ill about five years ago when my daughter got married, and I became sad because I have no son or husband, and my brother, God forgive him, would not help me. My sadness turned to illness. My sister took me to the doctor, but the more of the doctor's medicine I took the worse off I became. People said that I might be maʿzura. The asyad talked. They said that they are from Saudia, from the land of the Prophet. They told everyone that when I am not happy they make my whole body blue. They knew that my brother was not telling the truth when he refused to help me. The asyad from Saudia knew that I needed help. So, in order to show my brother that I needed help, they spoke to people through me and made them know of my need.

Relations of power differentials are not confined to male-female interactions. Women may find themselves subordinated to the authority of females, and men are likely to fall victims to the domination of more powerful males. On the basis of data collected in Fateha, it is hypothesized that *lamsa ardiya* (touch by supernatural beings), resulting in ʿuzr, would be a significant etiological category among both males and females who occupy a subordinate social role, which may change in a lifetime. According to this postulate, the frequency of possession illness among women, as among men, may be expected to vary in relation to different stages of the life cycle and the developmental cycle of the family. Thus ʿuzr would be less likely to affect women who assume the dominant role of mother-in-law, for example, and men who occupy the dominant status of older brother in a fraternal joint family household. In view of women's position of relative subservience and the greater restrictions imposed on them as a group, it is further hypothesized that women in particular are more likely to pursue the labeling *maʿzura*. They are more likely to solicit the sick role which, by definition, renders their otherwise deviant behavior legitimate. By so doing, they utilize one of the few mechanisms available to them for deviating from specified behavior, while at the same time invoking public recognition of the validity of their actions.

Data collected from one hundred households in the village lend support to the above hypotheses. According to the results of a survey designed to identify the social characteristics of persons who become afflicted with ʿuzr, the distribution was as follows. Of a total of 34 cases collected for 195 adult males and 208 adult females, 21 cases were reported for females, and 13 cases were reported for males. Closer analysis of reported cases reveals that of the 34 cases, 24 occurred among married persons, 7 among single individuals, 1 case for a widow, 1 case for a divorced woman, and, finally, 1 case for a woman temporarily separated from her husband because of constant quarrels with his mother.

In terms of status within the household, defined by relation to household head, the breakdown is as follows. Of a total of 34 cases, 5 afflictions occurred among household heads. Of these 5, 2 had had their first attack as children; 2 were childless, sterile males; and 1 had been diagnosed epileptic by a physician. Six cases were reported for wives of household heads. Of these, 4 were childless. Three cases were reported for daughters of household heads, 1 case for a son, 4 cases for brothers of household heads, 1 case for a sister, 1 case for a brother's wife, and 1 case for a brother's daughter. Only 1 case was reported for a mother-in-law, an old and weak woman who was at the mercy of her son's wife. A single case of ʿuzr affected a daughter's husband who resided with his wife's family. Finally, by far the largest group of sufferers from ʿuzr consisted of sons' wives in extended family households. This group consisted of 10 females.

To conclude, earlier studies of spirit possession in Egypt declare that this folk illness is particularly widespread among adult females

(Kennedy 1967, Fakhouri 1968). Since possession illness has also been reported among males (Nelson 1971), its reported, but not numerically validated, higher frequency among women cannot be attributed to an inherent biological predisposition. Neither can sex role be considered the only socio-cultural correlate. In the foregoing discussion it has been proposed that explanations for the differential incidence of ʿuzr should be sought in social relations of power differentials affecting both males and females. While it is suggested that women as a group are likely to be subservient to male authority, it is also noted that power relations are not static but are subject to patterned changes associated with the life cycle and the developmental cycle of the family. As the data cited in the foregoing analysis demonstrate, the incidence of ʿuzr is associated with deviation from culturally stipulated role behavior and is directly related to subservient status. The point to be stressed is that while ʿuzr offers a legitimate channel for temporary enhancement of social position and deviation from established norms, it does not result in a permanent modification of status. Strategies of indirect control, including illness, are subject to the confines of cultural and situational constraints.

Notes

1. *Folk illness* refers to maladies for which modern scientific medicine offers no explanation and for which specific cultural groups provide an etiology, diagnosis, and curing procedure (Rubel 1964).

2. Additional behavioral correlates of ʿuzr include reduced food consumption, loss of consciousness, reduced verbal communication, nonsensical utterances, disrespect toward superiors, reduced social intercourse outside the home, depression, and crying, as well as loss of ability to discipline children, to earn a living, to fulfill duty as wife, or (in the case of females only) to do housework.

3. Physical symptoms reported for ʿuzr are diffuse and variable. They may include any combination of nausea, headache, aches all over the body, trembling, hot-cold spells, coughing, chills, weight loss, swelling, loss of balance, vomiting, difficulty in breathing, lump in throat, diarrhea, fever, pain in joints, earache, watery eyes, back pain, dizziness, chest pains, and stomach ache.

4. The patterned opposition between the sexes is reflected in cases of ʿuzr. Females become possessed by male spirits while males succumb to the affliction of female spirits.

5. Although the healing ritual outlined here is the most common means of coping with possession illness, other procedures are also followed.

6. For an extended discussion of the consequences of these traits on female status, see Sanday (1973, 1974).

7. Vieille has pointed to the possible link between the differences in value between the sexes and what he refers to as the surmortality of small girls (1967:108). Data from Egypt show that for the last two decades, the female infant mortality rate surpasses that of males (Valaoras 1972).

8. Persons joining such processions sway in a rhythmic fashion to the loud singing of praises of God and the Prophet.

9. Male dominance is defined as "a situation in which men have highly preferential access, although not always exclusive rights, to those activities to which the society accords the greatest value, and the exercise of which permits a measure of control over others" (Friedl 1975:7).

10. Analysis of the differential frequency of ʿuzr is restricted to *adult* males and females who are believed to be actively involved in defining themselves as maʿzur and thus lending legitimacy to what would ordinarily be labeled deviant behavior. In other words, I believe that the disjunction between expected role performance and the personal needs of the individual prompts him or her to assume the sick role. In the case of children, by contrast, it is their adult relatives who define the nature of the affliction. Thus, while one of my female informants defines her son's illness as ʿuzr (although a physician defines it as epilepsy), the son (a student) does not believe that he is maʿzur and acknowledges the physician's diagnosis by attributing his seizures to a "nervous condition."

Bibliography

Ammar, Hamed. *Growing up in an Egyptian Village*. New York, 1966.

Angrist, Shirley S. "Review Essay: An Overview." *SIGNS: Journal of Women in Culture and Society,* 1 (1975):175–183.

Antoun, Richard. "On the Modesty of Women in Arab Muslim Villages: A Study in the Accommodation of Traditions." *American Anthropologist,* 70 (1968):671–697.

Beck, Lois Grant. "Women of a Tribal Aristocracy in Iran." Unpublished. Amherst, Mass., 1975.

Berque, Jacques. *Histoire sociale d'un village égyptien au XXème siècle.* Paris, 1957.

Blackman, W. S. *The Fellahin of Upper Egypt*. London, 1927.

Fakhouri, Hani. "The Zar Cult in an Egyptian Village." *Anthropological Quarterly,* 41 (1968):49–56.

Friedl, Ernestine. *Women and Men: An Anthropologist's View.* New York, 1975.

Kennedy, J. G. "Nubian Zar Ceremonies as Psychotherapy." *Human Organization,* 26 (1967):280–285.

Lewis, I. M. "A Structural Approach to Witchcraft and Spirit-possession." In *Witchcraft Confessions and Accusations,* ed. Mary Douglas. London, 1970.

———. *Ecstatic Religion: An Anthropological Study of Spirit Possession and Shamanism*. Baltimore, 1971.

———. "Patterns of Protest Among Non-Western Women." In *Configurations,* ed. R. Prince and D. Barrier. Lexington, Mass., 1974.

Maher, Vanessa. *Women and Property in Morocco.* Cambridge, 1974.

Meinardus, Otto F. A. *Christian Egypt: Faith and Life.* Cairo, 1970.

Mohsen, Safia. "The Egyptian Woman: Between Modernity and Tradition." In *Many Sisters: Women in Cross-Cultural Perspective,* ed. C. Matthiasson. New York, 1974.

Montague, Ashley. *The Natural Superiority of Women.* New York, 1975.

Morsy, Soheir. "The Changing Role and Status of Arab Women." Master's thesis. Michigan State University, East Lansing, Mich., 1972.

Nelson, Cynthia. "Self, Spirit Possession and World View: An Illustration from Egypt." *International Journal of Social Psychiatry,* 17 (1971) :194–209.

Oesterreich, T. K. *Possession and Exorcism.* New York, 1974.

Rubel, Arthur. "The Epidemiology of a Folk Illness: Susto in Hispanic America." *Ethnology,* 3 (1964) :268–283.

al-Saʿdawi, Nawal. *Woman and Sex* (in Arabic) . Beirut, 1972.

Sanday, Peggy. "Toward a Theory of the Status of Women." *American Anthropologist,* 75 (1973) :1682–1700.

———. "Female Status in the Public Domain." In *Woman, Culture, and Society,* ed. M. Rosaldo and L. Lamphere. Stanford, Calif., 1974.

el-Shamy, Hassan. "Mental Health in Traditional Culture: A Study of Preventive and Therapeutic Folk Practices in Egypt." *Catalyst,* 6 (1972) : 13–28.

Sweet, Louise. "In Reality: Some Middle Eastern Women." In *Many Sisters: Women in Cross-Cultural Perspective,* ed. C. Matthiasson. New York, 1974.

Valaoras, V. G. *Population Analysis of Egypt.* Cairo, 1972.

Vieille, Paul. "Birth and Death in an Islamic Society." *Diogenes,* 57 (1967) : 101–127.

Walker, Sheila S. *Ceremonial Spirit Possession in Africa and Afro-America.* Leiden, 1974.

31 The Theme of Sexual Oppression in the North African Novel

Evelyne Accad

The North African novels discussed here illustrate many of the problems experienced in particular by young North African women. Although the majority of their authors live in Paris and write in French and there is no proof that their works are read by the majority of even the literate people in the Maghreb, their realistic depiction of many aspects of North African life makes them significant. The laws, customs, and traditions governing the lives of couples are so restrictive that it is not surprising to find writers reluctant to deal openly with the theme of sexual oppression. Most have been able to do so only by emigrating to France, while the few others who have written thus in the midst of their culture have done so only at the expense of censure. But all of them are pioneers in what may be expected to be a growing trend toward social and sexual realism.

The theme of sexual oppression takes various forms, ranging from symbolic representation to concrete examples from everyday life. The symbolic representation includes images of women as life and death, East or West. This approach can be traced in the "new trend" novels of Kateb Yacine (Algerian, b. 1929) and Mourad Bourboune (Algerian, b. 1938). Concrete examples abound in most of the novels: inevitably tragic endings to adulterous love affairs; the isolation of women from society because of the absence through death or migration of their husbands; the fear old women have of being parasites because they can no longer procreate; the sadness with which the birth of girls is greeted; the view that marriage's prime function is procreation; the punishment of sexual dishonor by death; the general acceptance of such practices as polygamy, prostitution, slavery, and arranged marriages; and the enforced seclusion and veiling of women, all of which demonstrate the refusal of society to grant women the right to seek sexual fulfillment. The results of this oppression as they are offered in the novels, and sometimes corroborated in the lives of the writers themselves, range from suicide to insanity, from sickness to rebellion, from emigration to political engagement, from hypocrisy to religious piety, and from the death of the father (the authority figure) to the death of the female protagonist.

It is not possible in the space available here to cover all the novels and each of the individual problems in detail. The criteria for selecting those dealt with in this study are the frequency of a particular subject throughout all the novels, the popularity of a particular novel based on how well it sold, and the recognition given a novel by the critics. The basic subject of this study is marriage in the Maghreb countries, where it is seen as an economic settlement within a large family system, certainly not as an emotional understanding and commitment between two people who want to share a life together. Three aspects, all stemming from the traditional view of marriage, are analyzed: the notion of honor, the notion of arranged marriage, and the notion of procreation. Each aspect is analyzed separately, first in terms of traditional interpretation and then in terms of its treatment in the novels.

Honor has various highly valued codes in the Maghreb but is quite specific when it is linked to the sexual life of its people. A family's honor depends on its girls' virginity. To preserve the honor of one's female relatives means, above all, to protect them from premarital sexual intercourse. All precautions are taken to preserve virginity, which is intrinsically valuable, to be given only to its proper owner, the husband. When a girl reaches puberty, it is not unusual to see her quickly withdrawn from school before she has the chance to "dishonor" the family. As G. Tillion has pointed out in *Le harem et les cousins* (p. 203), the murder of a dishonored girl by her brother, though found in Morocco and Kabyle, is not as frequent in North Africa as it is in the other Arab countries. But even in North Africa, neither the law nor the society itself treats the defenders of this honor with much harshness. While the law asks only a lenient punishment for the defender of honor, society presses heavily on a brother to convince him he is unworthy and unmanly if he does not wash the honor of his family in blood. Other measures intended to secure a girl's virginity are her seclusion and her veil; both are means of separating women from the world where they might lose their honor and that of the family.

Assia Djebar (Algerian, b. 1936) deals with the theme of sexual oppression by seclusion in *Les impatients* (The impatient ones, 1958). (Biographical material on the authors is included in the appendix.) Her heroine, Dalila, is cloistered in the house, allowed to go out only occasionally to visit female friends, attend weddings, and go to the Turkish bath. Djebar also touches upon it in her third novel *Les enfants du nouveau monde* (Children of the new world, 1962), where the revolutionary male hero who is fighting the Algerian war for independence finds a small revenge by oppressing in turn his wife at home:

> Yes, to forget the French oppressor is almost easy, he thinks when he returns to his home at night and looks at his wife who will never be seen by the other, the all-powerful master outside. They say that she is "cloistered," but the husband thinks that she is "liberated" . . . this is why he considers her as his wife, not just a body he embraces without ecstasy, since it never meets the others' eyes in a dialogue (p. 17).

Another of Djebar's characters is Salima, a thirty-year-old teacher, imprisoned for her participation in the underground. While she is in prison, her past unfolds before her eyes. She remembers her father's death when she was fifteen, the only Muslim girl in school. She remembers feeling happy when he died, for he would otherwise have cloistered her like the other girls around her. Then there is Touma, a "loose" girl, semieducated in French schools, who must be killed by her younger brother Tewfiq to save the honor of his family. And Tewfiq must kill her before the *maquis* will admit him to their ranks.

Marguerite Taos (Tunisian Kabyle, b. 1913) deals with the theme in a different manner in *La rue des tambourins* (The road of the tambourines, 1960), where the social liberty of the heroine, Marie-Corail, is restricted by both of her parents—even by her mother who pretends to be an *evoluée*. The restrictions imposed upon her become even more severe when she reaches puberty: her parents control her every movement, allowing her to go only from school to home and then back again. Even her mother, who rebels against the old customs for her own benefit, decrees an opposite set of rules for her daughter: "In our country, at your age one already has a child at the breast and another one on the back" (p. 182). Both parents beat her severely when she disobeys, and her father high-handedly decides that she will be a teacher, opposing her study of art on the grounds that she would have to go to Tenzis every day and take the train alone. The treatment of his daughter compared with that of his sons, who are in France doing what they please, is dramatized to show how fathers decide the course of their daughters' lives without any consideration for the girls' wishes.

Zoubeida Bittari (Algerian, b. 1939) provides another example of this oppression in *O, mes soeurs musulmanes, pleurez!* (O, my Muslim sisters, cry! 1972), where Zoubeida, the heroine (the author herself), tells us of her childhood. She was born in a typical Muslim bourgeois family. She attended a French school where she had European girlfriends with whom she shared sports, games, and classes—unconscious that anything made her different from them. Suddenly, when she was twelve years old, there was a sense of panic and fear in the household. Zoubeida had reached a dangerous age—puberty. What would the neighbors say if she were allowed to continue going out, to school and to play sports? They would surely see her as unfit to be a wife. The only way to save her from scandal and a lost life was to take her quickly out of school and give her to a man she did not know.

The male writers do not emphasize this theme as much as the female writers, probably because it does not affect their lives as directly as other themes. Driss Chraibi (Moroccan, b. 1928) mentions it in his story *Le passé simple* (The past, 1954), where he describes his mother as being cloistered at puberty to be married off later. Albert Memmi (Tunisian, b. 1920) mentions it also in *Scorpion ou la confession imaginaire* (Scorpion or the imaginary confession, 1969), where he describes how his father beat his sister from head to toe with a heavy belt until she bled and was almost disfigured because he had found her kissing a man she loved. Her father forces her to marry a much older man who has a good job. Now that she has compromised her honor, she has to be married quickly.

The notion of arranged marriages is a direct result of the notion of honor. The fear of parents that their daughters may be deflowered before marriage, thereby dishonoring the family and making it impossible to marry them off, compels the parents to arrange for them a marriage when they are very young. This not only frees the parents of the terrible responsibility of having to protect the girls' virginity but of having to be in charge of them economically for the rest of their lives. Social pressure makes it very clear to women that marriage is the only desirable position in life. Furthermore, most North African girls do not marry the man of their choice, but rather one chosen by their parents. The reason given for this is that at that age a girl cannot know what she needs and that her parents are better judges of what will make her happy. Since marriage is a family affair, couples are made to feel that their elders should decide what is best for them. But as with the notion of honor, this practice has dangerous consequences. So much social pressure is applied to girls to have them accept arranged marriages that some of them resort to suicide as the only way out of an unbearable situation. As M'Rabet has pointed out in *Les Algériennes* (p. 149), every other day in Algiers some girl will attempt or commit suicide to avoid a forced marriage.

Custom also demands that at the time of the signing of the contract, the man has to pay a certain amount of money: the *mahr*. Formerly, the mahr was meant to protect the woman. Often, part of it had to be paid only if the husband divorced his wife, thus discouraging divorce. But it has acquired the taint of money, of transaction and bargaining. A woman has become a "thing" on which a price is placed. The amount varies quantitatively and qualitatively according to the individuals and their families. It depends not only on the quality and affluence of the girl but on the situation of the suitor and the value of the girl on the current marriage market.

The social pressures to marry girls who are virgins pushes men to take very young wives. In the countryside, fearful parents marry off their girls before they reach complete physical maturity. The girls have their first child when their own bodies are still growing and changing. And it is not enough for a woman to be physically a virgin, she must be psychologically a virgin as well. She must be unaware of any sexual sensations other than the ones her husband wants her to feel. This is one of the reasons he does not want her to be too educated.

Djebar's *Les enfants du nouveau monde* deals with this notion as well. Chérifa is the uneducated wife of Youssef, who is a merchant and also a member of the underground. But she has had her consciousness awakened through a first marriage, through three years of living with a man who had been forced upon her, "a man which everything in her had rejected." Every night for three years she had given herself to him like a cold statue, a possession worse than rape. Her decision to break from him had been her first act of rebellion, of taking consciousness of her own existence.

Another illustration can be found in Bittari's *O, mes soeurs musulmanes, pleurez!* Quickly taken out of school, Zoubeida is sold to a man she does not know. But worse than that, as she learns much later, she is not really sold because, the situation being urgent, her father had paid her husband to buy her so that the transaction would seem normal to the religious judge, to the neighbors, and to the relatives.

Among the male writers, Mouloud Feraoun (Algerian Kabyle, 1913–1962) describes the typical life of a Kabyle woman in *La terre et le sang* (The earth and the blood, 1953). There is the mother, Kamouma, who was married very young to a man of her parents' choosing, shifting merely from her father's authority to her in-laws' tyranny. There is also Chabha. At fifteen, she had been forced into marrying Slimane, a man fifteen years older than herself and whom she had not wanted. She had dreamed of someone different, someone she would love, but her parents had accepted the marriage proposal for her because the suitor had a good position and offered security. She had learned to respect him and they trusted each other. They made a "reasonable" couple, their caresses restrained and their gestures calculated, never undressing in front of each other except in darkness. Chabha's tragedy arrives when her cousin Amer returns from France. Passion awakens in her heart, leading her into the impossible situation that ends in the death of both her husband and Amer.

Another example is given by Mouloud Mammeri (Algerian Kabyle, b. 1917). In *La colline oubliée* (The forgotten hill, 1952), Mokrane and Aazi are married as strangers, since, as Mammeri comments, "the barbaric custom of joining two people who do not know each other is still in our tradition" (p. 18). The opening line of the novel is "Our springtime does not last," closely followed in subtle juxtaposition by "the springtime of our young women does not last either" (p. 11). With these lines, Mammeri attacks the Kabyle tradition that forces women from childhood to maturity by precocious marriages.

In *Le passé simple,* Chraibi shows us that the men are also oppressed by this practice. The son Driss feels pity for his father who, like his mother, is a victim of tradition: he has never really loved his wife, and he did not really marry her of his own free will or desire. In a moment of confidence, he admits to his son that he has taken concubines whenever he went on a pilgrimage:

> The time has come for settling the accounts, your brother is dead, my wife has died . . . One of the elements of my personal history . . . my behavior toward your mother and my wife was: authority, indifference, contempt . . . Did you ever stop to ask yourself why? Yes, why did I treat her like an animal? . . . Your mother, God keep her, was placed in my bed . . . you know about our traditions, the people most

concerned are never informed of the arrangements between the respective families (pp. 224–226, 231).

The evils of arranged marriages for boys as well as for girls are thoroughly explored by Abd al-Karim Ghallab (Moroccan, b. ?) in his novel *Dafanna al-madi* (We buried the past, 1967). The almost venal attitude of the mother in getting her son Abd al-Ghani married at an early age is exploited by Ghallab to show that not only girls but boys have no choice in their marriage. "And the months passed and Abd al-Ghani was totally unaware of the matter except that he knew that he was engaged to a faraway girl. He was engaged, in spite of himself, consenting or not. It was a matter with which he did not even argue" (p. 190).

There is also Aisha, the sister, who is to be married after the same fashion. It is interesting to note the advice that one of her brothers gives on the occasion of that arrangement:

> Do not get married to a man you do not know or do not approve of marrying. It is enough for you to have crucified the most important asset of your human personality: your confidence. Please do not let them crucify in you the most important human trait: choice . . . I will be behind you when you make up your mind, but I will not be with you if you give up (p. 236).

Though the brother is able to change the traditional outlook of his parents toward his sister's marriage, the novel does not present Aisha much alternative. She merely shifts her subservience from her father to her brother, who arranges her marriage with one of his friends.

Procreation, a notion whose importance is ingrained in both male and female in North Africa, is the prime function of marriage. A man whose wife has not delivered a child, or at least is not pregnant, within the year following their marriage sees his prestige considerably diminished. An average woman peasant has seven to ten children in her lifetime. A man whose wife cannot have male children, or any children at all, can very quickly divorce her, while a woman has not such rights over a sterile husband. It is the woman who is always accused of sterility.

Within a large family system, children are the best insurance against loneliness, economic and social dependence, and death. The more the male numbers of a family, the better its economic base. Perhaps this has psychologically as well as pragmatically determined the importance attached to bearing children. It has become a part of social thinking that beyond its economic values, the procreation of numerous children is a religious virtue, a divine gift granted to women. Their fulfillment of this role enhances their prestige and importance. So while women are treated as factories for producing the yearly offspring, their partial redemption lies in fulfilling this role successfully. At the same time, women unable to assume this function are regarded with disdain and contempt. Their integrity is questioned.

There are numerous examples of this theme by both male and female writers. In Assia Djebar's *La soif* (Thirst, 1957), one of the heroines, Jedla, attempts suicide because she has lost one child by miscarriage and fears she cannot have another. She has learned that her husband had a French mistress who bore him a son, and she is extremely jealous of something she cannot have. The theme of the novel is the "thirst" for children who will hold men close, for traditionally men and children are as necessary to women's lives as water. Jedla has been so well trained in her role as an Arab female that she thinks that a marriage without a child is sure to drive her husband away.

Such is also the fate of Zoubeida in *O, mes soeurs musulmanes, pleurez!* Although she is only twelve years old, she has to produce a child. The sex of the child is not even questioned: it has to be a boy. She gives birth to a baby boy after severe pain and almost dies from the physiological and psychological consequences of this experience. She is hardly more than a child herself.

The male writers use this theme repeatedly. In Feraoun's *La terre et le sang,* even Marie, the Frenchwoman who was married to Amer in his Kabyle village, feels she has gained a new dignity by being pregnant. The other women and the men of the village respect her more. Her mother-in-law takes hope, because the cycle of life, which is her only future, has not been broken. Her blood is not dead and will live again through a grandchild. Another woman in the novel, Chabha, is very unhappy because she cannot have a child. The peaceful understanding she has with a husband who had been forced upon her is shadowed by this childlessness. It is one of the reasons she so readily falls in love with Amer, bringing about her tragedy.

Procreation is also one of the themes in Mammeri's *La colline oubliée.* Aazi, the young bride, is persecuted because she cannot procreate. Her in-laws question her utility: "What can we do with a woman who cannot have children when we have only one son?" (p. 68). Under tremendous pressure, Aazi is desperate. She tears her hair and screams that she is not God who can create a child. Her mother-in-law especially insists that Aazi's sterility must be God's curse and punishment for some hidden sins she must have committed. Aazi's husband himself says:

> My mother in particular would insist that God blessed only the virtuous; she never came out and said it directly, but every time what she said made it apparent to us that Aazi's sterility was punishment for her sins. This idea of damnation, of uselessness, would sink into my wife's heart like a dagger. It would sink every day ever more deeply, would poison her joys, and when by some stroke of luck Aazi seemed to forget it for a while and relax, my mother would subtly shift the conversation back to that sensitive subject (p. 100).

Even the women of the village mortify poor Aazi and get a sadistic pleasure out of bringing her news of all the births in the district. Aazi tries all the known remedies against sterility—from following old women's recipes, to going on a prilgrimage to the tomb of Abdalrahman and evoking the *jinns* (spirits) through the *hadra* (a dance invocation to bring the situation to the spirits' attention and to ask their help to prevent a catastrophe). But it is of no use, and Aazi's situation with her in-laws becomes unbearable. She is repudiated by her father-in-law and returns to her mother.

Chraibi in *Le passé simple* deals with the theme of procreation in a much more violent and rebellious way. In his despair he even uses obscene language. The son Driss condemns his father for oppressing his mother and inflicting upon her pregnancy after pregnancy. She has to call her husband "master" and her relationship to him is truly that of a servant:

> She tried to prevent every catastrophe that threatened . . . my mother, tender and resigned, five feet tall, weighing ninety pounds . . . nothing other than a woman whose lord could chain her legs at will and over whom he had the power of life and death; the only thing that she knows how to do is to lay eggs and say "yes, my lord." She had always lived in houses with bars on the doors, and metal bars guarding the windows. From the balconies, only the sky was visible—and the minarets, symbols. One among God's creatures which the Quran has confined: "kiss them and kiss them again: through the vagina, it is more useful; then, ignore them until the next time of pleasure." Yes, this is how my mother was, weak, submissive, passive. She had given birth seven times, at regular intervals of two years (pp. 40–41).

But Driss also condemns his mother for blindly following old beliefs and superstitions. He gets very upset with her one day when he sees her all dressed up with *kohl* on her eyes and *henna* on her fingernails. She has just lost a child, who died because his father had beaten him, and is all set to seduce her husband in order to have another. Driss confronts her with her inconsistency. He shouts at her, calling her a "coffer of pregnancies" and despising her calculations (p. 124).

This theme is also dealt with by Albert Memmi in *La statue de sel* (The pillar of salt, 1966). Mordekhai, the hero, watches his mother tiring and aging after the several consecutive pregnancies that have considerably increased the size of the family, reducing the food on the table and the space in the house. Like Driss, he resents his father for it.

The novelists' treatments of three notions directly or tangentially connected with sex and the traditional oppressiveness of those notions in North Africa have been demonstrated here. Nowhere is sex seen as an act of enjoyment, an act fulfilling in itself, a rapport of mutuality of feeling, a sharing and giving. It is a role-playing in a contractual sense, and it is the many evils of this contractual sex that the novels emphasize. This literature is enlightening as an analysis of the social scene, and its emphasis on problems may awaken in some readers ideas for their solution.

Moving from the social and psychological aspects of the problems that are revealed by these novels to the socioeconomic and political dimensions, the picture becomes even more bleak. In general, the shift from a colonial status to a nationalist one has—with the primary exception of Bourguiba of Tunisia and those who follow him—resulted in a retreat to the precolonial view of life, a retreat to an even stronger insistence on the preservation of the traditional values. In the socioeconomic sphere, the chances for change largely depend on economic growth and on legislation supporting equal education and employment for men and women, because only with them can the basic problem of the economic dependence of women on men move toward a solution. Hopes for the general betterment of the lot of women, including the end of their sexual oppression, must hinge not so much on the political ideologies now strong in the Maghreb as on economic independence and progress.

Appendix

A few words about the authors dealt with in this study are appropriate.

Assia Djebar (Algerian, b. 1936) is a woman from a Muslim middle-class family who, by the age of twenty-six, had published three novels and obtained a *licence* in history from the Sorbonne. During the revolution, she taught in Tunis and Rabat, and now lives most of the time in France where she still writes and is a literary critic as well. She has published four novels.

Marguerite Taos (Tunisian, b. 1913) is the sister of the writer Jean Amrouche. They are from a Kabyle family converted to Christianity. She resided in France since 1945 where she hosted a radio program in the Kabyle language. She published two novels. She died in 1976 of throat cancer.

Zoubeida Bittari (Algerian, b. 1939) is a woman from a lower-middle-class family. She was forced to leave her country where she was persecuted and oppressed as a woman, and she has worked in France as a maid. She writes in simple, schoolgirl French and demonstrates the problems of sexual oppression as seen from the lower-middle-class point of view. She has published one autobiographical novel.

Driss Chraibi (Moroccan, b. 1928) comes from a middle-class family. He studied chemistry, then went into journalism. He lives in France and works for a radio company. He has published eight novels.

Albert Memmi (Tunisian, b. 1920) is a Jew who was raised in the ghetto of Tunis and is now living in France. He teaches sociology at the Sorbonne. He published three novels and various studies on oppression.

Mouloud Feraoun (Algerian, 1913–1962) is a Kabyle and the son of a peasant. He taught in Algiers, and published three novels. He was killed by the forces of the OAS (the secret French organization that endeavored to destroy the Algerian resistance movement) on the eve of Algerian independence.

Mouloud Mammeri (Algerian, b. 1917) comes from an upper-class Kabyle family. He has published three novels. He teaches sociology at the University of Algiers.

Abd al-Karim Ghallab (Moroccan, b. ?) is the president of the Writer's League in Morocco. He writes in Arabic. He has published one novel often compared to the trilogy of the Egyptian writer Naguib Mahfuz.

Bibliography

Bittari, Zoubeida. *O, mes soeurs musulmanes, pleurez!* Paris, 1972.

Chraibi, Driss. *Le passé simple*. Paris, 1954.

Djebar, Assia. *Les enfants du nouveau monde*. Paris, 1962.

———. *Les impatients*. Paris, 1958.

———. *La soif*. Paris, 1957.

Feraoun, Mouloud. *La terre et le sang*. Paris, 1953.

Ghallab, Abd al-Karim. *Dafanna al-madi*. Beirut, 1967.

Mammeri, Mouloud. *La colline oubliée*. Paris, 1953.
M'Rabet, Fadéla, *La femme algérienne, suivi de les Algériennes*. Paris, 1969.
Memmi, Albert. *Scorpion ou la confession imaginaire*. Paris, 1969.
———. *Statue de sel*. Paris, 1966.
Taos, Marguerite Amrouche. *La rue des tambourins*. Paris, 1960.
Tillion, Germaine. *Le harem et les cousins*. Paris, 1966.
Yacine, Kateb. *Nedjma*. Paris, 1956.

32 Women in Contemporary Persian Folktales

Erika Friedl

A description and evaluation of the position of women in Middle Eastern cultures hinge on the ideological framework and perception of the social scientist undertaking the research, and on the mode of collection and presentation chosen for the data. If the researcher is not a member of the same culture—which he or she usually is not—it is frequently charged that the collected data are prejudiced or misinterpreted. One possibility for avoiding this potential shortcoming is to concentrate on statements informants provide spontaneously, without challenge from a field worker, and without pressure to adhere to an alien conceptual frame like a questionnaire or a test. Folktales constitute exactly such data.

In tales, the plots, the characters, and the relationships among the actors are highly stereotyped and "simplified" compared with real events and people, but in a way that is understandable, acceptable, and meaningful to almost everyone who shares the same cultural background. If this were not the case, stories would lose their appeal or would be forgotten, or the irrelevent or incomprehensible parts would be changed. (In this way, the bad mother in the Brothers Grimm's "Hansel and Gretel" was first changed to a

---

I collected the tales between 1969 and 1971. Whenever certain practices in the tales are contrasted with "reality," that is, with actual practices in Boir Ahmad, I draw upon knowledge about the culture gained during a three-year period of anthropological field work in Boir Ahmad. The financial help of the Social Science Research Council and the Wenner-Gren Foundation for Anthropological Research for the field work underlying this study is gratefully acknowledged.

stepmother from whom such cruel behavior was easier to accept; later the episode was dropped altogether, and the children are usually simply said to have lost their way in the woods.) The figures in tales can be seen as ideal types, and as such they reveal what the people who tell the tales and listen to them feel about certain characters. Women, along with other kinds of people, are of course included; their proper place in the society is discussed, as are their relationships, conflicts, and fates, which all reflect norms and standards that are generally accepted in this particular culture. Moreover, the ideal types always include an indigenous evaluation of these traits as well.

The following analysis is based on forty-five tales from the tribal area of Boir Ahmad in southwest Iran, which I collected from oral tradition, and on ten tales from the same area and time period, collected by an Iranian physician (Lama'e 1970).[1] The narrators who told the forty-five tales collected by myself were five women, seven men, and three boys. The tales were recorded on tape, along with detailed observations on the narrators' and listeners' reactions, such as gestures, comments, and exclamations.[2]

The Boir Ahmadis are Lur-speaking, nomadic and transhumant sheep- and goatherders and farmers. Their mountains, herds, fields, camps, and villages, as well as their tribal organization, are reflected in the tales, and even modern features like schools, migrant labor, and the bureaucracy are included. This study, however, focuses only on what the tales reveal about the cultural images of women and is intended as an analysis, not an interpretation.

Storytelling in Boir Ahmad is a pastime activity and done by almost everyone at times. The more knowledgeable and animated a narrator is, the more listeners he or she will attract among kinsfolk and close neighbors, and some men and women are rather famous for their narrative skills. Tales are told mainly during informal gatherings on winter evenings. Lately, the radio and record player have become attractive entertainment for such occasions and the interest in storytelling is fading. Folktales and folksongs constitute by far the greatest body of oral traditions in Boir Ahmad. Bits and pieces of old heroic epics are remembered by some men, but these epics are considered "history" now and are no longer part of the active narrative repertory of the people.

Roles and Occupations

In the forty-five tales, women appear 122 times, and men 195 times; men outnumber women at the rate of about 3 to 2. While seven tales have no women at all, only one tale has no men. Women seem to appear slightly more often in tales told by a woman, but the sample of narrators is too small to allow a general statement about the relationship between sex of narrator and number of males and females in the tales. The only story in the collection that features no man was told by a woman.

A striking difference between the sexes appears when the tales' male and female figures are fitted into categories based on roles and occupations. Women act in altogether fourteen roles, seven of which are based on consanguineal or affinal kinship. Men, on the other hand, fill forty-three roles, of which six are based on kinship. Men's roles and occupations span a wide range of familiar traditional and modern occupations, from dragon and king to teacher, doctor, and even migrant worker. While the expanded work horizon for men has thus found its way into folktales, women teachers, midwives, and even schoolgirls have not yet been incorporated, although they are becoming a reality in Boir Ahmad.

As can be seen from tables 32.1 and 32.2, women act considerably more often as representatives of a kin group than in other contexts or than men. In fact, the relationship between kinship and others for women is just a reversal from the one for men. Except for maid, there is no occupational status described for women. If folktales continue to be a living art in Boir Ahmad, this can be expected to change in the near future. For now, the discrepancy between men's and women's roles reflects both a corresponding discrepancy in reality and also a greater reluctance to accept actual changes in the status of women than in the status of men.

In eighteen tales a woman is the center of the story; in five more a woman shares the focal position with a man; and in the other thirty-two a man is the hero. In some of these, women have important parts in an episode, usually as the friendly or hostile counterpart of the hero: as mother, fairy, good or bad wife, sister, or conspiratory "old woman." Of the forty-five tales, five feature animals as main characters, specified by title ("Uncle Fox") or other behavioral attributes as either male (three cases) or female (two cases). In one of these, the local version of our familiar "Wolf and the Seven Kids," the brave, clever, and energetic mother goat is referred to as "Uncle Goat" (*tata boz*) throughout the story (*tata* means father's brother or, by extension, a title of respect for men). Here, the fact that she stands on her own feet and takes matters in her own hands, relying on no one at all, not even for a fight or for building a house, overrides her femininity, as it were, and lets her score high on characteristics fitting for a man, and prompts the narrator (a woman) to call her "uncle."

Table 32.1. Kinship roles of women and men in fifty-five folktales.

Women		Men	
Role	Incidence	Role	Incidence
Daughter	30	Son	18
Wife	30	Husband	16
Mother	27	Father	13
Sister	9	Brother	5
Co-wife	5	Mother's brother	2
Stepmother	3	Sister's son	2
Mother's sister	1		

Table 32.2. Non-kinship roles and occupations of women and men in fifty-five folktales.

Women		Men			
Role	Incidence	Role	Incidence	Role	Incidence
Old woman	13	King/prince	34	Judge	2
Girl	8	Holy man	10	Migrant worker	2
Woman	8	Monster	9	Thistle-collector	1
Fairy	6	Vizier	8	Bath-keeper	1
Maid	4	Shepherd	8	Teacher	1
Neighbor	2	Horseman/rifleman	8	Carpenter	1
Bride	1	Man	7	Shoemaker	1
		Shopkeeper/trader	6	Hunter	1
		Servant	6	Guard	1
		Mullah	6	Musician	1
		Farmer	5	Neighbor	1
		Smith	4	Fate	1
		Headman	3	Darvish	1
		Jew	3	Manager of caravansary	1
		Host	3	Fisherman	1
		Guest	3	Miller	1[a]
		Lover	3	Tailor	1[a]
		Money-lender	2	Chauffeur	1[a]
		Doctor	2		

a. Mentioned, but not acting.

In four of the female-centered tales, nothing dramatic at all happens to the heroine: a woman fools her husband out of some desired food; Nut's mother asks various characters why Stone had hit Nut's head (to find that this will always be so); Old Woman catches Cat stealing milk and forces Cat to pay her back; Old Woman's yogurt is eaten by Rooster, but her subsequent complaints are in vain.

In the other tales focusing on a heroine, the female is a girl who, after abduction by a monster, after hardships caused by relatives, or after near destruction by other forces, is saved, that is, married (six cases), or else rediscovered by her husband (two cases) or by her family (two cases). In five instances, the heroine or the hero's female counterpart ends in destruction: two are punished by God for misdeeds and turned into animals, two female monsters are overcome and killed by their counterforce, the fairy, and one is persecuted by her stepmother and kills herself. Male heroes, in contrast, are never destroyed, save in two cases in which a monster as the counterpart of the heroine is killed. For men the happy end typically consists of a rise in status, either through the acquisition of wealth or through succession to a power position.

In the traditional hierarchy of power and authority underlying the tales, God stands at the apex, followed by the prophets. Next come kings and other foci of political power, and then men, women, and children. Animals stand at the bottom. In the tales a woman's fate is usually dependent on the actions of men who have authority over her, like a father or husband, while a man's fate is either directed by his own actions or the actions of one with superior power. Since a woman in general is subject to the authority of men, and in turn can wield authority only over children and animals, she is rarely in a threatening power position vis-à-vis a man, except if she is superhuman: a fairy or a cannibalistic wolf-girl.

Both male and female roles are largely stereotyped, and the behavior of the different types as well as the consequences of their behavior are highly predictable once the setting is specified. An ingratiated king will offer his savior his daughter. A youngest son or brother, who was cut short or insulted by his father or brothers, will leave his home and later return as a hero. Stepmothers are mean to their stepdaughters. Yet it seems that stereotypes of women generally are even more narrow than those of men. While a king, though stereotypically powerful and autocratic, can still be kind or threatening, demanding or generous, wise or in need of help, his beautiful daughter will inevitably be either good and complaisant to her father's wish, or bad and stubborn. Usually she is good.

While a male servant can be dedicated, loyal, resourceful, revengeful, tricky, or dangerous, a maid, if not just simply carrying out her master's will, is only bad and jealous. While the stereotypical old, poor man can be humble, desperate, kindhearted, generous, industrious, dedicated, or dumb, his counterpart Old Woman is usually simply greedy, hungry, and open for purchase for any service. This flatness in the characterization of female figures makes for a certain dullness of their parts, especially when a young woman, as a daughter or bride, stands directly within the realm of a man's authority. In these scenes—and they are by far the majority—she merely provides a background to the stage that is dominated by men. This happens even in some tales that center around a woman. Namaki, for example, forgets to lock the door at night, is stolen by a monster, and rediscovered by a rifleman; then the monster is tricked and killed by her family. Although she is the heroine, Namaki herself acts only once directly in the whole tale: she points out a strange cloud to her mother, who identifies it as the advancing monster.

Women develop a certain character of their own only when they are "alone," that is, without a father, brother, or husband. Old Woman, thus, is rather independent and free to do things a young, "proper" woman would not do. Another example is Mateti who, together with her six sisters, is abandoned by their father. From then on she acts with independence, bravery, daring, and resourcefulness, and she saves herself and her sisters from a dangerous monster. The story ends when the seven girls find husbands; they are back where they belong, under the protective power of men.

The other category of colorful female characters are "bad" women. Their actions too are usually out of the ordinary, being consequential for the plot, and their outrageous conduct is described in detail and with considerable emotional involvement on the part of the narrators. One of the most colorful women in the tales is Samanbar who uses (or rather misuses) her extraordinary beauty to trick masses of enchanted young men out of their money and her husband out of his magical devices. She makes herself a seemingly marvelous life, before the justice of the narrator catches up with her and makes an end to her immoral dealings.

The sex of the narrator does not seem to influence either the definition and description of role performance or the point of view that is taken when the story is told. Both male and female storytellers tend to identify with a male hero and to view the tale from a "male" point of view, even if the main character of the story is a woman. For example, in "The King's Son," which features a heroine and is told by a woman, a baby girl is abandoned at the order of her disappointed father, who had hoped for a son, and is found and raised by an eagle in a cliff. Up to this point, the story is treated perfunctorily and without any elaboration, although undoubtedly it has great dramatic potential. The plot really begins when a prince sees the girl and sends Old Woman to abduct her. Old Woman's tricky acting (she poses as blind and subsequently misuses the girl's pity and kindness) is described in detail, because it is of importance to the prince. The girl's reaction to the abduction, her feelings on departure from the eagle and the cliff and on arrival at her new surroundings (which later on prove to be dangerous) are not dealt with in a single word. Similarly, "Ali Pazanak" (told by a man) starts out with a heroine. A girl is abducted by a *jinn* (spirit) in the form of a mountain goat, is forced to marry him, bears him a son, is widowed under dramatic circumstances, is forced to marry her husband's brother, the Snake, and bears him a son too. All this takes less than one-sixth of the tale to tell. At that point, her two sons take over, and she is mentioned again only twice, in passing. Once she gives her sons some wanted information, and in the end her sons are said to take care of her. Even this statement, however, serves to show that the sons are good men who observe the duty of caring for old parents, rather than to say anything about her.

With very few exceptions, then, women, no matter where they actually stand in the plot, are defined primarily in terms of their significance to one or several men, while men are never discussed in terms of their significance to women.

Formal social status and material wealth of women in the tales are always dependent on the social and economic status of the men with whom these women are associated. The wife of a king is a *bibi* (lady), as long as she is actually with him. When she gets lost and is taken in by a poor fisherman, she becomes a poor woman selling flowers to her former husband's second wife, who, in turn, is raised from a maid to a bibi through her marriage with the king. The important criteria for a woman's status are affinity and descent, in that order. The daughter of a poor farmer can marry a king and thus become a bibi; the daughter of a king, married to a lame pauper, becomes a poor, insignificant woman. However, in the tales as in reality, the daughter of a king is much more likely to be married to a prince or rich man than is the daughter of a shepherd or craftsman. Thus, descent narrows the options for affinal relationships with men considerably. In old age a woman's status declines sharply with the declining status of her husband (for whom presence of mind, strength, and personal qualities will have been of more importance to his formal standing in the community), and if she survives him her status will finally depend on the status of the sons who take care of her and on the quality of that care. According to the tales, and corresponding with reality, there is not much Old Woman can hope for. In the tales, she seems to be largely on her own.

Wealth is intimately linked with status. No king is poor, and no pauper has high status. But a pauper rises quickly as soon as he obtains riches. With the exception of fairies, women have no wealth of their own, and have no honorable means of obtaining any. They do not even find treasures. A woman is not supposed or expected to acquire wealth, but she has to help her husband and father to display wealth in an appropriate and acceptable way in order to gain status for them, and thereby for herself. The lame hero in "Tambal" sends home the fortune he finds abroad, and his wife is described as having a good house built, carpets and the customary luxuries of life purchased, and servants hired, so that upon his return Tambal is already a made man in his community and does not have to begin proving his wealth. In "Najar," the wife, who is in a similar position to Tambal's wife, sends her returning husband a message to wait in the mountains outside the village. She sends him a fine suit to make sure that he will fit into his new stylish surroundings and organizes a welcome caravan in grand style. The former pauper enters his village as a truly noble man. In "Sadat," the thistle-collector's wife sells the precious stone her husband found in the desert, uses the money to upgrade their existence by buying food, rugs, lamps, and other amenities, and finally advises her husband to quit his arduous work and to settle down as the rich man he meanwhile had become. The people acknowledge his rise by calling him "Master Thistle-collector."

Inheritance, an important source of wealth and status for men in the tales and in reality, is of no significance to a woman. Nowhere is a girl described as inheriting anything from her father. If the father dies before she is married, her brothers take care of her in terms of physical welfare, protection, a husband, and status. This again is quite in accordance with actual practice. According to tribal law, a daughter does not inherit anything from her father. She gets a dowry (paid partly by the bridewealth the father gets from the groom) and perhaps some gifts in the form of jewelry and clothing, according to her father's means, but nothing else. Although contrary to Islamic law, this custom has not changed much. Currently, it is explained that upon the death of a father, the daughters renounce their share of the rightful inheritance for the sake of their brothers, who will have to make a living for themselves and their own families, while the daughters are taken care of by their husbands and are not in need of their share of the inheritance. The only woman in the tales who acquires wealth on her own is the beautiful "bad" lady mentioned above who proposes to sell herself to one of the many admirers who would bring her the most money. She seemingly thrives on this plan, but in the end is severely punished and loses all her wealth.

Aside from the parameters of status and wealth, the standing of individual women in their communities is not discussed in the tales. Factors of personal conduct are seldom mentioned in connection with a woman's position in public, and she is rarely seen against the background of the wider community. Her behavior is largely a private matter, and of consequence only to her immediate family. In the tales an unfaithful wife, for example, is not gossiped about or watched by suspicious neighbors. In one of the three relevant cases in the tales, the husband finds out about her affair with the help of his dog and rooster, in another he hides and watches his wife and her lover, and in the third he is alerted by his nephew who lives with him. Of all possible misdeeds by a woman, only murder is a transgression that involves the larger community in the tales. Eshei, Imam Hasan's bad wife who is said to have killed Hasan, in turn is killed by members of Hasan's paternal descent group. An unfaithful wife whose lover had been killed by her husband's nephew, is (unjustly) accused of this murder and lynched by the villagers.

This seeming indifference of a community to the personal qualities of a woman stands in sharp contrast to reality. Competence in housekeeping, efficiency in dealing with husband, children, and relatives, health and the ability to work, and any unusual personal abilities are noted, frequently discussed, inevitably evaluated, and result in overall attitudes toward a woman, marked by like or dislike, respect or disregard, envy or pity, dominance or submission. A woman's personal influence—and this is about the only influence she has since women usually do not fill positions in the power hierarchy—depends largely on these factors. Scoring high on these personal qualities in the eyes of the community can somewhat balance such disadvantages as being married to a man of low esteem or being childless. In the tales these variables for assessing a woman's personal standing are not very important, because women are viewed mainly as engaged in relationships within their own families and not as part of a wider community. As was seen earlier, most of the women's roles are based on kinship. Men, on the other hand, engage in many relationships, and the effect of their personal conduct and qualities on a community larger than the immediate nuclear family is much better elaborated in the stories.

Types and Characterizations

Of the fourteen roles women assume in the tales, seven can be singled out as being well-defined types: mother, stepmother, daughter, wife, co-wife, old woman, and fairy.

Mother is the least ambiguous and most straightforwardly positive female figure in the tales, regardless of whether she is mother to a son or to a daughter. Although a mother appears twenty-seven times in the tales, only once does she carry a negative image. In "Sadat" she lets her lover persuade her to cut open her sons' stomachs to recover the magic liver eaten by them, and thus causes her sons' flight and subsequent troublesome adventures. In one version of this tale, she is mildly punished for this misdeed in the end. In another version, told by a woman in Shiraz, the repenting mother is forgiven completely by her sons in the end (Christensen 1958:121). In two other instances where a mother causes her children's sufferings, this is not even evaluated as bad. A childless woman finds all her peas turned into children, but she does not know how to clothe and feed them all. The desperate woman kills all of them but one (and regrets it later, when she realizes how great a help little Nakhodak actually is). The fact that she deprived herself of the children she might have had is seen as its own punishment for her act of panic. In the other case, Bear threatens to kill a man and a woman for an offense, and the woman decides to sacrifice their children to him, comforting herself reasonably with the proverb: "As long as a tree has its roots [parents], it will grow branches [children] again!" The children flee and work themselves through the story, but the mother is not reprimanded. She, it was interpreted, acted out of dire necessity, and must be pardoned. Otherwise, mothers are caring, loyal, cautioning, and helpful and they stand by their children whenever they can, from mother "Uncle Goat" to the dead mother of the little girl who helps her endangered daughter despite the fact that the child, persuaded by another woman, had killed her. No other character in the tales, including any male one, is as unconditionally positive as the mother.

Just as mother is all good, father's wife (there is no term for stepmother) is all bad; she is always seen acting against a stepdaughter, but not a stepson. However, she only appears three times in the stories. Once, she is punished in the end (divorced by her husband, whose daughter's death she caused), and the other two times she gets by without a reprimand. This is understandable, because a daughter or stepdaughter will usually never be in a position to take revenge on a stepmother. This would have to be done by someone standing above the woman, like her husband. But men, as is seen below, are usually reluctant to take sides in quarrels among their womenfolk, and are not depicted as really guarding the interests of their daughters.

Daughter, together with wife, is the biggest category of female actors and represents the most passive and colorless group of females in the tales. There are some exceptions to this general statement, noticeably "bad" daughters who are disobedient toward their fathers or unchaste. But as mentioned before, as long as a girl is amiably associated with her father or her brothers, she has hardly a life of her own. Daughters, given their position in the hierarchy of authority and power, have practically no rights and are totally subject to the will of their parents, especially their father and/or brothers. Thus, in the tales, a baby girl is abandoned by her father, yet he is not reprimanded. The king's daughter is married off to a cripple and she does not protest. A daughter is dragged to death by a rope around her neck—allegedly on her father's orders, which she does not question. Another is married off to an ugly pauper by her father who wanted the fun of hearing three good jokes. No criticism is made of this arrangement—it is seen as absolutely legitimate.

In the tales daughters usually appear in the transitional period between their status as daughter and their next status as wife. It is then that they get the most attention, in real life as well as in the stories, and then that they are of most concern and significance to their fathers, to whom they are potentially a great asset. Without his daughter, Prophet Noah would not have been able to build his ship, because only by promising her to the various craftsmen could he procure their help, according to the legend. As far as other aspects of utility are concerned, daughters are said in the tales to keep house, bake bread, guard the herds, help their mothers, run errands, collect wild vegetables, berries, and flowers, and milk the goats; this is quite in accordance with reality. Also reflected in the tales is the common notion that a daughter is expensive to keep, like a luxury, for as a woman, she cannot work in the fields but still needs food and relatively expensive clothing (it is considered sinful to let a woman go around in rags). Her eventual usefulness as wife and childbearer will benefit only the family of her husband. The epitomy of desperate poverty is a man who has seven blind daughters. Such misery justifies the man's lying even to the king, in order to procure money for the care of his daughters.

The least stereotyped of all female characters in the tales is wife. Wives can range from the abovementioned fairy-wife—the good wife par excellence—to mean and treacherous ones, with many shades in between. A "good" wife is one who cares well for her husband, is faithful and obedient, keeps his interests in mind, and manages her house well. Conflict in the stories usually arises when a wife falls short on one or another of these duties. Three of the stories center around an unfaithful wife; in another an unfaithful wife has a major part. In comparison, an unfaithful husband is not mentioned once in the tales. Coupled with woman's unfaithfulness is neglect of the husband and the children. In fact, according to the tales, if a husband is being scoffed at or cut short in the allotment of food, it is always an indication of a woman's diverted interests. One tale starts out describing this condition: "A woman had a good husband who worked hard, yet she gave him only rye bread, and kept the scrambled eggs for her lover."

With the exception of fairy-wives, a wife is rarely ever discussed and is never of consequence for the plot, if she is not doing something wrong. No one mentions how the wife of the man who ordered his daughter's abandonment had reacted to his order. If she had disobeyed, the story would have proceeded differently; since she had not, she had done the right thing, and there was therefore no need to mention her at all.

By far the most frequent wifely misbehavior is disobedience. Eight times in the stories the events take a dramatic turn when a woman refuses to obey her husband. Twice, both times in joke-tales, the wife wins and the husband stands there fooled. Once, the wife manages to eat the chicken that was meant for the guests, and in the other case, a man with two wives finds himself sleeping in the mosque because each refuses him a bed for the reason that he has another wife and need not bother her. In the "serious" tales, ones that are not meant to prompt laughter, such behavior has grave consequences for the plot of the story and the ultimate fate of the woman: four times she is badly harmed and twice even destroyed.

Good wives are often mentioned. Usually they are complaisant and cooperative and fade into the background as soon as their brief moment of utility is over in the story. Mullah Nasreddin orders his wife to mourn for him and to organize a mock funeral, which she does. For a short paragraph she is the focus of attention, when she screamingly alerts the village to the mullah's alleged death. As soon as the funeral is under way, however, the "dead" mullah takes over again, his scheme succeeds, and the wife is not even mentioned again. Often a wife is mentioned only as an appendage to the hero. After having divorced his unfaithful first wife, one man "married a younger and more beautiful wife and lived happily ever after." Although this wife was mentioned in the tale, her only function was to round out the story and make it clear to the listeners that the hero from now on was well taken care of.

The role of a wife is very common in the stories, but the number of "significant" wives is small. Wives are more often than not viewed in negative terms, or at least in ambiguous ones. Only in three instances has a "good" wife a major part in the action of a tale: twice as a fairy, and once as a princess who, to save her own face, bails her coward husband out of trying situations in a splendid show of loyal bravery.

Co-wife, like stepmother, has a negative image and is not very frequent in the tales. Whenever co-wives appear, they stand in adversary positions to each other, either outrightly hostile and causing each other harm, or in opposition as in "The Seven Brothers," where one of the monster's wives is described as an unbeliever who gives the heroine bad advice and the other as a true believer who calls her co-wife a liar and helps the heroine. The stereotypical animosity between co-wives in the tales is extended to their children. Children of two mothers are expected to be in noncongenial competition with one another. Wolf-girl's father disregards his son's warnings about his daughter's dangerous habits, because "they are of two mothers," and, therefore, so he thinks, the son is just jealous.

In the everyday lives of most Boir Ahmadis, co-wives are of no particular relevance since polygyny is very rare. The few known cases of unpeaceful polygynous households, however, are gleefully recorded, feeding back into the general negative attitudes toward co-wives.

Old Woman is a favorite folk character in tales, jokes, and conversation. Old Woman is poor, ugly, suspicious, greedy, untidy, plagued by rheumatism, and hungry. Most remarkably, she is usually described as fending for herself, collecting cow dung and information, trading a favor here for a favor there, matchmaking, persuading, protecting, and always keeping in mind her own interests, for an old woman cannot afford to be generous with the meager resources she has. Old Woman is made fun of, in tales as in reality, yet her knowledge, her access to a wide range of people, and her willingness to do odd little transactions on the side make her quite valuable at times. Several of the heroes in the stories owe their success to the meddling of an old woman, like Hosein who is helped to a job that brings him near his captured master, or the prince for whom the old woman abducts the eagle-girl he had fallen in love with. Old women are beyond reward or punishment; they never get reprimanded for what they are doing. Their low status, hideous looks, and precarious economic circumstances are enough punishment for any sin, people jokingly say. Any old woman should, of course, be taken care of by one of her sons—usually the youngest—especially after the death of her husband; usually they are taken care of, but this is neither carried out nor looked forward to with great eagerness. As long as she can, Old Woman will try to get by on her own.

Fairies (*peri*), finally, are the most beautiful, kind, generous, loyal, and knowledgeable women one can dream of. They are absolutely perfect and can never do wrong. This, however, does not mean that they always fare well; human husbands disregard their good advice, or they are abducted and forced to marry. They possess magical powers and bestow miraculous gifts to humble, good people in trying circumstances. These gifts range from beauty for a poor newborn baby girl to the ability to walk on water, from a magic twig that turns people into donkeys to a new penis for a mutilated man. Only once is a fairy described as somewhat capricious and even dangerous: to test her abductor and delay her unwanted marriage to a suitor who had ordered her abduction, she sends the tale's hero away on nearly impossible errands, and she finally destroys her suitor with magically inflamed milk. Subsequently she marries the hero and proves a faithful, congenial wife.

Actually there are few people who strongly believe in the existence of fairies now. For some, they merged with the concept of angels; for others, fairies are mixed with jinns, that is, they are potentially dangerous and better not discussed. As symbols, however, they stand for beauty, fairness, and kindness, and many girls' names are built around the term for fairy, like Perijan (soul of a fairy) or Perigol (fairy flower). It is this image of a fairy that is most often encountered in the tales, especially when a fairy functions as a wife to a human man. According to the tales, the only perfect wives are fairy-wives.

Relationships

In the tales a woman's relationships within her nuclear family are by far her most important and most numerous ones. Maid, neighbor, bride, and unspecified females ("woman" and "girl") very rarely have an important part in a tale. (Fairy and Old Woman are the exceptions to this statement; they are the only major female characters who do not act primarily as members of a family.)

The most frequent relationship within a family in the tales is between husband and wife. A husband is described as having to provide his wife with the necessities of life, protect her, fulfill her sexual needs, and provide her with children. A poor man cannot afford to marry at all; a rich man may have more than one wife. A husband who presents his wife with ample food and clothing fulfills a major duty, and the virtue of hard work to procure these necessities is mentioned above, as for example in two cases in which the husband even works abroad to earn a better living for his wife. Not a single man in the tales shuns this duty, and two husbands make elaborate arrangements for their wives in anticipation of their own premature deaths.

Protection, as a husband's duty, is elaborated little in the tales and only in its effects on the wife. If a woman is not protected, her predicaments are described; if she refuses protection with an act of disobedience, she inevitably gets into trouble later. Aunt Bug, for example, is warned by her husband not to go out while he is at the mill stealing some wheat. Aunt Bug disobeys, takes a walk by the river, and promptly falls into the water. Her husband rescues her from this disagreeable situation, and, so the little story ends, "from now on he kept Aunt Bug in the house and brought her everything she needed personally so that she did not have to go out again." In "Ali Pazanak" the ram warns his wife not to cut off his left horn after his death. She disobeys, cuts off the left horn, and a snake is released who forces her to marry him.

Outright neglect of the duty of protection is not considered proper behavior for a husband, but the one man who actually engages in this behavior in the tales is not reprimanded. Khanzadeh is about to give birth in the wilderness, and her husband leaves her in search of something to wrap the child in. But he falls asleep someplace, and Khanzadeh is all alone. The neglectful husband is not rebuked. Instead, fairies come to help the destitute Khanzadeh and thereby amply compensate her husband's failure. This is the only incident of this kind. Usually and much more frequently it is the husband who trustingly and faithfully provides his wife with a living, while his wife deceives him.

Sexual needs and providing a woman with children are mentioned once in the tales. One little story's main theme is a man's inability to have intercourse with his wife, who, despite good intentions on her side, becomes dissatisfied and leaves the poor man. In the end, the good fairies help the husband and thus save the marriage. Another man, whose wives are barren, brings them seven magic oranges which they eat and as a result become pregnant. Otherwise, love, sexual desires, or even attractiveness or attachment between husband and wife are rarely commented on. Youth and beauty are mentioned as desirable features in a woman, and several princes are charmed by the good looks of a poor girl, but a "good" wife is much more valued as a marriage proceeds. To be counted a good wife, a woman must be obedient, industrious, strong, compatible, amiable, and wise. A listener to a tale, in which a vain woman cleans her dirty child with a piece of bread to spare her silken kerchief and is turned into a turtle as punishment, declared with great satisfaction that the father of the now motherless child would "find the child a better mother and himself a better wife."

Division of labor between husband and wife is pronounced and accounts for great interdependency, both in reality and in the tales. Women do not work in the fields and men have no part in the milk-processing. Women do not travel, build houses, or take part in public affairs; their husbands do not bake bread or do any housekeeping. A man needs his wife to feed him, wash his clothes, and prepare his bed, just as the wife needs her husband to bring home food—particularly grain and meat—and clothing and to provide a roof over her head, whether it is a tent or a hut. A wife usually has the say in the allotment of food her husband procures, and some foods, like eggs or wild vegetables, are fully under her control. Often the man is pictured as being completely at the mercy of his wife as far as his food is concerned. As mentioned above, any deprivation he experiences in this regard in the tales is usually an indication that he has lost the favor of his wife.

A woman is obligated to feed not only her husband, her children, and herself (in that order), but also any guests her husband may invite. In the tales this fact is mentioned several times, and twice it even accounts for much excitement. Mullah Nasreddin uses the rice mash he had ordered his wife to cook to fool his guests into believing that they had very bad dysentery (he puts it into their pants while they are asleep). Another time a pregnant woman, who had longed to eat her only chicken and finally kills it, finds herself almost deprived of it by her husband's invitation to several guests. Desperate, she scares off the unwanted visitors and eats the chicken all by herself, while her perplexed husband chases after the fleeing guests.

Twice in the tales a wife finds herself in a situation where she has to do things unfit for a woman, yet she has no choice because her husband's well-being depends on these acts. The unfeminine behavior is thus excused, but in both cases she has to conceal her identity. In "Wolf-girl," the fairy, whose husband is badly in need of help that only she can provide, dresses as a man and sets out on a journey. Hasan's wife kills the dragon that her clumsy husband should have killed, to save him and herself from embarrassment, but she has to do it secretly and pretend that her husband had done it.

An ideal husband is described only in the funny story of "Aunt Bug," where the bug sets out to find herself a suitable husband, one who would not hurt her too much when he beats her up. She finds her dream in Mouse, who promises to beat her only with his soft tail. The princess in "Hasan" falls for a self-proclaimed hero, as does another princess who is attracted to her cousin, "Isa the Hero," and who, the narrator says, "wanted very much to marry him." These are the only cases in the tales in which a woman is actually described airing an opinion with regard to her future spouse. In reality, a girl is considered to act in bad taste if she does discuss her opinion publicly. Preferences on reservations on her part have to be stated very cautiously—so subtly, in fact, that in tales they are not mentioned at all.

Conflicts between husband and wife are numerous, in the tales as well as in reality. It seems, however, that unfaithfulness and gruesome aberrations like murder are quite exaggerated in the tales. (As one informant explained, peaceful coexistence alone does not make an interesting tale.) Accusations of neglect, on the other hand, hurled in both directions, are frequent. Husbands reprimand their wives for disobedience and sometimes come down hard on them—in "Sadat," the hero turns his treacherous and disobedient wife into a donkey. Wives are frustrated because their husbands disregard their advice or otherwise act in what seems to be irresponsible fashion, but, unlike their husbands, they usually are powerless to retaliate or bring about much change. "Didn't I tell you!!" the fairy can only exclaim when her husband, despite her warnings, follows through with his plan only to find himself in great misery. Nevertheless, in no case is a woman described complaining about her husband. This can be seen both as a function of the lack of interaction between women and other people in the tales and as a function of the stories' being told from a male point of view. Thus, a husband will complain about the conduct of his wife, as, for example, the man who publicly accuses his wife of adultery and announces her divorce in front of his guests, but it would be seen as improper and not quite understandable if a woman were to talk about her husband. Even in the story about the pregnant woman and her chicken, which is one of profound disapproval of a husband's conduct from beginning to end, the wife never actually airs her dissatisfaction with him. In addition, the tale is funny, as are two others in which the husband is exposed as somewhat less than ideal, and is humiliated or outwitted by his wife. Stories that depict a husband as imperfect or as unable to control his wife cannot be taken "seriously."

The relationship between father and daughter is based on essentially the same basic principles as that between husband and wife. The father cares for his daughter, protects her, and marries her off; the daughter in turn is obedient and industrious and keeps her father's honor intact. In the tales the factors of authority and obedience have priority over any others, and just as in the relationship between husband and wife, here too the man's authority has almost no limits. A father can abandon his daughter (four cases in the tales), be oblivious to her bad treatment by the stepmother (three cases), marry her off to a most unfitting suitor (four cases), or put her into a room with a dog and a donkey—both very lowly and disgusting animals—to have the animals turn into exact duplicates of the girl. A father is never reprimanded for any of these acts in either words, comments, or the actual proceedings in the tales. All these actions, lamentable as they may be (and the narrator's gestures and exclamations while telling of these happenings left no doubt that they are lamentable), are legitimate as far as a father's power is concerned. In the tales none of these acts constitutes a misuse of authority. On the other hand, whenever a daughter disobeys her father's order, she is punished, just as is a disobedient wife. An unchaste daughter is killed by her father. A girl who ate from a certain remedy against her father's will becomes pregnant. Famekhanom is instructed by her brothers, who represent the father to her, never to eat the cat's food, but she does it nevertheless; the cat takes revenge, and Famekhanom comes to great harm. A princess contradicts her father, and he marries her to a lame man.

Offensive behavior in tales is as well-defined for a daughter as it is for a wife, while a father, it seems from the stories, can never do wrong. To balance this somewhat one-sided description, it must be noted that the relationship between father and son, as pictured in the tales, is not very different from that between father and daughter in this regard, with two exceptions. Sons are not married off, but choose their own spouses, and fathers are not worried about their chastity. Otherwise, sons are expected to be as strictly obedient as daughters, and the same sanctions apply to them as to their sisters.

Once in a while (three cases), a father shows a certain tender, but aloof, interest in a daughter. Once, a father, before leaving for his journey, asks each daughter what she would like him to bring for her. What marks him as aloof, however, is that he never realizes that one of his daughters is being misused badly by her stepmother. Another father defends his daughter against the accusations of being a wolf, but he never takes enough interest to find out what really is the matter with her.

Men are especially reluctant to interfere in their daughters' or wives' relationships with other women. To meddle in women's affairs, to take sides in their quarrels, is beyond the duty and dignity of a man. Therefore, conflicts between mother and daughter or between daughters, for example, do not ordinarily warrant a man's interference.

A daughter's place is with her father until she gets married. From then on she enters her father's house mainly as a visitor, unless the arrangement with her husband does not work out. In this case she can return home again and reactivate her status as a daughter, which means that she again works for her father. The disappointed woman who had just returned to her father and was milking his goats when she learns that her husband's problems with virility had been solved, kicks over the milk pail and says, "Let's go home! Am I stupid to milk my father's goats instead of my own?!"

The relationship between brother and sister, although again characterized by dominance and submission, is described as much more cordial and intimate than between father and daughter. In three cases, brothers actually serve as mediators between the sister and the father. In "Hasan," for example, the brothers of the stubborn princess, who has her mind set on marrying the hero, successfully plead on her behalf with the father. The only conflicts between brother and sister in the tales are caused by one sister's demonic nature, for which she is not even personally blamed. In two tales, the sister is a cannibalistic wolf-girl, who eats everyone in the camp until she is overcome by her brother's magic helpers. But in both cases, the girl, despite her destructiveness, is not depicted as hostile. In one of these tales she turns into a bird after her death and helps her brother solve a riddle that makes him a rich man. In the other, the brothers, full of joy about the birth of their baby sister, refuse to follow their dying father's advice to kill the baby, who is really a wolf. "How can we kill our only sister!" they exclaim.

The brother-sister relationship can be a fictive one, proclaimed to allow a young man to live under one roof with an unrelated girl.

Brother and *sister* in this case (in reality as in the tales) mean that they will treat one another like siblings, and brother will care for his sister honestly and make no sexual advances. In this way the hero in "Sawhead" adopts seven blind orphan girls, brings them game, is fed by them with the milk of their goats, and is helped by them to overcome his enemy.

In the absence of a father, the brother becomes the main protector of a girl. Famekhanom, who has no father or other male relative, leaves her mother in search of her lost brothers. She finds and stays with them, and both parties are very satisfied with the new arrangement. Famekhanom keeps house for them, and the brothers protect her against a monster's attacks.

Brotherly concern for a sister is taken so much for granted that it can be easily misused, according to one tale. The hero's unfaithful wife, asked why she fed him only rye bread (instead of the preferred wheat bread), says that it was the bad digestion of his sister somewhere far away that turned his wheat bread into rye bread. The man takes off immediately to find out what was wrong with his sister, just as his wife had hoped he would. The man's sister's son, who in turn represents his mother's concern and goodwill for her brother, returns with his uncle to set things straight for him.

Similarly close, but much less harmonious, is the relationship between sisters. In five of the nine cases in which sisters are described, they feel animosity toward each other. This animosity ranges in expression from greed and mockery toward a poor sister to a physical fight between Sun and Moon, in the course of which Sun gets the broom over her head (and is stuck with a halo ever since), and Moon's face gets marked forever with bread dough from the hands of her sister. In "Mateti" the seven abandoned and hungry sisters cast lots among themselves to determine which will have to be killed and eaten. Mateti, who is the one chosen, begs for her life with the promise to save her sisters. The youngest sister in another tale is teased by her sisters into staying behind in the mountains where she is abducted by a jinn. The only case in which two sisters are depicted as very amicable is in "Sadat," where the hero's maternal aunt makes a point of being very nice and hospitable to her sister's sons.

In reality, sisters stereotypically do not get along well as long as they are young. The older sister is responsible for the younger ones, who often get her into conflict with the mother. The young sister resents the older because she is bossy and makes her work for her. The older sister is jealous of the younger one, who gets more attention. Such reasons are cited when quarrels between sisters are discussed. As adults, however, sisters are said and expected to be very cooperative and congenial, to visit one another, pool resources, and keep in contact as much as possible. In times of distress, a sister customarily serves as the most reliable source for comfort and support, after the mother. Because it is mostly interaction between young sisters that is elaborated in the tales, the image of sisterly unrest is the prevalent one.

Parameters of Conduct

All the characters in the tales, their intentions and actions, are painted in black and white. People are either rich or poor, good or evil, to be admired, pitied, or scorned. Rarely is the situation left ambiguous. This makes it easy to identify with a hero, and to single out the most relevant criteria for "good" and "bad" conduct.

For the judgment of anyone's behavior, the all-encompassing criteria are the degree of one's acceptance of legitimate authority and the ability to use one's own power. For a woman, this means that she is judged according to the degree of her submission to father, brother, or husband; the more virtuous and "good" she is, the easier and more readily she accepts her dependent position. Rewards for complaisance, in the tales, are usually a smooth and tension-free life—so smooth, as a matter of fact, that a good tale cannot be made out of it. But in eleven cases a "good" woman, despite her morally correct reactions toward the authority of a man, fares badly. Complaisant daughters are given into marriage to unappealing men, stolen, sacrificed to dragons, dragged to death, killed by a servant, abandoned, or deprived of food. Sorely tried women like these are pitied in the tales but never revenged.

The most outstanding and potentially dangerous power a woman has over a man is her attractiveness, and she is forbidden to misuse it. Purposely confusing a man with one's beauty, playing with him, and being vain and overly concerned with one's looks are immoral acts in the tales. To use one's attractiveness as a weapon against a man, or even only to one's own advantage, is illegitimate and will be punished harshly. Samanbar, who capitalized on her looks and made fools of young men, is transformed into a donkey and set loose with the herd. An adulteress epitomizes such a misuse of power. It is up to a woman, first of all, not to inflame a man, and second, if a man other than her own husband does show an interest in her, she is not to encourage any advances but must resist them under all circumstances. An adulterous relationship is the woman's fault, not the man's, and accordingly it is the woman who is punished for it by death or divorce. Compared with other possible misconduct, like neglect of household, mistreatment of children, laziness, or bitchiness, those connected with defiance of authority or misuse of power in dealings with men are by far the most important ones in terms of occurrence, severity of implications for the plot of the tale, and gravity of rebuke.

Beyond matters of good and bad, the tales tell us that no mortal is spared hardship on earth. Women, however, seem to have a bit less to gain and a bit more to lose than anyone else. This is symbolized in the tale of the fairy who is caught and married to a human male and who cooks dinner for his forty guests while her fairy sisters are still free and fly around as doves, and in the story of Sparrow who steals the bride at a wedding and exchanges her for the musician's voice. Now Sparrow is happy because he can sing, as is the musician who gets a wife cheaply . . . and who thinks of asking the bride?

Notes

1. Lama'e is an Iranian physician who ran a health clinic in southern Boir Ahmad and who had schoolchildren write down tales they knew.
2. The tales in this analysis are used in their original version.

Bibliography

Christensen, Arthur. *Persische Märchen*. Düsseldorf-Köln, 1958.

Friedl, Erika. "Tales from a Persian Tribe." Unpublished. Kalamazoo, Mich., 1975.

Grimm, Brüder. *Märchen der Brüder Grimm*. Berlin, 1937.

Lama'e, Manuchehr. *Farhang-i amiane-yi asha'ir-i Boir Ahmadi va Kohgiluye* (in Persian). Tehran, 1349 [1970].

33 Being Female in a Muslim Minority in China

Barbara L. K. Pillsbury

On the Far Eastern periphery of Islam, in China, live somewhere between five and twenty-five million Muslim women, a far greater number of women than the total population of many countries in the Near Eastern heartland of Islam. There are Muslims in all provinces of China and mosques in all major cities. Publications of the People's Republic of China state the number of Muslims in China today to be more than ten million; the Nationalists on Taiwan allege there were fifty million Muslims in China before 1949 and say the low figure given by the Communist leaders results from and reflects their practice of discouraging religious expression. The true figure probably lies somewhere in between; but, in either case, this is a surprisingly large population about which Westerners are relatively ignorant.

In studying about the Middle East we learn immediately that, while Islam is a dominant element of society, not all Middle Easterners are Muslims and not all Muslims live in the Middle East. Often studies of non-Muslim cultures in the Middle East or of Muslim cultures outside the Middle East afford important insights.

This essay is based on data collected during and in conjunction with more than two years' ethnographic field work (1970–1972, 1975) among the approximately twenty thousand Muslims of mainland Chinese origin now living in the island province Taiwan. I am indebted to the Muslim women of Taipei for their hospitable cooperation and to Yih-yuan Li, director of the Institute of Ethnology of Academia Sinica, for its support of my work. I am also grateful to Conrad Arensberg, Margaret Mead, and Abraham Rosman for emphasizing to me the role of food taboos in the maintenance of social and ethnic boundaries, and to Elizabeth and Claude L. Pickens, Jr., for their reading of the manuscript.

The analysis of Muslim society in China provides precisely this kind of comparative perspective.

For centuries Muslim women in China have occupied a doubly subordinate status. Not only have they occupied a subordinate status in relation to men but also, along with Muslim men, they have occupied a subordinate status in relation to the Han Chinese majority.[1] The challenge of being female in China's Muslim minority is a double one: women must seek to achieve equality with men and also, along with Muslim men, they must achieve equality with the dominant non-Muslim majority. It may well be that Muslim women in many other societies where Muslims are a minority similarly occupy a doubly subordinate status. If this is so, a case study should increase our understanding of what it means to be female in Muslim minorities elsewhere in the world as well.

There are numerous problems in trying to learn about the position of Muslim women in traditional China and in present-day Communist society in the People's Republic of China. First, the position of women in pre-Communist China has been shrouded by male-oriented writing and reporting.[2] As in Chinese society and historiography in general, women have been typically relegated, both in fact and in the minds of male writers, to the supposedly unnoteworthy positions of wife, mother, daughter, mother-in-law, and daughter-in-law. Thus, there is far less information available about women in recent history than about men. This is especially true for Muslim women who, having long been outside the cultural mainstream of the dominant society, did not generally participate in the Chinese feminist movements of the early twentieth century.

Second, actual conditions on the post-1949 Chinese mainland were for a long time shrouded in secrecy. During the first two decades of the People's Republic of China, the only sources of information available to outsiders about its Muslim population were brief notices in the Chinese press about the struggles and purging of certain Muslim leaders, and reports by a handful of official foreign Muslim journalists of allegedly brutal treatment accorded their brethren by the "atheist" Communists. Only on Taiwan has it been possible for Westerners to conduct extended research and gather any substantive amount of data about the position of Muslims in present-day China.

The Muslim Minority

China's Muslims consider themselves descended from Arab, Persian, and Turkic merchants and mercenaries who came to China, some as early as thirteen centuries ago, by one of two routes. The first was the sea route to southeast Chinese port cities such as Canton where, long before the rise of Islam in Arabia, there already existed sizeable communities of traders from southwest Asia. The second was the land route, the so-called Silk Road, across Central Asia to Chinese Turkestan and even as far east as Peking.

Chinese Muslims, like Chinese in general, are anxious to explain—even if it means inventing—the origins of their institutions and traditions. They enjoy quoting the *hadith* of the Prophet Muhammad: "Seek knowledge, even unto China." One of their favorite founding myths explains how Islam supposedly came to China about 650 A.D. when the Prophet sent his mother's brother as an ambassador to the Chinese emperor. After examining the principles of Islam and finding them in harmonious accord with those of Confucianism, the emperor allegedly gave permission for the first mosque to be built in China.[3] Chinese Muslims today say that their Arab and Persian ancestors were referred to, literally, as "barbarian guests" and that they took native Chinese wives but raised their children as Muslims.

Throughout their first seven centuries in China the Muslims continued to be regarded as foreigners and were set apart by language, dress, dietary laws, and religious custom. In Canton and other cities special Muslim neighborhoods existed where *qadi*s were responsible for maintaining law and order.[4] In many rural districts Muslims lived in separate villages called *ying* (barracks), reflecting the large numbers of Muslims in military professions.

The Chinese emperors of the Ming dynasty (1368–1644), however, sought to sinify the non-Chinese peoples in China and prohibited foreign dress and the use of foreign languages and foreign names. With the cessation of migrations to China from the Middle East and the lessening of foreign influence in general, the Muslims in China slowly began to lose their alien status. A Chinese Muslim scholar outlines the sinification that took place among Muslims of "China proper"[5] as adoption of Chinese surnames, Chinese dress, Chinese food habits (such as use of chopsticks), and Chinese local dialects in place of Arabic and Persian as their lingua franca. For approximately the next five centuries the vast majority of Muslims in China remained completely isolated from the rest of the Islamic world. By the seventeenth century, when certain Chinese Muslims visited the Middle East, they discovered that the customs of Muslims in China had diverged markedly from those of their Islamic brethren in the heartland of Islam, and they set about to initiate reforms in China. These reforms eventually did bring China's Muslims back into closer conformity with orthodox Islamic tradition; nevertheless, many of their practices and much of their way of life still reflect the many centuries of sinification and the fact that they are a minority in the society of another of the world's major cultural traditions.

Muslim Women in Chinese History

More has been written, it seems, about the horses proudly owned and ridden by Muslims in China than about Muslim women. Only two Muslim women appear to have been included in the historical records of either China or Chinese Islam, and both are there as "wives" of Chinese emperors. The earlier of the two was Ma Huang-ho, wife of the first Ming dynasty emperor, Chu Yuan-chang (1328–1398). Empress Ma had a mosque built near the imperial palace and a troop of Muslim soldiers as her bodyguard (see Gamble 1921:98). Muslims today say she had considerable influence during the reign of her emperor-husband, particularly in leading him to set forth certain laws and directives to ease the hardships endured by the Muslims in a society of pork-eating pagan Chinese.[6]

The second woman was a Muslim "princess" from Dzungaria in what is now Sinkiang province in Chinese Central Asia. She was captured during the military conquest of Yarkand and taken with other spoils to Peking to become the "little wife"—that is, a concubine—of the Ch'ing dynasty emperor, Ch'ien-lung (1711–1799). Reputedly of immense beauty, she became known as Hsiang Fei, the "Fragrant Concubine," for she reportedly emanated a natural sweet perfume. Many Chinese Muslims today state proudly that her virtue and morality surpassed even her beauty and refer to her also as "The Concubine Who Never Succumbed," who never yielded to the emperor's advances. She supposedly was exceedingly unhappy in Peking and longed for her native home. The emperor, anxious to win her favor, built a Muslim quarter south of the Winter Palace and a tower inside the palace grounds from which Hsiang Fei could view her fellow Muslims in the nearby mosque and bazaars. It is said that the emperor even built her a Turkic-style bath. Yet, Hsiang Fei could not be persuaded and, furthermore, according to Muslim accounts, always carried a sharp weapon with which to threaten suicide or otherwise stave off the emperor's advances. Finally the emperor's mother, allegedly fearing for her son's safety and in any case thinking him far too fond of this Muslim princess, forced Hsiang Fei to suicide by self-strangulation while the emperor was away on ceremonial duties (see Bredon 1922; Hummel 1943:74). Although certain stories about her are undoubtedly legendary, many Chinese Muslims today are nevertheless proud that this Muslim woman nobly refused to stoop to become the concubine of a *kafir* (infidel) emperor (see Sun 1963: chap. 27).

Muslim Women in Twentieth Century Pre-Communist Mainland China

Muslim women in pre-Communist China proper do not seem to have experienced any form of institutionalized *purdah* or confinement, although some ritual separation of the sexes did exist. Among the most remarkable developments of Islam in China were women's mosques and female religious leaders. Of Peking's thirty-six mosques, for example, three were exclusively for women. In the city of Kaifeng women's mosques constituted more than half the total—eight of fifteen (Rhodes 1921:63–64). There, as in other large cities of China, Muslim women were led in prayer and educated in Islam and Arabic by female *ahungs*.

Ahung, the term of reference and address most commonly used today by Chinese Muslims for their religious leaders and teachers, comes from the Persian *akhund* which derives from a root meaning, primarily, "to instruct." Ahungs in most of China proper seem to have both taught the basics of Islam and led the communal prayer. Males attained this status after as many as thirteen years of study under a master ahung in a school attached to a mosque. In larger Muslim communities a kind of hierarchy (first rank, second rank, and so on) existed for male ahungs. Female ahungs, however, generally had fewer years and less formal kind of training. In many cases they were wives, sisters, or daughters of the male ahungs who performed parallel functions in mosques where *juma* (Friday) congregations were almost exclusively male. Women's mosques were explicitly designated as such, while mosques where males constituted virtually the entire body of worshipers were not designated as "male mosques" but merely as "mosques" (literally, "pure-and-true temples").

Where the concentration—or perhaps religiosity—of Muslims was not great enough to support a women's mosque, women customarily prayed at home. There is evidence that women's mosques did exist, however, in the cities of Hankow, Kaifeng, Nanking, Peking, Sama (on Hainan island), Shanghai, Shenyang, Tientsin, and in Shantung and Shensi provinces.[7] Chinese Muslims explain that the existence of separate women's mosques meant only separation for the "convenience" of prayer and not segregation in any sense of purdah. Muslims of both sexes point out that it is not quite seemly for men to perform prostrations behind women and vice versa.

Further evidence that Muslim women had a definite place in

public worship is provided by the seventeenth-century *Guide to the Rites of the True Religion,* that is, Islam (Broomhall 1910:231). No exception, it declares, can be made in the five daily prayers in favor of male or female. In the transliteration into Chinese of the Arabic names of every posture and every prayer, directions are given for modifications of prayer for female worship. To many Chinese Muslims the contrast in prayer position symbolizes the difference between male and female roles in society and the home. Men are to open up and spread out during prayer by placing their hands, knees, and feet relatively far apart in each prayer posture; in traditional society men were the ones to represent the family in virtually all matters outside the home. Women, praying, are to keep their arms and legs close to their bodies, just as in their activities they were to keep to the home. Indeed, the very term by which a man refers to his wife is *nei-jen* (inside person). While a man's chief Islamic duty seems to have been representing his family in public prayer, that of a woman has been to maintain a Muslim home and raise their children and grandchildren to be good Muslim adults.

Education for Muslim women was traditionally limited to the home and to women's mosques where they existed. Female ahungs in these mosques gave girls and women basically the same instruction in Islam as Muslim boys and young men received from male ahungs in the male-attended mosques, with the exception that girls generally received less intensive instruction and did not continue their studies as many years as did their male counterparts.

For both sexes this included the fundamentals of Islam as well as "Muslim language"—Arabic of the Quran and in some cases, Persian. In neither case did it include instruction in Chinese, which most Muslims of this period were neither able nor wanted to read or write. Muslims generally did not compete in the Chinese civil service examination system which embodied the main mode of education in China for centuries until its abolition in 1905. Until then, the Muslims, with their own mosque schools, remained outside the cultural and educational mainstream of the Chinese.

Only when the Chinese themselves began pushing for educational reforms did the Muslims ever so slowly start to establish "modern" schools, that is, schools offering a secular curriculum based on the European and American model. It appears that resistance on the part of the traditional sector of the Muslim population was directed not so much against education for Muslim women as against Muslim women and men alike "betraying the faith" by studying the written characters and culture of the idolatrous, pork-eating—

and, thus, somehow intrinsically inferior—Chinese. Despite initial resistance, Muslim schools were founded where girls as well as boys studied Chinese language, literature, history, and geography in addition to Islamic doctrine and Arabic. By the 1930s Muslim girls throughout China were attending schools on all levels, the most advanced of the Muslim "new curriculum" schools being the Ch'eng Ta Islamic Normal School for teacher training in Peking.

As for the economic position of Muslim women, few were employed outside the home prior to the mid-twentieth century. If they were, it has not been recorded. Training young Muslim women for secular teaching positions has been a modern development.

Chinese Muslim writers have often emphasized that it is the duty of women to maintain a "good Muslim household," as in a recent article, "I Remember Old Grandmother" (Hui-o 1970). This does not mean simply cooking and washing clothes, but responsibility for perpetuating and socializing children in the Muslim way of life. First and foremost in China, this implies preparing and eating "clean" or pork-free foods. Along with the "cleanliness" of food consumed goes cleanliness of home and self. Western observers have frequently commented that Muslim women "are a hardworking people and, compared with their Chinese sisters, are cleaner in their homes and also in dress" (Christie 1923:410). Also part of maintaining a Chinese Muslim household is the ready provision of hospitality, that is, food and accommodations to other Muslims who are traveling or otherwise away from home and who would in the absence of hospitality be obliged to patronize inns and restaurants where pork is served. This is one of the "inner meanings," say Chinese Muslims, of their most frequently quoted expression: "All Muslims under heaven are one family."

Reports conflict as to how extensively Muslims adopted the economically counterproductive Chinese custom of binding the feet of women. Many people, Muslim and non-Muslim alike, state they did not. One piece of "evidence" cited to "prove" that the empress Ma Huang-ho (mentioned above) was Muslim is that she had "big feet"—that is, natural feet. "Muslim women never had bound feet," numerous Muslim women insisted to me. "What other reason could explain why the wife of an emperor did not have dainty little bound feet?" Some writers say that if a Muslim woman's feet were bound, it was only loosely as token accommodation to the dominant Chinese tradition, or that, after death, relatives would "unbind, attempt to straighten, and put on stockings to cover the distorted feet in order to deceive Allah" (Botham 1926:172, 1938:360). Perhaps the best evidence that at least some Muslims in recent times did bind their daughters' feet is the fact that numerous Muslim women who are today in their sixties or older have "let-go bound feet"—feet distorted to about two inches shorter than normal by having once been bound before the practice fell into universal disfavor throughout China.

There are interesting parallels between binding the feet of women in China and the veiling of women in the Middle East.[8] Both practices were originally a sign of relatively high socioeconomic status in that they prevented a woman from performing arduous physical labor. According to Patai (1962:117), "The higher the social class to which the urban woman belonged the greater was the strictness with which she observed the rules of veiling." Actually, he says, "veiling was a mark of class distinction rather than a mere Muslim religious tradition." In China footbinding was first practiced by upper-class women but later became general. Only a pauper, obliged to preserve his daughter's ability to work, would not have her feet bound. According to sinologist Olga Lang (1946:45–46), "Bound feet kept women at home, made them safer, less movable property." This further parallels a statement by a Muslim author from North Africa about the *harem* as the place where a man kept his most respected and cherished possession—his wife—honoring her by protecting and sheltering her "like a precious, idle princess" (Djebar 1961:13).

Chinese Muslims who now live on Taiwan divide their map of China into three parts: China proper, where Muslims are a minority and most sinified; Sinkiang Province where over 90 percent of the population is Muslim, chiefly of Turkic stock and tradition; and the northwest (the provinces of Chinghai, Kansu, Ningsia, and Shensi) which lies between China proper and Sinkiang both geographically and in terms of "Muslimness" versus "Chineseness." According to the Muslims and to foreigners long resident in China, it appears that only in Sinkiang and the northwest, where conditions most approximated those of the Middle East, was there any form of veiling among Muslim women. Even then, in the northwest, the head covering was not a veil which could be used to cover the face but rather a hood which concealed all the hair while snugly rimming and exposing the face (somewhat like the traditional headwear of Roman Catholic nuns). Some Chinese Muslims point out that the Quran requires that not the face but the neck be covered. It seems that these hoods were most commonly worn by middle- and upper-class women when out in public and that they were most often white.[9]

In social relationships it appears that the greatest restriction on

Muslim women in China was not in the form of seclusion from men but rather derived from social boundaries between themselves and the non-Muslim Chinese. These boundaries have resulted in Muslim women in general being more confined to their homes than either Muslim men or non-Muslim women.

The chief reason for such boundaries and confinement has been the Muslim avoidance of pork, the most favored meat of the Chinese and the fat of which has been the standard cooking oil in all Chinese homes and restaurants. In most of the Middle East, where few pigs are even raised, the Islamic injunction against pork is of almost no consequence in daily social interaction. But in China, where pigs have been kept in virtually all Chinese farm homes as the chief source of fertilizer—and called for this reason in the official press a "national treasure"—and where, until recently, nearly all foods have been prepared in or otherwise polluted by lard, avoidance of the pig and its by-products has become the chief distinguishing mark of a Muslim and the major hindrance to comfortable relationships with the dominant Chinese society. Eating is a social exchange fundamental to social life in China. To issue invitations back and forth for meals is virtually indispensable to establishing and maintaining friendly relationships. Seldom does one enter a Chinese or Muslim home without being offered food or drink. But to exchange food and drink it is necessary to eat the same food. Muslims and Chinese do not. Muslim food is "clean" (*kan-ching*) ; Chinese food is "unclean." Among themselves the Muslims also use the Arabic word *halal* for food and kitchens that are in accord with Islamic dietary injunctions, just as the word *kosher* indicates food adhering to Judaic restrictions.[10]

Many Western observers have commented that the Muslim woman's social circle is limited and narrower than that of the Chinese woman (see, for example, Hutson 1920:260) . The pork taboo clearly seems to have been the major limiting factor, particularly in communities where Muslims were not numerous. One non-Muslim woman, for example, comments about a Chinese Muslim woman who used to visit "but never ate our food, or even drank our tea. She lived about fifteen miles from our city, and brought with her her own teapot and made her own tea, and ate her own bread" (Christie 1923:410) .

Muslim women say their social circles were much more limited in general than those of Muslim men whose business dealings brought them in greater contact with society at large. A social survey of Peking similarly concluded that since the Muslims "are unwilling to eat with those who are not of their faith, their religion is something of a barrier to social relationships, but it does not seem to interfere with business" (Gamble 1921:98–99). Relatively few women, however, engaged in business.

Marriage for a Muslim woman—as for her Chinese counterpart—was typically arranged by parents or some third party such as the ahung. Only rarely, however, was her husband-to-be a stranger, for most Muslims lived together in the same neighborhood or along the same street of a city or in the same section of a village and were acquainted from childhood. Criteria for a marriage partner differed from those of the Middle East as well as from those of the non-Muslim Chinese. Most Chinese Muslim women have never heard of such a thing as a marriage *preference* for their patrilateral parallel cousins (their father's brother's sons), the traditional ideal in much of the Middle East. Among Chinese, on the other hand, the ideal husband for a girl was her matrilateral cross-cousin (father's sister's son) and under no circumstance should she marry a man with the same surname as hers—a principle exactly opposed to that of the Middle East. Chinese Muslims, however, say such concerns were not important in selecting a husband for their daughters. What mattered was for the daughter to marry into a "good Muslim household," where the prospective son-in-law and his parents were all "good Muslims." This means not so much rigid adherence to Islamic duties of prayer, fasting, pilgrimage, or *zakat* as it does not eating pork, not worshiping idols or ancestors, and being a good person in general—one who is kind toward and provides for one's family.[11]

It was frowned upon and not common for a Muslim girl to marry out of the faith—that is, into a household of idol-worshiping, pork-eating Chinese pagans. Chinese girls, however, could and occasionally did marry into Muslim households, first undergoing a conversion ritual which is reported in many cases to have been less the spiritual acceptance of Islam than a physical process of purification—externally by baths and internally by drinking hot or alkaline water. The marrying in of Chinese wives is regarded by some as one of the chief reasons for the early expansion of Islam in China.

As for polygyny and divorce, there is little evidence to show that a Muslim woman of China proper had to share her husband with other wives and none indicating that she could be divorced by simple repudiation by her husband. In these regards Chinese Muslims seem to have been considerably influenced by Chinese attitudes and practices. According to Muslims from various parts of China, a childless Muslim couple usually adopted children rather than proclaiming the first wife barren and seeking a second wife for the husband. In fact, large-scale adoption by Muslims of non-Muslim children, particularly in times of famine, has been cited as another major factor in the historical growth of the Muslim population in China. In Sinkiang and the northwest, however, where conditions more closely approximated those of the Middle East, Muslim women did find themselves co-wives of wealthier men, and they could be divorced by repudiation.

The Chinese government made polygyny and concubinage illegal for all Chinese during the early 1900s. It seems, however, that laws were easier to make than to enforce and that the majority of Muslims continued to follow traditional patterns.

Since the Chinese mainland came under Communist control in 1949, changes in the lives of Chinese Muslim women have taken two separate courses depending on whether they stayed on the Communist mainland or fled as refugees to the island of Taiwan, the Republic of China or so-called "Free China." In both cases, however, they have been similarly obliged to leave their local Muslim communities and enter into the dominant Chinese society.

Muslim Women in the People's Republic of China

What is known about Muslims in mainland China today derives almost exclusively from the official Communist press and from reports of visiting foreign Muslims who, in many cases, have seen only what the government wanted them to see. Peking publications state that there are approximately ten million Muslims in China belonging to approximately eleven different ethnic groups. These are called "minority nationalities" or "national minorities," a fact reflecting the Soviet influence on the early Chinese Communist minority and religious policies. Largest of the eleven and said to number about four million are the Hui, usually translated into English as simply "Chinese Muslims." These are the Muslims of China proper who are most sinified, who speak Chinese, and who look in most cases like Chinese. Second largest are the Uighurs of Sinkiang, said to number almost four million. The others are, in order of decreasing size: Tuchia, Kazakh, Tunghsiang, Kirghiz, Salar, Tadjik, Uzbek, Paoan, and Tatar.[12]

Very little of this information concerns Muslim women in particular. Yet it is possible to hypothesize about their position in the People's Republic by patching together data on Chinese women in general (such as receiving eight weeks' paid maternity leave) with data on China's minorities in general and the Muslim minorities in particular.

The Chinese leadership has long been engaged in a carefully coordinated program of research, education, and political development among the minorities, including the extension of a certain amount of local autonomy in regions where minorities are concentrated. The motivation for this is summarized in an official publication that is distributed internationally in Arabic and other languages. According to *China Reconstructs* (1972:8),

> The purpose of national regional autonomy is to guarantee political equality for the national minorities and to give special consideration to the characteristics of the minority areas so that the policies and principles of the Party and government can be implemented more effectively. It also aims to give full scope to the minority people's initiative in participation in state life and the building of socialism, and to accelerate socialist revolution and construction in the minority areas. It is a necessary measure for promoting solidarity among the nationalities [and] consolidating the unity of the country.

"Special consideration" has been based on the leadership's appraisal of most of the minorities as lagging behind the Han Chinese in terms of "social development" and its consequent desire that they "make faster-than-average progress and catch up with the rest of the country." This necessitates a delicate balancing of encouragement and restraint on the part of the leadership, for it does not want to impede the process by pushing too hard and thereby inciting the minorities to opposition and rebellion, as occurred during the early years of the People's Republic. As a result, special health, educational, and social welfare programs have been implemented in the minority areas on the one hand, while on the other hand the minorities have been exempted from the nation's rapid schedule for land reform and are not obliged to adhere strictly to the nation's birth control programs.

Most of what has appeared in the Chinese press about Muslim women in particular has been limited almost exclusively to photographs and their captions. One, for instance, shows women praying in a Peking mosque wearing the white hoods mentioned above. Another shows a female clerk in the Ningsia Muslim Autonomous Region selling these white hoods—referred to in the caption as "national minority goods"—to another woman. Readers are told that Muslim girls, like boys, no longer get any education in the mosques but attend "Chinese schools" for their general education while receiving religious education at home.

Most Muslim women still marry within the Muslim community, according to some of its government-approved spokesmen (Whitehead 1971). Interviews with the leader of an Egyptian delegation to China and with Chinese Communist officials in 1973 and 1975 reveal that Islamic pork-free restaurants are still numerous in major cities and that many factories similarly provide pork-free and ritually pure food for their Muslim workers. These facts indicate that many Muslim women continue to bear the burden of maintaining Muslim kitchens in their homes and Muslim food habits in their children, or else must deal with rejection of those habits by children who are taught that many such religious practices are superstitions to be cast aside in the striving for the ultimate Communist society.

There is one item of unusual length, however, relating to Chinese Muslim women. This is an intriguing sixteen-page account titled "Mother of the Muslim People," which is summarized as follows:

> After the Lukouch'iao Incident in July 1937, the CCP [Chinese Communist Party] selected Ma Pen-chai to serve as leader of his fellow Muslims of Hopeh in the struggle against the Japanese. Accordingly, Ma led Muslim units attached to the 8th Route Army. After repeated attempts to defeat these Muslim units in battle, the Japanese and their Chinese puppets endeavored to blackmail him into surrender by capturing his 68-year-old mother and threatening her life. As both a filial son and a patriot, Ma's conscience was wracked by not knowing whether to put his mother's life above his country's interests. However, the mother put herself squarely on the side of the country and refused to capitulate to any of the various stratagems of the Japanese and the traitorous Chinese in their employ. The price of the patriotism was arrest, imprisonment, and execution; the reward was elevation to the status of "martyr" of the Muslim and Chinese people (Ch'en 1968:87).

This noteworthy account raises several interesting questions about which one can only speculate. One is the question of just who elevated this Muslim mother to martyr-hero status. Was it the Muslims themselves who first regarded her a hero and whose sentiments were given recognition by the Chinese Communist leadership? Or was it the Chinese leaders, anxious that both women and minorities should be active in and loyal to the new socialist state, who decided to create and hold up to the Muslims the example of one of their own people in order to inspire their allegiance to China's new society?

A second intriguing question stems from the fact that, traditionally, many Chinese taunted and mocked the Muslims for not eating pork and alleged the reason why was that their mother—that is, the apical ancestor from whom all Chinese Muslims are descended—was none other than a pig. During the first half of this century certain stories in the Chinese press about Muslims' being decended from a female pig resulted in numerous cases of civil disorder with irate Muslims smashing or setting afire bookstores, for instance, or forcing the offending periodicals out of publication. Perhaps, then, it was also to put an end to all the pig-mother stories—a gesture which would certainly please the Muslims—that the Communist leaders may have created the model of this imitable Muslim martyr-mother.

Muslim Women on Taiwan

Muslim women on Taiwan[13] who grew up on the Chinese mainland say the difference between themselves and women of the Chinese majority has little to do with the stereotypes of purdah and polygyny that became familiar in China following the adoption of Western-type education and its stereotyping of the Middle East. Instead, the main differences can ultimately be traced back to "dietary matters." This, in the phraseology of Chinese Islam, means none other than the avoidance of pork, an avoidance that has long stigmatized the Chinese Muslims and made them victims of mockery and insult.

"We Muslim women have one responsibility extra—but it is a major responsibility that complicates our lives in all regards," explains the mother of seven children who also cares during the day for the son of another Muslim family and has taken into her home a Muslim man who is without family. The responsibility means, first, providing halal—"clean"—food at home. This necessitates greater expenditure of time (for traveling by crowded city bus to the Muslim butcher shops instead of walking to the neighborhood market) and of money (since beef from cattle slaughtered according to Islam costs anywhere from about 10 to 100 percent more than either pork or "unclean" beef). Next it means ascertaining that family members will not need or be tempted to eat "unclean" food when "outside in society." This involves preparing lunches to be carried to work or school, but it moreover necessitates the arduous task—typically assigned to women—of educating the children to abide by Islamic restrictions and to reject all acquaintances, classmates, and social situations that would result in eating "unclean" food.

This latter aspect of the responsibility weighs particularly heavily for the large number of Muslims on Taiwan who believe their people to be facing forced absorption on the Communist mainland and gradual assimilation in the rapidly industrializing and Westernizing environment on Taiwan with its concomitant pressures to secularize that daily challenge their children. Mothers believe that if they have not adequately educated their children in the basics of Islam—and this becomes increasingly difficult given Taiwan's highly competitive and time-demanding public educational system—then they will marry out of the faith and fail to raise the next generation as practicing Muslims.

It is this set of factors that Muslim women say results in their being more confined to the home than are Chinese women in general. Many young Muslim mothers describe having reluctantly quit jobs they enjoyed because they or their husbands felt they were neglecting their "responsibility." But also influencing these decisions has been the fact that many women—more so than men—feel embarrassed and stigmatized whenever their dietary habits impinge on collegial lunches and socializing with Chinese co-workers, who tend to regard anyone who avoids pork as somewhat peculiar. If their families can make do without the extra income, then young Muslim mothers may well stop working "outside" and concentrate their energies in the home. The majority of Muslim women clearly feel it is the pork-eating society outside that confines them far more than do Muslim men per se.

Muslim women say the major changes the move from the mainland to Taiwan has brought are, first, living scattered about among non-Muslims; second, going to the mosque together with the men of the family; third, working outside the home for pay where the majority of co-workers and customers are not Muslim; fourth, seeing their children or grandchildren pass through the Chinese educational system, together with Chinese classmates, in many cases even through graduate school; and fifth, seeing some of those same children or grandchildren, who now desire to "marry for love," choose non-Muslim marriage partners.

The approximately twenty thousand Muslims on Taiwan do indeed live more dispersed than on the mainland, where many if not most resided in all-Muslim neighborhoods. In the mainland city of Sian, for example, these were even separated from surrounding Chinese residences by large gates that were closed at night (Thor 1918:35) . In the past each day was full of opportunities for Muslim women to chat and visit with one another, for, they say, their neighborhoods—even in large cities like Peking—had the intimacy of small Muslim villages. Now the women they meet on their streets and on their daily marketing rounds are not Muslims but pork-eating Chinese with whom they—out of habit—are not inclined to enter into friendships. Some women report that just after arriving in Taiwan they lived as far as twelve hours away from the nearest Muslim household.

The fact that Muslim women live so dispersed that their daily routines no longer provide them with opportunities to meet perhaps explains why so many, especially the older women, place such emphasis on being able to go to the mosques with the men. Taiwan's five mosques are regarded as meeting places where Muslims can congregate and stay in touch with one another. Taipei Muslim families have even shown a marked tendency over the past twenty-five years to move in closer to the city's two mosques (not far from which are also located the Muslim butcher shops). Women are still outnumbered at Friday prayer, but they are nevertheless there alongside the men and value the fact that custom now permits them to participate when they want.

Indeed, they are literally alongside the men during prayer at the large new Arabic-style Taipei Mosque, women to the left of a green curtain, men on the right. Or they are in rows behind, or on a special upstairs balcony which the ahung of the Taipei Culture Mosque takes great pride in having built for them. This separation, according to Muslims of both sexes, permits women to participate in public prayer without having to perform the prostrations "in front of the eyes of men." It also permits them to chat together and exchange the latest news and gossip—even during the ahung's sermon—about a new job or grandchild, a wedding or a funeral, travel or illness, the educational achievements of their children, and so on.

There are no women's mosques and no female ahungs on Taiwan but there are two organizations whose members are all women. These are the Chinese Muslim Women's Association and the Shih Niang (meaning something like "knowledgeable women"). This latter group exists primarily for the purpose of preparing for Islamic burial the bodies of deceased Muslim women.[14] Neither organization is autonomous but exists as a subgroup within two larger organizations (the Chinese Muslim Youth League and the Chinese Muslim Association, respectively) in which both women and men are members but which men dominate.[15]

The third difference cited above between life on the mainland and on Taiwan concerns Muslim women's employment outside the home. Life for most families in the early years after arrival on Taiwan was a scramble for survival that forced many women to seek ways of augmenting family income. Quite a few opened small restaurants or food stalls where they sold dishes typical to their native place. This is not surprising, for throughout China the

Muslims' special dietary restrictions have led them to specialize occupationally in food-related enterprises such as running restaurants and inns.

By about a decade later the more elderly among these women had returned to their traditional responsibilities of maintaining a good Muslim household. The settling-in process had been completed, their husbands or sons had found relatively steady sources of income, and children had been born to many of their families. The younger of these women, however, and particularly those whose children could be cared for by other family members, sought to remain in the labor force. Muslim female high school and university students look forward to working after graduation, and many who stop working to have children return to work as soon as the children can be left with a family member or another Muslim or be sent off to school.

The position of the woman in Muslim families on Taiwan continues to differ from that of Chinese women in general. Anthropologist Norma Diamond writes that Chinese women of Taiwan's urban middle class are backsliding and tend to be less educated and more satisfied by purely domestic roles than were their own more liberated mothers and even grandmothers (1973:212). Despite the complications mentioned above, this does not seem to be the case with the Muslim women for whom Chinese education has only relatively recently become more customary and available. This is illustrated by the stories of women of two Muslim families in Taiwan, taken from my own research.

Khadija Yang and her husband are both in their forties. They live comfortably in an apartment above a jewelry store in bustling downtown Taipei. Khadija's father, Abdul-Rahman, who has just proudly celebrated his eightieth birthday, lives with them. He was a jade merchant in Peking, a profession passed down from his ancestors who, according to family legend, had long dealt in the gems which passed between China and the Middle East via camel caravans of the Central Asian silk route. Both Khadija's parents were always very religious. Her mother, who died several years ago, was born at the turn of the century. She studied Islam and Arabic a few hours per week over a period of about ten years. She was able to read and write some phrases in Arabic but knew no Chinese characters. Khadija, born in 1925, attended a "Light of Islam" new curriculum Muslim junior high school and went on to graduate from a Chinese high school where a full "Chinese curriculum" was taught. Today she and her husband run the jewelry store owned by her father. When I last spoke with her she had just returned from an Asian trade fair in Malaysia at which she represented a Taiwan handicrafts export group. Her eldest daughter, Jemaileh, was at that time a university senior studying business administration and has since come to the United States for graduate school.

Amina Tieh, in her early thirties, lives with her husband, their two sons, ages four and six, and Mr. Tieh's seventy-year-old widowed mother. Amina's own mother completed a "pure-and-true" new-curriculum Muslim primary school where she learned to read and write Chinese characters. With her husband, an army general, she lived in Taipei until 1962 when they decided to retreat from city and military life. They now live in a little bamboo and thatch house forty-five minutes' hike up a mountain, where both work hard raising some eight hundred sheep and two hundred cattle. Amina took business courses at a vocational school after graduating from one of Taipei's best high schools. Some Muslims say they are traditionally more gifted at foreign languages than the Chinese. Amina speaks very good English and worked as an English-language secretary for an import-export firm before leaving work to have children. She would have liked to have had a girl but she was one of four children and her husband one of eight and she feels two is enough. When her second child was two years old she went back to work, leaving the children in the care of her mother-in-law and, alternately, her father's unmarried younger sister, age sixty-four. She is now a merchandise buyer for United States firms that export clothing from Taiwan and has made one business trip to the United States. It appears she is more steadily employed than her husband.

The trend toward more education and outside employment indicated by the three generations of women in these two Muslim families appears to be typical. Few if any Muslim women have had less education than their mothers, a bold contrast to the patterns described by Diamond for Chinese women. Most Muslim women today know less Arabic, however, than do their mothers. Arabic is taught, somewhat irregularly, in the mosques and is also offered as a regular course of instruction at Chengchi University, but few women "have time" to study it seriously. Two Muslim women, in contrast to numerous Muslim men, occupy high-level government posts; they are members of the Legislative Yuan and National Assembly, to which they were elected in the late 1940s.

In selection of a husband there are two prime differences from pre-1949 mainland customs. The first is the question of who selects the husband and the second is the fact that he might not be Muslim. Fewer Muslim women than men went to Taiwan in 1949. This was because many soldiers of lower rank had left their families behind, believing they would return to them in a matter of months.

Muslim women, however, went to Taiwan as members of families that lived close enough to the coast or were otherwise wealthy enough to afford the journey, or they were wives and daughters of government officials and military officers. Because of the shortage of Muslim women, many Muslim males eventually married Taiwanese women who converted, at least nominally, to Islam. Others waited for years until Muslim girls many years their junior were old enough to marry.

Traditionally, Muslim and Chinese marriages alike were arranged by parents or a third party. The modern ideal that Chinese young people have adopted from the West is "marriage for love," or selection of one's own mate. Marriage patterns on Taiwan represent permutations of the two. In urban Taipei it is generally true that, while a Muslim or Chinese girl may single out a partner on the supposed basis of love, her selection is still largely determined not by love but by the same traditional criteria that would have influenced her parents' decision had they been arranging the match. Such criteria include the proposed husband's health and "purity," appearance, adherence to niceties of Chinese etiquette, level of education and schools attended, and prospects for future employment (O'Hara 1962:64). For Muslims traditionally, and for conservative Muslims today, however, the criterion of being Muslim takes precedence over all the above.

Among young, not-yet-married Muslim women today, two attitudes can be discerned. Those of more religious background appear hopeful that from the circle of unmarried Muslim young men they will find one with whom they fall in love. Those of less religious background generally hope that the one with whom they fall in love will be Muslim or at least willing to convert and act sufficiently like a Muslim to receive parental approval. Hoping to satisfy both their own criteria as well as their parents' number one criterion of Islamic religiosity, Muslim women tend to marry later than other women on Taiwan. Some, as in the following example taken from my research, have not married at all.

Aisha Ma is thirty-nine years old and unmarried. At the university she met and began to fall in love with a non-Muslim boy. Her mother, opposed to such a husband for her daughter, suggested Aisha continue her education at a graduate school in Turkey where she would have Muslims rather than Chinese as classmates and thus more opportunity to fall in love with a Muslim. Aisha received a doctorate from the University of Istanbul but found no one to marry there. Upon return to Taiwan, she submitted to parental desires to have the ahung serve as matchmaker to find Aisha a Muslim husband. He presented numerous candidates including several retired soldiers at least twenty years older than Aisha. She was, by this time, however, too educated for any of them, for none of them had even a college diploma, and so she refused them all causing embarrassment to her mother and great loss of face to the ahung. Aisha now calls herself a "sacrifice to Islam," too educated either to accept any available Muslim man or to be satisfied in her present mediocre civil-service job and feeling confined by her limited social circles.

Aisha's case is by no means typical but it does illustrate, nevertheless, several common problems. Being female in a minority is for Aisha and many other upwardly aspirant young Muslim women too limiting in scope and opportunity. Not only do they feel disadvantaged relative to the dominant majority but they also feel dominated by men within the minority. It is the subordination to the dominant majority, however, rather than any subordination by Muslim men in the form of purdah or other strict confinement, that seems fraught with greater frustrations for the women in this Chinese Muslim minority.

Notes

1. *Chinese* as used throughout this paper refers to *Han* Chinese (those who are ethnically Chinese), and to their traditions, language, and so on. Despite a high degree of acculturation, Muslims in China consider themselves ethnically different and separate from the Han Chinese. Although they admit today that they are Chinese by citizenship, they generally continue to follow the traditional usage calling themselves *Muslim* rather than *Chinese*. See Pillsbury (1973:63–79, 1975) for fuller discussion of Chinese Muslim ethnicity.

2. This parallels somewhat traditional Chinese genealogy-keeping. Given the patrilineal social structure, women were not considered permanent members of their natal families and their names were therefore not recorded in their natal families' genealogies. In general, only after giving birth to a son was a woman recorded as having existed—by being written into her husband's family's genealogy as his wife.

3. Some Chinese Muslim traditions say the Prophet's mother's brother appeared to the emperor in a dream. Others, some inscribed in stone even, equate him with the Prophet's companion Sa'ad Ibn Abi Wakkas whose alleged "tomb" still stands in Canton (recently repaired and proclaimed as his tomb by the Chinese government), despite the fact that he never really traveled to China. The *Encyclopedia of Islam* emphasizes that the Chinese official dynastic histories are—like the unofficial accounts of the Chinese Muslims—full of legendary matter, "profoundly influenced by national pride and compiled with the usual Chinese lack of critical judg-

ment" (Hartmann 1913–34:840). Arabic sources, which provide an important check on the Chinese, are quite silent about many of these legends handed down in Chinese Islam.

4. The arrangement was similar to that underlying the *millet* system of the Ottoman Empire, with the difference being, of course, that in China Muslims were the minority rather than the majority.

5. *China proper* (*nei-ti*) is the expression Chinese Muslims use to designate all of China except the provinces where there is a high concentration of Muslims, namely Sinkiang (formerly called Chinese Turkestan) and those of "the northwest"—Chinghai, Kansu, Ningsia, and Shensi.

6. According to Haji Hikmet Ma Ming-dao, a Chinese Muslim professor of Turkish in the Department of Oriental Languages at Chengchi University in Taiwan, Chu Yuan-chang respected the Islamic pork taboo and ordered Chinese living in the vicinity of Muslims to abstain from raising pigs. He also promulgated a law—very possibly out of respect for the Islamic injunction against alcohol—stating that drunkenness would be severely punished. He maintained a Muslim kitchen in the palace in which all food was prepared according to Islamic dietary law, and had Quranic excerpts inscribed in prominent places in the imperial buildings. It remains to be determined, however, just how much of the emperor's sympathy with Muslim concerns was inspired by his wife rather than by the numerous Muslim men (such as Mu Yin) who also had influence with him (Claude L. Pickens, Jr., personal communication of July 12, 1974).

Certain Chinese Muslim scholars believe that the emperor may very well have been a Muslim himself but chose to "forget" this fact in order to advance his career in the dominant non-Muslim society. Among other arguments that support this hypothesis, Haji Hikmet points to the fact that it has traditionally been unusual for a Muslim woman to marry an idolatrous, pork-eating Chinese.

7. According to Pickens, who spent nearly three decades among the Chinese Muslims, women's mosques were a phenomenon of China proper. He recalls seeing none in northwest China, although he explains he was not specifically looking for them (personal communication of July 12, 1974).

8. These two practices appear to have met head on in northwest China where, in contrast to China proper, Muslims were dominant and some veiling did occur.

9. Pickens considers that black hoods were more commonly worn in public and reports that brides wore green hoods (personal communications of July 12 and September 28, 1974). This may reflect the great regional variation that has existed in Muslim practices in China.

10. Indeed, because the two dietary codes are so similar, Chinese Muslims visiting Europe and the United States know they are to seek out kosher restaurants and grocery stores which, in the absence of Muslim provisions, are also halal. In many ways, in fact, the position of Muslims in Chinese society parallels that of Jews in Europe and the United States. Largely because of the Muslims' high degree of acculturation, opinions

in China always differ as to whether they constitute a separate "race" or are merely people with a separate religion.

11. Some influences of Chinese ethics on Muslim attitudes toward marriage are outlined in the article, "A Chinese View of Mohammed's Marriages" (Mason 1921), based on a study of the life of the Prophet from Chinese sources.

12. Numbers of persons in each minority are given in official publications (such as *Nationalities in China,* 1961) as follows:

Hui	3,934,335	Salar	31,923
Uighur	3,901,205	Tadjik	15,014
Tuchia	603,773	Uzbek	11,557
Kazakh	553,160	Pao-an	5,516
Tunghsiang	159,345	Tatar	4,370
Kirghiz	68,862		

13. This information is based on interviews with women in 126 Muslim households on Taiwan. For further details, see Pillsbury (1973).

14. Virtually all Muslim funerals take place in the mosque, with burial in a Muslim cemetery. Chinese funeral parlors are scorned and avoided as infidels' places where the deceased is subjected to practices akin to idol-worship.

15. One might hypothesize that these women's groups exist within the larger male-dominated organizations simply to give women a chance to play a role. This is certainly true to a degree, as is also the case with two similar subgroups for young people. Another important factor, however, is that they in this way avoid the troublesome registration with the Ministry of the Interior which is required of all organizations and which their parent umbrella organizations have already carried out.

Bibliography

Bredon, Juliet. *Peking: A Historical and Intimate Description of its Chief Places of Interest.* Shanghai, 1922.

Botham, Olive. "Moslem Women of China." *Moslem World,* 16 (1926): 172–175.

———. "Moslem Women of China." *Moslem World,* 28 (1938): 360–364.

Broomhall, Marshall. *Islam in China: A Neglected Problem.* New York, 1966 (reprint).

Ch'en Ch'ing-po. "The Mother of the Moslem People." In *The Red Flag Waves: A Guide to the Hung-ch'i P'iao-p'iao Collection,* ed. Robert Rinden and Roxane Witke. Center for Chinese Studies Research Monograph, no. 3. Berkeley, 1968.

Ch'en Pao Fu K'an. *Hui-chiao Min-tsu Fu-nu Wen-t'i.* March 12, 28, 1925.

China Welfare Institute. "About National Minorities in China." *China Reconstructs,* 21 (1972):6–9, 37.

Christie, Mrs. William. "Moslem Women of Kansu." *Moslem World,* 13 (1923):410.

Diamond, Norma. "The Status of Women in Taiwan: One Step Forward, Two Steps Back." In *Women in China: Studies in Social Change and Feminism,* ed. Marilyn Young. Ann Arbor, Mich., 1973.

Djebar, Assia. *Women of Islam.* London, 1961.

Farjenel, F. "Extraits de 'Mispao' de Peking du 9 de la troisième lune: une dame sollicite un titre de noblesse." *Revue du monde musulman,* 3 (1907) :618.

Gamble, Sidney. *Peking: A Social Survey.* New York, 1921.

Hartmann, Martin. "China." In *The Encyclopedia of Islam,* ed. H. A. R. Gibb et al. Leiden, 1913–1934.

Hui-o, Wang. "Huai-nien Lao Nai-nai." *Chung-Kuo Hui-chiao,* 137 (1970) :19.

Hummel, Arthur W., ed. *Eminent Chinese of the Ch'ing Period.* Washington, D.C., 1943.

Hutson, James. "The Szechuan Moslem." *Moslem World,* 10 (1920) :251–261.

Lang, Olga. *Chinese Family and Society.* Hamden, Conn., 1968 (reprint).

Mason, Isaac. "A Chinese View of Mohammed's Marriages." *Moslem World,* 11 (1921) :189–190.

Nationalities Publishing House. *Nationalities in China.* Peking, 1961.

O'Hara, Albert. "Changing Attitudes toward Marriage and the Family in Free China." *Journal of the China Society,* 2 (1962) :57–67.

Patai, Raphael. *Society, Culture and Change in the Middle East.* Philadelphia, 1962.

Pillsbury, Barbara. "Cohesion and Conflict in a Chinese Muslim Minority." Ph.D. dissertation. Columbia University, New York, 1973.

———. "Pig and Policy: Maintenance of Boundaries between Han and Muslim Chinese." In *Minorities: A Text with Readings in Intergroup Relations,* ed. B. Eugene Griessman. Hinsdale, Ill., 1975.

Soderstrom, L. V. "The Mohammedan Women of China." *Moslem World,* 4 (1914) :79–81.

Sun, Shen-wu. *Hui-chiao Lun-tsung.* Taipei, 1963.

Thor, Mrs. J. E. "The Moslem Women of Sianfu, China." *Moslem World,* 8 (1918) :33–35.

Contributors
Index

Contributors

EVELYNE ACCAD teaches French Studies at the University of Illinois, Champaign-Urbana. She was born in Beirut and studied there and in the United States, receiving her doctorate in Comparative Literature from Indiana University. Two books are forthcoming: *Veil of Shame: The Role of Women in the Contemporary Fiction of North Africa and the Arab World,* and *Montjoie Palestine!* (English edition, *Last Year in Jerusalem*).

BARBARA C. ASWAD teaches Anthropology at Wayne State University. Her doctorate is in Anthropology from the University of Michigan. She has done field research in rural Hatay, Turkey, and in the Arabic community of the Detroit region. Her major publications include *Property Control and Social Strategies: Settlers on a Middle Eastern Plain* and *Arabic-Speaking Communities in American Cities* (editor and contributor), in addition to a number of articles.

ÜLKÜ Ü. BATES teaches Art History at Hunter College of the City University of New York. She was born in Romania of Turkish parents. She studied in Istanbul, the United States, and Germany, and her doctorate is in Art History from the University of Michigan. Her publications include a number of articles and book chapters on the subject of Middle East art history.

MANGOL BAYAT-PHILIPP teaches History and Middle East Studies at Harvard University. She was born in Iran and studied at the American University in Cairo and the University of London. She received her doctorate in History from the University of California at Los Angeles. She has taught at Pahlavi University in Iran, and has published a number of articles.

LOIS BECK teaches Anthropology and Middle East Studies at the University of Utah. She studied in the United States and at Pahlavi University in Iran. Her doctorate is in Anthropology from the University of Chicago. She has done field research on pastoral nomads and on tribal elite families in Iran. Her publications include book chapters and articles on Iranian nomads and on Muslim women, and she is coediting *Sex Role Asymmetry in Society*.

DAWN CHATTY spent eight years of her childhood in Syria and later returned to do research among Syria's pastoral nomads. She studied in the United States and the Netherlands and received her doctorate in Anthropology from the University of California at Los Angeles. She has recently taught at the American University of Beirut. Currently, she is teaching and doing research in Syria on a Fulbright grant. She has published a number of articles on pastoralism.

FATMA MANSUR COŞAR was born in Turkey and has conducted field research there. She studied in Beirut and London and received her doctorate in Government from Harvard University. She has published *Bodrum: A Town in the Aegean* and *Process of Independence* and is coeditor of *Turkey: Geographic and Social Perspectives.*

NOEL COULSON is Professor of Oriental Laws at the School of Oriental and African Studies, University of London. He is an M.A. (Arabic and Persian) of Oxford and a Barrister-at-law of Gray's Inn. He has spent many periods of research in Muslim countries, and has published *Succession in the Muslim Family, Conflicts and Tensions in Islamic Jurisprudence,* and *A History of Islamic Law.*

SUSAN SCHAEFER DAVIS teaches Anthropology at Trenton State College. She is completing her doctoral dissertation in Anthropology at the University of Michigan. She was in the Peace Corps in rural Morocco and later did research there. She has an article on a Moroccan woman in *Middle Eastern Muslim Women Speak.*

IAN C. DENGLER is a reseacher with the Office for History of Science and Technology at the University of California at Berkeley. He is finishing his doctoral dissertation in History there.

DAISY HILSE DWYER teaches Anthropology at Columbia University. She received her doctorate in Anthropology from Yale University. She has done field research in Morocco. She has written several articles about law, politics, and ideology in Morocco as well as a forthcoming book on sexual ideology as a social control mechanism.

MICHAEL M. J. FISCHER teaches Anthropology and Middle East Studies at Harvard University. His doctorate is in Anthropology from the University of Chicago. He has conducted research in Jamaica, and in Iran and India on Zoroastrians, Muslims, Jews, and

Bahais and on the training of Muslim religious leaders. His publications include articles on Jamaican and Iranian societies.

Erika Friedl teaches Anthropology at Western Michigan University. She was born in Austria and educated there and in Germany. Her doctorate is in Anthropology from the University of Mainz in West Germany. She has done many years of research in rural southwest Iran. Her publications include articles on the culture of Iranian villagers.

Mary-Jo DelVecchio Good teaches Medical Sociology in the Department of Psychiatry at the University of California at Davis. Her doctorate is in Sociology and Middle East Studies from Harvard University. She spent two years in Turkey with the Peace Corps, did sociological research in an Iranian town, and has been a consultant on rural health care projects in Iran with the World Health Organization.

John Gulick teaches Anthropology at the University of North Carolina at Chapel Hill. His doctorate is from Harvard University. He has conducted field research in Lebanon, Iraq, and Iran and is widely published. His major works are *Social Structure and Culture Change in a Lebanese Village, Tripoli: A Modern Arab City,* and *The Middle East: An Anthropological Perspective.*

Margaret E. Gulick has recently finished her master's degree in Sociology at the University of North Carolina. She has lived in Lebanon and Iran. She is the coauthor of a number of publications on her research in Iran and has co-compiled a bibliography on women in the Muslim Middle East.

Doreen Hinchcliffe teaches Law at the School of Oriental and African Studies, University of London. She is a Barrister-at-law, has a doctorate in Law, and has published articles on Islamic law and on the Iranian Family Protection Act.

Suad Joseph teaches Anthropology at the University of California at Davis. She was born in Lebanon and raised in the United States. Her research has focused on the politicization of religious sects in Lebanon. She completed her doctorate in Anthropology at Columbia University, and has published an article in *Middle Eastern Muslim Women Speak.*

Nikki Keddie taught History at the University of Paris (1976–1978), on leave from the Department of History of the University of California at Los Angeles. Her doctorate is in History from the University of California at Berkeley. She has done research on social history and on handicrafts in Iran. Her major publications are *Sayyid Jamal ad-Din al-Afghani: A Political Biography; Scholars, Saints, and Sufis: Muslim Religious Institutions since 1500* (editor and contributor); *An Islamic Response to Imperialism;* and *Religion and Rebellion in Iran: The Tobacco Protest of 1891–92.*

VANESSA MAHER teaches Anthropology in Italy. She was born in Kenya and educated in Tanzania and England. Her doctorate is in Social Anthropology from Cambridge University. She has conducted research in Morocco, in England in a working-class neighborhood, and in Italy among migrant workers. She has published a book entitled *Women and Property in Morocco* and a number of articles.

AFAF LUTFI AL-SAYYID MARSOT teaches History at the University of California at Los Angeles. She was born in Egypt and studied there and in the United States and England. Her doctorate is in Oriental Studies from Oxford University. She has published *Egypt and Cromer: A Study in Anglo-Egyptian Relations* and *Egypt's Liberal Experiment,* as well as numerous articles.

SAWSAN EL-MESSIRI teaches Anthropology at the American University in Cairo; she has a master's degree from this institution. She is completing her doctorate in Social Anthropology at Hull University in England. She was born in Egypt and has done research in Cairo and in a large industrial town in Egypt. She has published an article, and a book on Egyptian identity is in press.

JULIETTE MINCES was born in France and has done research in Algeria, Turkey, Egypt, West Africa, and France. She is the author of several books, including *Algeria: Failure of a Revolution* (coauthor), *Le nord, Un ouvrier parle, Les travailleurs étrangers en France,* and *L'Algérie de Boumedienne.*

SOHEIR A. MORSY teaches Anthropology at Michigan State University and has completed a doctorate in Medical Anthropology there. She was born in Alexandria, Egypt, and has had field research experience in Egypt, Algeria, and Lebanon. She has published an article on folk illness in Egypt.

KAMLA NATH is currently doing research in Sierra Leone on the work participation of women. She was born in New Dehli. She has a master's degree in Economics from the University of Punjab, has lectured at the University of Delhi, and has done studies on women in north India, Kuwait, and West Africa. She has published articles based on her work in India and has edited a UNESCO report on the education, training, and employment of Sierra Leone women.

BEHNAZ PAKIZEGI teaches Psychology at William Paterson College. She recently taught Psychology at Pahlavi University in Shiraz, Iran (part of her social-military service, required of all educated Iranian women [and *all* Iranian men]). She was born in Iran and completed her doctorate in Human Development at Cornell University.

CARROLL MCC. PASTNER teaches Anthropology at the University of

Vermont. She wrote her doctoral dissertation, in Anthropology at Brandeis University, on sexual dichotomization in an oasis community. She has conducted research in Pakistan among inland and coastal villagers, and has published a number of book chapters and articles on women and the institution of purdah and on the kinship, religious, and political structure of the Baluch.

EMRYS L. PETERS teaches Social Anthropology at the University of Manchester in England. He holds a doctorate from Oxford University. He has conducted field research in Libya and Lebanon among pastoral nomads and villagers. He has published numerous articles on this research, including an article on affinity in a Lebanese Maronite village in *Mediterranean Family Structures.*

THOMAS PHILIPP teaches History and Middle East Studies at Harvard University. He was born in Germany and was educated there and in the United States. He has done research in Cairo and Beirut; his doctorate is in Islamic Studies from the University of California at Los Angeles. He has taught at Pahlavi University in Iran, and has published a number of articles and a book entitled *Jurji Zaidan: An Intellectual Biography.*

BARBARA L. K. PILLSBURY teaches Anthropology at San Diego State University. She has done research in Egypt and among Muslims in Taiwan. Her doctorate is in Anthropology from Columbia University. She has written *Mosque and Pagoda: China's Muslim Minority,* is coauthor of *West Meets East: Life Among Chinese,* and has published articles on women's health and on Chinese Muslims. On leave from university teaching during 1977–79, she is working for the Near East Bureau of AID.

JANET ROGERS is a doctoral student at Michigan State University in Political Science and African Studies.

LAWRENCE ROSEN teaches Anthropology at Princeton University He has a doctorate in Anthropology and a J.D. from the University of Chicago. He has done research in Morocco and Tunisia and has published numerous book chapters and articles on Islamic law, Muslim-Jewish relations, and urban social organization. He is coauthor (with Clifford Geertz and Hildred Geertz) and general editor of a book entitled *Meaning and Order in Moroccan Society: Three Essays in Cultural Analysis* (in press), and editor of *The American Indian and the Law* (in press).

DANIEL SCHNEIDER is a doctoral student at the University of Wisconsin, Madison, in Political Science and African Studies.

NANCY TAPPER teaches Anthropology at King's College, University of London, and is completing work on her doctorate in Anthropology at the School of Oriental and African Studies, University of London. She has done research in Iran and Afghanistan among pastoral nomads, and has published several articles.

MARK A. TESSLER teaches Political Science at the University of Wisconsin, Milwaukee. He has studied in Israel and Tunisia, as well as in the United States, and has done research in Tunisia, Morocco, and Israel. His doctorate is in Political Science from Northwestern University. His major publications include *Arab Oil: Impact on the Arab Countries and Global Implications, Tradition and Identity in Changing Africa* (coauthor), *Survey Research in Africa* (coeditor and contributor), and many book chapters and articles. In press is the book *Three Nonassimilating Minorities: Jews in Tunisia and Morocco and Arabs in Israel.*

PAUL VIEILLE is a Sociologist who now holds a research position at the National Center for Scientific Research in Paris. He was born and educated in France. He has conducted many years of research in Iran and, as a consultant for UNESCO, was sent on missions in Syria, Lebanon, Saudi Arabia, Iraq, Tunisia, Algeria, and Morocco. He has published many articles and the following books: *Marché des terrains et société urbaine, Pétrole et violence,* and *La féodalité et l'état en Iran.*

ELIZABETH H. WHITE has been doing research in Indonesia and Pakistan on Islamic restrictions on women in the two countries. She was a member of the Peace Corps, a teacher, and a researcher in West Pakistan for over five years. She completed her doctorate in International Studies at the University of Denver. She has written articles on purdah.

NADIA H. YOUSSEF is a Social Demographer with the Population Research Laboratory of the Department of Sociology and Anthropology at the University of Southern California. She was born in Austria of Egyptian and Austrian parents. Her doctorate in Sociology is from the University of California at Berkeley. Her major publication is *Women and Work in Developing Societies,* and she has published several articles on the Middle East and Latin America.

Index